Praise for Michael Gorman's commentary on 1 Corinthians

"Michael Gorman provides us with an invaluable addition to our study of 1 Corinthians. His firm grasp of Paul's thought, his exceptional pastoral and missional sensibilities, and, of course, his masterful interaction with the text of this letter make this *the* go-to commentary for pastors, teachers, and students."

—**Joel B. Green**, Fuller Theological Seminary

"Michael Gorman's commentary is a treasure trove for anyone wanting to mine the riches of this fascinating letter to the church in Corinth. Not only does Gorman provide a wealth of background information and explanation of the text, but he also captures the spirit and heart of what Paul longs to communicate to this complicated community. Readers will encounter here both Paul's vision of God in Christ and the Spirit and his vision for the church. In addition to the insightful commentary, there are thought-provoking and practical questions for discussion, reflection, and application. This inspiring commentary is a gift for anyone studying, teaching, or preaching this letter."

—**Lucy Peppiatt**, Westminster Theological Centre (UK)

"Informed by a keen understanding of contemporary Pauline scholarship, Michael Gorman's commentary is a theologically rich, balanced, and accessible reading of 1 Corinthians. He engages with culturally, historically, and theologically diverse voices to bring the concerns of this ancient letter into conversation with challenges facing the church today. His reflections and questions at the end of each section function well as catalysts for classroom discussions and sermons. It is now my first choice for classroom use and the first recommendation I'll have for pastors teaching and preaching on 1 Corinthians."

—**Andy Johnson**, Nazarene Theological Seminary

"Once again, Michael Gorman has gifted pastors and teachers with an accessible commentary that takes seriously Scripture being 'written for our sake.' This is a deft guide through a theologically rich letter. The commentary will serve well all who long to live out the teachings of this sacred text."

—**Carla Swafford Works**, Wesley Theological Seminary

"True to the spirit of Paul and the diverse needs of readers, this masterful commentary demonstrates a holistic method of reading Paul, and transmits anew the dynamic theology of 1 Corinthians in restoring God's church and the world today. An excellent tool and a timely resource for students and teachers of the Bible."

—**K. K. Yeo**, Garrett-Evangelical Theological Seminary

"Someone once complained to me that the making of many books on Paul has no end, but the making of many books on Paul that helps pastors and teachers to proclaim the word of truth faithfully and to deliberate theologically on the issues they must confront in their settings *should* have no end. Gorman's theological-pastoral-missional commentary on Paul's theological-pastoral-missional letter to the Corinthians thoroughly and engagingly accomplishes this task. He not only unveils how what Paul wrote was 'written also for our sake' (1 Cor. 10:11), he spells out how what Paul wrote can help shape a body of believers in our era into a more faithful likeness of Christ."

—**David E. Garland,**
George W. Truett Theological Seminary, Baylor University

"Whereas many modern biblical scholars assert that the Christian creeds distort rather than illuminate the texts of Scripture, Michael Gorman masterfully shows how reading 1 Corinthians in light of the four marks of the church ('one, holy, catholic, and apostolic') brings out important elements of the text that continue to challenge believers today. Characteristically ecumenical, thoughtful, and lucid, this commentary represents the best of modern theological interpretation of Scripture, informed by the history of interpretation and attentive to the issues of our own day."

—**Isaac Augustine Morales,** OP, Providence College

Praise for Michael Gorman's commentary on Romans

"Michael Gorman's commentary is well written and based on a lifetime of study and teaching of Paul's letters. It will be very effective in undergraduate, seminary, and church groups who wish to engage with Paul's letter to the Romans in a faith-filled way."

—*Review of Biblical Literature*

"Romans commentaries are legion, but this one breaks the mold. Written for teachers and preachers, it is ready-made for a classroom setting. Immensely readable and practical, it features built-in reflection strategies, key points for staying connected to the letter's overarching argument and flow, sections devoted to deeper understanding of key terms and difficult ideas, and an introductory chapter that situates the letter within the larger scope of Paul's mission. This is not a commentary that hovers over every word or phrase. Plenty of others have accomplished that well. It is a theological and pastoral commentary that will edify the church and stimulate the classroom."

—*The Christian Century*

"Teachers, preachers, and group leaders will especially appreciate Gorman's reflections and questions offered at the end of each pericope's exposition, along with recommended resources for further reading, making this commentary an eminently helpful resource for both the church and the academy."

—*Religious Studies Review*

1 CORINTHIANS

A Theological, Pastoral, and Missional Commentary

MICHAEL J. GORMAN

WILLIAM B. EERDMANS PUBLISHING COMPANY
GRAND RAPIDS, MICHIGAN

Wm. B. Eerdmans Publishing Co.
2006 44th Street SE, Grand Rapids, MI 49508
www.eerdmans.com

© 2025 Michael J. Gorman
All rights reserved
Published 2025
Printed in the United States of America

31 30 29 28 27 26 25   1 2 3 4 5 6 7

ISBN 978-0-8028-8266-0

Library of Congress Cataloging-in-Publication Data

A catalog record for this book is available from the Library of Congress.

The section of the commentary called "Introducing Paul: His Life, Theology, and Spirituality" has been adapted from "Paul, His Life and Theology" in the *Paulist Biblical Commentary* © 2018 Paulist Press. Used with permission. All rights reserved.

Portions of this work draw on material first published in Michael J. Gorman, *Apostle of the Crucified Lord: A Theological Introduction to Paul and His Letters*, 2nd ed. (Grand Rapids: Eerdmans, 2017).

Unless otherwise noted, Scripture quotations are from the New Revised Standard Version (NRSV).

Scripture quotations marked NRSVue are from the New Revised Standard Version, updated edition. Scripture quotations marked CEB are from the Common English Bible. Scripture texts marked NAB are from the New American Bible, revised edition. Scripture quotations marked NIV are from the New International Version.

For the Church

and

in gratitude to and for the Friday night companions
in thirty-plus years of Scripture study, prayer, and mission

Contents

Preface	xvii
List of Abbreviations	xxiii

INTRODUCTIONS

1

INTRODUCING PAUL

3

Approaching Paul	3
Paul's Life and Ministry	6
Sources for Paul's Life and Theology	7
A General Chronology	7
From Persecutor to Apostle	9
Paul the Letter Writer	11
Paul's Theology and Spirituality	13
Human Condition, Divine Response	14
The Death and Resurrection of Jesus	15
Jesus as Lord and the Gift of the Spirit	16
Human Response to the Gospel	17
Paul's Spirituality	19
Conclusion	21
Reflections and Questions for the Introduction to Paul	22
Spiritual, Pastoral, Missional, and Theological Reflections	22
Questions for Those Who Read, Teach, and Preach	23
For Further Reading	23

vii

CONTENTS

Highly Accessible Books	23
Midlevel Books	24
More Technical Works	26

INTRODUCING THE COMMENTARY 27

INTRODUCING 1 CORINTHIANS 30

The Complex Character of 1 Corinthians	31
1 Corinthians as a Theological Text	31
The Fundamental Issue: The Cross (Christ Crucified) and the Spirit	31
Ecclesial Identity: Ongoing Conversion and the Marks of the Church	34
1 Corinthians as a Pastoral/Formational Text	38
1 Corinthians as a Liturgical Text	41
1 Corinthians as a Missional Text	43
1 Corinthians as a Contemporary Text	46
Summary	47
The Story behind the Letter	48
Paul's Mission	50
Divisions and Scandals: Chaos at Corinth	52
At the Root of the Chaos	55
The Letter as Paul's Response to the Chaos	57
The Story within the Letter	58
Paul's Bifocal Approach to Community Formation	60
Charismatic (Spirit-Filled/Spirit-ual) Community	63
Resurrectional, Charismatic Cruciformity	65
The Marks of the Church	67
One	68
Holy	69
Catholic	71
Apostolic	72
Participation/Koinōnia and the Marks of the Church	74
The Marks of the Church and the Character of God: Father, Son, and Spirit	77
The Marks of the Church and the Letter's Structure	79
For Further Reading and Study	82
Highly Accessible Books	82
Midlevel Works	83
Advanced/Technical Works	84

Contents

COMMENTARY WITH REFLECTIONS AND QUESTIONS   87

1:1–9   OPENING: SALUTATION AND THANKSGIVING   89

    1:1–3. Salutation: Senders, Recipients, and Greeting   89

      1:1. Senders   89

      1:2. Recipients   90

      1:3. Greeting   93

    1:4–9. Thanksgiving   95

    Summary of 1:1–9   98

    Reflections and Questions for 1:1–9   99

      Spiritual, Pastoral, Missional, and Theological Reflections   99

      Questions for Those Who Read, Teach, and Preach   100

    For Further Reading   101

1:10–4:21   ADDRESSING ECCLESIAL CHAOS: UNITY THROUGH
THE WISDOM AND POWER OF THE CROSS (*ONE* CHURCH)   102

    1:10–17. Divisions   103

      1:10–12. Paul's Appeal for Unity in the Face of Divisions   103

      1:13–17. Paul's Rhetorical and Historical Perspective
       as Theological Rejoinder   106

    Reflections and Questions for 1:10–17   108

      Spiritual, Pastoral, Missional, and Theological Reflections   108

      Questions for Those Who Read, Teach, and Preach   111

    For Further Reading   111

    1:18–2:5. The Word of the Cross and the Mission of God   111

      1:18–25. Christ Crucified as the Power and Wisdom of God   113

       1:18–20. The Cross as Divine Subversion   115

       1:21–25. The Cross as Divine Power and Wisdom   116

      Summary: The Cross as Divine Self-Revelation   118

      1:26–31. The Cross and the Composition of the Corinthian
       Community   119

       1:26–29. Divine Choice, Corinthian Constitution   119

       1:30–31. God as the Source of Life in Christ   122

      2:1–5. The Cross and the Shape of Paul's Ministry   124

    Summary of 1:18–2:5   127

ix

CONTENTS

Reflections and Questions for 1:18–2:5	127
Spiritual, Pastoral, Missional, and Theological Reflections	127
Questions for Those Who Read, Teach, and Preach	130
For Further Reading	131
2:6–3:4. Cruciform Spirituality and Corinthian Immaturity	132
2:6–16. Cross and Wisdom, Cross and Spirit in the Self-Revelation of God	132
2:6–13. The Revelation of God's Wisdom as Self-Revelation	134
2:14–16. The Spirit-ual and the Mind of the Lord	136
3:1–4. Division as Evidence of Spirit-Impoverishment	138
Reflections and Questions for 2:6–3:4	140
Spiritual, Pastoral, Missional, and Theological Reflections	140
Questions for Those Who Read, Teach, and Preach	141
For Further Reading	142
3:5–4:13. Ministers as Cruciform Servants in God's Church	142
3:5–9. God's Coworkers in God's Field	144
3:10–17. Workers on God's Building—God's Temple	146
3:10–15. Building on the Foundation	146
3:16–17. God's Temple	148
3:18–23. Wisdom and the Role of Leaders	150
4:1–7. Ministerial Accountability	152
4:8–13. Ministerial Cruciformity	154
Reflections and Questions for 3:5–4:13	157
Spiritual, Pastoral, Missional, and Theological Reflections	157
Questions for Those Who Read, Teach, and Preach	158
For Further Reading	158
4:14–21. Concluding Warning: Paul's Potential Parousia	159
Summary of 1:10–4:21	161
Reflections and Questions on 1 Cor 1–4 as a Whole	162
5:1–7:40 ADDRESSING MORAL CHAOS: HOLY LIVING BETWEEN CROSS AND PAROUSIA (ONE *HOLY* CHURCH)	164
Key Themes	165
Scripture-Based Distinctives in a Pagan World	166
Bifocal Existence in Christ	168

Contents

5:1–13. Incest and the Holiness and Witness of the Church	168
5:1–5. The Situation, the Individual, and Immediate Action to Take	168
5:6–13. The Situation and the Community	172
Summary	175
Reflections and Questions for 5:1–13	175
Spiritual, Pastoral, Missional, and Theological Reflections	175
Questions for Those Who Read, Teach, and Preach	176
For Further Reading	176
6:1–11. Lawsuits, the Justice of God, and the Witness of the Church	176
6:1–6. Lawsuits in the Community	179
6:7–11. Lawsuits and Cruciform Justice	183
6:7–8. The Lawsuits as Defeat and Injustice	183
6:9–10. The Unjust and the Kingdom of God	185
6:11. Transformation by the Triune God: Justification and Justice	186
Conclusion: Injustice and Justice in the Church	188
Reflections and Questions for 6:1–11	189
Spiritual, Pastoral, Missional, and Theological Reflections	189
Questions for Those Who Read, Teach, and Preach	190
For Further Reading	190
6:12–20. Sex with Prostitutes and the Temple of the Spirit	191
The Situation in Corinth and the Texture of the Passage	191
The Structure of the Passage	193
6:12–18a. Flee from Sexual Immorality!	195
6:18b–20. Glorify God with Your Body/Bodies	197
Summary	199
Reflections and Questions for 6:12–20	200
Spiritual, Pastoral, Missional, and Theological Reflections	200
Questions for Those Who Read, Teach, and Preach	204
For Further Reading	205
7:1–40. Confusion about Marriage and the Missional Call of God	206
Structure, Style, and Themes	206
7:1. The Subject: Sex More Generally	208

xi

7:2–16. Concrete Instructions about Marriage
   for Specific Situations   209
   7:2–5. Instructions to Married Believers about Sexual
     Relations in Marriage   209
   7:6–7. Paul's Preference for Singleness   211
   7:8–9. Instructions for the Unmarried and Widows   212
   7:10–11. Instructions for Married Believers
     about Separation   212
   7:12–16. Instructions about Mixed Marriages
     and Salvific Intentionality   213
7:17–24. Theological Reflections: The Persistence Principle and
   Vocational Contentment   215
7:25–40. Further Concrete Instructions and
   Theological Reflections   218
   7:25–28. Engaged Couples and General Principles   218
   7:29–35. Eschatology and Devotion   219
   7:36–40. Betrothed Men and
     Final Theological Reflections   221
Conclusion: Marriage Instructions and Theology   222

Reflections and Questions for 7:1–40   222
Spiritual, Pastoral, Missional, and Theological Reflections   222
Questions for Those Who Read, Teach, and Preach   223

For Further Reading   223

Summary of 1 Cor 5–7   224

Reflections and Questions on 1 Cor 5–7 as a Whole   225

8:1–14:40 ADDRESSING LITURGICAL CHAOS: THE CROSS, WORSHIP, AND SALVATION FOR ALL (ONE, HOLY, CATHOLIC CHURCH)   226

8:1–11:1 Meat Associated with Idols and the Church's Mission   227

8:1–13. The Problem of Idol Meat and Paul's Initial Solution   230
8:1–6. Slogan, Counterslogan, and Agreement   230
   8:1–3. Knowledge and Love   231
   8:4–6. One God, One Lord   232
8:7–13. Knowledge, Rights, and Cruciform Love   234
Summary   238

Reflections and Questions for 8:1–13   238
Spiritual, Pastoral, Missional, and Theological Reflections   238
Questions for Those Who Read, Teach, and Preach   240

Contents

For Further Reading	240
9:1–27. The Example of Apostolic Cruciformity and Salvific Intentionality within the Church	241
9:1–14. Paul's Apostleship: Apostolic Freedom and Rights	242
9:1–2. Paul's Freedom and Apostleship	243
9:3–14. An Apologia: Paul's Apostolic Rights	243
9:15–27. Christlike, Missional Accommodation as Freedom and Love	246
9:15–18. Paul's Sense of Obligation and Boast	246
9:19–23. Paul's Cruciform Ministry	247
9:24–27. The Goal of Eschatological Salvation	253
Summary	253
Reflections and Questions for 9:1–27	255
Spiritual, Pastoral, Missional, and Theological Reflections	255
Questions for Those Who Read, Teach, and Preach	256
For Further Reading	257
10:1–11:1. *Koinōnia* with and Imitation of Christ, and Salvific Intentionality outside the Church	257
10:1–22. Participation with Christ Is Exclusive	259
10:1–14. Flee from Idolatry! Learning from Israel	260
10:15–22. Exclusive Communion with Christ	264
10:23–11:1. Imitators of Christ via the Imitation of Paul	267
10:23–24; 10:31–11:1. Summary Admonitions	267
10:25–30. Eating Meat: Other Contexts	270
Summary	271
Reflections and Questions for 10:1–11:1	272
Spiritual, Pastoral, Missional, and Theological Reflections	272
Questions for Those Who Read, Teach, and Preach	273
For Further Reading	273
Summary of 1 Cor 8:1–11:1	274
Reflections and Questions on 1 Cor 8:1–11:1 as a Whole	275
11:2–14:40 The Church (Ekklēsia) Gathered for Worship	275
11:2–16. Prophetic, Prayerful Women and Men in the Assembly	277
Interpretation A: One Voice (Paul)	279
Interpretation B: Two Voices (Paul and Certain Corinthian Men)	282
Conclusion	284

xiii

CONTENTS

Reflections and Questions for 11:2–16   285
  Spiritual, Pastoral, Missional, and Theological Reflections   285
  Questions for Those Who Read, Teach, and Preach   286

For Further Reading   286

11:17–34. Abuse of the Lord's Supper   286
  11:17–22. The Problematic Situation: Not the Lord's Supper   288
  11:23–26. The Tradition of the Last Supper   292
  11:27–34. The Remedy for the Problematic Situation   295
  The Significance of the Lord's Supper   297

Reflections and Questions for 11:17–34   304
  Spiritual, Pastoral, Missional, and Theological Reflections   304
  Questions for Those Who Read, Teach, and Preach   305

For Further Reading   306

12:1–31. The Church as Christ's Richly Gifted Body   306
  Overview of Chapter 12   307
  12:1–3. Jesus Is Lord: The Criterion of Christian Authenticity   309
  12:4–11. The Gifts of the Triune God   311
  12:12–13. The Critical Point   314
  12:14–26. The Body   315
  12:27–31. The Body That Is the Church   318

Reflections and Questions for 12:1–31   319
  Spiritual, Pastoral, Missional, and Theological Reflections   319
  Questions for Those Who Read, Teach, and Preach   321

For Further Reading   321

13:1–13. The Rule (Criterion) of Cruciform Love in Eschatological Perspective   322
  13:1–3. Love's Necessity   326
  13:4–7. Love's Character   329
  13:8–12. Love's Permanence and Human Transformation   337
  13:13. Faith, Hope, and Love's Superiority   339
  Summary   341

Reflections and Questions for 13:1–13   344
  Spiritual, Pastoral, Missional, and Theological Reflections   344
  Questions for Those Who Read, Teach, and Preach   345

For Further Reading   346

14:1–40. Edification and the Use of Gifts in Worship   347

xiv

Contents

14:1–25. A Practical Theology of Gifts and Loving Edification	349
14:1–5. The Criterion: Loving Edification of the Body	349
14:6–12. The Necessity of Intelligibility for Edification	351
14:13–19. The Practical Consequence for Tongues Speakers	352
14:20–25. Missional Maturity in the Exercise of Gifts	354
14:26–40. Instructions for the Assembly's Worship	356
14:26–36. Order in Worship	356
14:37–40. Summary Exhortations	359
Reflections and Questions for 14:1–40	360
Spiritual, Pastoral, Missional, and Theological Reflections	360
Questions for Those Who Read, Teach, and Preach	361
For Further Reading	361
Summary of 1 Cor 11:2–14:40	362
Reflections and Questions on 1 Cor 11:2–14:40 as a Whole	363

15:1–58 ADDRESSING THEOLOGICAL CHAOS: THE APOSTOLIC WITNESS TO THE RESURRECTION OF CHRIST AND OF BELIEVERS (ONE, HOLY, CATHOLIC, AND *APOSTOLIC* CHURCH) — 364

The Presenting Problem: Some Are Denying the Resurrection of the Dead	366
Paul's Perspective	369
15:1–34. Christ's Resurrection and Its Consequences	371
15:1–11. The Common Creed: Christ Has Been Raised	372
15:1–2. The Gospel and the Corinthians	372
15:3–7. The Gospel in Four Acts	373
15:8–11. The Gospel, Paul, and the Corinthians	379
Believers' Participation in the Story/Reality of the Messiah	380
15:12–34. The Consequences of Christ's Resurrection as Fiction or Fact	382
15:12–19. The Consequences If Christ's Resurrection Is Fiction	383
15:20–28. The Reality of Christ's Resurrection and Its Consequences	385
15:29–34. Paul's *Peroratio*: Further Consequences If the Resurrection Is Fiction, and Concluding Admonitions	389

xv

CONTENTS

15:35–57. The Nature of Believers' Resurrection in Eschatological Perspective	392
15:35–50. The Nature of the Resurrection	392
15:35. Two Questions	392
15:36–41. An Analogy from Nature	393
15:42–49. The Analogy from Nature Applied to Bodily Resurrection	394
15:50. Conclusion to the Analogy and Its Application	395
15:51–57. The Final Victory	399
15:58. Concluding Exhortation	401
Summary	402
Reflections and Questions for 15:1–58	402
Spiritual, Pastoral, Missional, and Theological Reflections	402
Questions for Those Who Read, Teach, and Preach	405
For Further Reading	405
Summary of 1 Cor 15	406

16:1–24 CLOSING: THE APOSTOLIC WITNESS CONTINUES (ONE HOLY, CATHOLIC, AND *APOSTOLIC* CHURCH) — 408

16:1–4. The Ecumenical Collection for Jerusalem	408
16:5–9. Paul's Missional Plans	410
16:10–12. Concerning Timothy and Apollos	411
16:13–14. Summary Exhortations	412
16:15–18. Concerning Certain Corinthians	414
16:19–24. Greetings and Final Words	414
Reflections and Questions for 16:1–24	416
Spiritual, Pastoral, Missional, and Theological Reflections	416
Questions for Those Who Read, Teach, and Preach	417
For Further Reading	417

Acknowledgments	419
Index of Names	421
Index of Subjects	425
Index of Scripture and Other Ancient Sources	436

xvi

Preface

Like my previous commentary on Romans,[1] this volume is a midlevel commentary that has been prepared especially for pastors, students, and laypeople who want a careful exposition of the apostle Paul's first canonical letter to the Corinthians that stresses its theological content and considers its spiritual, pastoral, and missional implications for today. (Of course, I hope that biblical scholars and theologians will benefit from it as well.) This focus does not in any sense mean we will ignore the original message of Paul to his first audience, or the historical contexts and social settings suggested by the letter. It simply means that I engage 1 Corinthians as Christian Scripture and invite you to do the same.

"These things were written also for our sake" is Paul's basic principle for interpreting Scripture, and he would expect us to follow it in reading his own letters now that they are part of the Christian Bible.[2] I read, teach, and write about 1 Corinthians as a Protestant Christian who has spent more than thirty years in three interrelated ecclesial settings: as a professor in a Catholic seminary that also has an ecumenical graduate school; as a participant in an ecumenical Bible study and prayer group in our home; and as a teacher of adults in various kinds of churches, but especially Methodist. In each place, we have studied 1 Corinthians as a letter to and for us. After all, the letter's salutation names, with the Corinthians, "all those who in every place call on the name of our Lord Jesus Christ" (1:2).

Furthermore, designating this commentary as "theological, pastoral, and missional" means that these three aspects are inextricably related, even hy-

---

1. *Romans: A Theological and Pastoral Commentary* (Grand Rapids: Eerdmans, 2022).
2. See, e.g., Rom 4:23–24; 15:4; 1 Cor 9:10; 10:11.

xvii

PREFACE

phenated (theological-pastoral-missional), because Paul is a pastoral and missional theologian. First Corinthians is a project of what Scot McKnight calls "lived theology."[3] The apostle writes not merely about *thinking* Christianly but about *living* Christianly—about faith, hope, and love (1 Cor 13:13).

Moreover, therefore, the words "pastoral" and "missional" do not mean that either 1 Corinthians or this commentary is limited in usefulness to people identified as pastors or missionaries. Rather, it is Paul the pastor and missionary who, speaking in and through this letter, seeks pastorally to shape a Christlike, missional people. The goal of this commentary is to do the same. Another way of describing this approach is to say that doing theology is, or should be, an act of worship, of praise—both for the original doer/writer and for the reader/hearer. (I first learned this from the great Jewish scholar and spiritual writer Abraham Joshua Heschel.) Since theological commentary writing is, one hopes, doing prayerful theology, I have attempted to write this commentary, and now offer it, as a spiritual act, an act of worship. Theology is doxology; commentary writing, and commentary reading, is doxology.

As a Christian and a scholar, I am quite enamored with the apostle Paul and his writings. At the same time, I recognize what 2 Peter lamented years ago: "There are some things in them [Paul's letters] hard to understand, which the ignorant and unstable twist to their own destruction, as they do the other scriptures" (2 Pet 3:16). I therefore hope that this volume will illumine Paul's message in 1 Corinthians and identify some misinterpretations and offer, I trust, some new and helpful ones along the way.

However, as I sometimes tell my students about biblical interpretation, let whoever is without sin cast the first stone! As interpreters, we must approach the text with humility. In the words of Ellen Davis, "I begin with humility, for I follow Augustine in seeing this as the first virtue of Christian biblical interpretation. He compared Scripture to a large room; but its door is very low, so one has to stoop down in order to enter."[4] First Corinthians is a letter that feels very contemporary and seems to speak rather directly to our times, yet it is also

---

3. Scot McKnight, *Reading Romans Backwards: The Gospel of Peace in the Midst of Empire* (Waco, TX: Baylor University Press, 2019), xiii–xv. The essence of this lived theology, says McKnight, is "Christoformity," or Christlikeness (see 27–53). Although McKnight is writing about Romans, the same is true of 1 Corinthians. See also his *Pastor Paul: Nurturing a Culture of Christoformity in the Church* (Grand Rapids: Baker Academic, 2019).

4. Ellen F. Davis, "The Soil That Is Scripture," in *Engaging Biblical Authority: Perspectives on the Bible as Scripture*, ed. William P. Brown (Louisville: Westminster John Knox, 2007), 36–44 (here 38). The additional necessary "habits of mind and heart" for reading Scripture, writes Davis, are love and patience (37).

xviii

Preface

challenging and even confusing at points. My prayer is that this commentary will help those who wish to engage the letter to read it more intelligibly and charitably, and to embrace its call to participate in the life God offers in Christ by the Spirit more fully.

Unlike some commentaries, especially much longer ones, this commentary does not always deal with every word of every verse. It focuses on what scholars sometimes call *discourse units*, on the flow of the argument and the sense of the text, and on the theological content and significance of those various sections of the letter. The commentary also does not provide a list of all possible interpretations for every disputed word, verse, or topic—only for some. Some verses, words, and passages therefore receive more attention than others.

This volume also has a relatively modest number of footnotes and explicit references to other interpreters; the notes mostly explain or expand what is in the main text, and document quotations. My goal is to offer a sustained interpretation of the letter as a whole, often dialoguing with other interpreters behind the scenes, rather than on the pages or in the notes (with some exceptions). That is, this volume comments on the text, not on other commentators.[5] This approach should not, however, be labeled "popular." Rather, it aims to be accessible while also being robustly theological and grounded in solid scholarship.

Like my Romans volume, this commentary also has a distinctive format, with several elements that complement the observations about the text. At the end of the introductory sections of the commentary and at the end of each section of comments are further reflections, questions, and suggested reading. The reflections are a significant aspect of the commentary and should be read along with the exposition of the text to which they are connected. Since this commentary is not aimed primarily at scholars, I have generally restricted the reading suggestions to resources intended for, or at least accessible by, a broad readership. (A few more technical works are included and indicated as such.) Furthermore, although I have recommended important books on the biblical and theological topics raised by the letter, I do not necessarily agree with everything in every book listed. Finally, summaries appear after the commentary on chapters 1–4, 5–7, 8–10 (actually 8:1–11:1), 11–14, and 15, and occasionally after the comments on shorter units.

---

5. That said, those who compare this commentary with my commentary on Romans will note an increase in the number of notes, references to other interpreters, and overall length. This is due primarily to the great variety of topics that appear in this letter, and to my desire to explore in depth the (often unexplored or underexplored) theological dimensions of those topics.

xix

PREFACE

The default Scripture translation used in this commentary is the NRSV, although there are many references to other versions, especially the NIV, NAB (i.e., NABRE), the CEB, and the NRSVue (updated edition), as well as my own translations here and there.[6] I have, of course, worked with the Greek text even though it is only occasionally cited (in transliteration, such as *charismata*: "grace-gifts").

Of the making of books on 1 Corinthians there is no end. So what is the distinctive contribution of this commentary? Clearly, the general approach—evident in the subtitle—is theological, pastoral, and missional. I not only read 1 Corinthians with those emphases, but I also believe that is the kind of letter Paul actually wrote. As already noted, this approach does not ignore other aspects of the text (historical, rhetorical, etc.) but stresses these dimensions. Such an emphasis means that my conversation partners, both ancient and contemporary, explicit and implicit, will generally be people who are sympathetic to this way of reading the letter. I attempt also to interact with such interpreters from various cultures, and I do so out of a commitment to the global church, a commitment based in Paul's own ecclesiology. With these various conversation partners, I ask this: in light of God's mission, manifested most fully in Christ (the *missio Dei*, Latin for "the mission of God"), what should the church, empowered by the Spirit, believe (faith), do (love), and anticipate (hope)? This question is a contemporary version of the church's commitment to the fourfold sense of Scripture, and a short form of it appears in the sets of questions throughout the commentary.[7]

With respect to the specifics of my general theological approach, wise interpreters like Richard Hays and Joel Green have said that reading Scripture through the lens of the creeds of the church can help us ask questions about the text, and help us see things in the text, that otherwise we would not ask or see. *In this commentary, I especially read 1 Corinthians through the lens of the marks of the church enshrined in the Nicene (or Niceno-Constantinopolitan) Creed: one, holy, catholic, and apostolic.* First Corinthians, then, is a pastoral letter of Christian formation that urges the church then and now to be one, holy, catholic, and apostolic. These four marks of the church appear throughout the letter, not because Paul somehow knew the later creed but because the creed knew

---

6. I have chosen the NRSV, rather than the NRSVue, as the default version for two reasons: the NRSVue is still not widely used, and it was not even in print when I started work on this book.

7. Patristic and medieval interpreters often identified four senses of the text: literal, allegorical (doctrinal), tropological (moral), and anagogical (eschatological).

xx

Preface

Paul. That is, more specifically, the compilers of the creed understood, from Paul's letters and other New Testament writings, that the identity of the church could and should be characterized in this way.[8]

Not surprisingly, however, Paul has his own particular take on these four marks. They cannot be understood apart from his special focus on God's gifts of Christ crucified and raised, and of the indwelling Holy Spirit (Gk. *pneuma*). Thus the marks of the church will be unified in their fundamental christological and pneumatological shape. That is, the church's unity, holiness, catholicity, and apostolicity will be cruciform (cross-shaped) and charismatic (by which I mean empowered by the Spirit).[9] Or, we could say that the church will be resurrectionally cruciform: shaped by the indwelling of the resurrected Crucified One, present by his Spirit.

This emphasis on what I call "resurrectional cruciformity," or even "resurrectional, charismatic cruciformity," leads to two other specific distinctives in this commentary. First, it will note Paul's explicit and implicit use of a linguistic formula, or pattern, that expresses resurrectional, charismatic cruciformity as Christlike self-giving, life-giving love, a love that the Spirit reproduces in and among Christians. This pattern can be summarized as "Although [x] not [y] but [z]," generally meaning,

- › Although [x = possessing status, rights, or interests]
- › not [y = using the status, rights, or interests for selfish ends]
- › but rather [z = engaging in loving concern for others].

Such resurrectional, charismatic cruciformity is not a form of heroic, radical altruism focused (ironically) on itself but a form of love whose goal is life, salvation, and community.

Second, it will pay careful attention to how Paul thinks, and wants his addressees to think, *bifocally.* I use the term "bifocally" to indicate an approach to Christian theology and spirituality that looks both (1) *back* to the first coming of Jesus and all that is associated with that, especially for Paul his death and resurrection, and (2) *ahead* to Christ's second coming (Gk. *parousia*, or "royal

8. As I was completing this commentary, I became aware of an interesting, related article: Brian Rosner and Mark Simon, "Reading 1 Corinthians in Dialogue with the Apostles' Creed," *Journal of the Evangelical Theological Society* 66 (2023): 509–22.

9. As we will see in the commentary proper, the word "charismatic" comes from the Greek word *charisma*, meaning "grace-gift" or "manifestation of grace" but often translated as "spiritual gift." I use it also, however, simply to mean empowered by God's gracious Holy Spirit. One could also use the descriptor "pneumatic" (from *pneuma*, Spirit).

xxi

arrival/presence") and all that is associated with that, including the resurrection of the dead, judgment, and final glorification.

So what does "one, holy, catholic, and apostolic" in cruciform and bifocal perspective mean? Above all, like Romans and the other Pauline letters, 1 Corinthians is a letter about Spirit-enabled participation and transformation in Christ and his story, and thus in the reconciling, unifying, and sanctifying mission of God in the world—in anticipation of the fullness of the already-inaugurated new creation. That divine mission includes the creation of a worldwide communion of local bodies that constitute the one, holy, catholic, and apostolic *ekklēsia* (assembly/church), which participates in the *missio Dei* in Christlike ways as it lives between his first and second comings.

Abbreviations

BDAG	Danker, Frederick W., Walter Bauer, William F. Arndt, and F. Wilbur Gingrich. *A Greek-English Lexicon of the New Testament and Other Early Christian Literature*. 3rd ed. Chicago: University of Chicago Press, 2000
CEB	Common English Bible
DPL[2]	McKnight, Scot, Lynn Cohick, and Nijay K. Gupta, eds. *Dictionary of Paul and His Letters*. 2nd ed. Downers Grove, IL: IVP Academic, 2023
ESV	English Standard Version
KJV	King James Version
LCL	Loeb Classical Library
LNTS	The Library of New Testament Studies
MJG	author's translation
MT	Masoretic (Hebrew) Text
NAB	New American Bible, revised edition
NASB	New American Standard Bible
NET	New English Translation (NET Bible)
NETS	New English Translation of the Septuagint
NIV	New International Version
NJB	New Jerusalem Bible
NLT	New Living Translation
NRSV	New Revised Standard Version
NRSVue	New Revised Standard Version, updated edition
NTW	Wright, N. T. *The New Testament for Everyone*. 3rd ed. Grand Rapids: Zondervan, 2023
RSV	Revised Standard Version

Introductions

Introducing Paul

HIS LIFE, THEOLOGY, AND SPIRITUALITY

Paul, the Jew from Tarsus who had tried to destroy the fledgling Jesus-as-Messiah movement that became the Christian church, was early Christianity's most influential leader and thinker. His bequest to the church includes his apostolic example as well as his creative theology and profound spirituality. It is helpful to put his first canonical letter to the early Christian believers in Corinth into the larger context of his life and convictions.[1]

APPROACHING PAUL

There are various perspectives on Paul today, especially among scholars who have devoted their lives to studying the apostle. Within each perspective there

---

1. It is important to keep in mind the meanings of common words like "Christ," "Christian," "Christianity," and "church" when used in reference to Paul. "Christ" is not part of Jesus' name but simply means "Messiah," or anointed one (from Gk. *Christos*); as a royal honorific, it also means "King." "Christian"—a word that actually does not appear in Paul's letters—means (as a noun) a follower of Jesus the Messiah or (as an adjective) associated with the beliefs and practices centered on Jesus as the Messiah. "Christianity"—a word found nowhere in the Bible—therefore means something like the form of belief and practice centered on Jesus as the Messiah. And "church" (a common translation of the Greek word *ekklēsia*, meaning "assembly") refers to a, or the, community of Jesus-as-Messiah followers—or Christ-participants. Using such common English terms presents challenges, but completely avoiding them presents its own challenges, both practical and theological.

"Introducing Paul: His Life, Theology, and Spirituality" appeared in slightly different form in my *Romans: A Theological and Pastoral Commentary* (Grand Rapids: Eerdmans, 2022) and has been adapted from "Paul, His Life and Theology" in the *Paulist Biblical Commentary* © 2018 Paulist Press. Used with permission. All rights reserved.

is also diversity, not one single point of view. After listing some of the main outlooks on Paul and briefly describing a few general characteristics of each, I will highlight the approach taken in this commentary.[2]

- The *traditional perspective* on Paul, sometimes called the *traditional Protestant* or the *Lutheran* perspective, is the default position of many people. This perspective generally finds Paul stressing the individual's justification (right relationship with God) by faith rather than works; justification as a divine declaration of acquittal, as in a law court; substitutionary atonement, or Jesus' death in our place; and salvation history, or continuity between God's revelation to Israel and God's work in Christ. This approach to Paul is usually traced (rightly or wrongly) to John Calvin and Martin Luther. Contemporary proponents include Douglas Moo, John Piper, Thomas Schreiner, and Stephen Westerholm.
- The *new perspective* on Paul emerged in the 1960s through the early 1980s in reaction to the traditional perspective. It continues today, but in somewhat nuanced ways, due to critique from the traditional perspective and other quarters. Advocates have attempted to better understand first-century Judaism and Paul within it. Some new-perspective themes include the following:
  › Paul did not have a modern introspective guilt complex.
  › Judaism was not a religion of human effort, or works righteousness, but of *covenantal nomism*: keeping the law as a response to God's grace.
  › The center of Paul's theology was not justification but participation in Christ—the Messiah.
  › Justification is primarily about the inclusion of gentiles in the covenant community apart from keeping the Jewish law, especially the Jewish boundary markers of circumcision, kosher diet, and calendar (the Sabbath and other special days).

  Names associated with this perspective include Krister Stendahl, E. P. Sanders, James D. G. Dunn, N. T. Wright, and Scot McKnight.
- The *narrative-intertextual perspective* emphasizes Paul as both a narrative theologian—that is, there are discernible stories within and behind his letters—and a scriptural theologian—that is, Paul is primarily an interpreter of Israel's Scriptures (the Christian Old Testament). A key figure in this ap-

---

2. I draw heavily from my *Apostle of the Crucified Lord: A Theological Introduction to Paul and His Letters*, 2nd ed. (Grand Rapids: Eerdmans, 2017), 1–5, for this discussion. See also Scot McKnight and B. J. Oropeza, *Perspectives on Paul: Five Views* (Grand Rapids: Baker Academic, 2020).

proach is Richard B. Hays, and more recently Christoph Heilig stresses narrative in Paul.

- The *apocalyptic perspective* stresses that for Paul, God's apocalypse (revelation) in Christ is God's unexpected incursion into human history to rescue people, and eventually the entire cosmos, from the cosmic powers of Sin and Death.[3] Thus, traditional law court imagery for justification and salvation is insufficient, and the language of a continuous salvation history is in need of modification. Representative scholars include J. Louis Martyn, J. Christiaan Beker, Douglas Campbell, and Beverly Gaventa.
- The *anti-imperial perspective* contends that Paul's proclamation of the gospel was a critique of and an alternative to Rome—its emperor, gods, good news (gospel), values, and so on. Proponents of this perspective contend that Paul consistently undermines Roman claims and practices, presenting Jesus rather than Caesar as the true lord, and the Christ community as an alternative to the oppressive empire. Such claims, it is argued, affected people outside of Rome itself, whether in Corinth or Ephesus or wherever. Proponents of this view include Richard Horsley, Neil Elliott, and Sylvia Keesmaat.
- Similarly, the *postcolonial perspective* emphasizes how Paul has been misused by colonial powers (and others in power) to oppress people, and it works to reinterpret Paul in liberating ways. Proponents include Efraín Agosto, Roji T. George, Jeremy Punt, and Christopher Stanley.
- The *Paul within Judaism perspective* finds traditional and even new perspectives to be too influenced by their proponents' own Christian concerns, thus failing to understand Paul and his communities adequately. Proponents stress that Paul did not found something called Christianity to correct or replace Judaism. They contend that Paul remained firmly within Judaism as a law-observant Jew (though specifics are debated), even as an apostle of the Messiah among the nations. Paul's mission and message are manifestations of the variegated Judaism of his time. One of the ongoing areas of exploration is how best to understand and identify non-Jews in Christ (gentiles) in relation to Paul's new form of Judaism. Some leading advocates of this perspective are Paula Fredriksen, Mark Nanos, Anders Runesson, and Matthew Thiessen.
- Without at all denying Paul's Jewishness, the *social-scientific perspective* places primary emphasis on understanding Paul in his broader Greco-Roman context. Scholars working within this perspective use social history and other social sciences to attempt to understand Paul and his communities as concrete

3. When these words signify cosmic powers, they are often spelled with uppercase initial letters.

first-century social realities. Among the practitioners of this perspective are John Barclay, David Horrell, Margaret MacDonald, and Peter Oakes. Some of these scholars, especially John Barclay, find great theological significance in their analytical work.

- The *feminist perspective* on Paul brings women's questions and concerns to the study of Paul and the Pauline letters. Feminist interpreters look both critically and constructively at views of women expressed in the letters in their ancient contexts, and in the interpretation of those views from antiquity to today. First Corinthians has been a special focus of study from a feminist perspective (especially ch. 7, 11:2–16, and ch. 14). Lynn Cohick, Kathy Ehrensperger, and Lucy Peppiatt are a few of the scholars with these concerns.

- The *participationist perspective* stresses individual and community transformative participation "in Christ," especially in his death and resurrection, as the central dimension of Pauline theology. Its proponents resonate with early Christian interpreters of Paul and of salvation, who made statements like the following: "He [Christ/God] became what we are so that we could become what he is." Ben Blackwell, Susan Eastman, Nijay Gupta, Morna Hooker, and the present writer are among those within this perspective.

These various approaches to Paul—and there are more!—are not all mutually exclusive, though some are definitely in tension with others. Indeed, many interpreters work from more than one of these perspectives.[4] The present commentary comes from the participationist perspective but also shares certain concerns of other approaches, especially the new perspective, the narrative-intertextual perspective, the apocalyptic perspective, and the anti-imperial perspective. Readers of the commentary will undoubtedly notice the emphasis on participation, but also, as indicated in the preface, on related themes, especially unity, holiness (including justice), catholicity, and apostolicity.

PAUL'S LIFE AND MINISTRY

We have several kinds of sources for studying Paul. Nonetheless, dating his life and ministry with precision is notoriously difficult. At the same time, we can get a good general sense of the shape and character of his apostolic vocation.

4. For instance, N. T. Wright from the new perspective and the anti-imperial perspective; Richard Hays from the narrative-intertextual, apocalyptic, and participationist perspectives; and Beverly Gaventa from both apocalyptic and feminist perspectives. In addition, a critical aspect of interpretation is one's cultural location, which may be more significant in many global contexts than identification with one or another of the perspectives listed here.

Sources for Paul's Life and Theology

The most important sources for the apostle's life and theology are the seven letters he wrote that are universally, or nearly universally, agreed to be authored by him, including 1 Corinthians (see further below). Supporting evidence comes from the other six letters attributed to him but whose actual authorship is debated by scholars. These writings may—and I stress *may*—reflect less accurately or directly Paul's life and thought.

Another source is the Acts of the Apostles, written by Luke and thus more useful for Luke's own theology, and for his interpretation of Paul's life, than for Paul's theology per se. Scholars debate the degree of Luke's historical reliability, with some finding him more accurate in his description of the cities Paul evangelized than in his plotting of Paul's actual travels. (It is debated whether Luke was actually Paul's traveling companion.) My own approach finds Acts to be reliable and helpful for the interpretation of 1 Corinthians.

Yet another kind of evidence is more general: ancient Jewish and pagan writings, inscriptions and other archaeological remains, and other sorts of historical information that help us understand Paul in his context. For example, there exists something generally called the Gallio inscription, which is actually a collection of nine fragments of a letter from the emperor Claudius written in about the year AD 52. The fragments were found in the city of Delphi, about 125 miles northeast of Corinth. In the letter, Claudius mentions some advice he had received from Gallio, who was the Roman proconsul (governor) of Achaia (southern Greece) and is named in Acts as the official who dismissed charges against Paul in Corinth as an in-house Jewish dispute (Acts 18:12–17). Thus we seem to have an approximate date for Paul's visit to Corinth, since proconsuls generally served for two years (though Gallio's tenure may have been shorter).

Taken together, these sources reveal some highly significant aspects of Paul's life and theology, but they also leave open some questions. Although we cannot construct a full biography, and we cannot specify his precise position on every theological topic, there is sufficient evidence to describe and interpret both his life and his thought—sometimes quite precisely, sometimes more generally.

A General Chronology

Establishing a Pauline chronology is challenging, not only due to scholars' questions about the historical accuracy of Acts but also due to the general absence of references to datable historical events in Acts and especially in the letters. Moreover, unfortunately, none of the letters bears a date stamp. The references in Acts 18:12–17 to Gallio noted above may help us date Paul's original ministry in Corinth to the early 50s, but even this date and text are subject to scholarly argument.

A very general outline of Paul's life and ministry is possible by drawing on what we can glean from the letters, Acts, and other sources. It looks something like the following, with a range of dates normally given to indicate something of the range of scholarly reconstructions:

DATES	EVENT
ca. 5 BC–AD 10	Birth in Tarsus (followed by education in Tarsus, then Jerusalem)
ca. 30–36	Persecution of the Jesus-as-Messiah movement (the church)
ca. 32–36	Call/conversion/commission
ca. 33–39	Three years in Arabia and Damascus (Gal 1:17)
ca. 36–39	Initial Jerusalem visit with Cephas (Peter) and James (two weeks; Gal 1:18–19)
ca. 37–48	Early mission work in Syria, Cilicia, and possibly elsewhere (Gal 1:21; cf. Acts 9:30)
ca. 46–58	Evangelization especially in Asia Minor and Greece; writing of most canonical letters, including 1 Corinthians (in the middle to second half of this period)
ca. 47–51	Jerusalem meeting/council (Gal 2:1–10 = Acts 11:27–30? Acts 15?); earliest correspondence that has been preserved
ca. 50–52	Corinth mission of eighteen months (Acts 18; see Acts 18:11)
ca. 52–57	Ephesus mission of two to three years (Acts 19; see Acts 19:8, 10; 20:31), including possible imprisonment; 1 Corinthians was written from this city (1 Cor 16:8, 19) Additional three-month stay in Corinth (Acts 20:3)
ca. 54–59	Arrest in Jerusalem (Acts 21:27–36)
ca. 60–63	Imprisonment in Rome (Acts 28)
ca. 62–68	Possible release from Rome and further mission work and letter writing
ca. 62–68	Death

The transformation of Saul (his Jewish name)—or Paul (his primary secular name)—took place within a few years of Jesus' resurrection, but this sort of chronology suggests that we know very little of what happened to him for the next decade or so. It also places the main (undisputed) letters basically within the decade of the 50s (with the possibility that the Thessalonian correspondence was from 48 or 49). Apparently depicted in Acts 13–21 as three mission trips, this period started with ministry in the region or province of Galatia (central Anatolia, modern Turkey). It then focused on the Roman provinces of Asia (western Anatolia), Macedonia (northern Greece), and Achaia (southern Greece), all of which border the Aegean Sea (hence some call this period of Paul's life the Aegean mission). If Paul wrote some or all of the disputed letters, they would probably date from the 60s. (If he did not, some could derive from the late 60s to the 80s, and some from even later decades.)[5]

From Persecutor to Apostle

According to both Acts and the Pauline letters, Paul was a Pharisee (Acts 23:6; 26:5; Phil 3:5), a devotee of the Jewish law, who persecuted the Jesus-as-Messiah movement (e.g., Acts 8:1–3; 9:1–5; 1 Cor 15:9; Gal 1:13–14, 23; Phil 3:6; 1 Tim 1:13). For reasons that are not completely clear, he found the movement, which he later called "the church of God," or the "assembly [Gk. *ekklēsia*] of God" (e.g., 1 Cor 15:9; Gal 1:13), to be a threat both to the law that the Pharisees were committed to promote and to the people of the covenant who were guided by that law.

It may have been the movement's message of a crucified Messiah (see 1 Cor 1:18–25), its relaxed attitude to the Jewish law, or both (and more) that led Saul/Paul to want to "destroy" the church (Gal 1:13)—to seek its demise. It is highly likely that Paul found a mentor for his particular form of zealous sacred violence in the ancient figure of Phinehas (Num 25:6–13; Ps 106:30–31), who had killed an Israelite man and his Midianite consort, thus ending God's wrath against Israel's idolatry and impurity. (This does not mean Paul actually committed murder.)

---

5. One prominent scholar has argued solely from the letters themselves, without reference to Acts, that 1 and 2 Thessalonians were written in about AD 40 and the other eight Pauline letters to fledgling communities between 50 and 52, with 1 Corinthians dated to the spring of 51. See Douglas A. Campbell, *Framing Paul: An Epistolary Biography* (Grand Rapids: Eerdmans, 2014). His views have not yet won the day. On the other hand, a recent revisiting of the dating of all the New Testament documents insists on the indispensability of Acts when considering the Pauline letters. See Jonathan Bernier, *Rethinking the Dates of the New Testament: The Evidence for Early Composition* (Grand Rapids: Baker Academic, 2022), 133–44. Bernier argues for rather traditional dates for the main Pauline letters, as his interest in earlier dating lies with the Gospels. His summary (145): Galatians = 47–52; 1 and 2 Thessalonians = 50–52; 1 and 2 Corinthians = early and late 56; Romans = winter 56/57; and Ephesians, Colossians, Philemon, and Philippians = 57–59.

Again, both Acts and the Pauline letters relate (from different perspectives and with different details) Paul's unexpected encounter with the resurrected Jesus while in the midst of his persecuting activity: Jesus appeared to him (1 Cor 9:1; 15:8; Gal 1:15–16). This event took place, according to Acts 9 (retold in chs. 22 and 26), on the road to Damascus. It is generally known as Paul's conversion.

Many scholars, however, prefer to call the experience Paul's "call," since Paul did not cease being a Jew; he did not convert from Judaism to Christianity when he joined the Jesus-as-Messiah movement. Paul himself describes the experience as a prophetic call, echoing call narratives in Jeremiah and Isaiah (Gal 1:15–16; Jer 1:4–8; Isa 49:5–6). Nevertheless, if we define "conversion" as a radical transformation in belief, belonging, and behavior, then certainly Paul's call was also a conversion, as he himself implies (Phil 3:3–14). The initiative in this call/conversion was clearly not Paul's; Christ "took hold" of him (Phil 3:12 NJB).

Moreover, Paul's call/conversion was also a commission, a charge to preach the good news about Jesus as Messiah and Lord among the nations, or gentiles (the Greek word *ethnē* can mean either)—the polytheistic non-Jews throughout the Roman Empire.[6] He was appointed an apostle, one sent with the authority of the sender, like a representative, or ambassador, and spokesperson, or herald.[7] By virtue of God's grace, Paul believed, the former persecutor had been granted the privilege of seeing the resurrected Jesus and being called to apostleship (Rom 1:5; 1 Cor 15:9–10; Gal 1:15–17; Eph 3:7–8).

Some of the Hebrew prophets had promised a coming day in which YHWH's salvation would extend to the nations (e.g., Isa 2:2; 42:6; 49:6). Paul apparently saw the fulfillment of that promise above all in the ministry given to him and his colleagues. Although Paul's focus was to be the gentiles, the gospel was for both Jew and gentile (Rom 1:16–17). According to Acts, Paul frequently began his ministry in the synagogue, where he no doubt hoped to convince both Jews and Godfearers—gentiles who had affiliated with Judaism but had not become fully Jewish (i.e., for men, by circumcision). This meant, ironically, that Paul was sometimes rejected, and even persecuted, by his own people (e.g., Acts 17:1–9; 2 Cor 11:24–26).

Paul's life as an apostle was one of proclaiming the gospel by word and deed in unevangelized cities, which then served as epicenters of the gospel.

---

6. See Acts 9:10–16; 13:47; Rom 1:5; 15:15–21; 16:26; Gal 1:16; 2:1–10; Eph 3:1, 8; 1 Tim 2:7; 3:16; 2 Tim 4:17. The word *ethnē* is sometimes translated as "pagans."

7. I will use the term "apostle" throughout the commentary, though the significance of the term noted here should be kept in mind.

Major epicenters included Ephesus in the Roman province of Asia, located in western Anatolia, or Asia Minor (modern Turkey), and Corinth, located in the Roman province of Achaia, in southern Greece. Traveling on foot and by ship with coworkers, he was founder and then shepherd—often from a distance—of a network of small communities of Christ-followers (or better, from Paul's perspective, Christ-*participants*) whose mission was to bear witness to the lordship of Jesus in their city and beyond.[8]

Each community, or Christ assembly (*ekklēsia*), met in a house, or perhaps occasionally in a workshop, tavern, or other venue. These assemblies of Christ-participants are often called "house churches." The house church(es) in each city consisted of men and women, enslaved persons and free (or freed) persons, rich and poor, gentiles (mostly) and Jews (Gal 3:28).[9] But at Corinth, and almost certainly elsewhere, these Pauline communities looked especially like this: "Consider your own call, brothers and sisters: not many of you were wise by human standards, not many were powerful, not many were of noble birth. But God chose what is foolish in the world to shame the wise; God chose what is weak in the world to shame the strong; God chose what is low and despised in the world, things that are not, to reduce to nothing things that are, so that no one might boast in the presence of God" (1 Cor 1:26–29).

In order to imitate Christ's own self-emptying love, and to keep from being a burden to others, Paul himself eschewed status and power, working with his hands as a tent maker or leather worker (1 Cor 9:3–18; 1 Thess 2:9; 2 Thess 3:7–9; Acts 18:3). His apostolic life resembled Christ's in multiple ways, as he regularly suffered physical pain and deprivation, emotional distress, political torture, and imprisonment (Rom 8:35; 1 Cor 4:8–13; 2 Cor 4:7–12; 6:3–10; 11:23–33; 12:10). Paul's life became one of getting into what the late US congressman and civil rights activist John Lewis (1940–2020) called "good trouble."

Paul the Letter Writer

Paul's apostolic ministry meant he had ongoing concern for the churches he founded, as well as for other communities to which he was connected via associates, both men and women. In addition to occasional visits, Paul wrote letters in Greek (the common tongue in the Roman Empire) as a form of

8. We can and will also refer to Christ-followers or Christ-participants simply as "Christians," even though Paul himself does not use that term.

9. It should be noted that a "house" could have been anything from tenement housing (Lat. *insulae*) to villas. For more on the church in Paul's experience and theology, see my essay "Church," *DPL*[2] 116–28.

INTRODUCING PAUL

ongoing communal spiritual formation, pastoral care, and apostleship in absentia—sometimes even from jail (not unlike other political prisoners, such as Dietrich Bonhoeffer, the Rev. Dr. Martin Luther King Jr., and Lin Zhao).[10] As a self-described apostle, father figure, and mother figure (all at the same time), he corresponded expecting his addressees to read his letters aloud in the assembly and heed them.[11] Not everyone wanted to follow Paul, however, for he had opponents—who are often in view as he writes.

The New Testament contains thirteen letters bearing Paul's name. (Hebrews does not name its author, but it is almost certainly not by Paul despite its frequent association with him since the early years of the church.) Each letter is distinctive in terms of the situation addressed, rhetorical strategy employed, and specific theological content conveyed from within an overarching theological perspective. Seven of the thirteen are sufficiently similar to one another to be called the undisputed, or uncontested, letters, meaning that scholars almost universally agree that Paul authored them: Romans (the longest single letter), 1–2 Corinthians (the greatest amount of epistolary content sent to one community), Galatians, Philippians, 1 Thessalonians (probably the earliest letter, ca. 51), and Philemon.

To many scholars, the other six seem to reflect a situation, style, or substance that does not correspond to the historical Paul of the undisputed letters. These letters—2 Thessalonians, Colossians and Ephesians, and the Pastoral Epistles (1–2 Timothy, Titus)—may have been written by friends or disciples in Paul's name to adapt his teachings to new situations.

There is, however, ongoing debate about which letters, if any, are authored by someone other than Paul. Although this is not the place to discuss the question of authorship in depth, it is important to note that the notion of *authorship* in antiquity covered a broad range of practices, including the use of secretaries, who sometimes had considerable freedom.[12] Moreover, Paul's theology likely developed somewhat over time, and his pastoral approach varied from congregation to congregation. These factors, rather than non-Pauline authorship, may account for some of the unique features of the six contested letters.[13]

---

10. Bonhoeffer and King are well known. For the story of Lin Zhao, see the excellent biography by Lian Xi, *Blood Letters: The Untold Story of Lin Zhao, a Martyr in Mao's China* (New York: Basic Books, 2018).

11. For Paul's maternal dimension, see 1 Cor 3:1–3; Gal 4:18–19; 1 Thess 2:5–8.

12. My own view is that Paul is the author, in the broad sense of that word, of all the disputed letters except perhaps 1 Timothy and Titus.

13. For 1 Corinthians, Paul almost certainly employed a scribe, since he specifically says

PAUL'S THEOLOGY AND SPIRITUALITY

Paul understood his message—his "gospel," or good news—to be the power of God at work in the world for the salvation of all people (Rom 1:16–17, echoing 1 Cor 1:18–25). This gospel was in continuity with the good news promised and proclaimed by Israel's prophets, and then taught and embodied by Jesus. Paul's gospel—what he called "the gospel of God" (Rom 1:1; 15:16; 1 Thess 2:2, 8–9)—also stood in stark contrast to the Roman "gospel" of peace and salvation promised by the empire and proclaimed by those who perceived in Augustus and his successors the means to human flourishing.

The gospel Paul announced, which he paradoxically received both by divine revelation (Gal 1:11–12) and from those before him (1 Cor 15:3–4), focused on the crucifixion and resurrection of Jesus as being God's saving act of faithfulness to Israel and mercy to all, and this universal divine mission was evident in Paul's own missionary activity (see 1 Cor 9:19–23 and the narratives in Acts). Paul proclaimed this surprising gospel of a crucified Messiah (1 Cor 1:18–25) as God's apocalyptic (revelatory) and eschatological (end-time) act that brought about the prophetically promised new exodus, new covenant, new creation, and new age—the age of the Spirit.[14] Thus, N. T. Wright has rightly claimed that Paul's theology is a reconfiguration of Jewish theology in light of the Messiah and the Spirit.[15]

Scholars have debated how best to organize this theology; what, if anything, is at its center; and whether and how it developed over time. Here we will take a narrative approach, laying out the reshaped scriptural story of salvation Paul tells and how people are incorporated into it. Although Paul presents this story in the most cohesive way in Romans, it underlies and informs his other letters as well, not least 1 Corinthians. This is an important point, so we should dwell on it for a moment.

Writing to the Romans presented Paul with a unique challenge and opportunity: addressing a congregation he did not found and had never visited. This situation certainly accounts for the more systematic presentation we find in Romans.[16]

---

at the end of the letter, "I, Paul, write this greeting with my own hand" (16:21). In Romans, written from Corinth, Paul actually names his scribe, Tertius (Rom 16:22).

14. Paul does not frequently use the precise phrase "new . . . ," but it is nonetheless clear that he sees these prophetic visions fulfilled or inaugurated through Christ. For "new creation," see 2 Cor 5:17; Gal 6:15. For "new covenant," see 1 Cor 11:25; 2 Cor 3:6.

15. See N. T. Wright, *Paul: In Fresh Perspective* (Minneapolis: Fortress, 2005); *Paul and the Faithfulness of God* (Minneapolis: Fortress, 2013).

16. For more on Romans, see my *Romans: A Theological and Pastoral Commentary* (Grand Rapids: Eerdmans, 2022).

INTRODUCING PAUL

But we should not imagine that Paul suddenly began to think the things he says in Romans as he composed that letter, or that the (so-called) practical theology of 1 Corinthians became the (so-called) systematic theology of Romans during the relatively short period of time between the writing of the two letters. Rather, we should assume that much of Paul's theology was alive and well when he first evangelized and then wrote to the Corinthians, and that he actually shared much of that theology with them in person. We will have more to say about the intensely theological character of 1 Corinthians in the introduction to the letter.

As we consider the story Paul tells, it is critical to remember that he was not an armchair theologian; he was always concerned about the real-life implications of the gospel. In the words of Scot McKnight, "pastor Paul" had one main goal: forming communities of "Christoformity," or Christlikeness.[17] The gospel is something to obey, not just accept; to become (in the sense of embody), not just believe.[18] We should read, study, teach, and preach Paul's letters, including 1 Corinthians, today for the same purposes.

Human Condition, Divine Response

According to Paul the faithful Jew, the one true Creator God chose Israel to be the covenant people and thus the vehicle of divine blessing among the nations (gentiles). This God is an impartial judge who expects obedience from all people, whether through the law of Moses or through the unwritten law inscribed on human hearts (Rom 2:14–16). However, like the prophets, Paul believes that God finds Israel faithless and disobedient, and the gentiles idolatrous and immoral (Rom 1:18–3:20; 1 Cor 6:9–11). God has therefore promised to establish a new, effective covenant with Israel (Jer 31:31–34; cf. 1 Cor 11:25; 2 Cor. 3:6), and thus with and for all people, because Israel was called to be the source of blessing for all nations.

Paul characterizes the human condition as one marked by both sins (or transgressions) and Sin, a cosmic power that holds humanity captive (Rom 1:18–3:20). The two fundamental sins are failure to love, honor, and obey God (idolatry) and failure to love others (sexual immorality, injustice).[19] Not only gentiles but even God's people can succumb to these basic sins (e.g.,

---

17. See especially Scot McKnight, *Pastor Paul: Nurturing a Culture of Christoformity in the Church* (Grand Rapids: Baker Academic, 2019).

18. On becoming (embodying) the gospel, see my *Becoming the Gospel: Paul, Participation, and Mission* (Grand Rapids: Eerdmans, 2015).

19. See Rom 1:18–32; 1 Cor 6:1–20; 10:6–14.

1 Cor 10:1–22). Being under the power of Sin is like having an addiction that manifests itself in concrete acts. Without an intervention, the result is death, both a living death in the present and a future, permanent separation from God. Death itself, then, is also a power.

Human beings need a solution that deals with both problems: forgiveness for sins and liberation (redemption) from Sin—both an act of atonement and a new exodus. Only such a solution will restore people to full and abundant life (cf. John 10:10), to right covenant relations with God and others: love of God and love of neighbor. The law of Moses, despite its divine origin, cannot bring about this abundant life (Rom 3:20; 4:13; 5:12–21; 7:7–8:4; Gal 3:21).

In faithfulness to Israel and mercy to the gentiles, God has acted in righteousness, that is, with saving restorative justice, by sending Jesus the Jewish Messiah ("Son of God"), to effect salvation via his death and resurrection (known later, especially among Roman Catholics, as the "Paschal Mystery"—a wonderful term for all Christians).

The Death and Resurrection of Jesus

The death of Jesus the Messiah by crucifixion—Rome's most degrading and shameful form of capital punishment—has rich and varied meaning for Paul. We can think of it in terms of four Rs.

First of all, it is *revelatory*. It manifests the incarnate Son of God's faithful obedience to the Father and his freely chosen self-giving love for humanity (Rom 8:35–37; Phil 2:5–8; 2 Cor 5:14; Gal 2:20). It also discloses the Father's faithfulness and love, as well as God's counterintuitive and countercultural power and wisdom (Rom 5:1–11; 8:32, 39; 1 Cor 1:18–31). That is, the death of Jesus is both a Christophany (revelation of Christ) and a theophany (revelation of God).

Second, Jesus' death is *representative*. He dies as the faithful, obedient representative of God's covenant people and the single representative of all human beings. He is the second and last Adam, whose actions contrast with and counteract those of the first Adam (Rom 5:12–21; 1 Cor 15:21–22, 45–49). In his death, Jesus is the paradigmatic human, faithful to God and loving toward others. Moreover, Jesus dies not only as humanity's representative but also in their place and for their sins (Rom 5:8; 1 Cor 15:3; 2 Cor 5:14–15; Gal 1:4), fulfilling the role of Isaiah's suffering servant (Isa 52:13–53:12).

Third, Jesus' death is *redemptive*. Jesus died both to forgive sins and to liberate from the power of Sin (Rom 3:21–26; 1 Cor 6:20; 7:23). At the same time, as Paul knew from Scripture, it is the God of Israel who is the redeemer and liberator of the people of God. Jesus' death is ultimately an act of God.

INTRODUCING PAUL

Finally, Jesus' death, as an act of both God and God's Messiah, brings about human *reconciliation* with God (Rom 5:1–11; 2 Cor 5:11–21). In the Messiah's death, God has acted to restore humanity to that for which it was created: to right relations with God and others—to life! In doing so, God has kept the promise to Abraham that all the nations would be blessed through him (Gal 3:6–14). Above all, the death of Christ is God's act of amazing grace toward those who are God's enemies: sinful, rebellious people, unworthy of such love (Rom 5:1–11).

The death of Jesus is not a saving event, however, without his resurrection. The resurrection is God's act of vindicating and validating Jesus' death. Without it, Jesus is simply another crucified victim and would-be messiah whose death reveals Rome's victory, not God's. Without it, there is no forgiveness of sins, no eternal life, indeed no purpose to life other than hedonistic pleasure (1 Cor 15:12–34). Thus, the resurrection is more than a vindication and validation of the crucifixion, for the very purpose of the incarnation and the atonement was and is life—resurrection to new life.

Although Paul can resolve to know nothing but a crucified Messiah (1 Cor 2:2), he also wants everyone to recognize that the crucified Jesus is now the resurrected and exalted Lord who lives in and among his people by his Spirit, infusing his life into his body. At the same time, the exalted Lord always remains the crucified Jesus, whose resurrection power is, ironically, cruciform (cross-shaped). It is *that* kind of power that Jesus conveys to his people as the Lord: the power of humble love and self-giving service. The resurrection means that human beings can participate in the life of God manifested in Jesus the Son—both now and eternally.

Jesus as Lord and the Gift of the Spirit

When Paul speaks of Jesus as "Lord," which he understands as the most basic affirmation of faith in the gospel (Rom 10:9; 1 Cor 12:3; Phil 2:11), he once again means several things.

First, Jesus has been exalted to a position of participation in God's sovereignty, sharing the divine name, "Lord" (Gk. *kyrios*), and thus in the divine identity (Phil 2:9–11, interpreting Isa 45:23; 1 Cor 8:4–6). Second, Jesus is the one on whom people must call for salvation (Rom 10:5–13, interpreting Joel 2:32 [LXX 3:5]). Third, Jesus is worthy of obedience. To call on him and confess him as Lord means to pledge allegiance to him, to his way of faithfulness and love. Fourth, to name Jesus as Lord is to reject all other lords and gods and any participation in them (1 Cor 10:1–22). If Jesus is Lord, Caesar is not (as N. T. Wright has repeatedly put it), and neither is any other person or entity claiming rulership of the world, demanding ultimate devotion, or both. And finally, to affirm the lordship of Jesus is to allow the shape of his life to become the shape of ours.

God's action in the death, resurrection, and exaltation of the Lord Jesus is the climax in history of God's promises to Israel (2 Cor 1:20). In him (to repeat for emphasis), the new exodus, new covenant, new age, and new creation promised by the biblical prophets have been inaugurated, though in an utterly surprising way: via a crucified Messiah. Much Jewish thought at the time of Paul may be called *apocalyptic*, which is another term with many meanings. At the very least, however, it means that many Jews saw themselves as living in this age while anticipating the age to come. This age is characterized by sin, oppression, and injustice, while the age to come will be a time of righteousness, justice, and peace (Heb. *shalom*)—and these will be radically different from the righteousness, justice, and peace offered by the Roman Empire through its oppression and subjugation.

In Christ, Paul boldly claims, the new age has begun, but it is not yet here in its fullness. God's gift of the Holy Spirit—who is the Spirit of both the Father and the Son (Rom 8:9)—is at once the presence of God among the people of the Messiah and the guarantee of the fullness to come (2 Cor 1:22; 5:5; Eph 1:13–14). Scholars sometimes refer to this interim period, between Jesus' death/resurrection and his second coming (parousia, or "royal arrival/presence"), as the *overlap of the ages* (see 1 Cor 10:11). It is a time of *now but not yet*.

God's saving work will come to its ultimate conclusion, or telos, at the parousia (e.g., 1 Cor 1:7–8). This does not mean either the removal of the church from this world (as in the popular notion of the rapture) or the destruction of the world. Rather, the parousia signals a series of eschatological (end-time) events, including the resurrection of the dead, the final judgment, and the defeat of humanity's final enemy, Death (1 Cor 15:20–57; 1 Thess 4:13–18). It also signals the restoration of the entire cosmos to the wholeness intended by God (Rom 8:18–25; Col 1:15–20).

Human Response to the Gospel

We have thus far summarized Paul's understanding of God's redemptive action in the Messiah Jesus. Life comes to the spiritually dead only when there is a transformation—a resurrection, or revivification, as the prophet Ezekiel made clear (Ezek 37). But this grace and life do not convey automatically to human beings; there must be a response to the gospel of Christ crucified and raised.

For Paul (as today we say about real estate), location is everything. He understands humanity's sinful condition as being "in," or under the power of, Sin and thus being outside Christ and his sovereignty. When the gospel is proclaimed, the appropriate human response, enabled by God's grace, is twofold: faith and baptism. When faith and baptism occur, a person is brought from being outside Christ to being in Christ. Being "in Christ," Paul's basic term for what we would call being a Christian, means to be located within the resurrected Messiah by being in his body, the community or assembly of Christ-participants, and therefore under his lordship.[20]

In both faith and baptism (which probably occurred right after the public confession of faith), people begin a lifelong participation in Christ and his story by dying and rising with him (Gal 2:15–21; Rom 6:1–11). That is, to believe the gospel is to share existentially in God's saving act—Christ's death and resurrection, by which a person dies to an old way of life (which was, actually, a way of death) and is raised to new life. The four-part gospel Paul recounts in 1 Cor 15 (death, burial, resurrection, appearances) is a story into which believers are initiated, and it reflects the four-part story of Christ. (See comments on 1 Cor 15 in conjunction with Rom 6 in the commentary below.) Belief, then, entails participation in that saving event; participation entails devotion to Christ the Lord; and devotion entails obedience. Paul refers to all of this as the "obedience of faith" (Rom 1:5; 16:26), or what we might call believing allegiance.

Those who believe the gospel and are baptized into Christ the Lord (which means also into his body, the *ekklēsia*; 1 Cor 12) undergo a transformation—a metamorphosis—that Paul describes in many ways: they are, for instance, washed, justified, and sanctified (1 Cor 6:11). That is, they are forgiven of their sins (washed), restored to right covenant relations with God in the midst of God's people (justified), and set apart to live as part of God's covenant people (sanctified).

This is not a series of spiritual experiences but a unified act of God, who does the washing, justifying, and sanctifying. This transformation occurs, then, not by virtue of anyone's status or good deeds but only by God's grace and the response of faith described above (Rom 3:27–31; 4:1–25; Gal 2:15–21; Eph 2:1–10). Paul was fully aware of his own unworthiness and of God's mercy (1 Cor 15:8–10; Gal 1:11–16; 1 Tim 1:12–17)—and we should be too.

Believers, the faithful,[21] are now part of a new creation, remade for holy lives of righteousness, or godly justice (2 Cor 5:14–21). They (we!) are called

---

20. For more on the "in Christ" theme in Paul, see my article "In Christ," *DPL*[2] 476–82.

21. I will use these terms interchangeably, along with "Christ-participants," "Christ-followers," "Christians," and occasional longer descriptive phrases.

to leave behind idolatry, immorality, and injustice to experience the abundant life for which we were created. We are now in relationship with one God in three persons, as Christian theology would learn to say; we are, individually and corporately,

- children of God the Father (*Abba*; Rom 8:15; Gal 4:6; cf., e.g., 1 Cor 1:3; 8:6) and participants in the "church" or "assembly" (*ekklēsia*) of God (1 Cor 1:2; 10:32; 11:22; 15:9; 2 Cor 1:1; Gal 1:13);
- members of Christ and his body (1 Cor 6:15; 12:12–31; Rom 12:4–8) because the *ekklēsia* is the assembly of those "in Christ"; and
- the temple of the Holy Spirit (1 Cor 3:16–17; 6:19).

This relational matrix is one of many dimensions of Paul's early Trinitarian theology—the conviction that God exists as one being in three persons and that we relate to God as such (see also, e.g., 1 Cor 12:1–6; 2 Cor 13:13).[22]

The Holy Spirit supplies gifts for the *ekklēsia*'s common good (Rom 12:4–8; 1 Cor 12; Eph 4:7–16); produces "fruit," or Christlike virtues (Gal 5:16–26); and unites the community in faith, hope, and love (1 Cor 13:13; Gal 5:5–6; 1 Thess 1:3; 5:8) for faithful witness even in the face of opposition (e.g., Phil 1:3–2:18). The *ekklēsia* is a new family of brothers and sisters: male and female, enslaved and free, gentile and Jew (Gal 3:25–28). According to N. T. Wright, Paul "saw the church as a microcosmos, a little world, not simply as an alternative to the present one, an escapist's country cottage for those tired of city life, but as the prototype of what was to come . . . [when] the whole earth [would be filled] with his knowledge and glory, with his justice, peace and joy. Paul sees each *ekklēsia* as a sign of that future reality."[23]

Paul's Spirituality

Paul's spirituality, as we have already been seeing, is one of *participation* (location) and *transformation* (metamorphosis), both individual and corporate. In the words of Joshua Jipp, "the goal of human existence" is "sharing in the life of God," and Paul "was consumed with developing communities where persons-

---

22. Attention to the Trinity in Paul over the last two or three decades has mushroomed. For one approach, see Wesley Hill, *Paul and the Trinity: Persons, Relations, and the Pauline Letters* (Grand Rapids: Eerdmans, 2015). For references to some additional literature and to 1 Corinthians specifically, see my "Traces of the Trinity in 1 Corinthians," *Journal of Theological Interpretation* 15 (2021): 291–304.

23. Wright, *Paul and the Faithfulness of God*, 1492.

INTRODUCING PAUL

in-Christ could flourish in their shared lives with one another." [24] Those who have died with Christ and have been raised with him to new life are also inhabited by him, that is, by the Spirit—individually and corporately. *Spirit*uality means life in and with the Spirit. Such people may be called Spirit-ual.[25]

This is a relationship of *mutual indwelling*, or reciprocal residence: Christ/ the Spirit inhabits us, and we inhabit Christ/the Spirit. Those who move into Christ find that Christ has moved into them, so to speak. The situation is something like our relationship with the air/oxygen, which is both within and around us.[26] This reciprocal bond is true of both the *ekklēsia* as a community and each baptized individual (Gal 2:19–20; Rom 8:5–17). Paul refers to the resulting relationship in Greek as *koinōnia* with both the Lord and one another— participation, communion, partnership, solidarity (1 Cor 1:9; 10:16; Phil 1:5; 2:1; 3:10). This *koinōnia* should come to special expression at the Lord's Supper (1 Cor 10:16–22; 11:17–34; later called the Eucharist, "thanksgiving").

For Paul, the indwelling Christ is the one who lovingly gave himself on the cross. This means that Christ-filled individuals and communities will be characterized by a cross-shaped existence, or *cruciformity*. Cruciformity, which expresses the "mind of Christ" (Phil 2:5), means especially a life of self-giving love that looks out for the needs of others rather than oneself—precisely what Christ did in his incarnation and crucifixion (Phil 2:1–11). Because this cross-shaped life conforms to the story of Christ, it can be described as a *narrative* spirituality and a narrative form of participation. But because this is a *communal* rather than an individual spirituality, the gift of self to one another means that all benefit, all are cared for, all work together. Thus, for Paul the phrase "one another" is a critical dimension of his communal spirituality, a spirituality of "one anothering."[27]

---

24. See Joshua W. Jipp, *Pauline Theology as a Way of Life: A Vision of Human Flourishing in Christ* (Grand Rapids: Baker Academic, 2023), 1, 157.

25. Throughout this commentary I will often use the word "Spirit-ual" rather than "spiritual" to emphasize that Paul's theology and experience are not vaguely religious, otherworldly, or egocentrically interior but focused on the presence and power of God's Spirit.

26. The Greek word *pneuma* can signify both "breath" and "spirit." Another analogy is proposed by Matthew Thiessen: a sponge in a bucket of water, a situation in which the sponge is both soaked in and surrounded by the water (*A Jewish Paul: The Messiah's Herald to the Gentiles* [Grand Rapids: Baker Academic, 2023], 105–6).

27. See Rom 12:10, 16; 13:8; 14:13; 15:5, 7, 14; 16:16; 1 Cor 11:33; 12:25; 16:20; 2 Cor 13:11; Gal 5:13; 6:2; Eph 4:2, 25, 32; 5:21; Col 3:13, 16; 1 Thess 3:12; 4:9, 18; 5:11, 15; 2 Thess 1:3. Negative instances of improper "one anothering" are also listed: 1 Cor 6:7; 2 Cor 10:12; Gal 5:15, 26; Col 3:9; Titus 3:3.

Moreover, because the crucified Christ has been raised and indwells individuals and communities by virtue of the Spirit, cruciformity is, paradoxically, *resurrectional* and *charismatic*—infused with resurrection life and the power of the Spirit.[28] Resurrectional, charismatic cruciformity means that cross-shaped living embodies and passes on the transforming presence of God, by the action of the Holy Spirit, affecting both those who experience it firsthand and those with whom it is shared in community and in ministry to the world. The result is increased Christlikeness in every dimension of life.[29]

This transformation of thought and action, of mind and body (Rom 12:1–2) into Christlikeness is possible, then, only by the activity of the Holy Spirit (Gal 5:13–26; 2 Cor 3:17–18) and only in a community of mutual instruction and care. Paul refers to all believers as "saints" or "holy ones" (depending on the Bible translation; see, e.g., 1 Cor 1:2). His goal is for each individual and community in Christ to become holy (conformed to Christ) in anticipation of the final judgment (1 Thess 3:13; 5:23; 1 Cor 1:8).

Holiness, then, is not reserved for a special class of saints but is for all. It means being set apart for God's purposes and taking on God's character. Holiness is therefore the lifestyle of an alternative culture to that of the dominant culture (for Paul, the culture of Rome; for us, the dominant culture of the United States or wherever we live), the culture of those who do not know God (1 Thess 4:5). Holiness means knowing Christ by sharing both in his death and in the power of his resurrection (Phil 3:10–14), thus participating in, and extending, God's saving mission in Christlike ways.

Conclusion

As an apostle, Paul was simultaneously a community founder, a pastor, a father-mother figure, a spiritual guide or director, and a theologian—a pastoral theologian. At the end, moreover, he was probably a martyr who died at Rome in the 60s. In death as in life, his motto was, to paraphrase Phil 3:8–10,

---

28. One could also use the descriptor "pneumatic" (related to the Greek word *pneuma*, Spirit) instead of "charismatic."

29. On cruciformity, see the brief discussion in the preface above and my article "Cruciformity," *DPL*[2] 218–19. For more detail, see my book-length treatment: *Cruciformity: Paul's Narrative Spirituality of the Cross*, 20th anniversary ed. (Grand Rapids: Eerdmans, 2021). For emphasis on the resurrectional character of cruciformity, see my *Participating in Christ: Explorations in Paul's Theology and Spirituality* (Grand Rapids: Baker Academic, 2019), esp. 53–76.

"I want to know Christ and be found in him." It is a motto for all times and places, for all followers of Jesus.

Some people have thought and taught that there is a great difference between Paul and Jesus. The late eminent New Testament scholar James D. G. Dunn rightly contended for just the opposite: "Should we then speak of a gulf between Jesus and Paul? No! Should we deduce that Paul departed from or corrupted the good news which Jesus brought? No! Should we conclude that Paul transformed Jesus' message into something Jesus himself would not have recognized? No! . . . Paul, who may never have heard or seen Jesus for himself, nevertheless can be characterized as *one of the truest disciples of Jesus*, not simply of the exalted Lord Jesus Christ, but also of Jesus of Nazareth."[30]

Reflections and Questions for the Introduction to Paul

Spiritual, Pastoral, Missional, and Theological Reflections

1. Paul was **simultaneously a pastor, a spiritual guide or director, and a theologian (and more).** This multifaceted ministerial identity is worthy of study for those who fulfill any of those roles today, when the vocational complexity we see in Paul is often fragmented. He was also, obviously, a deeply spiritual (Spirit-ual) person who saw his life and ministry as an offering to God, in Christ, enabled by the Spirit.

2. As a pastor and pastoral theologian, Paul is worthy of study because he carefully **addresses the concrete needs** of the communities to which he writes with the promises and demands of the gospel.

3. As a spiritual guide or director, Paul is worthy of study inasmuch as his goal is the **transformation and formation of individuals and communities** into the likeness of the faithful and loving Messiah Jesus. This individual and community transformation both requires and produces a community life of "one anothering," for Paul is not a Western individualist.

4. As a (pastoral) theologian, Paul is worthy of study with respect to his being **both faithful to Scripture and creative** in interpreting it in light of the coming, death, and resurrection of Jesus—and applying that interpretation with contextual sensitivity to a variety of situations.

5. As a (missional) theologian and practitioner, Paul invites the communities he addresses **not merely to believe the gospel but to become (embody) the gospel and thus to advance the gospel.**

30. James D. G. Dunn, *Jesus, Paul, and the Gospels* (Grand Rapids: Eerdmans, 2011), 115.

6. As a Christian, Paul is worthy of study because of his **profound sense of being in Christ and having Christ within**, which means a life guided by the Spirit in daily worship of God and participation in God's mission, not as a lone ranger, but as part of the body of Christ.

7. The term **"resurrectional, charismatic cruciformity"** denotes the inseparability of cross and resurrection, and of cross and Spirit, that permeates Paul's letters, not least 1 Corinthians.

Questions for Those Who Read, Teach, and Preach

1. With which big ideas has Paul been associated in your experience and, as far as you know, in the history of the church? Are they similar to or different from those discussed in this introduction? What presuppositions about Paul do you (or do those to whom you minister through teaching or preaching) bring to the study of Paul and of 1 Corinthians?

2. What new information or perspectives about Paul did this introduction provide? How did you react to some of these? If you preach or teach, what challenges might you face in talking about these (or other) perspectives on the apostle offered here?

3. What is the historical and theological importance of understanding Paul's transformative experience as an appearance of Jesus? As a call and commission? As a conversion?

4. Which aspects of Paul's theology and spirituality/Spirit-uality do you find to be particularly significant in your context?

FOR FURTHER READING

Highly Accessible Books

Barclay, John M. G. *Paul: A Very Brief History*. London: SPCK, 2017.

———. *Paul and the Subversive Power of Grace*. Cambridge: Grove Books, 2016.

Barnett, Paul. *A Short Book about Paul: The Servant of Jesus*. Eugene, OR: Cascade, 2019.

Bird, Michael F. *Introducing Paul: The Man, His Mission and His Message*. Downers Grove, IL: IVP Academic, 2008.

Burnett, Gary W. *Paul Distilled*. Eugene, OR: Wipf & Stock, 2021.

deSilva, David. *Transformation: The Heart of Paul's Gospel*. Bellingham, WA: Lexham, 2014.

Fee, Gordon D. *Paul, the Spirit, and the People of God*. Grand Rapids: Baker Academic, 2023 (orig. Peabody, MA: Hendrickson, 1996).

Gorman, Michael J. *Participation: Paul's Vision of Life in Christ*. Cambridge: Grove Books, 2018.

———. *Reading Paul*. Eugene, OR: Cascade, 2008.

Kirk, J. R. Daniel. *Jesus Have I Loved, but Paul? A Narrative Approach to the Problem of Pauline Christianity*. Grand Rapids: Baker Academic, 2011.

Macaskill, Grant. *Living in Union with Christ: Paul's Gospel and Christian Moral Identity*. Grand Rapids: Baker Academic, 2019.

Matera, Frank. *The Spirituality of Saint Paul: A Call to Imitation*. New York: Paulist, 2017.

Thiessen, Matthew. *A Jewish Paul: The Messiah's Herald to the Gentiles*. Grand Rapids: Baker Academic, 2023.

Witherup, Ronald D. *101 Questions and Answers on Paul*. Mahwah, NJ: Paulist, 2003.

Wright, N. T. *Paul: A Biography*. New York: HarperCollins, 2018.

Midlevel Books

Barclay, John M. G. *Paul and the Power of Grace*. Grand Rapids: Eerdmans, 2020.

Bowens, Lisa M. *African American Readings of Paul: Reception, Resistance, and Transformation*. Grand Rapids: Eerdmans, 2020.

Burroughs, Presian R., ed. *Practicing with Paul: Reflections on Paul and the Practice of Ministry in Honor of Susan G. Eastman*. Eugene, OR: Cascade, 2018.

Byrne, Brendan. *Words of Faith: A Vocabulary of the Epistles of Paul*. Mahwah, NJ: Paulist, 2023.

Campbell, Constantine R. *Reading Paul as Christian Scripture: A Literary, Canonical, and Theological Introduction*. Grand Rapids: Baker Academic, 2024.

Campbell, Douglas A. *Paul: An Apostle's Journey*. Grand Rapids: Eerdmans, 2018.

———. *Pauline Dogmatics: The Triumph of God's Love*. Grand Rapids: Eerdmans, 2020.

Dunn, James D. G. *Jesus, Paul, and the Gospels*. Grand Rapids: Eerdmans, 2011.

Eastman, Susan Grove. *Oneself in Another: Participation and Personhood in Pauline Theology*. Eugene, OR: Cascade, 2023.

Fredriksen, Paula. *Paul: The Pagans' Apostle*. New Haven: Yale University Press, 2017.

Gorman, Michael J. *Apostle of the Crucified Lord: A Theological Introduction to Paul and His Letters*. 2nd ed. Grand Rapids: Eerdmans, 2017 (orig. 2004).

———. *Becoming the Gospel: Paul, Participation, and Mission*. Grand Rapids: Eerdmans, 2015.

———. *Cruciformity: Paul's Narrative Spirituality of the Cross*. 20th anniversary ed. Grand Rapids: Eerdmans, 2021.

Heilig, Christoph. *Paul the Storyteller: A Narratological Approach*. Grand Rapids: Eerdmans, 2024.

For Further Reading

Hill, Wesley. *Paul and the Trinity: Persons, Relations, and the Pauline Letters.* Grand Rapids: Eerdmans, 2015.

Hogan, Laura Reece. *I Live, No Longer I: Paul's Spirituality of Suffering, Transformation, and Joy.* Eugene, OR: Wipf & Stock, 2017.

Jipp, Joshua W. *Pauline Theology as a Way of Life: A Vision of Human Flourishing in Christ.* Grand Rapids: Baker Academic, 2023.

Legrand, Lucien. *Paul and Mission.* Maryknoll, NY: Orbis Books, 2023.

Longenecker, Bruce W., ed. *The New Cambridge Companion to St. Paul.* New York: Cambridge University Press, 2020.

Longenecker, Bruce W., and Todd D. Still. *Thinking through Paul: A Survey of His Life, Letters, and Theology.* Grand Rapids: Zondervan, 2014.

Matera, Frank J. *God's Saving Grace: A Pauline Theology.* Grand Rapids: Eerdmans, 2012.

McKnight, Scot. *Pastor Paul: Nurturing a Culture of Christoformity in the Church.* Grand Rapids: Baker Academic, 2019.

McKnight, Scot, Lynn Cohick, and Nijay K. Gupta, eds. *Dictionary of Paul and His Letters.* 2nd ed. Downers Grove, IL: IVP Academic, 2023.

McKnight, Scot, and B. J. Oropeza. *Perspectives on Paul: Five Views.* Grand Rapids: Baker Academic, 2020.

Moo, Douglas J. *A Theology of Paul and His Letters: The Gift of the New Realm in Christ.* Grand Rapids: Zondervan Academic, 2021.

Murphy-O'Connor, Jerome. *Paul: His Story.* New York: Oxford University Press, 2004.

Pitre, Brant, Michael P. Barber, and John A. Kincaid. *Paul, A New Covenant Jew: Rethinking Pauline Theology.* Grand Rapids: Eerdmans, 2019.

Prothro, James B. *The Apostle Paul and His Letters: An Introduction.* Washington, DC: Catholic University of America Press, 2021.

Reeves, Rodney. *Spirituality according to Paul: Imitating the Apostle of Christ.* Downers Grove, IL: InterVarsity Press, 2011.

Sanders, E. P. *Paul: The Apostle's Life, Letters, and Thought.* Minneapolis: Fortress, 2015.

Thompson, James W. *Pastoral Ministry according to Paul: A Biblical Vision.* Grand Rapids: Baker Academic, 2006.

Westerholm, Stephen, ed. *The Blackwell Companion to Paul.* Malden, MA: Blackwell, 2011.

Works, Carla Swafford. *The Least of These: Paul and the Marginalized.* Grand Rapids: Eerdmans, 2020.

Wright, N. T. *Paul: In Fresh Perspective.* Minneapolis: Fortress, 2005.

INTRODUCING PAUL

More Technical Works

Barclay, John M. G. *Paul and the Gift*. Grand Rapids: Eerdmans, 2015.

Campbell, Douglas A. *The Deliverance of God: An Apocalyptic Rereading of Justification*. Grand Rapids: Eerdmans, 2009.

Carr, Frederick David. *Being and Becoming: Human Transformation in the Letters of Paul*. Waco, TX: Baylor University Press, 2022.

Dunn, James D. G. *The Theology of Paul the Apostle*. Grand Rapids: Eerdmans, 1998.

Eastman, Susan Grove. *Paul and the Person: Reframing Paul's Anthropology*. Grand Rapids: Eerdmans, 2017.

Evans, Craig A., and Aaron W. White, eds. *Who Created Christianity? Fresh Approaches to the Relationship between Paul and Jesus*. Peabody, MA: Hendrickson, 2020.

Gorman, Michael J. *Inhabiting the Cruciform God: Kenosis, Justification, and Theosis in Paul's Narrative Soteriology*. Grand Rapids: Eerdmans, 2009.

———. *Participating in Christ: Explorations in Paul's Theology and Spirituality*. Grand Rapids: Baker Academic, 2019.

Gupta, Nijay K., Erin M. Heim, and Scot McKnight, eds. *The State of Pauline Studies: A Survey of Recent Research*. Grand Rapids: Baker Academic, 2024.

Hays, Richard B. *Echoes of Scripture in the Letters of Paul*. New Haven: Yale University Press, 1989.

Johnson, Luke Timothy. *Constructing Paul*. Vol. 1 of *The Canonical Paul*. Grand Rapids: Eerdmans, 2020.

———. *Interpreting Paul*. Vol. 2 of *The Canonical Paul*. Grand Rapids: Eerdmans, 2021.

Novenson, Matthew Y., and R. Barry Matlock. eds. *The Oxford Handbook of Pauline Studies*. Oxford: Oxford University Press, 2022.

Schnelle, Udo. *Apostle Paul: His Life and Theology*. Translated by M. Eugene Boring. Grand Rapids: Baker Academic, 2005.

Thate, Michael J., Kevin J. Vanhoozer, and Constantine R. Campbell, eds. *"In Christ" in Paul: Explorations in Paul's Theology of Union and Participation*. Grand Rapids: Eerdmans, 2018.

Thompson, James W. *Apostle of Persuasion: Theology and Rhetoric in the Pauline Letters*. Grand Rapids: Baker Academic, 2020.

Tilling, Chris. *Paul's Divine Christology*. Grand Rapids: Eerdmans, 2015.

Wright, N. T. *Paul and the Faithfulness of God*. Minneapolis: Fortress, 2013.

Introducing the Commentary

According to its subtitle, this volume is "a theological, pastoral, and missional commentary." What exactly does that mean? A few words to supplement those in the preface (to which the reader is referred) are in order.

Echoing Karl Barth, Beverly Gaventa claims that a theological reading is a reading for the subject: that is, God—and, we should add, all things in relation to God.[1] Richard Hays maintains that it is reading "with eyes of faith."[2] "Theological exegesis," he writes, "is not a 'method.' It is not a set of discrete procedures that could be set alongside, say, textual criticism or redaction criticism. Rather, theological exegesis is a complex practice, a way of approaching Scripture with eyes of faith and seeking to understand it within the community of faith."[3] Theological interpreters read the Bible as *Scripture*, as divine address and as divine instrument (2 Tim 3:16). Scripture is therefore a critical tool by which the Spirit "pulls us" into the life of the triune God,[4] both individually and corporately.[5]

Theological interpretation does not neglect historical and literary matters—not at all. But a theological commentary makes theological interests

---

1. See Beverly Roberts Gaventa, "Reading for the Subject: The Paradox of Power in Romans 14:1–15:6," *Journal of Theological Interpretation* 5 (2011): 1–12.

2. Richard B. Hays, "Reading the Bible with Eyes of Faith: The Practice of Theological Exegesis," *Journal of Theological Interpretation* 1 (2007): 5–21 (reprinted in his *Reading with the Grain of Scripture* [Grand Rapids: Eerdmans, 2020], 29–46).

3. Hays, "Reading the Bible," 11. Hays then offers twelve "identifying marks" of theological exegesis (11–15), many of which are echoed in my *Elements of Biblical Exegesis: A Basic Guide for Students and Ministers*, 3rd ed. (Grand Rapids: Baker Academic, 2020), 163–70.

4. Joel B. Green, *Seized by Truth: Reading the Bible as Scripture* (Nashville: Abingdon, 2007), 97.

5. See, e.g., Joel B. Green, *Why Salvation?* (Nashville: Abingdon, 2013), 11.

INTRODUCING THE COMMENTARY

primary, with historical, literary, and rhetorical concerns being, not ends in themselves, but means to the end of having a *theological* focus because exegesis is a *theological* discipline. A theological commentary is, therefore, not afraid of theological terms like "Trinity" and "Christian" and "theosis"; they are not anachronistic concepts, even if the terms that name them are not present, or not present in abundance, in the New Testament writings.[6]

A theological commentary does not see the theological traditions or creeds or practices of the church as hindering interpretation but—when used carefully—as aids to interpretation. This is the case because the tradition has been informed and formed by Scripture, such that there is a natural dialogical relationship between Scripture and theology, between Scripture and tradition, including the Christian creed(s).

Theological interpretation means reading with and for the church, which in turn means having a focus, not merely on ideas but on real life: the church's life together and its mission in the world. As for "pastoral," then, this word is a corollary to "theological." A theological commentary ought to address the needs of pastors and others in the church who preach and teach, and to bring out the contemporary significance of 1 Corinthians. Thus this commentary will include reflections on the meaning of the text in dialogue not only with biblical scholars but also with pastors, theologians, and others who contribute to the thought and the life of the church.

"Pastoral" therefore also means that both 1 Corinthians and this commentary are engaging in a pastoral activity: attempting to form a body of people called the church into a more faithful likeness of Christ in its spiritual and liturgical (worship) life together and in the world. Thus a pastoral commentary is, ultimately, for all the faithful, not only for those labeled "pastors."

So too with the term "missional." It does not refer exclusively, or even primarily, to those understood to be Christian missionaries or mission workers. If Scripture is an instrument by which the Spirit seeks to draw all people more deeply into the life of the triune God, it is also an instrument of the Spirit's sending God's people out. As we are pulled into the life of the God who is by nature missional, we are prepared to be dispatched into the world that God loved and loves. In other words, theological interpretation includes missional

---

6. In the words of Mikhail M. Bakhtin: "Semantic phenomena can exist in concealed form, potentially, and be revealed only in semantic cultural contexts of subsequent epochs that are favorable for such disclosure" ("Response to a Question from the Novy Mir Editorial Staff," in *Speech Genres and Other Late Essays*, ed. Caryl Emerson and Michael Holquist, trans. Vern W. McGee [Austin: University of Texas Press, 1986], 5).

Introducing the Commentary

interpretation, or missional hermeneutics—reading Scripture to discern and embody God's purposes in the world—the *missio Dei*.[7]

With respect to 1 Corinthians, the conviction that a theological-pastoral-missional approach is appropriate is a natural outgrowth of the view that this letter was, and is, itself a theological-pastoral-missional document. This view will guide our introduction to the letter, and the commentary on it.

7. See further my *Elements of Biblical Exegesis*, 170–76. The Latin phrase *missio Dei*, meaning "the mission of God," is commonly used to situate Christian mission within the activity of God.

Introducing 1 Corinthians

The great New Testament scholar Raymond Brown claimed that if one has time for in-depth study of just a single Pauline letter, it should be not Romans but 1 Corinthians.[1] This is quite a claim, since Romans is arguably—as I have suggested in my commentary on that letter—the most influential letter ever written, not only within Christianity but of all time and any place.[2] Moreover, according to many readers and interpreters of Paul's letter to the Romans, it is full of profound, universal Christian theology about the nature of sin, justification, the work of the Spirit, the place of Israel in God's plan, life in the Christian community, and so much more.

In comparison, 1 Corinthians can look like an annotated laundry list of responses to particular practical problems (division, sexual practices, worship wars, etc.) in one first-century church. Already in an early commentary on the letter, Ambrosiaster in the late fourth century begins by listing ten reasons Paul wrote 1 Corinthians, stopping after reviewing only chapters 1–7. "The other reasons," he adds, "will be brought to light in the body of the commentary."[3] These reasons are, of course, to address all the many issues at Corinth.

No one would say such a letter would be without value, since there are parallels to those ancient problems in the contemporary world. The letter is perhaps Paul's most practical and contemporary letter, which is why Raymond Brown commended it. In fact, it can be argued that those who interpret 1 Co-

1. Raymond E. Brown, *An Introduction to the New Testament* (New York: Doubleday, 1997), 511.

2. See Michael J. Gorman, *Romans: A Theological and Pastoral Commentary* (Grand Rapids: Eerdmans, 2022), 21–22.

3. Cited in Judith L. Kovacs, trans. and ed., *1 Corinthians: Interpreted by Early Christian Commentators*, Church's Bible (Grand Rapids: Eerdmans, 2005), 8–9.

rinthians today are preaching to modern (or postmodern) Corinthians.[4] But the original problems did not, and the analogous modern situations do not, necessarily generate great theological reflection. Or at least that's what many people seem to think about 1 Corinthians.

THE COMPLEX CHARACTER OF 1 CORINTHIANS

But nothing could be further from the truth. First Corinthians is a *pastoral* text with profound *theological* significance, a sort of mirror image of Romans, the *theological* text with profound *pastoral* significance. In fact, 1 Corinthians demonstrates the truth that difficulties and even dissensions in the church can generate great theological reflection and lasting theological insight. The rest of the introduction seeks to unpack this claim in some depth.

1 Corinthians as a Theological Text

The Corinthian community was Paul's problem child. The believers in Corinth managed to misunderstand just about everything Paul said and did, to their own detriment and Paul's utter astonishment. By the time Paul wrote the letter we call 1 Corinthians, the Corinthian church (or churches/assemblies, as there were almost certainly several small communities in Corinth) was, from the apostle's perspective, in utter chaos. In this letter, we have more (relatively) clear windows into an early Christian community than in any other New Testament writing. Although the letter does seem like a laundry list of problems and responses, the problems are the presenting symptoms of a more significant disease. (And it is worth noting, with Susan Eastman, that the laundry list comes from the Corinthians, not Paul, who diagnoses the disease.)[5]

The Fundamental Issue: The Cross (Christ Crucified) and the Spirit

What had infected the Corinthians was, most obviously, a divisiveness based on social and spiritual status. But even that was symptomatic of a much more fundamental problem: a failure to understand the real-life consequences of the gospel of "Jesus the Messiah—that is, Jesus the *crucified* Messiah" (1 Cor 2:2 MJG). Paul's goal became to convince the Corinthians to embody

---

4. See Fred B. Craddock, "Preaching to Corinthians," *Interpretation* 44 (1990): 158–68.

5. Susan Grove Eastman, *Oneself in Another: Participation and Personhood in Pauline Theology* (Eugene, OR: Cascade, 2023), 108.

the cross—that is, Christ crucified—in daily life in light of the past resurrection and soon return of their crucified Lord, and in the power of the Spirit whom they had come to know and love but misunderstand.[6] The fundamental Corinthian problem, in the words of Yung Suk Kim, was their "failure to embody Christ crucified."[7] The Corinthians are not cross-shaped, or cruciform.

It is not the case that Paul had never before thought about the implications of a crucified but living Messiah for life "in" that Messiah; Galatians, almost certainly written before 1 Corinthians, shows evidence of just those sorts of theological and spiritual connections (e.g., Gal 2:19–20). But Galatians deals fundamentally with only one difficult, divisive subject: whether gentile Christ-participants need to be circumcised and, if not (so Paul), how the Spirit of the crucified and resurrected Messiah addresses all the concerns that those promoting circumcision would have had.

The situation at Corinth was both similar to and different from the Galatian crisis. Paul's goal was once again connected to the basic question of practical Christian living, of spirituality (life in the Spirit), but now addressed to a much more complex and multidimensional situation. Paul raises the question of how one can know the presence of the Spirit of God (who is also, according to Paul, the Spirit of Christ) in a community or individual.[8] What exactly does it mean, in all the complicated aspects of the rough-and-tumble of daily life together, for individuals and communities to be in Christ, to be filled with the Spirit—*his* Spirit? After all, the Spirit is the sign of the new creation, as Paul had already said in Galatians, and of the new covenant, as he will make clear in his correspondence with the Corinthians.[9]

This question about the Spirit is central to both canonical letters to the Corinthians that have been preserved. In 1 Corinthians, the burning question seems to be a general one: "What does the multifaceted life of a Spirit-filled *community* look like?"—with some attention to the nature of apostolic ministry supplementing, and inextricably connected to, the focus on the community. In 2 Corinthians, the more specific critical issue appears to be this question:

6. Throughout this commentary, "the cross" often means "Christ crucified," as it did for Paul: "the word of the cross" (1:18 RSV).

7. Yung Suk Kim, *Christ's Body in Corinth: The Politics of a Metaphor* (Minneapolis: Fortress, 2008), 76.

8. For the Spirit specifically as the Spirit of Christ according to Paul, see Rom 8:9; Gal 4:6; Phil 1:19. Cf. Acts 16:7; 1 Pet 1:11.

9. For "new creation," see Gal 6:15; 2 Cor 5:17; for "new covenant," see 1 Cor 11:25; 2 Cor 3:6. Although the term "new covenant" does not appear in Galatians, it is clear that Paul is speaking of the new covenant anticipated by the prophets in that letter too.

What does the ministry of a Spirit-filled *apostle* look like?—with implications for all believers.[10]

In other words, 1 Corinthians is at least a letter about Christology (the theology of the person and work of Christ), pneumatology (the theology of the person and work of the Spirit), ecclesiology (the theology of the church, including the theology of ministry), and of course Christian spirituality, or Spirit-uality (the shape of Christian life in relationship to God and others).[11] Paul's primary theological and pastoral agenda is clear: *he wishes the Corinthians to become a resurrectionally cruciform charismatic community: a Spirit-filled church in the shape of Christ's cross.*

From Paul's perspective, the gap between the inspiring Spirit of the *resurrected* Messiah and the historical and ongoing reality of the *crucified* Messiah at Corinth had to be closed, and the two essentially merged. Resurrectional, charismatic cruciformity entails being empowered by the Spirit of the resurrected Christ to be shaped in the self-giving form of the crucified Christ.[12] This is because the resurrected, living Christ and the crucified Christ are one and the same; the cross is "the signature of the one who is risen."[13] The cross-shaped life is, therefore (paradoxically), the life of the resurrected, living Christ. Both aspects of this reality are present in the phrase "living sacrifice" (Rom 12:1).

Cruciformity is not a form of masochism; it is not a form of heroic self-sacrifice for the sake of self-sacrifice. Rather, this cross-shaped but life-giving

---

10. Interestingly, Thomas Aquinas (*Commentary on the First Letter of Saint Paul to the Corinthians*, Biblical Commentaries 38 [Green Bay: Aquinas Institute, 2012], prologue 2) thinks Romans is about grace, which "works in the seven sacraments"; 1 Corinthians is about those sacraments (especially baptism, matrimony, and Eucharist; C1, L2, para. 19), and 2 Corinthians is about the "ministers of the sacraments." Aquinas sees the discussion of the sacraments in 1 Corinthians ending in ch. 11, while ch. 12 begins Paul's discussion "about things pertaining to the reality signified in the sacraments," particularly grace and the (future) glory of the resurrection. The former (grace) is "contained" and "conferred" by the sacraments, but the latter (glory) is "signified" but not "contained" (C12, L1, para. 709).

11. This commentary sometimes uses the words "Spirit-ual" and "Spirit-uality," instead of "spiritual" and "spirituality" to stress what Paul stresses: the Spirit of God.

12. As indicated in the preface to this commentary, I sometimes use the word "charismatic," as here, not in reference to charismatic gifts or manifestations but simply to mean empowered by God's gracious Holy Spirit.

13. Ernst Käsemann, "The Saving Significance of the Death of Jesus in Paul," in *Perspectives on Paul*, trans. Margaret Kohl (Philadelphia: Fortress, 1971; repr., Mifflintown, PA: Sigler, 1996), 32–59 (here 56).

existence is the most fundamental work of the Spirit in individual believers and in the Christian community. Such a life is a major part of what it means to be a *charismatic* community—not just a community specializing in the gifts of the Spirit but one experiencing the cross-shaped work of that same Spirit: Christlike love in action. But the Corinthians, or at least many of them, did not grasp this theological truth and its practical implications.[14]

Ecclesial Identity: Ongoing Conversion and the Marks of the Church

But there is more—much more. First Corinthians has been described as a letter about social identity.[15] This is both insightful and correct, but it is also insufficient from a theological perspective. Theologically speaking, 1 Corinthians is a letter about *corporate conversion* in the sense of ongoing conversion, or sanctification.[16] More specifically, the letter gives concrete shape to the general exhortation that the Corinthians become a resurrectionally cruciform charismatic community. Theologically speaking, *1 Corinthians is especially a letter about the marks of the church*—its theological and spiritual identity.

In much of the Christian tradition, the Niceno-Constantinopolitan Creed (often called simply the Nicene Creed)[17] expresses the essential characteristics of the church in the words "one, holy, catholic, and apostolic."[18] Paul, of

14. For more on resurrectional cruciformity, see my *Participating in Christ: Explorations in Paul's Theology and Spirituality* (Grand Rapids: Baker Academic, 2019), esp. 53–76.

15. See, e.g., the work of J. Brian Tucker: *"You Belong to Christ": Paul and the Formation of Social Identity in 1 Corinthians 1–4* (Eugene, OR: Pickwick, 2010); *"Remain in Your Calling": Paul and the Continuation of Social Identities in 1 Corinthians* (Eugene, OR: Pickwick, 2011).

16. Brian Tucker, among some other practitioners of social identity theory and similar sociological approaches, would agree with this. See also, e.g., Stephen J. Chester, *Conversion at Corinth: Perspectives on Conversion in Paul's Theology and the Corinthian Church* (London: T&T Clark, 2003).

17. The precise origins of this creed are the subject of debate, but the text arises from the Council of Nicaea (325), supplemented by the Council of Constantinople (381), the first two ecumenical councils of the Christian church.

18. Even noncreedal Christians and churches should recognize these four qualities as faithful to the biblical text as a whole and thus appropriate for Christian theology. At the same time, there is no consensus among theologians and missiologists about precisely what these four marks do mean, or should mean. This commentary can hardly address that metaissue, but it can attempt to discern what Paul might have to offer on the question as he writes to the Corinthians. One other commentator on the letter, Pheme Perkins, also notes, briefly, that the letter addresses these four traditional, creedal marks of the church: *First Corinthians*, Paideia Commentaries on the New Testament (Grand Rapids: Baker Academic, 2012), 46–47. No one to my knowledge, however, has previously used these marks to guide the interpretation of the letter. For my earlier work from this perspective,

course, did not know this creed from later centuries, but he did desire that the *ekklēsia*—the assembly, or congregation, or church—at Corinth be

- *unified* by the one Spirit in the one Lord before the one Father;
- *holy*, in the sense of being an altercultural community with values and practices distinct from the world (the host culture) and yet one engaged with the world;
- *catholic*, both (1) in the sense of welcoming people of differing degrees of faith, ethnicities, genders, socioeconomic positions, and spiritual (Spirit-ual) gifts *and* (2) in the sense of being connected to a larger, global body;[19] and
- *apostolic*, or missionally oriented, both in imitation of Paul's Christlike love and in adherence to the apostolic faith he delivered to them, which means being absolutely Christocentric, for Christ is "the whole of the gospel," in the words of John Flett.[20]

In the letter (and thus in this commentary), each and all of these marks will be related to the overarching goal of the letter: the formation of a resurrectionally cruciform charismatic community. We will have much more to say about these marks later in this introduction, but for now, the main point is this: 1 Corinthians is a letter of profound, as well as practical, theology. This is because Paul was a practical, or pastoral, theologian. Both aspects of this characterization—the practical/pastoral and the theological—must be taken seriously when we read his letters.

In fact, this description of Paul is no more or less true with respect to 1 Corinthians than it is with respect to Romans. That Paul himself sees 1 Corinthians as serious theology is clear from his repurposing of aspects of it in the (allegedly) more theological Romans.[21] Furthermore, the number of theological topics that Paul explores in at least some depth in 1 Corinthians is rather stunning:[22]

---

see the essay "First Corinthians and the Marks of God's *Ekklēsia*: One, Holy, Catholic, and Apostolic," in *One God, One People, One Future: Essays in Honor of N. T. Wright*, ed. John Dunne and Eric Lewellen (London: SPCK; Minneapolis: Fortress, 2018), 167–90.

19. "Catholic" in the first sense does not mean inclusive without boundaries, a meaning that would contradict the mark of holiness, as texts like 1 Cor 5:1–13 make very clear.

20. John G. Flett, *Apostolicity: The Ecumenical Question in World Christian Perspective* (Downers Grove, IL: InterVarsity Press, 2016), 303.

21. For instance, the principles established in 1 Cor 8:1–11:1 are adjusted for a new situation discussed in Rom 14:1–15:13. Furthermore, the image of the variously gifted body of Christ in 1 Cor 12 and the poem to love in 1 Cor 13 reappear in abbreviated form, in the same sequence, in Rom 12:3–10.

22. After the first four bulleted topics, this list follows the letter as it unfolds.

INTRODUCING 1 CORINTHIANS

- unity
- holiness/sanctification
- catholicity
- apostolicity/mission
- ecclesiology (the church)
- eschatology (last things)
- the parousia (second coming)
- baptism
- Christology
- the cross
- cruciformity
- divine attributes
- power
- wisdom
- preferential option for the poor and weak/powerless
- the Holy Spirit
- the cross and the Spirit
- Christian maturity
- divine revelation
- ministry
- eschatological judgment
- excommunication
- soteriology (salvation)
- the Trinity
- justice
- ecclesial jurisprudence (church "law")
- conversion
- the human body
- sexuality
- marriage
- divorce
- celibacy
- vocation
- rights
- freedom
- freedom and love
- freedom and responsibility
- ministry and rights
- ministry and accommodation

- idolatry
- communion
- the Lord's Supper/Eucharist
- women and men/wives and husbands
- worship
- hospitality
- spiritual (Spirit-ual) gifts
- unity and diversity
- love
- the beatific vision
- the gospel
- Christ's resurrection
- the resurrection of the dead

Some interpreters have attempted to summarize or synthesize these various theological threads. Three examples follow.

Richard Hays:[23]

1. Christology
2. apocalyptic eschatology
3. embodied existence
4. the primacy of love
5. the transformation of power and status through the cross

Scott Nash:[24]

1. God as the sovereign and gracious Father
2. Christ as the crucified Lord
3. the Spirit as the enabler
4. the church as an eschatological community

Pheme Perkins:[25]

---

23. Richard B. Hays, *First Corinthians*, Interpretation (Louisville: Westminster John Knox, 1997), 9–11.

24. Robert Scott Nash, *1 Corinthians*, Smith & Helwys Bible Commentary (Macon, GA: Smith & Helwys, 2009), 37–42.

25. Perkins, *First Corinthians*, 28–38.

INTRODUCING 1 CORINTHIANS

1. turning away from idols to the true God
2. Scripture as the word of God
3. God's plan of salvation
4. Jesus tradition in Paul
5. Christian life in the Spirit
6. Christ's resurrection and ours
7. a believing community

The synthesis proposed in this commentary does not contradict any of these proposals (and may in fact complement or even incorporate some of them), but it is distinctive.

In sum, then, what is 1 Corinthians? *It is a theologically rich pastoral letter of community formation urging the church to be a resurrectionally cruciform charismatic community that is one, holy, catholic, and apostolic in character.* These are hardly minor aspects of the biblical text or of the Christian story. One church historian and missiologist has even said that we should envision the mission of God (the *missio Dei*) and the church's participation in it over the centuries as "cruciform apostolicity."[26]

Below we will briefly survey the main words in the italicized sentence above as indicative of key themes in the letter. But first we need to consider three dimensions of this theological text: its pastoral/formational, liturgical, and missional character.

1 Corinthians as a Pastoral/Formational Text

Because 1 Corinthians is a theological text in the sense described above, it can also be described as a *formational* text. The author's ultimate goal is pastoral: the formation, or transformation, of the recipients. In fact, as James Thompson has pointed out, Paul's overarching goal in all of his letters is community transformation, with the goal of communal blamelessness at the coming of Christ.[27] As Paul tells the Corinthians at the start of the letter: "[God] will also strengthen you [plural] to the end, so that you [plural] may be blameless on the day of our Lord Jesus Christ" (1:8). In the language of the Wesleyan tradition, we could describe the goal and the process as "moving on to per-

---

26. Scott W. Sunquist, "*Missio Dei*: Christian History Envisioned as Cruciform Apostolicity," *Missiology* 37 (2009): 33–46.

27. James W. Thompson, *Pastoral Ministry according to Paul: A Biblical Vision* (Grand Rapids: Baker Academic, 2006).

fection," a phrase that is reminiscent of Paul's own words in Philippians: "Not that I have already obtained this [resurrection from the dead] or have already reached the goal; but I press on to make it my own, because Christ Jesus has made me his own. Beloved, I do not consider that I have made it my own; but this one thing I do: forgetting what lies behind and straining forward to what lies ahead, I press on toward the goal for the prize of the heavenly call of God in Christ Jesus" (Phil 3:12–14).

Paul here is speaking for himself and for each and every Christian individual and community. This continuous transformation may be called "sanctification," but it means the growth in holiness of the community as a whole, as well as individuals. In many traditions, especially Roman Catholic, such continuous transformation is called "ongoing conversion." And it is one aspect of the larger reality that the Christian tradition has sometimes called "theosis" or "deification," or even "Christosis" or "Christification." These terms signify a Spirit-enabled process of becoming more like Christ the Son of God, and therefore more like God, in holiness now and eventually in glorification and immortality.

There is other language to express the same basic point. Scot McKnight, for example, calls Paul's pastoral goal "Christoformity."[28] Susan Eastman says Paul's formational goal, through the self-gift of Christ and the ongoing presence of God's Spirit in the community, is to "refocus his listeners' attention on the relational matrix that will guide, sustain, and transform them" into a community "constituted in love"[29]—that is, as 1 Cor 13 says, a community of faith, hope, and, above all, love.

This formational goal should not be interpreted merely as some sort of in-house communal perfection in Christian virtue but rather as a comprehensive transformation that includes increasing participation in the ministry and mission of the Spirit—the Spirit of Christ. Thus Paul has in mind a kind of corporate progress that we might call resurrectional, charismatic, cruciform, missional theosis. This (admittedly cumbersome) combination of words signifies becoming like God-in-Christ, not only by prayer and contemplation (important as they are) but also by Spirit-enabled participation in the divine mission—the *missio Dei* (see further below).

Such transformation toward blamelessness, Paul states clearly, is the work of God, particularly of the Holy Spirit. And yet individuals and communities

---

28. See Scot McKnight, *Pastor Paul: Nurturing a Culture of Christoformity in the Church* (Grand Rapids: Baker Academic, 2019).

29. Eastman, *Oneself in Another*, 108.

must be open to this divine work and willing to cooperate with the Spirit. Much of this work involves changes in understanding and attitude that will lead to changed behavior. Thus, Paul's pastoral task of community formation entails calling the Corinthians (and those who read the letter as Scripture) to a "conversion of the imagination."[30] First Corinthians "is best understood as an exercise, in epistolary form, in taking every thought captive to Christ and an exhortation to the Christians in Corinth to do the same in the concrete obedience of their ecclesial and social as well as personal and individual existence."[31]

This will be no easy task for Paul, for as he laments, "I could not speak to you as spiritual [Spirit-ual] people, but rather as people of the flesh, as infants in Christ" (3:1). Furthermore, he reminds the Corinthians, "I fed you with milk, not solid food, for you were not ready for solid food. Even now you are still not ready, for you are still of the flesh" (3:2–3a). The Corinthians are childish. Although anyone can feed a child, the image here seems to be a maternal one—Paul as mother trying to move his children toward maturity (see also the maternal images in 1 Thess 2:7–8; Gal 4:19–20). No mother wants a child to feed on milk alone forever.

Paul must engage the Corinthians, as both their mother-father (see also 4:15) and their brother (e.g., 1:10–11, 26; 11:33; 12:1) in Christ, in maternal-paternal and fraternal correction, often having to state or restate what should be obvious. He uses the question "Do you [plural] not know [*ouk oidate*]?" on ten occasions.[32] These phrases and other aspects of the letter's rhetoric are deliberative in character; that is, they are aimed at getting the Corinthians to think and then to change: to experience the conversion of the imagination— and of life—that God desires for them. To switch images, we could say that the Corinthians are spiritually diseased. As Gordon Fee has put it, Paul needs to perform "radical surgery without killing the patient."[33]

As noted in the preface to the commentary, two of the main ways Paul will express his surgical—that is, theological and pastoral—goal will be to engage in and encourage (1) bifocal thinking (looking both back and ahead) and (2) self-giving, life-giving love. These are discussed below in the section on the story within the letter.

---

30. Hays, *First Corinthians*, 11. (Hays uses this phrase in other publications as well.)

31. Kimlyn J. Bender, *1 Corinthians*, Brazos Theological Commentary on the Bible (Grand Rapids: Baker Academic, 2022), 5, alluding to 2 Cor 10:5.

32. 1 Cor 3:16; 5:6; 6:2, 3, 9, 15, 16, 19; 9:13, 24.

33. Gordon D. Fee, *The First Epistle to the Corinthians*, New International Commentary on the New Testament, rev. ed. (Grand Rapids: Eerdmans, 2014), 4.

1 Corinthians as a Liturgical Text

If it is important to remember that 1 Corinthians is a theological and pastoral/formational document, it is no less important to recognize its liturgical character, its focus on worship, as essential to its theological and pastoral character.[34] By "liturgical," I have three main things in mind.

First, part of the raison d'être of 1 Corinthians is to draw its addressees, past and present, more completely away from idolatry and more deeply into appropriate worship of the triune God.[35] Half of the letter—chapters 8–14—concerns attitudes toward, and behaviors in, cultic settings, both pagan and Christian. Several Christian liturgical practices for the gathered community receive special attention. These include especially baptism (1:13–17; 6:11; 10:2; 12:13; 15:29) and communion (the Lord's Supper, or the Eucharist: 10:1–22; 11:17–34). The practices also include prayer, glossolalia (speaking in tongues), and prophecy (11:2–16; ch. 14), as well as singing (14:15). Two other liturgical practices appear briefly in chapter 16: the greeting and the holy kiss (16:19–20). Worship is where formation occurs—the corporate conversion of the imagination, or resocialization and cultural renewal.[36]

Second, throughout the letter, we find both shorter and longer liturgical texts—words that were likely used in early Christian worship—and allusions to such texts. The following are examples of such texts (NRSV; emphasis added):

- "All those who in every place *call on the name of our Lord Jesus Christ*" (1:2).
- "*Grace to you and peace* from God our Father and the Lord Jesus Christ" (1:3).
- "*God is faithful*" (1:9).
- "Were you baptized *in the name of* Paul?" (1:13).
- "We *proclaim* Christ crucified" (1:23).
- "Our paschal lamb, Christ, has been sacrificed. Therefore, let us *celebrate the festival*" (5:7b–8a).

---

34. On this subject, see especially Rodrigo J. Morales, "A Liturgical Conversion of the Imagination: Worship and Ethics in 1 Corinthians," *Letter and Spirit* 5 (2009): 111–32. He suggests that liturgy "constitutes the 'substructure' of 1 Corinthians" (111).

35. See further John Paul Heil, *The Letters of Paul as Rituals of Worship* (Eugene, OR: Cascade, 2011), 28–49.

36. See Daniel J. Brendsel, "Socialization and the Sanctuary: The Arrangement of 1 Corinthians as a Strategy for Social Formation," in *Tending Soul, Mind, and Body: The Art and Science of Spiritual Formation*, ed. Gerald Hiestand and Todd Wilson (Downers Grove, IL: IVP Academic, 2019), 5–22. I owe this reference to my student Zack Holbrook.

INTRODUCING 1 CORINTHIANS

- "You were washed, you were sanctified, you were justified *in the name of the Lord Jesus Christ* and in the Spirit of our God" (6:11).
- "*For us there is one God, the Father,* from whom are all things and for whom we exist, *and one Lord, Jesus Christ,* through whom are all things and through whom we exist" (8:6; a christological reinterpretation of the Jewish Shema, Israel's declaration of God's oneness).
- "The cup of blessing that *we bless,* is it not a sharing in the blood of Christ? The bread that we break, is it not a sharing in the body of Christ?" (10:16).
- "For I received from the Lord *what I also handed on to you,* that the Lord Jesus on the night when he was betrayed [or "handed over"] took a loaf of bread, and when he had given thanks, he broke it and said, 'This is my body that is for you. Do this in remembrance of me.' In the same way he took the cup also, after supper, saying, 'This cup is the new covenant in my blood. Do this, as often as you drink it, in remembrance of me.' For as often as you eat this bread and drink the cup, you proclaim the Lord's death until he comes" (11:23–26).
- "I want you to understand that no one speaking by the Spirit of God ever says 'Let Jesus be cursed!' and no one can *say 'Jesus is Lord'* except by the Holy Spirit" (12:3).
- "For *I handed on to you* as of first importance what I in turn had received: that Christ died for our sins in accordance with the scriptures, and that he was buried, and that he was raised on the third day in accordance with the scriptures, and that he appeared to Cephas, then to the Twelve" (15:3–5).
- "*Our Lord, come!*" (16:22; *marana tha,* Aramaic words included in Paul's Greek text).
- "*The grace of the Lord Jesus be with you*" (16:23).

This accumulation of citations of and allusions to worship words suggests that Paul believes his pastoral work is accomplished in part by relentlessly reminding his audience of what they say and do already, such that their worship and their way of life may cohere more fully.

Third, then, in addition to matters of worship in the more restrictive sense of community gatherings and associated liturgical texts, there is the matter of worship in daily life. As Paul makes explicit in Rom 12:1–2 and assumes throughout his letters, worship in the narrow sense of gathering for praise, prayer, proclamation, and various other practices cannot be separated from worship in the broader sense of living appropriately as God's people in the world—as God's temple (see further below). Christian worship is not only a matter of what those who are gathered do in the assembly but also what they do, individually and corporately, when they are scattered.

The Complex Character of 1 Corinthians

Thus, at least certain ethical matters (questions of holiness) that are mentioned in passages outside of chapters 8–14 are to be dealt with when the community assembles (see 5:1–5; 6:1–8). Furthermore, "Flee from idolatry" (10:14 NIV), the urgent counsel to run away from any form of inappropriate worship, is one of two principal exhortations directed toward the avoidance of fundamental ways of breaking covenant with God (the other being "Flee from sexual immorality" [6:18 NIV]). In addition, cultic and liturgical images can be found at crucial points elsewhere in the letter, such as the highly significant image of the church and the individual believer as "the temple" of God/the Holy Spirit (3:16; 6:16)—the place where the God of Israel now resides, the focal point of God's presence in the world.

So what should we make of all this? For one thing, it suggests the critical role worship—in all its dimensions—played in Paul's pastoral ministry, in his theology, and in his practical understanding of the church. For those who read 1 Corinthians as Christian Scripture, this suggestion means, for us as well, that corporate worship is an essential, nonnegotiable aspect of Christian existence. It is where identity is shaped and formation occurs; where idolatry is named and resisted; where communion with Christ and others (both those nearby and those far away) takes place; where holiness is lifted up and embraced; where faith, hope, and love are taught and embodied; and especially where the Spirit of the living God and of the crucified and resurrected Christ is unleashed so that the community can glorify God and be edified. All of this is in preparation for a credible witness in the home and neighborhood and world.

1 Corinthians as a Missional Text

This last phrase, "a credible witness in the home and neighborhood and world," leads directly into the next aspect of 1 Corinthians to consider: its missional character.[37] It is often said that Paul must not have wanted the communities

---

37. See further Michael Barram, "Pauline Mission as Salvific Intentionality: Fostering a Missional Consciousness in 1 Corinthians 9:19–23 and 10:31–11:1," in *Paul as Missionary: Identity, Activity, Theology, and Practice*, LNTS 420, ed. Trevor J. Burke and Brian S. Rosner (London: T&T Clark, 2011), 234–46; Brian S. Rosner, "The Missionary Character of 1 Corinthians," in *New Testament Theology in Light of the Church's Mission: Essays in Honor of I. Howard Marshall*, ed. Jon C. Laansma, Grant Osborne, and Ray Van Neste (Eugene, OR: Cascade, 2011), 181–96; Michael J. Gorman, *Becoming the Gospel: Paul, Participation, and Mission* (Grand Rapids: Eerdmans, 2015), 212–60; and Scott Goode, *Salvific Intentionality in 1 Corinthians: How Paul Cultivates the Missional Imagination of the Corinthian Community* (Eugene, OR: Wipf & Stock, 2023).

INTRODUCING 1 CORINTHIANS

he founded to "spread the gospel" because he apparently never urges them to do so. Rather, it is claimed, spreading the gospel was the specific work of apostles and evangelists such as Paul and his colleagues, but not the task of the faithful in general.

I have written an entire book arguing against this (mis)interpretation of Paul and suggesting an expansive understanding of "mission" à la Paul.[38] This is not the place to rehearse the case made there but rather to indicate briefly what it means to call 1 Corinthians a missional text.

First of all, this letter is an instrument of Paul's mission in Corinth. In 1 Corinthians, Paul is continuing his mission of evangelizing, or gospelizing, the Corinthians—of getting them to believe and become (embody) the gospel. Paul may or may not think some of the Corinthians still need an initial conversion, but clearly he believes that they are, in general, spiritual children rather than adults (3:1–4).

Second, the letter also seeks to bear witness to and advance the mission of Paul and other Christians more broadly. Chapter 16 provides a synopsis of several aspects of this larger endeavor: Paul's collection for the saints in Jerusalem (16:1–4); his current work in Ephesus, planned activity in Macedonia, and possible additional visit to Corinth (16:5–9); the ministry of Timothy and Apollos (16:10–12); the ecclesial life of the Corinthians themselves (16:13–18); and the witness of the churches of Asia, including that of Aquila and Priscilla (16:19–20a).

Third, for Paul and for those who read his letter as Christian Scripture, 1 Corinthians is an instrument not only of the *apostolic* mission but of the *divine* mission. In Paul's mind, God's new-creation, new-covenant activity is at the heart of the divine rescue and renewal mission anticipated by the prophets. This activity, though centered in the gifts of Christ and the Spirit, is not merely a past event; it is an ongoing mission, one that takes place both *for* and *through* those who have already heard the gospel. What Christians do, says Paul, is to cooperate with God and one another in *God's* mission, the *missio Dei* (3:5–9).

Fourth, then, this letter articulates an ecclesiology that is not only about the internal life of the community but also about its witness in the world—to visitors to the assembly, to family members, to friends and neighbors. Paul was clear that the church was not to escape from the world—an impossibility—but to engage it: "I wrote to you in my letter not to associate with sexually immoral persons—not at all meaning the immoral of this world, or the

---

38. Gorman, *Becoming the Gospel*. On the Corinthian correspondence, see 212–60.

greedy and robbers, or idolaters, since you would then need to go out of the world" (5:9–10). To be apostolic is obviously to be missional, but a Christian individual or body cannot bear faithful witness if it does not embody a holy, altercultural way of life.

Although only a few texts are explicit about the witness to outsiders, the topic is, I suggest, assumed elsewhere. But here are a few texts about what Michael Barram calls "salvific intentionality" toward unbelievers (*apistoi*):[39]

TO VISITORS TO THE ASSEMBLY

If, therefore, the whole church comes together and all speak in tongues, and outsiders or unbelievers enter, will they not say that you are out of your mind? But if all prophesy, an unbeliever or outsider who enters is reproved by all and called to account by all. After the secrets of the unbeliever's heart are disclosed, that person will bow down before God and worship him, declaring, "God is really among you." (14:23–25)

IN THE FAMILY

And if any woman has a husband who is an unbeliever, and he consents to live with her, she should not divorce him. For the unbelieving husband is made holy through his wife, and the unbelieving wife is made holy through her husband. Otherwise, your children would be unclean, but as it is, they are holy. . . . Wife, for all you know, you might save your husband. Husband, for all you know, you might save your wife. (7:13–14, 16)

IN THE SOCIAL WORLD

If an unbeliever invites you to a meal and you are disposed to go, eat whatever is set before you without raising any question on the ground of conscience. But if someone says to you, "This has been offered in sacrifice," then do not eat it, out of consideration for the one who informed you, and for the sake of conscience—I mean the other's conscience, not your own. . . . So, whether you eat or drink, or whatever you do, do everything for the glory of God. Give no offense to Jews or to Greeks or to the church of God, just as I try to please everyone in everything I do, not seeking my own advantage, but that of many, so that they may be saved. Be imitators of me, as I am of Christ. (10:27–29a, 31–33; 11:1)

39. Barram, "Pauline Mission as Salvific Intentionality." It should be noted that each of these texts is open to various interpretations, but as a whole I think they articulate a concern for witness to unbelievers, as does Goode in *Salvific Intentionality in 1 Corinthians*.

45

INTRODUCING 1 CORINTHIANS

It is clear from this last text that Paul sees himself as a missional model for the Corinthians (10:31–11:1); he does not see participation in the *missio Dei* as his privilege and responsibility alone. In fact, the ultimate missional model is not Paul but Christ. But to the degree that Paul is Christlike, he, too, is a model for the Corinthians and for later Christian readers:

> For though I am free with respect to all, I have made myself a slave to all, so that I might win more of them. To the Jews I became as a Jew, in order to win Jews. To those under the law I became as one under the law (though I myself am not under the law) so that I might win those under the law. To those outside the law I became as one outside the law (though I am not free from God's law but am under Christ's law) so that I might win those outside the law. To the weak I became weak, so that I might win the weak. I have become all things to all people, that I might by all means save some. I do it all for the sake of the gospel, so that I may share in its blessings. (1 Cor 9:19–23)

To summarize, we may use the word "missional" in the sense rightly advocated by Michael Barram: as a descriptor of *all* of Paul's apostolic activity as he participates in the mission of God—and invites others to do the same in imitation of his imitation of Christ.[40] This activity includes what missiologists sometimes refer to as both the centripetal and the centrifugal aspects of the divine mission—internally oriented and externally oriented activities. But "missional" is also an especially apt word to summarize the particularly centrifugal (externally oriented) dimension of the church's life as Paul presents it in the letter. This concern for outsiders, or unbelievers, is one way in which both Paul and the *ekklēsia* are apostolic.

1 Corinthians as a Contemporary Text

As noted above, when reading this letter, one cannot help but see similarities to issues in the contemporary church and world: division, immorality and injustice, culture and worship wars, debates about central Christian convictions, and more. If we read this letter as Christian Scripture, or even as just interesting social and moral analysis and response, Paul is clearly addressing modern (or postmodern) Corinthians, as Fred Craddock put it.[41] This would seem to

40. Michael Barram, *Mission and Moral Reflection in Paul*, Studies in Biblical Literature 75 (New York: Lang, 2006).
41. Craddock, "Preaching to Corinthians."

46

be especially the case in places like Europe and North America but is true elsewhere as well. Filipino New Testament scholar Rolex Cailing says this:

> The Christian life is about transformation. Paul's answers and counsel to the issues raised in the Christ-assembly in Corinth may assist Asian Christ-assemblies in discovering a more genuine vision for community life and for leadership practices in the church. Paul's letters to the Christ-assembly in Corinth are still in many ways as relevant today as they were when he wrote them. *The competitive, social-climbing, status-obsessed, morally decadent society and cultural ideologies of the Greco-Roman world of Paul's time have remarkable parallels with some Asian cultures, and Paul offers timely teachings on how to remain faithful Christ followers in such a world.*[42]

We could certainly replace "Asian" with "Western" or "European" or "North American," and perhaps with other cultural identifiers. Neither Cailing nor I would suggest that all cultures and all individuals are similar to Greco-Roman culture and people, or that the church in every place is like the first-century church in Corinth. But if the shoe fits, as the saying goes, wear it. And it fits very often, and often very well. Of particularly grave concern today, throughout much of the world, is the abuse of power: political, cultural, religious. *Paul's concern to redefine power in light of the cross and to keep the resurrected Lord united to the crucified Messiah is critical in the contemporary context.*

Furthermore, even when the specific current situation is rather different from the Corinthian chaos, the call of God on the church persists: (1) to be one, holy, catholic, and apostolic, characterized by resurrectional, charismatic cruciformity, and (2) to look at everything bifocally, in light of the Paschal Mystery and the parousia. (See further below under "The Story within the Letter.") As Cailing says, 1 Corinthians is a text about engaging culture in light of the gospel.[43] First Corinthians is a letter for all times, places, and seasons.

Summary

We have seen that despite its appearance as a laundry list of Corinthian issues with responses to a variety of concerns, 1 Corinthians is a deeply theologi-

---

42. Rolex M. Cailing, "The Letters to the Corinthians," in *An Asian Introduction to the New Testament*, ed. Johnson Thomaskutty (Minneapolis: Fortress, 2022), 215–41 (here 215; emphasis added).

43. Cailing, "Letters to the Corinthians," 223.

cal, pastoral, liturgical, missional, and contemporary letter. So what precisely prompted the writing of this multidimensional apostolic missive? We turn now to the story behind 1 Corinthians.

The Story behind the Letter

"The trip to Corinth is not for every man," observed several ancient travelers, wary of moral or financial ruin in the city. Corinth had a reputation for trouble, and it was even the namesake for a verb. "To become Corinthianized" (Gk. *korinthiazesthai*) meant something like "to become thoroughly immoral and materialistic" or even "to fornicate." Corinth had the reputation that some US cities have, especially among non-Westerners.

From Paul's point of view, Corinth, like most other cities, demonstrated his Jewish conviction (see Rom 1:18–32) that gentiles majored in idolatry and immorality. Among the city's thriving industries was a fairly lively sex trade, some of which may have been inspired by the city's long association with Aphrodite and her temple.[44] Among the ruins of Corinth are also more than two dozen additional temples, statues, and monuments: to Apollo, Asclepius, Athena, Demeter and Kore, Serapis, the emperor and his family, and other gods. At nearby Isthmia are the ruins of a large temple to Poseidon, god of the sea.

Corinth was of considerable strategic importance for the spread of the gospel.[45] Located in the province of Achaia, on the isthmus that connects mainland Greece with the southernmost region, the Peloponnese, Corinth was a thriving, cosmopolitan, and commercial metropolis. It was especially known for its bronze products. The city was situated in an impressive spot, dominated by the massive Acrocorinth (site of the temple of Aphrodite), which rose nineteen hundred feet into the southern sky and overlooked a very large agora or forum at the heart of the city. Corinth was the "master of two harbors" (Strabo, *Geography* 8.6.20)—Lechaeum (or Lechaion), about two miles to the northwest on the Gulf of Corinth, leading to the Adriatic Sea; and Cenchreae, about six miles to the southeast on the Saronic Gulf, leading to the Aegean Sea. The two harbors were connected by the Diolkos, a track built in the sixth century BC on which goods and even small ships could be hauled between

---

44. In the Roman period, however, Aphrodite had several functions, including mother of the imperial family, and was not merely a sex deity. And whatever sacred prostitutes might have been associated with Aphrodite's temple in earlier times were not active in Paul's day.

45. For a brief overview, see B. W. Winter, "Corinth," *DPL*[2] 164–68.

the two ports. (Today a canal, conceived by several ancients—including Julius Caesar—and even attempted by Nero, but not completed until 1893, links the two gulfs.)[46] By these ports, Corinth controlled the Asia Minor–Italy trade traffic. The ports also permitted the east-west flow of religious and philosophical ideas, and their messengers. Corinth was "the passage for all of humanity" (Aelius Aristides, *Orations* 46.24).

Once a powerful Greek city-state, Corinth had been destroyed by Rome in 146 BC and was left largely dormant until 44 BC, when Julius Caesar refounded it as a colony of Rome (*Colonia Laus Julia Corinthiensis*, abbreviated "Corinth"). As in Philippi to the north, Latin (not Greek) dominated public spaces, yet everyday people largely communicated in Greek. Caesar populated the colony with enslaved people, freed enslaved persons, and other non-elite folks, such as immigrants, especially from the East. Veterans and others were settled there as well. It would not be inaccurate to describe some of the population, which may have numbered about eighty thousand,[47] as upwardly mobile, attempting to better themselves on the socioeconomic ladder. The natural drive of such people was further fueled by the highly competitive social environment that was common in the Roman Empire and that existed in an accentuated form within this rebuilt and constantly rebuilding city.

Indeed, Roman Corinth—Paul's Corinth—quickly became the chief city and capital of Achaia, and within the Roman Empire not far behind Rome and Alexandria in significance. The colony grew in prosperity, due in large part to its location. Scholars have long debated the socioeconomic characteristics of Corinth and other cities in Paul's day. But it is generally agreed that there was a tiny, powerful elite (maybe 2–3 percent of the populace), while 70–85 percent of the population lived in difficult economic situations: near, at, below, or far below subsistence-level existence. (It is difficult to assign percentages to this spectrum of poverty, but most experts agree that more than half of the people lived at, below, or far below the subsistence level.) That leaves about 10–20 percent of the population, known as the middling group, who were economically stable, with some surplus.[48]

Some craftsmen and merchants were among those with a bit extra, but

46. Following a revolt in Judea, the Roman general (and later emperor) Vespasian sent six thousand Jewish captives to work on Nero's project (Josephus, *Jewish War* 3.540).

47. Donald Engels, *Roman Corinth: An Alternative Model for the Classical City* (Chicago: University of Chicago Press, 1990), 33, 84, though data are sparse and perhaps more representative of the second century. Some scholarly estimates, however, go as high as 140,000.

48. For a general description of the makeup of the Corinthian church, see 1 Cor 1:26–29.

many struggled. Paul says that his financial condition varied from having plenty to being hungry (Phil 4:10–14), but abundance was probably not the norm. He tells the Corinthians—perhaps with a bit of hyperbole for rhetorical effect—that he and his coworkers lived at or below subsistence level themselves: "To the present hour we are hungry and thirsty, we are poorly clothed and beaten and homeless, and we grow weary from the work of our own hands" (1 Cor 4:11–12a).[49] In Corinth, nevertheless, Paul would have found plenty of opportunities for employment from normal requests for tent-making and leather work, and perhaps also from special requests for such events as the biennial Isthmian Games. Second only to the Olympiad, these games held at neighboring Isthmia were dedicated to Poseidon. They showcased talent not only in athletics but also in music, drama, and speech (rhetoric)—and were a living icon of the region's culture of competition. In fact, it comes as no surprise that the Corinthian believers had their own forms of competition and status-seeking.

Paul's Mission

It may have been this combination of the city's features—the challenge of idolatry and immorality, the poverty, the strategic location, and the opportunity for work—that led Paul, according to Acts 18:11, to spend eighteen months of his second mission trip (see Acts 15:36–18:22) in Corinth, almost certainly during the years 50–51 or 51–52. (Fairly precise dating is possible because of a reference in Acts 18:12–17 to the proconsul of Achaia, Lucius Iunius Gallio. Gallio is mentioned in a letter dating to circa AD 52 from the emperor Claudius, fragments of which were found at Delphi, about 125 miles northeast of Corinth.)[50] Paul was an urban missionary who helped make Corinth, like Ephesus, into an epicenter for the gospel. As an urban evangelist and pastor, he encountered all the social realities that characterized ancient Roman cities, including subsistence living or poverty for many; disparity between the elite and the nonelite, and between citizens and noncitizens; ethnic and political tensions; and so on.[51] What follows is a summary of Paul's mission according to Acts, with additional input from 1 Corinthians itself.

49. See also Rom 8:35; 2 Cor 6:4–5, 10; 11:27.
50. A few scholars think that Acts 18 merges two of Paul's visits to Corinth into one, which could make Paul's first visit about a decade earlier.
51. For an excellent overview of Paul's urban context, see D. A. Fiensy, "Urban Setting of Paul's Churches," *DPL*[2] 1094–1105.

The Story behind the Letter

Paul arrived alone in Corinth after little success in Athens (Acts 17:15–18:1), though that may have been more pleasant than the trouble he had encountered immediately before in Philippi, Berea, and Thessalonica (Acts 16:6–17:14). He met up with a man named Aquila and his wife Priscilla, two Jewish believers who had left Rome when Claudius expelled Jews, and who were also tent makers (Acts 18:1–4).[52] As usual, Paul preached in the synagogue, had minimal or no initial success, and then, joined again by Silas and Timothy, directed his efforts at the gentiles (Acts 18:5–6). Acts tells us that a Godfearer named Titius Justus, a synagogue official named Crispus, possibly another synagogue official (called Sosthenes), and many other Corinthians—almost certainly both Jews and (mostly?) gentiles—"became believers and were baptized" (Acts 18:7–8, 17; cf. 1 Cor 1:1, 14).

However, as in earlier locations, Paul was again opposed by certain Jews, who took the matter to Gallio the proconsul, or governor, but the proconsul dismissed the case as a matter of religious difference rather than Roman law (Acts 18:12–17). Nonetheless, Sosthenes was beaten in front of Gallio, who ignored the situation (Acts 18:17). This could explain why Sosthenes, who is most likely the named co-sender of 1 Corinthians (1 Cor 1:1), apparently accompanied Paul to Ephesus, where 1 Corinthians was written (1 Cor 16:8), though Acts does not mention Sosthenes as Paul's traveling companion.

First Corinthians testifies also to Paul's success as the community's founder, using the images of planter (3:6), foundation installer (3:10), and father (4:15). He was also quite obviously their teacher, or catechist. The letter explicitly reminds the Corinthians of traditions Paul passed on to them (e.g., 11:2, 23–26; 15:1–5), and it raises questions—such as "Do you not know?" (ten occurrences)—and makes statements that imply certain things have been taught.

During and after Paul's year and a half of evangelization and catechesis in Corinth, a vibrant, charismatic community developed that eventually included mostly gentiles (see 12:2) but also Jews, men and women, enslaved persons and free/freed persons. Some were people of means, intellect, and culture, though most were from various strata of the nonelite, lacking in such status indicators (1:26), to use the language of the social sciences. Together these people constituted the one *ekklēsia* (assembly, congregation, church) of God in Corinth (1:2).

It is quite possible that there were actually several different assemblies in the city (see the references to households in 1:16; 16:15), perhaps of different

---

52. The facticity and, if factual, the scope and significance of this expulsion are matters of scholarly debate, but they need not detain us here.

sizes and character. Whether one assembly or several, they met as a single body (14:23, "the whole church"; cf. Rom 16:23) for regular or occasional celebration of the Lord's Supper and worship together in the house of a wealthy believer (chs. 11–14), or at another venue with that person as the host.[53] For at least some time that host was a man named Gaius, whom Paul himself had baptized (1:14; Rom 16:23).

The baptized, then, became part of the assembly. Sociologically speaking, a Pauline *ekklēsia* was somewhat like a small association (Lat. *collegium*), but probably less formally structured than some such groups. Associations included neighborhood, ethnic, trade, and cultic groups. A Pauline assembly was similar to a Jewish association (the synagogue), and also to certain philosophical groups that stressed moral formation. The assembly also resembled an extended family—including the use of sibling language—but was not limited to an immediate family or single household. In spite of such similarities to other bodies, the Pauline *ekklēsia* was a unique entity with respect to diversity of composition and self-understanding—its basic character, practices, and purpose in the world.

But that uniqueness did not keep the Corinthian *ekklēsia*, or any early Christian assembly, from problems. The spirit of Corinth proved to be a powerful challenge to the work of the Spirit of God. We see aspects of that challenge throughout 1 Corinthians.

Divisions and Scandals: Chaos at Corinth

It may surprise some modern readers that baptism, and specifically who baptized whom, could become a major church issue. In retrospect, Paul may have wished that he had not actually baptized anyone, for the question of who baptized whom actually did become one of the causes for division in the community (1:13–14). Paul's departure from Corinth was followed by a very successful visit from the Alexandrian Jew Apollos, a bright and rhetorically powerful preacher (1:12; 3:4–6, 22; 4:6; 16:12; cf. Acts 18:24–19:1), and perhaps also a visit from Peter ("Cephas": 1:12; 3:22)—though this is by no means certain.[54]

---

53. Estimates on the size of the combined assemblies vary from about fifty to about two hundred. A group of fifty or so could meet in a large house; many more would likely require a different space.

54. Regardless of whether Cephas actually spent time in Corinth, he was clearly an important figure in the Corinthian church(es); see also 9:5; 15:5.

The Story behind the Letter

For a number of reasons, several sorts of divisions ensued along various lines. Some individuals and groups, possibly corresponding to assemblies organized according to their respective spiritual fathers (the preachers who converted and baptized them), aligned themselves with one apostolic figure or another—Paul, Apollos, or Cephas/Peter (1:12). They considered themselves in some sense to belong to their leader and to be that leader's devotees and servants (1:12; 3:4–5), perhaps in a sort of client-patron relationship. In addition to baptism, cultural and socioeconomic factors may have drawn people to one or another leader; perhaps observant Jewish believers claimed Peter, while the culturally and intellectually sophisticated rallied around Apollos. Some may have been critical of Paul, while others joined his party. Still others may have rejected all human allegiances ("I belong to Christ" in 1:12?) but nonetheless contributed to the factionalism.[55]

Other divisions, perhaps related to these, also appeared. Some Corinthians took fellow believers (lit., "brothers") to court (6:1–11). Some avoided the idol temples completely, while others ate within their precincts and may have mocked the scruples of others (8:1–13). Some treated the gatherings for the Lord's Supper like a banquet and drinking party (known as a symposium) for the wealthy and neglected the poor latecomers (11:17–34). Still others (or was it the same people?) looked down on certain members of the community, especially those who did not possess the more spectacular endowments of the Spirit like glossolalia (12:1–14:40).

At the same time, moral scandals had arisen. In addition to the lawsuits, a believer having sexual relations with his stepmother was tolerated, if not celebrated, by the community (5:1–8), and some believers were engaging the services of prostitutes (6:12–20). Many were confused about sex and marriage (7:1–40). An earlier letter from Paul, at least partly on sexual immorality, had confused the Corinthians still further when they mistakenly interpreted his admonition to avoid sexually immoral persons (i.e., fellow believers) as a call to avoid contact with their immoral *nonbelieving* friends (5:9–13).[56] Added to all this, some Corinthians were denying the resurrection of the dead (15:12), which, for Paul, had profound moral implications about sexuality and about life more generally.

---

55. Scholars have differed, and continue to differ, on the source of the divisions, and on the nature and the number of groups, or parties.

56. As noted below, the letter referenced in 1 Cor 5:9–13 is sometimes called letter A (i.e., Paul's first letter to the Corinthians), with our 1 Corinthians then being labeled letter B.

INTRODUCING 1 CORINTHIANS

Furthermore, a significant number of the believers appeared to be, in Paul's apt metaphor, "puffed up" (4:6, 18, 19; 5:2; 8:1; 13:4—too often translated blandly as "arrogant" or "proud") about whichever conviction or behavior or spiritual gift they were flaunting. Though we cannot know with certainty, it appears that many of these attitudes and actions were interconnected. A relatively small group of people, possessing significant status both socially and spiritually, and claiming special wisdom and knowledge, were likely exercising a disproportionate influence on the church as a whole.

The word "wisdom" (Gk. *sophia*) occurs seventeen times in the letter, and "wise" (*sophos*) eleven times, with nearly all of these occurrences found in chapters 1–3. In contrast, these terms are unusual in, or absent from, the other Pauline letters. The word "knowledge" (*gnōsis*) occurs ten times, accounting for nearly half of the occurrences in the Pauline corpus as a whole.[57] This is not to say that concerns about wisdom and knowledge were unique to Corinth or to the Corinthian believers; ancient Jews, Greeks, and Romans all sought to be wise and knowing. But at Corinth there was likely a special form of wisdom, a synthesis of the culture and the (misunderstood) gospel.

It is generally thought that these "wise" Corinthians were self-styled Spirit-filled people (*pneumatikoi*), sometimes called pneumatics, enthusiasts, or elitists, who were enamored of displays of powerful speech, especially in worship, and particularly in tongues-speaking. They also felt themselves enlightened and were apparently prone to a kind of moral libertinism in bodily matters such as food and sex ("all things are lawful": 6:12; 10:23) that was coupled with disdain for those of supposedly lesser spiritual or socioeconomic status. Most likely, this was a group of relatively powerful, elite men.

It is likely that the spirituality embraced by such people focused on the present possession of the glory and power of the Spirit, not on the paradoxical Pauline pattern of Spirit-enabled, resurrection-infused cruciformity. That is, from Paul's perspective, they separated the Spirit from the cross and thus, even if unintentionally, from Christ. This attitude may well have given rise to their critique, not only of "inferiors" in the community but of Paul as well.

The resulting situation was chaos, specifically what we might call a four-dimensional array of turmoil:

---

57. The word *sophia* is found once in Romans, three times in Ephesians, and six times in Colossians, while *sophos* appears four times in Romans and once in Ephesians. The word *gnōsis* occurs three times in Romans, six times in 2 Corinthians, and once each in Ephesians, Philippians, Colossians, and 1 Timothy.

54

The Story behind the Letter

- ecclesial chaos
- moral chaos
- liturgical chaos
- theological chaos

Paul will address these various forms of chaos in the letter.

At the Root of the Chaos

There have been many attempts to identify the root cause of the chaos—these sorts of Corinthian attitudes and behaviors. Perhaps the most interesting is the hypothesis that the Corinthians, or at least the Corinthian elite, were essentially Stoics, or "sub-Stoics" (Timothy Brookins's term). The Stoic values and attitudes of self-sufficiency, freedom, indifference, and neglect of the body (under the influence of Platonism), argues Brookins, appear in the letter as the norms of the Corinthian elite and self-styled "wise" (*sophoi*) and "spiritual" (*pneumatikoi*) who have made the Pauline gospel into a sort of Christian Stoicism. Paul himself, argues Brookins, also draws on philosophical, especially Stoic, themes and language—even some of what the Corinthians used—to correct their misguided interpretation of the gospel.[58]

This approach to 1 Corinthians has much to commend it. However, a similar reconstruction of the situation and a similar theological reading of its contents can occur without recourse to this specific, Stoic lens. I think it is more likely, overall, that the Corinthians naturally breathed in and absorbed currents (including Stoic ones) in the secular air, which contributed significantly to their misreadings of the Pauline gospel. (At the same time, I affirm that Paul's gospel is an implicit, and at times explicit, challenge to certain central Stoic claims.)[59]

---

58. See Timothy A. Brookins, *Reading 1 Corinthians: A Literary and Theological Commentary* (Macon, GA: Smith & Helwys, 2020). Brookins first argued for this sort of perspective on the Corinthians in his *Corinthian Wisdom, Stoic Philosophy, and the Ancient Economy* (New York: Cambridge University Press, 2014). Most recently, in *Rediscovering the Wisdom of the Corinthians: Paul, Stoicism, and Spiritual Hierarchy* (Grand Rapids: Eerdmans, 2024), he uses the term "sub-Stoics" for the Corinthian "wise." By this he means adherents to a Stoicism (its ideas and language) subordinated to faith in Christ according to their interpretation of Paul's gospel, a kind of philosophical school dedicated to Paul—whom they misinterpret.

59. See my *The Self, the Lord, and the Other according to Paul and Epictetus: The Theological Significance of Reflexive Language* (Eugene, OR: Cascade, 2023); see also C. Kavin Rowe, *One True Life: The Stoics and Early Christians as Rival Traditions* (New Haven: Yale University Press, 2016).

INTRODUCING 1 CORINTHIANS

We find similar situations today, when people (for example) who have never studied postmodernism articulate postmodern sensibilities and interpret their lives—including their Christian experience—in robustly postmodern ways, for better or worse. At the same time, whether in Corinth or today, certain teachers and leaders may be more knowledgeable about, and more deliberate in conveying, the intellectual ethos of the culture.

I think it is also critical to recognize that what the Corinthians said and did was, in fact, directly related to the gospel they had heard and received (see 15:3–5) and, especially, to the experience of the Spirit that the gospel offered. There were likely many forces at work to help the Corinthians reshape, and thus misshape, the significance of the Spirit's work. As noted above, Paul's goal is to reunite what the Corinthians have split apart: Christ and the Spirit, death and resurrection, cruciformity and resurrection power.

These sorts of spiritual divorces are perennial issues in the Christian church that may be partially explained by a specific cultural ethos, but at their foundation, they are (for Paul and for this interpreter) perversions caused by human sin and the cosmic power of Sin. The proper response is the reunification of that which should have never been divided. The proper response is the spiritual mission of preaching and practicing unity, holiness, catholicity, and apostolicity instead of division, immorality and injustice, inhospitality and favoritism, and neglect of the apostolic gospel. We will return to these central and remedial practices below.

The chaotic situation at Corinth, then, was a complex set of interrelated social, sexual, and spiritual problems that frequently pitted the supposedly enlightened, or elite and powerful, against the supposedly unenlightened, or nonelite and weak. Paul found out about these problems—this chaos—through both oral and written communications (1:11; 7:1; 16:17) from the church. From his new base of Ephesus (16:8), he responds by sending Timothy, who had helped him in Corinth (Acts 18:5), either ahead of or with the letter (4:17; 16:10–11). Paul had wished also to send Apollos, who wisely refused or discerned it not to be God's will (16:12).[60] And, God willing, Paul intends to visit the Corinthians himself, later, hopefully for an extended time after passing through Macedonia, in part to collect the Corinthians' contribution to the Jerusalem church (16:1–7).[61]

---

60. This "shows that for all his influence, Paul was not perceived, nor did he lead, in a highly authoritative way such that other believers felt they had to obey his every urging" (Michelle Rader, personal correspondence, October 22, 2023).

61. Second Corinthians makes it clear that this second visit did not go well. Paul eventually planned on a third visit (2 Cor 13:1).

56

The Story behind the Letter

But Paul's major response to the Corinthian situation is, of course, the letter, written from Ephesus, where he plans to stay until the late-spring feast of Pentecost (16:8–9). It was probably composed in the year 54 (give or take about a year). Some interpreters believe that the mention of Pentecost here and of Passover, by allusion, in 5:7 (the sacrifice of the paschal lamb) indicates that Paul is writing in the spring. But if he wishes to enter through the "wide door for effective work" that has been opened to him in the face of "many adversaries" (16:9), it is more likely that he is writing in the previous late summer or fall, looking ahead to more months, not weeks, in Ephesus.

The Letter as Paul's Response to the Chaos

The specific prompts that informed Paul and Sosthenes about the Corinthian four-dimensional chaos and led them to send this lengthy letter were two: (1) a visit from "Chloe's people" (1:11)—meaning perhaps her slaves, clients, family members, or colleagues—and (2) a letter from the Corinthians (7:1). In addition, Paul may have had other sources that fed him information about the situation (see, e.g., 11:18; 15:12; 16:17).

It is important to note that what we call 1 Corinthians (i.e., First Corinthians) is actually the second of at least four letters Paul wrote to the Corinthians. In 1 Cor 5:9, Paul mentions an earlier, greatly misunderstood letter. In addition, 2 Corinthians mentions a tearful, sorrowful letter (2 Cor 2:3–4; 7:8) written after the second, painful visit by Paul to Corinth, during which someone caused him distress (2 Cor 2:1, 5). This body of correspondence is sometimes designated as letters A, B, and C, as follows:

- letter A   the letter mentioned in 1 Cor 5:9;[62]
- letter B   1 Corinthians; and
- letter C   the tearful letter mentioned in 2 Cor 2:3–4 and 7:8.[63]

Following these letters, Paul writes one or more additional letters to Corinth:

- letter D   2 Corinthians (or parts of it).[64]

62. Although a few scholars believe that a part of letter A is preserved in 2 Cor 6:14–7:1, in my opinion the evidence does not favor this view.

63. This letter is sometimes identified with 1 Corinthians (extremely unlikely) or, somewhat more plausibly, 2 Cor 10–13.

64. If 2 Corinthians is one unified letter, as I would argue, then it can be termed let-

57

INTRODUCING 1 CORINTHIANS

Our concern, of course, is 1 Corinthians, which is almost certainly a single, coherent (if multipronged) letter.[65] In it, Paul seeks to form a community that is one, holy, catholic, and apostolic.

THE STORY WITHIN THE LETTER

First Corinthians is a well-crafted piece of deliberative rhetoric and corporate spiritual direction intended above all to strengthen, sanctify, and unify the community (1:8, 10) as a catholic and apostolic body.[66] The letter does this by urging every one of its members to "let all that you do be done in love" (16:14)—by which Paul means Spirit-empowered, Christlike, cruciform, self-giving, community-edifying, missional love. These two textual clues to the purpose of the letter (i.e., 1:8, 10 and 16:14), which serve as bookends to the whole collection of short, carefully crafted discourses within it, suggest also that its famous love chapter (ch. 13) is a crucial piece of Paul's argument. In its immediate context, chapter 13 addresses the problem of disunity through disregard for "weaker" brothers and sisters (today we might say "differently gifted"; see ch. 12, esp. vv. 22–24). But it also addresses the problems of unholiness and other community failings. In addition, the love chapter—as we will see in the commentary on it—also alludes to other problems addressed elsewhere in the letter.

Indeed, Paul seems to see many of the church's problems as a failure to love, especially a failure by those who possess certain social and spiritual status indicators to love those who lack them. Because most of the holders of such status indicators were, as elsewhere in the Roman Empire, most likely men, Paul's formational goal is in part to urge the powerful males at Corinth to be more like him and ultimately more like Christ—and thus also less Roman, less

---

ter D. Many scholars—though fewer now than in recent history—have contended that 2 Corinthians consists of perhaps three to as many as eight letters or parts of letters.

65. There are, however, some exceptions to this general consensus about 1 Corinthians. One proposal, e.g., finds parts of eight letters scattered throughout 1 and 2 Corinthians, four of which contributed to the formation of our 1 Corinthians: a letter about worship troubles, one about "body matters," one about unity, and one about anguish and tears. See Frank W. Hughes and Robert Jewett, *The Corinthian Correspondence: Redaction, Rhetoric, and History* (Lanham, MD: Lexington/Fortress Academic, 2021).

66. The goal of deliberative rhetoric was to elicit consideration of behavior and to persuade, dissuade, and exhort about that behavior moving forward. Among the many interesting features of this rhetorical gem of a letter is its use of wordplay. See Roy E. Ciampa and Brian S. Rosner, "Wordplay in 1 Corinthians," *Journal of Theological Studies* NS 74 (2023): 607–35.

patriarchal, and less (traditionally) male. In other words, they would become more truly and fully men as God intended them to be if they embodied resurrectional, charismatic cruciform love.[67]

At the heart of 1 Cor 13 and Paul's understanding of love is the part of v. 5 that reads "[love] does not insist on its own way" (NRSV), which is better translated as "love does not seek its own advantage" or "interests" (see CEB, NAB, NJB). This Greek idiom has already appeared in 10:24 and 10:33, where it explains what it means to be an imitator of Paul and, ultimately, of Christ (11:1). Similarly, in Phil 2 basically the same idiom appears (Phil 2:4, 21), as both a summary of the kind of humility and love that produce unity and a précis of the master story of Christ, who emptied and humbled himself (Phil 2:7–8). It is this sort of love that generates harmony and true holiness, and makes both catholicity and apostolicity possible.

Accordingly, when Paul calls the Corinthians to unity through the holiness of humility and love, he is telling them to live out the story of Christ crucified both in their community and in the wider world. After all, the apostle had "resolved to know nothing among you [the Corinthians] except Jesus the Messiah—that is, Jesus the *crucified* Messiah" (2:2 MJG). In fact, it was his preaching of the story of Christ crucified, "the power of God and the wisdom of God" (1:24), that had brought the Corinthians to faith, and God's Spirit—with whom they were so enamored—to them. Their previous personal and corporate stories had been rearranged by their encounter with God (the Father), Jesus, and the Spirit (6:11) in the message of Christ crucified, through whichever minister happened to be the ambassador (see 2 Cor 5:20).

Now their lives needed to be rearranged once again. Their resocialization had been incomplete. That is, their conversion had been incomplete and needed to be ongoing. The Corinthians' stories, ideologies, and spiritualities of wisdom and power needed to be deconstructed and reconstructed—reshaped by the story of Christ crucified. Their self-focused behavior was harming their siblings in Christ (8:1–13) and their witness to neighbors (10:23–11:1). In this sense, 1 Corinthians is not merely deliberative but *subversive*—subversive of the status quo even within the church, whose values are being turned topsy-turvy.

---

67. For an interesting, sophisticated treatment of this aspect of the letter, see Brian J. Robinson, *Being Subordinate Men: Paul's Rhetoric of Gender and Power in 1 Corinthians* (Lanham, MD: Lexington/Fortress Academic, 2019). Robinson argues that Paul undermines ancient ideas of masculinity by narrating his "weak" practices, self-identifying with nonpowerful images, and urging concern for the weak brothers and sisters. (One might suggest that all this is part of Paul's imitation of Christ.)

Yet the result of the reconstruction process would be a fuller partnership or "fellowship" (*koinōnia*) with God's Son (1:9; cf. 10:16), in anticipation of the conclusion of the divine story: the revelation and day of the Lord Jesus (1:7–8) and the resurrection of believers that day will bring (ch. 15). This is what holiness is for Paul: altercultural, resurrectional, charismatic (Spirit-empowered) cruciformity in expectation of the coming day of judgment and salvation and in service to the church and the world. It is participation in the life of Christ, the life of the Spirit, the life of God. Paul, as the community's founder and father, emphatically (repeatedly using the pronoun "I") calls the Corinthians to this ongoing conversion and *koinōnia*. It is such participation in the life of the triune God that will build unity.

But how does Paul work in the letter to convey the need for this ongoing conversion and its resulting holiness?

Paul's Bifocal Approach to Community Formation

One of Paul's most distinctive and theologically creative approaches to pastoral ministry is what we may call his bifocal pastoral, or practical, reasoning (Gk. *phronēsis*). Paul understands life in Christ to be an existence between the first and second comings of Jesus. This may be depicted graphically as follows:[68]

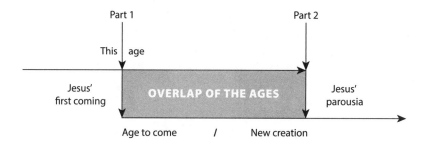

As Paul deals with both everyday dimensions of Christian existence and crises in the church, he constantly looks both back to Christ's first coming, and all it

---

68. A few scholars have questioned the appropriateness of this sort of graphic that insists on an overlap of ages. L. Ann Jervis, for instance, argues that existence in Christ is the new creation: *Paul and Time: Life in the Temporality of Christ* (Grand Rapids: Eerdmans, 2023). While it is true that Paul insists on the arrival of the new age and a new identity for those in Christ, the apostle also sees the ongoing reality and effects of the old age—which is therefore appropriately called "this" age (Rom 12:2 NRSVue; NAB). And this age can still negatively affect those in Christ, until it is fully replaced by the new age inaugurated by Christ.

entailed, and ahead to Christ's second coming, and all it will entail. The various aspects of these two comings play a large part in his practical moral reasoning, in his efforts at community formation, and in his attempts to get the churches to reason similarly on their own. He wants them to think bifocally.[69] With this image, then, I do not mean to suggest looking in one direction through two lenses (as with bifocal lenses in a pair of glasses) but rather looking simultaneously in two different directions—both back and ahead.

The key elements of the first coming to which Paul repeatedly refers are the incarnation, death, bodily resurrection, and exaltation of the Son. In addition, Paul associates the gift of the Spirit with the first coming, as well as our participation in that first advent by way of dying and rising with Christ in faith and baptism and receiving the Spirit. The key elements of the second coming include, in addition to the return of Jesus, the bodily resurrection of the dead, the final judgment, the liberation of the cosmos, the universal acknowledgment of Jesus as Lord and his submission to the Father, and glorification and eternal life for believers.

Some examples (in no sense exhaustive) of this bifocal approach are the following:

TOPIC AND PASSAGE	REFERENCES TO THE FIRST COMING (NRSV)	REFERENCES TO THE SECOND COMING (NRSV)
Division: power and wisdom (1:1–3:4)	- "Was Paul crucified for you?" (1:13). - "Christ [crucified] the power of God and the wisdom of God" (1:24; see all of 1:17–25). - "I decided to know nothing among you except Jesus Christ, and him crucified" (2:2). - "None of the rulers of this age understood this [Christ as the wisdom of God]; for if they had, they would not have crucified the Lord of glory" (2:8).	- "You are not lacking in any spiritual gift as you wait for the revealing of our Lord Jesus Christ. He will also strengthen you to the end, so that you may be blameless on the day of our Lord Jesus Christ" (1:7–8). - "But, as it is written, 'What no eye has seen, nor ear heard, nor the human heart conceived, what God has prepared for those who love him'" (2:9).

69. See, similarly, Hays, *First Corinthians*, 111 (though without the "bifocal" terminology): Paul "calls repeatedly for the Corinthian community to be resocialized into a pattern shaped by the gospel of the cross and illuminated by the eschatological setting of the church between the cross and the final day of the Lord." Hays says this with respect to 1 Cor 7–15, but he would no doubt agree that the pattern is present already in 1 Cor 1–6.

INTRODUCING 1 CORINTHIANS

Topic and Passage	References to the First Coming (NRSV)	References to the Second Coming (NRSV)
The nature of ministry (3:5–4:13)	- "I think that God has exhibited us apostles as last of all, as though sentenced to death, because we have become a spectacle to the world, to angels and to mortals. We are fools for the sake of Christ. . . . We are weak. . . . We [are held] in disrepute. To the present hour we are hungry and thirsty, we are poorly clothed and beaten and homeless, and we grow weary from the work of our own hands. When reviled, we bless; when persecuted, we endure; when slandered, we speak kindly. We have become like the rubbish of the world, the dregs of all things, to this very day" (4:9–13).	- "The work of each builder will become visible, for the Day will disclose it, because it will be revealed with fire, and the fire will test what sort of work each has done. If what has been built on the foundation survives, the builder will receive a reward. If the work is burned up, the builder will suffer loss; the builder will be saved, but only as through fire" (3:13–15). - "Therefore do not pronounce judgment before the time, before the Lord comes, who will bring to light the things now hidden in darkness and will disclose the purposes of the heart. Then each one will receive commendation from God" (4:5).
Incest (5:1–13)	- "Clean out the old yeast [leaven] so that you may be a new batch, as you really are unleavened. For our paschal lamb, Christ, has been sacrificed" (5:7).	- "You are to hand this man over to Satan for the destruction of the flesh, so that his spirit may be saved in the day of the Lord" (5:5).
Lawsuits (6:1–11)	- "In fact, to have lawsuits at all with one another is already a defeat for you. Why not rather be wronged [like Christ]? Why not rather be defrauded?" (6:7).	- "Do you not know that the saints will judge the world? And if the world is to be judged by you, are you incompetent to try trivial cases? Do you not know that we are to judge angels—to say nothing of ordinary matters?" (6:2–3). - "Do you not know that wrongdoers will not inherit the kingdom of God?" (6:9).
Sexual immorality (6:12–20)	- "You were bought with a price; therefore glorify God in your body" (6:20).	- "And God raised the Lord and will also raise us by his power" (6:14).

Topic and Passage	References to the First Coming (NRSV)	References to the Second Coming (NRSV)
Apostolic ministry (9:1)	- "For though I am free with respect to all, I have made myself a slave to all [like Christ in his incarnation and death], so that I might win more of them" (9:19).	- "Athletes exercise self-control in all things; they do it to receive a perishable wreath, but we an imperishable one" (9:25).
Love (13:1–13)	- "[Love] does not insist on its own way [or "seeks its own advantage," as Christ did not]" (13:5).	- "For now we see in a mirror, dimly, but then we will see face to face. Now I know only in part; then I will know fully, even as I have been fully known" (13:12).

This brief overview of the letter's contents, agenda, and bifocal approach leads naturally to a consideration of certain key themes in 1 Corinthians. We have already seen that there are many theological and practical theological topics in 1 Corinthians.[70] Of many that could be considered, we will focus on those that, with Paul's bifocal approach, will be emphasized in the commentary:

- charismatic community
- resurrectional, charismatic cruciformity
- the marks of the church (unity, holiness, catholicity, and apostolicity)
- *koinōnia*

Charismatic (Spirit-Filled/Spirit-ual) Community

The word "charismatic" means different things to different people. It can simply refer to someone in the public arena whose personality and energy attract admirers and followers. But the word itself comes from the Greek word *charisma*, meaning "favor" or "gift" or even "grace": (cf. *charis*, "grace," "gift"). The word appears sixteen times in the Pauline corpus, including seven in 1 Corinthians, of which five are in chapter 12.[71] In that chapter, the word is always plural (*charismata*) and could be translated as "manifestations/functions/gifts of [God's] grace." The plural form functions along with *pneumatika* (12:1; 14:1,

---

70. For other discussions of various themes, see, e.g., those mentioned in the earlier brief discussion of themes: Hays, *First Corinthians*, 9–11; Nash, *1 Corinthians*, 36–42; and Perkins, *First Corinthians*, 28–38.

71. See 1:7; 7:7; 12:4, 9, 28, 30, 31.

INTRODUCING 1 CORINTHIANS

37), which we could render as "manifestations/functions/gifts of the Spirit" (cf. *pneuma*, "Spirit").[72] That is, *Spirit*-gifts (probably the Corinthians' preferred term) are *grace*-gifts. In Christian circles today, the word "charismatic" refers to people and forms of worship that give special emphasis to the display of the gifts of the Spirit, especially the more dramatic ones, such as healing and speaking in tongues (glossolalia).

It is clear that the Corinthians put a lot of stress on the Spirit and on the gifts/functions of the Spirit, with special emphasis on glossolalia (see ch. 14). Paul does not in any way wish to denigrate these workings of the Spirit (see, e.g., 1:7; 14:1, 5, 12, 18, 39–40). Rather, he wants the community to remain truly charismatic—gifted with the Spirit and the Spirit's various gifts. In fact, the "Spirit/spirit" (*pneuma*) family of words occurs many times in the letter: *pneuma* appears forty times, *pneumatikos* ("Spirit-ual/spiritual," or "related to the Holy Spirit/human spirit") fifteen times, and *pneumatikōs* ("spiritually") once.

By "charismatic," then, I mean Spirit-filled and evidencing the gifts and functions of God's Spirit. Thus, with Paul, we may use the term "spiritual" or "Spiritual" or even "Spirit-ual." Nonetheless, it may help at times to use "charismatic" (to emphasize grace) because, it appears, the Corinthians used certain words in the *pneuma* word family to create division rather than unity, and to claim superiority rather than practice humility and love. Paul's goal was to remind them that the work of the Spirit is the work of grace, of transformation, of holiness, of unity:

- "Now we have received not the spirit of the world, but the Spirit that is from God, so that we may understand the gifts [*charisthenta*] bestowed on us by God. And we speak of these things in words not taught by human wisdom but taught by the Spirit, interpreting spiritual things to those who are spiritual" (2:12–13).
- "Do you not know that you are God's temple and that God's Spirit dwells in you?" (3:16; see also 6:19).
- "You were washed, you were sanctified, you were justified in the name of the Lord Jesus Christ and in the Spirit of our God" (6:11).
- "All these [gifts] are activated by one and the same Spirit, who allots to each one individually just as the Spirit chooses" (12:11).
- "For in the one Spirit we were all baptized into one body—Jews or Greeks, slaves or free—and we were all made to drink of one Spirit" (12:13).

---

72. In 12:1 the form of the word could possibly mean "people of the Spirit" who, then, have these various grace-gifts, though the usage in 14:1, 37 argues against this interpretation.

64

At the same time, the self-styled "spiritual" Corinthians (probably not the entire congregation) needed correcting to be *truly* spiritual/Spirit-ual:

- "Those who are unspiritual do not receive the gifts [lit., "the things"] of God's Spirit, for they are foolishness to them, and they are unable to understand them because they are spiritually discerned" (2:14).
- "And so, brothers and sisters, I could not speak to you as spiritual people, but rather as people of the flesh, as infants in Christ" (3:1).

Throughout the letter, Paul is not interested in taming the Spirit but in refocusing the Corinthians' understanding of what the Spirit is up to in their midst. He wants them to be a *cruciform* charismatic community. Their spirituality—including any sense of power and wisdom—must be in the shape of Christ crucified. It must be cruciform.

Resurrectional, Charismatic Cruciformity

For Paul, cruciform (cross-shaped) Christian existence is a life that embodies the humility, faithfulness, and self-giving love that Christ displayed in his incarnation and death. It is produced by the Spirit, who is the Spirit of the Father and the Son, in and among those inhabited by that Spirit. As we saw in the table above (in the column labeled "References to the First Coming"), Paul frequently names or alludes to Christ crucified as both the source and the shape, or norm, of Christian existence.

The term "*resurrectional, charismatic* cruciformity" highlights the paradoxical reality that it is the resurrected, living Christ who—by his indwelling Spirit—enables both individuals and communities to embody the story of his humility, faithfulness, and self-giving love. Moreover, this cruciform existence is resurrectional in the sense of being life-giving, both for the one(s) practicing it and the one(s) receiving it. The community at Corinth needs to learn that the Spirit they have come to know is the Spirit of *this* Christ. *The resurrected Lord remains the crucified Messiah.*

One way that Paul expresses this sort of Christlike love, either explicitly or implicitly, is through a linguistic formula, or pattern. This pattern can be summarized as follows: "Although [x] not [y] but [z]," which means something like the following:

- › Although [x = possessing status, rights, or interests]
- › not [y = using the status, rights, or interests for selfish ends]
- › but rather [z = engaging in loving concern for others].

INTRODUCING 1 CORINTHIANS

For instance, in chapter 9 Paul will claim the following:

> › Although [x] as an apostle he has the right to financial support from those to whom he ministers,
> › he has chosen not [y] to exercise that right
> › but has rather [z] worked with his hands to support himself and not burden others—an act of love.

The whole chapter is meant to urge the Corinthians to lovingly refrain from certain forms of meat eating that could do irreparable spiritual harm to others.

Such self-restraint is not, for Paul, a form of heroic individualism but rather one critical dimension of participating in a community of Christlike love empowered by his Spirit. Furthermore, although the "Although [x] not [y] but [z]" pattern is applicable to all—since everyone, no matter their station in life, has opportunities to act for their selfish advantage—it is especially applicable to those with unusual power, status, or rights.

In addition to this pattern and the example from 1 Cor 9, as well as the texts listed in the table depicting Paul's bifocality above, we should add several others that express resurrectional charismatic cruciformity, including some that are specifically related to the issue of Spirit-ual gifts:

- "Consider your own call, brothers and sisters: not many of you were wise by human standards, not many were powerful, not many were of noble birth. But God chose what is foolish in the world to shame the wise; God chose what is weak in the world to shame the strong" (1:26–27).
- "Knowledge puffs up, but love builds up" (8:1).
- "If food is a cause of their falling, I will never eat meat, so that I may not cause one of them to fall" (8:13).
- "To each is given the manifestation of the Spirit for the common good" (12:7).
- "God has so arranged the body, giving the greater honor to the inferior member" (12:24).
- "Those who speak in a tongue build up themselves, but those who prophesy build up the church" (14:4).
- "Since you are eager for spiritual gifts, strive to excel in them for building up the church" (14:12).

Once again, against some interpreters of the letter, we must stress that focusing on unity is not enough to understand what Paul and Sosthenes wish to accomplish. The Corinthians, or at least some of them, were *already* unified

66

The Story within the Letter

in their unspiritual or unholy ways. As Anthony Thiselton says, "it *would be a very serious mistake to imply that internal unity as an aspect of ecclesiology dominated*" the letter's contents. Thiselton rightly argues that Paul's agenda, as is seen in 1:26–31, is to place the whole community "under the *criterion and identity of the cross of Christ*" in order to effect a *"reversal of value systems."*[73] The reproclamation of grace, the cross and the resurrection, leading to a new "value system" characterized by love, is the community's need and Paul's message.[74]

The Marks of the Church

As noted several times already, one of the principal theological dimensions of 1 Corinthians that will be stressed in this commentary is what Christians have come to call the marks of the church: that it is called to be one, holy, catholic, and apostolic. Some interpreters have focused on one of these, normally unity or holiness, as the main concern of the letter. More promisingly for our purposes, other interpreters have sometimes noted the confluence of two or three of these marks in 1 Corinthians, without always using the language of "marks."[75]

For instance, Raymond Collins, while affirming 1:10 as the letter's formal thesis, refers back to 1:2 and argues that the substantive issue is "ultimately ecclesiological," with two focal points, unity and holiness: "How is the community one? How is the community distinct? How can it be one and distinct?"[76] These are critical questions, not only for the interpretation of this letter but also for the life of the church today, especially in a time of polarization both culturally and ecclesially. More recently, Brian Rosner and Mark Simon connect the letter and two marks, catholicity and holiness, in an essay on 1 Corinthians and the Apostles' (rather than the Nicene) Creed.[77]

---

73. Anthony C. Thiselton, *The First Epistle to the Corinthians: A Commentary on the Greek Text*, New International Greek Testament Commentary (Grand Rapids: Eerdmans, 2000), 33.

74. Thiselton, *First Epistle*, 33–34, 40.

75. For the following overview, I draw on my essay "First Corinthians and the Marks," 167–90.

76. Raymond F. Collins, *1 Corinthians*, Sacra Pagina (Collegeville, MN: Liturgical Press, 1999), 20, 27. Similarly, N. T. Wright, *Paul and the Faithfulness of God* (Minneapolis: Fortress, 2013), 390–96, esp. 394.

77. Brian Rosner and Mark Simon, "Reading 1 Corinthians in Dialogue with the Apostles' Creed," *Journal of the Evangelical Theological Society* 66 (2023): 509–22, esp. 518–19.

67

INTRODUCING 1 CORINTHIANS

In his *New Testament Ethics*, Frank Matera characterizes the two Corinthian letters as having three major ethical themes: "(1) the moral implications of being God's chosen and *sanctified people*; (2) the importance of building up the *community* of the church through *love*; and (3) the moral example of *his own life*."[78] That is, essentially, holiness, unity, and apostolicity. For catholicity, we can turn to Matera's *New Testament Theology*, in which he notes an implicit universal church in 1 Corinthians.[79]

As noted earlier, Pheme Perkins mentions the four marks explicitly in the introduction to her commentary.[80] But no one (to my knowledge) has previously read the letter, comprehensively, in light of the four creedal marks. Although Paul did not know these marks in a formal way as a quartet of ecclesial features, he nonetheless identifies them, we could say, instinctively. Knowing later Christian tradition about this quartet and using it as a lens through which to view 1 Corinthians allow us to perceive things we might not otherwise see.[81] The previous hints in this direction from other scholars demonstrate that doing so is not an artificial imposition on the letter.

We will first briefly trace each of these marks throughout the letter—that is, thematically—and show how they are connected to one another and to the character of God. Then we will consider each mark as especially emphasized in a particular part of the letter.

One

Paul devotes chapters 1–4 to the existence of *schismata* (1:10): "divisions" (NRSV, with other translations), "factions" (NJB), or "rival groups" (CEB). But the concern does not end when chapter 5 begins. The term appropriately reappears in 11:18—"I hear that there are divisions [*schismata*] among you"— and in 12:25 (quoted below).

Division is evidenced in other texts, too, including moral matters such as questions of how to deal with sexual conduct (5:1–11), litigation in the pagan courts (6:1–11), and concerns about marriage (ch. 7), as well as liturgical matters such as eating meat offered to idols (ch. 8), the dress and behavior of men

---

78. Frank J. Matera, *New Testament Ethics: The Legacies of Jesus and Paul* (Louisville: Westminster John Knox, 1996), 139 (emphasis added).

79. Frank J. Matera, *New Testament Theology: Exploring Diversity and Unity* (Louisville: Westminster John Knox, 2007), 123–26.

80. Perkins, *First Corinthians*, 46–47.

81. As stated in the preface, theological interpreters like Joel Green and Richard Hays have made this same point.

68

The Story within the Letter

and women at worship (11:2–16), and the celebration of the Lord's Supper (11:17–34), in which context 11:18 occurs. There is even division about the resurrection (15:12—"some" deniers).

Paul, of course, desires unity: "Has Christ been divided?" (1:13). Indeed, the entirety of chapter 12 is devoted to church unity:

- "For just as the body is one and has many members, and all the members of the body, though many, are one body, so it is with Christ. For in the one Spirit we were all baptized into one body—Jews or Greeks, slaves or free—and we were all made to drink of one Spirit" (12:12–13).
- "God has so arranged the body, giving the greater honor to the inferior member, that there may be no dissension [or "division"; *schisma*] within the body, but the members may have the same care for one another" (12:24b–25).

As the one holy temple of God's Holy Spirit (3:16), the *ekklēsia* is called to be a sort of *harmonious living liturgy* (see also Rom 12:1–2). The church *must* be unified because it *is* unified: it is the one *ekklēsia* and the temple of the living God. Paul issues a strong warning to those who cause division and thus risk destroying the temple, the community: "Do you all not know that you, as a body, are God's temple, and that God's Spirit dwells among you all? If anyone destroys God's temple, God will destroy that person. For God's temple is holy, and you all are that temple" (3:16–17 MJG).

Holy

"Holy," "holiness," and the related terms "sanctify," "sanctification," and "saint" are not popular words in the lexicon of many Christians today. Paul, however, uses this family of Greek words seventeen times in 1 Corinthians; most common is the adjective or noun *hagios* ("holy," "holy one," "saint") found twelve times.[82] The basic semantic sense of this word family is to be set apart from ordinary use for God's purposes as God's distinctive people (e.g., Lev 20:26). In contemporary idiom, we might use the language of God's creating an alternative culture, or community, to the reigning culture and way of life: an alterculture. The content of this alternative way of life is godliness, or Godlikeness: "You shall be holy for I, YHWH your God, am holy" (Lev 19:2 MJG).

---

82. Statistics and references: *hagios* twelve times (1:2; 3:17; 6:1, 2, 19; 7:14, 34; 12:3; 14:33; 16:1, 15, 20), *hagiazō* ("make holy," "sanctify") four times (1:2; 6:11; 7:14 [2×]), and *hagiasmos* ("holiness," "sanctification") once (1:30).

INTRODUCING 1 CORINTHIANS

The centrality of holiness to the letter is evident from the start; Paul writes to "those who have been made holy [*hēgiasmenois*] in Christ Jesus, the chosen holy ones [*hagiois*]" (1:2b MJG).[83] This community of holy ones is itself the holy temple of God (3:16–17), as we have just seen. This is the result of the action of the triune God: "You were washed, you were sanctified ["made holy"; *hēgiasthēte*], you were justified in the name of the Lord Jesus Christ and in the Spirit of our God" (6:11). The source and shape of this holiness is, not surprisingly, Christ crucified: "[He] became for us wisdom from God, and justice and holiness [*hagiasmos*] and redemption" (1:30 MJG). The task of the church at Corinth is to embody this Christlike holiness, this alternative way of being a human community. Such holiness must clearly manifest itself in the moral matters Paul addresses especially in chapters 5–7, but also in the liturgical matter of the Lord's Supper (11:17–34), and indeed in everything the church is and does. At the center of this kind of holiness will be Christlike love: "Let all that you do be done in love" (16:14).

This means that all operative Corinthian understandings of wisdom and power and rights must be deconstructed and reconstructed to correspond to the new narrative and new reality of Christ crucified that defines holiness and love. This transformation can be considered as the present dimension of theosis—of becoming Godlike by becoming Christlike.[84] Or, in the words of N. T. Wright, "*cruciform* 'divinization'" because the *ekklēsia* is "the *cross-and-resurrection-reshaped* people of God in the Messiah."[85] Paul's addressees, ancient and contemporary, need to learn that the distinctive feature of the Holy Spirit's work in this transformative process is the paradoxical union of power and weakness, of resurrection power and cruciformity.

The apostle's audiences need also to learn that holiness does not mean total separation from the world. In fact, it means active engagement with it, as it is called also to be apostolic (see below).

---

83. Most translations have "sanctified" (or "consecrated") rather than "made holy," though cf. CEB, "made holy."

84. Platonists, Stoics, and others—ancients and moderns alike—can claim to want to be like God. The critical questions are What is the character of God? and How do we know this character? Paul's answer is God's self-revelation, most fully in Christ. Here is a definition of theosis or deification I have used in several places (most recently in *Romans*, 29, n. 9): "transformative participation in the character, life, glory, and mission of God through Spirit-enabled conformity to the incarnate, crucified, and resurrected/glorified Messiah Jesus. It includes as one process what has often been seen in the Western Christian tradition as separate realities: justification, sanctification, and glorification."

85. Wright, *Paul and the Faithfulness of God*, 1023 and 375.

70

Catholic

A basic meaning of the word "catholic" is "comprehensive" or "universal." "Catholicity" in this context means a commitment to recognizing and practicing both a macro (global) and a micro (local) reality of the *ekklēsia* as a universal and an inclusive body.

As to *macrocatholicity*, Paul says the following: "To the church of God that is in Corinth, to those who are sanctified in Christ Jesus, called to be saints, together with all those who in every place call on the name of our Lord Jesus Christ, both their Lord and ours" (1:2). The universality of Jesus' lordship and of those who call on him as Lord could hardly be clearer. Specific practices discussed in the letter that refer to or assume a universal sense of the church include teaching about the following:

- Paul's "ways in Christ, as I teach them everywhere in every church" (4:17)
- divorce, with a command from the Lord (7:10)
- vocation, according to "my rule in all the churches" (7:17)
- the rights of apostles, with references to other apostles and the Lord's command (9:3–14)
- dress and behavior in the assembly, with a reference to "the churches of God" (11:2, 16)
- women's silence in the assembly (or possibly more general admonitions in the chapter), with a reference to "all the churches of the saints" (14:33–35)
- the collection for the church in Jerusalem, with instructions parallel to those given to "the churches of Galatia" for [the churches of] "Jerusalem" (16:1–4)

In addition, especially important are Paul's references to the traditions of the Last Supper and the church's christological affirmations that were handed to him and that he passed on (11:23–25; 15:3–5, a minicreed). These do not reflect local but rather universal, or ecumenical, convictions.[86] Such traditions are not merely sacred texts to be remembered and recited, for they contain within them mandates for certain practices that are constitutive of the church qua church. The church cannot be one or holy or apostolic if its practices are inconsistent with its catholic traditions.

Paul's concern for *microcatholicity* is found throughout the entire letter. It has the sense of deep and wide hospitality. For example: the inclusion of the

---

86. The word "ecumenical" comes from the Greek word *oikoumenē*, meaning "the inhabited earth" and often therefore, in Paul's day, the empire.

weak and those of no worldly esteem, because that is how and where God works (1:26–31); the need for self-denying love toward those with a weak consciousness (or self-awareness, or sensibility), because that is how Christ lived and died (8:1–13); the need to welcome those who have nothing at the Lord's Supper (11:17–34); the honoring of the weak (12:22–26); and the inclusion of all in the use of gifts in worship (14:26; cf. 11:4–5; 12:4–11).

For the church to be catholic, or universal, there must be unity, but that does not mean uniformity (as ch. 12 makes clear). We might call to mind a well-known Christian mantra: "In essentials, unity; in nonessentials, liberty; in all things, charity." But Paul would be very cautious, especially with the Corinthians—and their spiritual descendants—about the temptation to exploit the "liberty" part of that proverbial thought. "Catholic" does not mean inclusive without personal restrictions or community boundaries, for that would be a contradiction to holiness. For Paul, it is "in essentials, unity *and holiness*" that makes the church truly catholic and ecumenical, and those essentials are grounded in Paul's apostolic vocation and message.

Apostolic

Finally, we turn to the apostolic character of the church, and this in four ways.

First, throughout the letter, references are meant to ensure that the Corinthian community continues to believe what their father has taught them— much of which he did not invent but passed on, as we have just seen. Several texts (many of which we quoted in discussing the liturgical character of the letter earlier) reveal this concern:

- 8:6, widely recognized as an early christological reinterpretation of the Shema
- 11:23–25, the tradition about the Lord's Supper
- 12:3 ("Jesus is Lord"), the logical corollary of the reinterpretation of the Shema
- 15:3–5, the four-part christological creed
- 16:22 (*marana tha*; "Our Lord, come!"), an exclamation in Aramaic

Second, throughout the letter, we also find references to Paul's apostolic example, so that the community will not merely believe what their father taught them but also practice what he embodied of the gospel:

- "For though you might have ten thousand guardians in Christ, you do not have many fathers. Indeed, in Christ Jesus I became your father through the gospel.

The Story within the Letter

> I appeal to you, then, be imitators of me. For this reason, I sent you Timothy, who is my beloved and faithful child in the Lord, to remind you of my ways in Christ Jesus, as I teach them everywhere in every church" (4:15–17).

- "If food is a cause of their falling, I will never eat meat, so that I may not cause one of them to fall" (8:13).
- "We have not made use of this right [to financial support], but we endure anything rather than put an obstacle in the way of the gospel of Christ. . . . But I have made no use of any of these rights, nor am I writing this so that they may be applied in my case. . . . What then is my reward? Just this: that in my proclamation I may make the gospel free of charge, so as not to make full use of my rights in the gospel. For though I am free with respect to all, I have made myself a slave to all, so that I might win more of them" (9:12b, 15a, 18–19).
- "Just as I try to please everyone in everything I do, not seeking my own advantage, but that of many, so that they may be saved. Be imitators of me, as I am of Christ" (10:33–11:1).

It is clear that, for Paul, to be apostolic is not merely to be *Paul*-like but to be *Christ*like. That is what he claims in the quotations from chapters 4 ("in Christ Jesus") and 11 ("as I am [an imitator] of Christ"). And the descriptions of his actual or potential behavior in the other texts are deliberate echoes of christological texts such as Phil 2:6–8 (1 Cor 8:13; 9:12, 15, 19–23; 10:33).

Third, as noted above, there are clear indications in 1 Corinthians that Paul knows and expects the members of the community to be in close contact with nonbelievers in a spirit of "salvific intentionality," to use Michael Barram's helpful phrase. This includes relations in the social world, in the family, and in the assembly meetings themselves (see discussion above about the missional character of 1 Corinthians). The primary goal in these relationships with outsiders to the church and the faith is their salvation—their participation in the new life offered through faith, baptism, and participation in Christ's body.

Fourth, to be apostolic is to be supportive more broadly of the *missio Dei*, the mission of God in the world through his human coworkers. In chapter 16 of the letter, Paul speaks about his own missional activity and that of others in order to garner their participation (the collection for Jerusalem; 16:1–4), understanding (his ministry plans; 16:5–9), support (of Timothy, Apollos, and local leaders; 16:10–12, 15–18), and bonds of fellowship (16:19–24).

In 1 Corinthians, then, apostolicity—like unity, holiness, and catholicity—is actually a relational term, and specifically a term about being in relationship vertically with Father, Son, and Spirit, and horizontally with both fellow believers and outsiders. We turn now to briefly explore aspects of that set of relationships, or *koinōnia*, manifested in the letter.

Participation/Koinōnia *and the Marks of the Church*

Many modern interpreters focus on 1 Cor 1:10 as the stated purpose of the letter and (the quest for) unity as the letter's governing theme. This perspective echoes the words of the Muratorian Canon (or Fragment), which dates from the late second, or perhaps early fourth, century. It maintains that the purpose of 1 Corinthians is to prohibit the "heresy of schism."[87] Other ancient interpreters also found disunity as the root issue at Corinth. For example, in the fifth century, Theodoret of Cyrus wrote, "Paul was right to add the name of Christ here [to his appeal for unity in 1:10], because that is what the Corinthians were really rejecting."[88]

But this view overstresses unity at the expense of Paul's emphasis on conversion, holiness, and love, of which unity is the fruit. In fact, there are parts of the letter in which unity is not the only or main issue (see the letter outline below). It may be, in fact, that the word *koinōnia*, both with the Lord and (as a result) with one another, is a good summary of Paul's four-dimensional but integrated agenda.

Koinōnia is a word that has no perfect translation into English. It has to do with two or more parties having something significant in common and sharing their lives intimately. Accordingly, words like "fellowship," "communion," "sharing," "partnership,"[89] "companionship," "solidarity," and "participation" can all be used to indicate the nature of the vertical (people with God) and horizontal (people to people) relationships Paul seeks to foster. Anthony Thiselton tries to keep both elements together with the translation "communal participation."[90] More colloquially, one might think of *koinōnia* as "being in

---

87. Similarly, see Clement of Rome, esp. 1 Clement 1.1 and all of ch. 47 (written ca. AD 96). Division seems to have been part of the early Corinthian church's DNA. The most influential modern proponent of focusing on 1:10 has been Margaret Mitchell's *Paul and the Rhetoric of Reconciliation: An Exegetical Investigation of the Language and Composition of 1 Corinthians* (Louisville: Westminster John Knox, 1993).

88. Theodoret of Cyrus, *Commentary on the First Epistle to the Corinthians* 167, cited in Gerald Bray, ed., *1–2 Corinthians*, Ancient Christian Commentary on Scripture 7 (Downers Grove, IL: InterVarsity Press, 1999), 9.

89. Ancient usage of the word included references to business partnership, what we might call in this context "missional partnership."

90. Thiselton, *First Epistle*, 103–5, 750, 761–63.

sync"—with the triune God and with one another. *Koinōnia* language is covenant language: "I will be your God and you will be my people";[91] it speaks of an intimate mutual commitment, like marriage.

The word *koinōnia* appears only three times in 1 Corinthians, but these three occurrences are highly significant. Its first appearance is in 1:9, where it elicits two main English translations (italicized here):

- "God is faithful; by him you [plural] were called into the *fellowship* of his Son, Jesus Christ our Lord" (NRSV; NET has "fellowship with his son").
- "God is faithful, and you [plural] were called by him to *partnership* with his Son, Jesus Christ our Lord" (CEB; cf. NRSVue, NJB, NLT).

This verse concludes the opening segment of the letter (1:1–9) before the letter body begins at 1:10 and the unity theme is announced.[92] It serves as a summary of the first nine verses and, in effect, a summary of the letter as a whole. The community at Corinth—note the plural "you" embedded in the Greek verb *eklēthēte* ("you were called")—has been called by God to be in communion and partnership, together, with Christ. This is essential to their identity of being together "in" Christ, sanctified, or made holy, together with Paul and Sosthenes (1:1) and all others who confess Jesus as Lord (1:2).

This experience is not merely a feel-good social network or coffee hour but a partnership in mission—God's mission in Jesus. In other words, the word *koinōnia* includes within it the reality of being one, holy, catholic (universal), and apostolic. None of these marks stands alone in 1 Corinthians; they are all interconnected, as any good work on ecclesiology would affirm and as Paul tells us from the get-go.

The other two occurrences of *koinōnia* are in 10:16, which also elicits two main—but different—contemporary English translations (again italicized):[93]

- "The cup of blessing that we bless, is it not a *sharing* [*koinōnia*] in the blood of Christ? The bread that we break, is it not a *sharing* [*koinōnia*] in the body of Christ?" (NRSV, NRSVue; cf. CEB, NET).
- "Is not the cup of thanksgiving for which we give thanks a *participation* [*koinōnia*] in the blood of Christ? And is not the bread that we break a *participation* [*koinōnia*] in the body of Christ?" (NIV; cf. RSV, NAB, ESV).

91. See, e.g., Exod 6:7; Lev 26:12; Deut 29:13; Jer 7:23; 11:4; 30:22; Ezek 36:28; 2 Cor 6:16.
92. It is best to see 1:10 as indicating the theme of the first major section of the letter (1:10–4:21), rather than of the whole letter.
93. A few translations, following the KJV, use the word "communion."

The related word *koinōnos* ("partner," "participant") occurs in 10:18 and 10:20 (again, note italics):

- "Consider the people of Israel; are not those who eat the sacrifices *partners* [*koinōnoi*] in the altar?" (10:18 NRSV, NRSVue; cf. NET, RSV).
- "I imply that what pagans sacrifice, they sacrifice to demons and not to God. I do not want you [plural] to be *partners* [*koinōnous*] with demons" (10:20 NRSV, NRSVue; NAB, NIV, ESV have "participants").
- "Consider the people of Israel: are not those who eat the sacrifices *participants* in the altar?" (10:18 ESV; cf. NAB, NIV).[94]
- "But the sacrifices of pagans are offered to demons, not to God, and I do not want you to be *participants* [*koinōnous*] with demons" (10:20 NIV; cf. NAB, ESV).

In chapter 10, in the context of a discussion of idolatry and its effects, we learn that this participation in, and partnership with, Christ is an exclusive relationship. The church is called to flee from idolatry, which will destroy the very essence and character of the church. It cannot be unified as a holy, catholic, and apostolic (witness-bearing) community if it is involved in that which is precisely the opposite of those marks.

In fact, by using the related word *synkoinōnos* (*syn* = "with/co-" + *koinōnos* → "co-partner," "co-participant") in 9:23, Paul indicates that an appropriate apostolic lifestyle is critical to being involved in the gospel, the mission of God: "I do all things for the sake of the gospel, so that I may be a co-participant in it" (9:23 MJG).[95] If Paul is the model for the church's mission, there is a similar (if not precisely the same) need for the church to embody the gospel in order to advance the gospel as a participant in it—and thus in the *missio Dei*.

One final critical note about *koinōnia*: although the word does not appear in 1 Cor 13 or 15, the eschatological dimension of participation is clearly in view in those chapters. In chapter 13, we read, "When the complete comes, the partial will come to an end. . . . For now we see in a mirror, dimly, but then we will see face to face. Now I know only in part; then I will know fully, even as I have been fully known" (13:10, 12). This is certainly an apt description of the ultimate biblical, covenantal, relational understanding of knowing God:

---

94. CEB: "Look at the people of Israel. Don't those who eat the sacrifices *share* [*koinōnoi*] from the altar?"

95. The NRSVue, CEB, and NET have a similar translation, which is preferable to the NRSV's "I do it all for the sake of the gospel, so that I may share in its blessings" (similarly, RSV, NIV, ESV). No form of the word "blessing" itself appears in the text.

76

koinōnia in full.[96] And in chapter 15, participation culminates in the fullest form of life: "as all die in Adam, so all will be made alive in Christ" (15:22).

The Marks of the Church and the Character of God: Father, Son, and Spirit

In our discussion of the manifestation of the four marks of the church throughout 1 Corinthians, we have noticed that there are references to each mark in all sections of the letter, and that (for example) appeals for holiness and unity, or catholicity and apostolicity, appear in the same breath. We have now also seen that these four are interrelated aspects of *koinōnia*. This interrelationship is not coincidental or accidental; it is a function of Paul's unified vision of the church. This unified vision is no doubt rooted for Paul in what we may call the "unity of the virtues"; just as faith, hope, and love are distinct and yet ultimately belong together, and just as the dimensions of the fruit (singular!) of the Spirit (Gal 5:22–23) are distinct and yet manifestations of that singular "fruit," so also the four marks of the church are distinct yet inseparable: four in one.

Ultimately, this unity of the marks of the church, and of Christian virtues more generally, is grounded in the unity, or simplicity, of God.[97] We see this in 1 Corinthians when Paul speaks, explicitly or implicitly, of the unified activity—and hence, by extension, the unified being—of the Father, the Son, and the Spirit. But the marks are not only a unity pointing to the unity, or simplicity, of the triune God. The marks of the church are not *arbitrary* but *necessary* because they are grounded in the character of God. That is, the marks of the church are derivative: God is one, God is holy, God is catholic (i.e., universal and all-embracing), and God is apostolic (i.e., missional).[98]

We see this derivative relationship expressed in the phrase, "You [as my people] shall be holy, for I am holy" (e.g., Lev 11:45; 19:2; 1 Pet 1:16). We can expand this to say also, "You, as my people, shall be one, for I am one"; "You,

96. Interestingly, Paul's letter to the Colossians, preferring the notion of "fullness" (*plēroō* and related words) to *koinōnia*, indicates a similar present, ongoing, and eschatological fullness of participation in God, who dwelled and dwells fully in Christ. See Col 1:9–11, 19, 27; 2:9–10. The eschatological reality ("the hope of glory," 1:27; cf. 1:5, 23; 3:4) is a hope rooted in the present indwelling of Christ, which means therefore the indwelling of God.

97. I am grateful to my son, Rev. Dr. Mark Gorman, a systematic theologian, for his reminder of the importance of this truth.

98. See further D. Brent Laytham, "God Is One, Holy, Catholic, and Apostolic," in *God Is Not . . . Religious, Nice, "One of Us," an American, A Capitalist*, ed. D. Brent Laytham (Grand Rapids: Brazos, 2004), 117–38. Laytham writes, against the popular emphasis on the "invisible" church, that "the very purpose of the church is to be a vision of who God is and what God is not" (129).

INTRODUCING 1 CORINTHIANS

as my people, shall be catholic, for I am catholic";[99] "You, as my people, shall be apostolic, for I am apostolic." Because the God of Scripture is most fully revealed for Paul in the gift of Christ and the Spirit, these qualities will be especially associated, for him, with Christ and the Spirit.[100]

We will not, of course, find all of these precise phrases in 1 Corinthians, but the concepts are present:[101]

- Paul speaks of divine and human *unity* by asking, "Has Christ been divided?" (1:13), and by saying, "just as the body is one and has many members, and all the members of the body, though many, are one body, so it is with Christ" (12:12).
- He speaks of divine and human *holiness* by saying, "Be imitators of me, as I am of Christ" (1 Cor 11:1; see also 4:16), and by connecting the Holy Spirit as God's holy presence that makes both the ecclesial body and the individual believer's body God's holy temple (3:17; 6:19).
- Paul speaks of divine and human *catholicity* by reminding the Corinthians, at the start of the letter, that they are part of "all those who in every place call on the name of our Lord Jesus Christ, both their Lord and ours" (1:2), and at the end of the letter he says, somewhat mysteriously (but significantly), that eventually God will be "all in all" (15:28).
- And Paul refers to divine and human *apostolicity* when he describes both his and the Corinthians' missional engagement with others in christological language (see Phil 2:6–8): "For though I am free with respect to all, I have made myself a slave to all, so that I might win more of them" (1 Cor 9:19; cf. 10:24, 32–33). Ultimately, for Paul, it is God the missional God, who sent the Son and the Spirit (see Gal 4:4–6), who is the source of his, and all Christian, missional activity.[102]

---

99. That is, global or universal. But God's catholicity is more than that, entailing divine fullness, sufficiency, and inherent abundance. See Laytham, "God Is One," 134–35. See also Hans Urs von Balthasar, *In the Fullness of Faith: On the Centrality of the Distinctively Catholic*, trans. Graham Harrison (San Francisco: Ignatius, 1988), the original German title of which was simply *Katholisch*.

100. This is not to say that our unity and God's unity are precisely the same; we are speaking here by way of similarity of meanings, of analogical theological thinking.

101. Paul does refer to the Shema and offers a christological reinterpretation of it in 1 Cor 8:4–6.

102. My student Zach Watson has put this well: "Paul's missional drive is merely a reflection or an outgrowth of God's missional drive to save his people" (personal correspondence, September 1, 2022).

78

For Paul and for us, too, the theological and spiritual payoff of this reality—that the marks of the church are grounded in the character of God—is that "our salvation is *participation in the Triune life of the one God*."[103] This participation, as we have noted above, is what Paul refers to as *koinōnia* (e.g., 1 Cor 1:9; 10:16). Such *koinōnia* is not a static but a dynamic, transformative reality, which is why it is sometimes called "deification" or "theosis," as well as "Christification" or "Christosis"—words that signify a process. The point, once again, is that the church is called to be one, holy, catholic, and apostolic, not *accidentally* but *necessarily*. The power of the Spirit has been unleashed to make the church resurrectionally cruciform in specific ways: in Godlike, Christlike unity, sanctity, catholicity, and apostolicity. But, of course, the church can and does fail at this calling, as 1 Corinthians bears witness—as do church history, contemporary ecclesial life, and each of our own imperfect Christian lives.

The Marks of the Church and the Letter's Structure

Interpreters of 1 Corinthians have long wondered how it works as a document—how the various parts relate to one another. There is more than one legitimate way to understand the structure of any piece of writing, including this letter.[104] The approach taken here is based on both rhetorical and theological observations.

First, I have suggested that Paul is dealing with four forms of Corinthian chaos. We can now correlate these four forms of chaos with specific sections of the letter:

- ecclesial chaos (chs. 1–4, specifically 1:10–4:21)
- moral chaos (chs. 5–7)

103. Laytham, "God Is One," 132.

104. For a survey, see Matthew R. Malcolm, "The Structure and Theme of First Corinthians in Recent Scholarship," *Currents in Biblical Research* 14 (2016): 256–69. One insightful approach, at least partly compatible with the one offered here, is that of Roy Ciampa and Brian Rosner (*The First Letter to the Corinthians*, Pillar New Testament Commentary [Grand Rapids: Eerdmans, 2010], 21–28, esp. 24), who see 4:18–7:40 as "'Flee Sexual Immorality' and 'Glorify God with Your Bodies'" (i.e., moral chaos/holiness) and 8:1–14:40 as "'Flee Idolatry' and 'Glorify God' in Your Worship'" (i.e., liturgical chaos), bookended by treatments of wisdom and eschatology. Romanian scholar Corin Mihăilă proposes a chiastic (ABA') structure to each of the parts of the letter: "The ABA' Structure of Paul's Argumentation in 1 Corinthians: Love as a Unifying Theme," *Semănătorul (The Sower)* 4 (2023): 77–113, https://tinyurl.com/2emf4yx3. We will also note several instances of chiasmus in the letter.

INTRODUCING 1 CORINTHIANS

- liturgical chaos (chs. 8–14)
- theological chaos (ch. 15)

I further suggest that each of these forms of chaos and each main section of the letter can be understood as corresponding to one of the marks of the church that Paul seeks to inculcate at Corinth:

- ecclesial chaos (chs. 1–4): unity
- moral chaos (chs. 5–7): holiness
- liturgical chaos (chs. 8–14): catholicity
- theological chaos (ch. 15): apostolicity

As noted earlier, the four aspects, or marks, of the church are found throughout the letter, but they can also be seen as connected individually to the major emphasis of each of the main divisions of the letter. That is, Paul seeks to reform the church's identity and practices in four major movements. In the light of division, he wants them to be one; in the light of immorality and injustice, he wants them to be holy; in the light of mistreatment and exclusion, he wants them to be catholic; and in the light of resurrection denial, he wants then to be apostolic. These four movements are preceded by an important opening passage (1:1–9) and followed by an equally significant closing that continues the fourth movement's focus on apostolicity (ch. 16).[105]

This way of understanding the basic structure of the letter does not at all mean that Paul addresses only one mark at a time, because the marks (and the forms of chaos) are all interrelated and ultimately inseparable. Rather, each section of the letter can be seen as *stressing* one or the other of the four marks.

The following outline displays this structure in more detail:

1:1–9   Opening: Salutation and Thanksgiving
    1:1–3   Salutation: Senders, Recipients, and Greeting
    1:4–9   Thanksgiving

---

105. To those who might find this correspondence an artificial imposition on the text ("quite a coincidence—all four marks and in the creed's order," they might think): I am not arguing that Paul intended to treat, in order, marks whose existence and sequence in the later creed he did not know. Rather, I propose that aligning both the marks and their order with the letter contents and structure can open up the letter in new, insightful ways, both theologically and rhetorically. But this approach should not and need not hamstring or limit our interpretation.

80

The Story within the Letter

1:10–4:21 **Addressing Ecclesial Chaos: Unity through the Wisdom and Power of the Cross (*One* Church)**

 1:10–17 Divisions
 1:18–2:5 The Word of the Cross and the Mission of God
  1:18–25 Christ Crucified as the Power and Wisdom of God
  1:26–31 The Cross and the Composition of the Corinthian Community
  2:1–5 The Cross and the Shape of Paul's Ministry
 2:6–3:4 Cruciform Spirituality and Corinthian Immaturity
 3:5–4:13 Ministers as Cruciform Servants in God's Church
 4:14–21 Concluding Warning: Paul's Potential Parousia

5:1–7:40 **Addressing Moral Chaos: Holy Living between Cross and Parousia (One *Holy* Church)**

 5:1–13 Incest and the Holiness and Witness of the Church
 6:1–11 Lawsuits, the Justice of God, and the Witness of the Church
 6:12–20 Sex with Prostitutes and the Temple of the Spirit
 7:1–40 Confusion about Marriage and the Missional Call of God

8:1–14:40 **Addressing Liturgical Chaos: The Cross, Worship, and Salvation for All (One Holy, *Catholic* Church)**

 8:1–11:1 Meat Associated with Idols and the Church's Mission
  8:1–13 The Problem of Idol Meat and Paul's Initial Solution
  9:1–27 The Example of Apostolic Cruciformity and Salvific Intentionality within the Church
  10:1–11:1 *Koinōnia* with and Imitation of Christ, and Salvific Intentionality outside the Church
 11:2–14:40 The Church (*Ekklēsia*) Gathered for Worship
  11:2–16 Prophetic, Prayerful Women and Men in the Assembly
  11:17–34 Abuse of the Lord's Supper
  12:1–31 The Church as Christ's Richly Gifted Body
  13:1–13 The Rule (Criterion) of Cruciform Love in Eschatological Perspective
  14:1–40 Edification and the Use of Gifts in Worship

15:1–58 **Addressing Theological Chaos: The Apostolic Witness to the Resurrection of Christ and of Believers (One Holy, Catholic, and *Apostolic* Church)**

 15:1–34 Christ's Resurrection and Its Consequences

15:1–11	The Common Creed: Christ Has Been Raised
15:12–34	The Consequences of Christ's Resurrection as Fiction or Fact
15:35–57	The Nature of Believers' Resurrection in Eschatological Perspective
15:35–50	The Nature of the Resurrection
15:51–57	The Final Victory
15:58	Concluding Exhortation

16:1–24 Closing: The Apostolic Witness Continues (One Holy, Catholic, and *Apostolic* Church)

16:1–4	The Ecumenical Collection for Jerusalem
16:5–9	Paul's Missional Plans
16:10–12	Concerning Timothy and Apollos
16:13–14	Summary Exhortations
16:15–18	Concerning Certain Corinthians
16:19–24	Greetings and Final Words

It should be noted that although chapter 16 is not directly connected to the theological focus (resurrection) of chapter 15, it does continue the focus on apostolicity that is present in chapter 15.

Summaries of the letter may be found after the comments on chapters 1–4, chapters 5–7, 8:1–11:1, chapters 11–14, and chapter 15.

For Further Reading and Study

Highly Accessible Books

Agosto, Efraín. *1 y 2 Corintios*. Conozca su Biblia. Minneapolis: Augsburg Fortress, 2008.

Barnett, Paul. *1 Corinthians: Holiness and Hope of a Rescued People*. Rev. ed. Fearn: Christian Focus, 2000.

Clark-Soles, Jaime. *1 Corinthians: Searching the Depths of God*. Nashville: Abingdon, 2021. (with companion leader's guide and DVD)

McKnight, Scot. *1 Corinthians: Living Together in a Church Divided*. Grand Rapids: HarperCollins Christian, 2024.

Starling, David I. *UnCorinthian Leadership: Thematic Reflections on 1 Corinthians*. Eugene, OR: Cascade, 2014.

Tucker, J. Brian. *Reading 1 Corinthians*. Eugene, OR: Cascade, 2017.

For Further Reading and Study

Wright, N. T. *Paul for Everyone: 1 Corinthians*. Louisville: Westminster John Knox, 2004.

Midlevel Works

Bender, Kimlyn J. *1 Corinthians*. Brazos Theological Commentary on the Bible. Grand Rapids: Baker Academic, 2022.

Brookins, T. A. "Corinthians, First Letter to the." *DPL*² 169–81.

Calvin, John. *The First Epistle of Paul the Apostle to the Corinthians*. Translated by John W. Fraser. Grand Rapids: Eerdmans, 1960.

Chrysostom, John. *Homilies of St. John Chrysostom, Archbishop of Constantinople, on the First Epistle of St. Paul the Apostle to the Corinthians*. Christian Classics Ethereal Library. https://tinyurl.com/37mzyzh8.

Deasley, Alex R. G. *1 Corinthians: A Commentary in the Wesleyan Tradition*. New Beacon Bible Commentary. Kansas City: Beacon Hill, 2021.

Dunn, James D. G. *1 Corinthians*. T&T Clark Study Guides. New York: Bloomsbury T&T Clark, 2004.

Furnish, Victor Paul. *The Theology of the First Letter to the Corinthians*. Cambridge: Cambridge University Press, 1999.

Goode, Scott. *Salvific Intentionality in 1 Corinthians: How Paul Cultivates the Missional Imagination of the Corinthian Community*. Eugene, OR: Wipf & Stock, 2023.

Hays, Richard B. *First Corinthians*. Interpretation. Louisville: Westminster John Knox, 1997.

Kim, Yung Suk, ed. *1 and 2 Corinthians*. Texts @ Contexts. Minneapolis: Fortress, 2013.

Malcolm, Matthew R. *The World of 1 Corinthians: An Exegetical Source Book of Literary and Visual Backgrounds*. Eugene, OR: Cascade, 2013.

Murphy-O'Connor, Jerome. *St. Paul's Corinth: Texts and Archaeology*. 3rd ed. Collegeville, MN: Liturgical Press, 2002.

Nash, Robert Scott. *1 Corinthians*. Smith & Helwys Bible Commentary. Macon, GA: Smith & Helwys, 2009.

Perkins, Pheme. *First Corinthians*. Paideia Commentaries on the New Testament. Grand Rapids: Baker Academic, 2012.

Rosner, Brian S., ed. *The Wisdom of the Cross: Exploring 1 Corinthians*. Nottingham: Apollos, 2011.

Sampley, J. Paul. "The First Letter to the Corinthians." Pages 771–1003 in vol. 10 of *The New Interpreter's Bible*. Edited by Leander E. Keck. Nashville: Abingdon, 2002.

Talbert, Charles H. *Reading Corinthians: A Literary and Theological Commentary*. Macon, GA: Smyth & Helwys, 2003.

Thiselton, Anthony. *First Corinthians: A Shorter Exegetical and Pastoral Commentary*. Grand Rapids: Eerdmans, 2006.

Winter, Bruce W. *After Paul Left Corinth: The Influence of Secular Ethics and Social Change*. Grand Rapids: Eerdmans, 2001.

Witherington, Ben, III. *Conflict and Community at Corinth: A Socio-Rhetorical Commentary on 1 and 2 Corinthians*. Grand Rapids: Eerdmans, 1995.

Works, Carla Swafford. *1 Corinthians*. Commentaries for Christian Formation. Grand Rapids: Eerdmans, forthcoming.

Advanced/Technical Works

Adams, Edward, and David G. Horrell, eds. *Christianity at Corinth: The Quest for the Pauline Church*. Louisville: Westminster John Knox, 2004.

Brookins, Timothy A., and Bruce W. Longenecker. *1 Corinthians 1–9: A Handbook on the Greek Text*. Waco, TX: Baylor University Press, 2016.

Brookins, Timothy A., and Bruce W. Longenecker. *1 Corinthians 10–16: A Handbook on the Greek Text*. Waco, TX: Baylor University Press, 2016.

Brown, Alexandra. *The Cross and Human Transformation: Paul's Apocalyptic World in 1 Corinthians*. Minneapolis: Fortress, 1995.

Chester, Stephen J. *Conversion in Corinth: Perspectives on Conversion in Paul's Theology and the Corinthian Church*. London: T&T Clark, 2003.

Ciampa, Roy, and Brian Rosner. *The First Letter to the Corinthians*. Pillar New Testament Commentary. Grand Rapids: Eerdmans, 2010.

Collins, Raymond F. *First Corinthians*. Sacra Pagina. Collegeville, MN: Liturgical Press, 1999.

Conzelmann, Hans. *1 Corinthians*. Translated by J. W. Leitch. Hermeneia. Philadelphia: Fortress, 1975.

Fee, Gordon D. *The First Epistle to the Corinthians*. New International Commentary on the New Testament. Rev. ed. Grand Rapids: Eerdmans, 2014 (orig. 1987).

Friesen, Steven J., Daniel N. Schowalter, and James C. Walters, eds. *Corinth in Context: Comparative Studies on Religion and Society*. Boston: Brill, 2010.

Garland, David E. *1 Corinthians*. Baker Exegetical Commentary on the New Testament. Grand Rapids: Baker Academic, 2003.

Gorman, Michael J. "First Corinthians and the Marks of God's *Ekklēsia*: One, Holy, Catholic, and Apostolic." Pages 167–90 in *One God, One People, One Future: Essays in Honor of N. T. Wright*. Edited by John Dunne and Eric Lewellen. London: SPCK; Minneapolis: Fortress, 2018.

Harrison, James R., and L. L. Welborn, eds. *The First Urban Churches 2: Roman Corinth*. Atlanta: SBL Press, 2016.

Hay, David M., ed. *1 and 2 Corinthians*. Vol. 2 of *Pauline Theology*. Minneapolis: Fortress, 1993.

Martin, Dale B. *The Corinthian Body*. New Haven: Yale University Press, 1995.

Meeks, Wayne A. *The First Urban Christians: The Social World of the Apostle Paul*. 2nd ed. New Haven: Yale University Press, 2003 (orig. 1983).

Mitchell, Margaret M. *Paul and the Rhetoric of Reconciliation: An Exegetical Investigation of the Language and Composition of 1 Corinthians*. Louisville: Westminster John Knox, 1993.

Schowalter, Daniel N., and Steven Friesen, eds. *Urban Religion in Roman Corinth: Interdisciplinary Approaches*. Cambridge: Harvard University Press, 2005.

Thiselton, Anthony C. *The First Epistle to the Corinthians: A Commentary on the Greek Text*. New International Greek Testament Commentary. Grand Rapids: Eerdmans, 2000.

Commentary with Reflections and Questions

1:1-9
OPENING: SALUTATION AND THANKSGIVING

The rich opening of this letter sets the stage and the mood for what is to follow throughout the entire letter. Paul focuses particularly on the identity of the church, the *ekklēsia*, in both the salutation and the thanksgiving, in the hope that the Corinthians—and all Christian communities—will live up to their high calling. In fact, even as it anticipates later issues, the letter's opening is essentially a mini-ecclesiology (theology of the church). At the same time, the passage is highly theocentric and Christocentric. "God," that is, "God our Father" (1:3), is named six times (1:1, 2, 3, 4a, 4b, 9), while "Jesus Christ our Lord" (1:9) is mentioned (in various ways) in each verse, for a total of eleven times. As we will see, there are also indications Paul has the Spirit in mind. That is, Paul identifies the church theologically as the dwelling place of the holy triune God.

1:1-3. SALUTATION: SENDERS, RECIPIENTS, AND GREETING

The letter begins in typical fashion for an ancient, and specifically a Pauline, letter. Yet even these formalities are theologically rich.

1:1. Senders

Paul begins the letter by identifying himself, with emphasis on his divinely ordained apostleship, and Sosthenes as the letter senders. Paul's double emphasis on God's selection of him (despite Paul's unworthiness; 15:8-10)—*called* (that is, by God) to be an apostle of Jesus Christ *by the will of God*—is likely due to the fact that some Corinthians were not so sure of his divine appointment. If Sosthenes is the now believing Corinthian synagogue leader (*archisynagōgos*) mentioned in Acts 18:17, where we learn he was beaten up by some fellow Jews, his cosending (and perhaps cowriting) the letter as Paul's colleague, now in Ephesus, would strengthen Paul's hearing. Why? Because the apostle's popularity had likely diminished in some quarters following the advent of other preachers, especially Apollos. Yet ultimately, Paul understands the validity of his apostleship to lie not in the approval of Sosthenes, the Corinthians, or even himself, but only in the call of God (see 4:1-4).

Behind the probable strategic and rhetorical aspect of including Sosthenes as co-sender lies another highly significant theological and missional reality

89

OPENING: SALUTATION AND THANKSGIVING · 1:1–9

for Paul: ministry in general is not a lone-ranger affair, and colleagues are critical to forming and re-forming Christian communities.[1] Paul often calls his coworkers partners, fellow slaves, fellow soldiers, or fellow prisoners. But here, as in 2 Corinthians, Colossians, and Philemon, the co-sender is simply "the brother" (*ho adelphos*), usually translated "our brother."

Sosthenes is not an apostle, and though clearly Paul's colleague in the present task, he is above all a fellow sibling in Christ, and he has that relationship with both Paul and the Corinthians. (There is no reason to think Sosthenes is only Paul's scribe, or he would not be named at this juncture; cf. the scribe Tertius in Rom 16:22.) He is—practically and theologically—a source of deep connection between Paul and the community. Although this letter is generally referred to as *Paul's* first letter to the Corinthians, we will occasionally indicate that "Paul and Sosthenes" say such and such to keep the latter's important role in mind. That said, first-person-singular ("I" and "my") language prevails in the letter, such that we can conclude that Paul is clearly the principal author and the one whose teaching and concerns are primary.

1:2. Recipients

The Corinthian recipients are identified as "the church [Gk. *ekklēsia*: assembly, congregation, or community] of God that is in Corinth." This phrase echoes the biblical phrases "congregation/assembly [Heb. *qahal*] of YHWH" and "congregation/assembly of Israel," which suggests continuity with the people of God narrated in the Scriptures of Israel.[2] There is, however, a definite newness to this assembly because it does not *hope for* the Messiah but is actually *"in"* the Messiah—Christ Jesus. A major emphasis here, in light of what follows in the letter, is on this assembly belonging to God, not to any human

1. Paul's most frequent letter co-sender is Timothy (named as such in six Pauline letters—and as the recipient of two, 1 and 2 Timothy). Timothy played a role in the founding of the Corinthian community (Acts 18:5); is sent by Paul to the Corinthians (1 Cor 16:10–11); and is the co-sender of 2 Corinthians (2 Cor 1:1).

2. See the phrase "congregation/assembly of YHWH [*qahal YHWH*]" in, e.g., 1 Chr 28:8 (LXX *ekklēsia kyriou*). Paul uses the phrase "the church [assembly] of God" three other times in 1 Corinthians (10:32; 11:22; 15:9), and "churches [assemblies] of God" once (11:16). The singular form of the phrase occurs also in 2 Cor 1:1; Gal 1:13; 1 Tim 3:5, 15 ("living God"), and the plural form in 1 Thess 2:14; 2 Thess 1:4. "Churches [assemblies] of Christ" appears in Rom 16:16. The Septuagint (LXX) frequently translates *qahal* as *ekklēsia*, and some Jewish assemblies in Paul's day used the term *ekklēsia*. The word *ekklēsia* could also refer to various meetings and groups, including the civic assembly of a city, or citizens' council.

90

leader—not to the church's founder, any of its patrons, or one of its popular preachers/leaders.

But this assembly is not an isolated island, for there is but one Father, one Lord, one Spirit, and one body (cf. Eph 4:4–6). This particular body is a local manifestation of a widespread movement of communities that are in the Messiah Jesus and call upon him as Lord ("both their Lord and ours"; lit., "both theirs and ours")—that is, they call on Jesus as the source and the shape of their salvation, just as Israel called on YHWH.[3] The people called by God (1:2, 9), then, are those who call on the name of the Lord Jesus; the called *by* the Lord call *on* the Lord.

An appropriate term for this worldwide entity would be the "assembly of Christ assemblies"—a single universal reality constituted by many local assemblies that happen to be "in Corinth" or wherever.[4] As John Chrysostom said, "For if it [the church] be 'of God,' it is united, and it is one, not in Corinth only, but also in all the world: for the Church's name [*ekklēsia*, "assembly"] is not a name of separation, but of unity and concord."[5]

As such, Paul says twice, the Corinthians are called to be countercultural, or altercultural: set apart from the dominant culture for God's purposes. They are "sanctified" or "made holy" (MJG; CEB) in Christ Jesus and "called to be [God's] holy ones [*hagiois*] for God's purposes" (MJG; cf. NIV, NAB, NJB), images drawn from the Scriptures of Israel (see, e.g., Exod 19:6; Lev 19:2). The double occurrence of the passive voice ("sanctified"/"made holy" and "called")—known as the divine passive—indicates that an external power is at work: God himself. In fact, similar occurrences of the divine passive and the verbs "wash," "sanctify," and "justify" in 6:11 indicate that this is the cooperative activity of the Father, the Son, and the Spirit. Sanctification is the work of the triune God.

To be holy, then, is to be called and formed by God to be different, distinct, peculiar. The terms of this distinctiveness are not set by the holy ones; they are set by God. The real substance of holiness is likeness to God: "You shall be holy for I, YHWH your God, am holy" (Lev 19:2 MJG). God's people will be generous, faithful, merciful, just, and so on because those are divine characteristics. And, as Paul will say in 1:18–2:5, that divine holiness has a particular

3. See, e.g., 1 Kgs 18:24; 1 Chr 16:8; Pss 63:4; 86:5, 7; 116:2, 13, 17; Joel 2:32; and esp. Rom 10:12–14.

4. Similarly, Richard B. Hays, *First Corinthians*, Interpretation (Louisville: Westminster John Knox, 1997), 16–17.

5. Chrysostom, *Homilies on 1 Corinthians* 1.1 See Christian Classics Ethereal Library, https://tinyurl.com/mry36f6j.

OPENING: SALUTATION AND THANKSGIVING · 1:1–9

Christlike, cruciform shape to it, since it takes place "in Christ": you shall be cruciform for I am cruciform.[6] To be holy is to participate in the life of the holy one—and that leads to a distinctive mode of living.

Some English versions translate "holy ones" as "saints" (e.g., RSV, NRSV, NRSVue), but if this term is used, it must not be understood as some exclusive supercategory of Christians.[7] Rather, all the Corinthians—all Christian believers—are made holy and called to be holy. Paul's emphasis is on the community, not merely on individuals, though, of course, there is no holy community without holy individuals. They have been called no less than Paul has been called, he to apostleship, they to sainthood (!). As we will see, this actually means they have much in common.

The believers Paul addresses may be geographically located in Corinth (or in some other place), but their true identity derives, not from their geographical or social location but from their being "in" Christ (1:2, 4, 5).[8] That is, they have their being, individually and corporately, within the crucified Messiah, who is the wisdom and power of God (1:24). It is in him that Christians find protection, power, and purpose. "Christianity," wrote Dietrich Bonhoeffer, "means community through Jesus Christ and in Jesus Christ. No Christian community is more or less than this."[9] Christians live—or at least they should live—within the story of this particular Savior, not one they concoct on their own or borrow from their culture. (Of course, this is a significant issue at Corinth, and often in the church.)

Although the Corinthians are a community whose fundamental identity is being in the (invisible) crucified and resurrected Christ, and not in the (visible) culture of Corinth, they are not an invisible, mystical fellowship. They are the body of Christ (see esp. ch. 12), and the body of Christ "takes up physical space here on earth," for "the body of Jesus Christ can only be a *visible* body, or else it is not a body at all."[10] This body does not possess a holiness on its

6. See further my *Inhabiting the Cruciform God: Kenosis, Justification, and Theosis in Paul's Narrative Soteriology* (Grand Rapids: Eerdmans, 2009), esp. 105–28.

7. This is not to deny the value of having, formally or informally, a body of people in the church (whether currently or across time) known as "saints" in the sense of those especially graced by God. But that is not what Paul has in mind.

8. For more on being in Christ according to Paul, see my *Participating in Christ: Explorations in Paul's Theology and Spirituality* (Grand Rapids: Baker Academic, 2019) or, more briefly, "In Christ," *DPL*[2] 476–82.

9. Dietrich Bonhoeffer, *Life Together: The Classic Exploration of Christian Community*, trans. and ed. John W. Doberstein (New York: HarperCollins, 1954), 21.

10. Dietrich Bonhoeffer, *Discipleship*, Dietrich Bonhoeffer Works 4, trans. Barbara Green and Reinhard Krauss (Minneapolis: Augsburg Fortress, 2001), 225 (emphasis

own, but only by virtue of its being—and remaining—in Christ, as well as in Corinth or Madrid or Dar es Salaam or Chicago. He is the holy one of God and thus the source of sanctification (1:30).

But to be holy is not to be a holy huddle. Paul and Sosthenes write of communal holiness with a purpose, for scriptural holiness entails being set apart for a mission—the divine mission. The Corinthians (and we) may not be called to be *apostles*, but they (and we) are nonetheless called to be *apostolic*—missional, participants in the *missio Dei* (Latin for "the mission of God").[11] Such participation requires being set apart, being different: being salt and light, as Jesus put it (Matt 5:13–16).[12] Even the notion of calling on the Lord implies outreach to others, according to Isaiah: "And you will say in that day: Give thanks to the Lord, call on his name; make known his deeds among the nations; proclaim that his name is exalted" (Isa 12:4). Paul would agree.

1:3. Greeting

In 1:3, we find a typical Pauline greeting: "Grace to you and peace." This phrase Christianizes a common ancient epistolary greeting: *chairein*, meaning "Hello!" or "Greetings!"[13] It is not, however, a mere formality (even if it is a liturgical saying), much less a throwaway line. Rather, it is a succinct statement of the benefits of the gospel of God that have come, and will continue to come, to the Corinthians and to all who embrace that same good news. "These two include all other gifts."[14]

The word "grace" (*charis*)—also the basic word for "gift" in Greek—fundamentally means, for Paul, the outpouring of God's undeserved mercy and transformative power through the gifts of Christ and the Spirit. Paul bookends this letter with this greeting and another grace wish in 16:23. "Peace" (*eirēnē*)

---

added). It is interesting to think of the local implications of this for a house church in ancient Corinth. What did outsiders think about these house gatherings? What kinds of suspicions, or positive opinions, emerged? What kinds of interactions took place—or failed to take place—between the members of the house church and the neighbors? For a fascinating exploration of these sorts of questions, see Richard Last, "Christ Worship in the Neighbourhood: Corinth's *Ekklēsia* and Its Vicinity (1 Cor 14:22–5)," *New Testament Studies* 68 (2022): 310–25.

11. For the theme of God's calling, see also 1:24, 26 and 7:17–24.

12. On holiness and mission, see especially Andy Johnson, *Holiness and the* Missio Dei (Eugene, OR: Cascade, 2016).

13. This greeting is preserved in a letter that begins at 2 Macc 1:10: "Greetings [*chairein*] and good health."

14. Aquinas, *Commentary*, C1, L1, 9.

OPENING: SALUTATION AND THANKSGIVING
· 1:1–9

represents the Hebrew word *shalom*, indicating harmony in the fullest sense of that word, as promised by the prophets and brought to fulfillment in Jesus: peace with God, with others, and with the rest of creation.

Both Paul himself (3:10; 15:10) and the Corinthians (1:4) have already experienced the divine grace that is once again offered in 1:3, but it is not clear that peace reigns in chaotic Corinth. One of Paul's concrete goals in the letter will be to urge the Corinthians to practice God's peace more fully, as he explicitly says on occasion (7:15; 14:33; 16:11) and implies throughout the letter. This concern for peace will reappear in 2 Corinthians: "Put things in order, listen to my appeal, agree with one another, live in peace; and the God of love and peace will be with you" (2 Cor 13:11b). These words indicate that Paul's desires for grace, love, and especially peace are not merely friendly, but ultimately arbitrary, wishes; they stem instead from the very character of God. Several other times, Paul says God is "the God of peace" (Rom 15:33; 16:20; Phil 4:9; 1 Thess 5:23; cf. Heb 13:20); similarly, Jesus is "the Lord of peace" (2 Thess 3:16).

This connection between divine character and divine gift is reinforced when Paul identifies the source of grace and peace: "from God our Father and the Lord Jesus Christ." The word "from," of course, indicates that the source of grace and peace is this twofold but inseparable divine giver (see also 8:6). A giver can bestow only what the giver possesses; since God the Father and the Lord Jesus are themselves by nature full of grace and peace, they give what they *have* in the sense of who they *are*. The divine gift of grace and peace is ultimately self-gift.[15]

It may be puzzling, both here and elsewhere in the Pauline Epistles, that Paul does not mention the Spirit as the third divine partner in the giving of grace and peace. One might conclude—erroneously—that Paul is a binitarian, or at least an incipient binitarian, but clearly not Trinitarian. That the Spirit works together with the Father and the Son is, however, implied in the thanksgiving that follows in 1:4–9. There Paul mentions the *charismata*, or "manifestations/functions/gifts of [God's] grace," which are also called the *pneumatika*, or "manifestations/functions/gifts of the Spirit," in chapters 12 and 14.[16] And Paul

15. For grace as a characteristic of God the Father or Jesus, see 1 Cor 1:4 in this context, plus, e.g., Rom 5:15; 16:20; 1 Cor 16:23; 2 Cor 13:13; Gal 1:6, 15; Phil 4:23; 1 Thess 5:28; 2 Thess 1:12; 3:18; Phlm 25. See also the identification of Christ as "the grace of God" that has "appeared" (Titus 2:11).

16. The word *pneumatika* occurs in 12:1; 14:1; *charisma* (singular) appears in 1:7 and 7:7, while *charismata* (plural) occurs in 12:4, 9, 28, 30, 31. I agree with Hays (*First Corinthians*, 18) that it is likely that the Corinthians used the word *pneumatika* while Paul, stressing that the gifts are the result of grace and thus not the occasion for pride, preferred

94

makes it clear in chapter 12 that the source and goal of these gifts is the triadic divine reality of God the Father, Christ the Lord, and the Spirit (12:4–6) even while emphasizing the Spirit as the sovereign distributor of those gifts (12:7–11). If the Spirit is in partnership with the Father and the Son in the allocation of gifts, certainly the Spirit is at work in the circulation of grace and peace.[17]

1:4–9. THANKSGIVING

Paul resumes the theme of the gracious activity of God in the thanksgiving, even as he expands that theme. Certain key motifs of the letter appear in this expression of gratitude to God: the grace (*charis*) and faithfulness of God and Christ; spiritual wealth, particularly in speech and knowledge; manifestations/functions/gifts of grace (*charismata*); blamelessness (the result of holiness) as the church's telos (goal); the day of the Lord; and fellowship, or participation (*koinōnia*).

From beginning to end, the thanksgiving contains both passive-voice and active-voice verbs that stress the initiating and sustaining grace of God, providing its rhetorical and theological structure and substance.[18] The basis of Paul's constant thankfulness for the Corinthians is God's grace offered in Christ (1:4). It is God (or perhaps specifically Christ) who will "strengthen" or confirm them to their goal of being blameless at the coming of Christ (1:8). The theological basis for Paul's certainty about the Corinthians' reaching this goal is not *their* faithfulness, which appears to be in short supply, but *God's* faithfulness. Paul may cite a liturgical text to that effect in 1:9: "Faithful is God" (*pistos ho theos*). The God who called (1:9, echoing 1:2) will deliver the goods, so to speak—and specifically deliver the Corinthians to their ultimate end.

If divine grace is the overarching basis for Paul's gratitude, the apostle also acknowledges particular aspects of that grace. He emphasizes that God provided this grace *in Christ* (1:4), and that it is *in Christ* that God enriched the Corinthians in every imaginable way, including speech (*logō*; possibly "word" or even "reason") and knowledge (1:5). Location is everything for the apostle: Jesus the Messiah is where God is revealed (cf. 1:18–31), and Jesus the Messiah is where

---

the word *charismata*. That is, his language is likely a subtle means of spiritual correction and re-formation. Paul also uses the term "manifestation" (*phanerōsis*) in 12:7.

17. So why not explicitly mention the Spirit here or in the thanksgiving, and instead wait until ch. 2, where the Spirit floodgates open? It is possible that Paul wants to make sure the Corinthians, with their overly zealous focus on dramatic Spirit manifestations, understand the inseparable connections between the Spirit and both the Father and the Son (Christ crucified), which connections he is able to make in ch. 2.

18. In Greek, vv. 4–8 are all one sentence.

OPENING: SALUTATION AND THANKSGIVING

people receive the benefits of that divine self-revelation. God's participation in *our* life enables our participation in *God's* life. Paul is certainly sincere in his claim that God has enriched the Corinthians in and through Christ (see 2 Cor 8:9), but he also believes they have misunderstood and misused this spiritual wealth. (See the sarcastic exclamation in 1 Cor 4:8—"Already you have become rich!").

In due course, therefore, Paul will need to do some significant correcting of the Corinthians' mishandling of those rich gifts. In fact, the result of God's outpouring of grace was that the Corinthians lacked no "spiritual gift"—at least that's what many English translations say in 1:7 (e.g., NRSV, RSV, NAB, NIV, CEB, NET). But the word here is *charisma*, not a word containing an explicit reference to *pneuma* (Spirit/spirit). As noted above, Paul is referring to gifts that are manifestations or functions of divine grace: the Corinthians are lacking in no "grace-gift," though (once again) Paul will need to address some significant misuse of these gifts, including inappropriate pride, and ascriptions of honor and status, related to certain gifts and those who have them.[19]

Sandwiched between the references to abundance in God's gifts is a somewhat puzzling statement in 1:6 about "the testimony of Christ" having been "strengthened" (NRSV), or "confirmed" (CEB, NAB), among the Corinthians (*ebebaiōthē*). The immediate context suggests that Paul is referring to a divine confirmation of his testimony *to* or *about* Christ (NIV, CEB, etc.)—his preaching—in the form of the gift and gifts of the Holy Spirit (see also Gal 3:1–5; Rom 15:18–20). The theme of confirmation carries into 1:8, with God (or Christ) continuing the grace-filled activity to the very end because God is a faithful God (cf. Deut 7:9; Phil 1:6; 1 Thess 5:24; 1 Cor 10:13). Paul's expectation, therefore, is that by God's grace the Corinthians will be fully prepared for (what we call) the second coming of Christ by being blameless (1:8).

Interestingly, in v. 7 Paul does not use the term "second coming" or even "coming/presence" (Gk. *parousia*). Rather, he speaks of waiting for the day of the *apokalypsis*, or public revelation, of Jesus (1:7) and of "the day of our Lord Jesus Christ" (1:8).[20] The latter phrase is taken from the Scriptures of Israel, referring to YHWH's coming day of judgment (especially) and salvation;[21] it

19. Some translations simply have "gift" for *charisma* in 1:7 (e.g., NRSVue, ESV, NASB1995, KJV).

20. In the Pauline correspondence, the noun *apokalypsis* for Jesus' return is found also in 2 Thess 1:7; for the day/day of the Lord, see also 1 Cor 3:13; 5:5; 2 Cor 1:14; Phil 1:6, 10; 1 Thess 5:2, 4; 2 Thess 1:10; 2:2, 3; 2 Tim 1:12, 18; 4:8. A few manuscripts do have *parousia* instead of "day" in 1:8.

21. See, e.g., Isa 2:12; 13:6; Ezek 13:5; Joel 1:15; 2:1, 11, 31; 3:14; Amos 5:18–20; Zech 14:1–21; Mal 3:13–4:6; Mark 13:32; 2 Cor 1:14; 1 Thess 5:1–10; 2 Tim 4:7–8; 2 Pet 3:9–15.

96

is now transferred to the Lord Jesus in a remarkable act of attributing qualities and actions to Jesus that are reserved for Israel's God in Israel's Scriptures.

As elsewhere in Paul, the goal of waiting is not thumb-twiddling but growing in Christlikeness with the aim of being pronounced blameless at the judgment (1:8; cf. Phil 1:10; 1 Thess 3:13; 5:23–24).[22] Paul's eschatological mindset comes to a theological and liturgical climax at the end of the letter: "Our Lord, come!" (16:22b). There are powerful images and promises that precede this climactic prayer, such as the beatific vision (13:12) and the destruction of Death the final enemy (15:54–55), that explain the fervor of Paul's prayer.

What Paul implies in the thanksgiving is quite rhetorically and theologically clever: he affirms the Corinthians' spiritual prowess inasmuch as it is the work of God's grace, yet he reminds them that God's mission does not end with the granting of grace-gifts; it continues with the work of establishing the church as a holy and blameless people, participants together in Christ, and thus in God's mission in Christ, who will be ready for the judgment coming on the day of the Lord. This holy participation (*koinōnia*) as a community in Christ is what constitutes true fellowship with Jesus, God's Son (1:9).[23] It is *partnership* (so NRSVue; CEB; cf. NJB), not just intimacy or ecstasy, and because it is communion with the resurrected, crucified Christ, it will be an experience of joy but also of hardship, even suffering (Phil 3:10)—resurrectional, charismatic cruciformity. This solidarity with Christ and with one another is supposed to be especially expressed in the Lord's Supper, as described in 10:1–22 (where the word *koinōnia* appears twice in 10:16) and 11:17–34.

Having and deploying grace-gifts (or spiritual gifts), then, is not the be-all and end-all of Christian existence. The focus of the letter will be on how a *charismatic* (Spirit-endowed) community must live in order to be true to its identity as God's *countercultural, Christlike*, and *cruciform* community.

As already noted, the ecclesial focus of 1:1–9 is also densely theocentric. In addition to the frequency with which Paul mentions God and the/our Lord Jesus, there are actions and attributes articulated about both the Father and the

22. On this preparatory aspect of Paul's pastoral ministry, see especially James W. Thompson, *Pastoral Ministry according to Paul: A Biblical Vision* (Grand Rapids: Baker Academic, 2006).

23. Anthony C. Thiselton, *The First Epistle to the Corinthians: A Commentary on the Greek Text*, New International Greek Testament Commentary (Grand Rapids: Eerdmans, 2000), 103–5, speaks rightly of "communal participation." The Corinthians are "participants in the life of the Son" (Alex R. G. Deasley, *1 Corinthians: A Commentary in the Wesleyan Tradition*, New Beacon Bible Commentary [Kansas City: Beacon Hill, 2021], 49).

OPENING: SALUTATION AND THANKSGIVING · 1:1–9

Son. Some of these are explicit in active verbs, adjectives, and nouns associated with one or the other (or both) of the divine persons, while others appear in passive verbs: "called," "sanctified," "given," "enriched," and "strengthened." God the Father possesses a will, calls people to *koinōnia* and sanctification and mission, has an *ekklēsia* that stretches across the known world, sanctifies his called people, is worthy of thanksgiving, offers grace and peace, enriches and gifts his *ekklēsia*, and is faithful.

The Lord Jesus has apostles, is the locus of the Father's saving and sanctifying and enriching activity, is called on for salvation, is the dwelling place of the Father's called-out people, shares with the Father in offering grace and peace, is the subject of testimony, has communion with those who constitute the *ekklēsia*, strengthens the *ekklēsia* in preparation for his future revelation, and will in fact be revealed in the future.

With respect to the relationship between the Father and the Son, not only do they bestow grace and peace together, but things that the Scriptures of Israel attributed to YHWH are now attributed by Paul to Jesus: calling Jesus Lord, calling on the name of the Lord Jesus for salvation, and waiting for the day of the Lord Jesus. But for Paul, as Phil 2:9–11 indicates, none of this honoring of the Son detracts in any way from the honor due the Father.

SUMMARY OF 1:1–9

What we find in 1 Cor 1:1–9 as a whole, then, are two things: a foretaste of what is to come (e.g., gifts, eschatology) and a lot of theology in nuce. The theology is a sort of mini-ecclesiology, a brief statement about the nature of the *ekklēsia*, or Christian community, in relation to the Father, the Son, and (implicitly) the Spirit:

- It is created and sustained by God's grace in Christ and the work of God's Spirit.
- It does not belong to any human but to God alone.
- It exists in Christ and in communion and partnership with him.
- It is both local and global.
- It is one, holy (set apart from the reigning culture for God's use in that culture), catholic (universal), and apostolic (dependent on the teachings and example of Paul and his colleagues, and sharing in the mission of God).
- It is graced, gifted, enriched, strengthened, and confirmed by God, and it will continue to be so endowed by God as it anticipates final judgment and salvation at the revelation of Jesus.

98

Especially critical is Paul's insistence on the unity and holiness of the church, both in divided Corinth and throughout the world. *Despite its many problems and deficiencies, the church at Corinth is still the church of God,* a community in Christ, part of the one church across time and space. And that is true—as difficult to believe as it may be at times—of every Christian community.

REFLECTIONS AND QUESTIONS FOR 1:1–9

Spiritual, Pastoral, Missional, and Theological Reflections

1. What looks like a simple formality (the greeting) and brief introduction to this letter is **almost a systematic theology in miniature.** We find within 1:1–9 not only ecclesiology (and several dimensions of that—unity, holiness, catholicity, apostolicity) but also theology proper (the doctrine of God), Christology, pneumatology (implicitly), soteriology, sanctification and spirituality, eschatology, and probably more. Paul, it seems, cannot even think about what he needs to say, or summarize it, without speaking with great theological breadth. At the same time, throughout the letter, Paul will need to expand upon these themes and, in so doing, re-form the Corinthians' attitudes and practices.

2. Too many Christians, especially in the West or Global North, identify only with their particular expression, or brand, of Christian faith. This is a **functional denial of the unity and catholicity of the church** expressed in the opening of 1 Corinthians and throughout the letter. Especially important today is for Christians who are not subject to persecution to be aware of the peril—and faithfulness—of many other Christians around the globe.

3. "Every church a charismatic church" is the sort of **ecclesial mantra** Paul would agree with, meaning that every church has been, and will continue to be, graced with gifts, including the so-called spectacular gifts. But because such gifts have sometimes been the source of enormous divisions and incredible pride, Paul's emphasis in this letter on grace and diversity is critically important to the health of the church, both local and global.

4. The **tension between being called to be holy**, with the goal of blamelessness at the final judgment, on the one hand, and **the realities of human imperfection,** on the other, was and is perhaps the most obvious and disappointing aspect of Christian life, whether individual or corporate. That Paul can be so positive and hopeful about a church as chaotic and messed up (to put it colloquially) as the Corinthian assembly should give each of us and our churches hope—not in ourselves, but in the grace of God.

OPENING: SALUTATION AND THANKSGIVING   · 1:1–9

5. **Holiness has two fundamental, inseparable aspects:** (1) the quality of being Godlike (for Christians, that means Christlike) and therefore (2) the quality of being different, set apart, countercultural or altercultural. It involves coming out of Babylon, as Revelation puts it (Rev 18:4)—separating from the hegemonic (dominant) culture with respect to values and practices that are contrary to the gospel. At the same time, holiness entails being different for the purposes of God in the world, including the very culture from which coming out is required. Holiness, then, does not merely entail being distinct but involves a specific kind of distinction: sharing in the character, life, and mission of God.

6. A text that succinctly brings together some of the key themes in 1:1–9 is the following selection from the (Roman Catholic) Congregation for the Doctrine of the Faith, "Letter to the Bishops of the Catholic Church on Some Aspects of the Church Understood as Communion," cited in Pope John Paul II, "*Ut unum sint* [That They May Be One]: On Commitment to Ecumenism," no. 5: "The **Church is not a reality closed in on herself**. Rather, she is permanently open to missionary and ecumenical endeavour, for she is sent to the world to announce and witness, to make present and spread the mystery of communion which is essential to her, and to gather all people and all things into Christ, so as to be for all an 'inseparable sacrament of unity'" (emphasis mine).

Questions for Those Who Read, Teach, and Preach

1. Which aspects of Paul's description of the Corinthian church resonate with your experience of the church?

2. Why is it significant for the church to think of itself in relationship to the three-in-one God, Father, Son, and Spirit?

3. To what degree today does the church focus, or not focus, on being holy, and in what sense(s) is the word "holy" understood—and misunderstood?

4. Does Paul's vision of the church expressed in 1:1–9 comport with the notion of the church as a hospital for sinners? If so, how? If not, why not?

5. How do, or should, Christians navigate the natural tension between being both distinct from and yet involved in the world? What does it mean to be *in* but not *of* the world?

6. In sum, what does this passage urge the church to believe (faith), do (love), and anticipate (hope)?

100

For Further Reading

Johnson, Andy. "Holiness, Sanctification." *DPL*[2] 423–29.

———. *Holiness and the* Missio Dei. Eugene, OR: Cascade, 2016.

Thompson, James W. *The Church according to Paul: Rediscovering the Community Conformed to Christ.* Grand Rapids: Baker Academic, 2014.

Van De Walle, Bernie. *Rethinking Holiness: A Theological Introduction.* Grand Rapids: Baker Academic, 2017.

Weima, Jeffrey A. D. *Paul the Ancient Letter Writer: An Introduction to Epistolary Analysis.* Grand Rapids: Baker Academic, 2016.

1:10–4:21
Addressing Ecclesial Chaos:
Unity through the Wisdom and Power of the Cross
(*One* Church)

The theme of 1 Cor 1:10–4:21 is quite clear: unity, unity, unity (to which Paul actually refers three times in 1:10). But this clarion call for unity is not found in isolation.

Although many interpreters take 1:10 as the theme of the entire letter, it is better to see it as the theme text for this first major section of the letter. Verse 10 is formally separate from the announcement of the broader theme of ecclesiology found in 1:1–9, though unity is obviously a significant part of that ecclesial focus. Unity also relates directly and specifically to the strong emphasis on holiness and blamelessness in 1:1–9, for a divided church is not a holy and irreproachable church. Furthermore, although there is no explicit exhortation to love per se in chapters 1–4, chapter 13 has a description of love that is antithetical to the jealous divisions described in these early chapters. Similarly, in 8:1 Paul will proclaim that love "builds up," so when there is division and destruction, we can presume that love is lacking. And the exhortation to "let all that you do be done in love" (16:14) is relevant to every part of the letter, including these chapters. In other words, Paul's emphasis on unity in 1:10–4:21 is closely linked to his other concerns, especially about holiness and love.

Paul takes these unloving, unholy divisions *very* seriously, suggesting in 3:17 that they may result in the destruction of the church, in which case God would destroy the perpetrators.[1] His desire is that the Corinthians surrender their secular person-centered partisan spirit and refocus their boasting only in the crucified Lord (1:29, 31; 3:21). It is crucial also to note what Paul does *not* want—that is, for all the Corinthians to say "I belong to Paul" (see 1:12; 3:4–5, 22), for even if they should together imitate him as their father and as an imitator of Christ (4:16), he is their servant, not their lord. In the words of Thomas Aquinas, "the baptized are called Christians from Christ alone and not Paulians from Paul."[2]

One important dimension of this extended discourse on unity is its account of the intersection of three stories in 1:18–2:5: Christ crucified as the power-in-

---

1. The destruction (final judgment) of God's enemies is a frequent theme in the Scriptures of Israel, not least in the Psalms. See, e.g., Ps 92:7, 9.

2. Aquinas, *Commentary*, C.1, L.2, 24 (*baptizati a solo Christo denominantur Christiani, non autem a Paulo Paulini*).

weakness of God (1:18–25); the conversion of the Corinthians (1:26–31)—who were generally a group of nobodies (1:28); and Paul's rhetorically unimpressive, cross-shaped ministry (2:1–5). Based on these stories, another significant dimension of these chapters is a careful delineation of the nature of ministry in the church of God (3:5–4:13). In between the triad of intersecting stories and the discussion of ministry is a robust presentation of true Spirit-uality in contrast to what is prominent at Corinth (2:6–3:4). The chapter ends with a strong fatherly admonition (4:14–21).

1:10–17. Divisions

As Paul begins the body of the letter and four chapters on unity, he issues a fundamental, even classic, appeal for such unity in the very first verse of this passage. He then proceeds to briefly summarize the divided, chaotic context for that appeal in contrast to the historical and rhetorical context of his own ministry in Corinth.

1:10–12. Paul's Appeal for Unity in the Face of Divisions

Paul's initial call for unity, in 1:10, is an urgent appeal (*parakalō*; "I exhort"), because the situation in Corinth is the antithesis of what Paul believes, and he has just said to the Corinthians that there is but one church at Corinth, and it is God's church (1:2). Paul may be the Corinthians' father and apostle, but here he honors their essential commonality with him in Christ by twice addressing them as *adelphoi*, "(my) brothers and sisters" (1:10, 11).[3] He grounds his exhortation in the "name of our Lord Jesus Christ" (1:10), echoing the frequent references to Jesus as Messiah and, especially, Lord in 1:1–9. Paul issues this exhortation—it is not mere encouragement (so the CEB)—on behalf of Christ himself, drawing on both Christ's authority and his identity ("name"; cf. 1:2). Unity is what Christ wants (see also, e.g., John 17) and, in fact, requires of his church. This is an essential component of "the mind of Christ" (2:16).

But Christ's identity, or his mind, is not a blank slate onto which anything can be inscribed. Rather, the mind of Christ refers to Christ's desire for communal unity through conformity to him. Paul expresses the content of his appeal for unity in three phrases in 1:10:

---

3. The word *adelphos* occurs thirty-nine times in 1 Corinthians, twenty-seven of which are in the plural form.

- "that all of you be in agreement" (NRSV), or "agree in what you say" (NAB): *to auto legēte*
- "and that there be no divisions [*schismata*] among you"
- "but that you be united [*katērtismenoi*] in the same mind [*en tō autō noi*] and in the same purpose [*gnōmē*]"

This third phrase contains a form of a verb (*katartizō*) that suggests not a static reality but a dynamic process, and perhaps even a process of repair or reconstruction: "that you be knit together" (NRSVue) or "be restored with the same mind and the same purpose" (CEB). The sense is unity emerging from past and present disunity, and for a future purpose; that is, unity is not simply about internal cohesion but is also purposive, missional.

The language Paul uses here can be found in ancient political discourse about communal harmony. More important, theologically, is the text's similarity to the call for humility and unity through the mind of Christ in Phil 2:1–5, where Paul again finds multiple ways to articulate the need for unity:

If then there is any encouragement in Christ, any consolation from love, any sharing (*koinōnia*) in the Spirit, any compassion and sympathy . . .

> be of the same mind [*to auto phronēte*],
> having the same love [*tēn autēn agapēn echontes*],
> being in full accord [*sympsychoi*] and
> of one mind [*to hen phronountes*].

Do nothing from selfish ambition or conceit, but in humility regard others as better than yourselves. Let each of you look not to your own interests, but to the interests of others. Let this mindset [*touto phroneite*] be in your community, which is a community in Christ Jesus.[4]

The context of this passage (Phil 1:27–2:16) also implies that unity is necessary for mission. Paul expects the Philippians to be "standing firm in one spirit, striving side by side with one mind for the faith of the gospel" (Phil 1:27). The exhortation to unity continues in 2:1–4, cited above, before the Christ poem narrates Christ's mission (Phil 2:6–11). And the poem is in turn followed by the admonition to "shine like stars in the world" by "holding forth" (NRSVue) the word of life (Phil 2:15–16).

Although the explicit emphasis on Christlikeness in Phil 2 is only implicit in

---

4. NRSV, with v. 5 ("Let this mindset . . .") altered to my own translation.

1 Cor 1:10, the language in the two texts is quite similar. Moreover, the admonitions to Christoformity, and specifically cruciformity, found in Philippians are also scattered throughout 1 Corinthians as part of the larger message of how to express unity through humble, other-regarding love (see, e.g., 1 Cor 10:24; 10:32–11:1; 13:5). Despite the language of "sameness" in the passages from both letters, Paul's goal is not uniformity without difference (see 1 Cor 12). Rather, he seeks a unity that is both Christocentric and Christoform. The need for unity among God's people is also a theme in Paul's heritage, as the psalmist wrote: "How very good and pleasant it is when brothers and sisters live together in unity!" (Ps 133:1 NRSV alt.).

Paul has learned of the fractures and rivalries in the community (similar to those known in ancient Israel and in other ancient political bodies) from a visiting team, perhaps enslaved persons, clients, family members, or colleagues, related to a woman named Chloe (1:11). The situation has been made crystal clear to Paul. The slogans he attributes to the Corinthians in 1:12 are not necessarily verbatim statements but may be Paul's rhetorical, mocking paraphrases of their childish attitudes and behavior. Regardless of whether they are verbatim, these mottos represent a spirit of divisiveness and allegiance throughout the assembly ("each of you"; 1:12).

Four groups (regardless of whether they are precisely reflective of the situation) are named: adherents of Paul, Apollos, Cephas (Peter's Aramaic name), and Christ.[5] Such divisive competition—"fan loyalty"[6]—was common in the ancient world, especially among political factions but also among disciples of competing teachers. But such rivalry and schism contradict the gospel; they are a feature of spiritual immaturity and, indeed, of unredeemed humanity (see 3:1–4). The situation is, in the words of Robert Scott Nash, "lunacy."[7] The person who teaches someone the gospel or baptizes them is not their savior and lord.[8]

The Greek idiomatic phrase "I am of . . ." (see the KJV, NASB1995) in 1:12 is often translated as "I belong to . . ." (e.g., NRSV, NRSVue, RSV, CEB, NJB). But it has also been rendered as "I follow" (NIV, ESV) or "I am with" (NET,

---

5. There is no direct evidence that Cephas had been in Corinth, but since he is mentioned four times throughout the letter (1:12; 3:22; 9:5; 15:5), he clearly has some significance to the Corinthians, quite possibly indicating his having been with them.

6. Pheme Perkins, *First Corinthians*, Paideia Commentaries on the New Testament (Grand Rapids: Baker Academic, 2012), 49.

7. Robert Scott Nash, *1 Corinthians*, Smith & Helwys Bible Commentary (Macon, GA: Smith & Helwys, 2009), 87.

8. Aquinas claims that the Corinthians thought "they received a better baptism from a better baptizer, as though the virtue of the minister had an influence on the one baptized" (*Commentary*, C.1, L.2, 24).

NASB). This sort of phrase could be used to identify followers, children, enslaved persons, devotees of a god, political adherents, or clients, but in each case, there is a clear sense of both identity and committed belonging, or allegiance. This is why Paul will later stress that he and Apollos "belong to" the Corinthians (as their servants), not the other way around (3:22), because they are servants of the Lord (3:5–9; 4:1).

It is difficult to speculate with any degree of certainty about the specific character and composition of these various groups or parties—though it is certainly tempting to do so, particularly regarding those "of Apollos." According to Acts, Apollos was a Jew from Alexandria who was "an eloquent man, well-versed in the scriptures" who "spoke with burning enthusiasm" and "boldly" (Acts 18:24–26) in Ephesus. After some fraternal correction from Priscilla and Aquila (Acts 18:26), he went to Achaia (specifically, Corinth—19:1), after Paul had founded the church, with the commendation of the Ephesian believers. There "he greatly helped those who through grace had become believers, for he powerfully refuted the Jews in public, showing by the scriptures that the Messiah is Jesus" (Acts 18:27–28).

It is definitely possible that Apollos wowed certain Corinthians—especially the more educated or elite—with his rhetorical skill, and that this was the start of the community's rivalries, especially since Paul was, by his own admission, a weak presence and speaker (1 Cor 2:1–5; 2 Cor 11:6). This was something the Corinthians knew firsthand, and some exploited (2 Cor 10:1, 10). The Paul party, then, might have been largely a group of those identified by the elite as weak—materially, socially, spiritually, or all three. The Peter party might have consisted also of weaker members (from the perspective of the Apollos party), especially more observant Jews, but we cannot be sure. And as for those "of Christ" or "of the Messiah"—they are anyone's guess.

However we identify the parties, Paul's concern is not with the leaders—he does not blame Apollos or himself for the situation. In fact, he honors Apollos in multiple appropriate ways (1 Cor 3:5–6; 4:6; 16:12) and respects his brother's decision to postpone a follow-up visit to Corinth that Paul himself urged him to make (16:12). Paul's concern is with those participating in the groups in a contentious and divisive way.

1:13–17. Paul's Rhetorical and Historical Perspective as Theological Rejoinder

Having briefly stated his appeal in three ways and briefly rehearsed the situation in Corinth, Paul next uses a trio of rhetorical questions (1:13) to put preachers in their proper place and Christ in his:

- Has Christ been divided? (or, according to John Chrysostom, dismembered?)[9]
- Was Paul crucified for you? (or even, "Paul was not crucified for you, was he?!"; MJG)[10]
- Or were you baptized in the name of Paul?

Paul's implied answers are clear: Christ is one person/body; Christ, not Paul (or any of the preachers/teachers), was crucified for the Corinthians' redemption; and the Corinthians, though baptized *by* one preacher or another, were baptized *in* Christ's name (6:11) and *into* Christ (Rom 6:3; Gal 3:27)—not in the name of (or into) one of them. The passive voice of the last verb ("baptized") suggests both that the identity of the human baptizer is insignificant and that the ultimate baptizer is the triune God, the God who washes, sanctifies, and justifies (6:11), actions also expressed with divine passive verbs (recall such verbs also in 1:1–9).

There are additional theologically significant passive verbs to consider in connection with baptism. In baptism we are immersed into Jesus Christ and his story: crucified, buried, and raised to new life with him (Rom 6). Henceforth all who are baptized are in Christ and thus in his one body (1 Cor 12). For these reasons, Christ alone—no one and nothing else—is the sole source of the fundamental identity of all the baptized, and the sole focus of their allegiance.[11]

Paul next recalls, with some difficulty, those he baptized: Crispus, Gaius, the household of Stephanas, and *maybe* some others (1:14–16).[12] He is grateful that he baptized so few because no one can claim that he baptized them in his own name (1:15), which would be an act of heresy according to the triad of rhetorical questions. Apparently, he trusts those he names not to have ever made such a claim. He identifies them, not to grant them any special status, but to stress that the real work of an apostle is to proclaim the good news, to gospelize rather

9. The Corinthians have "cut in pieces Christ, and distributed His body" (*Homilies on 1 Corinthians* 3.5).

10. The Greek question uses the particle *mē* to indicate an expected negative answer.

11. On baptism in Paul, some recent works include Pontien Ndagijimana Batibuka, *Baptism as an Event of Taking Responsibility: A New Reading of Romans 5:12 to 6:23* (Carlisle: Langham, 2022), and Isaac Augustine Morales, *The Bible and Baptism: The Fountain of Salvation* (Grand Rapids: Baker Academic, 2022), 125–55.

12. Crispus was a synagogue leader (*archisynagōgos*), like Sosthenes (Acts 18:8); Gaius, at a later point, was host to Paul and the whole assembly (Rom 16:23); and the Stephanas household were "the first converts in Achaia" (1 Cor 16:15), while Stephanas himself (with Fortunatus and Achaicus) visited Paul in Ephesus (1 Cor 16:17–18). Although these people were probably among the few elite at Corinth (1 Cor 1:26), their status is of no consequence to Paul here.

than to baptize, and to preach in such an unobtrusive way that the power of Christ crucified—not some human "power"—might be unleashed (1:17).

This is not an instance of Paul dissing or dismissing baptism, but of assuring his audience then and now that the fundamental responsibility of an apostle is to proclaim the gospel (in deed as well as word) and thus to focus on Christ, rather than on any activity—even an appropriate, holy, and necessary one—that might draw inappropriate attention to the minister rather than to the triune God (see, again, 6:11) and the gospel of God.

Paul's critique of "eloquent wisdom" or (literally) "wisdom of word" (1:17; *en sophia logou*)[13] is that it does precisely the same sort of thing: it draws attention to the alleged power and prestige of the minister, and to some sort of human wisdom that such a minister claims to have. Such preaching, in terms of both form and, especially, content, renders the good news of the power and wisdom of the cross (1:18–25) null and void: emptied (*kenōthē*) and powerless. Phrases added to the word "emptied" in v. 17, such as "of its power" (NRSV) or "of its meaning" (NAB), are translators' attempts to fill out Paul's simple, stark language: *emptied*. That is, *anything that detracts from Christ's self-emptying on the cross (Phil 2:6–11) empties that self-emptying act.*[14] In 15:14, Paul will use the same "empty" word family to say that denying the resurrection also makes the gospel empty and vain.[15]

This critique of misguided understandings and practices of power explodes in the next section of the letter, in which the power of the Messiah's cross is elevated. That is, 1:18 picks up where 1:17 ends: focusing on the cross.

REFLECTIONS AND QUESTIONS FOR 1:10–17

Spiritual, Pastoral, Missional, and Theological Reflections

1. The **existence of cliques and personality cults** is obviously not merely a historical phenomenon limited to the church of first-century Corinth. Church di-

---

13. This is a challenging phrase to translate and is sometimes rendered "showy rhetoric" or "clever words" (CEB; similarly, NET). Form or appearance is one aspect of the problem, but Paul's emphasis is on the content, the alleged wisdom, as 1:18–25 makes clear.

14. I owe the wording of this insight to students in a seminar on the letter's theology, particularly Zack Holbrook.

15. "If Christ has not been raised, then our proclamation has been in vain [*kenon*; or "empty"] and your faith has been in vain [*kenē*; or "empty"]." But since Christ has been raised, Paul's work of proclaiming the crucified and resurrected Messiah by God's grace was not "in vain," or empty (*kenē*; 15:10).

108

visions focused on individuals can occur at local, denominational, and global levels. This does not mean that all theological traditions are inappropriate, however. "I am of Calvin" versus "I am of Wesley," for example, can mean either "Here are two competing figures, theologies, and ecclesial traditions that are at odds with each other" or "Here are two complementary figures who sincerely (though imperfectly) proclaimed the one Christ-centered gospel in different places and different ways, and their heirs can learn from one another."

2. Speaking of **John Wesley**, he once preached a sermon called "**On Schism**" (Sermon 75). The first text he considers is 1 Cor 1:10, and he traces the word *schismata* in the letter from there. In the sermon, he says in part the following (from para. 20–21; emphasis added):

> O beware, I will not say of forming, but of countenancing or abetting any parties in a Christian society! Never encourage, much less cause, either by word or action, any division therein. . . . Shun the very beginning of strife. Meddle not with them that are given to dispute, with them that love contention. I never knew that remark to fail: "He that loves to dispute, does not love God." Follow peace with all men, without which you cannot effectually follow holiness. . . .
>
> Happy is he that attains the character of a peace-maker in the Church of God. . . . Be not content, not to stir up strife; but do all that in you lies, to prevent or quench the very first spark of it. *Indeed it is far easier to prevent the flame from breaking out, than to quench it afterwards.* However, be not afraid to attempt even this: The God of peace is on your side. He will give you acceptable words, and will send them to the heart of the hearers.[16]

3. **Despite Paul's concerns in 1 Corinthians, perhaps the strongest case *for* division** in the church is the argument that an ecclesial body has departed from the true gospel, or from certain essential Christian teachings. The perpetual challenge for those who wish to remain committed both to Christian orthodoxy and orthopraxy (holiness), on the one hand, and to Christian unity, on the other, is twofold: (1) if and when diversity and disagreement move beyond the range of acceptable interpretations of Scripture and Christian tradition, and (2) if and when the resulting belief and behavior so thoroughly compromise the faith that unity is no longer possible. Ironically, it is Paul himself who raises such questions when he speaks of the impossibility of another gospel and of the possibility of pseudoapostles (e.g., Gal 1:6–9; 2 Cor 11:1–14). At the same time, it is precisely this sort of argument that has led to the numerous splits in the Christian church throughout history—many of which, in retrospect, look like mistakes.

16. "On Schism," Christian Classics Ethereal Library, https://tinyurl.com/59xrvw9c.

ADDRESSING ECCLESIAL CHAOS · 1:10–4:21

4. In 1964, the **Second Vatican Council** of the Roman Catholic Church produced a text called *Unitatis redintegratio*, which means "**restoration of unity**" but is known in English as the Decree on Ecumenism. The tone of restoration is also one we see in 1 Cor 1:10 with the verb *katartizō*, as explained above. Not surprisingly, the Decree on Ecumenism begins with a nod to our passage (emphasis added): "The restoration of unity among all Christians is one of the principal concerns of the Second Vatican Council. Christ the Lord founded one Church and one Church only. However, many Christian communions present themselves to men as the true inheritors of Jesus Christ; all indeed profess to be followers of the Lord but differ in mind and go their different ways, as if Christ Himself were divided [note referencing 1 Cor 1:13]. *Such division openly contradicts the will of Christ, scandalizes the world, and damages the holy cause of preaching the Gospel to every creature.*"

The last sentence of this quotation is, for many Christians, self-evidently true, whether the division is within a particular church or between churches (local), within a denomination or tradition (e.g., Episcopalians and Anglicans), or between global ecclesial bodies (e.g., Roman Catholics and Methodists or Orthodox). But the decree immediately expresses hope, and that hope is ultimately missional: "All . . . , though in different ways, long for the one visible Church of God, a Church truly universal and set forth into the world that the world may be converted to the Gospel and so be saved, to the glory of God."

5. The notion of **something emptying the gospel** seems to attribute a power greater than the gospel and greater than the power of God to the something in question—showy rhetoric or other forms of human power. But the issue is not that these things are actually more powerful than God, or God's gospel, or Christ crucified. The issue is that humans allow such misguided forms of power to influence them and thus, functionally, to disempower the true gospel. In the end, it is not the gospel that is overpowered and emptied per se, but it is humans who have submitted to another form of power in an act of exchange (on exchange, see Rom 1:18–25). The power of the gospel remains intact ontologically, so to speak, but its functionality is damaged by those who replace it with something that is actually inferior and, in fact, empty and powerless.

6. **Baptism is an essential aspect of Christian practice**, even though it is understood in widely different ways. But thanks to Paul, there are at least some basic agreements on fundamental aspects of the practice: above all, that we are baptized into Christ, into his death and resurrection. If Christian individuals and communities focused on unpacking that reality, much disunity might be overcome, and much spiritual depth and unity achieved. And it might ensure that more people who are baptized actually become disciples.

Questions for Those Who Read, Teach, and Preach

1. In your experience of the church, what kinds of divisions have existed, and what seems to have been their cause? How were these divisions addressed—if they were? In what ways do current divisions within the church resemble or differ from those that Paul observed and criticized in Corinth?
2. Assuming that baptism is something not to downplay but to understand rightly, what sorts of practical steps can the Christian church undertake to make that happen?
3. In what contemporary ways do forms of (allegedly) Christian teaching and practice, or forms of secular wisdom, contribute to the emptying of Christ crucified?
4. In sum, what does this passage urge the church to believe (faith), do (love), and anticipate (hope)?

FOR FURTHER READING

Adams, Kevin J. *Living under Water: Baptism as a Way of Life*. Grand Rapids: Eerdmans, 2022.

Armstrong, John H. *Costly Love: The Way to True Unity for All the Followers of Jesus*. Hyde Park, NY: New City, 2017.

John of Taizé, Brother. *Friends in Christ: Paths to a New Understanding of Church*. Maryknoll, NY: Orbis Books, 2012.

John Paul II. "*Ut unum sint* [That They May Be One]: On Commitment to Ecumenism." May 25, 1995. https://tinyurl.com/ymmbcvpv.

Morales, Isaac Augustine. *The Bible and Baptism: The Fountain of Salvation*. Grand Rapids: Baker Academic, 2022.

Olson, Roger E. *The Mosaic of Christian Belief: Twenty Centuries of Unity and Diversity*. 2nd ed. Downers Grove, IL: IVP Academic, 2016.

1:18–2:5. THE WORD OF THE CROSS AND THE MISSION OF GOD

"Wisdom" and "power" were likely key elements of the specialized vocabulary of the Corinthian elitists/enthusiasts. Both concepts certainly flourished in antiquity.[17] But how do these common topics—and common understandings of them, whether ancient or modern—align with the Christian gospel, or not?

---

17. Scholars debate the precise source of the Corinthians' fascination with wisdom and power, especially the former. Whether the kind of wisdom Paul critiques derives from

ADDRESSING ECCLESIAL CHAOS · 1:10–4:21

The book of Ecclesiastes says there is "a time to break down, and a time to build up" (Eccl 3:3). Sometimes, however, in the economy and chronology of God, both of these apparently antithetical activities must happen simultaneously. In 1 Cor 1:18–2:5, one of the most important texts in all of Paul's letters, Paul seeks to deconstruct the Corinthians' ideology of wisdom and power and, at the same time, to reconstruct it by replacing it with the "word of the cross" (1:18, literally), that is, with Christ crucified as God's wisdom and power (1:23–24). Paul presents his redefinition of these realities (1:18–25) and then offers two corroborations of the redefinition: the social makeup of the Corinthian community (1:26–31) and the shape of his own ministry (2:1–5).

In this process of deconstruction and reconstruction, Paul is offering the Corinthians, and us, a distinctively Christian way of knowing—in technical terms, "a new epistemology."[18] It is the epistemology of the cross. Paul is also offering a new, distinctively Christian doctrine of God, though it is clearly rooted in the Scriptures of Israel. The notion of a crucified (and then exalted) Messiah became, in the words of Wayne Meeks, "one of the most powerful symbols that has ever appeared in the history of religions"; moreover—and this is highly significant for 1:18–2:5 but also for 2:6–3:4—"belief in the crucified Messiah introduces a new and controlling paradigm of God's mode of action."[19]

Upon entering the world of this text, we must first of all keep in mind that crucifixion was a means, and the cross a symbol, of Roman domination, and of deterrence against any who would challenge that domination. Crucifixion was the worst form of death known to the ancients, something too horrific to name in polite conversation, but described by various writers:

- The Roman orator and statesman Cicero called crucifixion "a most cruel and ignominious punishment" and "the most miserable and most painful torture, appropriate to slaves alone" (*Against Verres* 2.5.64, 66).
- The Jewish writer Josephus, who knew of mass crucifixions of his coun-

---

the sophists (specialists in showy rhetoric—ostensibly powerful speakers), the Stoics, or another source is less significant than the basic fact that it does not derive from Scripture or the gospel.

18. Thompson, *Pastoral Ministry*, 125. Thompson considers this to be the focus of 1:18 to 2:16. Epistemology is the study, or theory, of human knowledge—its source, character, and limitations.

19. Wayne A. Meeks, *The First Urban Christians: The Social World of the Apostle Paul*, 2nd ed. (New Haven: Yale University Press, 2003 [orig. 1983]), 180.

112

trymen, referred to crucifixion as "the most wretched of deaths" (*Jewish War* 7.203).

- And the Roman rhetorician Quintilian, or (more likely) one of his disciples, reported, "When we crucify criminals the most frequented roads are chosen, where the greatest number of people can look and be seized by this fear. For every punishment has less to do with the offense than with the example" (*Lesser Declamations* 274).[20]

At the same time, crucifixions united those in power and those benefiting from that power. Lynchings served similar purposes in the American South.[21]

Rome used this mechanism of domination skillfully and effectively. In other words, the cross was a critical symbol and manifestation of Roman *power* and *wisdom*. Power and wisdom lay, supposedly, in the hands and crosses of the killers—in the crucifiers, not the crucified. Not so, says Paul, speaking like a prophet on behalf of God, the God whose true power and wisdom were likewise connected to the cross.

1:18-25. Christ Crucified as the Power and Wisdom of God

First Corinthians 1:18–25, though relatively brief, is one of the most powerful rhetorical, polemical, and theological texts not only in the Pauline corpus but also in the New Testament more broadly and the Christian tradition as a whole. It expresses crucial aspects of Paul's theological vision that, if followed, lead in one clear direction and, if neglected, lead almost inevitably to its direct and—I would say—dangerous opposite. The word (*logos*) of the cross, the "message" (so most translations) of the crucified Messiah Jesus, is the power of God released into the world, as Paul will again say in Romans: "For I am not ashamed of the gospel; it is the power of God for salvation to everyone who has faith, to the Jew first and also to the Greek. For in it the righteousness of God is revealed through faith for faith; as it is written, 'The one who is righteous will

---

20. Cicero, *The Orations of Marcus Tullius Cicero*, vol. 1, trans. C. D. Yonge (London: Bell & Sons, 1916), slightly altered; Josephus, *Jewish War* (Thackeray, LCL)—the word "wretched" could also be translated "miserable" or "pitiable"; Quintilian, *Lesser Declamations* (Shackleton Bailey, LCL).

21. See James H. Cone, *The Cross and the Lynching Tree* (Maryknoll, NY: Orbis Books, 2011), who calls a lynching "a family affair, a ritual celebration of white supremacy" that brought thousands of men, women, and children together (9). Yet, "the final word about black life is not death on a lynching tree but redemption in the cross—a miraculously transformed life found in the God of the gallows" (23).

live by faith'" (Rom 1:16–17 NRSV).[22] This divinely given, powerful *logos* of the cross is the antithesis of both Roman power and the humanly orchestrated wisdom of word (*sophia logou*) just mentioned in 1:17.

But perspective is everything; only those who are called (1:24; recall 1:9) and "are being saved" (1:18; cf. 15:2) can perceive the foolishness and weakness of Christ crucified as the revelation of God's wisdom and power (1:23–24). The ongoing process of salvation, of moving toward eternal life and glory—note that it is not yet complete ("being saved"; 1:18)—is the opposite of the normal human predicament. This predicament Paul calls "perishing": being in a situation of not knowing or loving God, and thus on the way to a permanent existence apart from God that can be characterized only as death. (Paul also returns to this subject, at length, in Rom 1:18–3:20.) Anticipating what 2 Cor 4:3–4 states explicitly, Paul here implies that God's saving work is first of all an opening of the eyes that results in a person's ability to perceive the truth.

The truth that the crucified Messiah—both the event and its proclamation— is the power of God has been called the "kerygmatic paradox," from the Greek word *kērygma*, "proclamation." It is arguably the most fundamental theological claim Paul makes in 1 Corinthians. *The most astonishing truth, or wisdom, in all of salvation history is the reality that the Davidic royal Messiah and the suffering servant, both described especially by Isaiah, are one and the same: Jesus of Nazareth.*[23] Furthermore, because this wisdom is a matter of divine revelation—not a revelation of facts but a self-revelation—this same rejected, resurrected, and regnant Jesus is rightly acknowledged as the "Lord of glory" (2:8).

This divine wisdom is decidedly not the wisdom of Jewish scribes or of gentile philosophers, teachers, and orators, whose purported wisdom does not truly reveal God and is therefore in fact foolishness (1:19–21). Those who are perishing, whether Jew or gentile, can only stumble over or laugh at the oxymoron—the "stumbling block" (*skandalon*)—of a crucified Messiah, God, or Lord (1:22–23; see also Gal 5:11). They desire instead the conventional proofs of power and wisdom such as miraculous signs or philosophical acumen. But, as John Barclay puts it, "the wisdom of God is not human wisdom enhanced, and the power of God is not a more powerful version of human power."[24] In fact, the wisdom of the cross is such a radical challenge to conventional

---

22. For the interpretation of this text, see my *Romans: A Theological and Pastoral Commentary* (Grand Rapids: Eerdmans, 2022), 67–72.

23. A similar point is made by Roy Ciampa and Brian Rosner, *The First Letter to the Corinthians*, Pillar New Testament Commentary (Grand Rapids: Eerdmans, 2010), 32.

24. John M. G. Barclay, *Paul and the Power of Grace* (Grand Rapids: Eerdmans, 2020), 115.

wisdom that we might call it an antiwisdom—which is in fact, paradoxically, true wisdom itself.[25]

1:18–20. The Cross as Divine Subversion

Paul begins this passage in 1:18 by connecting it back to his concern in 1:17 about emptying Christ's cross. Anything that is offered to replace the cross subverts it, annuls it. Verse 18 also interestingly combines "foolishness" and "power"; it serves as a thesis statement for the entirety of 1:18–25, hinting that Paul's main point will revolve around two pairs of opposites: foolishness versus wisdom and power versus weakness. But the cross-based, cross-shaped, cross-revealed reality of divine wisdom and power is not a self-evident reality; rightly perceiving it requires the eyes of faith, of being part of the community of those who have been called into Christ and are being saved. The word (*logos*) and wisdom of the cross are the logic of the cross, the counterintuitive logic of God.[26]

A word about the words "wisdom" and "power," and their cognates and opposites, is in order here because they appear throughout chapters 1–4:

TERMS	TEXTS
Wisdom (*sophia*)	1:17, 19, 20, 21 (2×), 22, 24, 30; 2:1, 4, 5, 6 (2×), 7, 13; 3:19
Wise (*sophos*)	1:19, 20, 25, 26, 27; 3:10, 18 (2×), 19, 20
Power (*dynamis*)	1:18, 24; 2:4, 5; 4:19, 20
Powerful (*dynatos*)	1:26
Be able (*dynamai*)	2:14; 3:1, 2 (2×), 11
Foolishness (*mōria*)	1:18, 21, 23; 2:14; 3:19
Foolish (*mōros*)	1:25, 27; 3:18; 4:10
Make foolish (*mōrainō*)	1:20
Weakness (*astheneia*)	2:3
Weak (*asthenēs*)	1:25, 27; 4:10

That humans would fail to see God's wisdom and power is nothing new, Paul avers, and God has been in the business of subverting human understanding

---

25. So David I. Starling, *UnCorinthian Leadership: Thematic Reflections on 1 Corinthians* (Eugene, OR: Cascade, 2014), 56.

26. See Timothy G. Gombis, *Power in Weakness: Paul's Transformed Vision for Ministry* (Grand Rapids: Eerdmans, 2021), 78–79.

ADDRESSING ECCLESIAL CHAOS

since at least the time of Isaiah, whom Paul quotes in 1:19: "The Lord said: Because these people draw near with their mouths and honor me with their lips, while their hearts are far from me, and their worship of me is a human commandment learned by rote; so I will again do amazing things with this people, shocking and amazing. *The wisdom of their wise shall perish, and the discernment of the discerning shall be hidden*" (Isa 29:13-14; Pauline quotation in italics).[27] Paul would agree with Isaiah (see Isa 29:9-12) that people—even those who self-identify as God's people—can be blind to divine realities. The process of sight restoration requires a course of unlearning that both the prophet and the apostle label "destruction." This is, in other words, serious business.

A triad of rhetorical "where" questions in 1:20 is not an inquiry about location; of course, Paul can find so-called wise people, scribes (or scholars or experts in the law), and debaters characterized as belonging to "this age." As a whole, these are the allegedly "wise," but the final rhetorical question—"Has not God made foolish the wisdom of the world?"—means that their wisdom is unwisdom, folly.[28] That is, through the cross and its dramatic aftereffects, God continues in the present the sort of subversive activity described by Isaiah. In fact, Paul alludes to yet another text in Isaiah: YHWH is the one "who frustrates the omens of liars, and makes fools of diviners; who turns back the wise, and makes their knowledge foolish" (Isa 44:25). The God of Scripture is the Great Subverter.

1:21-25. The Cross as Divine Power and Wisdom

The most recent and most significant divine subversion has occurred, Paul says, because human wisdom did not achieve its hoped-for goal of knowing God (1:21a; cf. Rom 1:19-22).[29] Human longing for God does not mean competence to search for God, much less success in the endeavor. This was (and is) no surprise to God, whose plan for human salvation involved the foolishness of preaching a foolish message, the opposite of human, worldly, this-age wisdom (1:21b). This claim leads Paul to one critical Greek sentence spanning three verses (1:22-24).

Some humans, particularly people of Paul's own tradition (Jews), ask for *powerful signs* that allegedly demonstrate divinity, or proximity to divinity,

---

27. This quotation, with the one from Jeremiah in 1:31, may be seen as the "twin pillars" of Paul's argument in this passage (Hays, *First Corinthians*, 26).

28. Both rhetorically and grammatically (by the presence of the particle *ouchi*), the expected answer to this last question is enthusiastically affirmative: Yes, that is precisely what God has done!

29. "Claiming to be wise, they [people, esp. gentiles] became fools" (Rom 1:22).

while others, particularly those not of Paul's tradition (Greeks/gentiles), look for *wisdom* as the demonstration of divinity, or proximity to divinity (1:22).[30]

But not Paul, and (hopefully) not the Corinthians or their spiritual descendants. "We" (1:23)—a reference to Paul and his colleagues (including Sosthenes), but also an implicit universal Christian reference—proclaim the crucified Messiah, which is the antithesis of standard forms of power and thus a "stumbling block" to those demanding powerful signs (cf. Rom 9:31–33). It is also the antithesis of standard forms of wisdom, and thus lunacy to those looking for normal expressions of wisdom. In fact, it is the abnormal, counterintuitive character of this divine power and wisdom that makes divine initiative, a divine call (1:24, echoing 1:2 and 1:9, and anticipating 1:26–29), necessary for accepting the crucified Messiah Jesus as divine power and wisdom. And this call can come to any and all, whether stumbling over misrepresentations of divine power or stymied by misconceptions of divine wisdom.

In 1:24, Paul calls Christ "the power of God and the wisdom of God." The context makes it absolutely clear that Paul is not referring to Christ in general terms, or to his life as a whole, but to the crucified Messiah.[31] Power and wisdom are not only two human and political qualities but also two essential divine attributes. To say that Christ crucified is the power and wisdom of God means that the cross not only tells us something about Christ but also reveals God. It is, in other words, both a *Christophany* and a *theophany*,[32] as I have said elsewhere: "'Christ crucified' (v. 23), then, is the embodiment of God's wisdom and power and, as such, undermines all competing claims to wisdom and power, whether from gods or mortals. The cross is subversive; it is an act of deconstruction and reconstruction, toppling conventional understandings of these two divine attributes (and of human sharing in them) and replacing them with a cruciform interpretation of both wisdom and power. Paradoxically, the crucified Messiah reveals divine power as (what appears to be) utter weakness, and divine wisdom as (what appears to be) utter folly."[33]

---

30. On Jews seeking signs, see also Mark 8:11–12; 13:3–8; Matt 12:38–45; 16:1–4; 24:1–3; Luke 11:14–16, 29–30; 21:5–7; John 2:18; 4:48; 6:30. On gentiles seeking philosophical wisdom, see Acts 17:16–34.

31. For a more general understanding of Christ as divine wisdom, see Colossians, esp. Col 2:3.

32. A theophany is a visible divine revelation or appearance and, in that event, an encounter with God. A Christophany, similarly, is a visible revelation of, and encounter with, Christ.

33. Michael J. Gorman, "The Cross as God's Self-Exegesis: Some Contributions from Paul and John," *Interpretation* 76 (2022): 15–26 (here 23).

The radical, subversive nature of God's activity in Christ crucified is summarized in 1:25: God's foolishness (or "God's idiocy")[34] and weakness are actually wisdom and power beyond human capability or imagining. Paul's concern, however, is not merely showy rhetoric versus simple preaching "but rather the paradoxical, world-shattering, commonsense-defying content of the gospel message vis-à-vis the world's common value judgments."[35]

Summary: The Cross as Divine Self-Revelation

In 1:18–25, then, we learn from Paul that the cross is the interpretive, or hermeneutical, lens through which God is seen; it is the means of grace by which God is known because it is an act of self-revelation. The cross is *theophanic*; it is *God's self-exegesis*.[36] The cross is the benevolent divine invasion of wisdom, power, and—as Paul will say in 1:30—justice, holiness, and redemption. In his death, Christ embodied the rightwising, sanctifying, redeeming character of God—and since God does that which God is, v. 30 reinforces the point of 1:18–25 that the cross is theophanic.

In addition, as the apostle implies throughout his correspondence (not least in 1 Corinthians), Christ crucified is the revelation of God as *love*. As the Rev. Dr. Martin Luther King Jr. repeatedly said, "That event on Calvary is more than a meaningless drama that took place on the stage of history. It is a telescope through which we look out into the long vista of eternity and see the love of God breaking forth into time. It is an eternal reminder to a power-drunk generation that love is . . . [the] most durable power in the world and that [it] is, at bottom, the heartbeat of the moral cosmos."[37] The great Roman Catholic theologian Hans Urs von Balthasar put it this way: "Being disguised

---

34. Scot McKnight, *The Second Testament: A New Translation* (Downers Grove, IL: InterVarsity Press, 2023).

35. Timothy A. Brookins, *Rediscovering the Wisdom of the Corinthians: Paul, Stoicism, and Spiritual Hierarchy* (Grand Rapids: Eerdmans, 2024), 67.

36. See further Gorman, "Cross as God's Self-Exegesis." The term "self-exegesis" comes from Udo Schnelle, *Theology of the New Testament*, trans. M. Eugene Boring (Grand Rapids: Baker Academic, 2009), 674, in his comments about John 1. It is a completely appropriate phrase here too.

37. Martin Luther King Jr., "Paul's Letter to American Christians," preached on June 3, 1958, to the Commission on Ecumenical Missions and Relations of the United Presbyterian Church, USA. See the Martin Luther King Jr. Research and Education Institute, https://tinyurl.com/3t937yjn. King preached the same sermon, with minor variations, on many occasions.

under the disfigurement of an ugly crucifixion and death, the Christ upon the cross is paradoxically the clearest revelation of who God is."[38]

Christian theology and practice, then, must be shaped by the counterintuitive reality of Christ crucified as the power and wisdom of God. Any human manifestation of power and wisdom must operate "in *God's own way*, for it corresponds with God's own nature as revealed in Christ and in the cross."[39] Any other type of power or wisdom, any other theology or practice, is a profound misrepresentation of God. It is, in other words, either blasphemy (misspeaking God) or idolatry (making something other than God into one's object of worship and allegiance).

A crucified Lord did result, and must result, in cruciform ministry and cross-shaped community. Paul turns next to these two realities, in reverse order: the resulting community before the ministry that established it.

1:26-31. The Cross and the Composition of the Corinthian Community

The first demonstration of Paul's radical thesis about the nature of divine wisdom and power revealed in Christ crucified is the makeup of the Corinthian church itself (1:26-31). But Paul and Sosthenes do not merely describe the church; they invite the Corinthians to engage in communal introspection. Specifically, they ask them to contemplate (lit., "see/look at" [*blepō*]; 1:26) their "call," harking back to the earlier mention of God's special, initial work in their community at the start of the letter (1:2), in the thanksgiving (1:9), and in the preceding passage (1:24). That which Paul is about to describe is no accident of Roman societal realities; it is the work of God. What precisely did God do? That is, what kind of people did God call?

1:26-29. Divine Choice, Corinthian Constitution

Paul does not describe the Corinthian who's who but the Corinthian who's not, because that was, and is, the Corinthian reality. Three times in 1:26 Paul uses the phrase "not many": "not many wise according to the flesh, not many powerful, not many of noble birth" (MJG). Scholars have (rightly) used this text to try to discern the social makeup of the Corinthian community, and although precise interpretations have varied, it is clear that this was not a com-

38. Hans Urs von Balthasar, *Mysterium Paschale: The Mystery of Easter* (San Francisco: Ignatius, 1990), 139.
39. Thiselton, *First Epistle*, 173.

ADDRESSING ECCLESIAL CHAOS · 1:10–4:21

munity primarily of elites but of quite the opposite, with few exceptions.[40] The Corinthians did not excel in the status indicators of secular wisdom, social or political or financial power, or family station.

Paul's point is not merely *sociological* but above all *theological*. His social description is (and should be for us) sociology in the service of theology. Verses 26–28 demonstrate that God is not impressed by status-quo wisdom and power—social, spiritual, or any other type—since God has called so few wise, rich, and noble but so many who are "low and despised" (1:28). Once again Paul makes his point in the form of a triple claim, with the phrase "God chose" (cf. Eph 1:4) in each claim: God chose the world's fools to shame the wise, God chose the world's weak to shame the strong, and God chose the world's nobodies to invalidate the somebodies (1:27–28)—reduce them to nothing.[41] Ironically, the crucifixion is an absolutely shameful reality, and yet it is through the shame of Christ crucified that God shames the worldly wise and powerful. The image of resurrection and new creation is present here as well, for God is the one who "gives life to the dead and calls into existence the things that do not exist" (Rom 4:17).[42]

These verses contain the cultural language of honor and shame but also the biblical, theological idiom of God's missional character: to bring down the high and mighty and raise up the lowly, as we see in the Scriptures of Israel, in Mary's Magnificat (Luke 1:46–55), in the teachings of Jesus, elsewhere in Paul (including 1 Cor 12), and in other parts of the New Testament. Perhaps Paul had words like these from the Psalms in mind:

> The LORD is high above all nations, and his glory above the heavens.
> Who is like the LORD our God, who is seated on high,

40. Paul's words suggest to many recent interpreters that the believers in Corinth are mostly nonelite, with some, or even many, near the subsistence level. Nonetheless, according to 2 Cor 8, the Corinthians as a whole were better off economically than the Jerusalem church and probably also than the Macedonian churches (e.g., at Philippi and Thessalonica). For an accessible, helpful discussion, see Carla Swafford Works, *The Least of These: Paul and the Marginalized* (Grand Rapids: Eerdmans, 2020), 12–33.

41. Although Paul uses Greek neuter-plural terms in these verses, he is clearly referring to people. The last verb of 1:28, *katargeō* ("reduce/bring to nothing," "abolish"), indicates a theme in the letter, appearing eight more times (2:6; 6:13; 13:8 [2×], 10, 11; 15:24, 26).

42. Paul uses almost identical Greek phrases to characterize both God's choosing of the Corinthian "things that are not, to reduce to nothing things that are" (*exelexato ho theos ta mē onta, hina ta onta katargēsē*; 1 Cor 1:28) and God's calling "into existence the things that do not exist" (*kalountos ta mē onta hōs onta*; Rom 4:17). I owe this connection to Michelle Rader.

who looks far down on the heavens and the earth?
He raises the poor from the dust, and lifts the needy from the
  ash heap,
to make them sit with princes, with the princes of his people.
(Ps 113:4–8)

The LORD upholds all who are falling, and raises up all who are
  bowed down. (Ps 145:14)

He may also have thought of Hannah, whose prayer echoes the words of Ps 113 (1 Sam 2:8), and who describes the Lord as the one by whom "the bows of the mighty are broken, but the feeble gird on strength" (1 Sam 2:4).[43] And perhaps Paul knew these words from Jesus: "I thank you, Father, Lord of heaven and earth, because you have hidden these things [i.e., his teachings] from the wise and the intelligent and have revealed them to infants" (Matt 11:25). This sort of theological claim from throughout Scripture—that God works with and for society's nobodies—might have made the average Corinthian feel honored, but there is also little doubt that some at Corinth (and some still today) would be offended by such theological thinking. Humans often assume that an omnipotent God must be on the side of the most powerful, an omniscient God on the side of the most intelligent.

But this is Paul's view: God works for and among the weak and foolish (according to human standards) because this is precisely the sort of God that God is—as demonstrated in the divine action on the cross, which the world evaluated as stupidity and weakness but which is in fact the wisdom and power of God. In his brief *Mémorial*, Pascal recounted his profound, joyful experience of the God of Abraham, Isaac, and Jacob—not the god "of the philosophers and the learned"—that led him directly to Jesus. (Pascal implicitly wished the same journey for others.)[44]

Paul would concur, as 1:18–25 makes clear, but would specify that the very personal God of Abraham, Isaac, and Jacob revealed in Jesus is the God of the cross.[45] The God revealed both in Christ's cross and in the Corinthian church has a preferential option for the poor and powerless, the bottom rung of soci-

---

43. See also Hays, *First Corinthians*, 32–35.

44. For the text of the *Mémorial* (just over two hundred words), see Christian Classics Ethereal Library, https://tinyurl.com/bd97nzst.

45. Pascal might actually agree with the Pauline emphasis, since he says this God "is only found by the ways taught in the Gospel." And Paul would agree with Pascal that the experience of this God brings unimaginable joy (see, e.g., Philippians).

ADDRESSING ECCLESIAL CHAOS   · 1:10–4:21

ety, and is again in the business of subverting the status quo by making some-bodies out of nobodies—and vice versa. This is not, however, some new God; rather, it is the God of Scripture, as we have seen (see also, e.g., Isa 57:15).

The eighteenth-century African American poet and preacher Jupiter Hammon knew the God of unexpected reversals well, and found in Paul's words in 1 Cor 1:26–29 an affirmation of Black enslaved peoples and a critique of their White oppressors. Similarly, the early nineteenth-century female preacher Zilpha Elaw drew on these verses to support her call to preach; she saw herself as a modern Paul, proclaiming the gospel of Christ crucified and challenging the racism of her day.[46]

This divine project of reversal has an ultimate purpose: to redirect human pride (honor, boasting) away from oneself and one's alleged status, significance, and self-importance. All of that disintegrates "in the presence of God" (1:29). The appropriate focus of one's redirected boast is spelled out in vv. 30–31.

1:30–31. God as the Source of Life in Christ

The truth that Christ's death and the incorporation of the Corinthians into Christ are divine acts leads Paul in v. 30 to spell out, succinctly, what that means. He begins by recalling the word "wisdom," reminding us that "God's wisdom is not a 'what,' but a 'who.'"[47] The crucified Christ is true wisdom, because he is the embodiment—the incarnate expression—of God's "righteousness" or "saving justice" (*dikaiosynē*); "sanctification" or "holiness" (*hagiasmos*); and "redemption" (*apolytrōsis*). These three terms (note yet another rhetorical triad), added to "wisdom," constitute a summary of Paul's unique interpretation of Christ's death and our participation in it.

Counterintuitively and paradoxically, Christ's death reveals the righteousness/justice of God and is an act of divine redemption (cf. Rom 3:21–26). That is, Christ's death is both *redemptive* and, as Paul has already said explicitly in 1:24, *revelatory*, the manifestation of the character and activity of God. And because that death is the action of God, it is *effective*; it accomplishes God's purposes for us (e.g., 2 Cor 5:18–21). Baptized into Christ's death, believers are cleansed, made just, and made holy (see 1:2 and esp. 6:11).

---

46. See Lisa M. Bowens, *African American Readings of Paul: Reception, Resistance, and Transformation* (Grand Rapids: Eerdmans, 2020), 46–47, 88–90, 95–97.

47. Susan Grove Eastman, *Oneself in Another: Participation and Personhood in Pauline Theology* (Eugene, OR: Cascade, 2023), 101.

1:30–31 · *God as the Source of Life in Christ*

That is, in and through Christ as the counterintuitive divine wisdom and unexpected revelation of divine justice (or "making-rightness"), God has redeemed and sanctified a people—set them apart to take on his character and serve his purposes. If the people of Israel rightly proclaimed, "YHWH is our righteousness/justice" (Jer 23:6 MJG) and rejoiced that YHWH proclaimed, "I am your salvation" (Ps 35:3), then Christians now proclaim, "Jesus Christ is our righteousness/justice and salvation."

This does not mean that Jesus *replaces* YHWH but that Jesus *embodies* YHWH and shares, in fact, in the divine identity. Thus, the adulation of Jesus does not compete with the praise of God; in fact, it honors God the Father (Phil 2:9–11). To be in Christ and share in his wisdom and justice is to share in nothing less than the wisdom and justice of God (cf. 2 Cor 5:21). In fact, it is to share in the very life of God. Verse 30 speaks of "the copiousness of the gift," writes Chrysostom, "as if he [Paul] had said, He gave unto us Himself."[48]

In 1:31, Paul turns to Jeremiah to reinforce the error, the folly, of boasting about human beings when God is the source of our life: "Thus says the LORD: Do not let the wise boast in their wisdom, do not let the mighty boast in their might, do not let the wealthy boast in their wealth; but let those who boast in this, that they understand and know me, that I am the LORD; I act with steadfast love, justice, and righteousness in the earth, for in these things I delight, says the LORD" (Jer 9:23–24 [9:22–23 LXX]).[49] Culturally and humanly speaking, pride in oneself or one's community is normal. Paul redirects the Corinthians to Scripture to stress that the only proper kind of boasting is in the Lord who acts with counterintuitive divine justice, not in oneself or any other human, or in human wisdom, power, or wealth. Paul could have quoted other scriptural texts as well, such as the Psalms: "My soul makes its boast in the LORD; let the humble hear and be glad" (Ps 34:2).

For Paul, "the Lord" can refer both to God the Father and to Christ the Son. To boast in the Lord is clearly to honor God the Father as the source of our life in Christ (v. 30). But in light of 1:18–25, Paul seems also to be interpreting the Jeremiah quotation in v. 31 to mean boasting in the crucified Lord Jesus, as he says explicitly in Galatians: "May I never boast of anything except the cross of our Lord Jesus Christ, by which the world has been crucified to me, and I to the world" (Gal 6:14). Pride of any other kind fails to recognize that those who are "in Christ Jesus" (1 Cor 1:30; recall 1:2, 4, 5) are there by the gracious

---

48. Chrysostom, *Homilies on 1 Corinthians* 5.4.
49. Similar language appears in Hannah's prayer in 1 Sam 2:1–10.

ADDRESSING ECCLESIAL CHAOS · 1:10–4:21

action of God displayed in the cross of his Son. There is therefore no place for pride in oneself or in any other human.

The apostle continues his witness to God's surprising way of salvation by reflecting on his own ministry.

2:1–5. The Cross and the Shape of Paul's Ministry

The second demonstration of the thesis in 1:18–25 is Paul's modus operandi as a preacher among the Corinthians. Not only did God not *choose* the wise and powerful, but God did not *use* the wise and powerful. These two realities are grounded in Christ crucified and inform us that Christ crucified is the *epistemological criterion* for discerning the activity of God—how we know what God is up to in the world, to put it colloquially.

By Paul's own admission, he was rhetorically and otherwise weak and fearful in public (2:1, 3–4; cf. 2 Cor 10:10; Gal 4:13–14). These features of his ministry were in stark contrast to those of most teachers, including Paul's successor Apollos, and they were probably the grounds for criticism of the apostle by some, or perhaps many, at Corinth. But weakness, though not what humans might want in a preacher or teacher, comports quite well with the word of the cross as the weakness of God that is stronger than human strength (1:25). For that reason, Paul did not shy away from recounting his own weaknesses and tribulations but rather boasted in them, which means in the weakness of the crucified Messiah: "If I must boast, I will boast of the things that show my weakness" (2 Cor 11:30). In that weakness, God's power and life are on full display (2 Cor 4:5–12; 12:5–10).

Paul's purpose in going to Corinth was to preach the "mystery" (2:1, *mystērion*; cf. the singular noun in 1 Cor 2:7 and the plural noun in 4:1) of God: that is, the gospel (cf. 1:17).[50] He likely uses the word "mystery" to suggest the counterintuitive character of this word of the cross, as he has just laid it out in 1:18–2:5. Because of its mysterious, counterintuitive, paradoxical character, Paul shunned "lofty" (2:1) and allegedly persuasive (2:4) words of wisdom. He took on neither the showy rhetoric of some rhetoricians (e.g., the Sophists) nor the alleged wisdom of the philosophers (e.g., the Stoics). To use the wisdom of this age would have been to subvert the strange wisdom

---

50. Some important manuscripts have "the testimony of God" (recall 1:6—"the testimony of" [or "to"] Christ) instead of "the mystery of God," and some translations follow those manuscripts (see RSV, NIV, NET, NRSVue). The content in either case is the gospel, even for the CEB's translation of "mystery of God" as "God's secrets."

of God. So "mystery" does not for Paul, or for Christians today, mean something to be puzzled out by human wisdom or special secretive knowledge, for it has already been revealed: the mystery is the self-revelation of God in the crucified Messiah.

For these reasons, Paul tells the Corinthians he "decided to know nothing among you except Jesus Christ, and him crucified" or, better, "nothing among you except Jesus the Messiah—that is, Jesus the *crucified* Messiah" (2:2 MJG).[51] Is this hyperbolic, shortsighted, or even disingenuous? Not at all. Rather, in this single sentence, we have not only an explicit statement uttered for a specific occasion but also, implicitly, a testimony to key aspects of Paul's overall understanding of God (theology proper), Christ's person and work, the Spirit, revelation and knowledge, the church, spirituality, morality, and ministry. Much about these is unpacked in this letter.

Paul's firm determination announced in 2:2 was not due to his (allegedly) failed focus on the resurrection in Athens, according to Acts 17, as many have suggested. Rather, Paul is telling the Corinthians two things. First, his decision to "know," to portray in speech and action, nothing but the crucified Messiah was grounded in his understanding of the divine mystery, the gospel. And second, he wanted the Corinthians to know that he had to embody in his ministry this counterintuitive truth—as he similarly informed the Galatians (Gal 6:14) and will spell out in more detail later in this letter (1 Cor 9).

The divinely inspired result of Paul's weakness and lack of worldly wisdom was a "demonstration of the Spirit and of power" (2:4), probably meaning both conversions and charismatic manifestations (cf. Rom 15:18–19; 1 Thess 1:5). The regular result of Paul's preaching of the cross seems to have been an outpouring of the Spirit and the Spirit's gifts (see also Gal 3:1–5). But the giving of such gifts was not, and should not be, separated from the gift of the power of the crucified Messiah. *This is a matter of both form and substance, of both ministerial modus operandi and theological content—of cruciform integrity.* The charismatic minister or community must also be cross-shaped.

Of course, Paul knows, and proclaimed to the Corinthians (15:3–9), that God raised Christ from the dead. He is present as the living Lord, known in the presence and work of his Spirit. But Jesus always remains the Crucified One, indicated in part by the use of the perfect participle *estaurōmenon* ("crucified")

---

51. The word *kai* ("and," "even," "also") that links "Jesus Christ" and "crucified" in 2:2 (e.g., "Jesus Christ, and him crucified"; NRSV) should be interpreted epexegetically, or explicatively, to mean "even" or "that is" rather than "and."

ADDRESSING ECCLESIAL CHAOS · 1:10–4:21

in 2:2, as in 1:23.[52] The cross is a permanent, not a temporary, part of Christ's identity, and cruciform existence is therefore always the mark of Christian ministry and community. As other parts of the New Testament also testify in various ways, the Resurrected One is identical to the Crucified One and bears the marks of that continuity and reality. (See, e.g., John 20:19–29, Luke 24:36–49, and Rev 5.) In the words of the German scholar Ernst Käsemann, writing in the wake of the Nazi era, the cross is "the signature of the one who is risen."[53]

As Käsemann implies and Paul knows well, because Christ has been raised and is alive (ch. 15), this cruciform existence is suffused with the life-giving Spirit and with Christ's resurrection life. Paradoxically, as we have already noted, cruciformity is *charismatic* (Spirit-enabled) and *resurrectional*: powerfully life-giving for those who practice it and those who benefit from it. As Dietrich Bonhoeffer put it, "Only as the cross of the risen one can his [Christ's] cross have power over us. The message of the one who was crucified is always already the message of the one who did not remain in death's bondage."[54]

Paul wants Christian faith never to rest on humans or human wisdom but only on "the power of God" (2:5). This is an echo of the apostle's words about not boasting in anyone but the Lord (1:29, 31), but it is also an echo of 1:18. Paul has concluded the unit 1:18–2:5 where it began, with reference to the power of God displayed on the cross and in the proclamation of the cross as the permanent mark of the resurrected Jesus. The phrase "the power of God" (1:18; 2:5) functions like a set of bookends for this section of the letter. The crucified Messiah is the definitive revelation of power and wisdom, divine and human.

Paul's cruciform understanding of wisdom and power indicts all other claims to either or both, whether those claims are personal, philosophical, political, or pious. It especially challenges all forms of imperial wisdom and power, whether at Corinth or elsewhere, including the manipulation of words through distortion or propaganda, as well as the manipulation of people through abusive religious, economic, military, or police power. Like Hannah and Mary, like the psalmists and prophets, Paul had received a word of rev-

---

52. The perfect participle in this context indicates the permanent and therefore present crucifiedness—the crucified reality—of the risen and reigning Lord.

53. Ernst Käsemann, "The Saving Significance of the Death of Jesus in Paul," in *Perspectives on Paul*, trans. Margaret Kohl (Philadelphia: Fortress, 1971; repr., Mifflintown, PA: Sigler, 1996), 32–59 (here 56). See also the strong emphasis on "the Resurrected Crucified One" in Stefan Alkier, *The Reality of the Resurrection: The New Testament Witness*, trans. Leroy A. Huizenga (Waco, TX: Baylor University Press, 2013).

54. Bonhoeffer, *Discipleship*, 257.

elation that God dwells among, sides with, and works through the nobodies of this world, not the wise and powerful. And like the Corinthians, Paul was living evidence of the reality of that revelation.

SUMMARY OF 1:18–2:5

In 1:18–2:5, Paul has woven together three stories: the stories of Christ, of the Corinthians' initial conversion to Christ, and of his own ministry as the means to that transformative experience. In each case, the means and the results were completely counterintuitive. The hallmark of the gospel is the powerful weakness and wise folly of God; this is old knowledge with a new twist. The cross reveals who God is and how God has worked and does work: in, through, and for the world's nobodies. Christ crucified is both the *revelation* of God and the means of our *redemption*; the cross is both the *source* and the *shape* of Christian salvation.

REFLECTIONS AND QUESTIONS FOR 1:18–2:5

Spiritual, Pastoral, Missional, and Theological Reflections

1. According to theologian Miroslav Volf, "In a world of violence, **the cross**, that eminently countercultural symbol that lies at the heart of the Christian faith, **is a scandal**. . . . There is no genuinely Christian way around the scandal. In the final analysis, the only available options are either to reject the cross and with it the core of the Christian faith or to take up one's cross, follow the Crucified—and be scandalized ever anew by the challenge."[55]

2. Fleming Rutledge offers these words: "Paul is willing to embrace his opponents' accusations of personal weaknesses and rhetorical dullness in order to make his point. One can see analogous situations in the church today. Preachers and teachers who are courageous and faithful in expounding the cross of Christ but lack the flashy, ostentatious style so much favored in this age of the sound bite find it difficult to gain a hearing. They are likely to be advised to improve their image and cultivate a more popular, even commercial, appeal. . . . Paul is adamant. **Razzle-dazzle does not serve the kerygma of the cross**."[56]

---

55. Miroslav Volf, *Exclusion and Embrace: A Theological Exploration of Identity, Otherness, and Reconciliation*, rev. ed. (Nashville: Abingdon, 2019), 16–17.

56. Fleming Rutledge, *The Crucifixion: Understanding the Death of Jesus Christ* (Grand Rapids: Eerdmans, 2017), 87.

ADDRESSING ECCLESIAL CHAOS

· 1:10–4:21

3. In the contemporary world, many people—including some self-identified Christians—**still find Christ crucified to be a stumbling block or offense**. Sometimes this is because the cross has been misunderstood and poorly preached as God's child abuse of his Son. Sometimes it is because those highlighting the cross have themselves used it as a cover for their own abuse of authority and power, whether domestic, religious, political, or military, completely missing the nature of the cross as the divine alternative to worldly power. But sometimes, the cross is experienced rightly as its inherently counterintuitive and thus offensive character—it is not what we expect or want because we want to remake God in our own image, and humans would never create a God whose power and wisdom were displayed most fully in weakness and folly.

    This claim that **the cross is a divine self-revelation**—a theophany—and the corollary notion of a cruciform God disturb or confuse many people, but it is also one of the most significant theological claims of recent decades. Commenting on 1 Cor 1:3 but anticipating the present section of the letter, Anthony Thiselton says the following: "The theme of the Christlikeness of God runs throughout the writings of [Eberhard] Jüngel and [Jürgen] Moltmann, who point to the decisiveness of the cross (1 Cor 1:18–25) for understanding God's being and identity. This is entirely true to Paul. Paul asserts simultaneously the unconditioned 'Almightiness' of God and the Christlikeness of God as known and revealed through the self-chosen 'weakness' of the cross. In this profound context the cross is no mere 'instrument' of salvation, but a revelation of the cruciform identity of God."[57]

4. Filipino social anthropologist Melba Padilla Maggay says this about Jesus' death on the cross: "In a mysterious way, what seemed like an act of supreme weakness and defeat proved to be **the disarming of principalities and powers**." She continues, "To embrace the ethic of the cross is to follow the same pattern. We exercise '*dominion*,' not primarily by capturing positions of power and influence, but by *servanthood* to the larger society."[58]

5. The reality of God's choosing the nobodies in the estimation of the world (or some parts of the world) and making them somebodies calls us to embrace the words of the late Kenyan Anglican theologian John Mbiti:

    > **Theology need not . . . be the monopoly of the comfortable, the secure, the highly educated, the rich**; it can come also from the songs and hymns

---

57. Thiselton, *First Epistle*, 83.

58. Melba Padilla Maggay, *Rise Up and Walk: Religion and Culture in Empowering the Poor* (Minneapolis: Fortress, 2016), 303.

of peasants as they till the ground; from the impromptu prayers of Christian parents as they nurse their sick child; from the unorganized sermons of the village catechist; from the charismatic leadership of an illiterate founder of an Independent Church; from the old man who is steeped in traditional religious life, who has been converted, together with his several wives and many children, to the Christian faith, and who is trying to make sense of it. . . . [Such theology] must be allowed a place in the Church universal.[59]

6. The theme of cruciform power and God's choosing of those considered nobodies also suggests that this passage should be seen in part as a **clear challenge to White supremacy and to Christian nationalism.** This passage is fundamentally an anti-racist text, and it is an absolute textual destroyer (in the prophetic and Pauline sense) of any form of Christian nationalism. The ministry and witness of the Rev. Dr. Martin Luther King Jr. was, on the other hand, a demonstration of true Christian power: the transformative power-in-weakness of the gospel.[60]

In **an imaginary letter from Paul** to the contemporary church in the West,[61] I have suggested that Paul might rephrase 1 Cor 1:23–25 in the following way: "We proclaim Christ crucified, a stumbling block to those who connect religion with political power, and foolishness to those who actually have secular status and power. But to those who are the called to bear witness to God's way of life, the crucified Christ is the power of God and the wisdom of God. For God's foolishness is wiser than the wisdom of those who seek to foster civil religion or Christian nationalism for the supposed good of God and country, and God's weakness is stronger than Western military, political, and economic strength."[62]

The integrity and mission of the church depend to a large degree, in certain contexts at least, on adhering (or not) to this understanding of divine power. *Fundamentally, Christian nationalism is a heresy that has annulled the cross and pushed the resurrection to its maximum, thereby completely distorting*

---

59. John S. Mbiti, "Theological Impotence and the Universality of the Church," in *Third World Theologies*, ed. Gerald H. Anderson and Thomas F. Stransky (Mahwah, NJ: Paulist, 1976), 6–18 (here 15; emphasis added). I am grateful to Joshua Barron for alerting me to this essay.

60. I owe this insight to one of my students, Rev. Dion Thompson.

61. This letter follows the example of the Rev. Dr. Martin Luther King Jr., who frequently preached a sermon entitled "Paul's Letter to American Christians" (quoted in the comments on 1:18–25).

62. Taken from my *Participating in Christ*, 245. I have added the words "or Christian nationalism" to the original text.

it; it has a resurrected, powerful savior and god without the cross as the revelation of God and the shape of salvation.

7. Many people, regardless of whether they are Catholic, have found the **spiritual exercises of Ignatius of Loyola** helpful. These include examen, or self-examination, exercises. My son Brian has adopted the Ignatian examen in a cross-centered way for use especially, but not only, during Holy Week, as follows (reprinted with his permission):

   › Acknowledge the Holy Spirit into your presence. (Pause)
   › Ask yourself: In what ways have I aligned myself with the Crucified One? Am I to be found among those where he is found? (Pause)
   › In what ways have I aligned myself with the imperial forces and systems that crucified him? How do I contribute to a culture of death? (Pause)
   › Pick one of these noticings (observations) to pray about. (Pause)
   › Pray for those who are being crucified in the world. (Pause)

8. The **Collect for the Third Sunday of Lent** in the Church of England Common Worship volumes contains these words: "Almighty God, whose most dear Son went not up to joy but first he suffered pain, and entered not into glory before he was crucified: mercifully grant that we, walking in the way of the cross, may find it none other than the way of life and peace."[63]

Questions for Those Who Read, Teach, and Preach

1. In what ways have Christians in both the past and the present replaced "the word of the cross" with some other message, thus subverting and even emptying the cross itself?

2. Who are the contemporary analogies for the (so-called) wise people, scribes, and debaters that Paul names? What forms of both "showy rhetoric" and pseudowisdom, often taken uncritically from the church's host culture, can be found in contemporary Christian circles, and what is the danger of such rhetoric and purported wisdom?

3. What are some of the understandings of power operative in the contemporary culture, and in the contemporary church? How does the word of the cross challenge these understandings?

4. Where and how does the preferential option for the poor and weak/powerless show up in contemporary Christian communities and ministries? Where does its opposite occur? How well or poorly does the church both minister

---

63. I am grateful to Rev. Philip Plyming for alerting me to this collect.

to and learn from the nobodies (persons without standard status indicators) in its midst?

5. In sum, what does this passage contribute to the church's goal of becoming one, holy, catholic, and apostolic?

FOR FURTHER READING

Bonhoeffer, Dietrich. *Discipleship*. Dietrich Bonhoeffer Works 4. Translated by Barbara Green and Reinhard Krauss. Minneapolis: Augsburg Fortress, 2001.

Bowens, Lisa M., and Dennis R. Edwards. *Do Black Lives Matter? How Christian Scriptures Speak to Black Empowerment*. Eugene, OR: Cascade, 2023.

Cen, Esther G. *Domination or Empowerment? A Power Discourse Analysis of 1 and 2 Corinthians*. Eugene, OR: Pickwick, 2023. (technical)

Cone, James H. *The Cross and the Lynching Tree*. Maryknoll, NY: Orbis Books, 2011.

Edwards, Dennis R. *Might from the Margins: The Gospel's Power to Turn the Tables on Injustice*. Harrisonburg, VA: Herald, 2020. (highly accessible)

Fitch, David E. *Reckoning with Power: Why the Church Fails When It's on the Wrong Side of Power*. Grand Rapids: Brazos, 2024. (highly accessible)

Gombis, Timothy G. *Power in Weakness: Paul's Transformed Vision for Ministry*. Grand Rapids: Eerdmans, 2021. (highly accessible)

Gorman, Michael J. *Cruciformity: Paul's Narrative Spirituality of the Cross*. 20th anniversary ed. Grand Rapids: Eerdmans, 2021.

Hengel, Martin. *Crucifixion*. Trans. John Bowden. Philadelphia: Fortress, 1977.

Hull, Cletus L., III. *The Wisdom of the Cross and the Power of the Spirit in the Corinthian Church: Grounding Pneumatic Experiences and Renewal Studies in the Cross of Christ*. Eugene, OR: Wipf & Stock, 2018.

Kennon, Jeff. *The Cross-Shaped Life: Taking on Christ's Humanity*. Abilene, TX: Leafwood, 2021.

Maggay, Melba Padilla. *Rise Up and Walk: Religion and Culture in Empowering the Poor*. Minneapolis: Fortress, 2016.

Matera, Frank J. *Preaching from the Cross: Paul's Theology of Proclamation*. Grand Rapids: Baker Academic, 2025.

Rutledge, Fleming. *The Crucifixion: Understanding the Death of Jesus Christ*. Grand Rapids: Eerdmans, 2017.

Senior, Donald. *Why the Cross?* Nashville: Abingdon, 2014.

Strait, Drew J. *Strange Worship: Six Steps for Challenging Christian Nationalism*. Eugene, OR: Cascade, 2024.

Teresa, Mother [Saint], and Brother Roger [of Taizé]. *Meditations on the Way of the Cross*. New York: Pilgrim, 1987. (highly accessible)

Volf, Miroslav. *Exclusion and Embrace: A Theological Exploration of Identity, Otherness, and Reconciliation*. Rev. ed. Nashville: Abingdon, 2019.

Whitehead, Andrew L. *American Idolatry: How Christian Nationalism Betrays the Gospel and Threatens the Church*. Grand Rapids: Brazos, 2023.

Whitehead, Andrew L., and Samuel L. Perry. *Taking America Back for God*. New York: Oxford University Press, 2020.

2:6–3:4. Cruciform Spirituality and Corinthian Immaturity

One of the most significant aspects of life in the early Christian communities was a palpable experience of the Spirit of God. This experience was not precisely the same from place to place, but there were certainly common dimensions, such as a sense of divine presence, power, and guidance. All of this was expressed in joyful worship, *koinōnia*, and (I would contend) concern for those outside the community.[64] From Paul's perspective, the work of the Spirit is absolutely essential to individual and corporate life in Christ. He does not question the presence of the Spirit in Corinth, but he does question many of the Corinthian practices that are allegedly signs of being spiritual, or Spirit-ual.

If the stories of Christ, the Corinthian community, and the Pauline modus operandi narrated in 1:18–2:5 all share a cruciform plot, what does that say to the problem at hand—the problem of divisions? Paul and Sosthenes turn next to answer that question, moving from the general (2:6–16) to the specific (3:1–4). The major theological issue at stake is really at the core of the entire letter: the relationship between the Spirit and being spiritual or Spirit-ual, on the one hand, and the word of the cross, on the other. It is a question of spiritual maturity/Spirit-maturity versus the fleshly, worldly, this-age immaturity that has gripped the Corinthian community. Paul's basic perspective will be this: that true spiritual wisdom

- comes from God through the Spirit of God—it is Spirit-ual;
- embraces the wisdom of Christ crucified; and
- subverts the Corinthian attention to leaders and its resulting divisiveness.

2:6–16. Cross and Wisdom, Cross and Spirit in the Self-Revelation of God

First Corinthians 2:6–16 is one of the more puzzling passages in the Pauline corpus. Careful attention to its context, however, helps. The upshot of 1:18–2:5, as

---

64. For the claim that the Pauline communities were inherently missional, see my *Becoming the Gospel: Paul, Participation, and Mission* (Grand Rapids: Eerdmans, 2015).

we have seen, is the rejection of human wisdom and power (the status quo) and the affirmation of Christ crucified as divine wisdom and power. Keeping this in mind, and recalling that Paul is still primarily concerned about divisions generated by infatuation with human wisdom (see 3:1–4), will assist in the interpretation of this puzzle. The frequent first-person-plural ("we") verbs in 2:6–16 are probably meant to include Sosthenes, Timothy, Apollos, and all Paul's faithful colleagues as truthful possessors and expositors of "the mind of Christ" (2:16).

This mind of Christ cannot be separated from the Father and the Spirit. It is important to note, once again, Paul's frequent naming of the persons of the Trinity:

- God, that is, the Father (2:7a, 7b, 9, 10a, 10b, 11), who is the Lord/YHWH (2:16)
- Christ (2:16b), who is called "the Lord of glory" (2:8) and implicitly "the Lord" in 2:16a
- the Spirit (2:10a, 10b, 13), who is God's Spirit (2:11, 12, 14)

That is, at the heart of this passage is not merely an anthropological question about human nature and human tendencies but a properly theological question about God, God's self-revelation, and human participation in God's life.

Central to this passage (2:6–16) and the following one (3:1–4) are two sets of contrasting terms: the natural, fleshly, unspiritual, merely human, on the one hand, and the spiritual, Spirit-ual, mature, on the other. Contrary to much popular interpretation of this passage, Paul is not affirming two levels of Christian maturity, spiritual and carnal. Rather, he is labeling a certain kind of (so-called) spiritual maturity as fraudulent, fleshly, and determined by worldly standards. Paul's goal in 2:6–16 is to affirm the reality of Spirit-inspired wisdom and to stress once again its connection to Christ crucified.

There is scholarly debate about the origin of these contrasting terms, but it is likely that Paul is picking up on the idiom and claims of the self-designated spiritually and socially elite in Corinth, who basked in their own version of spiritual maturity—a supposedly Spirit-inspired form of wisdom and power that had no connection to the cross.[65] In response, Paul contrasts divine and human wisdom (2:6–10), the need for both human and divine self-disclosure (2:11–13), and the necessity of having the Spirit to perceive the Spirit (2:14–16).

---

65. In *Rediscovering the Wisdom of the Corinthians*, Timothy Brookins argues emphatically for echoes of Stoic notions in this passage, beliefs that are at home in the Corinthian culture and *ekklēsia* (esp. 104–29, 206–35) but subverted by the apostle.

2:6–13. The Revelation of God's Wisdom as Self-Revelation

In 1:18–25 and 2:1–5, Paul had rejected mistaken forms of wisdom (*sophia*), but now he affirms in 2:6 that there is in fact a wisdom that can be shared with the mature (*teleiois*). Despite Paul's own talk of God's wisdom as "secret and hidden" (NRSV) or "a hidden mystery" (2:7 NRSVue),[66] and (again) contrary to popular, and sometimes scholarly, interpretation, Paul is not referring to some new form of secret wisdom reserved for the spiritual elite of his day or ours. Rather, he is once again referring to the wisdom of God that we know from 1:18–25 and 1:30: the wisdom of the crucified Messiah. It is not a new wisdom, for it was "decreed before the ages" (2:7), but it has now been revealed. In the world, however, and in the church infected with the world, there is no wisdom in the cross, and there is no connection between the powerful Spirit of God and the weakness of Christ crucified. But for God, proclaims Paul, wisdom and weakness go hand in hand, not in *contrast* to divine power but as the *manifestation* of that power, the work of the divine Spirit.

The danger in disconnecting the Spirit from the cross, Paul asserts, can be seen, ironically, in the crucifixion of "the Lord of glory" (2:8) by "the rulers of this age" (2:6, 8) who are "doomed to perish" (2:6). In fact, they are already "being reduced to nothing" (CEB; cf. NAB, NIV, NET). Paul uses the same Greek verb (*katargeō*) here that he used in 1:28 and will use again in the letter six more times. God is a God who renders powerless those who think they are powerful and important, and who are thought by others to be such. These "rulers" (*archontōn*) are the Roman political powers, though Paul likely assumes there are spiritual forces influencing them, just as there are demons behind idols (10:19–20).[67] Although Christ crucified truly is the revelation of God's wisdom, the Lord's crucifixion itself could be perpetrated only by those whose (so-called) wisdom failed to enlighten them about the identity of the one they executed. Now, for believers, failure to identify Christ crucified as the wisdom of God—with all the implications of that identification—reveals the *absence* of wisdom and of the Spirit, despite any and all claims to the contrary.

The crucified Messiah has become the fundamental criterion of wisdom, power, knowledge, and now Spirit-uality. This is a divine wisdom, an eternal mystery once hidden but now revealed (cf. Rom 16:25–27)—but not perceived by the murderous rulers of this age. The plan of God, through this

---

66. The phrase translated variously as "secret" or "mystery/mysterious" is *en mystēriō*.

67. For cosmic, spiritual powers, signified by a variety of Greek words, see 15:24; Rom 8:38; Eph 1:21; 2:2; 3:10; 6:11–12; Col 1:16; 2:10, 15.

counterintuitive form of wisdom, was to bring humans to "glory" (2:7; cf. 15:43; 2 Cor 4:17–18) by means of Jesus the Lord of glory. Paul could well have written to the Corinthians what he penned for the Colossians:

> I became its [the gospel's] servant according to God's commission that was given to me for you, to make the word of God fully known, the mystery that has been hidden throughout the ages and generations but has now been revealed to his saints. To them God chose to make known how great among the Gentiles are the riches of the glory of this mystery, which is Christ in you, the hope of glory. It is he whom we proclaim, warning everyone and teaching everyone in all wisdom, so that we may present everyone mature in Christ. For this I toil and struggle with all the energy that he powerfully inspires within me. (Col 1:25–29)

God's glorification project, accomplished through the Messiah's death and resurrection, is to bring humans to the fullness of life now and forever—transformation into Christ's likeness and into God's presence—a transformation that begins in the present and ends with eschatological metamorphosis; it is from glory to glory (2 Cor 3:18).

Had the rulers of this world known whom they were dealing with, they would not have crucified this glorious Lord.[68] Yet God the Great Subverter has turned their folly and their misuse of power into the means of salvation. And this salvation is beyond anything human beings can imagine, as Paul says in 2:9 by quoting a beautiful but not completely recognizable text, as only the first half (italicized) comes from Scripture (Isa 64:4 [64:3 LXX]): "'*What no eye has seen, nor ear heard*, nor the human heart conceived, what God has prepared for those who love him.'"[69] The mystery of the cross and of future salvation (glory) may be revealed, but they still retain—even after centuries of theologizing—their character as mystery: something humans can never completely understand or explain.

The next key theological claim Paul makes is how the mystery of God's unimaginable future has been revealed: by the probing Spirit of God (2:10). In vv. 11–13, he uses an analogy from human experience to make his point: "For what human being knows what is truly human except the human spirit that is within? So also no one comprehends what is truly God's except the Spirit of

---

68. Paul uses a contrary-to-fact conditional sentence: "if they had known [but they did not] . . . they would not have. . . ."

69. Scholars have debated the possible text(s) in play here.

God" (2:11). The reason the Spirit alone can teach about God and the things of God (2:12, 14) is thus quite simple: only a person's "spirit" knows and reveals the essence of that person. So too the "spirit" (Spirit) of God understands and reveals God.

The distinction in these verses between "God" and "the Spirit of God" implies both similarity and difference. Just as the spirit of a person is essential to that person's identity and thus reveals the person, but does not comprise the whole reality of that person, so also God's Spirit is essential to the being of God, such that the Spirit's revelatory action is *self*-revelatory. The Spirit of the Father, in bearing witness to the cross of the Son, who embodies God's power and wisdom, puts the world on notice that what happened on the cross was divine self-revelation. The cross, and nothing else, is the path to our future glory even as it was the path to Christ's own glory (cf. Rom 8:17, 29–35; Phil 3:21). And it is the very "Spirit that is from God," rather than "the spirit of the world," who has been given to believers (2:12) and who teaches and interprets the counterintuitive wisdom of God (2:13). *The Spirit reveals that the crucified Lord of glory reveals the mind of God.* This is the very heart of Paul's particular Trinitarian theology and experience.

2:14–16. The Spirit-ual and the Mind of the Lord

The inability, therefore, to connect the Spirit and the cross in theory and in practice reveals one's spirituality as something other than Spirit-uality (2:14; 3:1). Paul wishes to teach Spirit-determined things, by means of the Spirit, to those possessed by the Spirit (2:13). If, as he has repeatedly asserted, God's wisdom is revealed in Christ crucified, then God's Spirit and everything associated with the Spirit (e.g., charismatic gifts, including wisdom: 2:12–13; 12:8) must also reflect and point to Christ crucified.

This is ultimately both an ontological and a revelatory claim: Christ crucified is the definitive revelation of the divine reality—the inner spirit or fundamental identity, so to speak, of God. This divine reality cannot be discovered by human effort: "For who has known the mind of the Lord so as to instruct him?" asked the prophet Isaiah (Isa 40:13 LXX), whom Paul quotes in 2:16 (and in Rom 11:34). Scripture repeatedly affirms that "my thoughts are not your thoughts, nor are your ways my ways, says the LORD" (Isa 55:8). It is only by divine self-revelation and divine gift that a person can perceive the foolish wisdom of God (2:14).

Thus Paul contrasts two sorts of people, almost certainly meaning, in this context, not merely two types of people generally, but two types of people in the Corinthian *ekklēsia*. The first (v. 14) he calls *psychikos*, from the Greek word *psychē*, meaning "living being" or "soul." The second (v. 15) he labels *pneumatikos*, from the Greek word for "spirit/Spirit."[70] Translations differ significantly for these words, but the basic point is the difference between those living with, and according to, the Spirit of God and those who are not.[71] I suggest we use "natural" (NAB, ESV) or "merely human" (NTW) and "Spirit-ual" for the two different sorts of people.[72]

The *psychikos* or natural person is unable to understand or receive the things of the Spirit, while the *pneumatikos* or Spirit-ual person is able to discern such things and do so without fear of judgment by others, probably especially the *psychikoi* (2:14–15).[73] The contrast between the two, then, is a matter of having or lacking Spirit-enabled insight (philosophically speaking, it is a matter of epistemology).[74]

On their own, no one ancient or modern—not a Platonist, not a Stoic, not a Jew, and not even a Christian—would surmise that Christ crucified was the wisdom and power of God. This conclusion is not a matter of human wisdom discovering God, but a matter of divine self-revelation—of self-exegesis. When we encounter this Christ as the self-revelation of God made known by the very Spirit of God, and then embody this Christ, we are working with the grain of the universe, so to speak. For believers gifted with, and open to, the Spirit, what used to seem like error, nonsense, and folly becomes the truest truth and the wisest wisdom.

Most importantly in this context, the truly spiritual, or Spirit-ual, person is the one who makes the connection between cross and Spirit; this kind of person (and Paul and Sosthenes claim to be such) truly possesses the Spirit of God and therefore has "the mind of Christ" (2:16), the mind of the crucified Messiah (cf. Phil 2:5).[75] This "mind" is, to be sure, a way of thinking and

---

70. These words will return in 15:44–46.

71. In ch. 15, *psychikos* signifies the natural state of the created person, since Adam was made a living being or soul (*psychē*; 15:45).

72. The translation "unspiritual" (NRSV, CEB) for *psychikos* is helpful only if understood to mean "without the Spirit" (NIV)—un-Spirit-ual.

73. Some have suggested that 2:15 is a Corinthian quotation, in which case *pneumatikos* would be a self-designation expressing a spirituality of complete autonomy and nonaccountability. I think this is unlikely in light of 3:1–3.

74. See Andy Johnson, "Turning the World Upside Down in 1 Corinthians 15: Apocalyptic Epistemology, the Resurrected Body and the New Creation," *Evangelical Quarterly* 75 (2003): 291–309.

75. The clearly implied equation of "the mind of Christ" (2:16) with "the Spirit of God" (2:11–14) and "the mind of the Lord" (2:16) has, in turn, further profound Trinitarian

perceiving ("mindset") but also a corollary way of living. Having the mind of Christ does not, therefore, imply autonomy and nonaccountability but just the opposite: "we take every thought captive to obey Christ" (2 Cor 10:5). *To possess the mind of Christ means to be possessed by that mind.*

The implication of 2:16 is that the "we" in "we have the mind of Christ" refers not merely to Paul and Sosthenes but to anyone in Christ, any person gifted with the Spirit, as long as that person has not allowed the spirit of the world to functionally replace the Spirit of God. Paul is implicitly inviting the Corinthians to adopt the same mind in order to be truly Spirit-ual and receive the things of the Spirit in the present. This would be spiritual maturity (cf. 14:20). Matthew Thiessen has an insightful image for the gift of the "transforming *pneuma*": it is like receiving an "infusion of the Messiah's DNA," resulting in "pneumatic gene therapy."[76]

Such Spirit-ual people can also anticipate the incredible future—the ultimate glory—that God has planned for those who love God (2:9; cf. 8:3; 16:22). This is bifocal spirituality: looking back to redemption and ahead to final glorification.

3:1–4. Division as Evidence of Spirit-Impoverishment

Having established in 2:6–16 the connection between cross and wisdom, between cross and Spirit, and between cross and future glory as divine self-disclosure, Paul returns to his main pastoral point: that the divisions at Corinth, which effectively negate the cross (1:13), reveal the Corinthians' spiritual immaturity, their Spirit-impoverishment (3:1). They are not, as they might think (probably because of their many *pneumatika*, spiritual gifts or manifestations of the Spirit),[77] Spirit people or Spirit-ual (*pneumatikoi*). Rather, they are "people of the flesh" (3:1, 3 [twice]; *sarkinoi*, from *sarx*, "flesh") and "infants" (3:1).[78] Paul's characterization of them as *sarkinoi*, fleshly, is similar to *psychikoi*, which means merely human or natural but is even stronger.

For Paul, "the flesh" can refer to the body, to the sphere of normal human

---

implications. (Some manuscripts have "the mind of the Lord" instead of "the mind of Christ" in 2:16.)

76. Matthew Thiessen, *A Jewish Paul: The Messiah's Herald to the Gentiles* (Grand Rapids: Baker Academic, 2023), 110–11. He also says receiving the Spirit is "the equivalent of moral steroids" (128, 131).

77. Recall that it is likely that the Corinthians styled these manifestations as *pneumatika*, but Paul stressed that they are *charismata* ("grace-gifts," "manifestations of grace").

78. The word *pneumatikoi* is rendered "spiritual people" in many translations, while

existence, or to the anti-God, antihuman impulse within people. It is the second and third of these that are in view here: sadly, the Corinthians as a group are living as those without the Spirit of God and even in opposition to the Spirit (cf. Gal 5:13–26). Paul is no longer speaking in generalities as in 2:14–16; he is speaking directly to the Corinthians.

Amazingly, however, as at the start of the letter (1:1–9), Paul does not write the Corinthians off. He addresses them once again as his brothers and sisters who are in Christ (3:1; see also 1:10; 2:1). At the same time, he cannot address them as *pneumatikoi*—despite their many *pneumatika*—but only as *sarkinoi*. In a very real sense, they are unwittingly living an anachronism: they are subsisting in the old realm and former time of the flesh rather than flourishing in the new age of the Spirit—the Spirit, that is, of the crucified and risen Lord.

With the word *pneumatikoi* in 3:1, Paul means not merely people who claim to possess the Spirit or focus on having certain spiritual gifts but people actually defined and formed by the Spirit of God, people who walk according to the Spirit,[79] as opposed to those who are defined by and walk according to the flesh, or merely human ways (3:3, 4). In fact, Paul will use the word "walk" (*peripateite*) in 3:3, though many translations simply have a form of "behave" or "act." He asks, rhetorically, with the Greek grammar expecting an affirmative answer, "Are you not people of the flesh and walking according to mere human norms?" (MJG).

The same image of walking is often missed in translations of Pauline texts, including the related text in Gal 5:16: "But I say, walk [*peripateite*] by the Spirit, and do not satisfy fleshly desire" (MJG). The biblical tradition of two ways, rooted in Deut 30, is at work here: the way of death versus the way of life, the way of the flesh versus the way of the Spirit. Of course, the Spirit Paul has in mind, as we saw in 2:6–16, cannot be disassociated from the crucified Messiah.

Spiritual infancy and mother's milk *might* have been excusable when Paul first preached to the Corinthians, but no longer. Yet their mother/father in faith cannot feed them "solid food" (3:2) because they are still—as he says repeatedly in 3:1–4—(merely) human: baby humans, in fact.[80] The phrase "could

---

sarkinoi is variously translated as "people of the flesh" (NRSV, NET, ESV) or as "fleshly" (NAB, NRSVue), "carnal" (KJV), "unspiritual" (CEB), or "worldly" people (NIV).

79. The NIV has "people who live by the Spirit" for *pneumatikoi*.

80. Additional maternal imagery for Paul's self-understanding and ministry can be found in 1 Thess 2:5–8 and Gal 4:19–20. The image here is possibly that of a wet nurse, but it is more likely maternal. The milk–solid food contrast as a metaphor for immaturity versus maturity was not unique to Paul.

ADDRESSING ECCLESIAL CHAOS · 1:10-4:21

not speak" in 3:1 does not indicate Paul's inability to send communications but rather the Corinthians' inability to receive them, due to their infantile condition. Infancy here clearly means immaturity but also vulnerability—being in a precarious state.[81]

Allegiance to Paul or Apollos, rather than to Christ crucified, is a sure mark of spiritual infancy and hence vulnerability, even danger. The Corinthians' "jealousy and quarreling" (*zēlos kai eris*; 3:3) is childish bickering by supposed grownups, and clearly not the mature work of the Spirit. The reduction of four slogans in 1:12, focusing on Paul, Apollos, Cephas, and Christ, to just two in 3:4—Paul and Apollos—may suggest that the main practical issue in Corinth is division over these two figures (see also 3:5-6; 4:6). Cephas, however, will reappear with Paul and Apollos in 3:22, so he is not completely out of the picture.

Descriptions of people defined by the flesh and not the Spirit, by human rather than divine standards, certainly imply a precarious position far from Christ; yet Paul still calls such a community "the church of God" (1:2) and "God's temple" indwelt by God's Spirit (3:16). What does it mean to be this sort of body? And what is the role of individual leaders within it? These are the subjects Paul will address next.

REFLECTIONS AND QUESTIONS FOR 2:6-3:4

Spiritual, Pastoral, Missional, and Theological Reflections

1. When we look at 2:6-3:4 in connection with 1:18-2:5, we should notice that Paul has made **a very Trinitarian move**. He has spoken in 1:18-2:5 about Christ crucified as a theophany, a divine self-exegesis. He has spoken in 2:6-3:4 of the need for the Spirit of God to reveal God to us—an act of self-disclosure that is completely in sync with the divine self-revelation in the cross. This should not surprise us in light of Gal 4:4-6: "But when the fullness of time had come, God sent his Son, born of a woman, born under the law, in order to redeem those who were under the law, so that we might receive adoption as children. And because you are children, God has sent the Spirit of his Son into our hearts, crying, 'Abba! Father!'"

2. For Christians to behave like generic, un-Spirit-ual humanity is to subscribe existentially to the world's values, especially those of power and wisdom.

---

81. See Works, *Least of These*, 108-27. For Pauline concern about theological immaturity and vulnerability, see also Eph 4:11-16.

The Spirit given to all believers is the Spirit of *maturity* by virtue of being the Spirit of *cruciformity* and the Spirit of *community and unity*. In fact, it is by means of cruciformity that the Spirit produces both maturity and unity in Christ (Phil 2:1–4). But this does not occur, or does not occur sufficiently, in every Christian community. Corinthian immaturity is obviously not limited to ancient Corinth. Paul addresses similar concerns, providing similar perspectives, in Gal 5, where the "works of the flesh" include as many community-harming behaviors as behaviors often associated, in the Christian tradition, with "the flesh": "Now the works of the flesh are obvious: sexual immorality, impurity, debauchery, idolatry, sorcery, enmities, strife [*eris*, used also in 1 Cor 3:3], jealousy [*zēlos*, used also in 1 Cor 3:3], anger, quarrels, dissensions [*dichostasiai*, which also appears in some manuscripts of 1 Cor 3:3], factions, envy, drunkenness, carousing, and things like these" (Gal 5:19–21a NRSVue).

In Galatians, Paul also refers to participation in the cross explicitly as the antidote to the flesh (Gal 5:24) and implicitly as the expression of community concern and love (e.g., Gal 5:6, 13 in light of 2:19–20).

In other words, it appears that, for Paul, a common and critical diagnosis of the ecclesial condition is that **the church has a penchant for separating the Spirit from the cross, with varied but always disastrous consequences.** And the solution is to **reunite that which should have never been separated.**

3. At the same time, Christians affirm the activity of the Spirit in the world. Host cultures, by God's grace, can also provide good values to the church. One thinks, for instance, of ubuntu, the African notion of our interconnectedness. **The task of ecclesial and theological leadership** is, in part, to identify both the inappropriate and the appropriate values of their cultures, and to find ways to move people from the immaturity of the "merely human" to the maturity of the Spirit of the Father and the Son.

4. It is rather easy for Christians in relative comfort and even luxury to look down on those whose perspective on life is strongly eschatological, a hope for heavenly glory, such as that intimated by 2:9. But **for the persecuted and otherwise oppressed, such hope is what sustains them**, as it has sustained many enslaved people.[82]

Questions for Those Who Read, Teach, and Preach

1. What examples might there be today of the separation of the cross and wisdom? The cross and the Spirit? The cross and resurrection/future glory?

82. See, e.g., Bowens, *African American Readings of Paul*, 141.

2. What kinds of "foolishness" (as Paul would describe it) emerge from attempts at knowing God apart from divine self-revelation?

3. What misunderstandings of God occur, even in Christian circles, when secular perspectives on God—such as "I could never believe in a God who . . ."—determine the reality of God in which people believe?

4. What contributions can this passage make to contemporary Christian understandings of spirituality and spiritual formation?

5. In sum, what does this passage urge the church to believe (faith), do (love), and anticipate (hope)?

For Further Reading

Fee, Gordon D. *God's Empowering Presence: The Holy Spirit in the Letters of Paul*. Peabody, MA: Hendrickson, 1994.

———. *Paul, the Spirit, and the People of God*. Grand Rapids: Baker Academic, 2023 (orig. Peabody, MA: Hendrickson, 1996). (highly accessible)

Gorman, Michael J. *Cruciformity: Paul's Narrative Spirituality of the Cross*. Grand Rapids: Eerdmans, 2001.

Hull, Cletus L., III. *The Wisdom of the Cross and the Power of the Spirit in the Corinthian Church: Grounding Pneumatic Experiences and Renewal Studies in the Cross of Christ*. Eugene, OR: Wipf & Stock, 2018.

Keener, Craig S. *The Mind of the Spirit: Paul's Approach to Transformed Thinking*. Grand Rapids: Baker Academic, 2016. (technical)

Powery, Luke A. *Becoming Human: The Holy Spirit and the Rhetoric of Race*. Louisville: Westminster John Knox, 2022.

Rabens, Volker. *The Holy Spirit and Ethics in Paul: Transformation and Empowering for Religious-Ethical Life*. 2nd rev. ed. Minneapolis: Fortress, 2014. (technical)

Tebbe, Matt, and Ben Sternke. *Having the Mind of Christ: Eight Axioms to Cultivate a Robust Faith*. Downers Grove, IL: InterVarsity Press, 2022. (highly accessible)

3:5–4:13. Ministers as Cruciform Servants in God's Church

We have seen that Paul's desire for the church in Corinth (and everywhere, at every time) is unity, the primary focus of 1 Cor 1–4. But it would be simplistic to think that unity comes without effort, even without cost. For Paul, the quest for unity in the church involves a complex process of deconstruction and reconstruction. For most of the letter thus far, he has been engaged in deconstructing and reconstructing misguided notions of wisdom and power. Yet this has not been a merely theoretical undertaking; rather, it is one with immense practical consequences. If wisdom and power are redefined in light of Christ crucified, then those who think they are wise or powerful—or who are perceived by others to possess those attributes—must also be reconfigured in light of the crucified Messiah.

Paul, probably with the help of Sosthenes, now undertakes to re-form the Corinthians' understanding of apostles and other ministers of the gospel and thereby their understanding of the church. A misunderstanding of leaders that leads to factionalism, as we saw in 1:10–16 and 3:1–4, is ultimately a spiritual problem, and this spiritual problem is finally a problem of identity. To what or to whom do I, do we, belong? Who or what is the source of my, and of our, identity?

Paul attempts to transform a highly *anthropocentric* understanding of ministry and community identity into a robustly *theological* one. He inverts the Corinthian understanding of leaders that results in factionalism—a normal Corinthian and, indeed, human way of treating leaders—because God is the God of counterintuitive, even abnormal ways of leading, of expressing wisdom and power. That is, an appropriate theology of ministry and of the church is dependent on a proper understanding of God, and specifically a proper *Trinitarian* understanding of God. Paul has just provided the basics of such a theology in his discussion of God the Father, Jesus the Messiah, and the Spirit. God has been Paul's ultimate focus, and that will continue. The principal actor in the church is God, not Paul or any other church leader—then or now.

So what is Paul's basic perspective on the church and church leaders? Those who minister are servants of *God* and (by extension) of the church (3:5–9, 18–23), which is *God's* possession and project (3:9–15); neither it nor its members belong to anyone else (3:21–23). And because this divine project (field, building; 3:9) is in fact the dwelling place of God (temple; 3:16–17), if it is destroyed, the responsible parties will suffer the consequences (3:17).[83] These servants are ultimately answerable only to their Lord, who both equips and judges them (3:12–15; 4:1–7). Because the gospel of Christ crucified must be both preached and lived as the church's foundation (3:11), apostles live a cross-shaped existence (4:8–13).

---

83. The Qumran community (which produced the Dead Sea Scrolls), or at least its leadership council, also saw itself as both God's planting and God's temple (e.g., Rule of the Community [1QS] VIII, 5; XI, 7–8); see Paul Swarup, *The Self-Understanding of the Dead Sea Scrolls Community: An Eternal Planting, a House of Holiness* (London: T&T Clark, 2006).

3:5–9. God's Coworkers in God's Field

In 3:5–9, Paul offers an alternative to the Corinthians' misdirected zeal for human leaders, further developing his prophetic notion that believers should boast only in the Lord (1:31; 3:21). The theocentric tone of this passage is a startling contrast to the Corinthian attitude.

Paul begins with two brief introductory questions about the identity and role of Apollos and himself (3:5), picking up the same names mentioned in 3:4. Noticeably absent from 3:4 and 3:5–6, in contrast to 1:12, is Cephas, though he will reappear with Paul and Apollos in 3:22 (though not in 4:6). Thus we should not reduce the issue at Corinth to a battle between followers of Paul and followers of Apollos, even if the main focus here is on those two influencers. (It may well be that "those of Peter" exist, but, if Peter had never visited Corinth, he would not fit into the narrative Paul is about to recount.)

Paul and Apollos are servants (*diakonoi*; NAB "ministers"), *through* whom—not *in* whom—the Corinthians believed (3:5). Elsewhere Paul also characterizes himself and his colleagues as *diakonoi*, reinforcing the idea that to be apostolic is first of all to be a servant, an imitator or even an icon of Jesus the Servant (Rom 15:8; *diakonos*); apostles both represent and reveal him.[84] If they are servants, they are not lords and therefore not masters or owners of any group. In fact, the only true lord is *the* Lord, the one who assigned (3:5) both Paul and Apollos to their respective roles as divine instruments ("through [*dia*] whom"). Here "the Lord" probably refers to God the Father, rather than Jesus, as the word *theos* occurs five times in the following verses (3:6–9).[85]

Paul continues the thought of divine agency and human instrumentality by invoking the agricultural image of planting and watering (3:6). Where one "planted" (founded the church—Paul; see Acts 18:1–18) and another "watered" (nourished it—Apollos; see Acts 18:24–28), God caused the growth, so all credit goes to God alone (3:5–7).[86] The sense of the Greek verb at the end of

---

84. In Orthodox spirituality, an icon is a window into the divine life. In Mark 10:43–45, Jesus describes himself and his disciples as servants. For Paul and his colleagues as servants, see 2 Cor 3:6; 6:4; Eph 3:7. For others, see Rom 16:1 (Phoebe); Eph 6:21 (Tychicus); Phil 1:1 (unnamed); 1 Tim 3:8, 12 (more formal ministry); 1 Tim 4:6 (Timothy). See also 2 Cor 11:15, 23. Paul can also use the word *doulos* (slave) of himself and colleagues (Rom 1:1; 2 Cor 4:5; Gal 1:10; Phil 1:1; Col 4:12; 2 Tim 2:24), and of Christ (Phil 2:7), as well as other, related terms (e.g., 1 Cor 4:1: servants, or assistants, and stewards).

85. But the text of 2 Cor 4:5, which contrasts Paul and colleagues as slaves (*doulous*) with Jesus as Lord, leaves open the possibility that the "Lord" here is Jesus.

86. Paul once again engages in a little play on words, for the verb translated as "to wa-

144

v. 6 is something like "God was [continually] giving the growth"—that is, all through the different ministers, and perhaps even apart from those ministers, at different times. Verse 7 could be translated, "Thus neither the one who plants nor the one who waters is anything but only the growth-producing God!" (MJG).

To say such servants are not anything (3:7) is not meant to denigrate ministers. Rather, it is to say that God's servants are not in competition with one another but have a "common purpose" (3:8); Paul literally says they "are one" (so ESV; NIV "have one purpose"; NET "work as one"). At the same time, each is responsible for the specific tasks assigned by the Lord, for which they will receive "wages," an eschatological reward (3:8)—if they have been faithful (see 3:10–15). Paul's understanding of different but complementary tasks given by God anticipates the theology of gifts in chapter 12.

Paul concludes this passage with a succinct but significant statement of ministerial and ecclesial identity in v. 9. He refers to himself and Apollos as "God's coworkers" (MJG; *theou . . . synergoi*). It is not completely clear whether this means working cooperatively with *one another* as God's servants (so NRSV, NIV) or working with *God* (so NRSVue, CEB, NAB). Perhaps both are in view. If Paul and Apollos are one, then they are clearly working together even if they are not literally doing so.

But since the description of Paul and Apollos as "God's coworkers" is grammatically parallel to the descriptors of the Corinthians in terms of their relationship to God ("God's field, God's building"), there seems to be an emphasis on the pair's relationship to God. Furthermore, while Paul uses the term "coworker" (*synergos*) eleven other times, often with the qualifier "my" or "our," he does so only one other time in a phrase that includes the words "of God."[87] In 1 Thess 3:2, Paul refers to Timothy as "our brother and God's coworker in the gospel of Christ" (MJG; *synergon tou theou*). This similar phrase suggests that here in 1 Cor 3 Paul is describing ministry as working with God, who is the prime minister, so to speak. The implication is that all who serve God and others in the gospel are likewise God's coworkers.

Thus, although Apollos and Paul are one, Apollos is not merely Paul's coworker in ministry, or vice versa. Rather, they are one in their participation

---

ter" in 3:6–7 is the same verb translated as "fed you with milk" in 3:2. Paul may be implying that even the great rhetor Apollos could not do more than give the Corinthians the basics.

87. For *synergos* (coworker), see Rom 16:3, 9, 21; 2 Cor 1:24; 8:23; Phil 2:25; 4:3; Col 4:11; 1 Thess 3:2; Phlm 1, 24. The Greek preposition and prefix *syn*, meaning "with" or "co-," is an essential element in Paul's vocabulary of participation with Christ and one another.

in what could be called "the ministry of God" or (as it is commonly called) the *missio Dei*. In fact, the emphasis in the Greek text of v. 9 is on the word "God's"—*God's* coworkers! God is not merely the field or project supervisor but is actively involved as the one *causing* the growth and progress, allowing others to share in the work under his direction. Similarly, using the verb "cowork" (*synergeō*), Paul writes in 2 Cor 6:1 that he and his colleagues are "working together with" God (2 Cor 6:1; ESV).

At the end of 3:9 Paul turns succinctly to the identity of the *ekklēsia* with two metaphors: as God's field and God's building, with emphasis again on the word "God's." "You" (plural, of course), Paul tells the Corinthians and all Christian communities, are *God's* farm to cultivate and *God's* construction project to build (recall 1:2, "the church of God": *God's* church). The agricultural image has already been introduced in the previous verses; the architectural image will be developed in the following passage. The commonality between the two metaphors consists especially in (1) the essential characteristic of increase (growth, expansion), or transformation, and (2) the corollary need for people to give ongoing attention to the project.[88]

3:10-17. Workers on God's Building—God's Temple

Having developed the agricultural metaphor in the previous verses, Paul now annotates the architectural image (3:10-15) and specifies it (3:16-17). But in specifying the building as the temple of the Holy Spirit, Paul moves beyond metaphor to actual, existential identity: the church is not merely depicted as a building; it is the very dwelling place of God.

3:10-15. Building on the Foundation

Paul begins by attributing his work and his success to God's grace (3:10). This is both his sincere conviction, stated again in 15:10 and elsewhere in his letters, and his strategic reminder to the Corinthians that no one should boast in themselves or others. Paul's only boast about his ministry is this:

- "By the grace of God I am what I am, and his grace toward me has not been in vain. On the contrary, I worked harder than any of them—though it was not I, but the grace of God that is with me" (1 Cor 15:10).

---

88. In Col 2:7, Paul uses similar agricultural (or horticultural) and architectural images for individual Christians as well as the church as a whole: "rooted and built up in him [Christ] and established in the faith" (NRSV).

- "I will not venture to speak of anything except what Christ has accomplished through me to win obedience from the Gentiles, by word and deed" (Rom 15:18).[89]

Just as Paul planted and Apollos watered, so also Paul "laid a foundation" and another is (and still others may be) building on it (3:10). God's work continues.

But that is not all. In describing in 3:10 *what* he laid as a foundation and *how* he worked, Paul is not merely depicting and defending his own ministry (or that of Apollos or anyone else). Rather, all of 3:10–15 contains instructions and warnings to the Corinthians, to their various leaders, and to all actual or potential ministers in the church—to all who "build" in Corinth and beyond. The first teaching/warning is this: now that the foundation—Jesus Christ, that is, Jesus Christ *crucified* (recall 1:18–25; 2:2)—has been properly laid, it cannot be altered or replaced (3:11, alluding to Isa 28:16).[90]

"The church's one foundation is Jesus Christ, her Lord," as the hymn goes. Anyone who attempts to change that foundation with, say, a wise-teacher Jesus or a crusading, gun-toting Jesus has been forewarned that this is not merely wrong but actually impossible. There is no substitute for the crucified Jesus who, raised from the dead, now lives among his people through the presence of his Spirit (cf. Rom 8:9; Gal 4:6; Phil 1:19).

Paul says that his mode of starting the Corinthian building project, of laying the foundation, was as a "wise master builder" (3:10 NRSVue, CEB, NAB; *sophos architektōn*). The phrase can mean simply "skilled master builder" (NRSV; cf. ESV, NET, NJB), but the allusion to Corinthian claims to wisdom (*sophia*) and to the divine reconstruction of wisdom should not be missed. Paul worries—and warns—that the current builders in Corinth are botching the construction project.[91] John Chrysostom warns with an apt image, "Let us not then merely keep hold of Christ, but let us be cemented to Him, for if we stand apart, we perish."[92]

Those at Corinth who call themselves wise, or are called wise by others, but do not build on the foundation of Jesus Christ crucified as the wisdom of God are merely parroting some version of worldly wisdom, the wisdom of this age, which is actually foolishness. Paul has been not merely skilled but utterly

89. See also Eph 3:7–10; 1 Tim 1:12–17.

90. A different emphasis for a different purpose is found in Eph 2:20: "the foundation of the apostles and prophets, with Christ Jesus himself as the cornerstone."

91. Richard B. Hays, "Ecclesiology and Ethics in 1 Corinthians," *Ex Auditu* 10 (1994): 31–43 (here 37).

92. John Chrysostom, *Homilies on 1 Corinthians* 8.7.

wise. His wisdom is not that of the eloquent speaker or the philosopher but of the revealed wisdom of God in the cross of Christ and the self-exegetical work of the Spirit.

At the end of 3:10, Paul counsels any builder in God's construction project to engage in self-examination, using the same verb he used in 1:26 (*blepō*) to invite the Corinthians to consider their call. Those who build on Paul's initial ministry at Corinth—or who work anywhere in God's construction project—will be evaluated by God, on the coming "day," the day of judgment. The scriptural day of the Lord is now the day of the Lord Jesus (1:8), whose *apokalypsis* ("unveiling"; 1:7) or *parousia* ("royal arrival"; 15:23) will bring both judgment and salvation.[93] In apocalyptic imagery, that coming day is often depicted as a time of fire.

The judgment of God's workers, Paul says, will be according to the quality of materials used and the quality and durability of their workmanship (3:12–15). On that day, everything will be brought to light and tested (3:13; cf. 4:5). Construction with good materials (gold, silver, and precious stones, representing faithful work) will survive the divine judgment and be paid, or rewarded (3:14; cf. 3:8), while construction with lesser materials (wood, hay, and straw, representing less faithful work) will be burned up, destroyed (3:15). And foolish builders themselves will escape only by the skin of their teeth the flames that destroy their work (3:15)—that is, the divine judgment. It is difficult to imagine a more serious warning to all those who claim to minister as God's partners in God's church.

3:16–17. God's Temple

The implicit threat in these verses becomes explicit in 3:16–17, where Paul transforms the general architectural image into a sacred one—the church as God's temple (*naos*; cf. 6:19; 2 Cor 6:16). The word *naos* can refer to either a pagan temple or the temple in Jerusalem. It is possible that different Corinthians would hear one or the other sense, but more likely the former. Paul, on the other hand, may have had both senses in mind; the church stands in continuity with the ancient people of God (Israel) and in contrast to the people, and their gods, who do not know the God of Israel. A pagan temple would have housed a deity by placing its statue in the middle of the space; the temple in Jerusalem could not have a graphic representation ("graven image") of God, but it had symbols to represent God's presence (e.g., the holy of holies; the mercy seat).

---

93. See additional texts listed in the discussion of 1:8.

Now, in Christ, the people and the space have merged; the corporate body of Christ is the temple of God.[94]

"Do you [plural] not know?" in 3:16 means the Corinthians should have known and should have *acted on* that knowledge, on the reality of being God's temple.[95] God not only *owns* the church, as in the metaphors of the field and the building; God *inhabits* the church (see also Eph 2:21–22). The image is reality; Paul says, "You [plural] constitute God's temple, and God's Spirit has taken up residence among you [plural]" (MJG).

Translations (and teachers/preachers) should stress this communal, rather than individual, perspective by noting that "you" is plural; in colloquial American English, at least in the South: "Y'all are God's temple." Interpreters should also refer to the Spirit's presence as being "among you" (MJG) or "in your midst" (NIV) rather than "in you" (so most translations). To be indwelt corporately by God's Spirit is what it means to be this body, the body of Christ (see ch. 12). The church is the special dwelling place of the triune God.[96] (Paul will later also call the individual believer's body the temple of the Holy Spirit: 6:19.)

This claim about the church is quite an amazing assertion to make while there was an actual temple in Jerusalem. Paul is not saying something like "Christianity has replaced Judaism." Rather, he is saying that the prophetic promise—especially seen in Ezekiel—of a new temple (Ezek 40–48) and a renewed people, filled with the divine Spirit (Ezek 37), has come to fulfillment in the creation of the *ekklēsia*. That is, God will be in and among the people of God in a new way. From Paul's perspective, that renewal has taken place now in the gift of the Son of God and the Spirit of the Son (e.g., Gal 4:4–6). Hence, the people who are in Christ the Son and among whom Christ dwells are the temple of YHWH, the living God.[97] There are again strong hints of the Trinity here: a building whose foundation is Christ the Son, and which is in fact the temple of God where God's Spirit lives.

94. In John 2:12–22, the body of Jesus himself is identified as the temple. Given the close relationship between Christ and the church as his body (see esp. 12:12) in his theology, Paul may have thought about the link between these two instantiations of the temple, but he does not make that connection explicit.

95. See "Do you not know . . . ?" also in 5:6; 6:2, 3, 9, 15, 16, 19; 9:13, 24. Cf. 10:1; 12:1.

96. Paul unpacks this reality, without the explicit temple language, in Rom 8. That God inhabits the church in a special way does not contradict or conflict with the doctrine of God's omnipresence any more than God's presence in the tent or temple did.

97. Paul was not alone in identifying the community of God's people in this way. The Qumran sect (or at least its leadership council) did as well. And there are a few scriptural texts that identify the people themselves as God's dwelling place (e.g., Lev 26:11–12; Ps 114:2).

ADDRESSING ECCLESIAL CHAOS · 1:10–4:21

The Corinthians who were allegedly "wise" and focused on being "Spirit people" would have likely reacted with glee to this description of their community as the temple of the Spirit. But what self-styled wise, Spirit people often lack is the recognition that the privilege of being the locus of God's presence means that they must be Godlike—not in their own imaginations but according to the reality of God revealed in Christ crucified.

By moving from architectural image to divine-human reality, Paul has upped the ante, so to speak. If the temple is destroyed—which could well be the outcome of the divisions—the supposed builders will have become desecrators, and they will suffer the ultimate loss on the coming day (3:17). Church work is holy business in a holy place (3:17), and any who fail to see the seriousness of that truth, and its potential spiritual and eschatological consequences for themselves and for others, should find opportunities for paid or unpaid work elsewhere.

A final word about the *ekklēsia* as God's *holy* people, God's *holy* temple. If "holiness befits your house, O LORD" (Ps 93:5), then it clearly befits the people that constitute that house. Furthermore, if being holy means being set apart for God's purposes, and if the people of God have been called to be a "light," especially to the nations,[98] then to be the church is not to be a holy *huddle* but a holy *presence*, a holy *witness*, a holy *instrument* of God's grace: a proclaimer of the gospel in word and deed—even if only some are called to be apostles and evangelists per se. Such a missional, apostolic vocation would seem to be a significant part of what it means to be imitators of Paul's ways in Christ (4:16–17)—and to be filled with the same Holy Spirit that motivated and empowered him.

3:18–23. Wisdom and the Role of Leaders

The concern behind the warnings and admonitions that Paul articulated in 3:10–17 continues in 3:18–23, but the focus now is on what the Corinthians should do and think in order to avoid the negative judgment of God. Paul begins with a strong admonition against self-deceit (3:18), one of the most common and most dangerous human tendencies, often with dire consequences. This is both a word to the self-styled wise and a general admonition to the community. Returning to the theme of the reversal of human wisdom and God's counterintuitive wisdom that permeates the earlier chapters, Paul again

98. See Isa 42:6; 49:6; Matt 5:14–16; Luke 2:32; 8:16; John 1:5, 9; John 3:19–21; 5:35; 8:12; 9:5; 11:9; 12:35–36, 46; Acts 13:47; 26:23; Rom 2:19.

150

labels the wisdom of "this age" (3:18) folly. Therefore the wise must become fools to become truly wise.

This can mean only that the self-styled wise—and anyone else who has departed from Christ crucified as the source and substance of wisdom—must reconnect to the cross as the wisdom of God and thus take their place as servants accountable to the one and only Lord. Such a "conversion of the imagination" (as Richard Hays would put it) is necessary because the Lord sees through and subverts human wisdom, as Scripture teaches (3:19b–20, citing Job 5:13 and Ps 94:11). As Paul has already stated clearly (1:29), the community is not to boast in human leaders (3:21). Boasting, he has also already declared, can be only in the Lord (1:31).

In 3:21b–23, Paul offers a two-part theological rationale for not boasting in human leaders. It is first of all, as Paul says twice (vv. 21b, 22b), because "all things" are now the possession of the Corinthian believers, which includes both three people and five nonhuman entities (3:22). They are not owned but owners.

Beginning with the latter group, we are naturally puzzled, since it is hard to know how believers could possess the world, life, death, the present, and the future (3:22). Paul is likely reminding the Corinthians that since they belong to Christ (3:23), none of the forces of this world can do them ultimate harm; such forces, including the last enemy (Death; 15:26, 51–57) and the unknown future, are no longer to be feared as enslaved persons would fear a master. As the apostle says in Romans, "I am convinced that neither death, nor life, nor angels, nor rulers, nor things present, nor things to come, nor powers, nor height, nor depth, nor anything else in all creation, will be able to separate us from the love of God in Christ Jesus our Lord" (Rom 8:38–39).

More to the immediate issue of ecclesial division, the "all things" includes specifically Paul, Apollos, and Cephas, the three influential leaders in Corinth (3:22). In both v. 21 and v. 22, Paul actually says, more precisely, that "they are of you [plural]" or "they belong to you [plural]" (*panta hymōn*). This is precisely the opposite of what the Corinthians have been saying, or at least what Paul says their behavior communicates: "I am of Paul" or "I belong to Paul," and so on (1:12; 3:4). That is, Paul stresses, the leaders "belong" to the people (as servants), not the other way around. The leaders are not the Corinthians' spiritual gurus or masters who can demand or accept allegiance; they are not their spiritual patrons who can require or expect returns on spiritual blessings offered to their spiritual clients.

The second part of the theological rationale for not boasting in human leaders is the truth that the Corinthians actually *do* belong to someone (3:23). They are "of Christ," not "of" anyone else. They belong to Christ, who in turn belongs to God the Father. That relationship is the source of Christian identity, individual and corporate. The Corinthians are servants of Christ and Christ alone, who in turn is the servant of God. But this relationship also means that they are under the protection, the patronage, of Christ the Lord—and no one else. To accept these truths is to leave behind the wisdom of this age and embrace, or rather be embraced by, the wisdom of God.

4:1–7. Ministerial Accountability

To reinforce what he has said, and to answer his critics, Paul further develops the notion of minister as servant by using two appropriate word pictures in v. 1. The first is "servants" (so most translations), better understood as assistants or helpers (*hypēretas*). The second is "stewards" (*oikonomoi*) or household managers (CEB "managers"). Specifically, Paul and other ministers (Apollos, Cephas, Sosthenes, etc.) are Christ's assistants, which suggests that Christ (like God the Father in 3:5–10), not any human, is the main minister in ministry. Moreover, they are "stewards of God's mysteries" (4:1), a reference to their responsibility for all aspects of the gospel—its faithful dissemination, preservation, and embodiment in communities and individuals.

Stewards must "be found trustworthy," or "faithful" (NIV, CEB, NET; *pistos*; 4:2), by the householder, and Paul desires nothing more than approval from God for having engaged in faithful ministry (see 9:19–27). Household stewardship is an appropriate image in many ways, especially since it resonates with 3:10–15 about building on the foundation, which is Christ, with accountability. But the apostle also engages in a little play on words, for he has said that God's Spirit "dwells" (*oikei*) among the Corinthians (3:16), and his role is, in part, *oikonomos*.

Paul has already said that all God's coworkers will be judged (3:10–15)—that is, by God—on the day (3:13), yet apparently some pre-eschatological, human judging of Paul has already been occurring in Corinth. But any human judgment of Paul's ministry, even by the apostle himself, is inappropriate, for the only verdict that matters is the Lord's future judgment (4:3–5).[99] This attitude does not make Paul arrogant (see v. 6), for he clearly has examined himself and would try to correct any wrong he discovered (4:4a). Rather, what he likely means is not that he is perfect (see Phil 3:10–14) but that, as far as he knows, he has never strayed from knowing and proclaiming, in word and deed, "Jesus Christ crucified." Because God is the only rightful judge, this does not mean

99. This may be an echo of 2:15, if the sentiments there are Paul's own.

Paul is free of error or "acquitted" (4:4b); time will tell. But also precisely because God is the only rightful judge, the Corinthians should not engage in premature judgment "before the Lord comes," at which time all will be brought to light and God's servants will receive the Lord's commendation, or praise (4:5; cf. 3:13–14).

Paul then tells the Corinthians that everything he has said has been intended to apply to himself and Apollos—for the sake of the Corinthians (4:6). That is, Paul is not merely on the defensive but is looking out for the community's welfare. But this claim begins one of the most puzzling lines in all his letters: "I have applied all this to Apollos and myself for your benefit, brothers and sisters, so that you may learn through us the meaning of the saying, 'Nothing beyond what is written,' so that none of you will be puffed up in favor of one against another" (4:6). The source of this quotation is unknown and its meaning contested. But because the idea of "what is written" is, for Paul, a reference to Scripture, that is probably the sense here. The scriptural quotations about wisdom, boasting, and God in chapters 1–4 are applicable to all ministers of the gospel, and Paul has explicitly applied them to himself and Apollos. There is no competition between Paul and Apollos, and no exemption for either of them from scriptural expectations for ministry.

With this apostolic example of collegiality, unity-in-diversity, and accountability, Paul's bottom line is clear: the church can have no more divisive arrogance, no more being "puffed up" about him, Apollos, or anyone else (4:6b). Unfortunately, from Paul's perspective, arrogance is part of the Corinthian community's DNA, and he will reuse this vivid metaphor of being "puffed up" in reference to several other issues (see 4:18, 19; 5:2; 8:1; 13:4). The implication is that only the Spirit can alter the community's DNA.

Three rhetorical questions follow in 4:7, all using second-person-singular ("you") verbs, in contrast to the plural forms of the verbs in preceding and following verses. Rhetorically, Paul seems to be asking each individual reader/hearer to engage in self-examination. Those who recognize their own gifts, and the gifts of others, as gifts from God will not boast in themselves (see also 12:1–11; Rom 12:6–8). Recognizing God's grace is the antithesis of being puffed up, and the corollary to that recognition is humility (see, e.g., Rom 12:3; Phil 2:3)—a distinctive Christian virtue largely unknown in the pagan Corinthian environment.[100] (Its absenteeism is hardly restricted to the ancient world.)

---

100. On humility as a distinctive early Christian, and specifically Pauline, virtue, see Eve-Marie Becker, *Paul on Humility*, trans. Wayne Coppins (Waco, TX: Baylor University

ADDRESSING ECCLESIAL CHAOS · 1:10–4:21

The three rhetorical questions in v. 7 are a fitting conclusion to 4:1–7, but they are also an excellent segue into the next section.

4:8–13. Ministerial Cruciformity

Just in case the point about apostolic faithfulness and Corinthian arrogance is insufficiently clear, Paul turns in 4:8–13 to a massive rhetorical attack on the arrogance of elitist Corinthian spirituality by a spirited account of his own Christlike, cruciform life. Laced with irony but also with deep theology and spirituality, it is an oratorical tour de force with profound implications for Christian theology and praxis.

Paul begins in 4:8 with three sarcastic acclamations about the Corinthians: "Already you [plural] have all you want [or "are satisfied"]! Already you [plural] have become rich! Quite apart from us you [plural] have become kings [or "have begun to reign"]!" Even if only some are fully guilty as charged, all are responsible. The repeated "already" and the sarcastic imagery of satisfaction, wealth, and royalty suggest a Corinthian here-and-now spirituality, a kind of gospel of success and even power.[101]

The source of this Corinthian attitude has been debated. Does it derive from a rejection of future resurrection (see 15:12) that leads to a spirituality of present glory (the minority view)? Or does it perhaps reflect an Epicurean, Cynic, or Stoic mindset and language (the majority view)? Or is there a combination of factors? Whatever the specific source, it is clear that the Corinthians' fundamental issue, as Paul sees it, involves failure to understand the real-life implications of Christ crucified as the wisdom and power of God. The result is a *decoupled* spirituality that focuses on power in terms of Spirit- and resurrection-power untethered from the cross in both daily life and gathered worship. This seems to be the fundamental Corinthian error that manifests itself throughout the letter.[102]

Press, 2020). See also Dennis R. Edwards, *Humility Illuminated: The Biblical Path Back to Christian Character* (Downers Grove, IL: InterVarsity Press), 2023.

101. We find something similar in Rev 3:14–21.

102. The idea of a wise man being rich and reigning—and thus completely self-sufficient—was common in Stoicism, which is likely part of the influence on the Corinthians. Some have suggested that the Corinthians had an overrealized eschatology (spiritual resurrection now) that would diminish the significance of the cross. While this view is not currently in vogue, there is likely some truth in it that the phrase "decoupled spirituality" attempts to capture: the separation of the resurrected Lord (and his Spirit) from the crucified Messiah. That is, the Corinthians, or at least some of the Corinthians

Ministerial Cruciformity

After a sarcastic "wish you were reigning so we could reign with you" comment to conclude 4:8, Paul counters with his own narrative, the story of his ministry and that of his colleagues. He does so in large measure by using the rhetorical device of *synkrisis* (comparison; 4:10) to distinguish himself and his colleagues from the Corinthians. In fact, the entire passage is offered as a contrast to the supposed satisfaction, wisdom, power, wealth, and royalty in Corinth (4:8, 10). It is the earliest preserved catalog of sufferings in the Pauline correspondence.[103] It should be noted that Paul's catalogs of sufferings, including this one, list more than physical suffering. It would be better to call this list a catalog of cruciformity or even, more broadly, Christoformity. This ministerial life is one of participating not simply in Christ's *sufferings* but more fundamentally in Christ's *love*. Such love may, and often does, lead to some form of sacrifice or suffering, according to Paul.

This, then, is what it means for God's coworkers to know only Christ crucified (2:2):

- to live like criminals awaiting the death penalty or be made a spectacle (Gk. *theatron*), possibly like prisoners of war paraded in public and taken to an arena to participate as (defenseless) gladiators (4:9; cf. 2 Cor 2:14)[104]
- to be foolish, weak, and dishonored, rather than wise, strong, and honored (4:10; cf. 1:18–25)
- to suffer physically in various ways (4:11), including the following:
    - being thirsty and hungry, like Jesus (Matt 4:2; Mark 11:12; Luke 4:2; John 19:28)

(the elite men?), were so enamored with their self-proclaimed spiritual and social status that they could be rightly identified as focusing on the presence of the resurrected Lord by his Spirit without maintaining the Pauline connection between cross and resurrection. (At the same time, there have always been multiple reasons and ways to reject the counterintuitive wisdom and power of God.)

103. For other catalogs, see 2 Cor 4:7–12; 6:3–10; 11:23–33 and, more briefly or more focused, 2 Cor 1:3–11; 12:10; Rom 8:35. The variety of Paul's sufferings is quite stunning. Elsewhere (*Cruciformity: Paul's Narrative Spirituality of the Cross*, 20th anniversary ed. [Grand Rapids: Eerdmans, 2021], 286–87) I have divided them into the following categories: generalized pain and suffering; public disgrace and psychological pain; physical deprivation and pain; fatigue from physical labor; and political punishment and torture. We see all of these here.

104. The language of 4:9 could refer generally to theatrical entertainment but also to gladiatorial combat (Thiselton, *First Epistle*, 359), but the latter is more likely; see also 15:32. Corinth was a major setting for gladiator spectacles, the purpose of which was propaganda for Roman imperial power and values, such as the pursuit of honor and glory.

ADDRESSING ECCLESIAL CHAOS   · 1:10–4:21

- › being homeless, like Jesus (Matt 8:20; Luke 9:58)
  - › being struck (NRSV "beaten"), also like Jesus (Matt 26:67; Mark 14:65)[105]
- to engage in self-supporting manual labor (4:12a; cf. 9:14–15; 1 Thess 2:9; 2 Thess 3:8)
- to bless and endure when mistreated (4:12b–13, echoing the teaching of Jesus: Matt 5:3–12, 38–48; Luke 6:27–36; cf. Ps 109:28; Rom 12:14–21)
- to be treated like so much garbage and filth (4:13; cf. Lam 3:45)

Paul is not seeking pity. On the contrary, he is establishing his apostolic authenticity and authority, and these come precisely from his being conformed to Christ crucified, whose teaching (e.g., to bless when mistreated) Paul recalls here because it is fully in sync with the claim that Christ crucified is the powerful weakness of God. To know Jesus as the Crucified One is also to know him as the one who taught and lived in congruity with his own final fate. *There is no way to make Jesus into a teaching and serving Messiah in contrast to a dying and rising Messiah, or vice versa; he is always both, and his disciples are inseparably bound to the inseparable Jesus.*

Paul will return to similar themes about the Christlike shape of his ministry several times in 2 Corinthians and, to a degree, in Romans. If his lifestyle—*their* lifestyle, for the subject of all the verbs after "I think" in 4:9 is "we"—truly is what is appropriate for ministers of the gospel, he should succeed at establishing that authenticity and authority. In that case, the "wise" in Corinth—indeed the entire community—should both cease their arrogant divisions, which are full of boasts based on human forms of evaluation and self-evaluation, and renew their respect for Paul, who not only preaches but also lives the gospel of Christ crucified. And the Corinthians should follow suit (4:16).

In a sense, then, Paul is boasting, but *only in his conformity to the crucified Lord,* and thus ultimately he is following his own strong admonition about boasting in the Lord and not in any human (1:31; cf. 1:29; 3:21).[106] Amazingly, but not really surprisingly (if 1 Cor 1:18–25 is true), Paul attributes the shape of his ministry ultimately to the will of God (4:9), as he has already suggested in 1:26–31 and as he will develop at length in 2 Corinthians. *The experience of apostolic foolishness and weakness (4:10) is a manifestation of God's foolishness*

---

105. Paul uses the same verb (*kolaphizō*) in 4:11 for his own experience of being beaten that Mark (14:65) and Matthew (26:67) use for Jesus' being beaten in the presence of the high priest before his crucifixion.

106. This brief quasi-boast in cruciform ministry anticipates the similar but more extensive foolish boasting of 2 Cor 11:1–12:10.

and weakness in Christ—which is actually the manifestation of God's apocalyptic, counterintuitive, saving wisdom and power. Paul and his colleagues are content to be fools for Christ (4:10); it is the wisest thing one can do.

REFLECTIONS AND QUESTIONS FOR 3:5–4:13

Spiritual, Pastoral, Missional, and Theological Reflections

1. In 3:5–4:13, those in ministry are presented with **certain critical expectations**, such as cooperation with God and one another, careful attention to the church and its unity, faithfulness to the gospel, accountability, and Christoformity. Together with the Pastoral Epistles and certain key texts in the Gospels—not least John 13—this text offers **a sort of leadership manifesto** that remains relevant two millennia later. However, in light of the abuse of power by so many in church leadership, Paul's indifference to criticism needs to be tempered with the communal accountability he calls for throughout the letter, often implicitly focused on the powerful, and with the sort of expectations we find in 1 Tim 5:19-20: "Never accept any accusation against an elder except on the evidence of two or three witnesses. As for those [elders] who persist in sin, rebuke them in the presence of all, so that the rest also may stand in fear."

2. One of my students had this **reaction to 4:7-13** (used with the student's permission):

    > I had to come before God and repent of my boastful attitude and desperately seek His forgiveness. I was struck with the reality that even though I have proclaimed "Christ crucified," my life does not resemble Christ crucified. Not really. First Corinthians 4:7-13 was not just a list of Paul's tribulations, a lesson for the first-century church in Corinth, or even a message for the church in the U.S. today. God's Word was for me, a child of God whose pride has resulted in an improper perspective of grace and servanthood. Scripture came alive and pierced my heart. Even though I did not understand what to make of this passage, as genuinely as I was able to, I wanted (and still want) to live Christ crucified in today's context.

3. Timothy Gombis makes these two astute and relevant observations about Paul as minister and his **relationships with other ministers and with congregations**: "Because of our modern lenses, we may regard Paul as the great apostle, the 'senior pastor,' the 'CEO' or 'executive director' of his ministry team, but that is not how Paul identified himself. . . . [Rather, Paul] identifies his ministry partners as 'brothers' (1 Cor 1:1; Col 1:1), 'fellow workers' (1 Cor 3:9; Phlm 1, 23) and 'fellow slaves' (Col 1:7). Paul does not refer to

ADDRESSING ECCLESIAL CHAOS · 1:10–4:21

the Corinthians as 'mine,' or as 'my church,' 'my field,' 'my building.' This is instructive for pastors who have the common practice of speaking about 'my church,' and 'my people.'"[107]

4. In his book *UnCorinthian Leadership*, David Starling speaks of the "'**Corinthianization' of leadership**" as "the uncritical absorption and imitation of the mindset and power-structures of the surrounding culture." He then says this about wisdom and leadership in the church: "If the political wisdom of the world is about finding the powerful ones and attaching oneself to them by deal-making and alliances, God's wisdom works according to an entirely different formula."[108]

Questions for Those Who Read, Teach, and Preach

1. What contributions can the early chapters of this letter make to contemporary Christian understandings of ministry?

2. What kinds of ministerial competition and inappropriate pride in, or even idolization of, ministerial leaders occur in the contemporary church, and how can they be addressed and remedied?

3. In what ways might ministerial cruciformity, or Christoformity, be manifested today? How is its opposite manifested?

4. How can ministers and church leaders encourage each other to build practices and habits of humility, servanthood, and collaboration? How can they detect and resist habits of arrogance, narcissism, competition, and selfishness?

5. What contemporary organizational and leadership structures and attitudes may be more reflective of human wisdom than the mind of Christ?

6. In sum, what does this passage urge the church to believe (faith), do (love), and anticipate (hope)?

FOR FURTHER READING

Cen, Esther G. *Domination or Empowerment? A Power Discourse Analysis of 1 and 2 Corinthians.* Eugene, OR: Pickwick, 2023. (technical)

Coakley, Sarah. *Powers and Submissions: Spirituality, Philosophy and Gender.* Malden, MA: Blackwell, 2002. (technical)

Clarke, Andrew D. *A Pauline Theology of Church Leadership.* Edinburgh: T&T Clark, 2008. (technical)

107. Gombis, *Power in Weakness*, 113, 41.
108. Starling, *UnCorinthian Leadership*, 12, 49.

Edwards, Dennis R. *Humility Illuminated: The Biblical Path Back to Christian Character.* Downers Grove, IL: InterVarsity Press, 2023. (highly accessible)

Fitzgerald, John T. *Cracks in an Earthen Vessel: An Examination of the Catalogues of Hardships in the Corinthian Correspondence.* Atlanta: Scholars Press, 1988. (technical)

Gombis, Timothy G. *Power in Weakness: Paul's Transformed Vision for Ministry.* Grand Rapids: Eerdmans, 2021. (highly accessible)

Hellerman, Joseph. *Embracing Shared Ministry: Power and Status in the Early Church and Why It Matters Today.* Grand Rapids: Kregel, 2013.

McKnight, Scot. *Pastor Paul: Nurturing a Culture of Christoformity in the Church.* Grand Rapids: Baker Academic, 2019.

McKnight, Scot, and Laura Barringer. *A Church Called Tov: Forming a Goodness Culture That Resists Abuses of Power and Promotes Healing.* Carol Stream, IL: Tyndale, 2020. (highly accessible)

Plyming, Philip. *Being Real: The Apostle Paul's Hardship and the Stories We Tell Today.* London: SCM, 2023. (highly accessible)

Rosner, Brian S., Andrew S. Malone, and Trevor J. Burke, eds. *Paul as Pastor.* London: T&T Clark/Bloomsbury, 2018.

Starling, David I. *UnCorinthian Leadership: Thematic Reflections on 1 Corinthians.* Eugene, OR: Cascade, 2014.

Stott, John. *The Preacher's Portrait: Five New Testament Word Studies.* Grand Rapids: Eerdmans, 2017 (orig. 1961).

Tucker, J. Brian. *"You Belong to Christ": Paul and the Formation of Social Identity in 1 Corinthians 1–4.* Eugene, OR: Pickwick, 2010.

Wu, Siu Fung. *Finding God in Suffering: Journeying with Jesus and Scriptures.* Eugene, OR: Wipf & Stock, 2023.

———, ed. *Suffering in Paul: Perspectives and Implications.* Eugene, OR: Pickwick, 2019.

4:14–21. Concluding Warning: Paul's Potential Parousia

The somewhat surprising warning that concludes chapters 1–4 makes sense only if read in the context of Paul's sense of apostolic authority as the Corinthians' spiritual father and as an imitator of Christ (4:14–17; cf. 11:1). Paul is treating them, and warning them, as the children he *loves* (4:14). The governing image is family. Paul's desire is to admonish, not shame, them—a critical thing to say to his children in an honor-shame culture to which he has just referred in 4:10. The Corinthians may have many—even ten thousand (*myrious*)—"guides"

ADDRESSING ECCLESIAL CHAOS · 1:10–4:21

(NAB, RSV) or "guardians" (NRSV, NIV, NET; *paidagōgous*) in Christ, like Apollos and others who have come after Paul. But he is their unique father in Christ (4:15).[109] His invitation to imitation (4:16) is not about embracing him per se, or yielding to his power, but about embodying Christ crucified: "Be imitators of me, as I am of Christ" (11:1; cf. Phil 3:17; 1 Thess 1:6).[110]

In a culture that valued imitation (mimesis) of fathers and other formational and exemplary figures, Paul insists that the *real* figure to imitate is Christ Jesus.[111] But for Paul, imitation is inseparable from participation. In vv. 15–17, Paul's focus on being "in Christ" as the normal language of being a Christian is quite striking: the Corinthians and their guardians are in Christ (v. 15a), Paul is their father in Christ Jesus (v. 15b), Timothy is Paul's child "in the Lord" (v. 17a), and Paul's "ways" are in Christ (v. 17b). To imitate Paul is to be shaped by the Lord in whom the church, like Paul, lives. To be *in* Christ is therefore to become *like* Christ. His story has become Paul's story and must now become the Corinthians' story—and ours. From Paul's vantage point, his children have not been living up to that participatory privilege and responsibility.

Paul's warning is completely comprehensible if we recognize the gravity of the situation, at least from his perspective. Paul had sent (or perhaps is sending; cf. 16:10–11) his trusted colleague Timothy as a gentle reminder of Paul's Christoform ways (4:17).[112] Timothy is his beloved child (like the Corinthians), but Timothy (unlike the Corinthians!) is also faithful. Paul's catholicity is also in view in v. 17; his consistent teachings also further the unity, holiness, and apostolicity of the global *ekklēsia*. Some Corinthians, however, have inter-

109. A *paidagōgos* was not a teacher but an enslaved or hired person whose role, in loco parentis, was to keep a youth safe until he safely reached his physical and moral destination, especially school and adulthood. (In Gal 3:24–25, Paul calls the law a *paidagōgos* directing us to the Messiah.) Some translations (e.g., ESV, NAB, NASB1995) dilute the rhetorical power of v. 15 by translating *myrious* as "countless."

110. As we will see in the discussion of 8:1–11:1, there Paul is making deep connections between himself and Christ crucified. See also, e.g., Yung Suk Kim, "'Imitators' (*Mimetai*) in 1 Cor 4:16 and 11:1: A New Reading of Threefold Embodiment," *Horizons in Biblical Theology* 33 (2011): 147–70.

111. See Cornelis Bennema, *Imitation in Early Christianity: Mimesis and Religious-Ethical Formation* (Grand Rapids: Eerdmans, 2025).

112. Timothy is mentioned many times in the Pauline corpus and Acts: in addition to 1 Cor 4:17 and 16:10–11, see Rom 16:21; 2 Cor 1:1, 19; Phil 1:1; 2:19; Col 1:1; 1 Thess 1:1; 3:2, 6; 2 Thess 1:1; 1 Timothy; 2 Timothy; Phlm 1, and Acts 16:1–3; 17:14–15; 18:5; 19:22; 20:4. He is the (or a) co-sender of 2 Corinthians, Philippians, Colossians, 1 Thessalonians (with Silvanus), 2 Thessalonians (with Silvanus), and Philemon—six of the eleven Pauline letters not addressed to him.

160

preted Paul's failure to return to Corinth arrogantly, from Paul's perspective, being "puffed up" (4:18–19; cf. 4:6),[113] a situation perhaps exacerbated by the decision to send Timothy. The apostle therefore warns them that his absence is temporary and is no excuse for noncompliance. If the Lord wills, he will indeed be coming (4:19); the tone is reminiscent of the earlier talk of coming divine judgment. Paul would no doubt prefer to correct the Corinthians gently in love (4:21), as he counseled the Galatians to do for erring believers (Gal 6:1). But the other side of his fatherly personality will appear if his children disobey him—and ultimately God—in this crucial matter of church unity.

This strong response would not be a display of personal power but of divine power (4:20; cf. 2:4), not a form of bullying but of love—tough love, perhaps—a sort of family intervention. It would be a manifestation of the power of the kingdom of God (4:20), and that cannot be simply a rehash of Corinthian power, the power of this age. For "the kingdom of God . . . is justice and peace, and joy in the Holy Spirit" (Rom 14:17 MJG). But the kingdom is both now and not yet. The possibility of missing out on the future fullness of the kingdom is very real (1 Cor 6:9–10; Gal 5:21), and that is Paul's overriding concern for the Corinthians, as he told them at the start of the letter: "that you may be blameless on the day of our Lord Jesus Christ" (1:8).

SUMMARY OF 1:10–4:21

Throughout the comments on 1:10–4:21, we have focused on unity because that is what Paul has focused on. But it has been clear that the call for the church to be one cannot be separated from the call to be holy, catholic, and apostolic.

Furthermore, we can look back on these four chapters and clearly see Paul's bifocal approach, as noted in the table in the introduction to the commentary.[114] With respect to the divisions themselves, he looks back to the cross. He rhetorically denies that he was crucified for the Corinthians (1:13). He reminds them that he had focused, and continues to focus, on Christ crucified as the wisdom and power of God (1:18–25; 2:2), the one who was the embodiment of God's righteousness (saving justice), holiness, and redemption—a fact unknown to those who crucified the Lord (2:8). At the same time, he looks ahead to the ultimate salvation of the Corinthians on the day of the Lord Jesus (1:7–8), to the glorious but unimaginable future in store for those who love God (2:9).

---

113. Most translations flatten the image and speak of arrogance. But see the NAB for vv. 18–19: "inflated with pride . . . inflated people."

114. See pp. 61–63 above.

ADDRESSING ECCLESIAL CHAOS · 1:10–4:21

With respect to the issue of leadership and ministry per se, Paul reminds the Corinthians that true apostleship embodies the message and the death of the crucified Lord (4:9–13). Moreover, he reminds them that those who build (minister) will be accountable to the Lord on his coming day (3:13–15; 4:5).

In these four chapters, then, we see some of Paul's basic perspectives on God, Christ, church, spirituality, and ministry:

- God's desire is for the church, which is the temple of the Holy Spirit, to be unified.
- Proud allegiance to human leaders within the church, rather than to Christ, is divisive and destructive.
- The crucified Christ is, paradoxically, the wisdom and power of God; the cross is a theophany as well as a Christophany.
- Possession of the Spirit and spiritual maturity (true Spirit-uality) consist not in having and displaying humanly valued indicators of social or spiritual status but in living a life connected to the cross.
- The mark of apostleship, and of ministry in general, is faithfulness to God's call in word and deed through conformity to the crucified Christ and service to God's people.
- God's servants are accountable to God for the quality of their labor.
- The church does not belong to human leaders but to God.
- The one church of God must also be holy, catholic, and apostolic.
- Thinking theologically entails thinking bifocally, looking back on Christ's incarnation, life, death, and resurrection and ahead to his parousia, the final judgment, and eschatological glory.

REFLECTIONS AND QUESTIONS ON 1 COR 1–4 AS A WHOLE

1. A perennial challenge to the church is to acknowledge **the infiltration of "this age," the hegemonic (ruling) culture(s), into the church's beliefs and practices,** and to do something to stem the tide. In his book *Christ and Culture in the New Testament*, James Thompson says that in 1 Corinthians, Paul's task is "shaping a new kind of community," and this "begins with the theological foundation in 1 Corinthians 1–4, where he [Paul] draws a sharp dichotomy between the values of Christ and culture—between the old age and the new."[115] Thompson then goes on to list ten dichotomies between Christ and culture

115. James W. Thompson, *Christ and Culture in the New Testament* (Eugene, OR: Cascade, 2022), 54.

162

in 1:17 to 2:14 alone, mostly involving wisdom, power, Christ crucified, and spirit/Spirit. What dichotomies between the gospel and the contemporary ruling culture(s) exist today? How might they be appropriately addressed?

2. It goes without saying that the **kinds of problems noted in chapters 1–4 are still present** in Christian communities today: divisions and allegiances regarding ministers and other leaders based on theology, politics, worship preferences, and so on, as well as displays of (alleged) power and wisdom that are indebted to the ruling culture(s). Is anyone willing to say, as Paul does, that these sorts of divisions, allegiances, claims, and other behaviors are just as dangerous for church life and damaging to its witness as, say, sexual immorality? Are they as dangerous? Why or why not?

5:1-7:40
Addressing Moral Chaos: Holy Living between Cross and Parousia (One *Holy* Church)

Having dealt at length with Corinthian factionalism and the call to unity, Paul, with his co-sender Sosthenes, moves on to a new set of issues: the moral chaos and confusion within the church, and thus the call to holiness. Chapters 5–7 can be described as Paul's version of Israel's Holiness Code (Lev 18–20).[1] Not that Paul ever leaves the issue of divisions and the need for unity behind, for even in these matters of holiness (and even more so in the liturgical topics addressed in chs. 8–14), factionalism is very much part of the problem. Certain behaviors are causing other rifts and alignments within the church. And yet, at least from Paul's perspective, the church seems to possess a certain unity in its disunity—a certain common ability to misunderstand, or to be misled by those who misunderstand, the meaning of the gospel in daily life.

Nor is it the case that moral chaos is something completely separate from "liturgical chaos"—a phrase from the heading for chapters 8–14. If both the church and the individual believer can be called the temple of God (3:16-17; 6:19), then moral issues are in a very real sense liturgical matters—issues about the way God is honored, or not, and by whom, through either holy or unholy behavior. Furthermore, if liturgical settings, such as possible participation in pagan cultic activities (8:1–11:1) and celebration of the Lord's Supper (11:17-34), raise profound moral concerns, then worship matters are inherently moral issues—issues of holiness.

In chapters 5–7, Paul addresses four interrelated holiness issues brought to his attention in oral form (chs. 5 and 6—three issues) and written form (ch. 7—one multifaceted issue). For the people of Israel, ancient Jews, and early Christians—in principle if not always in practice—being God's *holy* people meant being set apart and distinctive; it meant, in a limited but substantive way, taking on the character of God. Holiness is what distinguishes the people of God from the not-people-of-God (e.g., Lev 20:26). To be holy means to be a "publicly identifiable people who embody God's very character in their particular social setting."[2] But the Corinthians are not acting like a holy people.

---

1. Paul Barnett, *1 Corinthians: Holiness and Hope of a Rescued People* (Fearn: Christian Focus, 2011), 77–78, 107.

2. Kent E. Brower and Andy Johnson, "Introduction: Holiness and the *Ekklēsia* of God," in *Holiness and Ecclesiology in the New Testament*, ed. Kent E. Brower and Andy Johnson (Grand Rapids: Eerdmans, 2007), xvi–xxiv (here xvii).

5:1–7:40 ·   *Key Themes*

Three principal features of these chapters unify Paul's description of the problematic matters and his responses to them: key themes, scriptural distinctives, and bifocal theologizing.

KEY THEMES

First of all, certain key words, word families, phrases, and general topics appear thematically throughout these chapters, especially in the three subjects treated in chapters 5 and 6. The three discourse units of those two chapters are structured chiastically (ABA'), and the structure reveals their interconnectedness:[3]

> A 5:1–13 Sexuality Issue: Incest and the Holiness and Witness of the Church
> > B 6:1–11 Justice Issue: Lawsuits, the Justice of God, and the Witness of the Church
> A' 6:12–20 Sexuality Issue: Sex with Prostitutes and the Temple of the Spirit

The fourth unit of chapters 5–7, "Confusion about Marriage and the Missional Call of God" (ch. 7), is materially related especially to the previous units in terms of sexuality, mission, or both.

For each of these moral issues, four aspects of the problem can be observed: (1) we can read Paul's description of the Corinthians' behavior; (2) we can discern possible Corinthian justifications of the behavior (sometimes more clearly than others); (3) we can see and sometimes almost feel Paul's strong reaction, with its corrective exhortation; and (4) we can analyze his theological rationale for that reaction.

The common word families and phrases in these three chapters include the following:

- holiness, explicitly in three of the four discourse units: 6:1, 2, 11, 19; 7:14, 34
- sexual immorality, in all four units: 5:1, 9, 10, 11; 6:9, 13, 15, 16, 18; 7:2
- judging (Gk. *krin-* family), in three of the units: 5:3, 12; 6:1, 2, 3, 4, 5, 6, 7; 7:37
- "Do you not know?" in three of the units: 5:6; 6:2, 3, 9, 15, 16, 19

---

3. Paul uses a chiastic structure elsewhere in the letter, most notably in 8:1–11:1 and chs. 12–14.

165

Scripture-Based Distinctives in a Pagan World

Second, these key themes indicate that standing behind these chapters is Paul's fundamental conviction that the pagan, secular, gentile world is characterized by the antithesis of holiness: idolatry, sexual immorality, and injustice.[4] This critical attitude is not unique to Paul but was fairly common among Jews of the diaspora in the Second Temple period (e.g., Wis 13–14). Frequently paired in Jewish antipagan polemic are idolatry and sexual immorality (*porneia*). This pairing also resonated with aspects of the Jewish tradition itself, such as the golden calf incident, to which Paul alludes in 10:7, as in Rom 1:18–27. And warnings against both idolatry (e.g., Deut 4; Isa 46) and sexual immorality (e.g., Lev 18; Prov 6:23–7:27) are found in Israel's Scriptures.

For Paul, these two sorts of sin are basic because they violate the two-part covenantal requirement of love for God and love for neighbor. Idolatry and sexual immorality, one sin against God and one against other people, were therefore aspects of his basic teaching of the gospel, the good news that meant liberation from addiction to other gods and to harmful relationships, as his earliest preserved letter indicates (1 Thess 1:9–10, about idolatry, and 1 Thess 4:1–8, about holiness, especially sexual holiness).

These two evils are such a threat to the earliest churches that Paul says the Corinthians must not merely avoid them but *flee* from them: "Flee [*pheugete*] from sexual immorality [*porneias*]!" (6:18 MJG) and "Flee [*pheugete*] from idolatry [*eidōlolatrias*]!" (10:14 MJG). Of course, *porneia* is not the only sin against one's neighbor; there are all sorts of injustices, and Paul will treat one of them in 6:1–11. But *porneia* receives the most attention in this part of the letter. What Paul had written to the Thessalonians about sexual behavior he could have also said to the Corinthians, and could (indeed would) say to all Christians:

> For this is the will of God, your sanctification: that you abstain from sexual immorality; that each one of you know how to control your own body in holiness and honor, not with lustful passion, like the gentiles who do not know God; that no one wrong or exploit a brother or sister in this matter, because the Lord is an avenger in all these things, just as we have already told you beforehand and solemnly warned you. For God did not call us to impurity but

---

4. See esp. Rom 1:18–32. Michelle Rader (personal correspondence, November 14, 2023) suggests that idolatry, sexual immorality, and injustice are concentric circles: brokenness/unholiness in relation to God, then in relation to self and certain others, and then in relation to the rest of humanity and the wider creation.

in holiness. Therefore whoever rejects this rejects not human authority but God, who also gives his Holy Spirit to you. (1 Thess 4:3–8 NRSVue)

In fact, much of 1 Cor 5–7 is an extended exposition of this basic Pauline teaching. With respect to sex, wrote the eminent scholar Larry Hurtado, "It is fair to judge that the impact of the distinctive stance of early Christian teaching involved a transformation in the deep logic of sexual morality." And according to theologian Beth Felker Jones, "Strange ideas about sex—odd ideas out of sync with those of the wider culture—marked Christians out from the very beginning."[5] But not always; *porneia* was not confined to the pagan world.

There has been significant scholarly debate about the meaning of the Greek word *porneia*. Prior to and apart from Jewish and Christian usage, it meant simply prostitution, but as a preeminent scholar on ancient Christian and Jewish sexuality says, *porneia* has "a wide range of meanings" in the New Testament, meanings that must be determined by context.[6] Generally, in Paul's writings, "sexual immorality" is the best translation of *porneia*, though specific types of *porneia* are discussed in different texts.

For Jews like Paul, *porneia* as a broad category would have included the sexual acts listed in Lev 18, which were intended to make the people of God distinct from the pagan world, originally the Egyptians and the Canaanites (Lev 18:3). The prohibited acts in Lev 18 (directed toward males but implicitly inclusive of all) consist of various forms of incest—particularly germane for 1 Cor 5:1–13—as well as same-gender sex and bestiality. Other scriptural texts forbid adultery, premarital sex; and prostitution (e.g., Deut 22:13–30; see also Exod 20:14; Lev 19:29; 20:10; Deut 5:18; 23:18), sometimes with the most serious consequence: death. Paul's outlook in 1 Cor 5–7 is greatly informed by scriptural themes and perspectives, even when direct quotations are absent. As already noted, some of these themes and perspectives are echoed in other Jewish and early Christian traditions (including the teaching of Jesus), to which Paul is indebted.

---

5. Larry W. Hurtado, *Destroyer of the Gods: Early Christian Distinctiveness in the Roman World* (Waco, TX: Baylor University Press, 2016), 171; Beth Felker Jones, *Faithful: A Theology of Sex* (Grand Rapids: Zondervan, 2015), 9. But to be fair to the ancients, not all gentiles were sexually obsessed and without morals, and there were pagan moralists who decried unbridled passion, whether within the imperial family or among the masses.

6. William Loader, *The New Testament on Sexuality* (Grand Rapids: Eerdmans, 2012), 142, esp. n. 115; cf. 246. He includes within *porneia* prebetrothal and premarital heterosexual sex (fornication) and homosexual relations as well as adultery, incest, and prostitution.

ADDRESSING MORAL CHAOS · 5:1–7:40

Bifocal Existence in Christ

Finally, also uniting these various problems in Paul's mind is his underlying conviction that believers have a bifocal existence as they live in Christ in the in-between time, the era between Christ's first and second comings.[7] That is, as we have already seen, they live with one eye fixed on Christ's past coming, suffering, death, resurrection, and exaltation, and another on his future parousia, with the bodily resurrection, final judgment, glorification, and liberation of all creation that day will entail. The Corinthians were apparently ignoring or downplaying both foci.

To live between these two events, and to be shaped by both of them, requires a process of careful community discernment guided by Scripture, the Spirit as the presence of the resurrected Lord, and, of course, the apostle. Here, then, we see Paul the pastor theologian carefully at work in grounding his response to each situation in the dynamic bifocal existence of the church in the overlap of the ages and inviting the Corinthians, and others who hear or read his letter, to do the same.

5:1–13. Incest and the Holiness and Witness of the Church

The first situation Paul and Sosthenes confront in this section of the letter is a real shock to them since it involves a kind of sexual immorality (*porneia*; 5:1) even the Corinthians' unconverted gentile (pagan) friends would not practice or condone. This is quite a claim (though it is true), since gentiles, as noted above, had a (generally well-deserved) reputation for all kinds of sexual activities. How sadly ironic that the pagan world, in this matter, was essentially holier than the Corinthian body of Christ.

5:1–5. The Situation, the Individual, and Immediate Action to Take

The specific form of *porneia* and the concrete situation according to 5:1–13 is this: one of the Corinthian believers is "living with [lit., "having," sexually] his father's wife"—that is, his stepmother (5:1). We do not know whether the father was living or deceased, but probably the latter. Such incestuous behavior was prohibited both by Roman law and custom and by Jewish Scripture, according to which the offender was worthy of cursing or even death.[8] Per-

---

7. See, similarly, Hays, *First Corinthians*, 111.
8. For scriptural texts, see Lev 18:8; 20:11; Deut 22:30 (cf. v. 22); 27:20. Jewish tradition

5:1–5 · *The Situation, the Individual, and Immediate Action to Take*

haps the man was one of the elite, even a community benefactor, so people were hesitant to criticize; or perhaps he offered a defense of his indefensible (to Paul) actions. All we can know with certainty is what Paul says about the community's reaction: rather than appropriately grieving about this believer's regression to, and even beyond, pagan practices, the church has become "arrogant" (NRSV) or "inflated with pride" (NAB, closer to the vivid Greek imagery of being "puffed up") about it (5:2a).

Being puffed up, as we saw in the discussion of unity, is not a minor problem at Corinth (see 4:6, 18, 19; 8:1; 13:4). This arrogance must have been reported to Paul; it is not merely his interpretation. And there is more than a subtle hint in Paul's words that the Corinthians are bearing witness badly by being so puffed up in spite of the fact that their pagan friends, neighbors, associates, masters (in the case of enslaved persons), and others would not approve of the situation. In fact, the implication is that the Corinthian community has become an *anti*witness to the gospel. The Corinthians need to change both their attitude and the situation itself.

Paul's remedy for the situation—issued four times—likely seems drastic at first: expulsion of the offending member from the church (5:2b, 5, 7, 13b). This judgment is what later church tradition has referred to with terms like "excommunication" and "disfellowship." Paul's warrant for this action is the Deuteronomic theme of "removing the evil from your midst," to which he refers in 5:13—though he uses the theme without citing its call for the death penalty that is found in many of Deuteronomy's texts as the means of removing the evil.[9] Paul's multifaceted rationale partially echoes reasons for exclusion from the community in Israel's Scriptures, such as covenant obligations, the call to holiness, corporate responsibility, avoiding contamination or pollution, and divine judgment.[10]

Paul clearly believes that his judgment has the approval of the Lord Jesus, whose apostle he is and for whom he speaks authoritatively (5:4b, and possibly also 5:4a). As Paul says in another letter to this community (2 Cor 13:10), this is not the kind of authority that is intended as a display of severity but as

---

echoed Scripture; e.g., Pseudo-Phocylides, from the first century before or after Christ, says explicitly, "Do not touch [i.e., sexually] your stepmother, inasmuch as she is your father's second wife" (Pseudo-Phocylides 179 MJG); so also Jubilees 33.10–13, with the threat of capital punishment. The *lex Julia* promulgated by Augustus in 18 BC prohibited marriage to a father's wife (Cicero, *Pro Cluentio* 5; Gaius, *Institutes* 1.63).

9. See further below.

10. Brian S. Rosner, *Paul, Scripture and Ethics: A Study of 1 Corinthians 5–7* (Leiden: Brill, 1994; repr., Grand Rapids: Baker, 1999), 61–93.

ADDRESSING MORAL CHAOS · 5:1–7:40

a means of edification—unless the unruly children disregard their spiritual parent. Thus, when the Corinthians assemble, with the physically absent Paul present in spirit (or in the Spirit; v. 3), they are to ratify this apostolic judgment by expelling the man from the community (vv. 3–5).

Verses 3–5 constitute a challenging passage in the Greek text. Within it, there is a particularly interesting phrase: "in the name of the [or "our"] Lord Jesus" (5:4a in the Greek, but sometimes included with 5:3). Because there is no punctuation in the Greek text, this phrase could be connected with more than one phrase in the rest of the text. The translation of the phrase in 5:3–4 includes at least three possibilities (emphasis added):

- *"I have already pronounced judgment in the name of the Lord Jesus* on the man who has done such a thing" (NRSV).
- *"When you gather together in the name of our Lord Jesus*, and I am with you in spirit . . ." (NET).
- "As for me, although I am absent in body but present in spirit, I have already pronounced judgment, as if present, on the man who has done such a thing *in the name of the Lord Jesus*" (MJG).

The first two translations fit the context and Paul's theology of his own authority and of the church quite well. The last interpretation seems, at first, unlikely and even unchristian. But this is precisely the point. As shocking as this last option is, it is grammatically and contextually possible. And it would explain to some degree how someone who self-identifies as a person in Christ would do such a thing and think he is doing it with the approval of Jesus. The man may have thought, like the people visiting prostitutes (6:12–20), that the Lord Jesus gives absolute freedom when it comes to the use of one's body. For Paul, however, this would be sin and slavery, not holiness and freedom—an example of taking the Lord's name in vain, among other transgressions. Furthermore, if the man is in fact doing this "in the name of the Lord Jesus," it may explain why Paul wants him, and him alone among the Corinthian problem children, gone in order to keep God's holy temple holy.

Whichever translation is correct (my preference being the third), Paul is convinced that when the Corinthians do assemble, "the power of our Lord Jesus" (v. 4b) will be with them to make this difficult decision take place. The power of the kingdom of God (4:20) can operate even without Paul being present. We cannot know whether anything like the process laid out in Matt 18:15–21 has been followed, but there is certainly an echo of these verses here: the presence of Jesus (Matt 18:20) and the need to separate the (unrepentant) sinner (Matt 18:17).

What are Paul's motives in rendering this judgment and saying, essentially, that it—not the man's incestuous relationship—is what reveals the Lord's will and power? The text makes it clear that he is focused on both the man and the community as a whole.

First, looking forward and considering the individual, Paul is concerned with the offending man's salvation on the day of judgment. This is the eschatological horizon of Paul's bifocal perspective. The man's behavior is a betrayal of his identity in Christ, and those who live in such a way, no matter their verbal confession or community affiliation, "will not inherit the kingdom of God" (6:9–10). (Since Paul says nothing about the woman, we can assume she is not a member of the community.) Paul hopes that removing this man from the sphere of the Lord Jesus and remitting him to the sphere of Satan (cf. 2 Cor 4:4; 1 Tim 1:20) will eventually terminate his behavior so that he will finally be saved (5:5). Paul is expressing an attitude of "salvific intentionality," and he hopes the community will share it.[11]

The stakes are clearly high.[12] Since salvation is, in Paul's theology, something experienced in Christ and thus in his body, we should assume that the practical means of the man's salvation is his repentance and subsequent readmittance to the Corinthian *ekklēsia*, which is anticipating corporate growth in holiness until the day of the Lord Jesus (1:8). Similarly, later ecclesial practices of excommunication and disfellowship have often had provisions for repentance and readmittance. (See also Job 2:6; 42:1–17.)

Paul's anthropological language in 5:5 is somewhat confusing: does he believe, in a dualistic way, in an evil flesh, the human body that can commit sexual sin, and a good, inner spirit that can be saved apart from the body? This is highly unlikely. For one thing, in the very next chapter, Paul will speak of proper sexual relations as the uniting of two into one flesh (6:16, citing Genesis and Jesus) and call the believer's body the "temple of the Holy Spirit" (6:19). Furthermore, in chapter 15, he will discuss the resurrection and transformation of the body. For another, in other contexts, Paul's understanding of "flesh" can be either neutral (life in the flesh) or negative (life according to the flesh), but it is not usually synonymous with "the body" for him.

---

11. See Scott Goode, *Salvific Intentionality in 1 Corinthians: How Paul Cultivates the Missional Imagination of the Corinthian Community* (Eugene, OR: Wipf & Stock, 2023), 11–19.

12. Although Paul does not tell us whether any in the community had already tried to dissuade this man from his way of life, the question is probably irrelevant to Paul in light of the community's arrogance, as he sees it. Paul also does not say whether the man could be readmitted to the community if he ended the relationship. However, the words of 2 Cor 2:5–11, regardless of whether they refer to this situation, reveal that Paul believed in repentance, forgiveness, and restoration.

ADDRESSING MORAL CHAOS · 5:1–7:40

As we saw in 1 Cor 3, the flesh has more to do with this age or this world—the sphere of those out of sync with God. Paul's hope that "the flesh" will be destroyed is similar to the sentiment expressed in Romans:[13] "We know that our old self was crucified with him so that the body of sin might be destroyed, and we might no longer be enslaved to sin" (Rom 6:6). It is also similar to his exhortation in Galatians, "Live [lit., "walk"] by the Spirit, I say, and do not gratify the desires of the flesh" (Gal 5:16), that precedes the list of the "works of the flesh" that are inappropriate for believers (Gal 5:19–21).[14] Since Paul quotes the leaven proverb that appears in 1 Cor 5:6 in Gal 5:9, too, he is likely thinking in the Galatian mode also here in 1 Cor 5.

But what about the salvation of the man's spirit? Once we see that there is no body-soul (flesh-spirit) dualism here, then we can conclude that the "spirit" is a reference to the man's true, en-Spirited self, liberated from domination by the flesh: that he will prove to be a Spirit-person rather than a flesh-person (see 2:13–3:5).

5:6–13. The Situation and the Community

Second, Paul is concerned about the community's attitude of toleration, though in fact he finds that they are more than tolerant; they are proud (5:2, 6; cf. Ps 52:1; 94:4). Instead, he avers, they should be penitent and mournful. Their pride would likely stem from belief in an extreme libertinism (after all, Paul preached a gospel of freedom) that held that what one does sexually, with one's body, has no impact on one's relationship with God (see 6:12–20). The Stoic Epictetus, in *Discourses* 4.1.1, had said this: "He is free who lives as he wills."

No doubt this was a common sentiment in Corinth. In this man they had living proof of their liberation, but it was an understanding of liberation at odds with the gospel and reflective instead of pagan culture. Paul's Jewish version of "one bad apple spoils the whole barrel" (5:6), using the image of leaven, assumes both that the behavior is wrong and that it is dangerous to the church.[15] Western readers may not fully grasp the concern for contamination,

---

13. The Greek text of v. 5 lacks the possessive pronoun "his," but that is not uncommon and merely means that Paul could be referring to "the flesh" generically or, much more likely, "his" (the man's) flesh. The same is true of the reference to "the" or "his" spirit.

14. In Gal 5, the sins of the flesh are as much relational and social in character as they are bodily or sexual.

15. Leaven was the leftover dough (sourdough) that was used as an agent of fermentation and mixed with new dough. The Greek word should not be translated as "yeast."

or pollution of the community, expressed in this image; an individual's sin and impurity can render the whole body unholy, impure, and unhealthy.

Drawing on a phrase that appears several times in Deuteronomy, Paul urges the community to "remove the evil person from among you" (5:13 NET; *exarate ton ponēron ex hymōn autōn*). Yet unlike the book of Deuteronomy and some postbiblical texts, but like certain other postbiblical Jewish writings, Paul's call does not include the death of the evildoer.[16] In fact, as we have seen, it intends his salvation.

The leaven analogy serves not only to illustrate the spread of impurity but also to connect the whole issue to Christ crucified as "our paschal lamb [who] . . . has been sacrificed" (5:7, interpreting Exod 12:21–28). Now Paul, in the other dimension of his bifocal mode, is looking backward. Believers, Paul suggests in reflecting on Christ's past death, live in a permanent state of Passover, during which time only unleavened bread may be eaten. (See Exod 12 for the original Passover, and Deut 16:1–8 for the ongoing ritual.)

The leaven to be removed (see Exod 13:7) for the proper ongoing communal celebration of Christ's death is not a baking component but "malice and evil" (1 Cor 5:8). It is significant that Paul does not merely say, "Get rid of all the sexual immorality." The present situation allows Paul to speak more broadly about the church's need to take all forms of sin (see 5:11) seriously. This is, in part, what it means to be the people marked out from others by the blood of the lamb, the called and sanctified church of God in Christ, the *holy* temple of the *Holy* Spirit. This holiness must be manifested in the normal activities of daily life and in special times of assembly for the remembrance of Christ's paschal sacrifice, the Lord's Supper (10:14–21; 11:17–34).

At this juncture, Paul inserts a parenthetical comment to clarify an important and relevant principle from a previous letter: "not to associate with sexually immoral persons [*pornoi*]" or with other kinds of evildoers, such as the greedy, idolaters, and so on (5:9–11). The apostle is probably borrowing again from Deuteronomy and its practices worthy of judgment, with a focus on the actual problems at Corinth.[17] What Paul meant was not that the community should disassociate itself from all sinful nonbelievers (an existential impossi-

---

16. See Deut 13:5; 17:1–13; 19:15–21; 21:18–21; 22:20–24; 24:7; many translations render the Hebrew as "purge the evil"; the LXX (and thus Paul) says "the evil one." As noted above, one Jewish text that retains the requirement of capital punishment is Jubilees, which pronounces a curse on all who commit the unforgivable sin of lying with their father's wife, a curse that is confirmed by all the "holy ones" (Jubilees 33.10–13).

17. *Porneia*, greed, and idolatry were often mentioned together in Jewish critiques of sinful behavior; naming the greedy here may also anticipate the litigants described in 6:1–11.

ADDRESSING MORAL CHAOS

bility then or now) but that it should distance itself from flagrant hypocrites within the church, professing believers who were still living as idolatrous and immoral pagans—like the man with his stepmother (5:11; cf. 2 Thess 3:6).

Refraining from table fellowship with such people, avers the apostle, is an appropriate form of community discernment, or judgment (5:11–12). The "table" in question is the one found in the community's assemblies, which included both everyday food and the Lord's Supper (see the discussion of 11:17–34). Paul is in effect saying, "While someone is essentially in the state of being *outside* Christ, keep that person from participating in the community gatherings as if they were *in* Christ."[18] Paul's admonition not to eat with such people is at first rather stunning, given that he had criticized Cephas (Peter) for withdrawing from table fellowship with gentile believers (Gal 2:12). Paul would not, however, have judged himself to be hypocritical, for in Christ the boundary marker is not circumcision (so Cephas, for a time) but "keeping the commandments of God," as he will say in 7:19.

Paul's rejection of disassociation from "outsiders" (5:12–13) is at least implicitly also a call to associate with them in normal relations and with their spiritual health and salvation in view (see 10:23–11:1). The Christian community dynamic of being *in* the world but not *of* the world is at play in this passage. So is the reality that the *world* can often be in the *church*. Ultimately, Christian holiness is also about Christian witness and mission—or apostolicity. The church cannot have integrity in its witness if what it wrongly practices is not even done by people in the secular world.

This is almost certainly the unexpressed, and perhaps even the most basic, reason Paul calls for the man's expulsion but does not call for the removal of anyone else in the pages of this letter. Not only the incestuous man but also the tolerant, puffed-up church has become an antiwitness. In a sense, then, the entire church's salvation is in the balance. A radical cancer requires radical surgery, though that metaphor works only part way because there is the hope in Paul's mind for the man's restoration—and for the community's growth in holiness and witness.[19]

---

18. Certain other Jewish texts similarly require holiness for participation in community meals.

19. Even if community exclusion for incest was practiced elsewhere in Paul's day, it would not have been for the same theological reasons.

Summary

Paul's concern in 5:1–13 is for both the man's ultimate salvation and the congregation's spiritual health, that is, the effect of an individual's flagrant sin on both that person and the community. This whole passage is a highly rhetorical but also thoroughly theological effort to drive home the importance of the principle of communal holiness—which includes separation from evil—and its application to the issue at hand. It was a difficult word then, and it is certainly no easier twenty centuries later.

REFLECTIONS AND QUESTIONS FOR 5:1–13

Spiritual, Pastoral, Missional, and Theological Reflections

1. On the subject of not judging outsiders, Chrysostom commented that it was **"superfluous to speak the precepts of Christ to those who [know] not Christ Himself."**[20] Rather, by implication, the church's mission is to proclaim the good news and to speak of Christ. Because we cannot separate Christ from his teaching, such proclamation will necessarily involve witnessing to his teaching. However, the church does not primarily try to convince others to be good apart from discipleship but to embrace and follow Jesus, from whom all good derives. At the same time, paradoxically, since the world is always better off when its actions resemble those of Jesus rather than those of say, the reigning political powers, Christians need not shy away from hoping for, or celebrating, Christlike actions on the part of non-Christians.

2. **In an age of radical toleration**, especially of sexual behavior, the Christian church needs to take seriously the theological perspectives articulated in this passage.

3. One of the most serious offenses within the Christian church has been **the plague of sexual abuse, especially of minors**. It has been not only tolerated but covered up in a mindset that is not dissimilar from being puffed up, even if other factors are in play. Often church leaders are resisting structures and means of accountability that are now accepted by non-Christians as essential to protecting the vulnerable from sexual exploitation. Thus, no one can doubt the harm such abuse has done to the church's witness, in addition to the harm to so many individuals. This situation demonstrates that in addition to the flagrantly sinful individual harming the church, the flagrantly sinful church harms individuals. The failure of accountability cuts both ways.

---

20. John Chrysostom, *Homilies on 1 Corinthians* 16.2.

Questions for Those Who Read, Teach, and Preach

1. Because tolerance is a nearly unassailable virtue of the highest order, at least in Western cultures, and because excommunication or disfellowship has sometimes been abused in Christian circles, does it have any place in the contemporary church? If so, in what kinds of circumstances and with what guardrails so it is not misused? If not, what are the possible consequences of having no accountability for egregious sin?
2. How do church communities discern the difference between arrogant sexual sinners (who need discipline) and struggling sexual sinners (who need pastoral care and gentle correction, or restoration—Gal 6:1)? What difference does that make in how the community treats them?
3. How does a Christian community discern the differences among sexual abusers, the sexually exploited, and the sexually immoral when the surface behavior can sometimes appear to be similar, especially from a distance? What sorts of approaches to ministry does each group need?
4. In sum, what does this passage urge the church to believe (faith), do (love), and anticipate (hope)?

For Further Reading

Hays, Richard B. *The Moral Vision of the New Testament: Community, Cross, New Creation; A Contemporary Introduction to New Testament Ethics*. San Francisco: HarperCollins, 1996.

Jones, Beth Felker. *Faithful: A Theology of Sex*. Grand Rapids: Zondervan, 2015. (highly accessible)

Loader, William. *The New Testament on Sexuality*. Grand Rapids: Eerdmans, 2012.

Rosner, Brian S. *Paul, Scripture and Ethics: A Study of 1 Corinthians 5–7*. Leiden: Brill, 1994. Repr., Grand Rapids: Baker, 1999. (technical)

Smith, David Raymond. *"Hand This Man Over to Satan": Curse, Exclusion, and Salvation in 1 Corinthians 5*. London: T&T Clark, 2008. (technical)

Thompson, James W. *Moral Formation according to Paul: The Context and Coherence of Pauline Ethics*. Grand Rapids: Baker Academic, 2011.

6:1–11. LAWSUITS, THE JUSTICE OF GOD, AND THE WITNESS OF THE CHURCH

The theme of judging (5:12–13) continues in 6:1–11; now, however, Paul writes about inappropriate, audacious judging—as in "How *dare* you?!" (the tone of

6:1). Some members of the community in Corinth are suing other members in the Roman courts of the city (6:1, 4, 6).[21] They are acting just like normal Corinthians, or at least like normal elite Corinthians. Some scholars believe for good reasons that the elite were taking the nonelite (and legally more vulnerable) to court, where judges would normally side with the more powerful. But regardless of whether that is true, Paul's concerns would apply to anyone in the community taking legal action.

The passage is another rhetorical tour de force, as Paul pulls out all the stops to make his point that those who have been justified—made just and brought into the community of the just by means of Christ's death and their participation in it—cannot practice injustice. Paul rather sarcastically refers to the Corinthians' own claim to wisdom (6:5). He uses the "Do you not know?" question three times (6:2, 3, 9). He makes points by way of rhetorical questions and with sentences that could be questions or, more likely, exclamations. (There are no punctuation marks in the original.) He rhythmically repeats small words like "nor" (6:9–10) and "but" (6:11) that are striking in Greek but not always translated into English. And, in contrast to his fatherly statement in 4:14 about not shaming the Corinthians about their divisiveness, here he unashamedly shames the Corinthians (6:5).

Most significantly, Paul has creatively constructed the passage around four interrelated sets of words:

- the "judgment" word family: nine occurrences (in vv. 1–7)
- the "justice" word family: five occurrences (in vv. 1, 7–9, 11)
- the "holy" word family: three occurrences (in vv. 1, 2, 11)
- the word "brother" (*adelphos*; i.e., Christian sibling): four occurrences (in vv. 5, 6, 8)

Unfortunately, most translations, especially the NRSV, fail to convey these interconnections (the NAB is better than most), this "deft wordplay."[22] A new translation, with added boldfaced type, will help to bring out the interconnections of key words and word families in this passage:

21. The plural verbs in key parts of the passage (esp. vv. 7–8) probably indicate that there is more than one case, though it could be that Paul is making general statements or blaming the entire community for the action of one individual.

22. Hays, *First Corinthians*, 98. The Holman Christian Standard Bible captures a bit of the linguistic interconnections: "Why not rather put up with injustice? Why not rather be cheated? Instead, you act unjustly and cheat—and you do this to believers!" (1 Cor 6:7b–8; similarly, the NJB).

ADDRESSING MORAL CHAOS · 5:1–7:40

Does any of you dare, when you have a grievance against another, to take it for judgment [*krinesthai*] before the **unjust** [*tōn adikōn*] and not before the **holy ones** [*tōn hagiōn*]? Do you not know that the **holy ones** [*hoi hagioi*] will **judge** [*krinousin*] the world? And if the world will be **judged** [*krinetai*] by you, are you unworthy of the least matters in need of **judgment** [*kritēriōn*]? Do you not know that we will **judge** [*krinoumen*] angels—so why not everyday matters? If you have everyday matters in need of **judgment** [*kritēria*], then, do you seat [i.e., as judges] those who have no standing in the assembly/church?[23] I say this to your shame! Can it really be that there is no one among you wise enough to **judge a matter** [*diakrinai*] between **brothers** [*adelphou*]? But instead a **brother** [*adelphos*] brings a **judgment** [*krinetai*] against a **brother** [*adelphou*]—and this before **unbelievers** [*apistōn*]!

It is already completely a defeat for you that you have such legal **judgments** [*krimata*] among yourselves. Why not rather **be treated unjustly** [or "**endure injustice**"; *adikeisthe*]? Why not rather be defrauded? But you yourselves **inflict injustice** [*adikeite*] and defraud—and this to **brothers** [*adelphous*]! Do you not know that **the unjust** [*adikoi*] will not inherit the kingdom of God? Do not be deceived! Neither sexually immoral persons [*pornoi*], nor idolaters, nor adulterers, nor passive or active male same-sex partners, nor thieves, nor the greedy, nor drunkards, nor revilers, nor robbers will inherit the kingdom of God. And these things some of you used to be. But you were washed, but you were **made holy** [*hēgiasthēte*], but you were **made just** [*edikaiōthēte*] in the name of the Lord Jesus Christ and in the Spirit of our God.

There is a lot going on here. At one level, the questions at hand are: Why would you sue a sibling? and Why can't the family settle family matters? At the same time, other significant questions arise: What is the nature of Christian community? What does it mean to be washed/baptized, sanctified, and justified, to live as a holy people in light of Christ crucified, to practice justice in biblical and specifically Christian rather than pagan, secular, Roman terms? As we will see, justice in light of Messiah Jesus is both in continuity with and a new development of biblical justice; it is both prophetic and cruciform. And once again, Paul theologizes bifocally, looking back to the cross and ahead to the final judgment and the kingdom of God.

Implicit in Paul's response is the negative witness of the members of the *ekklēsia* who are airing their dirty laundry not only in public but in court.

---

23. The second half of v. 4 could be translated as an imperative, "[you should] seat as judges the persons of no account in the church." See discussion below.

6:1–6. Lawsuits in the Community

Rather than being a witness to the gospel, they are (like the community as a whole, according to 5:1–13), an unholy *anti*witness.

6:1–6. Lawsuits in the Community

Paul begins by describing the situation in anything but calm language, using a series of questions and an exclamation or two to express his horror at siblings suing siblings. He calls the pagan court system that is the venue for such suits the sphere of the "unjust" (*adikōn*, 6:1 MJG; NAB) and "unbelievers" (6:6).[24] Paul does not only mean, however, that the court system is unjust and unfair because it is not composed of Christian lawyers and judges. There is more to it than that—outsiders, those in the world who follow merely human values (recall 2:6–3:4), are now described *as the unjust*, among whom are the administrators of Rome's (so-called) justice. The implicit corollary? This kind of suit is an act of injustice.

Roman justice was in fact generally rife with bribery and partiality toward the powerful. Therefore the justice of Rome is not, and cannot be, the justice of God, or of God's people. The people of God have always had a different way to pursue justice:

> You shall appoint judges and officials throughout your tribes, in all your towns that the LORD your God is giving you, and they shall render just [*tsedheq*; LXX *dikaian*] decisions for the people. You must not distort justice [*mishpat*; LXX *krisin*]; you must not show partiality; and you must not accept bribes, for a bribe blinds the eyes of the wise and subverts the cause of those who are in the right. Justice, and only justice [*tsedheq*; LXX *dikaiōs to dikaion*] you shall pursue, so that you may live and occupy the land that the LORD your God is giving you. (Deut 16:18–20; cf. Exod 18:13–27; Deut 1:9–18)

But biblical justice is not just a legal matter. The great Jewish theologian and spiritual writer Abraham Joshua Heschel claimed that "the fundamental experience of the prophet is a fellowship with the feelings of God" and that "to be a prophet means to identify one's concern with the concern of God."[25] The Scriptures of Israel insist that one of the things God cares most about is justice (Heb.

---

24. For *adikōn*, CEB has "aren't just," NRSV "unrighteous"; cf. 6:9.

25. Abraham J. Heschel, *The Prophets*, two vols. in one (Peabody, MA: Hendrickson, 2007 [orig. 1962]), 1:26; and *Between God and Man: An Interpretation of Judaism* (New York: Free Press, 1997 [1959]), 126.

mishpat; LXX *krima* and related words) and the related reality of righteousness (Heb. *tsedheq, tsedhaqah*; LXX *dikaiosynē*). This is not just a matter for courts and kings. Neighbor love is to be expressed in justice, or making things right, especially for the vulnerable, such as the poor, widows, and orphans:

- "He [the LORD] has told you, O mortal, what is good; and what does the LORD require of you but to do justice [*mishpat*; LXX *krima*], and to love kindness, and to walk humbly with your God?" (Mic 6:8).
- "Learn to do good; seek justice [*mishpat*; LXX *krisin*], rescue the oppressed [LXX *adikoumenon*], defend the orphan, plead for the widow" (Isa 1:17).
- "Let justice [*mishpat*; LXX *krima*] roll down like waters, and righteousness [*tsedhaqah*; LXX *dikaiosynē*] like an everflowing stream" (Amos 5:24).

Filled with God's Spirit, Jesus the Messiah both preached and practiced biblical justice, as he announced at the start of his ministry, quoting from Isa 61: "The Spirit of the Lord is upon me, because he has anointed me to bring good news to the poor. He has sent me to proclaim release to the captives and recovery of sight to the blind, to let the oppressed go free, to proclaim the year of the Lord's favor" (Luke 4:18–19).

Of course, both the prophets and Jesus realized that humans—even God's people—do not always practice justice. Although such sin is not surprising, it elicits some of the harshest criticism from both the prophets and Jesus:

- "How the faithful city [Jerusalem] has become a whore! She that was full of justice [*mishpat*; LXX *krima*], righteousness [*tsedheq*; LXX *dikaiosynē*] lodged in her—but now murderers! . . . They do not defend the orphan, and the widow's cause does not come before them" (Isa 1:21, 23c).
- "Woe to you, scribes and Pharisees, hypocrites! For you tithe mint, dill, and cumin, and have neglected the weightier matters of the law: justice [*krisin*] and mercy and faith [or "faithfulness"; MJG]. It is these you ought to have practiced without neglecting the others" (Matt 23:23; cf. Luke 11:42).

So too with Paul and justice: expectation and critique. For many people, however, the phrase "Paul and justice" does not spring to mind as a natural theological pair. Yet "justice" is in fact a critical term for the apostle, who is as concerned about justice as were the prophets and Jesus.[26] As we have already

---

26. For further discussion of Paul and justice, with consideration of this passage, see my *Becoming the Gospel*, 212–60.

noted, and as the translation offered above indicates, much of Paul's argument in 6:1–11 turns on the words "justice," "unjust," and "justified/made just." And as we will see shortly, the counterintuitive justice of God is revealed—as we should expect—in Christ crucified rather than in the courts of the unjust unbelievers.

Equally critical for Paul are the terms he uses to characterize the community: they, in contrast to the unjust outsiders, are the *holy* ones (6:1, 2); Paul is echoing what he said at the start of the letter: the Corinthians have been made holy and are called to be holy (1:2). And Paul will also remind them in 6:11 that the baptisms they all experienced (and about which they have wrangled) made them holy and just (often simply translated as "justified"), made them into a community set apart to act differently from the people of "this age." As believers rather than unbelievers (the implication of 6:6), they are just or righteous—or at least they should be.

But the word "believers" is not actually in the text of this passage. Paul's emphasis is on the reality that this is a community of *siblings*; they are family, brothers and sisters (*adelphoi*; 6:5, 6, 8). Translations that obscure this reality with words like "believers" in reference to members of the community (e.g., the NRSV in vv. 5–6 and 8) miss one of Paul's most important points.[27]

With his bifocal approach to life in Christ, in 6:2–3 Paul looks ahead to the second coming of Jesus and, specifically, the eschatological scenario of the final judgment. He calls upon the Jewish apocalyptic conviction, shared by Jesus and then received and passed on (Paul implies) by the early church, that God's people assist God on the judgment day, judging both the world (humans) and angels.[28] This future role in the divine judgment is quite ironic, since at present Paul, his coworkers, and no doubt others have become "a spectacle to the world, to angels and to mortals" (4:9). There is quite a role reversal on the horizon.

How then, Paul wonders, can the Corinthians not engage in appropriate judgments about comparatively small (6:2; even "trivial": NRSV, NIV, NET, CEB), everyday matters within the community rather than taking them to the pagan courts (6:3–4)?[29] To use an analogy from baseball: the Corinthians, Paul

27. In 6:6, for instance, NRSV has "a believer goes to court against a believer," but the NRSVue, CEB, NAB, NIV, and most other versions use "brother and sister" or "brother." NET uses "Christian."

28. See, e.g., Wis 3:8; Matt 19:28; Luke 22:30; cf. Dan 7:22.

29. A typical Jewish argument from lesser (mundane judgments) to greater (eschatological judgment) is operative here: how can the Corinthians not do the former if they are destined for the latter?

implies, may not be qualified for the big leagues if they cannot play little-league ball. There is at least a mild threat in this interrogation. And there is certainly shame (6:5). There is also scriptural precedent for intracommunity judgment: Moses appointing judges for the assembly of God's people (e.g., Deut 16:18, quoted above), and certain parts of the stories in the book of Judges.

The second half of v. 4 is usually interpreted as a reference to those pagan courts, as in the NRSV: "do you appoint [lit., "seat"] as judges those who have no standing in the church?" (RSV: "those who are least esteemed"; NIV: "those whose way of life is scorned in the church?"). If this is the correct interpretation, then "appoint/seat" is clearly used in a figurative sense (NIV: "ask for a ruling from"), since, of course, the church does not appoint the judges in the secular courts.

It is also possible, however, that Paul is not asking a question but making a request. (The Greek text has no punctuation.) The long descriptive phrase "who have no standing in the church" is actually just a form of the same Greek verb used in 1:28 to characterize the "despised in the world" (NRSV)—the nobodies God chose.[30] In other words, we might understand v. 4 this way: "If you have everyday matters, why not seat as judges some of those least esteemed persons in the church?" (MJG). With this interpretation, Paul could be being a bit sarcastic (given his lack of sympathy for Corinthian wisdom), but more likely he is being completely serious: the nonelite and marginalized would make good judges. Quite a role reversal again.

Although the first interpretation is more common, I think the second is correct. But however we understand the second half of v. 4, these questions, exclamations, or admonitions lead Paul also to the Corinthians' self-designation as a community of the "wise" (6:5), to continue to make his first point. The eschatological judgment, Paul seems to imply, will require great wisdom. A community and family allegedly endowed with wisdom should be ashamed of their failure to adjudicate everyday, trivial wrongs by an internal (church) "court" presided over by some of the wise—and if not, then some of the wiser poor. The implicit proposal about how to deal with such cases reflects practices in Jewish communities of Paul's day, indebted to the biblical examples. Instead, at Corinth, siblings are judging—suing—one another.[31]

---

30. The verb is *exoutheneō*, related to the word *ouden*, "nothing."
31. In addition, certain other groups in Paul's day also frowned on litigation instead of internal dispute settlement.

6:7-11. Lawsuits and Cruciform Justice

But that solution—to handle such matters internally—is necessary but not sufficient for Paul. He now turns to an incisive analysis of the lawsuits themselves and of the individuals and communities that pursue them. The very existence of such litigation—no matter who wins or loses—is a comprehensive "defeat" for the community (6:7; "for you," plural), not just for the litigants. That is quite a charge, so what does Paul see at stake in such matters?

6:7-8. The Lawsuits as Defeat and Injustice

The existence of these suits is not a lose-lose situation simply because the litigated matters are everyday or trivial, and hence not worth the trouble, as some have suggested. Instead, Paul goes to the heart of the matter by asking two essentially synonymous rhetorical questions in 6:7—why not rather suffer injustice (*adikeisthe*), and why not rather be defrauded (or cheated)? To both ancient and contemporary people, the suggestion inherent in these questions is offensive and may (ironically) sound unjust, even if the words and example of Jesus himself are Paul's inspiration. Jesus taught nonretaliation: "if anyone strikes you on the right cheek, turn the other also; and if anyone wants to sue you and take your coat, give your cloak as well" (Matt 5:39b–40; cf. 1 Pet 3:9). And he practiced what he preached (e.g., Luke 23:34).

Paul expects the justified to suffer injustice rather than inflict it, because that is what Jesus the paschal lamb did on the cross (5:7; cf. Isa 53:7–9) at the hands of the unjust Romans who crucified "the Lord of glory" (2:8). That is, with his bifocal approach to life in Christ, he now looks back at the first coming of Jesus, to his teaching, example, and death. Paul has already alluded to Jesus' teaching and cross as the inspiration for his own cruciform lifestyle: "When reviled, we bless," he writes; "when persecuted, we endure; when slandered, we speak kindly" (4:12–13).[32] That is, *a different "law" is at work in the Christian community: the law, the pattern, the paradigm of the Messiah* (9:21).

Paul will allude to Christ crucified again in connection with injustice in chapter 13: love does not seek its own interest (13:5) or rejoice in injustice/wrongdoing (*adikia*; 13:6), in the courts or anywhere else. To endure injustice is to imitate Paul imitating Christ (cf. 11:1). And Paul will later tell the Corinthians that such Christlike behavior would also be imitating God the Father: "God was in the Mes-

---

32. See also Paul's explicit prohibitions of vengeance: 1 Thess 5:15; Rom 12:14, 17–21. In both of these letters, retaliation is forbidden toward both insiders and outsiders ("all").

siah, reconciling the world to himself, *not counting their trespasses against them*" (2 Cor 5:19 MJG). Those trespasses obviously included sins against God.

But Paul goes still further in 6:8: by pursuing justice, *how* and *where* the world defines pursuing justice, actually means that siblings are practicing injustice and engaging in fraud.[33] The community that has been justified and therefore called to be just (6:11) according to the gospel is *practicing* injustice (*adikeite*) rather than *enduring* injustice. Here again, some translations mask this all-important point. This is not simply a matter of being "wronged" instead of wronging others (e.g., NRSV). Rather, Paul is saying that those who used to live as part of the unholy and unjust world have now returned to that old way of life in spite of the fact that through their baptism they have been made into a community of holiness and justice. They resemble the king's slave who, forgiven a debt of ten thousand talents, holds a fellow slave accountable for a hundred denarii (Matt 18:21–35). They have experienced a sort of deconversion, a repaganization, that must be reversed. Paul is portraying a common, legal activity (litigation) as injustice and fraud. That it is done to a family member makes it worse, but the familial context alone does not determine the act's significance. *Injustice and fraud, or robbery, are ungodly—literally*: "For I am the Lord, who loves justice [*dikaiosynēn*] and hates spoils obtained by injustice [*adikias*]" (Isa 61:8a LXX; NETS alt.).

We could summarize Paul's message in this passage by using the pattern from Phil 2:6–8 discussed in the introduction to the commentary: "Although [x] not [y] but [z]," which means the following:

> › Although [x = possessing status, rights, or interests]
> › not [y = using the status, rights, or interests for selfish ends]
> › but rather [z = engaging in loving concern for others].[34]

According to Philippians, this meant the following:

> › Although [x] Christ was in the form of God,
> › he did not [y] exploit that equality with God for his own advantage,
> › but rather [z] emptied himself by becoming human and humbled himself to the point of death on a cross.

Applied to the Corinthians, this christological pattern would mean this:

---

33. Paul also uses the latter verb ("defraud, cheat") in 7:5 to refer to withholding marital relations.

34. See further the discussions in my *Cruciformity*, esp. 155–267.

> ‣ Although [x] you have the right according to Roman law to sue fellow members of the *ekklēsia* in a Roman court, and this is a normal Corinthian practice,
> ‣ do not [y] do so, because it demonstrates your community's lack of wisdom, love, holiness, and the Spirit, and is unloving, unjust, and unchristlike,
> ‣ but rather [z] find judges within the community to settle the matter (6:1-6), or endure the injustice (6:6-8).

We will see Paul appeal to this pattern later in the letter as well.

It is certainly possible that Paul's greatest concern is about the elite, or strong, suing the nonelite, or weak, in the community. This would certainly be in keeping with what Paul has said about the divine preferential option for the poor and weak (1:18-31) that will reappear in 8:1-11:1 and 11:17-34. There can be little doubt that Paul wants to hold in check the exercise of elite power. But it is interesting, indeed significant, that Paul does not explicitly limit his concern about injustice to a sort of class warfare. Rather, his concern is that Christian family love has been replaced by injustice, no matter who is involved.

6:9-10. The Unjust and the Kingdom of God

This failure of familial love to the point of injustice points to another critical question. Paul's bifocal perspective shifts again to the eschatological horizon. Do those who engage in this *adikia* (injustice) realize that the *adikoi*—the unjust—will be excluded from inheriting the kingdom of God when it comes in its fullness (6:9, 10; cf. Gal 5:21)? Practicing injustice essentially annuls the justification wrought by God; it is a return to the realm of the unjust, and it jeopardizes one's future inheritance of the kingdom of God (6:9).

"Kingdom" or "reign" or "realm" of God language is rather rare in Paul's letters, even if the concept is not. The phrase "the kingdom of God" appears five times in 1 Corinthians (here in 6:9, 10; 4:20; 15:24, 50). It can imply for Paul both the present reality (e.g., 4:20; Rom 14:17) and the future reality (e.g., here, 1 Cor 15, and Gal 5:21) of God's reign—and sometimes both (perhaps 1 Thess 2:12; 2 Thess 1:5). The unjust litigants, if they remain *adikoi*, will suffer the same fate as those named in the so-called vice list of 6:9-10, in which the first group named is the *adikoi*—those who practice injustice.

It is common to appeal to 1 Cor 6:9-10 to identify the worst kinds of sinners, those who will not "go to heaven." This is misguided in several ways. First of all, Paul does not speak about the Christian's future eschatological reality as "going to heaven" but as "inherit[ing] the kingdom of God" (6:9; also 15:50; Gal 5:21)—a reference to eternal life under divine rule that, canonically speaking, involves the merger of heaven and earth (esp. Rev 21-22). Second, the apostle's primary purpose here is not to condemn *outsiders* but to remind *insiders*—Christians—from where they have come, what they have become, and what they are to continue to become: "And this is [lit., "these things are"] what some of you used to be" (6:11), so don't go back! That is, Paul's reminder is also a warning. Third, then, the list is a reminder of God's grace in transforming sinners like the Corinthians (and all subsequent Christians) into holy and just people, or at least into people on the way to holiness and justice. We all come from somewhere.

This does not, however, mean that Paul is nonchalant about the contents of the list; he is quite serious about these sinful practices (just as he is in texts like Rom 1:18–32 and Gal 5:19–21). Once again, as in 5:11, this is probably a selective list drawn from Deuteronomy and Leviticus but focused first of all—after the spotlight on the main issue of injustice in 6:9—on the two fundamental errors of idolatry and sexual immorality, and then on the topic of greed/theft. (These are the three common elements in the lists in 5:9, 5:11, and 6:9–10.)

The translation of the fourth and fifth terms in 6:9, which name two specific aspects of sexual immorality, is notoriously difficult and hermeneutically significant: *malakoi* and *arsenokoitai*. The latter term almost certainly means what its etymology ("male" + "bed") suggests: simply "men lying with men," that is, (male) homosexual behavior generally, as prohibited in Lev 18:22; 20:13. The former term is more difficult and may mean male prostitutes, or, more likely, the passive partner in male homosexual relations. Hence Paul is referring to "both participants in same-sex intercourse" (CEB), meaning "passive or active male same-sex partners" (MJG; cf. CEB note).

Same-gender relationships were of various kinds in antiquity, both exploitative and consensual, both casual and long-term. As in Rom 1:26–27, Paul joins fellow Jews of his day in condemning same-gender sexual relations. That said, to make the condemnation of same-sex relations the sole or primary point of these verses is to miss the main point of both the reminder and the warning.

6:11. Transformation by the Triune God: Justification and Justice

Some of the Corinthians, of course, "used to be" (6:11a) among the sexually immoral, idolaters, unjust and so on. But the Corinthians have been transformed by virtue of their experience of baptism, sanctification, and justification—not three separate events but one unified act of God, expressed three times in the passive voice, specifically the divine passive.[35] God has (1) washed them, or cleansed them from sin in baptism; (2) sanctified them, or made them holy—

---

35. For the connections among baptism, justification, and sanctification as one event of salvation, see also Gal 2:20; 3:27 and Rom 6. See esp. Rom 6:13, 17–18: believers are

set them apart for him and his purposes, and remade them into godly people; and (3) justified them, or made them just, re-created to practice the justice of God by sharing in the counterintuitive divine justice displayed in Christ crucified (see 1:30). Holy living, including the work of justice, is not a *supplement* to baptism and justification but the *actualization* of baptism and justification.

For Paul, being justified (*edikaiōthēte*) means more than what the common language of "being counted righteous" or even "being put right" might be understood to mean. Justification, for Paul, powerfully maintains its inherent linguistic connection, in English as in Greek, to the semantic field of "justice." He says, in effect, in justification/baptism you were made just, as you were transferred out of the pagan community of the unjust (see 6:1, 9) and incorporated into the community—indeed the *family*—of the just. Justification means that the unjust have been liberated from injustice to be just and to live justly. Justice is inherent in justification. *The justified are also the justice-ized.*

This transformation is God's doing, a saving act with human mediation: "in the name of the Lord Jesus Christ and in the Spirit of our God." Human ministers, of course, mediate the divine grace, but, as we saw in chapters 1–4, their role in baptism is not to be stressed. The wording "in the name . . ." suggests a Trinitarian theology of baptism, and perhaps a Trinitarian formula used by the apostle or other ministers, though slightly different from the one in Matt 28:19.[36]

But people need to live into and out of the transformative divine grace experienced in the sanctifying event of justification and baptism, the event of personal faith and public affirmation/incorporation into the body of Christ. To be sure, this justification is pure gift, an unmerited act of sheer divine grace, yet from start to finish the gift demands and offers complete identification with the cross of Christ, not only as the basis of a right relationship with God but as the very shape of that relationship.[37]

Baptism—as well as the inseparable corollaries of sanctification and justification—"implies a *break*," as Dietrich Bonhoeffer said.[38] For Paul, the Corinthians' behavior is a sign of no break, or at least an incomplete break requiring ongoing conversion. (The Corinthians are certainly not unique in this.) When believers act unjustly, betraying their identity and forsaking the cross of their Lord, they engage in a dangerous anachronism that reveals them to be more like pre-Christ than

---

to present themselves to God as slaves of justice (*dikaiosynē*) rather than Sin, and their bodily members to God as weapons of justice (*dikaiosynēs*) rather than injustice (*adikias*).

36. See further my "Traces of the Trinity in 1 Corinthians," *Journal of Theological Interpretation* 15 (2021): 291–304.

37. See further John M. G. Barclay's books, *Paul and the Power of Grace* and *Paul and the Gift* (Grand Rapids: Eerdmans, 2015).

38. Bonhoeffer, *Discipleship*, 207.

post-Christ people; "used to be" (v. 11) has become "still are." The justified must now practice the justice of God, which will mean not returning evil for evil; it will mean blessing when cursed, even within the family. Otherwise the falsity of their claim to justification and sanctification will be revealed on the coming day.

Conclusion: Injustice and Justice in the Church

For Paul the sort of legal action happening in the Corinthian church is at least a four-dimensional failure: a failure of wisdom (6:2–6); of family care and obligation (6:5–8); of cruciform love and justice (6:2–8); and of conversion—baptism, justification, and sanctification (6:9–11).[39] The Corinthians should have known better, corporately as well as individually, as the triple "Don't you [all] know?" of 6:2, 3, and 9 indicates. *Ultimately, 1 Cor 6:1–11 tells a tragic, ironic tale of injustice within the family of the just.*

As counterintuitive as it may seem, Paul's rhetorical question—"Why not rather endure justice instead of inflicting it?"—is actually an expression of justice, of cruciform justice, of God's justice. Refusing to pursue justice in the legal sense of that term does not mean that justice is denied. According to Paul, the community still needs to learn to settle disputes in the pursuit of family harmony and in the pursuit of justice as the embodiment of such harmony. Yet this must be done without appealing to the pagan courts and without denying the principle of absorbing rather than inflicting injustice. The balance between these two tensive principles of pursuing justice/harmony and blessing when cursed was, is, and always will be a difficult one to sort out.

In other words, *Paul's words do not mean that the community as a community can neglect those who are being treated unjustly.* That, too, would be a form of injustice on the part of the community as a whole. The call to forgive is not an excuse for injustice. *The church cannot be one, holy, catholic, and apostolic when it promotes, tolerates, or covers up its own injustice or that of particular members.* If it does so, it is no longer the community of the just, which is what God has intended it to be: "For our sake, God made him who knew no sin (Christ) to be sin, so that in him we would become the justice (*dikaiosynē*) of God" (2 Cor 5:21 MJG).

There is also a significant, if implicit, missional dimension to the issue of lawsuits. Taking fellow Christian family members to court is a certain kind of witness—an *anti*witness. It proclaims that Christians do not really possess a

---

39. Similarly, Chrysostom writes, "[It] is a twofold crime, perhaps even threefold or fourfold. One, not to know how to bear being wronged. Another, actually to do wrong. A third, to commit the settlement of these matters even unto the unjust. And yet a fourth, that it should be so done to a brother" (*Homilies on 1 Corinthians* 16.8).

transformative gospel that allows them to deal with conflict and even injustice in a way that is different from the secular world. It proclaims that the teaching and the cross of Jesus do not really constitute the norm for Christian existence. And it proclaims that the counterintuitive, transformative grace and power of God do not, and perhaps cannot, offer hope to a world bent on violence, retaliation, and other acts of injustice, often, sadly, in the very name of justice.

If, on the other hand, Christian communities develop internal, substantively Christian ways of dealing with conflict and injustice, and if the teaching and model of Jesus (and of Paul) guide Christian action, there will be a true and powerful witness to the gospel.

REFLECTIONS AND QUESTIONS FOR 6:1–11

Spiritual, Pastoral, Missional, and Theological Reflections

1. **Western culture, especially US culture, is incredibly litigious,** and that characteristic is also, unfortunately, deeply ingrained in much of the Christian community. Churches sue the denominational entities to which they belong, and vice versa. Christians sue one another. And so on. Paul's teaching in 1 Cor 6 is either unknown or ignored (more often the latter, I suspect) in many Christian circles.

   The goal of litigation is often described as "justice," but it nearly always also has an element of retribution. What can individual Christians and churches, who (at least theoretically) reject vengeance, do? At the same time, various forms of Christian mediation exist, and sometimes these can be helpful to all parties involved.

2. I once had a student whose young daughter died after a routine surgery became lethal due to errors on the part of the anesthesiologist. It was a clear case of **medical malpractice, yet the Christian parents decided not to sue but to forgive.** This is one of the most powerful embodiments of this passage I have ever personally known. In a more well known case, the reaction of the Amish community in Nickel Mines, Pennsylvania, to the shooting of ten school-age girls in 2006 was a potent witness to the gospel that impacted both the church and the wider world.

3. If the secular courts and normal processes, whether then or now, often favor the rich and powerful, God in Christ favors the poor and vulnerable. To say the church has not always sided with God in this sort of matter would be an understatement. It is unfortunately often the case that internal Christian courts, whether formal or informal, whether local or regional or global, fail to deal appropriately with matters that come before them. They frequently favor the powerful and thus also the perpetrators of injustice, rather than the

victims. That is why **the wisdom of the cross is so critical to justice in the church**: it favors the weak and vulnerable, not the powerful and connected.

4. Many people in so-called Christian or Christianized communities and countries **completely misunderstand baptism**. Symbolic of this is the practice—still rare, thankfully—of (literal) drive-through baptisms. But many baptisms are, at least metaphorically, drive-through events. Baptism, however, is supposed to make public and communal that which is first of all personal and individual but cannot remain so. Baptism is a parabolic enactment of one's faith (or one's parents' faith) in the holistic sense of belief, commitment (allegiance to Christ and his church), and behavior. A church that practices any form of drive-through baptism, literal or metaphorical, is on its way to becoming a Corinthian congregation, if it is not already one.

Questions for Those Who Read, Teach, and Preach

1. In what ways does Corinthian law-court activity resemble that of the contemporary culture, and the contemporary church? What Christian ethical principles and practical applications can be drawn from this situation and Paul's response to it?

2. Not pursuing justice for oneself, at least as justice is often understood, just seems *wrong*. How might Paul respond to this concern? Is this approach to justice ultimately unjust?

3. Since the time of Paul, sexual immorality and abuse within the church have harmed both people, especially the vulnerable, and the church's public witness. What can churches and individual Christians do to counteract these various forms of damage and minimize them going forward? Since these are not trivial matters, should they sometimes be handled in the secular courts?

4. In sum, what does this passage urge the church to believe (faith), do (love), and anticipate (hope)?

For Further Reading

Adams, Kevin J. *Living under Water: Baptism as a Way of Life*. Grand Rapids: Eerdmans, 2022.

deSilva, David. *Transformation: The Heart of Paul's Gospel*. Bellingham, WA: Lexham, 2014. (highly accessible)

Gorman, Michael J. *Becoming the Gospel: Paul, Participation, and Mission*. Grand Rapids: Eerdmans, 2015. (esp. 212–60)

———. *Inhabiting the Cruciform God: Kenosis, Justification, and Theosis in Paul's Narrative Soteriology*. Grand Rapids: Eerdmans, 2009.

Guthrie, G. H. "Baptism." *DPL*[2] 69–74.

Hays, Richard B. *The Moral Vision of the New Testament: Community, Cross, New Creation; A Contemporary Introduction to New Testament Ethics*. San Francisco: HarperCollins, 1996.

Jones, L. Gregory. *Embodying Forgiveness: A Theological Analysis*. Grand Rapids: Eerdmans, 1995.

Keller, Timothy. *Generous Justice: How God's Grace Makes Us Just*. New York: Viking, 2010. (highly accessible)

Morales, Isaac Augustine. *The Bible and Baptism: The Fountain of Salvation*. Grand Rapids: Baker Academic, 2022.

Rosner, Brian S. *Paul, Scripture and Ethics: A Study of 1 Corinthians 5–7*. Leiden: Brill, 1994. Repr., Grand Rapids: Baker, 1999. (technical)

Ruth, John L. *Forgiveness: A Legacy of the West Nickel Mines Amish School*. Harrisonburg, VA: Herald, 2007, 2011 (with afterword). (highly accessible)

Thompson, James W. *Moral Formation according to Paul: The Context and Coherence of Pauline Ethics*. Grand Rapids: Baker Academic, 2011.

Thurian, Max, ed. *Ecumenical Perspectives on Baptism, Eucharist and Ministry*. Geneva: World Council of Churches, 1983.

6:12–20. Sex with Prostitutes and the Temple of the Spirit

The list of the unjust (*adikoi*), sexually immoral (*pornoi*), idolaters, and others in 6:9–10 may have prompted Paul to return to another specific problem of sexual immorality (*porneia*, as in 5:1) also reported to him. In considering this text, we need to remember the ancient pagan, Jewish, and early Christian attitudes toward sexual conduct discussed above in the introduction to chapters 5–7. Sexual immorality and idolatry were, for Jews like Paul, the hallmark sins of gentile existence. Paul called on the body of Christ to use their bodies in distinctive, holy ways. The specific problem addressed in this brief passage brings forth from Paul a profound theology of Christian sexuality.

The Situation in Corinth and the Texture of the Passage

The sexual chaos at Corinth included not only a man sleeping with his stepmother (5:1–13), but also a man or (more likely) men having sex with prostitutes (6:12–20). Whether these were prostitutes at a brothel, sacral harlots (associated with a temple), or after-dinner guests at the homes of some of Corinth's elite has been debated. (An infamous contingent of prostitutes at Aphrodite's temple, on the Acrocorinth, was active only in pre-Roman times, if the ancient reports are accurate.) The mention of food in 6:13 may suggest the association of sex and food at a temple banquet or a dinner party in a private home—a common connection in the ancient world. It is more likely than not, however, that the situation involved once again one or more elite males at Corinth, who would have had the economic means or social occasions for such activities.

It is interesting to note, however, that Paul does not even hint that he is addressing a sexual matter until practically the end of 6:13, and he does not mention the word "prostitute" until 6:15.[40] Rather, he begins with the root cause of the activity and its fundamental justification; it is the fruit of a libertine ethic summarized in a Corinthian slogan of sorts that Paul quotes back to the church: "All things are permitted for me" (6:12 NRSVue, twice; cf. 10:23). In this and succeeding chapters, Paul will have quite a bit to say about the apparently innocuous but deceptively significant word "all things" (Gk. *panta*).

Most scholars believe that a good deal of this passage consists of Corinthian slogans (perhaps perversions of Paul's own teachings) and of Paul's rebuttals, though there is debate over which of the phrases might represent the Corinthian position—or at least the position of those who used the services of prostitutes. (Unfortunately, Paul did not provide quotation marks to indicate such things.) It was not uncommon in ancient rhetoric to quote those with whom one disagreed, sometimes indicating that a quotation is present (and sometimes its source) but not always.

When there appear to be such quotations, or even a manufactured conversation, called a diatribe, an interpreter must try to look at the back-and-forth movement of the dialogue to determine who is actually speaking in each sentence. In 6:12–20, there are some lines that sound like the Paul we know from the rest of the letter and the rest of his correspondence, and there are lines that sound more like the popular culture of Corinth that has infiltrated the *ekklēsia* there. If these are not the exact words of certain Corinthians, they are at least good summaries of their convictions.

Regardless of whether the Corinthians were Stoics or interpreted their faith in a Stoic manner, as some have argued, cries of freedom were common-

---

40. The CEB's "someone who is sleeping around" in v. 15 is probably too general, though this translation would not affect Paul's response. A note offers this alternative: "Or *a prostitute*; commonly, women who sell their bodies to multiple sex partners but includes those who are sexually immoral."

place in their culture, coming not least from the Stoics. For example, the Stoic Epictetus wrote, "He is free who lives as he wills, who is subject neither to compulsion, nor hindrance, nor force, whose choices are unhampered, whose desires attain their end."[41] We see this sense of absolute autonomy in 6:12, and the remaining verses make it clear this autonomy is being expressed in sexual practices. Subsequent verses also reveal a kind of unpauline dualism in which the activities of the body carry no obvious moral or spiritual significance. The dominant words Paul pens in the passage, therefore, are *porneia/pornoi* ("sexual immorality"/"the sexually immoral") and *sōma* ("body").[42]

Observing this back-and-forth between the Corinthians and Paul leads us to consider the structure of our text.

The Structure of the Passage

Paul's negative response to the libertinism and dualism, though it has the tone of a scolding ("Do you not know?" occurs once again, as in 6:1–11, three times: 6:15, 16, 19), is a carefully structured piece that draws on the diatribe's rhetorical devices to make some highly significant theological points. This passage is absolutely crucial to understanding Paul's ethic generally and his sexual ethic specifically.

The passage is composed as two consecutive but parallel arguments (6:12–18a and 6:18b–20), each consisting of the following four elements:

- Corinthian slogans
- Paul's counterslogans
- Paul's theological correction and claims (introduced by "Do you not know?")
- Paul's pastoral exhortation

The following table, which uses the NRSVue text but has minor alterations, especially to indicate the quotations and to emphasize key phrases, shows these parallel elements:[43]

---

41. Epictetus, *Discourses* 4.1.1 (Oldfather, LCL).

42. As noted in the introduction to chs. 5–7, there is scholarly debate about the meaning of the *porn-* word group. In my judgment, the NRSVue, CEB, NIV, and NJB rightly render *porneia* in 6:13, 18 as "sexual immorality" and *pornoi* in 6:9 as "the sexually immoral." The NRSV, wrongly, renders *porneia* as "fornication" (too narrow) and the NAB simply as "immorality" (too broad); they each translate *pornoi* as "fornicators" (too narrow).

43. Adapted from Michael J. Gorman, *Apostle of the Crucified Lord: A Theological Introduction to Paul and His Letters*, 2nd ed. (Grand Rapids: Eerdmans, 2017), 299.

ADDRESSING MORAL CHAOS

PARALLELS IN 1 COR 6:12–18A AND 6:18B–20

	6:12–18A (NRSVUE ALT.)	6:18B–20 (NRSVUE ALT.)
Corinthian Slogans	12a—"All things are permitted for me." 12c—"All things are permitted for me." 13a—"Food is meant for the stomach and the stomach for food, and God will destroy both one and the other."[44] *Note: Many translations have "lawful" instead of "permitted" in v. 12, but the issue is not legality. For v. 13a, the NRSVue has a footnote indicating that the quotation may extend to "the other," as I have done here (and as the NIV has done).*	18b—"Every sin that a person commits is outside the body." *Note: Failing to recognize this sentence as a Corinthian slogan, many translations (e.g., NAB, NIV, NJB, RSV) render this verse as something like "Every other sin . . . ," inserting a word ("other") that is absent from the Greek text to try to make some sense of it as Paul's idea.*
Paul's Counterslogans	12b—"But not all things are beneficial [sympherei]." 12d—"But I will not be dominated by anything." 13b—"The body is meant not for sexual immorality but for the Lord and the Lord for the body." 14—"And God raised the Lord and will also raise us by his power." *Note: In v. 13b, some translations have either "fornication" or "immorality" rather than "sexual immorality."*	18c—"But the sexually immoral sin against their own bodies." *Note: Some translations have either "fornicator" or "immoral person" rather than "sexually immoral person." The NRSVue's phrase "the body itself" is better rendered "his own body." The plural pronouns are used here (so also CEB) because the generalization can apply to both men and women.*
Paul's Theological Correction and Claims ("Do you not know . . . ?")	15—"*Do you not know* that your bodies are members of Christ? Should I therefore take the members of Christ and make them members of a prostitute? May it never be!" 16—"*Do you not know* that whoever is united to a prostitute becomes one body with her? For it is said, 'The two shall be one flesh.'" 17—"But anyone united to the Lord becomes one spirit with him."	19—"Or *do you not know* that your [plural] body [singular] is a temple of the Holy Spirit within you, which you have from God, and that you are not your own?" 20a—"For you were bought with a price."

44. That is, implicitly (see v. 13b), *sex : body :: eating : stomach*, or, "sex is to the body as eating is to the stomach."

	6:12–18A (NRSVUE ALT.)	6:18B–20 (NRSVUE ALT.)
Paul's Pastoral Exhortation	18a—"Flee from sexual immorality!" *Note: "Flee from" (so also NET, NIV) better translates the Greek* pheugete *(NRSVue "Shun"; some translations have "Avoid").*	20b—"Therefore glorify God in your [plural] body [singular]."

As the table indicates, some of the main interpretive issues in this passage are the following:

1. Which lines represent the Corinthians' (or some Corinthians') perspective, and which represent Paul's?
2. How should the Greek word family *porn-* be translated? As a reference to immorality, sexual immorality, or fornication?
3. How should the first word in v. 18 be translated—as "Shun," "Avoid," or "Flee from"?
4. Are the phrases "your [plural] body [singular]" in v. 19 and v. 20b references to the individual body or to the corporate body, the body of Christ—or both?

Readers of English translations should keep in mind that all occurrences of the words "you" and "your" in this passage are second-person-plural pronouns. Furthermore, therefore, the imperatives are second-person-plural verbs (e.g., "Flee" = "All of you must flee!").

6:12–18a. Flee from Sexual Immorality!

The first argument (6:12–18a) focuses on the misunderstanding of sex as an unrestricted activity that is similar to eating. Paul answers the twice-quoted slogan of absolute libertinism in 6:12, "All things are permitted for me" (NRSVue) or "I have the right to do anything" (NIV), with two criteria of authentic freedom. First, the free action must be beneficial (6:12a; probably here primarily beneficial to the self, but in 10:23 to others). Second, it must not enslave or rule over the individual (6:12b). Such brief responses could have been offered by other ancient moralists, but Paul introduces more specifically theological rejoinders and develops them succinctly but vigorously.

Paul sets out to answer the implicit analogy of sex to eating and the belief that the entire body will one day be destroyed (6:13a), thus permitting sexual indulgence without moral or spiritual consequences. He rebuffs the notion that sexual indulgence, which is actually, he claims, sexual immorality (*porneia*), is what the body is intended for, saying instead that the body is intended "for the Lord, and the Lord for the body" (6:13b). The language of mutuality and union (v. 17) is covenantal, describing a two-way commitment that is mirrored in certain ways in Christian marriage (6:16b; 7:2–4). From the believer's side, the body and bodily activities are to be used to honor and demonstrate devotion to the Lord. In developing this idea, Paul relies on his own teaching that believers are members of Christ's body (6:15; cf. ch. 12, esp. vv. 12, 27; Rom 12:4–5) and on the Genesis narrative that says sex makes a man and a woman one flesh (6:16; see Gen 2:21–25, quoted also by Jesus: Mark 10:7–8; Matt 19:5–6).[45] Believers are, analogously, united to Christ: "one spirit with him" (6:17).

Paul does not say that having sex with a prostitute is a form of unfaithfulness to one's wife, if one is married. Undoubtedly he thinks it is, but that is not his focus here. Bodily union with a prostitute—sexual immorality—subverts not a physical but an existing spiritual union, which is displayed in concrete bodily activity, between Christ and the believer (cf. 2 Cor 11:2–3; Eph 5:29–32). Paul is likely echoing the notion that Israel was the Lord's bride (Ezek 16; Hos 1–3). Moreover, the believer's body is not destined for destruction (6:13a, the Corinthian view) but for resurrection (6:14; cf. 15:35–50; 2 Cor 4:14), just like Christ's. In other words, whether in life or death, the believer is in a relationship with the Lord that is expressed through the body (see also Rom 6:12–13, 19). *Bodies matter.* For these reasons, believers must flee from sexual immorality (6:18a); it derails them from the goal of their existence.

The translations of the English words rendered here as "sexual immorality" (*porneia*; 6:13b, 18) and "flee" (*pheugete*; 18a) are important. For *porneia*, "immorality" is too broad and "fornication" too narrow. As for "flee," Thomas Aquinas wisely says this: "Other vices are overcome by resisting, because the more a man considers and deals with particulars, the less will he find in them anything in which to take delight, but more to be cautious about. But the vice of fornication [i.e., sexual immorality] is not overcome by resisting, because the more a man considers the particular case the more is he inflamed; but it is overcome by fleeing, i.e., by avoiding entirely all unclean thoughts and all occasions whatsoever, for it is said: *flee from the land of the north* (Zech 2:6)."[46] Perhaps Paul has the story of Joseph in mind (Gen 39:7–20). The Genesis

---

45. Sexual union with a prostitute is a physical bond that is a pseudomarriage, since Genesis tells us that the sexual union makes one body out of two.

46. Thomas Aquinas, *Commentary on 1 Corinthians*, C.6, L.3, 306.

narrator tells us that Joseph fled from Potiphar's wife when she tempted him, and the Septuagint text (LXX) uses the same Greek verb we find in 1 Cor 6:18a: *pheugō* (Gen 39:12, 18).

The Corinthians' deficient spirituality of freedom and of sex meant that they thought anything goes, and therefore that all sexual urges may be satisfied. After all, if our genitalia are meant for sex and they will one day be destroyed, then carpe diem—hook up (to put it colloquially) as often as one wants, and with whoever will satisfy those urges. Although Paul does not say this explicitly, it is clear from the context of this passage that such behavior (both using people by paying for sex and unconstrained sexual activity more generally) is unloving and thus unjust; *porneia* is a form of *adikia*. Furthermore, so-called sexual freedom is, rather, a form of slavery; sex can become an idol, and addiction to that deity is the opposite of freedom. Once again, bodies matter, because they are destined for resurrection (6:14), not destruction.

That Paul twice asks, "Do you not know?" (vv. 15, 16), suggests either (1) that he specifically taught the Corinthians the content found in those verses as part of his catechesis on sexuality, or (2) that he expected the Corinthians to be sufficiently spiritually and theologically wise to draw those conclusions from their knowledge of Scripture and the gospel. The same is true with respect to the content of 6:19 in the next argument.

6:18b–20. Glorify God with Your Body/Bodies

The second argument (6:18b–20), parallel to the first but briefer, further develops Paul's perspective on the significance of the body. The corollary of erroneous disregard for the body's spiritual significance is the belief that sin does not involve the body and, therefore, that no bodily activity can be a sin (6:18b). That is the misguided Corinthian error, expressed in another slogan, Paul needs to correct. As shown in the table above, the idea of "every *other* sin" (NAB; cf. NIV) being outside the body is not something Paul did or would say; the word "other" is not in the Greek text. (Because this is so important and so often not known, I repeat for emphasis: *the word "other" is not in the Greek text.*) The inclusion of this word in translations is a desperate attempt to interpret Paul's words as his own. But they are not; they come from the Corinthians. Paul's own point is that lots of bodily actions, including especially some sexual ones, can be sins—indeed, sins against the body (6:18c).

But how can one "sin" against the body, as Paul claims in his counterslogan? Only if the body is associated with God, which is precisely the point of 6:19-20. "Do you not know?" is Paul's way of expressing disappointment in

ADDRESSING MORAL CHAOS

the Corinthians' failed memory and impoverished spirituality. One's body is God's temple, filled with God's Spirit, and it does not belong to oneself (6:19). It is not yours! It belongs to another.

Here Paul refers to Christ's cross as the act of God's purchasing the believer, like the redemption of an enslaved person (6:20a; cf. 7:22–23; Rom 3:24), referring both to the general ancient practice of redemption and to YHWH's redemption of Israel. The Lord had declared to Moses, "Say therefore to the Israelites, 'I am the LORD [YHWH], and I will free you from the burdens of the Egyptians and deliver you from slavery to them. I will redeem you with an outstretched arm and with mighty acts of judgment. I will take you as my people, and I will be your God. You shall know that I am the LORD [YHWH] your God, who has freed you from the burdens of the Egyptians'" (Exod 6:6–7).

As in 6:11, Paul employs the passive voice—"you were bought with a price" (6:20)—to indicate divine action, and once again all three persons of the triune God are involved in the saving act. God the Father is the one who made the purchase, the redeeming death of the Son (cf. 1:30) was the cost, and the Holy Spirit is God's gift, not of a separate entity or impersonal force but of God's very own self (see 2:11–12).

Henceforth the purchased person (or community) belongs not to self but to the redeemer, to live in loyalty to the new master or lord. The fact that Paul uses the imagery of slavery, purchase, and (therefore) new ownership is important. It implies that one is always a slave to someone or something; true freedom consists of belonging to the right owner. Christ's death, and identification with it in faith and baptism, effects the necessary change of ownership. God himself is now the rightful, all-benevolent lord "whose service is perfect freedom."[47] For these reasons, believers are not only, negatively, to flee from immorality (6:18a) but also, positively, to glorify God in God's dwelling place—their bodies (6:20b). The two exhortations belong together.

There is possibly an interesting twist to this interpretation: as noted above, in 6:19 and 6:20, Paul actually speaks of "your [plural] body [singular]," not "your bodies [plural]." So is he telling the Corinthians as a whole that their one (corporate) body does not belong to them and that they should glorify God in their one (corporate) body—the church? Although this is possible and the idea echoes 3:16–17, the emphasis here seems to be on the many individual bodies, and the Greek can mean that. To be sure, these bodies are connected

---

47. A phrase from the Book of Common Prayer (first published in 1549) that may go back another thousand years.

198

to Christ as part of his (one) body (v. 15), but it is various individuals who have been going to prostitutes and defiling their individual temples.

For Paul, then, both the individual (6:19–20) and the community (3:16–17; 2 Cor 6:16) are God's temple; salvation means that whole persons, bodies and all, are incorporated into the one body of Christ as the locus of divine worship (cf. Rom 12:1–2). This is more than simply a cultic metaphor or an analogy; it is reality and foreshadows 12:12. As in 6:11, the saving reality of God's grace and the Corinthians' experience of it are decidedly Trinitarian: each Corinthian body, as well as the Corinthian body as a whole, has been transformed into the temple of the Spirit, belonging to God because of the redemptive death of Jesus.

In and through Christ, God has made his human creation into his special dwelling place. There is no higher honor, or corollary responsibility, proclaims the apostle.

Summary

Throughout this passage, Paul implicitly reasons in a cruciform manner. Sexual immorality and cruciform love cannot co-exist, for *porneia* is at best a form of self-love and self-indulgence that harms others and radically diminishes the holiness of the individual, the so-called partner, and the community (the body of Christ). At the same time, such self-indulgence is the opposite of what Christ displayed in his incarnation and death for us. In other words, once again the "Although [x] not [y] but [z]" pattern is implicitly operating:

- Although [x] the dominant view may be that you have the right to do whatever you want with your body, and that your bodily activity cannot harm your relationship with the Lord,
- do not [y] engage in sexual relations apart from marriage, or in other forms of sexual immorality,
- but rather [z] flee from sexual immorality and honor God with your bodies.

It is critical to note that *the body itself is not evil and is not the problem*; it is how one understands the nature and purpose of the body, and then uses it accordingly, that is the issue. In the same way, *sex itself is not evil and is not the problem* (despite what some Corinthians apparently concluded; see 7:1–5); it is how one understands the nature and purpose of sex that is the issue.

Paul also explicitly reasons bifocally, invoking both the consequences of Jesus' past death and the hope of believers' future resurrection. Bodily activity *does* matter and *does* have spiritual consequences because of both the present and the future status of the body in relation to God. The individual's body is the locus of spirituality (cf. Rom 6:12–23; 12:1) and the focus of redemption (cf. Rom 8:23); it is also part of a larger body and temple, the communal body of Christ and temple of God's Spirit. Bodily freedom, therefore, cannot be understood as anything less than belonging to the right lord (God, not self) and honoring that Lord in and through the Lord's temple.

Human bodies, to summarize, have both a present purpose and a future destiny that some Corinthians' sexual behavior betrays. So much of this Corinthian error is related to denying future bodily resurrection (see 15:12), which also implies at least a misunderstanding, if not a corollary denial, of Christ's resurrection (6:14a; 15:1–34). As John Chrysostom said many centuries ago, there is a reciprocal influence between belief and behavior: "This is what the Devil is earnest for, not only that the Resurrection may be disbelieved, but good works also may be done away with. For those who do not expect that they shall rise again and give an account of the things which they have done, will not quickly apply themselves to virtue; will in turn come to disbelieve the Resurrection entirely: for both these are established by each other; vice by unbelief, and unbelief by vice."[48]

Paul's theology of the body, rooted in his theology of the cross and resurrection and his bifocal approach to the spiritual life, challenges ancient and modern claims suggesting that human beings, or at least those who claim the name of Christ, have inalienable rights to the control and use of their bodies and to the sexual practices of their choosing. For Paul, nothing could be further from the truth. In fact, such freedom is both slavery and idolatry.

REFLECTIONS AND QUESTIONS FOR 6:12–20

Spiritual, Pastoral, Missional, and Theological Reflections

1. Apart from the specific matter of sex, we learn much about Paul's theology in this passage, especially about the **nature of Christian freedom and the importance of the human body**. This biblical theology of the body and of freedom subverts ancient and modern claims that we have inalienable rights

---

48. Chrysostom, *Homilies on 1 Corinthians* 17.3, altered for gender inclusivity. Unlike Chrysostom, Paul does not explicitly mention the future judgment in 6:12–20, but it has been a theme of the letter thus far and is a central aspect of the future dimension of Paul's bifocal theologizing.

to the control and use of our bodies and to the sexual practices of our choosing. However, as strong as Paul can be on matters of human sexuality, he never sees sexual sin in isolation. It is not the worst or only sin, neither in 1 Cor 6 nor in Rom 1.

Nor does Paul see the body in isolation. Many sorts of sin, particularly sexual sin, involve and affect more than the body. Because a person is an integrated whole, a psychosomatic unity, **all aspects of a person**, however they are conceived (e.g., body, mind, heart, spirit, soul), are **involved and affected in sexual sin.**

2. **Christian freedom is not absolute.** Even activities that do not seem to harm anyone else must be judged by two criteria: (1) Does it help? That is, does it further growth in Christlikeness? (2) Does it enslave me, or does it make me free to be that which I am called to be as a disciple and a member of the body of Christ? (Actions that might harm another person are subject to still further criteria, as we will see especially in 8:1–11:1.)

   Christian freedom, furthermore, is a question of belonging to the right lord. Christians are not their own lords, the masters of their own fate, for they belong—heart, mind, soul, and body—to the God whose Son has bought them at a tremendous cost. In a highly sexualized culture, whether that of the ancient Greco-Roman world or that of the postmodern West, sex becomes a deity, the focus of existence and even devotion for many people, driven by uncontrollable passion. This is the religion of the hookup culture. The wisdom of the ancient Jewish document Pseudo-Phocylides is worthy of consideration: "*Erōs* is not a god but a passion that destroys all" (Pseudo-Phocylides 194 MJG).

   Those in ministry with people, particularly young adults, who struggle with and are constantly being taken in by cultural claims about unbounded sexuality and sexual behavior have found how such misguided concepts of sexual freedom deeply hurt and damage bodies, relationships, and images of self.

3. **The body, then, is absolutely critical** to the doctrine of salvation and to Christian spirituality. Christians are not Platonists or docetists or gnostics who think the body is of no consequence. The body is meant for the Lord, and the Lord cares for, and cares about, the body. The body is the locus of spirituality, of service to God and others. Its actions are the concrete manifestations of its being the temple of the Holy Spirit.

4. **With respect to sex itself**, it would be difficult to find another subject—except perhaps lawsuits—about which Paul and contemporary Western cultures, including much of Western Christian culture, **differ more profoundly.** For example, the American Lutheran minister Nadia Bolz-Weber wrote a best-

selling book called *Shameless: A Case for Not Feeling Bad about Feeling Good (about Sex)*.[49] Reacting against the Christian purity movement and similar approaches to sexuality, Bolz-Weber proposes a contemporary practical theology of sexual exploration and freedom.

Bolz-Weber surmises that the church's obsession (as she sees it) with sexual purity is likely due to its desire for holiness. But she then raises the question of what holiness actually is: "Holiness is when more than one become one, when what is fractured is made whole." Therefore, "when two loving individuals, two bearers of God's image, are unified in an erotic embrace, there is space for something holy. Two spirits, two bodies, two stories are drawn so close that they are something together that they cannot be alone. There is unity." Holiness is distinct from purity, she then argues, "because holiness is about union *with*, and purity is about separation *from*." Real holiness, she insists, is on display in the Gospels, when Jesus touches bodies; thus, she implies, the richest form of holiness "is sensual and embodied and free from shame and deeply present in the moment and comes from union with God."[50]

Nadia Bolz-Weber's understandings of both holiness and human sexuality are seriously deficient, but her sentiments have been welcomed by many because they reflect—or elicit—a view that is increasingly common in the church: human sexuality is simply a matter of eroticism that is (allegedly) inherently holy. This view is theological cover for a Corinthian-like ethic of radical autonomy and self-realization through sexual pleasure. Holiness in Bolz-Weber's definition lacks its most basic biblical content: that it involves being set apart and distinctive and, for humans, taking on the character of God. Furthermore, a simplistic sharp distinction between holiness as "union *with*" and purity as "separation *from*" is at odds with Paul (and the New Testament as a whole). The sexual holiness to which Paul calls the church and the popular sexual holiness proffered by Bolz-Weber are antithetical to each other.

5. It is rather ironic, in the face of perspectives like that of Bolz-Weber, that some secular philosophers are once again extolling **the virtue of chastity** in relation to the pursuit of personal and spousal happiness; to the practices of

---

49. The following discussion is taken from my essay "Recovering Sexual Holiness in 1 Corinthians 6: Spiritual, Theological, and Missional Implications," in *The Holy People of God: Identity, Context, Challenges*, ed. Svetlana Khobnya et al. (Eugene, OR: Pickwick, 2024), 22–34.

50. Nadia Bolz-Weber, *Shameless: A Case for Not Feeling Bad about Feeling Good (about Sex)* (New York: Convergent, 2019), 19, 20, 26, 27.

temperance, prudence, and justice; and to issues of objectification, power dynamics, reproduction, and sexual autonomy.[51]

6. The early Christian text called the Epistle to Diognetus, dating probably from the late second century, says this about the **Christian alterculture**, which echoes our text and its predecessor, 1 Thess 4:3–8, quoted in the introduction to chapters 5–7: "Christians are not distinguished from the rest of humanity by country, language, or custom. . . . They marry like everyone else, and have children, but they do not expose their offspring. They share their food but not their wives. They are in the flesh, but they do not live according to the flesh" (Epistle to Diognetus 5.1, 6–8).[52]

7. C. S. Lewis wrote this in **defense of desire for the reward of heaven** promised in the gospel: "It would seem that Our Lord finds our desires not too strong, but too weak. We are half-hearted creatures, fooling about with drink and sex and ambition when infinite joy is offered us, like an ignorant child who wants to go on making mud pies in a slum because he cannot imagine what is meant by the offer of a holiday at the sea. We are far too easily pleased."[53]

8. **Dietrich Bonhoeffer** offers the following analysis of *porneia*, unfortunately mistranslated as "fornication": "**Greed is related to fornication. An insatiable desire is what both have in common.** . . . Fornicators and greedy people are nothing but desire. Fornicators desire to possess another human being. The greedy desire to possess the things of this world. . . . Those who create their own god and their own world, those who allow their own desire to become their god, must inevitably hate other human beings who stand in their way and impede their designs."[54]

9. One of the most difficult ethical issues for Christians and others is **abortion**. It is nearly impossible to read 1 Cor 6:12–20 without also thinking about that complex and controversial subject. The popular claim about bodily autonomy, expressed in phrases like **"my body, my choice,"** is fundamentally an

---

51. Eric J. Silverman, ed., *Sexual Ethics in a Secular Age: Is There Still a Virtue of Chastity?* (New York: Routledge, 2021).

52. The translation is from Michael W. Holmes, *The Apostolic Fathers: Greek Texts and English Translations*, 3rd. ed. (Grand Rapids: Baker Academic, 2007). It is likely that the text implies more than the rejection of the obvious (adultery, bigamy) and serves as a generic statement about sexual morality. On Jewish and Christian rejection of infanticide, exposure, and abortion, see my *Abortion and the Early Church: Christian, Jewish, and Pagan Attitudes in the Greco-Roman World* (Downers Grove, IL: InterVarsity Press; Mahwah, NJ: Paulist, 1982; repr., Eugene, OR: Wipf & Stock, 1998).

53. C. S. Lewis, "The Weight of Glory," in *The Weight of Glory and Other Addresses* (Grand Rapids: Eerdmans, 1965), 1–15 (here 2).

54. Bonhoeffer, *Discipleship*, 265.

unchristian position, if we take Paul seriously. This mantra has also been used for other issues that apparently have no connection to abortion, such as vaccinations and the use of certain kinds of drugs. During the pandemic that began in 2020, especially as the US Supreme Court reconsidered the famous *Roe v. Wade* decision, one could see the exact same text—"My body, my choice"—in the same place (Washington, DC) used by people on opposite ends of the cultural, religious, and political spectrum to make different points: no vaccine mandates, no abortion restrictions.

For Christians, our bodies are not our own, as Paul says specifically in our passage. The modern/postmodern idol of complete freedom and choice is part of the mentality of this world/age/culture that Paul challenges us to challenge (Rom 12:1–2) because it is not freedom but slavery. *So Paul speaks a word of true sexual liberation.* Moreover, as Paul makes clear in 1 Cor 6:12–20, sexual acts (and their consequences) involve more than one person, more than one body. Whatever one's final position on abortion, one must at least admit that there is more than one body involved; a new, bodily life is growing inside another. In other words, as a matter of intellectual honesty, we must move beyond the talk of individual bodily autonomy.

Paul would say that we, like the Corinthians, live in a culture—and sometimes a Christian community—that idolizes irresponsible notions of freedom. He would also agree (see Rom 3:9–20) that we live in a culture of violence. He would even concur, I suggest, that we live in an "interlocking directorate of death" from abortion to guns to the death penalty to the Pentagon and war, as the late Fr. Daniel Berrigan said.[55] We obviously do not live in a culture that is even remotely "pro-life" in the broad sense of this term.

A truly pro-life position will not be advocating for unfettered gun rights while decrying unfettered abortion rights—or vice versa. Christians need a consistent ethic.

10. The theological truth that one's body is not one's own has **implications beyond matters associated with sexual behavior**. Diet, exercise, avoidance of harmful drugs, and more—all of these contribute to appropriate care for that which is the temple of God's Spirit.

Questions for Those Who Read, Teach, and Preach

1. What are some contemporary manifestations, both in the realm of sexuality and beyond, of the spirit of unbridled freedom?

55. Interview by Lucien Miller, *Reflections* 2 (1979): 1–2.

2.   What does this passage say, both in what it affirms and what it critiques, about the relationship between sexuality and spirituality?

3.   What sorts of unhealthy and unchristian attitudes and practices are at work in the contemporary hypersexualized culture? How might this passage speak to such a culture (recalling that the culture of Roman Corinth was also hypersexualized)?

4.   What is the appropriate relationship between fleeing from sexual immorality and maintaining healthy relationships with other people in ministry and in daily life?

5.   How might Paul respond to those who support extreme sexual freedom as an expression of the quest for justice?

6.   In sum, what does this passage urge the church to believe (faith), do (love), and anticipate (hope)?

For Further Reading

Brower, Kent E., and Andy Johnson, eds. *Holiness and Ecclesiology in the New Testament*. Grand Rapids: Eerdmans, 2007.

Gooder, Paula. "Body." *DPL*[2] 77–83.

———. *Body: Biblical Spirituality for the Whole Person*. London: SPCK, 2016.

Hays, Richard B. *The Moral Vision of the New Testament: Community, Cross, New Creation; A Contemporary Introduction to New Testament Ethics*. San Francisco: HarperCollins, 1996.

Hurtado, Larry W. *Destroyer of the Gods: Early Christian Distinctiveness in the Roman World*. Waco, TX: Baylor University Press, 2016.

Jones, Beth Felker. *Faithful: A Theology of Sex*. Grand Rapids: Zondervan, 2015. (highly accessible)

———. *Marks of His Wounds: Gender Politics and Bodily Resurrection*. New York: Oxford University Press, 2007. (technical)

Loader, William. *The New Testament on Sexuality*. Grand Rapids: Eerdmans, 2012.

May, Alistair Scott. *"The Body for the Lord": Sex and Identity in 1 Corinthians 5–7*. London: T&T Clark, 2004. (technical)

Rosner, Brian S. *Paul, Scripture and Ethics: A Study of 1 Corinthians 5–7*. Leiden: Brill, 1994. Repr., Grand Rapids: Baker, 1999. (technical)

Silverman, Eric J., ed. *Sexual Ethics in a Secular Age: Is There Still a Virtue of Chastity?* New York: Routledge, 2021.

Thompson, James W. *Moral Formation according to Paul: The Context and Coherence of Pauline Ethics*. Grand Rapids: Baker Academic, 2011.

ADDRESSING MORAL CHAOS · 5:1–7:40

7:1–40. CONFUSION ABOUT MARRIAGE AND THE MISSIONAL CALL OF GOD

Beginning with chapter 7 and continuing, it appears, through chapter 15, Paul responds to written queries from the Corinthian assembly: "Now concerning the matters about which you wrote" (7:1). The phrase "now concerning" also appears several other times (7:25; 8:1; 12:1; 16:1, 12), generally indicating topics about which the Corinthians sought Paul's input. But sometimes the phrase probably simply represents a shift in Paul's own thinking and writing.

It seems clear from 5:1–13 and 6:12–20 that the believers in Corinth were generally confused about the place of sexuality in the lives of those who belong to Christ. Because bodies matter, and thus sexual behavior matters, Paul's rather long response to Corinthian questions in chapter 7 seeks to set out some general principles about marriage, and also to address the specific situations of certain groups within the church. This response is likely building on instructions about sexual holiness and marriage given in person, as Paul seems to have regularly taught about these matters (see 1 Thess 4:3–8). Among the many fascinating aspects of this chapter is the constant theme of husband-wife mutuality and equal male-female responsibility with respect to marriage (see further below),[56] as well as the concrete, specific character of Paul's instructions.

At the same time, this chapter is much more than an advice column. In fact, it expresses a fundamental Pauline principle that should not be overlooked: *remain as you were when you were called by God*—what can be called the *persistence principle*. We will see that this principle has a deeper theological basis than simply "Jesus is coming soon" or "marriage is a cure for uncontrollable sexual urges." Furthermore, we will also see that it is not a hard-and-fast rule but one with considerable contextual flexibility.

Structure, Style, and Themes

After an opening sentence that sets the conversation in motion (7:1), the chapter is structured chiastically (like chs. 5–6, 8:1–11:1, and chs. 12–14) in three main sections:

---

56. Similar equality appears in connection with prayer and prophecy in worship (11:4–5).

> A Concrete Instructions about Marriage for Specific Situations (7:2–16)
>   B Theological Reflections: The Persistence Principle and Vocational
>   Contentment (7:17–24)
> A' Further Concrete Instructions and Theological Reflections (7:25–40)

Structurally, this chiasm points to vv. 17–24 as critical to the entire chapter.

Stylistically, it should be noted that Paul employs quite a few second-person imperatives ("you, or you all, do this") as well as third-person imperatives ("let them, or him/her," meaning essentially "they, or he/she, should"). This does not mean, however, that Paul is issuing ad hoc orders without a solid theological basis. Even when he does not have a direct command from Jesus (see 7:10–12) or from Scripture, he is thinking and writing theologically in terms of the gospel and the saving mission of God. Among the significant theological topics and themes in this chapter are the following:

- holiness, particularly sexual holiness (vv. 1, 34, 36) and self-control (vv. 9, 36–37)
- bifocal spirituality: daily life in light of Christ's death and his parousia
  - › looking back to Christ's teachings (vv. 10, 12, 25) and death (v. 23)
  - › looking ahead to the parousia and associated events (vv. 26, 29–31)
- the nature of devotion to the Lord and of freedom in him (vv. 5, 22–23, 29–35, 39)
- salvific intentionality in daily life, particularly in marriage (vv. 12–14, 16)
- divinely given calls, vocations, and gifts (vv. 7, 15, 17–24)
- vocational contentment regarding one's station in life (7:17–24)
- persistence, or staying put, often expressed with the verb "remain" (Gk. *menō*; vv. 8, 11, 20, 24, 40; cf. v. 26, without that verb) but also as "don't leave" (vv. 12–13)
- equality in Christ, in the spirit of Gal 3:28
  - › Jew and gentile (vv. 18–19)
  - › slave and free (vv. 21–23)
  - › male and female (vv. 2–4, 10, 12–16, 28a, 32–34)
- marriage and singleness as good gifts/blessings (vv. 7, 38, 40), with the latter preferred (vv. 6, 8, 26–28, 32–35, 38, 40)
- marriage as a form of Christian community and discipleship (7:32–35)
- mutuality in marriage (vv. 2–4, 10, 12–16, 32–34)

The theme of man-and-woman mutuality in marriage is particularly striking:

ADDRESSING MORAL CHAOS · 5:1–7:40

Verse(s)	Aspect of Mutuality
v. 2	man and woman should have (sexually) his/her own spouse
v. 3	same conjugal rights
v. 4	mutual bodily authority
v. 10	neither should separate/divorce
vv. 12–13	each should stay with a consenting unbelieving spouse
v. 14	each sanctifies an unbelieving spouse
v. 15	each may allow an unbelieving spouse to separate
v. 16	each might save an unbelieving spouse
v. 28a	neither sins if they marry
vv. 32–34	an unmarried man or woman seeks to please the Lord; a married man or woman seeks to please his/her spouse

Such equality in the realm of sexual behavior and marriage is radical in a culture that generally allowed and even expected immense sexual freedom for men, married or not. No less radical is the claim, implicit throughout the chapter (as in 6:12–20), that marriage alone is the proper place for sexual relations for Christians.

We turn now to the concrete instructions and theological principles themselves.

7:1. The Subject: Sex More Generally

Paul begins by saying the Corinthians wrote inquiring about subjects related to these words: "It is well for a man not to touch [a euphemism for "have sex with"] a woman." This sentence is almost certainly to be attributed not to Paul but to (some of) the Corinthians, as the quotation marks in the NRSV, NAB, (updated) NIV, and many other translations indicate.[57] There were moralists within the Greco-Roman world who called for men not to indulge their libido

---

57. The original NIV's rendering of "touch" as "marry" is a complete mistranslation; the updated NIV, "have sexual relations with a woman," is more accurate (so also CEB, NET). The failure of the NJB and NAS (like the KJV and the original NIV) to put these words in quotation marks perpetuates the erroneous impression that Paul, rather than some of the Corinthians, opposed sex per se. It is possible that Paul is quoting back to the Corinthians their rendering of what he said about preferring celibacy, but if so, the Corinthians have radically misunderstood him as supporting sexless marriage. (Ciampa and Rosner think the euphemism is more specific and refers to sex for selfish gratification; if so, then Paul partially agrees: *First Letter to the Corinthians*, 272–75.)

208

(as we saw in 6:12–20) but to suppress it. It is possible, then, that some Corinthians who misunderstood Paul *thought* he said precisely this.

Paul's own teachings about sex—as something for Christians to treat very differently—may have generated some questions about the propriety of sexual activity, even in marriage, and also about marriage itself. Is marital sex a form of *porneia*? Is marriage sinful? It is quite possible that the Corinthians knew specifically of Paul's view that union with Christ and union with a prostitute are mutually exclusive (6:15–17)—and then interpreted that mutual exclusivity to mean union with Christ and union with *any* human, even one's spouse. Or perhaps they interpreted his singleness, referred to both in this chapter (explicitly in 7:7, 8) and in chapter 9 (see 9:5, 15), as a fundamental part of the call to imitate him imitating Christ (see 11:1).

These questions and concerns were not theoretical. It appears they arose not only from talking about Paul and his teaching but also from actual strong opinions and related practices that had emerged in the Corinthian community. Some of the believers concluded that sex was basically permissible for anyone with anyone (e.g., even with relatives or prostitutes, as seen in chs. 5 and 6), while others—those quoted in 7:1—thought it was not permissible *at all* for brothers and sisters in Christ, the holy ones, even in marriage (see also 1 Tim 4:3).[58] Both perspectives misunderstood Paul and were shaped by different impulses within Greco-Roman culture.

7:2–16. Concrete Instructions about Marriage for Specific Situations

The apostle proceeds in the rest of the chapter to address misunderstandings about sex and marriage and to provide theologically grounded instruction about marriage itself. In vv. 2–16, Paul offers instructions about marriage to people in various life situations.

7:2–5. Instructions to Married Believers about Sexual Relations in Marriage

In 7:2–5, Paul rejects the notion that sexual abstinence is appropriate for married believers, except perhaps occasionally for special periods of prayer (7:5).[59] Similar guidelines are found in other Jewish writings of the time. As the table

---

58. That is, "Christian *freedom* means any and all sex is permitted" versus "Christian *holiness* means no sex, not even in marriage." Another view of the situation is that the Corinthians agreed that spousal sex was not for pleasure, but some said sexual pleasure could be sought with others (e.g., prostitutes, slaves, or mistresses), while others disagreed. See Ciampa and Rosner, *First Letter to the Corinthians*, 250.

59. Some manuscripts add "and fasting."

above suggests, Paul clearly sees marriage—and sex within it—as an exclusive relationship of mutuality, another standard Jewish perspective.[60]

Paul expresses this mutuality in a series of parallel, proverb-like third-person ("they"/"them") sentences in vv. 2–4. The primary (if implicit) theological basis of this relational reciprocity is the equality of the sexes in Christ (Gal 3:28). In addition to the symmetrical sentences themselves, Paul uses words such as "likewise" (vv. 3, 4), "one another" (v. 5), "by agreement" (v. 5), and "come together again" (v. 5) to express the mutuality. This claim of mutuality in marriage, especially with its language of mutually having "authority" over one another's body (7:4), would be shocking in a patriarchal society.[61] A man's wife is his equal partner, not his property, asserts Paul.

Paul not only expects husbands (as well as wives) to fulfill the appropriate conjugal needs of their spouses, but—in contrast to much of the pagan world—he also expects them not to engage in sex with other people.[62] Commenting on this passage, especially v. 4, Chrysostom offers advice to married people tempted to extramarital sexual activity: they should say, "My body is not mine, but my wife's," or "My body is not mine, but my husband's."[63] Theologically, this language of obligation and ownership is, at bottom, actually the language of covenant—of mutual commitment and enduring love, analogous to the covenantal relationship between believers and their Lord (6:13, 15–17). It in no way legitimizes forced sex or rape, the antithesis of sexual mutuality and love.

Although the word "love" does not actually appear in these verses, Paul is describing one aspect of the other-centered love he extols in chapter 13 (see also 7:33–34, which is both a description of and an implicit prescription about mutual care in marriage). In fact, the "Although [x] not [y] but rather [z]" pattern of cruciform love once again appears to be operative:

60. Eph 5:21–33 is often interpreted as a text advocating patriarchal hierarchy or even domination, but it also suggests mutuality in marriage—with rhetorical bookends (vv. 21, 33) stressing that mutuality.

61. Ciampa and Rosner (*First Letter to the Corinthians*, 281) find one ancient parallel, indeed precedent: Song 2:16; 6:3; 7:10.

62. The grammar and vocabulary of 7:2 (cf. 1 Thess 4:4) indicate that each person should have sexual relations with one's own spouse, never another's. Some exceptions to the general cultural norm of "anything goes" in the sexual arena, at least for free males, did exist. Paul's contemporary Musonius Rufus, a leading Stoic, opposed sex outside marriage; believed like Paul in mutuality in marriage with respect to the body and sex; stressed total mutual marital devotion; and held that marriage has two goals, procreation and *koinōnia*, or companionship ("On the Chief End of Marriage"). Some ancient writers commended sexual relations *only* for procreation.

63. Chrysostom, *Homilies on 1 Corinthians* 19.2.

> ‣ Although [x] you have the power and, according to some, the right or even the spiritual obligation to withhold sexual relations from your spouse,
> ‣ do not [y] do so, or do so only for appropriate short, mutually agreed-upon times,
> ‣ but rather [z] normally, in self-giving love, give your spouse his or her conjugal rights because you belong to one another equally, spiritually and bodily.

Underlying this implicit call to love is the scriptural teaching that man and woman become one flesh (6:16; Gen 2:24; Matt 19:5–6; Mark 10:8; Eph 5:31), which rules out sex with mistresses, slaves, prostitutes, other men, and boys.

Furthermore, Paul realistically sees abstinence from sex within marriage as an invitation to temptation and *porneia* (7:2, 5), such as that seen in the cases narrated in 5:1–13 and 6:12–20 and the list in 6:9–10. In fact, the reality of sexual temptation is actually the practical and rhetorical starting point of this section: "because of cases of" *porneia* (v. 2). Thus Paul finally turns in v. 5 from axioms about mutuality to direct instruction: don't "deprive" (or even "rob, defraud") one another except temporarily,[64] by mutual consent, for spiritual purposes. Having sex in marriage is not at all committing the sin of *porneia*, as some might fear. But abstention can lead to such sin.[65]

7:6–7. Paul's Preference for Singleness

Verses 6 and 7 of this chapter can be read as connecting with what precedes or with what follows. (One can even link v. 6 to vv. 1–5 and v. 7 to vv. 8–9.) But it is better to see these verses as a quasi-independent unit that presents one key guiding principle for the instructions that follow. That is, the word "this" at the start of v. 6 looks forward, not backward, but it looks forward only to v. 7.

Having clarified his position on sex in marriage, Paul makes his preference about marriage itself known in these two verses. Although singleness (celibacy) and marriage are both gifts (*charisma*; 7:7),[66] Paul's way of celibate singleness is preferable, he believes. Why? Later he will write that it allows for undistracted devotion to the Lord's work (7:32–35). That is, Paul is not an *opponent* of sex but a *proponent* of dedication to Christ.

---

64. Paul uses the same verb in 6:7b regarding lawsuits.

65. Because the implicit virtue operative here is Christlike covenantal love, Paul would never countenance forced sexual relations, even in the context of mutual marital obligations.

66. The same word used of "spiritual gifts" or "manifestations of grace" (*charis*) in 1:7; 12:4, 9, 28, 30, 31.

Importantly, however, the apostle stresses that what he says is not a command but a concession (v. 6), a sort of middle ground between an inflexible call for celibate singleness and a blanket endorsement of marriage as the Christian norm. He will repeat his preference in vv. 8, 26–28, 32–35, 38, 40, so it definitely provides one of the fundamental perspectives on marriage as he moves forward with practical instructions. Yet Paul should not be misunderstood as someone who sees marriage as merely a solution for uncontrollable sexual desire. No, marriage is first of all a gracious gift from God. As chapters 12–14 make clear, Paul has a similar view of speaking in tongues and prophecy: each is a gift of God's Spirit and grace, but the latter is preferable to the former.

7:8–9. Instructions for the Unmarried and Widows

Paul's next set of (very brief) instructions is for "the unmarried and the widows" (v. 8), and it is clearly his own perspective: "I say" are the first words in the Greek text. The Greek word for "unmarried" (*agamoi*) can refer to men or women; the word "widows" (*chērai*) refers only to women. But Paul might implicitly include widowers in this instruction, while not naming them, since there were far fewer widowers than widows.[67] Essentially, then, Paul is counseling all unmarried and widowed believers to remain single (cf. vv. 39–40), like himself—unless their passion is out of control (v. 9; cf. v. 36).[68] The apostle famously offers a vivid image commonly used in the ancient world to express such passion: "it is better to marry than to burn with sexual desire" (v. 9 NET; cf. Prov 6:27–28). Paul is *not* imagining burning in hell.

This is the first allusion to the principle of persistence, or staying put ("remain as you are"; 7:26). But—we must recall vv. 6–7—this is not a command, and celibacy is a gift of the Spirit that not all have. To repeat for emphasis, *Paul is not saying that marriage is simply the solution to an uncontrollable libido.*

7:10–11. Instructions for Married Believers about Separation

Returning in 7:10–16 to the subject of married believers, Paul begins with a firm directive (in contrast to v. 6). He charges both men and women who are married to fellow believers (7:10–11) not to initiate a separation or divorce (in

---

67. Some scholars understand "the unmarried" to be widowers, but this is unlikely.

68. Encouraging even *widows* to remain single probably implies the existence of a support system (see Rom 12:13; Gal 6:2) within the church such that remarriage is not a financial necessity or expectation.

context, the terms are interchangeable). The ideal of celibate singleness could have suggested to some Corinthians that they should divorce their spouses. While the persistence principle is perhaps operative in the background, the explicit basis of Paul's instruction is not himself, as in v. 8, but the Lord's "command" ("not I but the Lord"; v. 10). Paul is referring to the teaching of Jesus preserved in Matt 5:31-32; 19:3-9; Mark 10:2-12; Luke 16:18.

As with the subject of sexual relations discussed in 7:3-4, the fundamental similarity of expectations for both men and women is striking. Its basis is not just in Paul's theology of male and female equality in Christ but also in the teaching of Jesus: "Whoever divorces his wife and marries another commits adultery against her; and if she divorces her husband and marries another, she commits adultery" (Mark 10:11-12). For Paul, echoing Scripture, Jewish tradition, and Jesus, marriage is a gift of grace and a covenant; as such, it is not to be ended: "Therefore what God has joined together, let no one separate" (Matt 19:6).

Paul, like Jesus, is strict but not inflexible in giving this instruction. For Jesus, with respect to divorce, there was an "exception clause" for *porneia* (Matt 5:32; 19:9).[69] Paul does not tell us what might be an appropriate cause for separation in this context, but *porneia* is certainly a possible justification, since Paul is passing on Jesus' teaching. However, if a woman (there is no explicit exception clause for a man) does seek a separation/divorce, she may aim for reconciliation but not marriage with another (v. 11; see 7:39 for the case of spousal death).

7:12–16. Instructions about Mixed Marriages and Salvific Intentionality

As for "the rest" (v. 12)—the spouses of nonbelievers (7:12-16)—Paul now has no direct word from Jesus but only his own counsel, as in v. 8. This is because Jesus addressed a different situation, with all Jewish followers. But especially as gentiles became believers and (often) their spouses did not, surely some must have wondered whether the mixed marriage was detrimental or impure. It is possible that Paul's earlier letter that included an admonition not to associate with sexually immoral persons (see 5:9-11), which was seriously misunderstood, may have also raised questions about such a marriage. Some believers might have wanted to leave their unbelieving spouses to marry fellow

---

69. The meaning of *porneia* in Matthew is disputed: sexual immorality, unfaithfulness, unchastity, or illicit marriage.

ADDRESSING MORAL CHAOS · 5:1–7:40

believers. One can make good, spiritual, even Pauline (see 2 Cor 6:14–7:1) arguments for such impulses.

Paul instructs both men and women not to seek divorce if the unbeliever consents to stay married (7:12–13). The effect of the unbalanced union is from unholiness toward holiness, and not vice versa, thereby positively affecting children as well as the unbelieving spouse (7:14), who may actually become a believer (7:16). "Holiness is, as it were, contagious," writes Richard Hays. This does not mean that the unbelieving spouse and children are automatically saved but that they are set apart to experience God's saving work through the believing spouse/parent, who is, after all, holy—a holy temple of the Spirit (6:11, 19). The mixed marriage has become a "sacred environment."[70]

There is scholarly debate about the tone of Paul's words in 7:16. They are actually questions in Greek, but should they be understood optimistically or pessimistically about a spouse's coming to faith? "How do you know as a wife if you will save your husband? Or how do you know as a husband if you will save your wife?" (CEB). The hopeful interpretation would interpret the questions to mean this: Do you know what could happen if you stay in the marriage—the conversion of your spouse! (See the NRSV and NRSVue, which turn the questions into statements.) The doubtful interpretation would understand the queries to mean this: How do you know whether you will ever save your spouse?

In light of the immediate context and Paul's overall missional emphasis, the optimistic interpretation is the much stronger.[71] The apostle advocates for personal witness to the unbelieving spouse. Paul himself is the model here, trying to "win" or "save" as many people as he can (9:19–23). Of course, it is neither Paul nor the believing spouse who actually saves anyone; humans are the agents of God's saving activity. A mixed marriage, then, can be a place of Christian witness. The Christian spouse is to act with "salvific intentionality"—a desire for all to be brought to salvation in Christ.[72] (A similar dynamic is at work in, e.g., 10:23–11:1—the case of having meals in the homes of unbelievers.)

In a sort of parenthesis to his main point (7:15), Paul does note an exception: if the unbelieving spouse initiates divorce, the believer is not bound

---

70. Hays, *First Corinthians*, 121, 122. Paul may be drawing on Jewish thinking and language about betrothal as an act of sanctification in the sense of setting apart (Goode, *Salvific Intentionality in 1 Corinthians*, 28–30).

71. See especially Goode, *Salvific Intentionality in 1 Corinthians*, 20–43. The language of salvific intentionality is from Michael Barram (see next note).

72. Michael Barram, "Pauline Mission as Salvific Intentionality: Fostering a Missional Consciousness in 1 Corinthians 9:19–23 and 10:31–11:1," in *Paul as Missionary: Identity, Activity, Theology, and Practice*, ed. Trevor J. Burke and Brian S. Rosner, LNTS 420 (London: T&T Clark, 2011), 234–46. See also 1 Pet 3:1.

214

to maintain the union. He or she, now no longer "bound," is possibly free to remarry, though Paul is not explicit about that.[73] Once again, the apostle holds men and women, Christian brothers and sisters, to the same standards. Despite the missional possibilities within a mixed marriage, the divine desire for "peace" (7:15; cf. Rom 14:19) suggests that the voluntary departure of an unbelieving spouse is better than domestic warfare—which is not a positive Christian witness. We can guess that, in such situations, the church would be called to pray for both parties to experience the peace of God.

7:17–24. Theological Reflections: The Persistence Principle and Vocational Contentment

The apostle next shifts gears to offer in 7:17–24 a crucial theological rubric, the center of his entire discussion, within which to view marriage as well as other aspects of daily life. This rubric is one of Paul's catholic, or universal, instructions (v. 17b).[74] It consists of two inseparable parts. First, there is what we may call the persistence principle, or a "preferential option for staying put."[75] Second, there is a call for what we may call vocational contentment (referring to the transforming call of God, not a career), within which Paul views marriage and all other stations in life.

The apostle's bottom line is basically this: *Stay as you were when God called you into the body of Christ* (7:17, 20, 24; see also 7:27). The symmetrical structure of 7:17–24 reinforces this point:

v. 17	*Remain as you are.*	v. 20
v. 18	specific examples	v. 21
v. 19	theological rationale	vv. 22–23
	v. 24 summary	
	Remain as you are.	

73. In certain Christian traditions, especially the Roman Catholic Church, the words of 7:15 are sometimes called the "Pauline privilege." According to the Roman Catholic Code of Canon Law (canon 1143), this means that a legitimate marriage between two originally unbaptized persons can be dissolved if one spouse is baptized but the other remains unbaptized and wishes to end the marriage. Under those circumstances, the baptized spouse is free to marry another person, at which time the first marriage is dissolved. (The baptized person cannot initiate the dissolution and remarry.)

74. See also 4:17; 11:16; 14:33–35.

75. The phrase comes from Michelle Rader. The Greek verb *menō*, "remain," appears in vv. 20, 24.

ADDRESSING MORAL CHAOS · 5:1–7:40

This acceptance of, and even positive attitude toward, life situations is not a version of Stoic apathy toward external things that cannot affect one's inner self—things that don't matter (*adiaphora*). Rather, Paul offers a robust theological basis: he explicitly affirms that God calls people from every station. Moreover, the context implies that God has a task for them in their particular situation, for what Paul has just said about having a missional perspective in mixed marriages (vv. 15–16) can transcend that specific station to include all life situations.

The "call-" word family (*kaleō*; *klēsis*) occurs nine times in 7:17–24 and continues a theme from the beginning of the letter (1:9, 26) and already reannounced, also in connection with marriage (7:15). Believers are to look back, remember their call, and live into it—literally "walk" in it (v. 17; *peripateitō*), a verb that implies purpose and movement, not ho-hum toleration. It implies trust in the God who apportions to each.

As Paul will say explicitly in 7:29–31, there is also a fundamental eschatological perspective underlying this acceptance of one's station. Here, however, the emphasis from the "call" language is the irrelevance of all social distinctions for a community that encompasses people from all life situations (see also Gal 3:28): gentiles and Jews (7:18–19) as well as enslaved persons and free persons (7:21–22), but also—as seen in both previous and following verses—male and female, married and single.

The irrelevance of circumcision or uncircumcision (7:18–19) is an important Pauline theme.[76] The peculiar words about undoing circumcision in v. 18 refer to an actual, if occasional, surgical practice (e.g., 1 Macc 1:15) called epispasm, meant to reverse the circumcision through restoration of the foreskin. It was intended to increase a man's status and acceptance in a gentile-dominated environment where nudity was the norm for athletics. Paul says both, "Don't get circumcised" and "don't be epispasm-ed."[77] What marks people in the Messiah is not the state of their genitals but obedience to God's commands (7:19): expressing their faith in love (see Gal 5:6), the hallmark of the new creation (Gal 6:15).

---

76. See especially both Galatians (esp. 2:1–21; 5:1–12; 6:12–16) and Romans (esp. 2:25–29; 3:27–31; 4:1–22; 14:1–15:13). Some interpreters argue that the phrase "Circumcision is nothing, and uncircumcision is nothing" in 7:19 is not a general principle about the equality of gentile and Jew in Christ but is rather directed simply to gentiles: For you gentiles, circumcision is nothing, and uncircumcision is nothing, so don't try to get circumcised if you are not, or uncircumcised if you are. This interpretation is a case of special pleading that goes against the major Pauline theme of equality in Christ that is on display here.

77. McKnight, *Second Testament*.

The main theme of staying put is repeated in vv. 20 and 24. Paul is leveling the playing field and asserting that God did call, and does call, people in all social stations and that therefore none of those stations is better or worse than any other. As a general principle (with occasional exceptions, as in vv. 11, 15), there is no need to change, no reason to want to change—and a mission to bloom where one is planted.

The one sticky point here is Paul's word about enslaved persons, particularly 7:21. The verse ends with a Greek verbal construction that contains the verb "to make use of" and an adverb that can mean either "more" or "rather." Does Paul mean, "much more make use of your enslaved condition," or, "rather, use the opportunity for freedom"? Translators and other scholars are divided:

- "Were you a slave when called? Do not be concerned about it. Even if you can gain your freedom, make use of your present condition now more than ever" (NRSV, NRSVue; cf. NAB, NJB).
- "Were you a slave when you were called? Don't let it trouble you—although if you can gain your freedom, do so" (NIV; cf. RSV, CEB, ESV, NET).

The scholarly debate is endless, and some have declared the problem insoluble. In light of Paul's letter to Philemon, however, an argument can be made that Paul would want slaves to be free.[78] Moreover, in 7:23, which echoes 6:20, Paul does not merely reinforce the persistence principle but clearly implies that *ownership by another human is not appropriate for one purchased and owned by God through the death of his Son*: "You were bought [note the divine passive] at a price; do not become slaves of human beings" (NIV). Paul is not proslavery, for (like women), slaves are persons, not property (economic or sexual). Certain Black Americans in the eighteenth and nineteenth centuries, such as Lemuel Haynes—the first ordained Black American—understood this theological truth and preached against the proslavery interpretation of 7:21.[79]

Yet there were enslaved persons in the Corinthian church and in other early Christian communities who could not obtain their freedom. Thus Paul announces another theological truth: the paradox that all enslaved persons are

78. See especially Stephen E. Young, *Our Beloved Brother: Purpose and Community in Paul's Letter to Philemon* (Waco, TX: Baylor University Press, 2021). It is important to note that in Philemon, Paul addresses a master; here he addresses enslaved persons. The larger discussion of Paul and slavery needs also to consider Col 3:18–4:1 and Eph 5:21–6:9, but they are beyond the scope of this commentary.

79. Bowens, *African American Readings of Paul*, 52–54.

freed—liberated—persons in Christ, and all free persons are Christ's enslaved persons (7:22). There is a liberation from the powers of Sin and Death that no master can take away. Likewise, to call Jesus Lord is to be freely enslaved to him and his ways of faithfulness and love.[80] Thus, like husbands and wives, enslaved persons and masters are already equal in Christ, and yet there is an inherent penchant in the apostle's theology toward liberation and liberty. In both the Christian household and the Christian community as a whole, such equality had to be both revolutionary and difficult to implement.

7:25–40. Further Concrete Instructions and Theological Reflections

The last third of this chiastically structured chapter is also chiastically shaped:

> A   Engaged Couples and General Principles (7:25–28)
>   B   Eschatology and Devotion (7:29–35)
> A' Betrothed Men and Final Theological Reflections (7:36–40)

In 7:36–40, Paul returns to the general topic of unmarried believers considered in vv. 25–28 and earlier in vv. 8–9. The last two verses (vv. 39–40) might feel somewhat like an afterthought, but they contain much theological substance.

7:25–28. Engaged Couples and General Principles

The explicit topic of 7:25–28 is (in Greek) *parthenoi*: literally, "virgins" (e.g., NRSV, NAB, NIV).[81] That is, the subject is those who have never married (CEB, NET) or perhaps the "betrothed" (ESV, in light of vv. 36–38). Indeed, since both men and women are addressed, it may be best to see engaged couples as the group Paul has in mind. And he will return with more instructions for engaged men in vv. 36–38.

In 7:25, as in 7:12, Paul says he has no teaching from Jesus, but now he claims that by the mercy of the Lord (i.e., Jesus), his own counsel is trustworthy (cf. v. 40; 4:2). That counsel is, as expected, "remain as you are" (7:26b). Using the imagery

---

80. In Rom 6 (vv. 6, 16–22), Paul uses slavery to God and righteousness (versus slavery to Sin) as a basic image of Christian existence, and in Gal 5:13 as a basic image of relationships within the Christian community.

81. A form of *parthenos* occurs in vv. 25, 28, 34, 36, 37, 38. The word usually refers to a young, especially virgin, woman, but can occasionally signify a chaste or virgin man.

of being "bound to" or "free from" a wife, in v. 27 Paul specifically tells married and unmarried men not to reverse their situation. Though his focus is on the unmarried, Paul reiterates both his basic principle and his earlier prohibition of divorce from vv. 10–11, creating a symmetrical, comprehensive mandate for men.

That said (and here we see Paul's flexibility), those who marry do not sin—neither the directly addressed man ("you" singular) nor the indirectly addressed virgin young woman (7:28a; cf. v. 36).[82] As noted earlier, the concern about marriage as sinful was almost certainly raised by some Corinthians.

Most importantly, Paul provides two practical (but also theological) rationales for his counsel: "the impending crisis" (v. 26) and the avoidance of distress (v. 28). The meaning of the former phrase has been warmly debated, but it is likely a reference to the messianic woes (persecution, etc.) expected before the parousia.[83] Both reasons are amplified in the following verses.

7:29–35. Eschatology and Devotion

In 7:29–35, Paul continues his pastoral guidance within that eschatological perspective. He believes that because in Christ the new age has begun (see 2 Cor 5:17), "the present form of this world"—its taken-for-granted structures and institutions, including marriage and slavery—"is passing away" (7:31). The result should be nonconformity to this age (see Rom 12:1–2) and thus a profound relativizing of all human commitments and relationships: marriage, life's shared highs and lows, the purchase and use of goods, and so on (7:29–31). Paul's succinct exhortations are counterintuitive, even shocking.

This relativization, a spiritual cousin of the vocational contentment discussed in 7:17–24, is necessary not only because the time—that is, the time between the first advent and the parousia—has been contracted (7:29),[84] but also because in Christ the future has already invaded the present. That is to say, Paul's perspective on the social structures of this age is indebted as much to the *quality* of the present time as it is to the *quantity* of time remaining. The imminence of

---

82. Both CEB and NET interpret "free from a wife" in v. 27 to mean divorced, which would imply that v. 28 allows remarriage after divorce. But the immediate context suggests that the bound or free language means simply married or unmarried.

83. Some translations and other interpreters render this as a "present" crisis (NAB, NIV, CEB, ESV), which has sometimes been understood to be a famine and its consequences. But a looming, eschatological crisis makes more sense in context (cf. NRSV, NET), unless Paul is referring to all the difficulties present in the overlap of the ages.

84. This is probably a better interpretation of the Greek, rather than "has grown short," or something similar, as in most translations.

ADDRESSING MORAL CHAOS · 5:1–7:40

the parousia is less important than the presence of the new in the midst of the old, during this overlap of the ages (10:11). At the same time, it is true that final salvation "is nearer to us now than when we became believers" (Rom 13:11).

We now see clearly what really drives Paul's passion for singleness. There are two main things, as we have already observed: eschatology and devotion. Related to Paul's desire for the Corinthians' devotion is his pastoral concern for their good (7:28b, 32a, 35). Marriage *is* a distraction from total devotion to the Lord, because married people—whether male or female—are (appropriately) occupied with another person in a way that is not true of single people; they are "anxious" about the affairs of the world and about pleasing their spouse (7:32–35).[85] The verb "please" here refers to loving devotion in imitation of Paul and, ultimately, Christ (10:33–11:1; Rom 15:1–3) that seeks the good and edification of the other (8:1; 10:23–24; 13:5). That is, *marriage is a form of Christian community and discipleship.*

Thus, Paul's words about pleasing do not mean that only unmarried believers are concerned about the Lord's affairs and wish to please him. Paul's either-or proposition is hyperbolic to make his point about the demands of marriage, which means a married person's interests or priorities are divided—literally, that *person* "is divided" (7:34). Nor does Paul imply that only the unmarried can or should be "holy in body and spirit" (v. 34; recall 6:12–20), only that this is (or should be) the primary motive of the unmarried.

Even though the institutions of this world are indeed passing away, the *ekklēsia* and its individual participants are not called to stop caring for others. The *relativizing* of relationships noted in 7:29–31 does not mean the *renunciation* of them. Husbands and wives still have marital relations (7:2–5); Christians are still called to weep with those who weep and rejoice with those who rejoice (12:26; Rom 12:15; Phil 2:17–18). Possessions must be used, but not overused, or abused, or allowed to become the possessors rather than the possessed: "I will not be enslaved by anything" (6:12 RSV).

Nor are believers, married or not, supposed to abandon the world and live in some kind of holy huddle. Rather, it is clear throughout the letter—including right in this chapter (7:10–16)—that the church is always to engage nonbelievers and to do so with an attitude of salvific intentionality. As Paul has already acknowledged, it is impossible to "go out of the world" (5:9–10). But it is not

---

85. The distinction between "unmarried woman" and "virgin" (most translations) in v. 34 may indicate that the former term refers to the previously married. But it more likely refers to the never married, while the latter term means "fiancée" or "betrothed" (ESV); see vv. 36–38.

220

merely impossible; to do so would be inappropriate, hardly reflecting the life Paul led or the modus operandi of the incarnate Lord he attempts to imitate.

The last verse of this section (7:35) is critical: throughout this chapter, what Paul has been teaching has been for the Corinthians' benefit (*symphoron*), for "not all things are beneficial" (6:12; *sympherei*). The apostle is always in formational and missional mode, striving for the welfare (*symphoron*) of everyone he encounters (10:33). Looking out for what benefits others is at the heart of Christian love (13:5). Thus, Paul's pedagogical motive is love, not control. His opponents and detractors then and now may not agree with him, but that is clearly how he sees his mission and ministry.

7:36-40. Betrothed Men and Final Theological Reflections

Paul wraps up this chapter with instructions continuing on from vv. 25-28, followed by a brief but theologically rich concluding remark about the permanence of marriage and the question of remarriage.

Interpreters have been divided about the identity of those addressed in 7:36-38 concerning behavior toward their "virgins" (*parthenoi*, as in vv. 25, 28, 34). Some, especially in the patristic period, have thought of it as involving fathers who are wondering whether to seek marriage for their virgin daughters. But most see the situation as involving engaged couples. The man is addressed directly and given two options: if strong passions are causing improper behavior toward his fiancée,[86] then the couple should marry and will not be sinning (v. 36; cf. vv. 9, 28). But if he has heartfelt determination to behave appropriately, he can continue in a nonsexual, nonmarital relationship with her (v. 37).[87] *Both options are good*—and it is important to emphasize this truth (recall the "gift" language of 7:7)—even if the latter is better (v. 38). To repeat, Paul does not see marriage simply as a remedy for a hyperactive libido. But the call for holiness means that certain behaviors cannot continue.

In 7:39-40, Paul concludes his discussion of marriage with words that seem to once again address widows (see 7:8-9), but his concerns are actually larger. He makes at least five final theological claims about Christian marriage, naturally with echoes of scriptural and other Jewish themes:

86. The Greek word in v. 36 that seems to signify strong passions indicates *some sort of* great increase, but it could refer, instead, to the woman and mean something like "if she is past the bloom of youth" (NET).

87. The word *kardia* ("heart") appears twice in 7:37 in idiomatic phrases, so many recent translations have words like "mind" or "resolve," but see ESV: "established in his heart . . . determined this in his heart."

- It is between a man and a woman (no polygamy, polyamory, or same-gender marriage).
- It is a lifelong bond—that is, covenant—unto death.
- It is blessed by God.
- Remarriage is permissible after a spouse's death, even if remaining single is preferable and results in greater blessing (cf. v. 8).
- Christians are to marry Christians.

Paul's stipulation that widows remarry only believers ("only in the Lord"; 7:39) simply makes explicit his assumption about believers marrying only believers that permeates the chapter.

The apostle closes with the suggestion that his counsel here (and implicitly throughout the chapter), even when not based on the teachings of the earthly Jesus, derives from his Spirit-inspired apostolic wisdom (7:40; cf. v. 25; 2:12–13, 16).

Conclusion: Marriage Instructions and Theology

As noted in the introduction to this chapter, Paul's practical instructions are replete with explicit and implicit theological claims about holiness, salvific intentionality, vocation, persistence, equality in Christ and mutuality in marriage, the gift-quality of both singleness and marriage, and the bifocal perspective that wraps all of this together.

The chapter is about both Christian marriage and Christian celibate singleness. Marriage, in short, is a highly theological and spiritual bond of love, not to be entered into lightly. It is not merely a concession to sexual overdrive, for it is above all a divine gift and blessing, a mode of Christian community and discipleship. And so also is Paul's preference of celibate singleness, for equally deep spiritual and theological reasons. It can enable a different sort of devotion to Christ. But both forms of Christian holiness have their place in the church and its participation in the *missio Dei*.

REFLECTIONS AND QUESTIONS FOR 7:1–40

Spiritual, Pastoral, Missional, and Theological Reflections

1. Despite the common accusation that Paul is patriarchal, if not misogynist, the **equality of male and female spouses**, especially in 7:2–16 and 7:32–35, is quite striking. It should help to put to rest such accusations, or at least to

create a significant balance to texts that seem to suggest the legitimacy of the accusations.

2. A famous text about Saint Anthony the Great, one of the desert fathers, goes like this: "Someone asked Abba Anthony, '**What must one do in order to please God?**' The elder replied, 'Listen to what I tell you: whoever you may be, always have God before your eyes; whatever you do, do it according to the testimony of holy Scripture; and, in whatever place you live, do not easily leave it.'"

3. The **theological depth of 1 Cor 7**, as noted especially in the introduction and in the last two sections of the discussion above, is not to be missed. Paul's instructions reveal not a person making off-the-cuff pronouncements or offering an odd view of sex and marriage. Rather, this is **the work of a profound and sensitive pastoral theologian.**

Questions for Those Who Read, Teach, and Preach

1. In an age (at least in the West or Global North) when sex and even marriage are seen as vehicles of self-gratification and self-actualization, to be terminated when the self is no longer satisfied, what can Paul's understanding of sex and marriage offer the church and the culture?

2. If Paul does not issue either an inflexible call for celibate singleness or a blanket sanction of marriage as the Christian norm, how might his perspective on the benefits of singleness be received and practiced today?

3. How should the reality that "the form of this world is passing away" affect Christian decision making about the use of time, energy, finances, and other resources?

4. In sum, what does this passage urge the church to believe (faith), do (love), and anticipate (hope)?

For Further Reading

Bergsma, John S. *The Bible and Marriage: The Two Shall Become One Flesh.* Grand Rapids: Baker Academic, 2022.

Deming, Will. *Paul on Marriage and Celibacy: The Hellenistic Background of 1 Corinthians 7.* Grand Rapids: Eerdmans, 2004.

Glancy, Jennifer A. *Slavery in Early Christianity.* Exp. ed. Minneapolis: Fortress, 2024 (orig. 2002).

Instone-Brewer, David. *Divorce and Remarriage in the Bible: The Social and Literary Context.* Grand Rapids: Eerdmans, 2002.

ADDRESSING MORAL CHAOS · 5:1–7:40

Jervis, L. Ann. *Paul and Time: Life in the Temporality of Christ*. Grand Rapids: Eerdmans, 2023.

Jones, Beth Felker. *Faithful: A Theology of Sex*. Grand Rapids: Zondervan, 2015. (highly accessible)

Levering, Matthew. *Engaging the Doctrine of Marriage: Human Marriage as the Image and Sacrament of the Marriage of God and Creation*. Eugene, OR: Cascade, 2020.

Loader, William. *The New Testament on Sexuality*. Grand Rapids: Eerdmans, 2012.

Rosner, Brian S. *Paul, Scripture and Ethics: A Study of 1 Corinthians 5–7*. Leiden: Brill, 1994. Repr., Grand Rapids: Baker, 1999. (technical)

Tucker, J. Brian. *"Remain in Your Calling": Paul and the Continuation of Social Identities in 1 Corinthians*. Eugene, OR: Pickwick, 2011.

Works, Carla Swafford. *The Least of These: Paul and the Marginalized*. Grand Rapids: Eerdmans, 2020. (see esp. 34–51)

Young, Stephen E. *Our Beloved Brother: Purpose and Community in Paul's Letter to Philemon*. Waco, TX: Baylor University Press, 2021.

SUMMARY OF 1 COR 5–7

In these three chapters Paul has articulated some basic principles for individual and corporate holiness between the first and second comings of Christ. These include the following:

- Belonging to God's new, holy community entails leaving the immoralities and injustices of one's former life and the pagan world behind.
- Life in Christ means having a bifocal vision: shaping present existence in light of the past (ministry, teachings, death, and resurrection of Jesus) and the future (parousia, bodily resurrection, and judgment).
- The selfish pursuit of avenging wrong in pagan courts—or anywhere else, including the church—is itself an act of injustice and a betrayal of the gospel, and yet the church must be a place that pursues and practices cruciform justice.
- Sexual behavior in particular is a matter in which sanctification must be expressed; sexual immorality endangers both the individual believer and the community.
- Believers' bodies, which will one day be raised, do not belong to believers for their indulgence but to God for God's glory, and, within marriage (in a narrower sense), to their spouses.
- God calls people from all stations of life into fellowship in the body of Christ.
- Marriage, for believers, is a permanent bond of mutuality in Christ and poten-

224

tially a witness to nonbelievers. It is neither a sin nor a simplistic solution to uncontrollable sexual urges. It is a grace-filled gift (as is celibate singleness), though it is also a distraction from total devotion to the Lord and one of the institutions that will end with the passing of this age.

REFLECTIONS AND QUESTIONS ON 1 COR 5–7 AS A WHOLE

1. It is sometimes thought that Christians must **choose between personal holiness and outreach, or between evangelization and justice.** These chapters reveal that such choices are unnecessary, indeed theologically misguided. What kinds of connections between these pairs are present in these chapters? How do these connections—or separations—manifest themselves in the church today?

2. We have seen that these chapters constitute a kind of Christian holiness code, but holiness is never realized in isolation. How do these chapters also manifest the **relationships among holiness, unity, catholicity, and apostolicity?**

8:1–14:40
ADDRESSING LITURGICAL CHAOS:
THE CROSS, WORSHIP, AND SALVATION FOR ALL
(ONE, HOLY, *CATHOLIC* CHURCH)

If pagan culture provided (and provides) many opportunities for immorality and injustice, it afforded (and affords) no fewer for idolatry and related practices. As the temple of the one true God (3:16–17) located in the midst of many other temples and their various activities, the church at Corinth found itself interacting, both directly and indirectly, with the explicitly cultic dimension of Greco-Roman culture: devotion and sacrifice to various deities. Problems arising from some dimensions of that interaction, and of the general worship life of the Corinthian community, are addressed in chapters 8–14. Within these chapters, Paul seeks to quell the liturgical chaos in Corinth with pleas for both centripetal (inwardly oriented) and centrifugal (outwardly oriented) hospitality and inclusivity, or catholicity. This catholicity is inseparable from unity, holiness, and apostolicity; they all come together in these chapters.

First Corinthians 8–14 is the crossroads of Paul's ecclesiology and his ethics. Because this section of the letter is quite lengthy (seven chapters), we will consider it in two parts: essentially chapters 8–10 (actually 8:1–11:1) and chapters 11–14 (actually 11:2–14:40). It is unfortunate that the division of the letter into chapters during the Middle Ages did not end chapter 10 with the words of 11:1, which are clearly the culmination of the argument of chapters 8–10: "Become imitators of me, as I am of the Messiah" (MJG).

Chapters 8–10 provide a double preparation for chapters 11–14, and chapters 11–14 a double response to chapters 8–10.[1] The horizontal failure of love and the vertical sin of idolatry on display in the earlier chapters are countered with calls for a catholic love and holy worship in the later ones. But chapters 8–10 are not just a setup for what follows; their own theological importance is especially clear from Paul's reuse of the themes and principles enunciated there to address a related, but different, matter at length in Romans 14:1–15:13.[2]

Several times in chapters 8–14, Paul again structures his argument in an ABA' (or chiastic) pattern. He does this in short passages, such as 10:23–11:1, and in large blocks of text, such as chapters 8–10 and chapters 12–14. This pattern suggests that Paul grants special pride of place to the fulcrum of each

---

1. Although these words are my own, I owe the basic point to Roy Ciampa.
2. See Gorman, *Romans*, 266–84, esp. 267–68.

of these arguments. This is especially the case for the larger segments, such that we must pay special attention to chapters 9 and 13.

At Corinth, the most influential people were all in favor of unbridled freedom, as we would expect (recall 6:12—"All things are permitted for me"; NRSVue). In chapters 8–14, Paul seeks a kind of order and unity to the community's liturgical life that is fully open to the Spirit and therefore fully grounded in Christ crucified, because, as we saw in chapters 1–4, the two are inseparable. Speaking as one charismatic (Spirit-filled person) to others, Paul can argue not only that freedom and *order* are compatible but also that freedom and *love* are compatible. In fact, freedom and love are not only compatible, but they are two sides of the same coin. Such liberating, resurrectionally cruciform behavior must guide each and every Spirit-filled person in Christ, and the community as a whole, in their interactions both inside and outside the church. That sort of life is at the heart of a catholic church.

8:1–11:1
Meat Associated with Idols and the Church's Mission

In 8:1–11:1, Paul and Sosthenes once again address Corinthian factionalism, and yet again the divisions affect both the church's life together and its external witness. These divisions may correspond to the parties or cliques described in chapter 1, or to the implicit divisions associated with the unholy practices addressed in chapters 5–6, or to both. But what seems to be especially the case in 8:1–11:1 and, probably, in at least some of the previously noted problems is an overarching divide between the socially and (allegedly) spiritually elite and the nonelite. The issue this time is not allegiance to leaders, or lawsuits, or sexuality, but the eating of meat ("food" in some translations) offered to, or perhaps generally associated with, idols, either in the precincts of pagan temples (the primary issue, 8:10; 10:18–21) or in private homes (10:23–30).

The issue of idolatry, like sexual immorality (recall 5:1–13; 6:9–11, 12–20; 7:1–5), was at the forefront of every Jewish ethical mind, including Paul's. This was not necessarily the case for gentile converts to the Jesus-as-Messiah-and-Lord movement, even if they had been instructed in these matters as part of their earliest formation.

Temples to various deities dotted the landscape of ancient cities such as Corinth. These temples could be found downtown, near and around the agora, or forum, as well as on the city's acropolis, as many people know because of the famed Parthenon on the acropolis in Athens. In Corinth, there was at least one temple, to Aphrodite, on its towering Acrocorinth. Near and around the agora were several other temples. The most famous, the iconic symbol of ancient Corinth, was probably originally dedicated to Apollo but later repurposed as a temple of the imperial cult. Several other temples of the imperial cult(s) were also present, including one dedicated to Octavia, sister of Augustus, and one connected with Roma, the Senate, and the emperor. There was also a sanctuary of Asclepius (an Asclepeion) and other buildings, sites, and fountains dedicated to deities.

The temples varied in size, but the larger ones generally shared the following features:

- a cult statue, as well as different sorts of gifts offered to the deity, inside the temple
- an altar, where priests offered sacrifices, in front of the temple
- a porch in the front and often also in the back
- columns on four, or sometimes two, sides
- dining areas on the side or in the back[3]

In addition, meat markets would be in the vicinity to sell the leftover sacrificial meat, since only some was actually set aside for the various deities.

Jews abhorred the practice of eating this cultic meat as idolatrous, and they were forbidden from eating it in any form anywhere: not at a sacral meal at the pagan temple; not at other occasions in the dining rooms in the temple precincts; and not at home, where additional leftovers, purchased at the temple market, might also be prepared. It appears that the early church generally expected gentile converts to avoid such meat (Acts 15:28–29; 21:25), though the issue was sometimes contested (Rev 2:14, 20).

The Corinthians are split. There is a group of self-styled possessors of knowledge (8:1, 10), brandishing their knowledge that idols do not really exist and their consequent freedom and right to eat whatever, whenever—even on the temple grounds (8:1–6, 9–11). There is also a group that Paul himself labels "weak" (8:9), people with a weak conscience or consciousness (8:7, 12) who lack the knowledge of the other group. The brothers and sisters in this group associate such meat eating with actual idolatry (8:7a). Seeing other believers consume this kind of meat, especially at a pagan temple, they might be tempted also to eat and thus (from their own perspective) to commit idolatry (8:7b–10). We will refer to the two groups neutrally as the meat eaters, or temple diners, and the non–meat eaters, or nondiners.

3. For example, the Asclepeion had three dining rooms.

Paul's response to the situation is as complex as it is creative. He packs a kind of one-two punch. His first move is to affirm the meat eaters' monotheistic theology but challenge their knowledge-based ethic of personal rights, calling instead for an ethic of others-oriented love (ch. 8). After offering himself as an example of the alternative ethic he proposes (ch. 9), he returns to the theological issue, warning the meat eaters that participation in a pagan sacral meal is in fact a kind of idolatry, a fellowship with the demonic (10:1–22). Thus he says that dining in the temple precincts is potentially (in fact, likely) spiritually injurious to others and definitely injurious to oneself. It can *cause* idolatry, and it *constitutes* idolatry.

The flow of this three-part argument reveals another chiastic structure:

A Temple dining and the salvation of your siblings: love, not rights (ch. 8)
  B Paul as example of forgoing rights (ch. 9)
A' Temple dining and your own salvation: flee idolatry (10:1–22)

This argument is followed by a brief coda (10:23–11:1) that reiterates Paul's ethical principles and grants permission, though not blanket permission, to eat meat bought at the temple market in private homes with nonbelievers; that is, in a potentially missional setting. The great importance Paul attaches to the principles and arguments developed in these chapters is evident from their being repurposed (with significant modifications for a new situation) in Rom 14.

It is no surprise that some of the key words in these chapters are related to Paul's deep concern about the temples and idolatry:

- *eidōlothyton*, "(food/meat) sacrificed to idols"—a Jewish and Christian term (8:1, 4, 7, 10; 10:19)[4]
- *hierothyton*, "meat sacrificed to a deity," the term used by others (10:28)
- *eidōleion*, "idol's temple" (8:10)
- *eidōlon*, "idol" (8:4, 7; 10:19; see also 12:2)
- *eidōlolatrēs*, "idolater" (10:7; see also 5:10, 11; 6:9)
- *eidōlolatria*, "idolatry" (10:14)

No less significant, however, is the appearance of a word family we have seen before (1:25, 27; 2:3; 4:10): "weak-":

4. Although various foods could be offered as sacrifices to deities, and thus called *eidōlothyta*, 1 Cor 8:13 indicates that meat (*kreas*) is the primary food (*brōma*) at issue in Corinth.

229

ADDRESSING LITURGICAL CHAOS

- *asthenēs*, "weak" as a noun, that is, "weak ones" (8:7, 9, 10; 9:22 [three times])
- *astheneō*, a verb used as a noun, that is, also "weak," "weak ones" (8:11, 12)

Once again Paul will display a preferential option for the powerless, specifically those he calls "the weak"—to whom he will give preference also in 12:22–26. And an important word that is critical to these chapters is *exousia* (previously used only in 7:37), often mistranslated as "freedom" or "liberty" but rightly rendered as "right" (8:9; 9:4, 5, 6, 12 [twice], 18).

In other words, although the "just-" (*dikaio-*) word family does not occur in these chapters, Paul sees the unqualified assertion of rights and the failure of love as another example of Corinthian *adikia* (injustice), this time explicitly toward the weak. In addition to the "weak-" word family, Paul also once again uses familial language: *adelphos* appears four times in 8:11–13.[5] That is, Paul is speaking about inappropriate power relations among siblings; *it is the language of an extreme form of family dysfunction to the point of severe damage and possible destruction.*

8:1–13. The Problem of Idol Meat and Paul's Initial Solution

Addressing a new issue ("Now concerning"; 8:1), probably also revealed to Paul in the letter he received, the apostle begins by naming and challenging the position of some Corinthians who are eating in certain temple precincts, assured of their knowledge and hence their right to do so, without considering the potential effect of their behavior on others. Chapter 8 identifies the Corinthian situation, the attitude and practice of some Corinthians, and Paul's theological argument for a different attitude and practice.

8:1–6. Slogan, Counterslogan, and Agreement

In the first half of the chapter, Paul does three things. He names the presenting problem (consuming idol meat), identifies with slogan and counterslogan the core issue (love versus knowledge), and recites the shared belief (one God, one Lord) that is central to this chapter and also to chapter 10.

---

5. Unfortunately, few translations actually render all four (if any) occurrences as "brother(s)" or "brother(s) or sister(s)."

8:1-3. Knowledge and Love

Following the pattern devised in chapter 6, Paul begins chapter 8 by quoting what appears to be a Corinthian slogan, "All of us possess knowledge," or perhaps even "*We know* that all of us possess knowledge" (emphasis added), and refuting it with a counterslogan: "Knowledge puffs up, but love builds up" (8:1a). The "know" word family appears six times just in vv. 1–3. Paul does not specify what the Corinthians say they know, but that will become clear in 8:4. For now, Paul's point is that knowledge is different from, indeed inferior to, love. Knowledge "enhances status."[6] "Love builds up"—that is, it edifies others; it is other-centered and community-oriented, rather than self-centered.[7] As Susan Eastman says, "The short phrase 'love builds up' thus summarizes the thrust of all Paul's exhortations regarding the flourishing of the church."[8]

The earlier language of being "puffed up," meaning arrogant (4:6, 18, 19; 5:2), and especially its later reappearance in the love chapter—it is the last word in 13:4—reinforce the knowledge-love antithesis. A life governed by absolute certainty about one's knowledge, especially theological knowledge, leaves little room for humility, much less for concern about others who have a different perspective. In this instance, the Corinthians represented by the slogan in v. 1, the meat eaters (probably the socially and spiritually elite), assume that everyone knows what they supposedly know. (That is not the case, as the chapter will show.) Paul refers to such a person as one "who possesses knowledge" (8:10), meaning something like "a know-it-all."

Ironically, those who *think* they know actually do not possess the knowledge they think they have because they have not known rightly (8:2; cf. Gal 6:3). The Greek actually says, "as it is necessary to know," or "as one ought to know" (see NIV, NAB, ESV). Knowledge, in other words, carries with it a moral responsibility for its possession and use. And its first responsibility, even before it can be other-centered, is to be God-centered (8:3). The most fundamental human knowledge is not a relationship with facts or truth claims but a relationship with God, and it is a relationship of love. And to love God means being in the wonderful but also humbling position of being intimately known by God. Perhaps Paul had Ps 139 in mind:

---

6. McKnight, *Second Testament*.

7. In 8:10, Paul will use the same Greek verb, *oikodomeō* ("build up"), sarcastically to characterize the potential consequences of the situation at hand—building up people to practice idolatry.

8. Eastman, *Oneself in Another*, 105.

O LORD, you have searched me and *known* me.

You *know* when I sit down and when I rise up; you *discern* my
thoughts from far away.

You *search out* my path and my lying down, and *are acquainted* with
all my ways.

Even before a word is on my tongue, O LORD, you *know* it
completely.

You hem me in, behind and before, and lay your hand upon me.

Such *knowledge* is too wonderful for me; it is so high that I cannot
attain it. (Ps 139:1–6; emphasis added)

Paul does not mean in 8:3 that love *generates* God's knowledge of us, but rather that love for God is evidence that one is known by God (see also Gal 4:9). A love relationship with God/the Lord (see also 2:9; 16:22) exists by God's/Christ's initiative.[9] "That is the syntax of salvation," comments Richard Hays eloquently.[10]

This love relationship with God, this knowledge of God, always remains imperfect, but it can also be *dangerous* if it is not a humble knowledge, and if it does not issue in love for others. Love, not knowledge, is the primary element in any relationship with both God and others, as the double love commandment—which undergirds these verses—also affirms.

If God's thoughts are not our thoughts (Isa 55:8–9), then humility about knowing anything, and most especially about knowing God, is not only prudent, but it is possibly lifesaving. Knowledge is "not only imperfect, but also injurious, unless there were another thing joined together with it"—namely, love.[11] That said, some theological claims are so basic as to be nonnegotiable.

8:4–6. One God, One Lord

With the critical perspective about the meaning and morality of knowledge in mind, Paul returns in 8:4 to the specific topic at hand, meat sacrificed to idols,[12] and to two more quotations from the Corinthians: "no idol in the cosmos [really exists]" and "no God [exists] but one" (MJG). That is, the Corinthi-

9. See also Rom 5:5, 8; 8:28, 35–39; 2 Cor 5:14; 13:13; Gal 2:20; Eph 2:4; 5:2, 25; 6:24; 1 Thess 1:4; 2 Thess 2:16; 3:5.

10. Hays, *First Corinthians*, 138.

11. John Chrysostom, *Homilies on 1 Corinthians* 20.2.

12. As noted earlier, 8:13 implies that meat is the main concern, though other foods could also be offered to the gods.

ans deny the existence of idols and affirm the one God of Jews and Christians. The latter quotation is an echo of the first words of the Shema—"Hear, O Israel: The LORD is our God, the LORD alone" (Deut 6:4 NRSVue)—and the former phrase its corollary.[13] The Corinthians have clearly been taught some basic scriptural truths.

Although the "we know" of 8:4 could be part of the Corinthians' slogan, the phrase more likely indicates Paul's agreement with them. But even if "we know" represents the Corinthians' voice, Paul in fact shares the theological knowledge the meat eaters possess. Of course, there are many *so-called* gods and lords all around Corinth and the rest of the world (8:5), but "for us" there is but one God and one Lord (8:6).

The meaning of "for us" is not simply subjective, as if there are merely two opposite opinions: "they think that, but we think this." Rather, this is knowledge that is true knowledge, nonnegotiable. Because it really is true that there is only one God and one Lord, Jews and Christians don't worship other (so-called) deities. Therefore, the Christ cult is exclusive (as Paul will say in ch. 10). But this is true knowledge that is known *rightly* only when it is used *lovingly*, not as a hammer to beat others over the head or as a badge of honor to humiliate them.

In 8:6, then, Paul returns to the Shema that he and the Corinthians agree about, now in order to give it a particularly christological reinterpretation. The Greek Bible he knows does not contain the name YHWH in the Shema, but it has the words *kyrios ho theos hēmōn kyrios heis estin*, or "The Lord our God is one Lord" (NETS).[14] Paul takes this Greek version of the basic Jewish affirmation of YHWH as the one God and reads it, in light of Christ, dyadically as referring to one *theos* and one *kyrios*. Instead of "many gods and lords," there is but one God and one Lord, and instead of one "person" who is both God and Lord, there is

- "one God, the Father," the source ("from whom") of all creation and the goal, the telos ("for whom") of our existence, and
- "one Lord, Jesus Christ," the agent ("through whom") of all creation and the agent ("through whom") of our existence.[15]

---

13. The precise translation of the Hebrew in Deut 6:4 has been debated; see below for how the Greek Bible (LXX) rendered it. In the context of Deut, the emphasis is clearly on YHWH as the sole deity: "there is no other" (Deut 4:34, 39), and Paul retains that emphasis while reinterpreting it.

14. Or perhaps, "The Lord is our God; the Lord is one" (MJG).

15. See also Col 1:15–17.

Structurally, the text has an elegance of simple parallelism that looks like this (with the extra English words added in translations, for clarity, removed):

But for us	and
one God, the Father	one Lord, Jesus Messiah
from whom all things	through whom all things
and we for him	and we through him

The interpretive move that Paul makes in this text has almost certainly not been invented by him; rather, he is echoing the perspective and especially the worship of other early Christian communities who have been calling Jesus "Lord" since the start of the movement.[16] Paul's letters embody this conviction in many ways, not least in the opening words of his letters: "Grace and peace to you from God the Father and the Lord Jesus Christ." This does not mean that Paul affirms two lords or gods. Rather, Paul is affirming what some have called "christological monotheism," the inclusion of Jesus in the identity, and thus in the worship, of the one God. There is therefore no competition between the Father and the Son; each one, each divine person, is recognized by Christians as included in the Shema, and yet each can be identified by prepositions as having distinct actions that can be attributed, or appropriated (the technical term), to that specific person: "from and for" for God the Father, and "through" for Jesus the Lord.[17]

8:7–13. Knowledge, Rights, and Cruciform Love

The temple diners and Paul may confidently know that the polytheists' gods and lords do not actually exist, but some of the recent converts at Corinth are not so sure (8:7a). Why not? Because they have come from a culture (and perhaps a personal life) of regular meat eating in the temple precincts as an aspect of actual devotion to actual deities, and they cannot break that habit (8:7b). For them, eating idol food is inherently participating in the deity's cult. This is not due to a weak "conscience," as nearly all translations say in 8:7b, but

---

16. On this, see especially Larry W. Hurtado, *Lord Jesus Christ: Devotion to Jesus in Earliest Christianity* (Grand Rapids: Eerdmans, 2005). For a different view of 8:6, see Thomas Gaston and Andrew Perry, "Christological Monotheism: 1 Cor 8.6 and the Shema," *Horizons in Biblical Theology* 39 (2017): 176–96.

17. A similar relational dynamic that includes all three persons of the Trinity may be seen in 12:1–11.

to a weak consciousness, or self-awareness, or sensibilities—they do not have the right knowledge that could keep them from defilement.[18]

The Corinthian "weak," then, do not have a *weak* but a *robust* conscience, unlike the temple diners. Their weakness is not a moral infirmity but (perhaps) a matter of Christian immaturity, and yet they are not the most spiritually immature people in Corinth. That honor goes to the meat eaters who are flaunting their knowledge without love. Some interpreters have suggested that the meat eaters feel a need to participate in temple banquets in order to maintain status with peers or patrons. Paul would see this as pursuing selfish interests at the expense of others, rather than practicing love, and (at least implicitly) compromising their Christian witness.

In 8:8, there are two sentences that could be those of Paul, or the meat eaters, or a combination—one sentence coming from each. The NRSV and NRSVue, alone among English translations, attribute the first line to the Corinthians by placing it in quotation marks: "'Food will not bring us close to God.'" English translations universally imply that the second sentence—"We are no worse off if we do not eat, and no better off if we do" (NRSV)—comes from Paul. But is that correct?

We do know that Paul, echoing Jesus, believes all meat is the creation of the one God and is itself good (10:26; cf. Mark 7:19b). He therefore does not believe that eating or abstaining from food per se affects one's relationship with God (see Rom 14), "for the kingdom of God is not food and drink" (Rom 14:17). Thus Paul *might* actually say all of v. 8: that food will not bring us closer to God and that eating is essentially a nonessential, as the Stoics would say (i.e., it is one of the *adiaphora*, or matters that don't matter).

Yet it is more likely that all of v. 8 expresses Corinthian attitudes. The words restate the Corinthian separation of eating from spirituality we saw in 6:13 and the consequent apathy about it. Paul's view is different: this matter of eating *does* matter—not, at least for now, because it involves *food* but because it involves *people*, and specifically brothers and sisters in Christ. Moreover, it also involves what Paul perceives as a question of attitude, and specifically the temple diners' conviction that they have an *unqualified right* to eat this food in these places.

We hear Paul's voice again in v. 9. The key word Paul uses in that verse is *exousia*, usually mistranslated as "freedom" or "liberty," but the context makes it certain that Paul means "authority" or "right."[19] Richard Hays calls *exousia*

---

18. See Thiselton, *First Epistle*, 640–44.

19. The basic meaning of *exousia* is "right," "power," or "authority." Here in 8:9 the

ADDRESSING LITURGICAL CHAOS

the Corinthians' "buzzword."[20] This alleged right is Paul's concern in 8:9, and it suggests that no matter whose words are cited in 8:8, the conclusion the meat eaters have drawn from the position expressed in those words is highly problematic: a lifestyle grounded in personal autonomy and individual rights—entitlement. This takes us back to the beginning of the chapter.

The counterslogan in 8:1 summarizes Paul's whole attitude toward the *behavior*, or ethic, of the Corinthian knowledgeable meat eaters. The right way of acting that the Corinthians must exercise is the one revealed in the crucified Christ: not focused on knowledge but on love for others, expressed as actions for their edification. An ethic grounded in "knowledge" focuses on individual *freedom* and the exercise of one's *rights* that are thought to derive from that freedom. An ethic of cruciform love, on the other hand, seeks to build up the other, taking account of the impact of one's behavior on others. This is, paradoxically, true freedom.

Negatively, Paul's alternative ethic means not becoming a "stumbling block" (*proskomma*) to the weak (8:9), who, if they see "you" eating (lit., "reclining [at table]") in the idol's temple, might be "edified" or "built up" (NAB) to practice idolatry (8:10).[21] Paul uses the same verb (*oikodomeō*; "build up") as in 8:1, only in a sarcastic way. *This is the wrong kind of edification!* These people are one's siblings in Christ (8:11–12), brothers and sisters for whom Christ died! As in 6:1–11, this is also a family matter.[22] One might expect outsiders who fear the repercussions of anyone not honoring the civic deities to pressure new or weak believers—emotionally, socially, economically, or even physically—to return to their former cultic practices. But no one expects what is essentially betrayal from a brother or sister.

Actually, the act would be even graver than betrayal. To harm weak siblings

---

connotation is inherent or even inalienable right—the possession of power and authority that derives from the possession of some status. The ESV has "right"; NIV, "rights." Unfortunately, "liberty" is more common: it renders *exousia* in 8:9 in NRSV, NRSVue, NAB, NET, and many more, while others have "freedom." Paul knows the word for "freedom," *eleutheria* (see 10:29), but does not use it here. He will speak of being "free" (*eleutheros*) in ch. 9 (9:1, 19) only in conjunction with the ongoing *exousia* theme (9:4, 5, 6, 12 [twice], 18). Paul sees freedom as the source of rights but will specifically affirm that freedom is something one sometimes exercises, paradoxically, by lovingly enslaving oneself in the giving up of one or more rights.

20. Hays, *First Corinthians*, 150.

21. Paul makes the same point, with the same stumbling-block metaphor, in Rom 14:13, 20–21. Similar is Jesus' warning in Mark 9:42 (= Matt 18:6): "As for whoever causes these little ones who believe in me to trip and fall into sin, it would be better for them to have a huge stone hung around their necks and to be thrown into the lake" (CEB). See also Lev 19:14.

22. Gk. *adelphos* ("brother," "sibling") occurs in 8:11, 12, 13 (2×).

236

is to *destroy* them (8:11; recall 3:17) by means of one's so-called knowledge.[23] If they resume their previous idolatry, they will no longer be participating in Christ, the locus of salvation (see 10:1–22). Knowledge, used improperly, has become an instrument of death. This is sin, *mortal* sin, so to speak. "Your" behavior—note how personal Paul gets with the singular pronoun (*se*) in 8:10–11—is spiritually killing someone(s) for whom Christ was killed. And inasmuch as these brothers and sisters are members of Christ's body (see ch. 12, esp. 12:12; cf. 6:15), sinning against them is sinning against Christ (8:12).

The notion of sinning against Christ's body in this way has several senses. Causing mortal harm to another "member" of the body is an attack on the body itself as a whole—a process of dismembering. But since the attacker is also a member of the body, he or she is engaging in self-harm as well as other-harm. Moreover, the "other," the "weak" one who may be harmed, is not just a member of a social entity referred to metaphorically as "the body of Christ." The sin against such a person is not *like* a sin against Christ but is *in fact* a sin against Christ because—and only because—that person is in Christ and Christ is in that person. In this sense, that person is Christ—as Jesus himself taught his disciples in the parable of the sheep and the goats (Matt 25:31–46). Since an attack on the weak may be spiritually fatal, in effect (Paul might say) those guilty of this kind of sin are again crucifying the Son of God (cf. Heb 6:6).

Positively, charismatic cruciform love (as the alternative to other-harm/Christ-harm/self-harm) means forgoing the exercise of a right for the welfare of the other, especially when the other is, or is perceived to be, "weak." This basic Christian Spirit-ual practice derives directly from the content of the gospel itself, and indeed from the powerfully weak actions of both God and the apostle narrated in 1:18–2:5. The sort of life that is willing to forsake rights out of love for others is what Paul means to encourage by offering himself as an example of what he would do: become a voluntary vegetarian for life (8:13).[24]

Of course, this assertion is not really a statement about the value of vegetarianism per se; it is a statement about the missional call to a cruciform life that is life-giving—resurrectional—not only for those who benefit from such a life but also for those who live such a life. Moreover, such a life is not just for Paul, his colleagues like Sosthenes, and other apostles but for all. The explicit call to become imitators of Christ by becoming imitators of Paul will appear in 11:1, but it is already implicitly issued here. This kind of life is truly catholic, or universally oriented toward the welfare of all.

---

23. Again, Paul makes the same sort of point in Rom 14:15, 20.

24. Cf. Rom 14:13b, 20; Mark 9:42 and parallels; Lev 19:14.

Summary

The current behavior of the meat eaters, as Paul sees it, is totally and inappropriately self-centered. It shows no love, no concern for the spiritual health and well-being of other brothers or sisters (the non–meat eaters) and for the grave temptation ("stumbling block") that the behavior poses to these weaker believers. In fact, the unloving exercise of this knowledge and right becomes— even if the knowledge is correct and the right legitimate—*sin*, indeed *mortal* sin. After all, Paul has already instructed the Corinthians about God's siding with the weak in the cross (1:18–31), and he will tell the Romans that Christ died for us when *all* were weak (Rom 5:6). Ironically, the strong Corinthian meat eaters demonstrate their moral weakness—their sin—in the very act of exercising their alleged strength.

The gravity of this situation leads Paul to issue a challenge in the form of a claim: *he would forgo the exercise of an inalienable right for the good of others.* In so doing, he is not only siding with the weak, but he is effectively becoming weak (see 4:10; 9:22). And he demonstrates the credibility of his claim, while offering a living example of such love and such strength in weakness, in the autobiographical chapter that follows.

Both that next chapter, as we will see, and this one display the need for self-giving love rather than the exercise of rights if that exercise will harm, rather than help, others spiritually:

> - Although [x] you possess the right to eat whatever the one true God has created,
> - do not [y] exercise that right if it might wound the weak, or even cause their spiritual destruction, for that would be unloving, unchristlike, and unpauline,
> - but rather [z] be willing, in love, to refrain from using that right and even never to eat meat again in order to prevent anyone from falling away from Christ.

This is catholic, Christoform neighbor love, community concern, and salvific intentionality.

Reflections and Questions for 8:1–13

Spiritual, Pastoral, Missional, and Theological Reflections

1. In what is an astounding theological move in this chapter (continued in ch. 9), **Paul denied not the existence of rights (or "authority"—*exousia*) per se but the absolute right to use rights.** What Paul does deny is the propriety of any

behavior that fails to consider the effect of its action on others, particularly actions that could seriously endanger the well-being and even salvation of another or others. Since love builds up, while knowledge puffs up, Paul urges believers who *know* to be believers who *love*. There are times when, for the good of others (and ultimately oneself, too), rights must not be exercised.

At the same time, **Paul's position can never be taken as a legitimation of the denial of basic human rights to others**, especially the poor and marginalized or those perceived as the enemy. To do so would be a complete repudiation of everything we have seen in this letter, particularly God's preferential option for the powerless. The issue for Paul is not the *existence* of rights but the *abuse* of rights, even the *idolization* of rights.

2. Christians in the West or Global North, especially in the United States, live in **a culture of rights.** In the United States, the absolute right to abortion, primarily on the political left, and the absolute right to gun ownership and use, especially on the political right, are part and parcel of the cultural ethos. (For abortion, see the reflections on 6:12–20.)

In an essay entitled "Can a Christian Own a Gun?"[25] New Testament scholar David Lincicum has argued that the gun is "an instrument of cultural formation"; that buying a gun is "a sort of ritual of initiation"; and that a gun "transforms one into a new category of person, 'a gun-owner,'" such that the threat of limiting guns in any way is a threat to an owner's "very sense of self" (126).

Lincicum contends that "the gun [specifically as a means of self-defense or defense of others] is a temptation to arrogate life-destroying power to the wielder and should be resisted by those who follow in allegiance to a crucified Messiah" (116). He grounds his argument above all in the New Testament's call to imitate Christ in the way of the cross (119–20), and in that vein also in Paul's message in 1 Corinthians and Romans. Paraphrasing Rom 14:15, which echoes 1 Cor 8:11–13 and 9:12, Lincicum avers (124) that Paul might say this to American Christians: "For if, for the sake of owning a gun, your brother or sister is grieved, you are no longer walking according to love; do not for the sake of mere gun ownership destroy that one for whom Christ died." (See further reflections along these lines after the commentary on chapter 9.)

3. In Asian (and, for example, Asian American) contexts, this passage has often raised the question of **ancestor worship, or ancestor veneration/reverence**

---

25. David Lincicum, "Can a Christian Own a Gun?," in *God and Guns: The Bible against American Gun Culture*, ed. Chrisopher B. Hays and C. L. Crouch (Louisville: Westminster John Knox, 2021), 113–28. Page numbers are indicated in parentheses. A popular version of his argument is "Do Not Destroy the One for Whom Christ Died," *Presbyterian Outlook* 205/6 (2023): 22–27.

(which is what it is for most people today, according to scholars). One of the leading experts on this topic is K. K. Yeo, whose influential work is worthy of note for this matter and beyond.[26] Yeo's basic position on such culturally sensitive issues is that they must be engaged with both **knowledge and love**, the latter requiring openness and a desire to find common ground. Furthermore, according to Yeo and others, while the practice of such customs can spring from both positive (e.g., love, respect) and negative (e.g., fear) sentiments, ultimately the Christian gospel affirms the former and provides an alternative to the latter. The challenge for Western Christians may be to note distinctive cultural practices that require a similar kind of sensitive blending of knowledge and love.

Questions for Those Who Read, Teach, and Preach

1. How might Paul's response to the issue of eating meat associated with idols inform a contemporary theological understanding of such topics as freedom, rights, and love?
2. In what ways can the lack of self-giving, self-restraining love described in this chapter occur in the church today?
3. How can Christians affirm the existence and significance of rights, especially for the weak and marginalized, without allowing them to become disconnected from the Spirit-ual practice of resurrectional cruciformity?
4. How does Paul's valuing of weakness challenge the human/American idolization of strength and power? How might we revise our assessments of the value, competency, or perspective of people our communities or culture judge to be weak?
5. In sum, what does this passage urge the church to believe (faith), do (love), and anticipate (hope)?

For Further Reading

Capes, David B. *The Divine Christ: Paul, the Lord Jesus, and the Scriptures of Israel.* Grand Rapids: Baker Academic, 2018.

Eastman, Susan Grove. "Love's Folly: Love and Knowledge in 1 Corinthians." Pages 96–109 in *Oneself in Another: Participation and Personhood in Pauline Theology.* Eugene, OR: Cascade, 2023.

26. See, e.g., K. K. [Khiok-Khng] Yeo, "The Rhetorical Hermeneutic of 1 Corinthians 8 and Chinese Ancestor Worship," *Biblical Interpretation* 2 (1994): 294–311 (an essay that summarizes a longer work and has itself been reprinted elsewhere).

Edwards, Dennis R. *Humility Illuminated: The Biblical Path Back to Christian Character*. Downers Grove, IL: InterVarsity Press, 2023. (highly accessible)

Fotopoulos, John. *Food Offered to Idols in Roman Corinth: A Social-Rhetorical Reconsideration of 1 Corinthians 8:1–11:1*. Tübingen: Mohr Siebeck, 2003. (technical)

Hurtado, Larry W. *Destroyer of the Gods: Early Christian Distinctiveness in the Roman World*. Waco, TX: Baylor University Press, 2016.

———. *Lord Jesus Christ: Devotion to Jesus in Earliest Christianity*. Grand Rapids: Eerdmans, 2005. (technical)

9:1–27. THE EXAMPLE OF APOSTOLIC CRUCIFORMITY AND SALVIFIC INTENTIONALITY WITHIN THE CHURCH

When Paul writes autobiographically, he writes paradigmatically. On the surface, 1 Cor 9 sounds like a self-defense of apostolic rights, which in part it is. Paul uses the Corinthian buzzword *exousia* ("right") from 8:9 six times (9:4, 5, 6, 12 [twice], 18).[27] But the fundamental purpose of Paul's assertion of rights is to show that he, like the Corinthian elite, had legitimate rights that could be deliberately suppressed as an act of cruciform love and, ultimately, of true freedom (cf. 1 Thess 2:1–12). In this chapter, with a flood of rhetorical questions, Paul accomplishes the following:

- establishes his apostleship and apostolic rights (9:1–14, minus 12b)
- narrates his renunciation of them as a fundamental part of his apostolic identity and Christlike modus operandi (9:15–18 plus 12b)
- explains his two motives for doing so—to win others through Christlike freedom and love (9:19–23), and to ensure his own participation in the eschatological victory (9:24–27)
- implies that he does all of this as an example to the Corinthians of both cruciform love and salvific intentionality[28]

Within the larger argument of 8:1–11:1, Paul offers himself as an example with respect to both internal and external concerns, or what missiologists sometimes refer to as the centripetal (inner-oriented) and centrifugal (outward-oriented) aspects of mission. Centripetally, his missional aim is to prevent the Corinthians from doing anything that might cause a fellow (espe-

---

27. See Hays, *First Corinthians*, 150, for the term "buzzword."

28. Barram, "Pauline Mission as Salvific Intentionality"; Goode, *Salvific Intentionality in 1 Corinthians*.

ADDRESSING LITURGICAL CHAOS   · 8:1–14:40

cially weaker) believer to leave Christ and return to idolatry (esp. 8:1–13). Centrifugally, his missional goal is to prevent the Corinthians from doing anything that might give someone reason not to leave idolatry behind in order to enter Christ and the church (esp. 10:23–11:1). Only with such a two-dimensional missional vision can the church be truly catholic, and apostolic, seeking with Paul to save "as many as possible" (9:19 NAB).

Chapter 9 begins with Paul's apologia for, or self-defense of, his apostleship and its corollary rights. But it moves organically and fairly quickly toward an explanation of his decision not to exercise those rights—à la Christ.

9:1–14. Paul's Apostleship: Apostolic Freedom and Rights

Was Paul a legitimate apostle? Was his modus operandi of self-support by manual labor (described later in this passage), rather than receiving payment from his students or support from a patron—like a normal teacher or philosopher— appropriate? Did his overall demeanor make him trustworthy and credible? None of these questions received a rousing yes from the Corinthian community as a whole. Paul was being criticized and judged (9:3, and recall 4:1–6).

To some, especially any elite in the community, his manual labor as a preacher-teacher would have been an embarrassment, a matter of public shame—like a message of divine humility, self-enslavement, and crucifixion. Cicero, for instance, speaks representatively for the elite by referring to "craftsmen, shopkeepers, and all such dregs of the cities." He declares, "Unbecoming to a gentleman . . . and vulgar are the means of livelihood of all hired workmen whom we pay for mere manual labor, not for artistic skill; for in their case the very wages they receive are a pledge of their slavery."[29]

The situation for Paul only grew worse by the time he wrote 2 Corinthians, in which he has to finally go into a full-blown defense of his apostolic credentials, especially his overall weakness, including his self-humbling by working with his hands (see 2 Cor 10–13).[30] Although the main purpose of 1 Cor 9 is to offer his ministerial modus operandi as an example for the Corinthians, Paul also uses it to establish the legitimacy of his apostolic existence and the call to that apostleship announced all the way back in 1:1.

---

29. Cicero, *Pro Flacco* (*In Defense of Flaccus*) 18 (MJG) and *De officiis* (*On Duties*) 1.150 (Miller, LCL, slightly alt.).

30. See esp. 2 Cor 10:1, 8–10; 11:5–11, 22–33; 12:5–10, 13, 15, but also parts of 2 Cor 1–7.

242

9:1-2. Paul's Freedom and Apostleship

The chapter's first two verses are steeped in first-person-singular language: "I" and "my." As in 1:13, in 9:1 Paul employs rhetorical questions, four in number this time, and all expecting an affirmative response according to the rules of Greek grammar. He cleverly begins by asserting his own freedom—a freedom he never renounces—and thereby identifies his common status with the meat eaters and others in Corinth boasting of their freedom. But his freedom is also unique, because it is apostolic freedom. And Paul is nothing if not an apostle (1:1, 17; 4:9; 15:9).

The two proofs of his apostleship offered here are his having seen the resurrected Lord Jesus (9:1a; see also 15:8-11; Acts 22:17-18; 26:16) and his having fathered the Corinthian church (9:1b-2; cf. 4:15). The Corinthian believers are the "seal" (9:2), the proof, of his apostolic call, his having been commissioned by Christ to found new communities of gentiles and Jews alike.[31] Paul, as he often does, emphasizes that both his apostolic ministry and his very apostolic identity are "in the Lord" (9:1, 2; cf. 4:17)—the same kind of phrase that characterizes the Corinthians (e.g., 1:2, 4, 30; 3:1; 4:10, 15) and all Christian believers. Yet with apostleship come certain rights, for which Paul gives a brief defense in 9:3-14 (minus the parenthesis in 9:12b) to those who would judge him.

9:3-14. An Apologia: Paul's Apostolic Rights

Paul begins the defense (v. 3; Gk. *apologia*) of his apostolic rights, against his critics, by once again employing rhetorical questions, indeed a long series of them in rapid-fire succession. But now the language moves from "I" to "we." The first three questions (9:4-6) seek to establish, from apostolic precedent and practice, two basic rights for himself and his co-apostle Barnabas:[32]

1. to financial support especially in the form of "food and drink" (9:4, 6 and further developed in 9:7-12a, 13-14)
2. to spousal companionship on mission trips—literally "a sister-wife" (*adelphēn gynaika*; 9:5)[33]

---

31. Cf. 2 Cor 2:2-3.

32. For the relationship between Paul and Barnabas and their joint ministry, see Acts 9:27; 11:19-30; 12:25; 13:1-15:41; Gal 2:1-13.

33. That is, a "Christian" (NAB)—a believing wife.

ADDRESSING LITURGICAL CHAOS
·8:1–14:40

The first right (food and drink) receives the lion's share of attention because it is directly relevant to the Corinthian issue addressed in 8:1–11:1. The latter right (spousal companionship) is of little relevance to that issue, though it does reinforce his position in chapter 7 that marriage is a blessing, not a sin. But the main point in 9:4 is that Paul and company are equal to other apostles (cf. 9:12a), and that their apostolic rights extend beyond economics.[34] Most importantly, the word "right" is taken directly out of the Corinthians' own idiom and playbook (see 8:9), and, as noted above, it is used in this chapter six times (9:4, 5, 6, 12 [twice], 18).

Next Paul yet again uses rhetorical questions, combined with the teaching of Moses and Jesus, to offer three warrants for his right to financial support for meals and other expenses:

- "human authority" (9:8a) or common practice, both secular and religious
- the law (9:8b)
- the command of Jesus (9:14)

It is clear that Paul wants to emphasize this right to support as strongly as he possibly can.

Like a soldier, an apostle does not pay his own way, and like a vineyard planter or shepherd, he benefits from his labor (9:7). This sort of normal secular practice is enunciated as a religious principle in Deut 25:4, Paul says, interpreting (in good rabbinic fashion) the prohibition of ox-muzzling as a word about apostolic rights as well as animal rights (9:8–10; cf. 1 Tim 5:18). Here Paul reveals perhaps his most basic principle of scriptural interpretation: that all Scripture was written "for our sake" (9:10a; cf. 10:11; Rom 15:4).

Thus sowing "spiritual good" should reap some "material benefits," and specifically from those among whom the spiritual sowing has occurred (9:10b–11; cf. 2 Tim 2:6).[35] This image builds on the agricultural analogy used in 3:5–9,

---

34. The list of those having the right to bring their wives along is interesting: the other apostles, the Lord's brothers (see, e.g., Matt 13:55; Mark 3:31–35; John 2:12; Gal 1:19), and Cephas (Peter). Cephas is the only one named, probably because he is personally known, somehow, to the church, and he is mentioned in the letter three other times (1:12; 3:22; 15:5). Perhaps the Corinthians even hosted Cephas and his wife. James, also named in 15:7, would be among the Lord's brothers. Since Barnabas is implicitly a named apostle here (v. 6), and in 15:5–7 Paul seems to distinguish "the Twelve" from "all the apostles," the apostles discussed here are clearly not equivalent to the Twelve (see also Rom 16:7 and perhaps 1 Cor 4:9).

35. See the similar argument in Rom 15:26–27 for participation in the Jerusalem collection.

244

even using the same verb, "plant" (*phyteuō*). The specific image of planting a vineyard (v. 7) suggests that Paul sees his work in continuity with the scriptural designation of God's people as God's vineyard.[36] If others (Apollos? Cephas?) have exercised this rightful claim to financial support vis-à-vis the Corinthians, why not also Paul (and Barnabas), asks Paul in 9:12a.

A further illustration of this principle of financial and food support is provided by the priests in the Jewish temple (9:13).[37] The final authoritative word comes from Jesus himself in 9:14, an echo of the mission teaching preserved in Matt 10:10 and Luke 10:7: laborers deserve food/pay. (Some of Paul's detractors might say he is disobeying Jesus by not taking support. Paul could argue, however, that the Lord's command lays a nonnegotiable responsibility on those who would be giving, not receiving, support.) Paul's inherent, inalienable right as an apostle is grounded in the highest and most self-evident authorities.

"*Nevertheless. . . .*" Paul's great interruption to all the assertions about his apostolic right to support appears first in 9:12b before its development beginning in 9:15. He has not used this right and is not seeking to exercise it now. Rather, Paul (with his colleagues; 9:12b) has refrained from using the right so as not to create any obstacle for the spread of the gospel (9:12b; cf. 8:9, 13; Acts 20:33-35). Instead, Paul implies, as he reminded the Thessalonians, too, they labored "night and day, so that we might not burden any of you while we proclaimed to you the gospel of God."[38] From Paul's perspective, this practice was an act of love: the phrase "we endure everything" (v. 12, NAB; *panta stegomen*) is precisely how Paul will describe love in chapter 13: love "endures all things" (13:7; *panta stegei*). As we will see more fully in 9:19, this is Christlike, cruciform love.

That is, Paul looks back, but he also looks forward—he lives and thinks bifocally. Both here in v. 12 and later in v. 18, Paul alludes to his own eschatological framework from chapter 7: not to fully use the things of this world (7:31). Living within this framework produces love, with the ultimate goal of sharing the gospel by embodying the gospel, and by not getting in the way of that powerful, dynamic good news. Any potential critics, as well as the meat eaters, need to know and embrace this motive: maintaining the integrity of the gospel and seeking the salvation of others.[39]

---

36. E.g., Isa 5:1-7; Ps 80:8-10. Cf. Mark 12:1-12 and parallels; John 15:1-8.

37. See, e.g., Lev 6:14-18; Num 18:1-19, 29-32; Deut 18:1-8.

38. 1 Thess 2:9; cf. 2 Thess 3:8-9.

39. Paul did indeed have his critics about this practice, and he therefore defends it,

ADDRESSING LITURGICAL CHAOS · 8:1–14:40

9:15–27. Christlike, Missional Accommodation as Freedom and Love

Since embodying the gospel is critical to sharing the gospel, Paul now moves from a defense of apostolic rights to a self-description of his ministry, unpacking v. 12b. In doing so, he leaves behind the general principles and wider apostolic perspective of 9:3–14 and returns to the first-person-singular language of 9:1–2. But he also concludes this section with a metaphor that is applicable not only to himself but also to all with ears to hear.

9:15–18. Paul's Sense of Obligation and Boast

In 9:15, Paul restates his personal decision to forgo his right to financial aid. His decision not to accept support while evangelizing in Corinth (and, implicitly, elsewhere), with its consequent lifestyle, has now become Paul's "ground for boasting" (9:15) and his "reward" (9:18). He would rather *die* than be deprived of this boast (9:15), so no one is going to deprive him of it—literally "empty [*kenōsei*] his boast." *This is not hyperbole.* Paul's honor is at stake. The "empty" word family is a critical one in this letter: the cross and resurrection, the very heart of the gospel—and the faith, life, and preaching associated with that display of divine grace—must never be emptied. To prevent this sort of emptying of the gospel requires, in Paul's view, his life of self-emptying.

Paul has freely chosen this lifestyle, this modus operandi, this basis for boasting, but to evangelize has been given to him as an obligation (9:16), as a "stewardship" (NAB, ESV) with which he has been entrusted (9:17; cf. 4:1–2). That is, the Lord has charged him to minister, and he would be a poor steward of the gospel and displeasing to his Lord (that is the sense of the word "woe") if he did otherwise (9:16). Paul's self-description is reminiscent of the prophet Jeremiah's: "within me there is something like a burning fire shut up in my bones" (Jer 20:9).

His "reward," or pay (*misthos*), Paul says, is to evangelize "free of charge," not making use of the very right he has (9:18); his reward is to accept no reward (from humans)—though there will be a final divine reward for him if he is faithful (9:24–27). Explicitly echoing 9:12 and 7:31, and alluding to 8:9–13, Paul declares that he practices what he preaches about not making full use of normal things and standard rights. As an apostle, then, he has no choice but

---

adamantly, in 2 Cor 11:5–15. Interestingly, especially in light of 1 Cor 9:14, when Paul briefly describes his practice in Acts, he quotes a rather famous but otherwise unattested saying of Jesus, "It is more blessed to give than to receive" (Acts 20:35).

to proclaim the gospel, but to do so free of charge, when he has the right to be paid, is an admirable sacrifice, something to be proud of. Or is it?

9:19–23. Paul's Cruciform Ministry

Repeatedly in this letter, Paul has condemned pride and counseled boasting only in the Lord. Has he now contradicted himself? No! Verses 19–23 demonstrate that Paul's renunciation of financial support is his way of embodying Jesus' cruciform faith and love. It is essential to his mission of participating in God's saving work, attempting to "win"/"save" (9:19–22) all kinds of people. It is his way of "boasting in the Lord." It is therefore a free but also, for him, a necessary choice. Verses 24–27 will confirm that Paul is convinced that only in embodying such Christlikeness will he himself also be guaranteed salvation.

The concrete meaning of this cruciform existence is provided in 9:19, the theological centerpiece of the chapter. In this verse, read with vv. 12, 15, 18, and 20–22, we see Paul succinctly telling his own story in a way that rhymes with the teaching and story of Jesus. The Gospels tell us that Jesus responded to the request of James and John for positions of eschatological privilege by offering himself as a servant, a slave (*doulos*), and calling his disciples to be like him: "You know that among the Gentiles those whom they recognize as their rulers lord it over them, and their great ones are tyrants over them. But it is not so among you; but whoever wishes to become great among you must be your servant, and whoever wishes to be first among you must be slave of all [*pantōn doulos*]. For the Son of Man came not to be served but to serve, and to give his life a ransom for many" (Mark 10:42b–45; cf. Matt 20:25b–28; Luke 22:25b–27). In 9:19, Paul echoes both the "slave" (*edoulōsa*) and the "all" (*pantōn, pasin*) language of Jesus' words.

More specifically, Paul's self-description is told in three stages that parallel the story of Jesus found in the first half of the poem in Phil 2:6–11 (vv. 6–8), Paul's "master story."[40] Similar to several earlier passages, including 8:1–13, these verses once again suggest a narrative pattern of "Although [x] not [y] but rather [z]":

> › Although [x = possessing status, rights, or interests]
> › not [y = using the status, rights, or interests for self-benefit]
> › but rather [z = others-oriented self-giving/self-enslavement].

---

40. Beginning with *Cruciformity*, I have argued that Phil 2:6–11 is Paul's master, or foundational, story from which his apostolic identity and his most basic ethical teaching derive.

Like Jesus, Paul possessed a particular status, and thus certain rights associated with that status, but rather than exploiting them for his own advantage and interests, he voluntarily took the form of an enslaved person for the benefit of others, indeed "all."[41] Especially critical is the parallel between Christ's *self*-emptying into slavery and *self*-humbling (Phil 2:7–8) and Paul's *self*-enslavement (1 Cor 9:19):

PARALLELS BETWEEN PHIL 2 AND 1 COR 9

	PHIL 2	1 COR 9
[x] Possession of status, rights, or interests	"though [x] he [Christ Jesus] was in the form of God" (6a)	- "For though [x] I am free with respect to all" (19a) - "though [x] I myself am not under the law" (9:20b)
[y] Decision not to use the status, rights, or interests for self-benefit	"[he] [y] did not regard equality with God as something to be exploited" (6b)	- "Nevertheless, we [y] have not made use of this right" (12b) - "But I [y] have made no use of any of these rights" (15a) - "so as not [y] to make full use of my rights in the gospel" (18c)
[z] Others-oriented self-giving/self-enslavement	- "but [z] emptied himself, taking the form of a slave [*doulou*], being born [lit., becoming] in human likeness. And being found in human form" - "he [z] humbled himself and became obedient to the point of death—even death on a cross" (7–8)	- "I [z] have made myself a slave [lit., "enslaved myself"; *emauton edoulōsa*] to all, so that I might win more of them" (19b–c) - "but we [z] endure anything [lit., "all things"] rather than put an obstacle in the way of the gospel of Christ" (12c) - "To the Jews I [z] became as a Jew, in order to win Jews. . . . To the weak I [z] became weak. . . . I [z] have become all things to all people, that I might by all means save some" (20–22)

41. Commentators have observed for centuries these parallels between Paul and Jesus. For example, in about 386 in his *Letters to Priests* 54, Ambrose of Milan interpreted 1 Cor 9 in light of Phil 2 (Saint Ambrose, *Letters, 1–91*, Fathers of the Church [Washington, DC: Catholic University of America Press, 1954], 293–95).

The Christ poem offered here, with its "Although [x] not [y] but [z]" structure, is not only about Christ's preincarnate, incarnate, and postincarnate status. Paul can make widespread use of this story for himself and his communities because it is a *missional* story, the narrative of Christ's acts for human salvation. In context (Phil 1:27–2:18), it is also an implicit call to participate in the missional activity of God manifested in Christ, the self-giving, suffering servant of God.[42] That is, *Phil 2:6–11 is a missional Christology for a missional people*, and Paul has understood that well.

Paul's missional activity involved manual work. Manual labor such as tent making or leather work (see Acts 18:3) was associated with enslaved persons and disdained by the Greco-Roman elite, although Jews generally did not share that attitude. Paul's working with his hands and renouncing financial support from the whole church, or from some wealthy patron(s), no doubt engendered criticism, especially from the elite Corinthians. Paul, however, sees his refusal of financial support, and his self-lowering to the point of menial labor and enslavement, as analogous to the self-abasement of Christ from equality with God to the slavery of human life and a shameful death on the cross, as one would execute a slave. Such downward mobility is counterintuitive and unexpected of both deities and free persons, ancient or modern. What is going on?

Like Christ, Paul acted for the salvation of all, motivated ultimately by love.[43] He accommodated himself to any and all (9:20–22)—Jews ("those under the law"), gentiles ("those outside the law"), and especially the *weak* (9:22a; cf. 8:11).[44] In fact, although he became *as* a Jew, *as* one under the law, and *as* one outside the law (9:20–21), he did not merely become *as* a weak person but specifically became weak (9:22).[45] This is a general description of Paul's conformity to the gospel of God's powerful weakness in Christ (1:18–25) with which Paul has already said he was in sync by virtue of his weakness when he first evangelized the Corinthians (2:1–5). And, of course, focusing on the weak is immediately relevant to the main reason Paul has written this chapter:

---

42. For elaboration on this approach to the poem, see my *Becoming the Gospel*, 106–41.

43. Phil 2:6–11 does not mention love or salvation explicitly, but both are implied in context.

44. Paul's missional concern for both Jews and gentiles appears also throughout Romans, including Rom 9–11.

45. This leads naturally to Paul's saying he became all things (not "as all things") in v. 22b, but that does not detract from the significance of the shift from "became as" to "became" when he mentions the weak.

ADDRESSING LITURGICAL CHAOS

· 8:1–14:40

to undergird his exhortation about love for weak siblings in chapter 8. (A form of the word "weak" appears five times in 8:7–12.)[46]

It is noteworthy that Paul does *not* complete the parallelism with "weak" by saying he became, or became as, the "powerful" or "strong" to win such people, for that would mean (in this context, at least) not working with his hands, which for him would be a betrayal of the gospel. Rather, he implies, the gospel is for the elite and powerful, but only if they accept it as the paradoxical status-reversing power-in-weakness that it is.

As for becoming as a Jew/one under the law and as a gentile/one outside the law (9:20–21), there has been significant scholarly debate. These verses do not mean that Paul stopped being Jewish or that he was, in Christ, neither a Jew nor a gentile.[47] To be sure, his fundamental identity is being "in Christ," or "in the Messiah." His primary guide is not the law of Moses in all of its details but the "law" of Christ (see below). Yet even in this letter, he quotes that very Mosaic law and shows evidence of his commitment to it—to the torah and all the Scriptures of Israel. The question is how observant was Paul the messianic Jew, and what kinds of practices and flexibility could his identity as a Christ-following Jew entail, especially as a Jewish apostle of the Jewish Messiah in and to the gentile world?[48]

This debate cannot be addressed or resolved here, but Paul's words suggest that he felt both a freedom and an obligation to adapt himself *to some degree* to the cultural practices of the people to whom he was ministering. Paradoxically, as a self-enslaved apostle, he experiences immense freedom, and as a free slave (so to speak), he has immense obligations. That which grants him this freedom and obligation, especially vis-à-vis his fellow Jews, is this: any freedom from the law (*nomos*) Paul has by virtue of being in Christ is met with the reality of being "under Christ's law," or *in* Christ's law (9:21; *ennomos* [*en* + *nomos*] *Christou*)—because he is in Christ.[49] What does that mean?

The attitude Paul exhibits here is clearly that of "salvific intentionality," a culturally sensitive, purposive, missional posture in all situations. The apostle's

---

46. See also Rom 15:1, where Paul calls all to "bear with the failings of the weak" (RSV, NIV, NET, ESV) or "be patient with the weakness of those who don't have power" (CEB).

47. See, e.g., Phil 3:5–8; Rom 9:1–5.

48. Some interpreters have wondered whether Paul would have eaten idol meat like, and even with, gentiles; chs. 8 and esp. 10, taken together, make it clear that he would not. But he was likely otherwise flexible about participating in meals.

49. Note the wordplay in 9:20–21: something like "under law" (Jewish), "lawless" (gentile), or "in-lawed to Christ." See also Gal 6:2: "Bear one another's burdens and thus you will fulfill the law of the Messiah [*ton nomon tou Christou*]" (MJG).

goal is to "win" (five times in 9:19–22)—that is, "save" (9:22)—"as many [people] as possible" (NAB).[50] (The verb "save" [*sōzō*] that Paul uses here is the same verb used twice in 7:16 for believers possibly saving unbelieving spouses.) And this salvific intentionality is universal in scope and comprehensive in its embodiment, as Paul eloquently says in 9:22b: "I have become *all* things [*panta*] to *all* people [*pasin*], that I might by *all* means [*pantōs*] save some" (emphasis added). Paul's becoming "all things to all people," however, does not mean that he had a disingenuous or chameleonlike ministry. Rather, his inconsistency was in fact his consistency, his constant self-emptying his way of fulfilling God's law by embodying Christ's law. His ministry was characterized by inculturation/contextualization that was manifested in cruciform flexibility and empathy.

In context, then, the "law" (*nomos*) of Christ refers to the pattern—we should say the *missional* pattern—demonstrated in the table above. It is best understood as Christ's narrative pattern (i.e., paradigmatic story) of self-enslavement or Christ's narrative pattern of faith (= obedience) and love. Yet the coherence of this pattern with Jesus' calls to obedient, servant (missional) discipleship (e.g., Mark 10:45, quoted above) makes it clear that this pattern is not to be seen as something in contrast to Jesus' teachings. As indicated in the table above, the pattern/law (*nomos*) can be summarized as the "Although [x] not [y] but [z] pattern." Jesus *did* that, but he also *taught* it.[51]

Yet there is also a twist to this poetic story from Philippians and Paul's use of it. The Greek word in Phil 2:6 that is usually translated "though" or "although" is actually an interpretation of the Greek participle "being" (*hyparchōn*) that occurs in that verse: "being in the form of God." This may be understood in at least three ways:

1. *temporally*: simply as "while being in the form of God" = "while he was in the form of God"
2. *concessively*: with most translations and commentators, as "although/though being in the form of God" = "although/though he was in the form of God"

50. This seems to be the intent, and the realistic hope, of Paul's expressed desire to win "the more" or "many" (9:19) and "some" (9:22). Naturally, he believes that he is not the actual savior but the agent of God's activity. The words "I have become *all* things to *all* people, that I might by *all* means save *some*" in 9:22 (emphasis added) apparently struck some early Christians as containing a non sequitur, since some manuscripts say, "that I might by all means save all."

51. For more on the coherence of Jesus and Paul, see my *Death of the Messiah and the Birth of the New Covenant: A (Not So) New Model of the Atonement* (Eugene, OR: Cascade, 2014), 77–131.

ADDRESSING LITURGICAL CHAOS · 8:1–14:40

3. *causally*: with a few interpreters, "because of being in the form of God" = "because he was in the form of God"

The first option, unlike the second and third, does not capture the poem's dramatic tenor. But which of options two and three is correct? It can be plausibly argued that either "although" or "because" is legitimate. It can also be argued, however, that both are legitimate and can work together: *although* we do not expect deities to empty themselves and humble themselves in becoming human and being crucified, in a mysterious way that is what Christ did precisely *because* he was in the form of God. He did what he did *despite* human expectations and, simultaneously, *because* that is what it means truly to be God.[52]

So too with Paul according to 1 Corinthians. The Corinthians, like many of us, would not expect an apostle—a commissioned, authoritative representative of Christ—to work with his hands as a bivocational, or tent-making, pastor/evangelist. Like Christ, however, Paul did what he did in forgoing financial support and working with his hands both *despite* his status (and the expectations of others) and *because of* his status as an apostolic imitator of Christ. In 9:19, Paul even imitates the grammar of Phil 2:6 with a similar participle: "For *though* being [*ōn*] free with respect to all, I have made myself a slave to all; and, simultaneously, *because of* being [*ōn*] free with respect to all, I have made myself a slave to all" (MJG). This is what it means, for him, to truly be apostolic à la Christ. In not doing what he could have done but rather doing something radically unexpected to observers, he revealed his true identity. Paul forsakes rights *because* that is of the essence of Christlike apostleship.

This should not be interpreted as the height of arrogance or as a critique of others (e.g., those named in 9:5). Paul is simply saying that refraining from exercising a legitimate right, as an act of freedom and love, is not the antithesis of a minister's identity or any Christian's identity any more than it is the antithesis of Christ's identity. Rather, it a powerful expression of that identity—and especially something for certain Corinthians to embrace in their situation. To refrain from temple dining would be an expression of their true identity in Christ, an embodiment of life-giving, resurrectional cruciformity in step with Paul (e.g., Cor 4:11).

Paul writes in 9:23, "I do all things [*panta*] for the sake of the gospel, so that I may be a co-participant in it" (MJG).[53] This is love in action—bearing all

---

52. See the argument in the first chapter of my *Inhabiting the Cruciform God* (9–39).

53. The word translated "co-participant" is *synkoinōnos*: *syn* = "with/co-" + *koinōnos* = "participant" → "co-partner," "co-participant." For a similar translation, see NRSVue,

things (*panta*; 9:12; 13:7) for the salvation of others—but it also impinges on his own salvation. Consistently embodying the Christlike "Although/Because [x] not [y] but [z]" pattern in a variety of ways—doing "all things [*panta*]"—is Paul's way of *really* sharing in the gospel and its blessings as a co-participant in it: not the "material benefits" (9:11) he is due as an apostle but the "imperishable" wreath of final salvation (9:25).

9:24–27. The Goal of Eschatological Salvation

Paul concludes this chapter with words that represent both his own ultimate goal of eschatological salvation—note the continuation of the first-person "I" language in 9:26–27—and his desire for his addressees to arrive at the same goal: "Run in such a way that you may win" the prize (9:24b).[54] This double focus means that Paul does not literally mean, in v. 24, that only "one" of them will reach eternal glory.

Like a runner or boxer who practices self-control and bodily enslavement (9:27, using the verb *doulagōgō*, an echo of *doulos* in 9:19), as one would witness at the biannual Isthmian Games near Corinth, Paul enslaves himself as Christ Jesus enslaved himself. This is his form of athletic discipline; his activity in practice and in competition is purposeful (v. 26). In doing this, Paul does not *renounce* his freedom but *exercises* it in acts of love. But if Paul did not embody the gospel, he would be "disqualified" from the main event (9:27) and would not receive the imperishable wreath, an athletic metaphor for immortality (9:25; cf. 15:42–54);[55] *he would not be saved*. Let those who have ears (like the meat eaters) hear.

Summary

In this chapter, Paul has defended his apostolic rights, defended his right to *renounce* those rights, and offered himself to the Corinthians as an example of the renunciation of personal rights for the benefit of others. His is a life of

---

CEB, NET. (The NRSV's "I do it all for the sake of the gospel, so that I may share in its blessings" [cf. RSV, NIV, ESV] unfortunately substitutes a form of the "blessing" word group for the actual word group "participation.") It is not completely clear what *synkoinōnos* implies. Co-participant with the Corinthians? With all believers? With fellow apostles? With the Lord? Perhaps all of the above.

54. For pressing on toward the goal of final salvation, see also Phil 3:12–14; 2 Tim 4:7–8.

55. Athletes at Isthmia and elsewhere were sometimes awarded crowns of withered celery or pine.

both self-giving and self-denial, but both are paradoxically (as Jesus promised—Mark 8:34–37) self-fulfilling. As always, Paul reasons bifocally, looking back to Christ's incarnation, teaching, example, death, and resurrection, and ahead to the day of judgment, resurrection, and life eternal.

The exemplary, Christlike nature of Paul's apostolic ministry is, from one perspective, the focus of this chapter. At the same time, the universality of the Christian gospel is robustly portrayed here too. That is, this chapter is about the *catholicity* of the gospel and the corollary *catholicity* of Christian ministry and mission. Even the little word "all" (Gk. *pas, panta*, etc.)—employed numerous times in this chapter—is profoundly indicative of this catholicity.

> For although and because I am free with respect to *all people*, I have made myself a slave to *all people*, so that I might win more of them. . . . To the weak I became weak, so that I might win the weak. I have become *all things* to *all people*, that I might *by all means* save some. I do *all things* for the sake of the gospel, so that I may be a co-participant in it. Do you not know that in a race *all the runners* compete, but only one receives the prize? Run in such a way that you may win it. *All athletes* exercise self-control in *all things*; they do it to receive a perishable wreath, but we an imperishable one. (9:19, 22–25 NRSV alt.; emphasis added)

This is the apostolic, catholic church. Paul is not speaking only autobiographically; he is speaking paradigmatically, both to the Corinthians and to all who hear his words as divine address. The paradigm is an *ethical* paradigm, yes, but also, and just as importantly, a *missional* paradigm of cultural flexibility and adaptability, both for individuals and for communities.

Efraín Agosto, writing on 9:19–23, captures Paul's attitude and practice in a highly insightful way from the perspective of his Latino context. By his willingness to engage all kinds of people, Agosto writes, Paul "crosses various borders in his ministry (in addition to the geographic ones) to establish his communities and secure them. Thus an image that is important for understanding Latino/a reality today—'border'—becomes a metaphor for Paul's pragmatic missionary approach. . . . He gives up certain rights and security in order to carry out this mission: he crosses borders. To complete the argument of the rest of 1 Corinthians 8–10, Paul is asking, 'Why shouldn't the "strong" do so as well?'"[56] But this sort of border-crossing is more than a strategy for effective

56. Efraín Agosto, "An Intercultural Latino Reading of Paul: The Example of 1 Corin-

evangelization; it is consonant with the mission of Christ and thus with the *missio Dei*—indeed, with the very character of God. It was and is, after all, the triune God who is the ultimate border crosser.

REFLECTIONS AND QUESTIONS FOR 9:1–27

Spiritual, Pastoral, Missional, and Theological Reflections

1. Perhaps the main claim this chapter makes is that in order **to** *advance* **the gospel, Christians must** *embody* **the gospel.** This can occur only in specific contexts, each of which requires the sort of cruciform flexibility and intercultural engagement that characterized Paul's salvific intentionality and activity.

2. Another critical aspect of this chapter, as with chapter 8, is **the possibility of an idolatry of rights.** As Anthony Thiselton put it succinctly, "We should not allow anything to obscure the force of this chapter for the current debates about 'autonomy' and 'the **right** to choose.'"[57] Thiselton does not specify which debates he had in mind, but we should not think only of abortion.[58] Let's consider the right of self-defense.

   I agree with Richard Hays that "there is not a syllable in the Pauline letters that can be cited in support of Christians employing violence."[59] But how would Paul structure an argument with someone who claims the right to use violence in self-defense, as most Christians do?

   In 1 Cor 9, Paul appeals to several possible sources that Christians might use (Scripture, church tradition, common sense) to build the case for the existence of certain rights, just as Christians today might appeal to various sources, and not necessarily only Christian ones, to build the case for something like self-defense, and thereby the right to use violence in self-defense, or the right to participate in a war understood to be in national self-defense.

   Paul might be willing, for the sake of argument, to grant the existence, and the Christian appropriation, of the just-war tradition and thus of the right to

---

thians 9:19–23," in *1 and 2 Corinthians*, Texts @ Contexts, ed. Yung Suk Kim (Minneapolis: Fortress, 2013), 49–63.

57. Thiselton, *First Epistle*, 676.

58. The following is adapted from my book *Participating in Christ*, 46–47. For a way of thinking with Paul about abortion, see the reflections on 6:12–20.

59. Richard B. Hays, *The Moral Vision of the New Testament: Community, Cross, New Creation; A Contemporary Introduction to New Testament Ethics* (San Francisco: HarperCollins, 1996), 331.

self-defense. But then he would almost certainly turn the logical consequence of accepting that tradition, with its implicit right, on its head:

> Although [x] you have been wronged, and although you do have an authoritative tradition that gives you the right of self-defense as a last resort,
> do not [y] make use of that right and thereby return evil with evil,
> but rather [z] continue in practices that overcome evil with good. (See Rom 12:17–21.)

3. To the pragmatic, Paul (or at least this argument put on his lips) will sound naive. After all, human beings are not God; they cannot overcome evil at will. Of course not, Paul would say. But then he would add that this is not the point. Christian existence requires conformity to the pattern of God's action in the Messiah, sometimes meaning **relinquishing rights** established by recognized authorities, even when logic and moral intuition seem to say otherwise.

4. That Paul would actually construct such an argument to counter something like the standard arguments for self-defense (including even natural law) seems quite clear from 1 Cor 9, where he offers just this type of christological moral reasoning. In a moral universe like ours (especially in the West or Global North) that is so dependent on the establishment and exercise of rights, with respect to abortion, gun ownership, warfare, and much more, **Paul offers a uniquely Christocentric and theocentric way of moral reasoning that we neglect to our own detriment.**

Questions for Those Who Read, Teach, and Preach

1. How does Paul's model of self-support as a form of imitating Christ apply to ministry today—if it does?

2. If Paul's ministry is characterized by inculturation/contextualization that was manifested in cruciform flexibility and empathy, what do those terms actually mean? What would a ministry characterized by these pastoral practices look like today?

3. How should Christians understand and apply Paul's voluntary renunciation of certain rights and his critique of the unrestrained exercise of one's rights in rights-based cultures of today? Is it wrong for people who have particularly experienced oppression to assert their rights in the public square or the church? How do Christians discern when it is right to assert rights and when rights should be given up or sublimated on behalf of others? Are there differences between the social context of Paul's day and our day that make a difference to this question?

10:1–11:1 · *Koinōnia with and Imitation of Christ, and Salvific Intentionality*

4. In sum, what does this passage urge the church to believe (faith), do (love), and anticipate (hope)?

FOR FURTHER READING

Agosto, Efraín. "An Intercultural Latino Reading of Paul: The Example of 1 Corinthians 9:19–23." Pages 49–63 in *1 and 2 Corinthians*. Texts @ Contexts. Edited by Yung Suk Kim. Minneapolis: Fortress, 2013.

Barram, Michael. "Pauline Mission as Salvific Intentionality: Fostering a Missional Consciousness in 1 Corinthians 9:19–23 and 10:31–11:1." Pages 234–46 in *Paul as Missionary: Identity, Activity, Theology, and Practice*. LNTS 420. Edited by Trevor J. Burke and Brian S. Rosner. London: T&T Clark, 2011.

Burke, Trevor J., and Brian S. Rosner, eds. *Paul as Missionary: Identity, Activity, Theology, and Practice*. LNTS 420. London: T&T Clark, 2011.

Goode, Scott. *Salvific Intentionality in 1 Corinthians: How Paul Cultivates the Missional Imagination of the Corinthian Community*. Eugene, OR: Wipf & Stock, 2023.

Hock, Ronald F. *The Social Context of Paul's Ministry: Tentmaking and Apostleship*. Minneapolis: Fortress, 1980. Repr., 2007.

Rudolph, David J. *A Jew to the Jews: Jewish Contours of Pauline Flexibility in 1 Corinthians 9:19–23*. 2nd ed. Eugene, OR: Pickwick, 2016.

Schnabel, Eckhard J. *Paul the Missionary: Realities, Strategies, and Methods*. Downers Grove, IL: InterVarsity Press, 2008.

Wells, Samuel. *Incarnational Mission*. Grand Rapids: Eerdmans, 2018. (highly accessible)

10:1–11:1. *KOINŌNIA* WITH AND IMITATION OF CHRIST, AND SALVIFIC INTENTIONALITY OUTSIDE THE CHURCH

In chapter 8, Paul had summoned the Corinthian knowledge-driven, meat-eating temple diners to replace their self-centered, unqualified exercise of rights with love for their siblings in Christ, for whom he died. With its language of idolatry, stumbling, and destruction, that summons also contained a subtle but unmistakable warning to the meat eaters themselves, yet the clear focus was on the real or possible harm done to others.

That strong admonition led to chapter 9, and to Paul's assertion of his own rights as a preface to a description of his ministry as inclusive of a deliberate Christlike renunciation of those rights for the salvation of others. The chapter ended with a warning about possible disqualification from the spiritual mar-

ADDRESSING LITURGICAL CHAOS · 8:1–14:40

athon that is discipleship. Paul's language of loving concern and action for all is not merely autobiographical but paradigmatic. *Forgoing legitimate rights to safeguard or encourage the salvation of others—of all—is inherently catholic and missional; it is a fundamental form of embodying the gospel and is not to be ignored.*

Paul will return to the general admonition to look out for the needs and interests of others in 10:23–24 and 10:31–11:1, where he once again quotes the Corinthian slogan "all things are permitted" (NRSVue) and, once again, counters with his own words. The instructions in the last part of chapter 10 focus on situations in private homes. But before Paul can get to that subject and to a final set of general, missional exhortations, he must return to the topic of idolatry. The warning implied in chapter 8 is not yet complete, so in 10:1–22 Paul wants the Corinthians to reconsider the issue of idolatry. This time attention will be given not to the impact of temple dining on others but on the temple diners themselves.

Perhaps Paul thinks the Corinthians will be open to careful self-examination now that he has shown them the ethical error of their ways. But perhaps not; maybe the elite Corinthians, at least, still despise him, not only for acting like an enslaved person but for admitting, in effect, to disobeying Jesus (see 9:14). In any case, Paul wants the Corinthians, especially the temple diners, not to test Christ (10:9), as their ancestors did, by flirting with, or even engaging in, demon-inspired idolatry.

Rather, the Corinthians are called to be Christ's new-covenant partners in an exclusive relationship of participation, or communion (*koinōnia*), with him (10:15–22). The language of *koinōnia* picks up Paul's term *synkoinōnos* ("co-participant") in 9:23. The *koin-* word family, along with the related verb *metechō* ("participate, share"), dominates the latter part of chapter 10:

> The cup of blessing that we bless, is it not a sharing [*koinōnia*; NIV "participation"] in the blood of Christ? The bread that we break, is it not a sharing [*koinōnia*; NIV "participation"] in the body of Christ? Because there is one bread, we who are many are one body, for we all partake of [*metechomen*] the one bread [NIV, "share the one loaf"]. Consider the people of Israel; are not those who eat the sacrifices partners [*koinōnoi*] in the altar? What do I imply then? That food sacrificed to idols is anything, or that an idol is anything? No, I imply that what pagans sacrifice, they sacrifice to demons and not to God. I do not want you to be partners [*koinōnous*; NAB, NIV, ESV "participants"] with demons. You cannot drink the cup of the Lord and the cup of demons.

258

You cannot partake of [*metechein*; CEB "participate in"] the table of the Lord and the table of demons. (1 Cor 10:16–21 NRSV)[60]

Another word that recurs throughout 10:1–11:1 is, once again (as at the end of ch. 9), "all." It has several significant functions: to describe the experiences of God's people as a whole, ancient and contemporary; to simultaneously suggest a warning in light of the ancestors' experiences; and to serve as part of a related admonition about true freedom that is central to this letter:

> I do not want you to be unaware, brothers and sisters, that our ancestors were *all* under the cloud, and *all* passed through the sea, and *all* were baptized into Moses in the cloud and in the sea, and *all* ate the same spiritual food, and *all* drank the same spiritual drink. For they drank from the spiritual rock that followed them, and the rock was Christ. . . . Because there is one bread, we who are many are one body, for we *all* partake of the one bread. . . . "*All things* are permitted," but not *all things* are beneficial. "*All things* are permitted," but not *all things* build up. (1 Cor 10:1–4, 17, 23; NRSV alt.; emphasis added)

10:1–22. Participation with Christ Is Exclusive

In 10:1–22, Paul draws on Israel's past as a lesson (10:6, 11, 18) for the Corinthian church to strengthen the implicit warning at the end of chapter 9: even those who are baptized and participate in the Lord's Supper are not immune from idolatry and may not receive the (eschatological) prize. Paul's use of the exodus–wilderness–golden calf narrative from Exodus, Numbers, and Deuteronomy suggests that even former pagans in the Corinthian church, who are now identified as the Israelites' descendants, had been taught these major biblical stories about "our ancestors" (10:1; cf. Gal 3:7). For Paul, the Scripture narratives not only speak to but also prefigure the church; Israel's story is also now the Corinthians' story, for the Corinthians have been incorporated into it. The bottom line? The Corinthians, and all who engage this letter as Scripture, must likewise flee from idolatry because participation in Christ is an exclusive relationship.

---

60. See also 10:30: "If I partake [*metechō*] with thankfulness, why should I be denounced because of that for which I give thanks?"

10:1–14. Flee from Idolatry! Learning from Israel

The language Paul uses in vv. 1–14 is primarily that of *typology*. Events and characters in the story of Israel are "types" of the Corinthians and their experience. The Greek words usually translated as "example(s)" in 10:6 and 10:11 are the noun *typoi* (v. 6) and the adverb *typikōs* (v. 11). Some translations, including the RSV and NLT, have "warning," that is, "negative example." But there is more to "types" than examples or warnings. The notion is one of prefiguration, of earlier characters representing, or prepresenting, later characters. The earlier characters are more like archetypes, but archetypes with specific recurrences that are of interest to the people considering the *typoi*, the archetypes. (It may be useful to think of patterns and analogies, or correspondences.) One helpful interpretation renders 10:6 and 10:11 as follows:

> Now these things happened as typifications of *us*, so that we might not become desirous of evil things, as some of them desired evil. (10:6)

> Now, these things were happening to them archetypically and were written down for our exhortation, (we) on whom the ends of the ages have come. (10:11)[61]

According to Paul in 10:1–4, the church's Israelite ancestors—*all* of them ("all" appears five times in these four verses)—had every spiritual experience imaginable (10:1–4), like the Corinthians themselves. They were in God's presence and under divine protection (the cloud; Exod 13:21–22), and they were rescued from bondage in Egypt (through the sea; Exod 14:21–29). Paul describes these experiences in the language of participation as being "baptized into [*eis*] Moses" (10:2), which prefigures baptism into Christ and the presence of his Spirit, the Spirit of God: "For in the one Spirit we were all baptized into [*eis*] one body—Jews or Greeks, slaves or free—and we were all made to drink of one Spirit" (12:13).

Furthermore, the Israelites shared in a common spiritual (*pneumatikon*) food and a common spiritual (*pneumatikon*) drink (10:3–4), references to the manna (Exod 16; Num 11) and water from a spiritual rock (Exod 17:1–7; Num

---

61. Timothy A. Brookins and Bruce W. Longenecker, *1 Corinthians 10–16: A Handbook on the Greek Text* (Waco, TX: Baylor University Press, 2016), 5–6. Thiselton renders *typoi* as "formative models" (*First Corinthians*, 731–49).

20:2–13) provided in the wilderness.[62] The repetition of "spiritual" surely resonated with the Corinthians' own experience and language, on which Paul has already drawn (2:13, 15; 3:1; 9:11).[63] In addition to foreshadowing baptism and the gift of the Spirit, these ancient experiences also clearly prefigure the Lord's Supper. That is, the Israelites "eucharistized" (or "communionized") with spiritual food and drink.[64] In fact, they "drank from . . . the Rock [who] was Christ" (10:4). This is perhaps a surprising interpretation of Christ as the rock in Exod 17 (vv. 1–7), but an appropriate one if he is the preincarnate Son of God, if the Lord God is Israel's rock in the wilderness,[65] and if both God the Father and Jesus are rightly called "Lord." That is, Paul is not merely engaging in metaphor or allegory; he really believes Christ was present with the Israelites, the means of divine sustenance in the wilderness, without claiming that Christ was literally a rock.[66]

Nothing could have been more spiritually or liturgically nourishing and catholic (shared by "all") than the Israelites' experiences that Paul recounts. But none of that experience mattered (or matters, Paul implies), if its result is not faithful living, for "God was not pleased with most of them, and they were struck down" (10:5; see Num 25:1–9). Paul is not simply telling an ancient story; it is a story with a purpose, for the events are types: "so that we might not desire evil as they did" (10:6). The ancestors' error, from which their spiritual and sacramental experiences did not protect them, was specifically to become both idolatrous—specifically expressed in inappropriate eating and drinking—and sexually immoral (10:7–8; see, e.g., Exod 32; Num 25:1–2).

---

62. Other references to these significant experiences are found in Pss 78, 105, and 106.

63. We should recall that Paul could not treat the Corinthians as "spiritual" or "Spiritual" people (*pneumatikois*; 3:1) even though they had received the Spirit and plenty of "spiritual gifts" (*pneumatika*).

64. The first evidence we have of the Lord's Supper (communion) being called the Eucharist (Gk. *eucharistia*, "thanksgiving") is Didache 9, which probably dates from the late first century.

65. E.g., Deut 32:4, 15, 18, 30–31. See also Ps 78:35 in light of 78:15–16, 20; Ps 95.

66. Augustine famously wrote, "All symbols seem to personify the realities of which they are symbols. 'So,' St. Paul says, 'The rock was Christ,' because the rock in question symbolized Christ." See Augustine, *City of God* 18.48 (*The City of God, Books XVII–XXII*, Fathers of the Church [Washington, DC: Catholic University of America Press, 1954], 168). Apparently other Jews had understood the rock in the wilderness to be a traveling rock or well; see, e.g., Ciampa and Rosner, *First Letter to the Corinthians*, 450–51. Some recent interpreters have suggested that Christ inhabited the rock in a spiritual way as a sort of preincarnation.

ADDRESSING LITURGICAL CHAOS · 8:1–14:40

Such idolatry and immorality were common in the pagan world, not infrequently occurring simultaneously. And as we have already noted several times, Jews often thought of idolatry and sexual immorality as the basic sins of that gentile world. Yet here Paul does not cite pagan behavior but rather the activity of the chosen people, the liberated, God-surrounded, divinely fed communicants who should have known better. He has already shown that some of the Corinthians have committed *porneia* (5:1–13; 6:12–20). He is now warning them that any such behavior (sexual immorality and idolatrous eating and drinking) can lead to disaster. *Their own spiritual and sacramental experiences do not provide immunity from sin or exemption from its consequences.*

In 10:7–10, Paul refers to several incidents in the Scriptures that are such types of self-inflicted spiritual destruction and the resulting divine judgment. Unlike the repetitive "all" of 10:1–4, we now have the word "some" in each verse. Paul alternates between the second-person-plural imperative form ("Do not"; 10:7, 10) and the first-person-plural imperative ("Let us not" or "We must not"; 10:8, 9).

- First, Paul appeals to the golden calf incident, and in 10:7 specifically quotes Exod 32:6 from the narrative of that event.[67] Idolatry is specifically named, and sexual immorality implied.
- Second, in 10:8 Paul recalls the combination of sexual immorality involving the women of Moab and idolatry with their god Baal of Peor, recounted in Num 25, this time stressing the immorality. Numbers tells us that twenty-four thousand of God's people "fell" in one day (Num 25:9; Paul has twenty-three thousand).
- Third, Paul mentions the testing and complaining that occurred in the wilderness of the Negeb, which resulted in destruction by serpents (10:9; see Num 21:4–9).
- Fourth, Paul alludes to incidents of grumbling or complaining that resulted in more destruction, perhaps thinking of Num 14, though a "destroyer" is not specifically named there. Maybe Paul is thinking of the angel of death from the exodus narrative (Exod 12:23).

Paul recounts these incidents in a highly organized way, with a clear pattern applied to each admonition, though only one verse actually contains a marked scriptural quotation (10:7):

67. Paul alludes to the golden calf incident in Rom 1:18–27 too. Other ancient Jewish writers also referred to it.

262

1 Cor Text (NRSV Alt.)[68]	Admonition	Type (negative example)	Old Testament Text
10:7	"Neither become idolaters as some of them did"	"as it is written, 'The people sat down to eat and drink, and they rose up to play'"	Exod 32 (32:6 quoted)
10:8	"Neither let us indulge in sexual immorality as some of them did"	"and twenty-three thousand fell in a single day"[69]	Num 25 (see esp. 25:1, 9)
10:9	"Neither let us put Christ to the test, as some of them did"	"and were destroyed by serpents"	Num 21:4–9 (see esp. 21:4–6)
10:10	"Neither complain as some of them did"	"and were destroyed by the destroyer"	Num 14:2, 36; 16:41–49; Ps 106:24–27 (see also Exod 12:23)

Out of these accounts and the warnings associated with them come several admonitions: do not desire evil, do not succumb to idolatry or sexual immorality, do not put Christ to the test or complain. (The thought of putting Christ to the test in v. 9 comes from the earlier identification, in v. 4, of Christ as the rock present in the wilderness.)[70] In 10:11, echoing 10:6, Paul repeats the main point—these things happened to the Israelites, but they happened to them *typologically* and were therefore recorded for *our* instruction. We are those "on whom the ends of the ages have come" (10:11).[71] That is, the Corinthians and Paul—and all who read the letter as Scripture—live at the intersection of the old and the new ages, the overlap in which, through Christ, the new way of life of the age to come can be lived in the present.

But such a life requires attention and care; God's people must stay alert so

68. I have slightly altered the text of the NRSV to show the nature of the imperative verbs and the repeated use of the particle *mēde*, "neither," which connects these four narratives and admonitions together.

69. As noted above, Num 25:9 says twenty-four thousand. The discrepancy could be due to various reasons, but it is of no significance.

70. It is perhaps surprising that Paul says the ancestors tested Christ, rather than the Lord or God. In fact, some New Testament manuscripts actually have "the Lord" or even occasionally "God," but the best texts read "(the) Christ."

71. Or perhaps "the culmination of the ages" (NIV).

ADDRESSING LITURGICAL CHAOS

· 8:1–14:40

as not to arrogantly think themselves to be in fine shape and then fall (10:12), like the many thousands of Israelites. They must rely on God, who is faithful (10:13; cf. 1:9), to deliver them from these sorts of common tests or temptations (10:13). The word "common" is significant: idolatry and sexual immorality are always options, everywhere and at all times. God may not test beyond his people's limits, but they must play their part in experiencing God's act of faithfulness: they must be faithful too. Specifically, they must "flee from idolatry" (10:14 NIV), which is parallel to "Flee from sexual immorality!" (6:18 NIV). These are the two great temptations to break covenant relations with God, test Christ, and reenact the wrong stories of one's fathers and mothers.

It is not at all clear that the Corinthians as a whole understood the necessity of *fleeing* from idolatry. To the rationale for that strong admonition Paul turns next.

10:15–22. Exclusive Communion with Christ

In 10:15, Paul invites his audience, whom he calls "sensible," or even "wise" (*phronimois*), to think carefully and critically with him. Even though he referred to the Corinthians as wise in 4:10 (*phronimoi*), he did so sarcastically while calling himself and his coworkers foolish. But perhaps now Paul is thinking like Isaiah: "Come now, let us argue it out, says the LORD: though your sins are like scarlet, they shall be like snow; though they are red like crimson, they shall become like wool" (Isa 1:18). Maybe he hopes the Corinthians will hear him out and think through the logic of their shared experience of *koinōnia* in the Lord's Supper.[72] After all, Paul has announced at the very start of the letter that the Corinthians, and all believers, have been called into communion—*koinōnia*—with Jesus (1:9).[73]

Paul begins in 10:16 with two rhetorical questions about the Lord's Supper in which Greek grammar indicates that the queries expect affirmative responses:[74] "The cup of blessing that we bless, is it not a participation [*koinōnia*] in the blood of Christ? The bread that we break, is it not a participation [*koinōnia*] in

---

72. Or perhaps Paul is thinking more in the mode of Isaiah from verses just before Isa 1:18: "Wash yourselves; make yourselves clean; remove the evil of your doings from before my eyes; cease to do evil, learn to do good; seek justice, rescue the oppressed, defend the orphan, plead for the widow" (Isa 1:16–17).

73. For a fuller discussion of *koinōnia* and the Lord's Supper, see the comments on 11:17–34.

74. That is, they use the particle *ouchi*.

264

the body of Christ?" (NAB).[75] Paul must be appealing not only to the common experience of blessing the cup and breaking the bread, rooted in the meal we call the Last Supper (and thus also in the Passover Seder),[76] but also to the common understanding of that experience as *koinōnia*: participation, or sharing, in the blood of Christ and the body of Christ. That is, the Supper is a profound act of identification with the death of Christ—his once-and-for-all self-sacrifice— and a concomitant renewal of faith and baptism as immersion into Christ: his death, his body, his story.[77] *That* is part and parcel of communion.

Paul is not just reasoning philosophically or hypothetically with the Corinthians. He could not expect an affirmative answer to the rhetorical questions in 10:16 if this perspective were not already the Corinthians' point of view as well as Paul's. This suggests that this understanding of the Lord's Supper was part of the instructions the apostle gave about the Supper when he passed on to the Corinthians the tradition given to him (11:23–26).

Furthermore, the vertical *koinōnia* with Christ is complemented by a horizontal *koinōnia* and unity, as one body, with all who partake of the one bread/ loaf (10:17, twice). The threefold "one" in 10:17 (similar to the threefold emphasis on unity in 1:10) is rhetorically powerful.[78] Theologically, the overall claim is this: *paradoxically, the broken body of Christ, manifested now in the broken bread, is precisely that which makes the one body and makes the body one; in its brokenness lies the power to make whole.* Thus, this participation in Christ only takes place in community, as an event of sharing and solidarity. The vertical and horizontal aspects of *koinōnia* are inseparable, a truth that is critical to what Paul will discuss regarding the malpractice of the Lord's Supper in 11:17–34. Anthony Thiselton therefore translates *koinōnia* as "communal participation."[79]

Verse 18 serves a dual role in Paul's unfolding argument as it invites the Corinthians to careful consideration of Israel (lit., "Israel according to the flesh")

---

75. "Participation" is also used in NIV, RSV, and ESV, while NRSV, CEB, and NET have "sharing."

76. See references to the bread and cup in the Last Supper accounts in Mark 14:22–25; Matt 26:26–29; Luke 22:15–20. There is considerable scholarly debate about the connection, or lack thereof, between the Last Supper and the Seder; I side with Thiselton (*First Epistle*, 754–70) that there is a strong link.

77. On the uniqueness and singularity of Christ's sacrifice, see especially the Letter to the Hebrews.

78. On being one, an important Pauline theme, see also, e.g., 1 Cor 12 (esp. v. 27); Rom 12:4–5; Eph 4:13, 16; Phil 2:2; Col 3:15.

79. Thiselton, *First Epistle*, 750, 761–63.

ADDRESSING LITURGICAL CHAOS · 8:1–14:40

in the form of another rhetorical question expecting an affirmative response.[80] First, in 10:18 Paul once again deploys the interpretive strategy of typology, only this time a positive type is put forth: consumers of Israel's sacrifices were participants (*koinōnoi*) in the altar, that is, partakers of the sacrifice (Lev 7:9, 15), prefiguring the *koinōnia* of the Lord's Supper. Second, in 10:18 Paul makes a critical connection between eating sacrifices and *koinōnia*—solidarity, fellowship, communion, participation.

At first blush, this could sound like Paul is saying that there is something real about idols and the food sacrificed to them. In 10:19, however, Paul uses yet another pair of questions, now with an explicit answer in v. 20, to state emphatically that there is no there there, so to speak.[81] Neither idols nor idol offerings have any significance in themselves. That is, Paul does not now contradict his earlier claim in chapter 8 that idols do not exist (8:4–6). Rather, with other Jews of his time, he claims that there is something real behind an idol, namely, a demon, an evil spirit or hostile semidivine being (10:20–21). Idolatry is not evil because the gods exist but because the worship of them is part of the great cosmic battle against the worship of the one true God. Similarly, the book of Revelation (Rev 12–13) posits the power of Satan behind the Roman Empire and emperor, and behind the imperial cult, with its sacrifices and other expressions of devotion to the imperial idol.[82]

Moreover, as a general principle, Paul is claiming that whenever one participates in any kind of worship, particularly a sacral meal, one becomes an intimate partner (*koinōnos*) with the deity, as was the case in Israel (10:18)—or, if the deity does not exist, with the demonic power behind it (10:20–21). This was true of Israel's sacred meals, it is true of meals in pagan temples (often called "the supper of _____ [a god]"), and it is true of "the table of the Lord" or "the Lord's supper" (10:17, 21; cf. 11:20). For Paul, "participation" is the very heart of the spiritual and cultic, or liturgical, life. To participate in the worship of idols is to follow in Israel's footsteps by sacrificing to demons (Deut 32:17, partially cited in 10:20: "They sacrificed to demons, not God, to deities they had never known"). And Paul does not want anyone reading his letter to be in such a partnership.

---

80. This seems to imply, with 10:1, that the Corinthians are now part of the "Israel of God" (Gal 6:16), the people of God that includes believing Jews and gentiles alike.

81. More technically, Thiselton says that, in modern parlance, idols possess no "ontological existence or metaphysical reality," and, in postmodern idiom, they are "social constructs" (*First Epistle*, 773).

82. Elsewhere, the Pauline correspondence suggests a connection between evil earthly and evil cosmic powers (e.g., Eph 1:21; 2:2; 6:12).

266

The conviction driving Paul's argument here is that, unlike the demonic idols but like YHWH in relation to Israel, Christ exercises an exclusive and total claim over his body, his community, as expressed in the sharing, or participation (*koinōnia*), which is the Lord's Supper (10:16–17, 21; hence it is called "communion"). Paul emphasizes this point as bluntly as he possibly can, with two "You cannot" sentences in 10:21: "You cannot drink the cup of the Lord and the cup of demons. You cannot partake of the table of the Lord and the table of demons."[83] The new sacrifice in the temple of the Holy Spirit (the *ekklēsia*) is the only one for Christians.[84] *The act of communion with the Lord Jesus is, therefore, the ultimate act of nonidolatry. It is participation understood as complete allegiance and worship.*

With a final pair of rhetorical questions expecting a negative response (v. 22), Paul closes out this argument against the Corinthians eating food sacrificed to idols in the precincts of a pagan temple. The Lord is still a "jealous" God (Deut 4:24; 5:9; 6:15; 32:16–21), so Christians cannot partake of the Lord's Supper and the suppers of the gods. If we were to think otherwise, we would be supposing that we are stronger and wiser than God. But, instead, Paul might remind his addressees, "my thoughts are not your thoughts, nor are your ways my ways, says the Lord" (Isa 55:8).

10:23–11:1. Imitators of Christ via the Imitation of Paul

Returning finally to the place where he began this discussion of food, idolatry, and love (8:1–13), Paul now summarizes his main points in two short, proverb-like sections (10:23–24; 10:31–11:1) that surround a brief discussion of the one subject not addressed so far: eating meat in contexts other than pagan temple precincts (10:25–30). In other words, 10:23–11:1 is another chiastically structured passage.

10:23–24; 10:31–11:1. Summary Admonitions

The summaries of Paul's main points about freedom and love are quite clear and emphatic. The apostle begins by citing and rebuffing a version of the Corinthian slogan we saw in 6:12, "All things are permitted for me" (twice; NRSVue). It is now quoted in a more general form, "All things are permitted"

---

83. See also the general principle in 2 Cor 6:14–16 and a similar problem in Israel's history according to Mal 1:6–14.

84. Ciampa and Rosner, *First Letter to the Corinthians*, 159.

ADDRESSING LITURGICAL CHAOS

(10:23, again twice; NRSVue). Interestingly, the fundamental Corinthian arguments for both unrestricted sex and unrestrained food consumption are the same: the (alleged) autonomy of the Christian, an autonomy derived from a general cultural norm that has infiltrated the *ekklēsia*.

Paul's twofold rebuttal in 10:23 begins with the first response from 6:12 (NRSVue), "Not all things are beneficial," and is followed by a parallel phrase, "Not all things build up." It is clear now that Paul is focused on the effects of behavior on the other, or on the community, not oneself (the focus of 6:12). The verb translated as "are beneficial" (*sympherei*) will appear yet again in 12:7 to indicate the common good, and the related noun *sympheron* occurs in 10:33 to refer to the advantage, or benefit, of others rather than self. In other words, Paul is calling for that fundamental virtue of not seeking one's own interests or advantage but that of others—that is, the virtue of love (13:5).[85] Similarly, building up, or edification, was said in 8:1 to be what love does: "knowledge puffs up," while "love builds up." That is the litmus test of Christian behavior with respect to others: does it express love in the sense not merely of warm feelings (as important as they are) but of seeking the good of that individual or the community?

So Paul's one-word answer about Corinthian behavior toward others is "love!" Somewhat surprisingly, the word itself does not occur in these verses, but its content is everywhere. This one-word response is given more specific, but not unexpected, shape in four maxims, found in 10:24 and 10:31–11:1. These maxims are meant as substitutes for the misguided Corinthian slogans in v. 23 and as amplifications of the brief rejoinders there. Paul's alternatives stress the criterion of loving, missional other-centeredness:

- **10:24:** "Do not seek your own advantage [NIV, "good"] but that of the other [NAB, "neighbor"]." See also 10:33, quoted below, and 13:5; Phil 2:4, 21; Rom 15:1–4. This is an exhortation to community care and reciprocity.
- **10:31:** "So, whether you eat or drink, or whatever you do, do everything [*panta*; "all things"] for the glory of God." See also 6:20; Col 3:17. This is an exhortation to a comprehensive approach to daily life as worship (see Rom 12:1–2). As with sexual behavior (6:20), what and how one eats and drinks in relationship with one's neighbor is also an expression of one's relationship to God and God's glory.
- **10:32–33:** "Give no offense to Jews or to Greeks or to the church of God, just

---

85. The *symph-* word family was commonly used in Greek to urge community harmony. Paul gives it a theological, specifically christological, interpretation.

268

as I try to please everyone ["all people"] in everything ["all things"] I do, not seeking my own advantage [NIV, "good"; NAB, "benefit"], but that of many, so that they may be saved." See also 10:24, quoted above, as well as 9:19–23; 2 Cor 12:19. This is an exhortation to a truly catholic ("all") and missional perspective and praxis both outside and inside the *ekklēsia*.

- 11:1: "Be [lit., "become"] imitators of me, as I am of Christ." See also 4:16; Phil 3:17. This is an exhortation to missional Christoformity—not an expression of hubris or self-promotion.

In sum, these maxims call on the Corinthians to glorify God in their eating, or noneating, by living a life dedicated to the welfare—that is, the salvation—of the other, even to the point of renouncing the exercise of status and rights, as an imitator of their spiritual father and, ultimately, of their Lord. Once again, the "Although [x] not [y] but [z]" pattern is implicitly operative, with the [y] and [z] components explicit in phrases like "Do not . . . but" (10:24) and "Give no offense . . . but" (10:32–33).

The Greek phrase "Become [*ginesthe*] imitators of me" (MJG) in 11:1, usually translated simply as "Be imitators," tells us that living out these maxims is an ongoing process of transformation—transformation not into the image of Paul per se but into the image of Christ. Jesus is the ultimate apostle (Rom 8:3; Gal 4:4). Paul, his colleagues, and other believers are, in turn, his ambassadors (2 Cor 5:20).

Imitation was a highly significant aspect of ancient ethics, Jewish as well as pagan, and it appears in various ways throughout the New Testament writings, including Paul's. But we must distinguish Paul's spirituality from a simple ethic of imitation, even *imitatio Christi*. Paul's focus is on the activity of the living, indwelling Messiah, by the Spirit—who is the Spirit of both the Father and the Son. The living Lord Jesus, who is identical with the crucified Messiah (as discussed in the comments on 1:18–2:5), enables individuals and communities he indwells to become like him. They will engage in acts of Spirit-enabled *nonidentical repetition* that constitute their individual and communal narratives. Those narratives will be fundamentally shaped like those of Paul and, ultimately, of Christ, yet also different in details, varying from time to time and place to place. This is the essence of resurrectional, charismatic cruciformity.

It is clear that Paul sees the maxims listed above as much more than off-the-cuff rejoinders to the Corinthians. They are deeply theological and widely applicable in many different settings, both within the church and outside the church (as we will see in considering 10:25–30). Paul's universal, catholic con-

ADDRESSING LITURGICAL CHAOS · 8:1–14:40

cern is prominent, and for him the centripetal and centrifugal dimensions of mission are clearly inseparable. Once again, as well, the vertical and horizontal aspects of covenant fulfillment are inextricable: looking out for one's neighbor and glorifying God; giving no offense to anyone and imitating Christ.

Since Paul has already warned about being a stumbling block that might undo someone's salvation (8:9), it comes as no surprise that his motivation for this others-centered life is people's salvation. But now the scope of that salvation has grown from "the church of God" to include "Jews or Greeks," meaning anyone outside the church (10:32; cf. 1:22–24). As in Romans, Paul divides the non-Christ-following world into Jews and Greeks/gentiles.[86] The "do no harm" exhortation of 10:32 means that all believers have a missionary mandate to live and work for the salvation—new and eternal life in Christ— that they have experienced themselves. Paul wants the Corinthian believers to "develop what we may call a 'missional consciousness' in every aspect of their individual and corporate lives. . . . To cultivate a purposive, missional posture—a 'salvific intentionality.' . . . It is this salvific intentionality that links Paul's comprehensive mission to that of the Corinthian church."[87]

10:25–30. Eating Meat: Other Contexts

In between the two sets of maxims found in 10:23–24 and 10:31–11:1, Paul turns in 10:25–30 specifically to two related matters: eating meat sold in meat markets and eating meat in the homes of nonbelieving gentile acquaintances. The theme of salvific intentionality continues.

The first issue is the eating of meat sold in the markets, which were generally associated with temples, to be consumed at home (10:25–26). The Corinthian believers are free to eat such meat because it is part of God's good creation, as Scripture attests (10:26, quoting Ps 24:1).[88] If invited to the home of an unbeliever for a meal, they may eat the meat set before them, without asking questions, since the meal is neither in the temple precincts nor (Paul assumes) a sacral meal (10:27).

If, however, someone identifies the meat as sacrificially offered to a god—as *hierothyton*, or sacred meat (because for the non-Christian friend it is not idol meat, *eidōlothyton*)—the Corinthians should seek not to be a stumbling block (for believer or unbeliever) by eating the meat. Abstaining is a way of disasso-

---

86. See Rom 1:16; 2:9–10; 3:9, 29; 9:24; 10:12; cf. Gal 3:28; Col 3:11.
87. Barram, "Pauline Mission as Salvific Intentionality," 236–37 (emphasis added).
88. See also Ps 50:13; 89:11; Rom 14:14, 20; Mark 7:18–19.

270

ciating themselves from any hint of idolatry (10:28–29a, patterned on the "not [y] but [z]" maxims in 10:24 and 10:32–33) and looking out for the salvation of the friend or associate. The concern is for the other's *syneidēsis*—the person's awareness or sensibilities (10:29a, as in 8:7). That is, believers have both a personal and a missional interest in such a setting. One can only imagine how interesting—or possibly distressing—the resulting conversation could be.

This discussion still leaves, however, 10:29b–30: "For why should my liberty be subject to the judgment of someone else's conscience? If I partake with thankfulness, why should I be denounced because of that for which I give thanks?" The first-person-singular ("my," "I") language is significant. If 10:28–29a is read as a kind of parenthesis, Paul may be reasserting his own position from 10:25–27 that one's freedom to eat meat should not unnecessarily be curtailed. That is, in a private home, when no questions are raised, there is no reason to hesitate for anyone's sake.

But there is a better interpretation of vv. 29b–30. Although it may sound like Paul is speaking personally and articulating his own position, the first-person language is a rhetorical device. The ideas, if not the precise words, represent a Corinthian perspective on freedom we have come to expect. Paul is putting into "I/my" language what is a logical, individualistic Corinthian response to his call for self-restraint and missional other-centeredness, not to *affirm* it but to *refute* it. His own view is contained in the maxims: Christlike love, salvific intentionality, avoidance of idolatry, glorification of God.

In 10:29b–30, then, we find the perspective of a person and culture whose basic ethical position asserts autonomy and rights. Paul's missional drive leads him in a different direction, shaped by Christ, and he desperately hopes the Corinthians (whether of the first or the twenty-first century) will follow. In the larger subunit at hand (10:23–11:1), Paul preserves Christian liberty by advocating either the use of rights or the renunciation of rights, whichever befits and advances the gospel by serving others and glorifying God.

Summary

If catholicity is arguably a prime theme of chapters 8–14, it emerges in 8:1–11:1 in various ways, perhaps best summarized in the words "no offense to Jews or to Greeks or to the church of God" (10:32). That is, catholicity is inherently apostolic, missional. Positively, this means looking out for the interests, needs, salvation, and spiritual flourishing of all people, both outside and inside the *ekklēsia*. And surprisingly, this concern appears again in the little word "all": not all things are beneficial, not all things edify; all things for the glory of God.

ADDRESSING LITURGICAL CHAOS · 8:1–14:40

Reflections and Questions for 10:1–11:1

Spiritual, Pastoral, Missional, and Theological Reflections

1. It is ironic but true that **the consumption of food and drink** can express the deepest communion with fellow Christians, with Christ, with the poor, and with nonbelievers, and yet, especially in excess, can also express idolatry and provoke sexual immorality.

2. Two writers to consider on **the general nature of idolatry**:
   › Poet and spiritual writer Kathleen Norris:

   I no longer think idolatry is a problem of primitive people in a simpler time, those who worshipped golden calves in fertility rites. I have only to open a newspaper to contemplate the wondrously various ways in which idolatry is alive in the here and now.[89]

   › Biblical scholar and theologian Stephen Fowl:

   I am convinced that it is never any believer's immediate intention to engage in idolatry. Rather, idolatry is the result of a number of small incremental moves: a set of seemingly benign or even prudent decisions; a set of habits and dispositions—often acquired through subtle participation in a wider culture; a set of influential friendships. All of these work in complex combinations gradually to direct our attention slowly and almost imperceptibly away from the one true God towards that which is not God.

      Further, detecting such deviations is difficult because such turning away from God is rarely total. It appears much more common that our turning away from God still allows us to keep God in view, in our peripheral vision.[90]

3. More specifically, on the particular character of idolatry in the West or Global North:

   It has often been said that the most common idols in the West are Power, Sex, and Money; with this I am not in any profound disagreement. However, inasmuch as these idols are connected to a larger vision of life, such as the American dream, or the inalienable rights of free people, they become part of a nation's civil religion. I would contend, in fact, that the most alluring and dangerous deity in the United States is the omnipresent, syncretistic god of nationalism mixed with Christianity lite: religious beliefs, language, and practices that are superficially Christian but infused with national myths and habits. Sadly, most of this civil religion's practitioners belong to Christian

---

89. Kathleen Norris, *Amazing Grace: A Vocabulary of Faith* (New York: Riverhead Books, 1998), 92.

90. Stephen E. Fowl, *Idolatry* (Waco, TX: Baylor University Press, 2019), 3–4.

churches, which is precisely why [the book of] Revelation is addressed to the seven *churches* (not to Babylon), to all Christians tempted by the civil cult.[91]

What this quotation describes briefly (and there is much more detail in the book) as "civil religion" is better described, as of the publication of the present book, as **Christian nationalism. This term is perhaps the most dangerous oxymoron in the history of the English language,** even if the distorted theology behind it is not new but goes back many centuries. (Hence a better term is *so-called* Christian nationalism.) As recent events have demonstrated, it can be both fiercely pro- and fiercely antigovernment. Though hardly limited to the United States, it can arguably be described as the most potent—and dangerous—religious force in the United States. Ironically, especially in light of Stephen Fowl's words cited above, it is an idolatry that for some does not involve turning *away* from God, and specifically from Jesus, but rather turning more intensely *toward* Jesus. Or so it is thought. Yet it is nonetheless idolatry, because the Jesus allegedly worshiped is another Jesus, not the Jesus of the Gospels or Paul. Christian nationalism, as Paul himself would say, is a perversion of Jesus and the gospel (2 Cor 11:4; Gal 1:6–9).

Questions for Those Who Read, Teach, and Preach

1. What sorts of idolatry are currently operative today? If idolatry is common but (generally?) unintentional, what can Christians do to identify and avoid it for themselves, for other Christians, and for the wider public?

2. What is the proper Christian response to Christian nationalism and to those involved in it?

3. Since food and drink can both express communion and provoke sin, how should contemporary Christian communities understand and practice various forms of eating and drinking today, in their specific cultures?

4. How can one maintain an attitude of salvific intentionality without becoming either mercenary or manipulative?

5. In sum, what does this passage urge the church to believe (faith), do (love), and anticipate (hope)?

FOR FURTHER READING

Beale, G. K. *We Become What We Worship: A Biblical Theology of Idolatry*. Downers Grove, IL: InterVarsity Press, 2008.

91. Michael J. Gorman, *Reading Revelation Responsibly: Uncivil Worship and Witness; Following the Lamb into the New Creation* (Eugene, OR: Cascade, 2011), 56.

Cavanaugh, William. *The Uses of Idolatry*. New York: Oxford University Press, 2024.

Fowl, Stephen E. *Idolatry*. Waco, TX: Baylor University Press, 2019.

Goode, Scott. *Salvific Intentionality in 1 Corinthians: How Paul Cultivates the Missional Imagination of the Corinthian Community*. Eugene, OR: Wipf & Stock, 2023.

Goppelt, Leonhard. *Typos: The Typological Interpretation of the Old Testament in the New*. Trans. Donald H. Madvig. Grand Rapids: Eerdmans, 1982. (technical)

Hays, Richard B. *Echoes of Scripture in the Letters of Paul*. New Haven: Yale University Press, 1989. (technical)

Hurtado, Larry W. *Destroyer of the Gods: Early Christian Distinctiveness in the Roman World*. Waco, TX: Baylor University Press, 2016.

Strait, Drew J. *Strange Worship: Six Steps for Challenging Christian Nationalism*. Eugene, OR: Cascade, 2024.

Whitehead, Andrew L. *American Idolatry: How Christian Nationalism Betrays the Gospel and Threatens the Church*. Grand Rapids: Brazos, 2023.

Summary of 1 Cor 8:1–11:1

Since 1 Cor 8:1–11:1 is such an important and substantive unit, some summary words are in order:

- Those who live in Christ cannot order their lives according to an ethic of unrestrained freedom based on knowledge—even correct theological knowledge—that stresses self-interest and rights without regard for the impact of behavior on others.

- The truest expression of freedom is not the unrestrained exercise of rights but the free decision, out of loving concern for others, not to exercise even legitimate rights. True freedom, in other words, is freedom from the tyranny of the self; it is self-giving love. For those who pattern their lives after Christ, such freedom may also, paradoxically, be an obligation.

- Thus, salvific intentionality—concern for the salvation of others, both within and outside the church—should guide Christian decision making.

- Even apparently correct theological knowledge can be destructive and dangerous when used carelessly or selfishly.

- Allegiance to the Lord Jesus is an exclusive devotion and *koinōnia* that leaves no room for association with idolatry.

- The church has been woven into the story and the stories of Israel, within which and from which it must learn how to be God's people: one, holy, catholic, and apostolic—all at once.

REFLECTIONS AND QUESTIONS ON 1 COR 8:1–11:1 AS A WHOLE

1. One of the main contributions of these three chapters is the **challenge they pose to normal understandings of such key philosophical, theological, and practical topics as freedom, rights, and love.**

   How could the interrelationship among these three topics be summarized from these chapters? How could their interconnectedness contribute to the often-polarized discussions of these and related topics in the church and the wider culture?

2. It is once again clear that **the marks of the church—one, holy, catholic, and apostolic—are also inseparable from one another.**

   How do these four marks appear as a unified whole in these chapters? How can they be kept together in contemporary Christian theology and praxis?

11:2–14:40
*The Church (*Ekklēsia*) Gathered for Worship*

If 1 Cor 8:1–11:1 is focused in large measure on the negative, namely, how *not* to worship—vertically through acts of idolatry and horizontally through acts of self-centeredness—then 11:2–14:40 is focused on the positive, namely, how *to* worship. This is not to say that the problems in Corinth have been left behind, because there is still plenty of controversy and chaos recounted in these chapters. Nonetheless, Paul, assisted by his colleague Sosthenes, concentrates on re-forming the church's corporate worship, in ways that better exhibit the cross of Christ and the work of the Spirit. In so doing, they hope the Corinthians and their spiritual heirs will be more catholic (universal, inclusive) and more unified, holy, and apostolic in their worship of the one true God, Father, Son, and Spirit (see, e.g., 12:4–5)

These four chapters provide more light on early Christian worship than any other part of the New Testament. It appears that when the *ekklēsia* actually gathered together, which probably happened at least weekly, on the "first day of every week" (1 Cor 16:2),[92] it did so both to share food (a *deipnon*) and to engage in related cultic and community-building (edifying) activities

---

92. That is, Sunday, or possibly Saturday evenings, since the Jewish Sabbath ended at sundown. But most interpreters take the reference to "the first day" to be Sunday, since gentiles would be following the Roman, not the Jewish, calendar.

ADDRESSING LITURGICAL CHAOS   · 8:1–14:40

(a *symposion*).[93] The evidence from these chapters of 1 Corinthians, from other parts of the letter, and from the remaining Pauline letters bears witness to numerous practices, many of which probably occurred regularly in the group's gatherings:

1. an entrance ritual of initial participation in Christ and his body by immersion (baptism) for new converts (e.g., 1 Cor 1:14–16; 6:11; 12:13; Rom 6; Eph 4:5)
2. the Lord's Supper, focused on sharing one cup and one loaf (1 Cor 11:17–34)
3. prayer, that is, individuals—both men and women—speaking *to* God on behalf of the assembly (e.g., 1 Cor 11:2–16; 1 Thess 5:17–18; Eph 6:18; Phil 1:9), including intercession, praise/blessing, and congregational "Amens" (1 Cor 14:16; Eph 5:20)
4. prophecy/revelation, that is, individuals—both men and women—speaking *for* God to the assembly (1 Cor 11:2–16; 14; 1 Thess 5:19–21), subject to communal testing and discernment (1 Cor 14:29–33; 1 Thess 5:21)[94]
5. the exercise of additional *charismata/pneumatika* (grace-gifts/Spirit-ual gifts) such as glossolalia (tongues-speaking), tongues interpretation, and healing (1 Cor 12, 14)
6. active participation by those present (1 Cor 14:26–31)
7. the recitation of acclamations, such as "Jesus is Lord" (1 Cor 12:3; Phil 2:11) and *marana tha* (= "Our Lord, come!"; 1 Cor 16:22; cf. Rev 22:20); creed-like texts (e.g., 1 Cor 15:3–8; Phil 2:6–11); and other liturgical material (e.g., 1 Cor 11:23–25)
8. the singing of psalms and hymns (1 Cor 14:15, 26; Eph 5:19; Col 3:16)
9. mutual care, including the sharing of participants' joys, sufferings, and practical needs (Rom 12:9–13; 1 Cor 12:22–26; Phil 2:1–4; 1 Thess 5:11–15)
10. the reading and interpretation of Scripture (e.g., Rom 15:4)
11. the reading and interpretation of apostolic correspondence (1 Thess 5:27), including letters originally sent to other assemblies (Col 4:16)
12. teaching, including moral admonition, both from leaders and among participants (1 Cor 14:26; Eph 5:16)
13. preparation for ministry (Eph 4:11–13)
14. the exercise of discipline and dismissal (1 Cor 5:1–13)
15. the extension of forgiveness and, in extreme cases, reacceptance/readmission (2 Cor 2:5–11; Eph 4:32; Col 3:13)[95]

93. For these terms, see the discussion of 11:17–34.
94. There may have been some (local?) restrictions on women's participation; both 1 Cor 14:33b–35 (see discussion below) and 1 Tim 2:11–15 are difficult texts to interpret.
95. I am not suggesting, as some interpreters think, that the person described in

276

16. the collection of funds for internal needs (Rom 12:13; Gal 6:2?), apostolic mission work (Rom 15:24, 28–29; Phil 4:10–19), and support of other churches (Rom 15:25–28; 1 Cor 16:1–4; 2 Cor 8–9; cf. Gal 2:10)

17. the welcoming of nonbelieving visitors and believing guests (Rom 12:13; 1 Cor 14:16, 21–25; Phlm 22)

18. the exchange of holy kisses (Rom 16:16; 1 Cor 16:20; 2 Cor 13:12; 1 Thess 5:26)

We turn now to 11:2–14:40 itself. The major sections of these chapters are the following:

11:2–16 **Prophetic, Prayerful Women and Men in the Assembly**
11:17–34 **Abuse of the Lord's Supper**
12:1–14:40 **Spiritual Gifts in the Body of Christ**
    12:1–31   The Church as Christ's Richly Gifted Body
    13:1–13   The Rule (Criterion) of Cruciform Love in Eschatological Perspective
    14:1–40   Edification and the Use of Gifts in Worship

11:2–16. Prophetic, Prayerful Women and Men in the Assembly

Few passages in the Pauline letters are as vexing for the interpreter as 11:2–16, which has been debated for centuries. The difficulty of certain words, the complicated—some would say tortured or inconsistent—logic of thought and interrelationship of sentences, and the veiled (no pun intended) references to ancient social phenomena are just some of the interpretive issues. The result is a complex set of variables that has given rise to numerous reconstructions of the social setting and thus to various overall interpretations. Some people delight in Paul's alleged call for women to be subordinate to men; others find Paul's statements offensive and oppressive; still others conclude that the passage must be a later interpolation (addition) similar in spirit to 1 Tim 2:9–15.

Within this interpretive morass, one very important aspect of 11:2–16, about which all interpreters should be able to agree, is often overlooked: Paul assumes without hesitation or discussion that women, like men, may pray and prophesy in worship (11:4–5, 13). Women speak both *to* God on behalf of the assembly (prayer) and *for* God (prophecy) to the assembly (11:4–5). No matter what else we conclude, we must stress that in this respect, men and

---

2 Cor 2:5–11 is the person described in 1 Cor 5:1–13. But the person Paul has now forgiven has been subject to serious punishment by the Corinthian majority (2 Cor 2:6).

women are equal in Christ. Here we have echoes of various texts penned by Paul, especially Gal 3:28 ("no longer male and female; for all of you are one in Christ Jesus") and the discussion of reciprocity in marriage (1 Cor 7:1–16).

Paul may also have this prophetic promise in mind: "Then afterward I will pour out my spirit on all flesh; your sons and your daughters shall prophesy, your old men shall dream dreams, and your young men shall see visions. Even on the male and female slaves, in those days, I will pour out my spirit" (Joel 2:28–29). The Spirit empowers women as well as men, young and old, slave and free. Paul certainly treated women with respect and as coworkers in his own ministry, and in recognizing their hosting and leading house churches.[96]

The first half of chapter 11 raises many specific questions, among which we may note the following:

- Does the text describe male-female or husband-wife relationships—or a little of both? (The Greek words for "man" and "woman" can also mean "husband" and "wife.") Are these relationships descriptive of all people or just believers?
- What is the significance of the word "head" in these verses—in both literal and nonliteral senses? Does it have multiple meanings in the text? (Some possible nonliteral meanings include "authority," "source," "most prominent figure," and "contrast or complement to the body.") Is the character of each of the three relationships of headship (man-woman, Christ-man, God-Christ) precisely the same?
- Does the passage interpret male-female or husband-wife relationships as hierarchical, reciprocal, or both?
- Does the text refer to the practice of wearing some article of clothing (e.g., toga, hood, veil, or head covering—though none is explicitly named), to hairstyles (loose or bound), or to both? Which of various possible cultural practices does the text reflect?
- Does Paul *propose* or *oppose* the clothing or hairstyles mentioned?
- Does every line in the text represent Paul's own views? If so, does he *contradict* himself or *qualify* himself as the passage moves forward? If not, is he possibly once again quoting some Corinthians?
- How does this passage relate to other passages in the letter and elsewhere in Paul?

How are we to put together all these variables and answer these difficult questions? We will not address all of these issues in detail; that would take

96. See, e.g., Rom 16; 1 Cor 16:19; Phil 4:2–3; Col 4:15.

at least a book. Rather, what follows are two different basic interpretations of this passage. Both interpretations proceed on the assumption that Paul is not incoherent or inconsistent. Any interpretation must be offered with due humility and tentativeness.

Interpretation A: One Voice (Paul)

What follows is my own amalgam and reinterpretation of various proposals that have been made about this passage. I offer it in the best possible light but will also point out certain serious difficulties with it.

It appears to many scholars that some women in Corinth felt that the gospel (i.e., life in Christ and the Spirit) emancipated them, at least when they were at worship, from their culture's normal public expressions of (1) female distinctiveness from men or (2) sexual modesty—and perhaps both. These women expressed this gospel-rooted emancipation in the assembly by uncovering their heads or letting their hair down, thereby emitting cultural signals of maleness, sexual looseness, or both. Since Paul has already addressed instances of *male* sexual freedom (5:1–13; 6:12–20), perhaps these women were merely seeking gender equality.[97]

Paul seeks to redress this practice, not by putting women in their place (i.e., under the authority of men) but by reminding male and female believers alike of the ongoing need for culturally appropriate signs of gender identity and modesty, as well as the reality of equality and interdependence in the church. Interpreters are divided over whether this gender identity by virtue of creation should be understood as gender hierarchy (i.e., male superiority or prominence) or simply differentiation. In either case, it could be argued that the creative tension in Paul's mind between the two realities of creation/culture and redemption/Christ produces the difficulties and near inconsistencies in the passage.

On this reading, Paul opens and closes the passage (11:2, 16) by appealing to the importance of apostolic tradition and universal custom (catholicity) in certain matters (cf. also 11:23–26; 15:3–7), including this one. He commends the Corinthians for maintaining the traditions he handed on to them intact, which is (on any reading) a bit of an odd statement since the two specific traditions he later names—the Last Supper (11:17–34) and the gospel's emphasis on the resurrection (15:1–12)—have been undermined by certain Corinthians.

---

97. I owe this observation to Michelle Rader.

ADDRESSING LITURGICAL CHAOS

Moreover, Paul then goes on to correct the Corinthians' misappropriation of his teaching, as he has done before in this letter.

The basic teaching he seems to recall and wants to have properly interpreted has to do with three relationships of headship: Christ to man or (more likely) husband, husband to wife, and God to Christ (11:3). These forms of headship can be understood in either specifically hierarchical (head as authority) or in more generally relational (head as source or contrast/complement) terms. Recent scholarship definitely favors the latter. In either case, the relationship implies that the "head" can be shamed or disgraced by the behavior of the other (11:4–5), who is the "glory" (*doxa*) of the corresponding head (11:7).[98]

These somewhat confusing more theological remarks about headship and glory envelop the concrete practice at issue: the appropriate head covering or hairstyle for men and women at worship. (The context focuses on, but is also broader than, husband-wife relations.) If a man prays or prophesies with his head covered (11:4)—as contemporary males with sufficient social status to lead rites in pagan temples often did (ancient statues and coins bearing witness)—he shames his head (Christ), perhaps by treating Christ like a pagan deity, drawing attention to himself, or dressing in an inappropriately effeminate way.[99]

On the other hand, a woman who prays or prophesies with her head uncovered (or her hair unbound)[100] disgraces her head (her husband), perhaps by failing to maintain her gender identity, her sexual modesty, or both; she has become a loose woman, so to speak, and she might as well adopt the most culturally radical sign of rejecting her femaleness and modesty: a shaven head (11:5–6), the sign of a prostitute. The head covering or bound hair, then, is a sign of chastity, a symbolic barrier to sexual advances. It is possible that a woman's uncovered head or loose hair in worship would be associated also with the frenzied activity of women in certain pagan cults.

At first glance, the next few verses (11:7–10), which appeal to the Genesis creation narrative, sound like the most hierarchical and patriarchal sentences in the passage, and they well may be. But modern translations can actually create more forceful impressions along these lines than what the text actually says.

---

98. Because the cultural dynamic in play here is honor versus shame, the key term *doxa* should be rendered as "glory" (so most translations) or at least something like "reflection of glory" (cf. NJB), not simply "reflection" (NRSV, NRSVue).

99. In some cults, men did not cover their heads, so the precise reference and analogy cannot be discerned with certainty.

100. Although none of the standard English versions translates the phrase this way, some interpreters have suggested it.

For example, "*but* [Gk. *de*] woman is the glory of man" (11:7b NAB, NIV) can be translated "*and* woman . . . ," while woman's creation "*for* man" (11:9 NAB, NIV) or "*for the sake of* man" (NRSV) is better rendered "*on account of* [Gk. *dia*] man."

These nuances may suggest that the relationship of man to woman is not primarily one of superiority but rather of source, as 11:8 states. The enigmatic references to a sign of "authority" and to "angels" (11:10) are probably intended to reinforce the need for order in the assembly, where angels were apparently thought to join with humans in the worship of God. (Another possibility is that women must not sexually tempt angels, like those in Gen 6:1–4, according to Jewish tradition.)

One potential problem with this reading, however, is that it possibly (some would say definitely) includes a one-sided misinterpretation of Genesis, for in Genesis it is not merely man who is the image of God (1 Cor 11:7) but "male and female" (Gen 1:27). However, since it is difficult to believe that Paul disagreed with Gen 1:27, it is possible that the succinct phrase in v. 7b could actually mean that woman as well as man is created in God's image: "he is the image and glory of God, while woman [also the image of God] is the glory of man" (MJG; tentative paraphrase).[101]

If we assume that the entire passage represents Paul's thinking, regardless of whether hierarchical tendencies are present in 11:7–10, the ultimate significance of any such tendencies is countered by the reciprocity and equality affirmed in 11:11–12. In the Lord (Christ), men and women are thoroughly interdependent (11:11; recall 7:1–16); the gospel makes them equals (cf. Gal 3:28; cf. Col 3:11) who build one another up through prayer and prophecy. This gospel affirmation is supplemented by a reminder that even in the ongoing creation of humanity through childbirth, man comes from woman, and both from God (11:12)—an explicit egalitarian affirmation that at the very least modifies 11:8 and reinterprets 11:3 to rule out a hierarchical understanding of its headship language.

The conclusion of the passage, according to this overall interpretation, is a final admonition in the form of an invitation (11:13), grounded in an appeal to nature (11:14–15) and church custom (11:16). Women/wives must pray with their

---

101. See also, similarly, Cynthia Long Westfall, *Paul and Gender: Reclaiming the Apostle's Vision for Men and Women in Christ* (Grand Rapids: Baker Academic, 2016), 61–105, who speaks of Eve's "double identity" (65) as both image of God and glory of Adam, the latter due to being created directly from him. This interpretation is not new; it can be found, for instance, in Aquinas, *Commentary on 1 Corinthians* C.11, L.2, 607.

ADDRESSING LITURGICAL CHAOS · 8:1–14:40

heads covered (or hair bound). In sum, according to this reading of the passage, Paul affirms both (1) culturally appropriate expressions of gender identity (distinctiveness and sexual modesty), grounded in creation, and (2) gender equality and interdependence, grounded in both creation and Christ. Truly Spirit-filled worship respects these principles and embodies the order that is appropriate to the worship of God and the edification of the community (cf. 14:33, 40), even as both men and women pray and prophesy in the assembly. Nothing should distract from such full and holy participation in the church's worship.

Interpretation B: Two Voices (Paul and Certain Corinthian Men)

Interpretation A has a lot to commend it, but it also has some issues. For instance, it seems to some interpreters to pit creation against new creation in Christ, and possibly to pit Paul the hierarchicalist against Paul the egalitarian. In addition to such internal tensions, if not outright contradictions,[102] within this passage and in comparison to other texts in Paul, there is at least one additional significant problem with interpretation A. In 11:16, Paul does not advocate for the practices, or at least some aspect of the practices, he has been discussing. He does not say, "we have no *other* practice—nor do the churches of God" (NIV, emphasis added; cf. RSV, NET), but rather, "we have no such custom, nor do the churches of God" (NRSV, NRSVue; cf. NAB, CEB).[103] In other words, the principle of catholicity means *rejecting* some aspect of Corinthian practice. This suggests that Paul is not in 100 percent agreement with what seems to be said, or referenced, in the previous verses.[104]

As we have seen in earlier parts of the letter, when scholars note language that seems to contradict Paul's clear position on a topic, they often (rightly) posit Corinthian attitudes, even slogans, in the text (recall parts of 6:12–20; 7:1; 8:8; 10:29b–30). Some scholars have suggested that the patriarchy reflected in

---

102. One (not uncommon) version of interpretation A finds Paul to be confused and confusing and resorting to emotion and tradition when reason fails: Jouette Bassler, "1 Corinthians," in *Women's Bible Commentary*, rev. and updated ed. (3rd ed.), ed. Carol A. Newsom, Sharon H. Ringe, and Jacqueline E. Lapsley (Louisville: Westminster John Knox, 2012), 557–65 (here 562–63).

103. As in some translations of 6:18, the word "other" has been added despite its absence from the Greek text.

104. It also makes one wonder whether Paul is at times being sarcastic, perhaps here at the end of the passage (v. 16a) or back at the beginning (v. 2): "I commend you because you remember me in everything and maintain the traditions just as I handed them on to you" (cf. 11:19).

282

1 Cor 11:7–9 in particular is a distortion of Gen 1:27. Moreover, they contend that vv. 7–9 are in stark contrast to some of the surrounding verses, to the male-female mutuality of chapter 7, and to texts like Gal 3:28. In this view, Paul's own perspective is found primarily in 11:11–16, which begins with the word "Nevertheless" or "However" (Gk. *plēn*): in the Lord (Christ), there is male and female interdependence, and there is no need for hair restrictions other than the natural difference between male short hair and female long hair.

One important voice in this sort of reinterpretation is that of Lucy Peppiatt.[105] She argues that the problem at Corinth is not with certain *women* but with certain *men*, men who are trying to force women to wear head coverings because of their allegedly derivative and subordinate status that renders them in need of a "covering" in God's presence. According to Peppiatt, it is this practice Paul rejects by saying that such a practice is not the custom in the Christian assemblies (11:16); it is not *catholic*. Peppiatt argues that 11:3 shows Paul is seeking to correct the Corinthian men's misinterpretation of his original teaching about men and women. She attributes the words in 11:4–5 to these powerful men. In 11:6, she finds Paul's sarcastic rhetorical remark in response to their comparison of a woman's uncovered head to a shaven head: the (abusive, absurd) thing to do is shave their heads! Peppiatt further attributes 11:7–10 to the men, finding in those verses both poor scriptural interpretation and poor theology, which results in the misguided practice of requiring women to have a head covering.

Paul's main response, in 11:11–16, comes in two parts, according to Peppiatt.

First, in vv. 11–12, Paul speaks of interdependence in the Lord and reminds the Corinthians that the ultimate source of all is God. Paul is robustly God-centered, not male-centered. This harks back to his reminder that God is the "head" of Christ, and it helps to clarify Paul's original teaching about headship summarized in 11:3—it is a question of source. Moreover, in 1 Cor 15:28 Paul will affirm that God will be "all in all"; that is, everything ultimately comes from and will return to God. "Headship," then, does not mean a chain of command; in Christ there is no male-female subordination but cruciform mutuality, as chapter 7 has already made clear regarding marriage and chapter 12 will confirm with respect to life in the assembly.

Second, in vv. 13–16, Paul invites the Corinthian men to reconsider their position and realize that a woman already has appropriate glory and covering:

---

105. See Lucy Peppiatt, *Women and Worship at Corinth: Paul's Rhetorical Arguments in 1 Corinthians* (Eugene, OR: Cascade, 2015) and her more accessible *Unveiling Paul's Women: Making Sense of 1 Corinthians 11:2–16* (Eugene, OR: Cascade, 2018).

her hair. Thus, they should stop imposing a practice that is not the custom in the churches. It would be uncatholic.

Although the jury is still out on interpretation B, it has much to commend it. It eliminates possible internal contradictions in the text, providing a coherent reading of the passage as almost a dialogue—similar in rhetorical character to 6:12–20. It also removes the apparent tension between 11:2–16 and 7:1–16, and between the words in this passage and Paul's actual practices with respect to women. It also rescues Paul from what could be a poor reading of the creation narrative. Furthermore, it offers a positive interpretation of a text that has arguably done much damage to women and to male-female relationships.

At the same time, interpretation B has a few problems. To name just one, Peppiatt's analysis of v. 3 is debatable, and thus the proposed break between v. 3 (Paul) and vv. 4–5 (the Corinthian men) is thrown into question.[106]

Nevertheless, even if the last word on this passage has not been spoken, interpretation B is a significant alternative to interpretation A and is especially helpful in this respect: it is a reading of the passage that aligns with both what we know about Paul regarding women (see especially Rom 16) and what we think we know about the nature of the problems at Corinth—often, it appears, caused by elite males.[107] Further nuancing of such an interpretation may be necessary, but an attractive foundation has been laid.

Conclusion

The two sorts of interpretations described above are clearly incompatible with each other. At the same time, each has its own problems. I have indicated my

---

106. The problem of v. 3 is a technical matter of Greek that can be stated only in general terms here. Peppiatt interprets the infinitive form (*eidenai*) of the verb "to know/understand" (*oida*) in 11:3 not as "I want you to understand" (NRSV and most translations) but as "I wish/want you to have understood/known" (*Women and Worship at Corinth*, 86–87). This interpretation changes the entire character of the passage from a monologue to a rather sharp interchange. The overall interpretation may still be correct, but its basis in the translation of v. 3 is shaky.

107. Of course, there are a few passages in the Pauline correspondence that sound hierarchical or dismissive of women. We will consider 14:33–36 in due course. Eph 5:21–33 (regardless of whether by Paul himself) should be read in a cruciform and egalitarian way (see my *Cruciformity*, 261–66); 1 Tim 2:11–15 (again, regardless of whether by Paul) is complicated and continues to be subject to close scrutiny. See, e.g., Sandra L. Glahn, *Nobody's Mother: Artemis of the Ephesians in Antiquity and the New Testament* (Downers Grove, IL: IVP Academic, 2023).

own leaning toward B, but any honest interpreter should recognize that certainty about many aspects of this text, at this time, is probably not possible. Yet whichever overall interpretation of this puzzling passage one finds most persuasive, some form of A or B, there are in fact two points of absolute certainty, one theological and one practical:

- Theologically, in Christ the Lord, men and women, including husbands and wives, have a relationship of interdependence and, in some real sense, equality.
- Practically, this means that both men and women are invited and expected to pray and prophesy in the assembly at worship.

REFLECTIONS AND QUESTIONS FOR 11:2–16

Spiritual, Pastoral, Missional, and Theological Reflections

1. The various interpretations of this challenging passage provide **a good example of several issues in scriptural interpretation generally**: how to manage our biases and presuppositions, how to engage with new perspectives, how to understand and evaluate the significance of cultural contexts, how to read both carefully and canonically, and much more. Especially critical is the need for interpretive humility when dealing with texts that have so many variables.

2. With respect to the **significance of cultural context** for interpretation, all interpreters, but especially those who favor interpretation A, would do well to heed the words of the Ghanaian scholar John D. K. Ekem. After noting both the various challenges in our passage and the presence of various ethnicities and customs in Corinth, he concludes as follows:

> The Greek of 11:16 can also be interpreted as suggesting that there is no universal policy on this matter, and that it should be carefully handled within each specific cultural setting. . . . The question of head covering/hair-do, whatever its legitimacy in the Corinthian context, should not be treated legalistically and worse still, be allowed to degenerate into a fruitless bone of contention. Each community should handle the matter judiciously, guided by the principle of propriety. . . . Underlying 1 Cor 11:2–16 is the profound thought that decent orderly worship can occur within a multi-cultural context. Paul's argumentation in this intriguing passage can be understood as a plea for the cultivation of propriety by the worshipping community, mindful of divine-human relations as well as cultural sensibilities regarding male-female relations.[108]

---

108. John D. K. Ekem, "Does 1 Cor 11:2–16 Legislate for 'Head Covering'?," *Neotestamentica* 35 (2001): 169–76 (here 175).

ADDRESSING LITURGICAL CHAOS · 8:1–14:40

This perspective suggests that head coverings for women might be a sign of suppression or control in certain contexts but of respect in other contexts. It would seem most appropriate to show respect to someone who is gifted to pray or prophesy in the assembly.

3. The **rediscovery of an egalitarian Paul** has been slow in coming in certain circles. It is worth pondering whether that is due to exegesis or to something more ideological.

4. As with 1 Cor 12 and 14, this passage raises the question of **how best to acknowledge the gifts** given to all who are in Christ and to give space for their **exercise in the church's worship.**

Questions for Those Who Read, Teach, and Preach

1. What difference for preaching and teaching this passage does each of the overall interpretations (A, B) offer? Is there something of value in each?

2. What are the positive aspects of this text for preaching, teaching, and church life?

3. How have (allegedly Pauline) negative attitudes toward women affected the church's life and mission?

4. In sum, what does this passage urge the church to believe (faith), do (love), and anticipate (hope)?

FOR FURTHER READING

Gupta, Nijay K. *Tell Her Story: How Women Led, Taught, and Ministered in the Early Church*. Downers Grove, IL: IVP Academic, 2023. (highly accessible)

Peppiatt, Lucy. *Unveiling Paul's Women: Making Sense of 1 Corinthians 11:2–16*. Eugene, OR: Cascade, 2018. (highly accessible)

———. *Women and Worship at Corinth: Paul's Rhetorical Arguments in 1 Corinthians*. Eugene, OR: Cascade, 2015.

Westfall, Cynthia Long. *Paul and Gender: Reclaiming the Apostle's Vision for Men and Women in Christ*. Grand Rapids: Baker Academic, 2016.

11:17–34. ABUSE OF THE LORD'S SUPPER

First Corinthians 11:17–34 is of particular importance because it is the only discussion, in conjunction with 10:15–22, of "the Lord's supper" (11:20) in the Pauline letters.[109] Banquets of various kinds were common in the ancient

---

109. Following scholarly convention, I will capitalize "Supper" in the phrase "the

world, as in ours. There were private social banquets, collegium (club or association) banquets, philosophical banquets, sacrificial banquets, and more in the pagan world, as well as banquets in Judaism.[110] Most, if not all, of these banquets had a cultic dimension (devotion and sacrifice to a deity), though some more so than others.

The Corinthian believers naturally conducted their meetings and meals according to the models at hand, probably especially those of the ancient cultic collegium and the private dinner. In general, banquets had two parts, the meal itself (Gk. *deipnon*) plus the after-dinner time of discussion, entertainment, and especially drinking called the symposium (Gk. *symposion*). A symposium could take place on its own too.[111] Dining and divisiveness sometimes went hand in hand. A century after Paul, Lucian of Samosata makes fun of the culture of the *symposion* by describing a *deipnon*, with various philosophers among the guests, that devolved into drunkenness, intellectual quarreling (*eris*, as in 1 Cor 1:10; 3:3), food fights, and physical altercations with bloodshed.[112]

For Christ-participants in Corinth, the second stage of the banquet, the symposium, contained certain ritual elements and worship, including praise and prophecy (see 11:2–16; chs. 12–14). This time of worship was, or was supposed to be, the Christian substitute for the after-dinner discussions and other activities that would take place in a home or association gathering—without the drunkenness, division, and violence, of course.

In 1 Cor 11:17–34, however, Paul presents this Supper as something much more than a typical Greco-Roman banquet with only a few minor adjustments. The Lord's Supper is a bifocal event of solidarity (*koinōnia*), commemoration, and proclamation that brings spiritual blessing in remembrance of Christ's saving death and in anticipation of his parousia and the eschatological banquet of salvation. From Paul's perspective, however, the Corinthians have created an event of division, amnesia, and betrayal that warrants divine wrath. It looks a lot like something the god Dionysus (Bacchus) would host. The Corinthians are therefore *not* celebrating the Supper of the crucified, present, and coming Lord, no matter what they *think* they are doing.

Lord's Supper" (and in the short form, "the Supper") except when citing a text, like the NRSV, that uses the lowercase "supper."

110. See Dennis E. Smith, *From Symposium to Eucharist: The Banquet in the Early Christian World* (Minneapolis: Fortress, 2003); R. Alan Streett, *Subversive Meals: An Analysis of the Lord's Supper under Roman Domination during the First Century* (Eugene, OR: Pickwick, 2013).

111. Smith, *From Symposium to Eucharist*, 27, 31.

112. Lucian, *Symposium* (also known as *The Carousal*).

ADDRESSING LITURGICAL CHAOS

In the Greco-Roman world, meals expressed and created social boundaries. It is thus no surprise that eating seems to have been a problem in Corinth, as in other early Christian communities; Paul has already spent three chapters on the subject (8:1–11:1).[113] As in those chapters, Paul does not explicitly use a word from the "just-" (*dikaio-*) family, although the combination of factionalism and self-interest is indeed a matter of injustice. The meal has become a direct assault on those in the community "who have nothing" (11:22), an infliction of injustice against the weak and vulnerable. If *idol* worship is anathema for Christians (10:1–22), so also is its close cousin, *false* worship: worship that is fundamentally self-interested and fails to issue in care for others. Paul's concerns echo those of Isa 58:

> Look, you *fast* only to quarrel and to fight and to strike with a wicked fist. Such *fasting* as you do today will not make your voice heard on high. . . . Is not this the *fast* that I choose: to loose the bonds of injustice, to undo the thongs of the yoke, to let the oppressed go free, and to break every yoke? Is it not to share your bread with the hungry. . . . If you offer your food to the hungry and satisfy the needs of the afflicted, then your light shall rise in the darkness and your gloom be like the noonday. (Isa 58:4, 6–7a, 10; emphasis added)

For the Corinthians, we could replace Isaiah's word "fast" with the word "feast."

Paul addresses the abuse and injustice at the Supper in three steps, with another chiastic structure:

A The Problematic Situation (11:17–22)
  B The Tradition of the Last Supper (11:23–26)
A' The Remedy for the Problematic Situation (11:27–34)

The following comments begin with a relatively brief examination of each of these three sections, after which there is a fairly extensive treatment of Paul's theology of the Lord's Supper that incorporates both what he says here and what he had previously said in chapter 10. Paul is in a joint pedagogical and disciplinary mode, and in that mode he is once again profoundly, if succinctly, theological.

11:17–22. The Problematic Situation: Not the Lord's Supper

Paul begins his instructions by contrasting his commendation of the Corinthians in 11:2 with his criticism concerning their conduct of the Supper (11:17,

113. See also, e.g., Rom 14:1–15:13; Gal 2; Rev 2:12–17.

288

22). Verses 17–22, then, are bracketed by the phrase "I do not commend" (or "praise"; CEB, NAB) you. This *inclusio*, though perhaps understated for effect, drives home the main point of this section: sharp criticism of the standard Corinthian practice. The problem seems to be the norm, rather than the exception, for Corinthian gatherings; Paul speaks three times in these verses about the way the Corinthians "come together" (11:17, 18, 20). He will reuse the same verb in vv. 33 and 34. These are the times when the *ekklēsia* gathers as such (11:18), "in one place" (11:20; CEB, NAB); this Supper must not be treated as a private meal at home (implied by v. 22).

The Corinthians' coming together is "not for the better but for the worse" (11:17). This catastrophe results in judgment (11:34)—both Paul's (11:17, 22) and the Lord's (11:27–34). Something that ought to benefit the community is actually hurting it. The specific manifestation of harm is the existence of divisions—*schismata* (11:18; the same word is used in 1:10). Paul's reaction, again rather understated for rhetorical effect, is that this is just another variation on the Corinthian theme of factions: "to some extent I believe it" (11:18).[114] But the muted belief expresses, in context, the apostle's very deep concern. Paul sees the divisions as a necessity—the language hints at divine necessity; the chaos is a way of manifesting those who are genuine, tested and proven, so to speak (11:19).[115] Paul is somehow confident that something good may yet come from this chaos.

But before that can happen, he must assess the situation bluntly. The Supper is, or is supposed to be, "the Lord's" in at least three ways:[116]

- Jesus, as the risen Lord, is the *host* (and, as host, invites all sorts of people, especially those considered poor and weak).
- Jesus, again as the risen Lord, is the *guest of honor* (who is treated as such only when the meal is properly, hospitably practiced).[117]

114. Richard Hays describes Paul's attitude as one of "mock disbelief" (*First Corinthians*, 195).

115. A similar sentiment appears in 1 John 2:19.

116. See also Smith, *From Symposium to Eucharist*, 77–79, on the dimensions of ancient sacred meals.

117. An interesting parallel to the god as both host and guest can be found in the cult of the popular Greco-Egyptian god Sarapis (or Serapis); see, e.g., Philip A. Harland, "An Invitation from the God Sarapis: Banqueting with the Gods," *Ethnic Relations and Migration in the Ancient World*, last modified February 11, 2023, https://tinyurl.com/ms4phwbc. A papyrus invitation contains the words, "The god [Sarapis] calls you to a banquet being held . . . tomorrow from the 9th hour."

ADDRESSING LITURGICAL CHAOS   · 8:1–14:40

- Jesus, the risen Lord who is also the crucified Messiah, is the *meal* (consisting of his body broken and his blood shed).

But when the Corinthians are assembling, it is not to eat *the Lord's* Supper (11:20). *Jesus is no longer the host, the guest, or the meal.* There are no qualifiers like "not only" or "not really" (so NRSV, NET)—simply "it is not." Period. Paul does not mince words. Instead, he insists, each one goes ahead with *his own* supper (11:21). Or perhaps we should translate this as "his or her own," though it may be the case that elite males are the principal culprits. Nonetheless, Paul is counting the whole community culpable.

The concrete problem according to 11:20–22 seems to be something like the following:[118] all the believers, representing a variety of socioeconomic groups, are assembling at the large house of one wealthier member-patron, probably Gaius (see Rom 16:23; 1 Cor 1:14), or elsewhere under his patronage. Those with more wealth, leisure, and status—perhaps the host's friends and associates—are arriving early for the evening gathering, which includes a nice meal, while those lower on the socioeconomic ladder are arriving much later after working into the evening. The early birds are not waiting for the latecomers but joining the patron for what amounts to a private dinner and symposium, with some over-indulging in alcohol and no one showing concern about the needs of the poor who must come late. Slaves would not normally have participated, or participated fully, in any banquet, though they often purchased and served the food, and sometimes washed guests' feet. Were such things happening at Corinth?

Even a very large house would normally have only one or two dining rooms (*triclinia*),[119] which would not accommodate everyone, so the poorer late-comers and slaves are forced to eat separately from the wealthier members, perhaps in the atrium or in other rooms, and to scrounge for leftovers. This event has therefore lost all connection with the teaching Paul had given the Corinthians (11:23–26) and has come to resemble a typical dinner party of the Corinthian elite, at which such a situation would be perfectly normal.

Yet even some pagans knew that the host of a meal should treat all participants as equals. Pliny the Younger (ca. AD 61–113) writes of his negative experience at a meal and his own very different practice:

---

118. Since Paul does not provide a lot of information, scholars differ on various details about the situation.

119. A *triclinium* was a dining room with a couch along each of three sides. Many of these couches would hold only three people each, so the number of guests in a *triclinium* was quite limited.

I found myself dining the other day with an individual with whom I am by no means intimate, and who, in his own opinion, does things in good style and economically as well, but according to mine, with meanness and extravagance combined. Some very elegant dishes were served up to himself and a few more of us, whilst those placed before the rest of the company consisted simply of cheap dishes and scraps. . . . My neighbour, reclining next me, observing this, asked me if I approved the arrangement. Not at all, I told him. "Pray then," he asked, "what is your method upon such occasions?" "Mine," I returned, "is to give all my visitors the same reception; for when I give an invitation, it is to entertain, not *distinguish*, my company: I place every man upon my own level whom I admit to my table." "Not excepting even your freedmen?" "Not excepting even my freedmen, whom I consider on these occasions my guests, as much as any of the rest."[120]

It is possible that the Corinthians have not only made the meal into an expression of divisions rather than unity but also completely abandoned the ritual dimension of the Lord's Supper, the special cup and bread that were supposed to be the heart of the experience and its deepest expression of unity. Paul's dissatisfaction is not hidden; in 11:22, he poses four rhetorical questions:

- First, a biting, even sarcastic, rhetorical question about the Corinthians possibly not having private homes for private meals: "What! Do you not have homes to eat and drink in?" This does not mean that the assembly's gatherings were in, say, shops alone rather than homes, or that there was no meal at the gatherings. Rather, these gatherings had to be distinct both from private meals at home and from the cultural norm for segregated banquets by expressing *koinōnia*: unity, holiness, and catholicity.
- Then, a bluntly accusatory question that identifies what Paul claims the Corinthians are actually doing: showing contempt for God's church and shaming those who have nothing—the very kinds of people God has chosen (1:26–28).[121] Those God has called to shame (*kataischynē*) the powerful (1:27b) the powerful are now shaming (*kataischynete*)—a reversal of God's reversal![122]

---

120. Pliny the Younger, *To Avitus* (*Ep* 2.6; Harvard Classics trans.)

121. The phrase "those who have nothing" (*tous mē echontas*) in 11:22 echoes the phrase "things that are not" (NRSV) or "those who count for nothing" (NAB) in 1:28 (*ta mē onta*), and almost certainly refers to the same people—the majority of the Corinthian believers.

122. Most translations have a form of the verb "humiliate" rather than "shame," but the NET captures the Greek verb well: "Or are you trying to show contempt for the church of God by shaming those who have nothing?"

ADDRESSING LITURGICAL CHAOS · 8:1–14:40

Like other forms of division, this is, or at least closely approximates, church destruction (see 3:16–17).

- Next, a deliberative question, born of frustration—"What should I say to you?"
- And then right away, returning to the statement of 11:17, "Should I commend you?"—to which Paul replies succinctly but firmly in the negative.

Paul's rhetoric of judgment is grounded in the traditional biblical concern for the poor and needy, especially at meals, that we see expressed in the Old Testament prophets, Jesus, and James.[123] Paul is just as concerned about social justice as these predecessors; in fact, his concern is amplified by the gospel he preaches, the gospel and its consequences rehearsed in 1:18–2:5. The breaking of fellowship with others, especially the weak, inherently entails breaking fellowship with Jesus; the two fundamental divisions of the covenant—love for God and love for neighbor—are inseparable.

To correct the expulsion of the Lord, the grave injustice, and the attempted destruction of the church, Paul turns to the tradition about the Supper.

11:23–26. The Tradition of the Last Supper

In recounting the content of the tradition about Jesus' last meal with his disciples, Paul uses language that reflects the standard Jewish concept of formally receiving and passing on sacred tradition: in Greek, the verbs are *paralambanō* ("receive") and *paradidōmi* ("hand on/over"), both used in 11:23. But unlike the similar language about the tradition of Jesus' death, burial, resurrection, and appearances in 15:1–8, here Paul specifically identifies the source of the tradition: Jesus himself. Moreover, Paul identifies the time at which Jesus instituted this Supper with the same verb for "handing on/over," *paradidōmi*—that is, on the night Jesus was "betrayed" (NRSV and most translations) or "handed over" (NAB).[124] Given his use of the verb elsewhere (Rom 4:25; 8:32), Paul likely understands the agent here to be not Judas or other humans but God the Father.[125]

A few scholars think that Paul means he received the tradition directly from Jesus in a revelation (see 2 Cor 12:1, 7). But the language (see also 1 Cor 15:3)

123. See, e.g., Isa 25, 55; Luke 14:7–24; Jas 2:1–7.

124. The verb *paradidōmi* is used throughout the Gospels and in Paul to refer to Jesus' being handed/delivered over or betrayed. Interestingly, Paul also uses it to describe a key aspect of Christlike ministry: "we are always being given up [or "handed over"] to death" (2 Cor 4:11).

125. For the Old Testament background, see esp. Isa 53:6, 12; in both verses of the LXX, the verb *paradidōmi* is used, with 53:6 naming the agent specifically as "the Lord."

makes it much more likely that the words of Jesus came to Paul via certain disciples (Peter and James?) or more general oral traditions about Jesus, perhaps in gatherings of other early Christian assemblies. What is critical is that Paul is clearly placing a lot of weight on this tradition and especially its source. The implication is that neither Paul nor the Corinthians nor anyone else has the freedom to distort the practice of the Lord's Supper, because it comes from the Lord himself.

The account of the Last Supper with what are now sometimes called the words of institution appears in all three Synoptic Gospels, but Paul's version is more like Luke's (see Luke 22:15-20) than Matthew's or Mark's. Three key similarities between Luke (alone) and Paul are the following phrases:[126]

- "[My body] given for you [*hyper hymōn*]" (Luke 22:19b) and "my body that is for you [*hyper hymōn*]" (1 Cor 11:24)[127]
- "Do this in remembrance of me" (Luke 22:19b; 1 Cor 11:24, 25)
- "the new covenant in my blood" (Luke 22:20b; 1 Cor 11:25; cf. Exod 24:5-8)

The acts of Jesus narrated in the tradition (vv. 23b-25) are straightforward:

- taking the bread (before the meal? during the meal?)
- giving thanks
- breaking the bread
- identifying the bread as his body "for you"—plural, meaning "all of you" and "for your sins" (see 15:3)
- directing that this be enacted as a remembrance of him
- similarly taking the cup (after the meal, and probably also again giving thanks)
- identifying the cup as "the new covenant in my blood"
- directing that this be enacted, whenever it is enacted, as a remembrance of him

In the view of many scholars (including me), Jesus and, by extension, the early church (including Paul), understood this meal as a reinterpretation of the Passover Seder.[128] But this is debated, as there are elements noted here

---

126. A few manuscripts of Luke omit 22:19b-20, and some scholars think that the parallels listed here are actually due to Paul's language being added to Luke's Gospel after it was produced. I side with the scholars who find Luke 22:19b-20 to be original to Luke.

127. Some manuscripts have "broken for you" rather than simply "for you" in 11:24.

128. See, among others, Thiselton, *First Epistle*, 755-68, 871-88.

that would be part of other Jewish and even non-Jewish meals. No matter the sort of meal, the acts listed above and their accompanying words express the reality of Jesus' death for others—body given/broken, blood shed—and its twofold consequence: benefiting those for whom he dies and inaugurating the new covenant promised by the prophets.

Each of the actions and words listed above could receive detailed analysis. Some have been extraordinarily theologically controversial and theologically determinative, especially "This is my body" (v. 24). Rather than offering a word-by-word discussion, this commentary presents a synthetic theological reading of the Lord's Supper as a whole below (see pp. 297–303).

Following the recital of Jesus' acts and interpretive words, in 11:26 Paul adds what is probably his own interpretation of the eating and drinking at the Lord's Supper that arises organically from the tradition.[129] The Last Supper has become the Lord's Supper, a regular occurrence, not a onetime event or annual remembrance (like Passover). It is a proclamation of Jesus' death until he comes (again), until the parousia. Paul is, of course, devoted to proclaiming the crucified Messiah in word and deed (see 1:18–25; 2:1–5). The eschatological horizon included here appears also in Luke and the other Synoptic Gospels (Luke 22:16, 18; Matt 26:29; Mark 14:25). The Supper "mingles memory and hope."[130] Paul is again theologizing in a bifocal way: looking back to the cross and ahead to the parousia as he situates himself and his addressees in the present, shaped by the past and the future.

After considering Paul's solution to the crisis, we will consider more fully the meaning of this tradition as Paul inherits and interprets it. But what is immediately clear is this: an act that is meant to proclaim (CEB: "broadcast") the death of Jesus must not, cannot, contradict the fundamental purpose and significance of that death. Jesus' death "for you"—for the Corinthians, for us, for all—is the ultimate *catholic* act, the establishment of a new covenant and thus of a new-covenant community for Jews and gentiles, women and men, rich and poor.

This meal, then, is supposed to be a momentous celebration of a momentous event, the fulfillment of prophetic promises for a new exodus (e.g., Isa 43:16–21; 51:9–11) and a new covenant (e.g., Jer 31:31–34; 32:40), effected not by the death of animals (Exod 24) but by the death of God's Son, the Passover lamb (1 Cor 5:7). Although Paul uses the term "new covenant" only

---

129. It is possible that 11:26 is part of either the words of Jesus or the tradition Paul received, but it is more likely Paul's own succinct interpretation.

130. Hays, *First Corinthians*, 199.

here and in 2 Cor 3:6, the reality of the new covenant pervades his writings.[131] Can the Corinthians do worse than break that covenant?

11:27–34. The Remedy for the Problematic Situation

In 11:27–34, the Corinthian church receives strong words of condemnation, warning, and instruction concerning their behavior. Paul's solution to the eucharistic crisis at Corinth is multifaceted. In a word, it is "Wait!" or perhaps "Welcome [all]!" (11:33; cf. Rom 15:7): wait for and welcome all in order to eat the *Lord's* Supper—*together*. But there is more to Paul's response than that; his solution is inseparable from a preliminary but critical word of judgment. It is a message that takes up the first six verses (11:27–32) of this last section; the apostolic judgment of 11:17–22 is now clearly divine judgment. And with God's judgment, there is also, as always, hope.

In those six verses, the apostle wraps two general statements about accountability for taking part in the Supper in an unworthy manner (11:27, 29) around an admonition to therefore engage in self-examination before participating (11:28; see also 2 Cor 13:5). He then diagnoses the illness and dying at Corinth as a sign of divine judgment (11:30, 32) that, with appropriate community self-judgment, could have been avoided (11:31).[132] The community is "answerable" for the cross (11:27) and judged by the Lord; Paul explains the Corinthian debilitation and death as a consequence of their grave misbehavior—they are like the Israelites in the wilderness, where many died (see 10:1–11). In fact, the warnings from chapter 10 about idolatry and sexual immorality have been transferred to the sin of injustice toward the weak.

But there is, so to speak, a silver lining in all of this. Paul uses three different verbs in 11:32 to say that when the Lord *judges* us, he is *disciplining* us so that we will *not be condemned* as the world will be. In other words, the Corinthians have an opportunity to get their act together.

What would that mean? The answer is in 11:33–34, as Paul says, "So then" or "Therefore. . . ." (1) When you meet as the church of God, wait for and thereby welcome *all*—not some, but everyone, especially those who have nothing (11:33). (2) Do not consider this event to be primarily a meal, which you can have at home, but rather a communal celebration and proclamation

---

131. See especially Brant Pitre, Michael P. Barber, and John A. Kincaid, *Paul, A New Covenant Jew: Rethinking Pauline Theology* (Grand Rapids: Eerdmans, 2019).

132. The verb referring to death in v. 30 is the present tense of the verb "to sleep"; although it could mean "are dying" (NAB), it more likely means "have died" ("are sleeping").

ADDRESSING LITURGICAL CHAOS · 8:1–14:40

(11:34). *There may be some food, but the food is not the main course: Jesus is.* To consume him—his body and blood—means to share in his death by sharing in the life of the community, not by gorging oneself on food and drink.

This passage raises several significant exegetical and theological questions, especially about unworthy participation, self-examination, discerning the body, and divine punishment/discipline. But a few controversial aspects are actually quite clear as long as we read the passage as a whole and don't just pick a verse out of context.

First, whatever else it means, to participate unworthily in the Supper (v. 27) clearly means to mistreat others, especially the poor, in the way the Supper is celebrated. The ultimate catholic Christian ritual cannot be exclusive about which members of the community are welcome.

Second, whatever else it means, Paul's call to self-examination (v. 28) is not a polite invitation but a strong admonition. It is both an *individual* call ("let each person examine himself or herself"; 11:28 MJG)[133] and a *communal* call ("if we judged/discerned ourselves"; 11:31). Each of us and all of us must look at what is done and how it is done.

Third, whatever else it means, discerning "the body" (v. 29) refers to seeing the gathered *ekklēsia*—the whole church, meaning each and every participant—for what it is: the one body of Christ (see ch. 12). (At the same time, those who have typically dismissed the interpretation of discerning the body as a reference to the communion bread, as Christ's body, need to look again at the connection between bread and community that appears when chapter 10 is read alongside 11:17–34.) The ultimate feast of catholicity is inherently a celebration of unity, or at least it should be. Paul has already criticized the (allegedly) wise Corinthians for their failure at discernment (6:5), but he will also say that God does indeed gift the gift of discernment (12:10) and expects it to be used in the assembly (14:29).

And finally, whatever else it means, divine punishment (vv. 30–32) has a disciplinary and salvific telos, both for the individual and for the community. This is a theme that runs throughout Scripture.

Like Paul with additional instructions (11:34b), the present commentary has still more to say about what Paul himself teaches, implicitly or explicitly, about the multivalent significance of the Lord's Supper.

---

133. See also, similarly, CEB, NAB, NET, RSV. The NRSV and NRSVue have "Examine yourselves," rightly capturing the imperative force but masking the individual focus.

296

The Significance of the Lord's Supper

As we have seen, Paul had handed on to the Corinthians the tradition about Jesus' Last Supper that he received. In response to the chaos at Corinth, he interpreted this tradition theologically and practically with respect to the present Lord's Supper, first rather briefly in 10:15–22 and then at greater length here in 11:17–34. So what can we say about this Lord's Supper in summary?

It may be helpful to reflect briefly, first, on the variety of attitudes toward and practices of the Lord's Supper in the Christian church(es). For some Christians, it is perhaps the most central act of their faith, in which they partake weekly or even daily. For others, it is significant but not central to their spiritual life; they may partake monthly or even quarterly. Christian traditions name and interpret the Lord's Supper differently. It is communion, or holy communion, or the Eucharist, or the Most Blessed Sacrament, or simply the Lord's Supper. For some, it is fundamentally a memorial; for others, it is (or is part of) a feast, a love feast; for many, it also involves the presence of Jesus in some way or another; and for many, it additionally constitutes a sacrifice.[134]

For Paul, the Lord's Supper is, in some sense, all of these things, though not necessarily precisely in the way it has been variously interpreted by later Christians. But it is also much more; the Lord's Supper is a complex, multivalent event.

1. First of all, the Lord's Supper is *an act of worship*, and specifically worship of the God of Israel by worshiping God's Messiah Jesus. This is the case because Jesus is Lord (8:6; 12:3; and many other texts), sharing in the identity of YHWH and thus in the worship due God alone (cf. Phil 2:9–11). The communion (*koinōnia*) with Christ Paul describes (10:16–21) is not first of all a sentiment but the antithesis of idolatry. As such, it is inherently worship, meaning absolute, exclusive devotion in both ritual and daily life. The Supper regularly reinforces the pledge of allegiance to Jesus made in baptism.
2. Furthermore, the Lord's Supper is not a sequence of private meals but a *communal event of* koinōnia: *solidarity, fellowship, communion, participation,*

---

134. This is not the place for a description of all the various interpretations. For brief but accurate summaries, see Ted A. Campbell, *Christian Confessions: A Historical Introduction* (Louisville: Westminster John Knox, 1996); for longer explanations, Michael Welker, *What Happens in Holy Communion?* (Grand Rapids: Eerdmans, 2000). But perhaps this short exposition of Paul's understanding will contribute in a small way to his own stated goal of ecclesial catholicity and unity.

mutuality.[135] This communion is with Christ, the risen and present host of the meal, and therefore necessarily with one another, for the people are Christ's body (cf. 8:12; 10:16-17; ch. 12) and God's church (11:22; cf. 1:2; 3:16). Our individual union with Christ (6:17) is never in isolation.[136] "For this much is certain: there is no community with Jesus Christ other than the community with his body."[137] Western individualism, even about communion/the Eucharist, needs to engage the challenge of more communitarian cultures, such as those of Africa. Because African Christians take family meals seriously, they also "take the covenantal and communal dimensions of the Lord's Supper seriously."[138]

Moreover, there needs to be a special solidarity with "those who have nothing" (11:22), for they are the special object of God's calling in Corinth (1:26-31). Paul believes the real presence of Jesus in this meal is especially (though not exclusively) in the members of his body; Christ and church (= people) are inseparable for him (cf. 8:12).

Accordingly, the warning against eating and drinking "without discerning the body" (11:29) is first of all about discerning and honoring the church members as the body of Christ. At the same time, however, there is something unique about the one loaf and this one cup (10:16-21; 11:24-26), which are inseparable from the one body of Christ that they create and symbolize. The communion elements are thus also inseparable from Christ himself. In this sense, at least, Jesus is present in the bread and cup.

The practice of the Lord's Supper must correspond to this mysterious reality of Christ's presence and to the earthy means of communal participation in it (11:27-29). Communing in an unworthy manner (11:27) and without discerning the body (11:29) means above all doing so without seeing the interconnections among Christ, cross, community, concrete practices, and communion elements. There is communion with Jesus only if the identity of Jesus is embodied in practices that reflect his life-giving death for all; otherwise Jesus is absent, and the meal is not the Lord's Supper (11:20). In other words, this event of *koinōnia* is inherently an event of *agapē*.

---

135. The word *koinōnia* does not appear in 1 Cor 11:17-34, though its presence and sense are carried over from ch. 10.

136. Thus, if we use the language of theosis/deification, even it must be understood as both individual and corporate.

137. Bonhoeffer, *Discipleship*, 216.

138. J. Ayodeji Adewuya, "Revisiting 1 Corinthians 11.27-34: Paul's Discussion of the Lord's Supper and African Meals," *Journal for the Study of the New Testament* 30 (2007): 95-112 (here 109).

If *koinōnia* entails mutual love, then the Lord's Supper is an occasion for both receiving and giving. We receive Christ and we give our lives to Christ at each Supper, deepening the relationship of mutual indwelling that began at the initial moment of faith and baptism (see Gal 2:19–20; 3:27–28). Similarly, we receive from and give to one another. This means that all participants are equal as both givers and receivers—the table is a place of hospitality, harmony, and peace, of honoring one another, a place of noncompetitiveness and reciprocity. All status is gone at the foot of the cross and at the table where that cross is remembered.[139]

3. Related to the Supper as event of *koinōnia* is its *paradoxical character as both exclusive and inclusive, or catholic.* As James Thompson puts it, "While the Lord's Supper, according to 10:14–21, is an exclusive act, in 11:17–34, it is also an inclusive act."[140] This paradoxical character makes perfect sense in light of its being the (singular) Lord's Supper, which excludes all other lords and all devotion to other lords but includes all who are in fact devoted to this one true Lord.

4. The Supper is also an *event of memory.* First of all, the Last Supper has been remembered and handed on. More importantly, the words of institution focus on the phrase "in remembrance of me" (11:24, 25), that is, reliving the significance of Jesus' death and thus experiencing its significance once again. The remembering occurs in physical actions—breaking, eating, drinking—rather than merely mental ones. That is, this event of memory is not one of simply *recall* but of *reenactment.* Remembering for Jews was never merely recollecting; it meant faithfully responding to God and God's past saving actions (especially the exodus), which are made present and effective once again in the act of faithful remembrance in ritual, in worship (see, e.g., Exod 12:14).[141] In his death, Christ the paschal lamb gave himself for sins to effect the new exodus (5:7) and establish the new covenant in which his followers now live.

---

139. The theme of mutuality in communion has been especially prominent in certain Chinese Christian leaders and theologians. See, e.g., Xiangjiao Meng, "Rethinking Eucharistic Communion: A Theology of Harmony—a Study of the Lima Document," *Religions* 14, no. 8: 988 (2023): 1–13, https://tinyurl.com/44ayksz6.

140. James W. Thompson, *Apostle of Persuasion: Theology and Rhetoric in the Pauline Letters* (Grand Rapids: Baker Academic, 2020), 156. It should be noted that Paul's notion of the meal's inclusive, catholic character does not mean that it is open to non-Christ-followers; if it were, it would negate the exclusive dimension of the meal.

141. "This day shall be a day of remembrance for you. You shall celebrate it as a festival to the LORD; throughout your generations you shall observe it as a perpetual ordinance" (Exod 12:14).

To remember Christ's self-giving in death is to participate in it as a present reality, to live faithfully and appropriately in the shadow of the cross. It is the kind of remembering intimated by the spiritual "Were You There?"[142]

5. Additionally, the celebration of the Lord's Supper is an *act of (new-) covenant renewal.* If Jesus' "cup" is "the new covenant in my blood" (11:25; Luke 22:20; cf. Exod 24:8), then drinking the cup together is a corporate act of receiving, or ingesting, Jesus' death and thereby reaffirming the community's participation in the new covenant. It is the community's way of repeatedly renewing the baptismal experience of dying and rising with Christ into the new life of that new covenant (cf. 6:11; Rom 6). The gospel tradition to which Paul refers also suggests, as does Romans, that this baptismal reality is not a onetime experience but an ongoing reality. It means serving rather than seeking honor (Luke 22:24–27), and it may involve suffering (Mark 10:38–39). Participants in the meal, such as the Corinthians, may not be aware that this act of covenant renewal implicitly means a whole-hearted commitment, possibly to the point of suffering and even martyrdom.[143]

6. For Paul, the ritual is an *act of proclamation*—a parabolic sermon on Jesus' mission and on the gospel (cf. 15:3–5). This means that, for Paul, not only unbelievers but also believers need to have Christ crucified proclaimed to them. A community that forgets the cross forgets its identity—its origin as well as its present shape. A community decoupled from the cross will inevitably marginalize the weak. It is only by constantly repreaching the cross in tangible ways (with bread and cup) that Christ-participants will be reminded and enabled to embody the love that the cross proclaims (11:1; ch. 13). This proclamation (11:26) must be not only with words but also with deeds, and not only at the meal but in daily life.

7. Thus the Supper is an *act of embodiment and integrity.* The death of Jesus inaugurates the new covenant, but the reality of that inauguration is manifest only when the community embodies the Spirit-filled life that the new covenant brought into being. That is why the Supper requires individual and communal self-examination (11:28, 31). In this sense, the Supper is an iconic moment, a window into the community's life—and therefore, hopefully, its communal and cruciform faith, love, and hope (1 Cor 13:13), its hospitality to the weak whom God in Christ has welcomed.

142. Noted by the (late Anglican) Thiselton, *First Epistle,* 877.

143. There are few metaphors that convey a more intimate and participatory relationship with someone or something than those involving liquids, either consumption (drinking) or cleansing. Both Paul and the gospel tradition use each metaphor to convey the totality of entering into relationship with Christ.

Once again, we see the "Although [x] not [y] but [z]" pattern at work, and we especially see here its *communal* character:

> Although [x] your culture grants you certain rights and privileges at meals based on your social status, and you have instinctively transferred that right to the practice of the Lord's Supper,

> do not [y] selfishly practice those so-called rights and privileges at the Supper of the Lord—who died for all equally—and thereby shame the poor and fail to be the body of Christ,

> but rather [z] wait for and welcome one another, and eat the Lord's Supper together worthily, as one body.

8. The Lord's Supper is thus also an act of subversion of the status quo and of embodying the preferential option for the weak (the poor and powerless)—an event of God's counterintuitive peace and justice.[144] "If you offer your food to the hungry and satisfy the needs of the afflicted, then your light shall rise in the darkness and your gloom be like the noonday" (Isa 58:10). If the typical Corinthian banquet entails reinforcing Roman cultural norms, neglecting the poor and weak, and honoring other so-called gods and lords (including the emperor), then this meal is, or is supposed to be, the antithesis of all that. When it is not, then the *ekklēsia* that practices it is in grave danger of no longer being what it claims to be.

9. This leads to yet another dimension for Paul: his emphasis on the forward-looking character of the meal; it is a *foretaste of the future messianic banquet, an event of hope as well as memory*. It is a present experience of blessing and spiritual sustenance (10:3–4, 16–21) in anticipation of the eschatological fullness of salvation—the new creation not merely inaugurated but consummated.

10. Furthermore, it must not be forgotten that the Lord's Supper is actually a meal in the present; it is *an act of consuming Jesus*. The menu does not consist merely of fish and fruit but of the Lord himself—spiritually but really and truly. The meal's bread is the Lord's body and the cup the Lord's blood. Paul would likely say that we need not precisely define the word "is" in these phrases to understand that we are receiving Jesus when we commune with him in the company of others. This reality of ingesting Jesus should be understood as the flip side of putting on Jesus like clothing (Rom 13:14; Gal 3:27). Together, they express the reality of mutual indwelling, or reciprocal residence: Christ in us, and we in Christ. In each case, the result should be

---

144. See especially Streett, *Subversive Meals*, 202–87; William T. Cavanaugh, *Torture and Eucharist* (Malden, MA: Blackwell, 1998).

ADDRESSING LITURGICAL CHAOS · 8:1–14:40

that those who eat and wear Jesus should become more and more like the one consumed and worn.

Regardless of whether Rev 3:20 is a reference to the Lord's Supper, it is clear that every church and every Christian must continually re-receive Jesus into its, or his or her, life. This is obviously the case for those like the Christians of Corinth and Laodicea who have effectively excommunicated Jesus, but it is true for all who name Christ as Lord.

11. Moreover, while the Lord's Supper is an act of consuming Jesus, it is also the case that the Supper is *an act of consuming actual physical elements: the bread and fruit of the vine*. The elements are "the work of human hands," as some communion liturgies say. The Eucharist is an occasion for enjoying the company of other believers, diverse yet unified. It is also a time to express gratitude for the gift of cultivating crops like wheat and grapes that make the meal possible. And it is also a time for the Christian community to commit itself to supporting healthier ways of food production and distribution so that neither the poor nor the earth suffers from degradation. Such a commitment is an appropriate embodiment of the self-giving, others-regarding love that is remembered in the Supper.[145]

12. Although Paul does not use the term, we should also understand the Lord's Supper as a *sacrament*. By "sacrament," here I mean simply a *liturgical event of grace*, a sign and means of divine beneficence, which utilizes common entities (like bread and wine) to convey God's uncommon grace.[146] If judgment is the outcome of wrongheaded practices of the Supper, then its opposite, grace, is implicitly the outcome of appropriate practices. God works in and through the community's remembrance of, and participation in, the fundamental act of grace: God's reconciling work in Jesus' death (Rom 5:1–11; 2 Cor 5:14–21).

13. Furthermore, we should understand that what happens at the Lord's Supper is in some sense *a sacrifice*. It is both parallel to and *an alternative to* the sacrifices that would take place at a pagan temple (10:18–20) inasmuch as Christ's sacrifice (see 5:7–8) is being remembered and experienced afresh. Both the cup and the body are offered not to pagan deities but to the true Lord, while simultaneously being consumed by the participants like a sacrificial offering in Israel's temple or, of course, the Passover lamb (10:18).[147] The Supper is the

145. On this aspect of communion/the Eucharist, see (among others) Presian Renee Burroughs, *Creation's Slavery and Liberation: Paul's Letter to Rome in the Face of Imperial and Industrial Agriculture* (Eugene, OR: Cascade, 2022), 277–81.

146. Since this is not the place for detailed discussion of how various ecclesial families have interpreted the Lord's Supper, I use the word "sacrament" in a general sense.

147. That is, the Eucharist understood as sacrifice does not mean that "a sacrifice in

time at which each member of the church, and the church as a body, is called to re-present themselves to God as a living sacrifice (see Rom 12:1–2). And that means a life of participation in the sacrificial life and death of the living Lord Jesus—a life of Spirit-enabled resurrectional cruciformity.[148]

14. Finally, the Lord's Supper is an event of *witness and mission*. This is not the place to enter into a debate about precisely who should receive the eucharistic elements and when. It should be stressed, however, that by its very nature as communion with Christ and one another, this is a family meal for the body of baptized, faithful Christ-participants, to which others who wish are invited as witnesses (see, similarly, 14:21–25 about the public use of Spirit-ual gifts).[149] What nonbelievers witness, therefore, is critical to their own spiritual journey toward Christ. Do they see true communion or disunity, neglect of the weak, and other practices antithetical to the gospel? Certainly Paul was implicitly concerned about this.

Furthermore, what precisely should those who partake of the Lord's Supper do *after* partaking in it? Already in the late fourth century, John Chrysostom railed against Christians who left the Lord's table and went out of the church only to once again neglect the poor.[150] If the Supper is the first place to practice participating in Christ worthily by not neglecting the poor, it is not the last.

It should be obvious that enacting all of these aspects of the Lord's Supper would require of the Corinthians (and probably most other Christian communities) radical transformation. But this transformation can take place only by doing the Supper, for in the reconceived, ongoing practice itself is the hope of change. As Michael Rhodes puts it, the Lord's Supper is *formative* feasting.[151] As the church aspires toward this multivalent formative practice within the

addition to Christ's death" is being made but that "Jesus' death and the meal are united—the meal is the sacrificial feast of the same sacrifice made at the cross" (Michael Barber, personal correspondence, December 8, 2023).

148. For a fuller interpretation of the sacrificial dimension of the Lord's Supper in Paul from a Roman Catholic perspective, see Pitre, Barber, and Kincaid, *Paul, A New Covenant Jew*, 211–50.

149. In other words, Paul does not give us explicit directions on the appropriate age for the baptized to begin to participate in the Lord's Supper. However, his directions in 5:1–13 do suggest that there may be times when baptized believers could be excluded from communion.

150. Chrysostom, *Homilies on 1 Corinthians* 27.6–7.

151. See Michael J. Rhodes, *Formative Feasting: Practices and Virtue Ethics in Deuteronomy's Tithe Meal and the Corinthian Lord's Supper* (New York: Lang, 2022).

ADDRESSING LITURGICAL CHAOS
· 8:1–14:40

context of a comprehensive time of worship—and carries that practice outside of the meal context—it will become the sort of people who feast, and live, not for the worse but for the better (see 11:17).

In sum, the Supper reminds the church that both its life and its preaching must be cross-centered (looking back) until the parousia (looking forward). When it is not, the new-covenant event of memory, integrity, hope, and witness to the gospel devolves into one of forgetfulness, betrayal, condemnation, and refutation of the gospel. A bifocally oriented means of *grace* has become an occasion for *judgment*. As the book of Revelation would put it, let those who have ears to hear listen to what the Spirit is saying to the churches.

Ultimately, then, the Lord's discipline is an invitation, and is always for the community's good, so if the Corinthians can really examine themselves to discern their true identity and then act as the body of the crucified and resurrected Christ that they are, they will not ultimately be condemned. They will consume the "medicine of immortality" and become what they eat, both now and in the age to come.[152] Otherwise, sadly but inevitably, they will share the final fate of those who persist in unbelief (11:32)—and they will bear poor witness to those people, perhaps even driving them away and deeper into unbelief.

Reflections and Questions for 11:17–34

Spiritual, Pastoral, Missional, and Theological Reflections

1. The phrase **"You become (or are) what you eat"** has many possible meanings with respect to healthy diet and other forms of input into our material and spiritual selves. But when associated with the Lord's Supper, it involves consuming Jesus in the totality of what Paul has said about him, and about the significance of the meal. With Paul's sort of understanding, it is difficult to overestimate the significance of the Supper. But it has that importance only in the context of a community's wider worship and life together.

2. Yet **the Lord's Supper is often poorly understood, taught, and practiced,** especially in certain Protestant and nondenominational contexts. Paul's theology and spirituality of the Supper undergird Ambrosiaster's late fourth-

152. The phrase "medicine of immortality" goes back to the early second century: Ignatius of Antioch, *Letter to the Ephesians* 20.

century characterization of it as "spiritual medicine," a phrase for all Christians to take seriously.[153]

3. Repeatedly citing Augustine's work on the Gospel of John, Thomas Aquinas agrees with Augustine that the sacrament (the Lord's Supper) is the **sacrament of unity and love**.[154] As such, it should be received both "spiritually and sacramentally" to avoid participating unworthily and thus incurring divine judgment.[155] To eat both sacramentally and spiritually is to "share in the reality of the sacrament, namely, charity through which ecclesial unity exists." To receive sacramentally but not spiritually is to receive "in such a way that they do not have the reality of the sacrament, i.e., charity."

4. The prominent Orthodox theologian John Zizioulas offers this poignant summary of the Eucharist/communion: "It is not by accident that the Church has given to the Eucharist the name of 'Communion.' For in the Eucharist we can find **all the dimensions of communion**: God communicates himself to us, we enter into communion with him, the participants of the sacrament enter into communion with one another, and creation as a whole enters through [us] into communion with God. All this takes place in Christ and the Spirit, who brings the last days into history and offers to the world a foretaste of the Kingdom."[156]

Questions for Those Who Read, Teach, and Preach

1. Which aspects of the Lord's Supper identified in the discussion above are particularly relevant in the present context? What could a particular church do to incorporate these key aspects into both the Lord's Supper and all of its activities that involve food?

2. How might the interpretations of the Lord's Supper according to Paul offered above help in ecumenical conversations about it?

3. Gorging oneself or getting drunk at a typical Christian worship service today is highly unlikely. But in what ways might we resemble the Corinthians in

---

153. Cited in Gerald Bray, ed., *1–2 Corinthians*, Ancient Christian Commentary on Scripture 7 (Downers Grove, IL: InterVarsity Press, 1999), 111.

154. E.g., Aquinas, *Commentary on 1 Corinthians* C.11, L.4, 630; C.11, L.5, 654; C.11, L.7, 691.

155. Aquinas, *Commentary on 1 Corinthians* C.11, L.7, 698.

156. John D. Zizioulas, *Communion and Otherness: Further Studies in Personhood and the Church*, ed. Paul McPartlan (New York: T&T Clark, 2006), 7.

ADDRESSING LITURGICAL CHAOS · 8:1–14:40

the way we celebrate communion or worship more generally? How might contemporary Christians and churches neglect the poor in their midst today?

4. In sum, what does this passage urge the church to believe (faith), do (love), and anticipate (hope)?

For Further Reading

Adewuya, J. Ayodeji. "Revisiting 1 Corinthians 11.27–34: Paul's Discussion of the Lord's Supper and African Meals." *Journal for the Study of the New Testament* 30 (2007): 95–112.

Alikin, Valeriy A. *The Earliest History of the Christian Gathering: Origin, Development and Content of the Christian Gathering in the First to Third Centuries.* Leiden: Brill, 2010. (technical)

Baptism, Eucharist and Ministry. Geneva: World Council of Churches, 1982.

Cavanaugh, William T. *Torture and Eucharist.* Malden, MA: Blackwell, 1998.

Gorman, Michael J. *The Death of the Messiah and the Birth of the New Covenant: A (Not So) New Model of the Atonement.* Eugene, OR: Cascade, 2014.

Hunsinger, George. *The Eucharist and Ecumenism.* Cambridge: Cambridge University Press, 2008.

Martin, Jessica. *The Eucharist in Four Dimensions: The Meanings of Communion in Contemporary Culture.* London: Canterbury, 2023.

Rhodes, Michael J. *Formative Feasting: Practices and Virtue Ethics in Deuteronomy's Tithe Meal and the Corinthian Lord's Supper.* New York: Lang, 2022. (technical)

Scott, Margaret. *The Eucharist and Social Justice.* Mahwah, NJ: Paulist, 2009.

Smith, Dennis E. *From Symposium to Eucharist: The Banquet in the Early Christian World.* Minneapolis: Augsburg Fortress, 2003.

Streett, R. Alan. *Subversive Meals: An Analysis of the Lord's Supper under Roman Domination during the First Century.* Eugene, OR: Pickwick, 2013.

Thurian, Max, ed. *Ecumenical Perspectives on Baptism, Eucharist and Ministry.* Geneva: World Council of Churches, 1983.

Wainwright, Geoffrey. *Eucharist and Eschatology.* 3rd ed. Peterborough: Epworth, 2003.

Welker, Michael. *What Happens in Holy Communion?* Grand Rapids: Eerdmans, 2000.

Williams, Rowan. *Being Christian: Baptism, Bible, Eucharist, Prayer.* Grand Rapids: Eerdmans, 2014.

12:1–31. The Church as Christ's Richly Gifted Body

The theme of the oneness and catholicity of the community centered on Christ crucified that Paul articulates in 11:17–34 provides the springboard into the next topic: spiritual, or Spirit-ual, gifts in the body of Christ. This topic spans three chapters, the first two providing a framework within which the particular problem of glossolalia (speaking in tongues) in the gathered assembly can be specifically addressed in the last. Gifts, Paul says, are provided by God to unify and edify the church and must always therefore be publicly exercised in constructive, Christlike love and with an appropriate degree of order. The apparently uncontrolled charismatic worship in Corinth did not measure up, in Paul's view, to the God, Christ, and Spirit of the gospel.

As with 8:1–11:1, Paul structures chapters 12–14 chiastically:

A The Church as Christ's Richly Gifted Body (ch. 12)
   B The Rule (Criterion) of Cruciform Love in Eschatological Perspective
     (ch. 13)
A' The Use of Gifts in Worship (ch. 14)

In addition, as again with 8:1–11:1 (and elsewhere), Paul's "Although [x] not [y] but [z]" pattern is present in these three chapters as a whole. It may be summarized as follows:

› Although [x] as members of the body of Christ you have been given certain gifts that some of you think are more significant or spiritual than other gifts in the body,
› do not [y] be puffed up about such gifts or use them publicly without regard for other believers or visitors to the assembly,
› but rather [z] value the gifts that might appear "weaker" or less significant, and lovingly exercise your gifts in public for the good of the community and any nonbelievers present.

Overview of Chapter 12

Chapter 12 carries on the theme of the church as one diverse body formed by the cross, developed first in 1:18–2:5 and then in 11:17–34 (see esp. 11:29, with its "body" language). As Christ's body, Paul declares, the church should be a community of "diversity and interdependence."[157] But he also describes the church as a paradoxical combination of equality and hierarchy. On the one hand, there is an *equality* of gifts, with a corollary interdependent unity-in-diversity. On the other hand, there is a *hierarchy* of gifts, based on their ability to edify others, not to enhance the self. There follows from this hierarchy a

157. Hays, *First Corinthians*, 213.

307

corollary hierarchy of members in the body, based on their weakness, not their power. This arrangement is simply not normal. The *ekklēsia* is to be "an alternative community, or 'space,' with a distinct ethos," within whatever culture it exists.[158]

Language about the body was commonly used in antiquity by people such as Aristotle and Plato as a metaphor for community and political structures. (Even today we use phrases like "the body politic.") That idiom, then, is not unique to Paul; neither is his focus on interdependence. What is unique is his rejection of power and status, and his prioritizing of the weak members of the body, both of which amount to an inversion of the Greco-Roman (and the Corinthians') status quo. In each case, the hierarchy Paul constructs reflects Christ crucified: the values of love and weakness. Such is the work of the Spirit.

The body of Christ is a cross-shaped body, "a collective participation in *Christ crucified*," as Yung Suk Kim puts it.[159] Yet this body is, paradoxically, full of resurrection life: a people that incarnates the self-emptying, self-giving Messiah who is the incarnation of the self-giving, life-giving God (1:18–2:5). For Paul, "the body of the Messiah" is more than a well-used metaphor; it means that the crucified, resurrected, and exalted Jesus is present in and through his church. As the body of Christ, the church continues, in a sense, the incarnation and thus the *missio Dei*. By the power of the indwelling Christ (i.e., the Spirit), the story of Christ is reenacted in the church as a whole and in each individual member.

A word about the word "member" (Gk. *melos*) is important here. Paul does not conceive of the *ekklēsia* as an organization (or even a modern church!) that one joins and from which one receives a membership card or certificate. Rather, he depicts the church here as Christ's body and human beings who have been connected to it by baptism as integral components—spiritually connected body parts (recall 6:15, 17). Thus they are members as in "bodily members" like limbs and organs (the primary meaning of *melos* in Greek), not as in "dues-paying club members."

Another key word in this chapter and beyond is "spiritual/Spirit-ual gifts." Paul uses two different terms to refer to such gifts, each indicating their origin: *pneumatika* (12:1; 14:1) and *charismata* (12:4, 9, 28, 30, 31), meaning "gifts or

---

158. Rolex M. Cailing, "The Letters to the Corinthians," in *An Asian Introduction to the New Testament*, ed. Johnson Thomaskutty (Minneapolis: Fortress, 2022), 215–41 (here 234).

159. Yung Suk Kim, *Christ's Body in Corinth: The Politics of a Metaphor* (Minneapolis: Fortress, 2008), 21.

manifestations of the Spirit" (*pneuma*; possibly the Corinthians' own designation) and "gifts or manifestations of grace" (*charis*)—sometimes therefore called "charisms." Both designations are significant, but there can never be a true gift or manifestation of the Spirit unless it comes from and expresses the reality of grace, and specifically the Christ-gift, the ultimate manifestation of God's grace.[160]

12:1–3. Jesus Is Lord: The Criterion of Christian Authenticity

Paul does not want the Corinthians or subsequent recipients of his words to be ignorant of or misinformed about gifts or manifestations of the Spirit (12:1). What he will have to say should be taken with the utmost seriousness as divine instruction, not merely human opinion, and common Christian practice (see 14:36–38). But before addressing the divine source and community-oriented purpose of the gifts in some detail through the "body" language, Paul introduces the most basic criterion of all Christian existence, which is the common early confession "Jesus is Lord": *Kyrios Iēsous* (12:2–3).

For Paul, of course, this means that the *crucified* Jesus is (the now resurrected) Lord. It also means that the honor, allegiance, devotion, and worship due to YHWH as the Lord (*Kyrios* in the LXX) are to be shared with Jesus—which can only be right, true, and nonidolatrous if Jesus shares in the divine identity. Paul's repeated connection of scriptural YHWH texts to Jesus underscores this reality (see esp. 1 Cor 8:6; Rom 10:12–13; Phil 2:9–11). The gospel reveals that the God of Israel, as the sole source of salvation and the only one worthy of our obeisance, is inseparably connected to Jesus as Savior and Lord—and vice versa.

Believing and confessing that Jesus is Lord is not merely an intellectual affirmation; it is a personal and public commitment to obey this Lord; it is a promise of exclusive loyalty, a pledge of allegiance.[161] Moreover, this confession is not something that happens once; it is the ongoing reality of life in Christ. And because it is so serious and so all encompassing, it can be sustained

160. It is possible, but less likely, that the form of the word for "gifts or manifestations of the Spirit" in 12:1 refers more generally to "spiritual things." It is also possible that it refers to spiritual/Spirit-ual "people" rather than spiritual/Spirit-ual "gifts" or "things." But in light of 14:1, where the referent of the same word is clearly the "gifts/manifestations," not generic "things" or "people," the word in 12:1 should be understood as "gifts or manifestations of the Spirit."

161. See Matthew W. Bates, *Salvation by Allegiance Alone: Rethinking Faith, Works, and the Gospel of Jesus the King* (Grand Rapids: Baker Academic, 2017).

ADDRESSING LITURGICAL CHAOS · 8:1–14:40

and nurtured only by God's grace and the support of a community of like-minded people, a family of faithful siblings.

This confession of Jesus, and the reality to which it attests, is the most basic and essential characteristic of that community, distinguishing it from all forms of paganism. During their life as pagans, or unredeemed gentiles (*ethnē*; 12:2), which most of the Corinthian believers were, these men and women were led into the worship of gods that are not gods, only mute idols (12:2). Paul here briefly echoes a common prophetic sentiment:

> What use is an idol once its maker has shaped it— a cast image, a teacher of lies? For its maker trusts in what has been made, though the product is only an idol that cannot speak! Alas for you who say to the wood, "Wake up!" to silent stone, "Rouse yourself!" Can it teach? See, it is gold and silver plated, and there is no breath in it at all. But the LORD is in his holy temple; let all the earth keep silence before him! (Hab 2:18–20; for extended critiques of idolatry, see Ps 115; Isa 44)

Although the Corinthian believers were (for the most part) pagans/gentiles, Paul says "when you used to be" *ethnē*; they are now part of something new, the *ekklēsia* of God (see esp. 10:32). They are technically still gentiles, or Greeks (as opposed to Jews),[162] but they have a new fundamental identity, and they now belong to the one true God of all, the God who *can* speak, *has* spoken, and *does* speak. They have been liberated from the most fundamental spiritual error, idolatry: the lure of making nongods into God.

If "Jesus is Lord," then no other (so-called) lord is worthy to be thought of, or spoken of, as the recipient of a person's or a community's devotion and allegiance—not any ruler ancient or contemporary, not any god ancient or modern, not any person or profession or pastime. Moreover, no speech or behavior that contradicts this confession can be inspired by the Spirit, even if the speaker claims to be Spirit-filled (12:3). The reference to a curse in v. 3 uses the Greek word *anathema*. This could be a hypothetical acclamation used here for rhetorical effect in contrast to "Jesus is Lord." If, as is more likely, it is an actual statement, its precise meaning is not clear. It could refer to any of the following:

- people cursing Jesus: "Jesus *be* cursed."
- people confessing the opposite of Jesus' lordship: "Jesus *is* cursed"—perhaps because of having been hung on a tree.[163]

162. For "Greeks," see also 12:13 and 1:22, 24.
163. See Gal 3:13, though the word *anathema* is not used there.

- people using Jesus' name to pronounce a curse: "I curse you in the name of Jesus."[164]

Conversely, all who sincerely utter the claim that Jesus is Lord and thereby pledge allegiance to him—no matter what Spirit-ual gift they do or do not possess—are Spirit-filled members of the body of Christ.

12:4–11. The Gifts of the Triune God

Paul's specific take on this early acclamation of Jesus' lordship is actually Trinitarian: it means that the crucified Jesus who was raised from the dead to the position of Lord by God the Father is present here and now by the Spirit. The import of this perspective becomes clear in 12:4–11, where Paul indicates that the work of the Spirit is actually the work of the triune God, who determines the distribution and purpose of the "varieties of gifts," that is, gifts of grace (12:4; *charismatōn*—see also Rom 12:6). In vv. 5–6, these grace-gifts are also called forms of *diakonia* ("ministries" [CEB] or "services" [NRSV]) and *energēma* ("workings" [NAB] or "activities" [NRSV, CEB]).

The divine triad of the Spirit, the Lord (Jesus), and God (the Father) is the starting place for Paul's reflections on the gifts (12:4–6).[165] Subsequently, he focuses on the Spirit as the person of the Trinity to whom the gifting activity is appropriated (12:5–11). We learn here (and elsewhere) that Paul's superficially binitarian theology of 8:4–6 is actually Trinitarian, inclusive of the Spirit.

The word for the Spirit, *pneuma*, occurs twelve times in the chapter, eight of them in vv. 4–11. The Spirit is explicitly named as the source of four gifts (wisdom, knowledge, faith, healing—vv. 8–9) and implied, of course, for the rest. Furthermore, Paul twice names the Spirit as *the same* Spirit, in vv. 4 and 11, forming an *inclusio* for this passage. This same Spirit—not different Spirits/spirits, and certainly not human leaders—gives the grace-gifts to the various members of the community (12:4, 7–11). Jesus, as the Lord and as the one whose body is constituted by the church, is served by these ministries (12:5). And God (the Father) produces or activates (*energōn*) these activities (12:6). As in his discussion of ministries of planting and watering—"God gave the growth" (3:6)—Paul is robustly theocentric. All of this divine activity means

---

164. Thiselton (*First Corinthians*, 918–24) lists a dozen different interpretations. Paul later utters *anathema* concerning those who have no love for the Lord (16:22).

165. This is the most succinct and explicit Trinitarian text in the letter, and it has been recognized as such since the earliest commentators on the letter. See also the Trinitarian starting point for the discussion of gifts in Eph 4:4–6.

ADDRESSING LITURGICAL CHAOS

that spiritual gifts are just that—gifts, the result of divine grace, not human worth or importance—and are not intended to be self-serving. (Paul will unpack this truth later in the chapter and especially in ch. 14.)

As with the Spirit, Paul stresses that it is the *same* Lord and the *same* God who is involved with each and every one of the members of the body and their various grace-gifts (12:5–6). We see, in the language of Trinitarian theology, that Paul is affirming the reality of God's indivisible external (*ad extra*) actions, or inseparable operations. This truth is reinforced by Paul's saying that both God (the Father; v. 6) and the Spirit (v. 11) produce (*energeō*) the gifts. Paul the Trinitarian monotheist emphasizes that there is one God (theologically speaking, an affirmation of divine simplicity) who exists in three persons as an eternal divine community of unity-in-diversity.[166] He expects a parallel unity-in-diversity in God's people.

Every believer ("to each") has a gift, "a manifestation of the Spirit for the common good" (12:7), though not all have the same gift. Some of the possibilities are listed for the first time in 12:8–11, as well as 12:28–30 (NRSV):

- the utterance of wisdom (though implicitly not the kind the Corinthians claim to have): v. 8
- the utterance of knowledge (again, implicitly not the self-centered forms of knowledge operative in Corinth; see also 14:6): v. 8
- faith (beyond that required for justification): v. 9
- gifts of healing: vv. 9, 28, 30
- the working of "powers" or "powerful deeds" (NRSVue; "miracles" in many translations): vv. 10, 28
- prophecy/prophets (see also ch. 14; Rom 12:6; Eph 4:11) = speech to the assembly from God through a human messenger for general or particular communal edification: v. 10
- the discernment of spirits (cf. 1 Thess 5:19–21): v. 10
- various kinds of tongues (see also ch. 14) = glossolalia of different kinds, probably angelic and possibly also human languages (13:1; cf. Acts 2:1–18), as spoken or sung prayer/praise to God (14:2, 14–17):[167] vv. 10, 28, 30

166. In other words, the three members of the divine triad, or persons of the Trinity, are equally active and equally responsible for what happens in the church. Their unified activity (theologically speaking, the economic Trinity) implies something other than three separate parties—an ontological unity (the immanent Trinity).

167. Scholars have various understandings of glossolalia or "tongues": other human languages, angelic/heavenly languages, unique prayer language(s), or even nonsensical sounds.

- the interpretation of tongues (see also ch. 14); the interpretation of glossolalia: vv. 10, 30
- apostles (apostleship) (see also Eph 4:11; those sent to proclaim the gospel): v. 28
- teachers (teaching) (see also 14:6; Rom 12:7–8; Eph 4:11) = instructors within the assembly: v. 28
- forms of assistance (see also *diakonia* and acts of mercy in Rom 12:7–8) = probably material aid/relief: v. 28
- forms of leadership (see also Rom 12:8; 1 Thess 5:12): v. 28

It should be noted that in both 12:10 and 12:28–30, tongues and their interpretation appear at the end of the lists, no doubt because this gift was the most problematic and least edifying, at least from Paul's perspective, in Corinth. It should also be noted that these good gifts from God are nonetheless *not* the most important dimension of Christian existence (see 13:1–3), and they are temporary manifestations of God's presence and power (13:8).

The list of gifts from chapter 12 is not an exhaustive inventory, as Romans and Ephesians demonstrate (Rom 12:6–8; Eph 4:11). In fact, the emphasis on the more spectacular gifts of healing, miracles, and tongues indicates that there is a definite Corinthian flavor to this list. It is important also to distinguish between the gifts of the Spirit, which are variously distributed and no one has them all, and the singular, variegated "fruit" of the Spirit (Gal 5:22–23), which is a package deal intended to be manifested by all believers.[168]

It should also be noted that similar displays of speech and power attributed to deities were known throughout the ancient world. (One well-known example is the famous oracle of Apollo at Delphi, near Corinth in Greece, where a priestess called the Pythia prophesied.) Whatever the actual causes of such phenomena and whatever their similarities to the gifts Paul identifies, Paul has a particular critical perspective: every gift is given as a "manifestation of the Spirit for the common good" (12:7; not a vague "some benefit" [NAB]),

---

168. In addition, in some Christian traditions, most notably Roman Catholic, gifts of the Spirit are also found in Isa 11:2. Defined in the *Catechism of the Catholic Church* (sections 1830–31) as wisdom, understanding, knowledge, counsel, piety, fortitude, and fear of the Lord, they are understood as "permanent dispositions" that make us "docile in following the promptings of the Holy Spirit." These gifts should be understood as a singular set of dispositions for all Christians, similar to the fruit of the Spirit in Gal 5, which the *Catechism* notes in the same context (section 1832) as "perfections that the Holy Spirit forms in us as the first fruits of eternal glory." The *Catechism* calls the sorts of gifts found in 1 Cor 12 "special graces" or (appropriately) "charisms" (sections 799–801; 951; 2003).

ADDRESSING LITURGICAL CHAOS · 8:1–14:40

for communal edification (see also 14:26; Eph 4:12). Thus the use of any gift requires cruciform love, and this love will be reciprocal so that all benefit from one another's gifts.

This requirement is a bedrock principle of Paul's perspective on the topic of gifts, and arguably the main point of chapters 12–14. The noun for "common good" Paul uses in v. 7 (*sympheron*) is related to the verb he uses in 6:12 and 10:23 in response to Corinthian slogans about absolute freedom; the criterion of communal benefit is operative, then, throughout the letter.[169] In addition, Paul repeatedly stresses that it is the one Spirit, the *same* triune God, who is manifest in the various gifts precisely for this common good and, as he will say later, to avoid divisions (12:25).

This reality of the diversity of gifts but unity of source (God) and purpose (edification of the community) creates a fundamental equality in the church, which Paul now addresses with the language of a "body." After announcing the main point of his comparison between the human body and the body of Christ (12:12–13) as Spirit-generated unity-in-diversity, Paul first gives an extended description of the human body (12:14–26), which is obviously an implicit description of the church. He then gives a partial explicit application of it to the church (12:27–31). As noted above, the image of a body here is more than simply a metaphor; the crucified and exalted Messiah is present in the world by means of the Spirit-inhabited people who have been baptized into him.

12:12–13. The Critical Point

In 12:12, Paul makes his critical point in this chapter clear: "Christ" (*ho Christos*) is like the human body by virtue of its being constituted as many members but one body (cf. 10:17; 11:29).[170] Paul clearly means the *church* as the body of Christ, but the fact that he says it is *Christ*, rather than the church, that is body-like is more than rhetoric or a linguistic slipup. It suggests a very close connection between Christ and the church, such that the words attributed to Teresa of Avila—"Christ has no body, hands, feet, or eyes but yours"—make perfect sense. In the words of Richard Hays, "by identifying the many members of the church directly with Christ, Paul seems to press beyond mere analogy to make an ontological equation of the church with Christ (cf. v. 27)."[171]

---

169. The *symph-* word family was commonly used in Greek to urge community harmony. Paul gives it a theological, specifically christological, interpretation.

170. See also Rom 12:4–5; Eph 4:4; 5:30.

171. Hays, *First Corinthians*, 213.

314

This identification of Christ and the church is an essential part of the theological basis for the bodily unity-in-diversity of the church. It is also part of the basis for the concern and care that the body's members have for one another, as we have already seen in this letter: "when you thus sin against your brothers or sisters . . . you sin against Christ" (8:12 MJG; see further 12:21–26 and cf. Acts 9:4). The *existential* basis for Paul's claim about the church as one body with many members is the common work and gift of the Spirit in bringing diverse people together as one. The emphasis on "one" in these two verses is noteworthy: one body is mentioned three times, one Spirit twice.

Paul identifies two fundamental aspects of the church's relationship to the Spirit: (1) baptism (immersion) into one body by (or "in") the Spirit (cf. Gal 3:28) and (2) drinking of the Spirit. These liquid images and realities are profoundly participatory: immersion in the Spirit (in whom we now live) and drinking of the Spirit (who now lives in and among us).[172] Together they suggest a mutual indwelling or reciprocal residence, similar to Paul's "in Christ" and "Christ in/among" us language. (See also the discussion in the comments on 11:17–34 about mutuality in the images of consuming Jesus as the flip side of putting on Jesus like clothing [Rom 13:14; Gal 3:27].)

It is especially interesting that although Paul's focus in these chapters is Spirit-ual gifts, the unity-in-diversity to which he points encompasses ethnic and socioeconomic distinctions (12:13, possibly taken from an early baptismal liturgy). The absence of a word about gender distinctions (unlike the parallel in Gal 3:26–28 but like Col 3:11) may be accidental, or it may be related to the issues in 11:2–16 and 14:34b–36. Whatever the reason, it is clear that Paul included women among the gifted (11:5) and thought of them as equals to men (ch. 7).

12:14–26. The Body

The word "Spirit" has done its duty and will not appear in the remainder of the chapter, though, of course, the Spirit is still operative; Paul now focuses not on the who behind, but the what of, the gifts. His use of the image of the body conveys four interconnected main points, three conventional and one unconventional. The conventional points are these:

172. See also the liquid metaphor of the Spirit being "poured out" (Joel 2:28; Acts 2:17–18). Liquid analogies with respect to the Spirit also appear in John 7:37–38. Some interpreters have associated drinking of the Spirit with the Lord's Supper, but that is highly unlikely.

ADDRESSING LITURGICAL CHAOS
· 8:1–14:40

- bodily unity-in-diversity (12:14, 20)
- the necessity of all parts (12:15–19, 21)
- the solidarity, or mutual interdependence, of all parts (12:26)

Feet, hands, ears, eyes, and the nose all are necessary; there can be no body without diverse bodily parts (12:14). Paul proceeds to make some obvious claims about the necessary diverse functions and "members" in human bodies, using the literary device of personification (12:15–16, 21) and rhetorical questions (12:17, 19) to do so. So too, Paul implies, the church as the body of Christ consists of people with various backgrounds and gifts, all of whom are necessary for the activity of the body (12:19), and all of whom need one another and should care for one another (12:25–26). No one should feel inferior (as if to say, "*I'm* not needed"; 12:15–16) or superior (as if to say, "*you're* not needed"; 12:21). This arrangement is the work of God, not humans (12:18).

The unconventional point in 12:14–26 appears at this juncture and constitutes the first of Paul's two kinds of cruciform hierarchy described in this chapter (the second occurring in vv. 27–31). Not only are feelings of inferiority or superiority inappropriate, but in the church the apparently "weaker" members are actually "indispensable," and the "less honorable . . . less respectable [or "less presentable"; NAB]" ones are treated with greater honor and respect (12:22–24a).[173]

"*God* has so arranged the body, giving the greater honor to the inferior member" (12:24b; emphasis added). This preferential option for the weak and powerless, then, is also by divine arrangement, just as Paul said in 1:26–31. It is intended to preempt dissension (*schisma*; 12:25a, as in 1:10; 11:18) by counter-culturally showering *more* attention on those of *less* status so that all will receive equal care (12:25b), a very un-Roman thing to do. In fact, it is also arguably a very un-American, and probably generally a very unhuman, thing to do. But therein lies the irony: *if the crucified Christ and the cruciform existence he elicits are in fact the expression of true humanity, then treating the weaker members of any body with the most honor is one of the most profoundly human activities a person or community can engage in.* It is also the antithesis of how the Corinthians have been acting, on the one hand, and the embodiment of the divine justice that Paul has been enunciating since at least chapter 6, on the other.

But having weaker members—or those that "seem" to be weaker—in the community is not just an opportunity for self-giving care for them or for feeling good about being a just community; such members are *indispensable*, "the

---

173. There is likely here an allusion to the sexual organs as the "less honorable" bodily parts.

316

most necessary" (CEB; 12:22); without them, the body is not fully the body. They not only *have* gifts, but they *are* gifts. For instance, when people with disabilities—who are actually, from Paul's perspective, differently abled—are neglected rather than included and celebrated for their gifts, the body of Christ itself is disabled.[174]

In the church of God, then, the undervalued people and gifts are actually the most valuable. This reality should not divide the church but unite it, because it is God's way of doing things, God's way of preventing or undoing dissension (12:25a). The church, in other words, is a community of profound reciprocity, or "one anothering." In the words of John Barclay, "everyone [in the community] is bound to everyone else, both in gift and in need. . . . as gifts circulate, everyone is constantly in the process of both giving and receiving."[175] *Grace-gifts are meant to foster a circle of grace.* But Corinthians and others do not always understand, or practice, these truths.

Moreover, when one member of the church, weak or not, suffers either ill or good fortune, the entire church stands (or should stand) with that member, irrespective of that member's status in worldly terms (12:25b–26, using the Greek verbs "cosuffer" and "corejoice" in v. 26).[176] This is precisely what the community that embodies the Lord's Supper should do. To be part of a body is to rejoice and to suffer as one, to participate in one another's lives in deep ways—practical, emotional, spiritual. But to do so across normal ethnic, socioeconomic, and other humanly drawn lines is a significant challenge and even, to many people, abnormal.

Yet this is the abnormal normalness of the God of the cross. Only the cruciform church can be a catholic church, joyfully multicultural and more attentive to the weak than to the powerful.[177] The God of the cross mixes things up in a radical way, but the Corinthians, it would seem, have not gotten it so far. (Have their spiritual descendants?) This new "body" to which Paul bears witness is a far cry from the bodies known to his addressees: the culture of Roman Corinth and indeed the Roman Empire as a whole, including its political structures (and those that emulate them later).

---

174. I borrow the words at the end of this sentence from Amberle Brown, cofounder of the Banquet Network, https://tinyurl.com/3p6vtaxa, a ministry of inclusion for those with disabilities. See "Amberle's Story," YouTube video, https://tinyurl.com/7judz3fz.

175. Barclay, *Paul and the Power of Grace*, 127. Barclay points out the danger of one-way gifts as potential acts of patronizing and power plays (129).

176. See also Rom 12:15. The verb "cosuffer" (*sympaschō*) occurs also in Rom 8:17; "corejoice" (*synchairō*) also in 1 Cor 13:6 and Phil 2:17, 18.

177. See especially Kim, *Christ's Body in Corinth*.

ADDRESSING LITURGICAL CHAOS · 8:1–14:40

12:27–31. *The Body That Is the Church*

Paul follows his discussion of the first cruciform hierarchy (greater honor to the weak) with a second, this one quite explicitly mentioning the church as the body of Christ: greater importance to the gifts that edify (12:27–31). Once more, this is God's doing (12:28). In vv. 29–30, Paul again uses rhetorical questions, this time seven brief ones (all grammatically expecting a "no" answer),[178] to stress the diversity of gifts and their distribution to various members of the body. The number seven may be accidental, or it may be deliberate to represent the theme of universality and completeness.

Although there is a diversity of gifts, and not all have the gifts that might signal greater status, there are for Paul "greater gifts" (12:31a), and these are to be enthusiastically pursued, collectively. The admonition, as in 14:1, appears as a plural verb—"you all should be zealous for these gifts" (MJG).[179] But the primary point is that all of these gifts are manifestations of grace; Paul does not use the word *pneumatika* but only *charismata* in vv. 28, 30, and 31. The cruciform hierarchy he envisions within this communal working of divine grace is reflected in 12:28–29, where apostles, prophets, and teachers clearly rank higher than those who possess the more spectacular gifts (such as healing), including—at the very bottom—those who speak in tongues. And, significantly, just before tongues is "forms of leadership"—undoubtedly a blow to many in Paul's audience, ancient or modern.[180]

This is a direct attack by Paul not on the gifts (for they are, after all, from God and are therefore worthy of passionate pursuit) but on the Corinthians' inappropriate overvaluing of the less valuable gifts, especially tongues. As Paul will say explicitly in chapter 14, the greater gifts are those that edify others (e.g., 14:4–5), thereby most exhibiting love (8:1) and most conforming to the crucified Messiah. In fact, every gift is to be exercised in love—which will be

---

178. That is, they all begin with the particle *mē*.

179. The verb in both 12:31 and 14:1 is *zēloute*. By form, this verb could be either an indicative, describing what the Corinthians already do, or an imperative, signifying what they should do. In context, it is almost certainly the latter, especially in light of 14:1, which is clearly an exhortation: "Pursue love and be zealous for the Spirit-ual gifts, especially that you might prophesy" (MJG). There is also a parallel situation with the verb *zēteite* ("seek") in 14:12—where the Corinthians are described as "zealous" (*zēlōtai*) for the gifts but need to seek to abound in them for the community's edification—and another in 14:39, again with *zēloute*.

180. I owe this insight to Michelle Rader. The word's meaning is debated; it might signify administrators or those who provide guidance.

the point of chapter 13, as anticipated by the phrase "a still more excellent way" at the close of chapter 12 (12:31b). Love is the modus operandi for believers' exercise of the gifts.

Paul, then, is contending for the church as an ongoing manifestation of Christ in the world. The cross, as we saw in 1:18–25, is not only a Christophany and a theophany but also an ecclesiophany—a revelation of the church's character. Now we see the flip side of that reality: the cruciformly constructed church is a Christophany. Indeed, when Paul affirms in this last part of the chapter that the church *is* Christ's body (12:27), he is saying (as we noted above with respect to 12:12) that, in a significant way, the church is Christ. That is an astounding claim with an equally astounding corollary set of responsibilities in the world.

At the same time, Paul does not make a total identification of the church and Christ, for he identifies Christ as the one who "died, yes, who was raised, who is at the right hand of God, who indeed intercedes for us" (Rom 8:34) and who will "descend from heaven" (1 Thess 4:16). There is therefore something of a mystery here: we are Christ and yet we are not Christ. But the mystery is, in some ways, not all that mysterious: ultimately what makes the church Christ in some profound sense is its embodiment of Christ's love, which is depicted in the next chapter.

REFLECTIONS AND QUESTIONS FOR 12:1–31

Spiritual, Pastoral, Missional, and Theological Reflections

1. This passage should be **placed in conversation** with texts like John 17, Jesus' prayer for unity among his disciples and their spiritual descendants, and Rev 7, about the multiethnic, catholic reality of the church. In context, each text also carries missional implications.

2. Richard Hays says this about the **unity-in-diversity** of the body of Christ in Paul: "The creative imagination of God is so many-faceted that God's unitary power necessarily finds expression in an explosion of variegated forms."[181]

3. In the Christian theological tradition, the **Spirit is often associated with love;** it makes sense that Paul will tell us in the next chapter that love is the modus operandi for Spirit-ual gifts.

4. Christians from many contexts have **bemoaned the divisions in the body of Christ**. The Rev. Dr. Martin Luther King Jr. famously proclaimed this in his frequently preached "Letter to American Christians": "There is another thing

181. Hays, *First Corinthians*, 210.

ADDRESSING LITURGICAL CHAOS · 8:1–14:40

that disturbs me to no end about the American church—you have a white church, and you have a Negro church. You have allowed segregation to creep into the doors of the church. How can such a division exist in the true body of Christ? You must face the tragic fact that when you stand at eleven o'clock on Sunday morning to sing 'In Christ There Is No East or West,' you stand in **the most segregated hour** of Christian America."[182]

More recently, in India Pathipati Victor Paul has called for an "inclusive liberative ecclesiology" in which the church would be liberated from the "caste ridden society" and the largest percentage of its members, the Dalit (poor, rural) Christians, would be treated justly in an "authentic Church—the body of Christ," with a liberating effect on the community as well.[183]

5. Asian New Testament scholar Rolex Cailing, writing from the Philippines, makes the following critical point about **success and status** that is applicable to many cultures and churches: "In a culture that judges people by reputation and achievements, Paul is counterintuitive: Christ followers have to resist the lure of living for professional recognition and achievement."[184]

6. Of particular importance to the contemporary church in reflecting on and embodying 1 Cor 12 is the **role of people with disabilities**, whether physical, emotional, or intellectual. In a church oriented toward power and performance, such people may be sidelined or otherwise neglected. In a church oriented toward the cruciform hierarchy articulated in this chapter, however, those with disabilities need to be honored, and will be honored, in significant, altercultural ways. But what does that mean practically? A general vision statement like the following, from the Banquet Network, is a starting place:

> The Banquet Network is the result of God inspiring a convergence of men and women to live out His heart and passion for people with disabilities. We are driven by Luke 14, and many other Scriptures, in which God reveals His love and compassion for the sick and suffering in this world. We know that people with disabilities, like all people, are indispensable members of the Church (1 Cor. 12) and we want to see the Church reflect this truth more faithfully. We believe that every church—even smaller congregations—can do something to invite people with disabilities to "the banquet." We have many dreams, but most of all, we dream that more people and families affected by special needs and disabilities would be invited to the banquet of salvation.[185]

7. In a similar vein, the late John Stott commented,

---

182. King, "Paul's Letter to American Christians."
183. Pathipati Victor Paul, *Exploring Socio-Cultural Aspects of Pauline Ecclesiology: A Study of Paul's Term "in Christ"* (New Delhi: Christian World Imprints, 2018), 92.
184. Cailing, "Letters to the Corinthians," 235.
185. "Who We Are," The Banquet Network, https://tinyurl.com/ymjzujx2.

I sometimes hear old people, including Christian people who should know better, say, "I don't want to be a burden to anyone else. I'm happy to carry on living so long as I can look after myself, but as soon as I become a burden I would rather die." *But this is wrong.* We are all designed to be a burden to others. You are designed to be a burden to me and I am designed to be a burden to you. And the life of the family, including the life of the local church family, should be one of "mutual burdensomeness [referring to Gal 6:2]."[186]

Questions for Those Who Read, Teach, and Preach

1. What are the implications of being the body of Christ, and of its having "cruciform hierarchies," for Christian theology and practice today?

2. In what ways do the challenges of unity and diversity manifest themselves in the contemporary church? What insights does chapter 12 offer in considering these challenges?

3. Most churches tend either to ignore or to overemphasize the so-called spectacular Spirit-ual gifts. What is a proper balance toward the practice of gifts such as glossolalia and healing?

4. Is it theologically appropriate, with commentators such as Anthony Thiselton, to understand "gifts of healing" (plural) to include both sudden and gradual, both physical and mental, and both prayer-induced and medicine-induced healing?[187]

5. In sum, what does this passage urge the church to believe (faith), do (love), and anticipate (hope)?

FOR FURTHER READING

Adewuya, J. A. "Gifts of the Spirit." *DPL*[2] 361–67.

Banks, Robert J. *Paul's Idea of Community: Spirit and Culture in Early House Churches.* 3rd ed. Grand Rapids: Baker Academic, 2020.

Barton, Sarah Jean. *Becoming the Baptized Body: Disability and the Practice of Christian Community.* Waco, TX: Baylor University Press, 2022.

Bates, Matthew W. *Salvation by Allegiance Alone: Rethinking Faith, Works, and the Gospel of Jesus the King.* Grand Rapids: Baker Academic, 2017.

Bonhoeffer, Dietrich. *Life Together: The Classic Exploration of Christian Community.* Translated and edited by John W. Doberstein. New York: HarperCollins, 1954.

---

186. John Stott, *The Radical Disciple: Some Neglected Aspects of Our Calling* (Downers Grove, IL: InterVarsity Press, 2010), 110.

187. Thiselton, *First Epistle*, 948.

ADDRESSING LITURGICAL CHAOS

Edwards, Dennis R. *Humility Illuminated: The Biblical Path Back to Christian Character*. Downers Grove, IL: InterVarsity Press, 2023. (highly accessible)

Hardwick, Lamar. *How Ableism Fuels Racism: Dismantling the Hierarchy of Bodies in the Church*. Grand Rapids: Brazos, 2024.

John of Taizé, Brother. *Friends in Christ: Paths to a New Understanding of Church*. Maryknoll, NY: Orbis Books, 2012.

Johnson, Luke Timothy. *Miracles: God's Presence and Power in Creation*. Louisville: Westminster John Knox, 2018.

Kim, Yung Suk. *Christ's Body in Corinth: The Politics of a Metaphor*. Minneapolis: Fortress, 2008.

Koenig, John. *Charismata: God's Gifts for God's People*. Philadelphia: Westminster, 1978.

Moltmann, Jürgen. *The Church in the Power of the Spirit: A Contribution to Messianic Ecclesiology*. Translated by Margaret Kohl. Minneapolis: Fortress, 1993 (orig. 1977).

Thompson, James W. *The Church according to Paul: Rediscovering the Community Conformed to Christ*. Grand Rapids: Baker Academic, 2014.

Twelftree, Graham H. *Paul and the Miraculous: A Historical Reconstruction*. Grand Rapids: Baker Academic, 2013.

Yong, Amos. *The Bible, Disability, and the Church: A New Vision of the People of God*. Grand Rapids: Eerdmans, 2011.

13:1–13. The Rule (Criterion) of Cruciform Love in Eschatological Perspective

Paul desired that the members of the body of Christ practice love both among themselves and outside the *ekklēsia* in their daily public lives. As he wrote in his earliest preserved letter, "may the Lord make you increase and abound in love for one another and for all [i.e., outsiders], just as we abound in love for you" (1 Thess 3:12). Susan Eastman observes that the "theme of love [*agapē*] runs through 1 Corinthians like a red thread."[188] But the garment it sews is on full display in chapter 13.

Few passages of the Bible are read as often, or read as often out of context, as 1 Cor 13. It has nothing to do with marriage, at least not explicitly, though it is heard most often at weddings. It does provoke thought and questions. What is love? An emotion? A physical act? Does it have any synonyms? What are its characteristics? Is it "all you need"? Why do people sometimes name their

188. Eastman, *Oneself in Another*, 97.

children Charity or Love? People want to understand love, and to experience it, embody it, live it.

Scholars have debated exactly what genre of writing we have here. It is best understood as a poetic encomium, or discourse in praise of a virtue, full of striking images and memorable phrases. Paul intends the chapter to be an encomium in praise of the "more excellent way" (12:31) of exercising Spirit-ual gifts—and of living as believers more generally—by the Spirit in light of Christ crucified. It is a bridge between 1 Cor 12 and 1 Cor 14, sitting in the middle of the chiastic (ABA') structure for chapters 12–14 noted in the introduction to chapter 12. Paul has discussed love before, especially in relation to the question of treating others with respect to the issue of eating idol meat: "Knowledge puffs up, but love builds up" (8:1b).[189] He now returns to the subject to unpack its meaning more fully, to offer love as the essence of a rule of life for Christian community.[190]

Chapter 13 contains both an *antidescription* of the Corinthians and an *antidote* for their self-centered and self-destructive behavior, both individually and corporately. Thus, like most encomia, it has a definite hortatory function. Love—*agapē*—is the norm of life in the body of Christ, and that especially includes its gathered life at times of eating and worship. In this chapter, Paul addresses the following:

- love's necessity (13:1–3)
- love's character (13:4–7)
- love's permanence (13:8–12)
- love's superiority (13:13)

Other ancient encomia in praise of virtues address similar aspects of the virtue.

Despite the absence of any explicit reference to God, Christ, or the Spirit, the *agapē* described in this chapter is clearly the fruit of the Spirit (cf. Gal 5:22),

---

189. See also 4:21 about Paul's love and 2:9; 8:3 about our love for God. In addition, as we will see below, love is the implicit subject of 10:23–11:1, which echoes 8:1b. The vivid image of being "puffed up" (arrogant) found in 13:4 occurs also in 4:6, 18–19; 5:2; 8:1a.

190. "Rule" in this context is being used in the sense of a monastic rule, meaning "guideline(s) for life together." The church is a *koinōnia* of *agapē*. Some interpreters of 1 Cor 13 wrongly take it to be nothing more than a manipulative call for obedient imitation of Paul's way. To be sure, Paul believes he embodies Christ's love and believers should imitate his imitation of Christ (4:16; 11:1). But he is not bullying or manipulating the Corinthians.

the sort of love that God has for the world (e.g., Rom 5:6–8) and Christ demonstrated in his death on the cross (e.g., Gal 2:20). First Corinthians 13 is then a profound testimony to the love of the triune God that we find throughout Paul's writings and the rest of the New Testament.[191] It is one of Paul's ways of implicitly saying that God is love (see 1 John 4:8, 16) and of proclaiming what kind of God we mean when we utter those words.[192] That divine love is also, of course, manifested in the Scriptures of Israel. The attributes of God named in the Psalms and elsewhere anticipate 1 Cor 13—for instance, "The Lord is merciful and gracious, slow to anger and abounding in steadfast love" (Ps 103:8; 145:8).[193]

At the same time, it is clear that Paul's driving concern in chapter 13 is human love, specifically Christian love, and even more specifically Corinthian love. Yet such human love is ultimately a reflection of the love of God and, thus, of the God who is love. To love in this way is thus to be simultaneously the most human and the most divine a person or community can be—that is, most like what we were created to be and most like the creator who created us. "Works of love directed towards one's neighbour are the most perfect manifestation of the interior grace of the Spirit," claims Pope Francis.[194]

Such Christlike, cruciform love is not merely a *possible* or *optional* work of the Spirit, but it is the sine qua non of the Spirit's activity. In other words, when cruciform love is absent, so is the Spirit, and when the Spirit is present, so is cruciform love. Paul, therefore, is not merely taking existing material and repackaging it in a new form. The *agapē* he portrays here is distinctively Pauline.

It is critical to observe that love—*agapē*—is not one of the *pneumatika*, the *charismata*. Rather, as noted in the discussion of 12:31, it is the modus operandi for the exercise of the gifts—the way they should be practiced. To be sure, grace is needed to act with Christlike love—in fact, *power* is needed. Cruciform love is indeed the work of the Spirit, but it is not one of the gifts like teaching or glossolalia, distributed to some but not to all. As the first and most

191. The *agapē* word group occurs nearly 150 times in the Pauline letters.

192. Although there is no precise equivalent in the Pauline correspondence to the Johannine phrase "God is love," Paul "would have approved" of that statement (so, rightly, Douglas A. Campbell, *Pauline Dogmatics: The Triumph of God's Love* [Grand Rapids: Eerdmans, 2020], 54). See esp. 2 Cor 13:11, where Paul describes God as "the God of love and peace."

193. See also, e.g., Exod 34:6; Ps 86:15; Joel 2:13.

194. Pope Francis, *Evangelii gaudium* (*The Joy of the Gospel*), para. 37 (2013).

important aspect of the fruit of the Spirit according to Gal 5:22, it is produced by the Spirit in all believers—or at least it is supposed to be.

The Corinthians, like the Galatians and some (most?) of Paul's later readers, need to be more open to the Spirit's work of love. For that reason, Paul will also return to the subject of love as the defining mark of the Christian community at the end of the letter: "Let all that you do be done in love" (16:14). As we have seen, "all" is a significant word in this letter. Love is the sine qua non not only of life in community but also of life in the world, the life of Christian mission. "Christ's love compels us" (2 Cor 5:14 NIV). Paul would agree with another Johannine text: Jesus says, "By this everyone will know that you are my disciples, if you have love for one another" (John 13:35).[195] *Agapē* is both catholic and apostolic, and it both unifies and sanctifies.

But this love chapter is not only about love per se; it puts love (and other aspects of Christian faith) in eschatological perspective and is in fact a chapter about eschatology—the last things. As such, it both anticipates and complements the discussion of the resurrection of the body and new creation in chapter 15. In the present chapter, Paul stresses the relational and epistemological (having to do with knowledge) dimensions of eschatology.

Growth in love for others is part of the process that takes us, eventually, into the very presence of God, to see God "face to face" and to "know fully, even as I have been fully known" (13:12; cf. 8:3)—that is, known by God (another instance of the divine passive). This is not mere content knowledge, even knowledge of gospel truths, but personal knowledge of the God who already knows us fully, as Ps 139 so eloquently sings:

> O LORD, you have searched me and known me.
> You know when I sit down and when I rise up; you discern my
>   thoughts from far away.
> You search out my path and my lying down, and are acquainted with
>   all my ways.
> Even before a word is on my tongue, O LORD, you know it
>   completely.
> You hem me in, behind and before, and lay your hand upon me.
> Such knowledge is too wonderful for me; it is so high that I cannot
>   attain it. (Ps 139:1–6)

---

195. Furthermore, like Jesus in John (John 17:23), Paul sees unity as critical to Christian witness.

ADDRESSING LITURGICAL CHAOS

The promise of the gospel is that the way of love pursued in this life leads ultimately to the total, wonderful knowledge of God, in the life to come, for which the psalmist longs. But even now, through love, that knowledge is attainable in part. We can refer to the process as the *redemption* of knowledge, for knowledge unredeemed, unshaped by God's love—as Paul has told the Corinthians more than once—is not healthy for individuals or communities.

Once again, Paul is thinking in a bifocal manner: looking back at the cross that reveals the love of God and that shapes and reshapes the Christian community, and ahead to the eschatological climax. In fact, a community of Christlike love anticipates that climax.

13:1–3. *Love's Necessity*

Paul insists in chapters 12 and 14 that Spirit-ual gifts/grace-gifts are good and necessary. But the artfully constructed opening of this intervening chapter gets right to the main point with words that are simultaneously blunt and poetic: glossolalia, or any other Spirit-ual gift, that is not practiced with love erases any status the person might have and makes him or her "nothing" (13:2). The use of first-person "I" language may be partially autobiographical, but it is especially a rhetorical device to draw the hearer/reader in and identify with the claims being made. The repetition of the phrase "but do not have love" is also rhetorically powerful. Each time it follows an "if" clause stating the condition and precedes what is essentially a "then" clause, spelling out the consequence of failing to love:

VERSE	IF ...	BUT ...	THEN ...
1	"If I speak in the tongues of mortals and of angels"	"but do not have love"	"I am a noisy gong or a clanging cymbal"
2	"And if I have prophetic powers, and understand all mysteries and all knowledge, and if I have all faith, so as to remove mountains"	"but do not have love"	"I am nothing"
3	"If I give away all my possessions, and if I hand over my body so that I may boast"	"but do not have love"	"I gain nothing"

Also rhetorically powerful are three other aspects of this triad of spiritual scenarios:

- First, there is the increasing seriousness of the conditions, from spiritual speech to incredible spiritual power/insight/faith to absolute spiritual self-divestment.

326

- Second, there is the fourfold repetition of the word "all": all mysteries, all knowledge, all faith, all possessions.
- Third, there is the repetition of "nothing," signifying existential ("I am") and material ("I gain") bankruptcy. Paul's strong language has a sharp but pastoral point: it is not to drive the Corinthians (or us) to despair but to our knees.

In 13:1, the language of human and angelic languages is in part a reference to glossolalia. It seems to imply that glossolalia is angelic speech, but that is a matter of debate among both scholars and practitioners. Loveless, self-centered expressions of glossolalia, whatever its precise linguistic character, is nothing but percussive noise (perhaps like that of frenzied worshipers in the cult of Cybele) that is of no benefit whatsoever to the musical ensemble that is the body of Christ (13:1).[196] In fact, spiritual giftedness of any kind without love is painful for others to experience.

It can also be detrimental to the gifted one. According to 13:2, possessing legitimate, God-given prophetic powers, comprehension of mysteries, and knowledge,[197] or even having the radical faith called for by Jesus,[198] makes one a spiritual null set if love is absent. We know that "knowledge," like spiritual gifts more generally, is an issue already raised by Paul, one of the sources of arrogance and disunity in the community, addressed in chapter 8. But the mention of "mysteries," a word for Paul that refers above all to the gospel (see 2:1; 4:1; 15:51), reminds us that even right knowledge of the gospel (correct theology) or claims to extraordinary insight into divine inscrutabilities can be had, and manifested, without love.[199]

Finally, even the absolute self-surrender of one's possessions or one's body in order to boast (or possibly to be burned), apart from love, merits nothing (13:3).[200] In fact, doing something as radical as offering one's possessions or oneself completely to God for the purpose of boasting, rather than for the

---

196. Cybele was the Great Mother deity whose cult often included ecstatic and wild rituals.

197. See, e.g., 1:5; 12:8–10; 14:1–40.

198. See Matt 17:20; 21:21; Mark 11:23; cf. Luke 17:6; 1 Cor 8:9.

199. For mysteries as a reference to the gospel, see also Rom 11:25; 16:25; Eph 1:9; 3:3–5, 9; 6:19; Col 1:26–27; 2:2; 4:3; 1 Tim 3:9. In 1 Cor 14:2, the mysteries spoken in tongues may refer to the gospel or, more likely, to the Corinthians' witness to heavenly mysteries—so that may be the sense here too.

200. Whether the purpose of handing over one's body is to "boast" (NRSV, NRSVue, NAB, NIV mg.), "to be burned" (NRSV mg., NRSVue mg., NJB), or "to [experience] hardship" (NIV) does not affect the main point of v. 3. The different translations are due to differences in the Greek manuscripts. But if "to be burned" is in fact what Paul wrote, he is likely picking up a Jewish theme of martyrdom by fire.

purpose of serving God and others in love, is about as spiritually impoverished as one can imagine; hence the appropriateness of the quasi-financial image of gaining nothing in v. 3 (see also Matt 6:1–4). Even concern for the poor can be prideful and self-serving.

But buried in the Greek of this verse is an allusion to love as the right motive for self-giving: the language of "handing over" one's body uses an important Greek verb (*paradidōmi*) that Paul employs to describe Christ's loving act of self-gift in his death: "And the life I now live in the flesh I live by the faithfulness of the Son of God, who loved me by giving himself [*paradontos heauton*] for me" (Gal 2:20 MJG).

So what is the positive point in all this? It is that love, as described by Paul in this chapter, is the hallmark of all believers' activity at all times. *Agapē* is absolutely necessary, spirituality's sine qua non.

DR. KING ON LOVE ACCORDING TO PAUL

The Rev. Dr. Martin Luther King Jr. was an admirer of the apostle Paul. He frequently drew on certain key texts from 1 Corinthians, especially chapters 12 and 13.[201] From at least 1956 until at least 1962, he preached various versions of a sermon entitled "Paul's Letter to American Christians" more than fifteen times, eventually publishing it in his 1963 collection of sermons *Strength to Love*.[202] Toward the end of that sermon, he offered an updating of 1 Cor 13:

> I must say to you, as I said to the church at Corinth, that I still believe that love is the most durable power in all the world. . . .
>
> So, American Christians, . . .
>
> you may have the gift of prophecy and understand all mysteries. You may be able to break into the storehouse of nature and bring out many insights that men never dreamed were there. You may ascend to the heights of academic achievement so that you will have all knowledge. You may boast of your great institutions of learning

---

201. See the discussion in Bowens, *African American Readings of Paul*, 238–62.

202. The published form is in Martin Luther King Jr., *Strength to Love* (New York: Harper & Row, 1963; repr., Minneapolis: Fortress, 2010), 127–34 (145–53 in the 2010 ed.). A version from 1958 can be found at "Paul's Letter to American Christians," Online King Records Access, https://tinyurl.com/yc39wzrw. I quote from it here.

and the boundless extent of your degrees. But all of this amounts to absolutely nothing devoid of love.

Yes, America, you may give your goods to feed the poor. You may give great gifts to charity. You may tower high in philanthropy, but if you have not love, it means nothing. You may even give your body to be burned and die the death of a martyr. And your spilled blood may be a symbol of honor for generations yet unborn, and thousands may praise you as history's supreme hero. But even so if you have not love, your blood was spilled in vain. . . .

This is the thing that must keep the church moving, and America, let me say to you that this is the meaning of the cross. That event on Calvary is more than a meaningless drama that took place on the stage of history. It is a telescope through which we look out into the long vista of eternity and see the love of God breaking forth into time. It is an eternal reminder to a power-drunk generation that love is [the] most durable power in the world and that [it] is, at bottom, the heartbeat of the moral cosmos. Only through achieving this love can you expect to matriculate into the university of eternal life.

13:4–7. Love's Character

This *agapē* that is spirituality's sine qua non is described in 13:4–7, which Chrysostom called an "outline of [love's] matchless beauty."[203] English translations, however, are normally unable to represent a critical aspect of Paul's characterization of love, especially when rendering vv. 4–5.[204] For instance, many translations begin v. 4 with "Love is patient; love is kind." In the Greek text of 13:4–7, however, there are no adjectives ("love is *x*"), only a series of verbs and verbal phrases, saying in proverb-like form that love "acts patiently," "performs acts of kindness," and so on.[205] That is, love is more than a feeling or emotion; it is an action word. It is not something to pin down but to observe

203. John Chrysostom, *Homilies on 1 Corinthians* 33.1.

204. One exception is the KJV tradition.

205. The word *agapē* appears twice in 13:4 (three times in some manuscripts), but in 13:5–7 there are only verbs and verbal phrases with "love" as the obvious subject. Two of these verbs appear nowhere else in the New Testament: *chrēsteuetai* = "perform acts of kindness" (13:4) and *perpereuetai* = "heap praise on oneself" (13:4); several others are rare.

329

ADDRESSING LITURGICAL CHAOS · 8:1–14:40

on the move. Scot McKnight tries to capture this creatively: "Love patiences, love graces, doesn't zeal."[206] This does not mean that love is detached and unemotional, only that sentiment alone does not constitute Christian love.

In these verses, there are two positive verbs/verbal phrases, then eight negative, and then five more positive. But there is also variety in the way these items are presented: a sequence of nine, one after the other (vv. 4–5); a pair of opposites (v. 6); and a set of four pithy concluding phrases, each referencing "all things" (v. 7; Gk. *panta*).[207] The thrust of the alternating positive and negative phrases is that "love does *a* but does not do *b*," and so on. Love, then, includes a set of practices with corollary restraints.

Furthermore, according to these verses, love clearly does the opposite of what the Corinthians do, and the Corinthians do the opposite of love. Throughout the entire paragraph, there are allusions to various parts of the letter—some phrases explicitly repeating words, others referring more implicitly to situations—that show that Paul thinks of the Corinthians essentially as an unloving bunch. At the Lord's Supper, they act with impatience; they envy one another's leaders, status, and gifts; they display arrogance about their own spiritual and social status, and even about some of their immorality; some act rudely and shamefully in legal and sexual matters; some practice resentment and even injustice. Few if any are marked fundamentally by the kind of faith, hope, and endurance that God's love generates (13:7). Their story, from Paul's perspective, is not yet one of basic appropriate Christian living, much less cruciform love.

Following is a table showing the correspondences between the description of love's actions here in chapter 13 and the rest of the letter.[208] The texts from the rest of the letter consist almost exclusively of negative descriptions of the Corinthians. This antidescription of the Corinthians is a listing of characteristics of love that are antithetical to the Corinthians' behavior. In the right column are the aspects of love implied by the negative aspects of what love is not. These negative statements are like the prohibitions in the Decalogue (such as "Thou shalt not steal") that similarly imply positive exhortations.[209]

---

206. McKnight, *Second Testament*.

207. Some interpreters take "all things" to mean always (e.g., NIV, NJB; Ciampa and Rosner, *First Letter to the Corinthians*, 648–51).

208. This table is adapted from Gorman, *Cruciformity*, 224–26.

209. See Patrick D. Miller, *The Ten Commandments* (Louisville: Westminster John Knox, 2009), 7–8; Miller cites John Calvin: "if he [God] commands this, he forbids the opposite; if he forbids this, he enjoins the opposite" (*Institutes* 2.8.8).

13:4–7 ·   *Love's Character*

"Love" Statements from 1 Cor 13:4–7 NRSV (unless otherwise indicated), MJG	Descriptions of the Corinthians' Behavior from Elsewhere in 1 Corinthians NRSV (unless otherwise indicated)	The Implicit Positive Corollaries of the Negatives in 1 Cor 13:4–7
13:4		
"is patient [*makrothymei*]" MJG: "acts patiently/ with forbearance"	"When you come together, it is not really to eat the Lord's supper. For when the time comes to eat, *each of you goes ahead with your own supper*, and one goes hungry and another becomes drunk. What! Do you not have homes to eat and drink in? Or do you show contempt for the church of God and humiliate those who have nothing? . . . So then . . . when you come together to eat, *wait for one another*" (11:20–22, 33; emphasis added).	
"is kind [*chrēsteuetai*]" MJG: "performs acts of kindness"	No verbal parallels per se, though it is possible that Paul intends a play on words with the Greek word for Christ (*Christos*)—"acts in Christlike ways." Such Christlike, kind acts could include several, such as forgoing meat consumption (8:1–13) and litigation (6:1–11), and waiting for those who have nothing (11:17–34).	
"is not envious [*ou zēloi*]" MJG: "does not act jealously"	"As long as there is jealousy [*zēlos*] and quarreling among you, are you not of the flesh, and behaving according to human inclinations?" (3:3).	Seeks harmony and unity in the body
"[is not] boastful [*ou perpereuetai*]" MJG: "does not heap praise on itself"[210]	"What do you have that you did not receive? And if you received it, why do you boast as if it were not a gift?" (4:7; see also 1:29–31; 3:21; 5:6; and "[is not] arrogant" below).	Acts with humility and with awareness of God's grace
"[is not] arrogant [*ou physioutai*]" NET: "is not puffed up"	"I have applied all this to Apollos and myself for your benefit . . . so that none of you will be puffed up [*physiousthe*] in favor of one against another" (4:6).	Demonstrates humility and a sane sense of one's limitations and deficiencies

210. So BDAG.

ADDRESSING LITURGICAL CHAOS · 8:1–14:40

"Love" Statements from 1 Cor 13:4–7 NRSV (unless otherwise indicated), MJG	Descriptions of the Corinthians' Behavior from Elsewhere in 1 Corinthians NRSV (unless otherwise indicated)	The Implicit Positive Corollaries of the Negatives in 1 Cor 13:4–7
MJG: "does not allow him- or herself to get puffed up" (colloquially: "does not act as God's gift to the world")	"Some of you, thinking that I am not coming to you, have become arrogant [*ephysiōthēsan*]. But I will come to you soon, if the Lord wills, and I will find out not the talk of these arrogant people [*pephysiōmenōn*] but their power" (4:18–19). "It is actually reported that there is sexual immorality among you. . . . And you are arrogant [*pephysiōmenoi*]!" (5:1–2a). "Knowledge puffs up [*physioi*], but love builds up" (8:1b).	
13:5		
"[is not] rude [*ouk aschēmonei*]" MJG: "does not behave shamefully/ dishonorably" NIV: "does not dishonor others"	"If anyone thinks that he is not behaving properly [*aschēmonein*] toward his fiancée, if his passions are strong, and so it has to be, let him marry as he wishes; it is no sin. Let them marry" (7:36; see also 5:1–2, 6:12–20, 11:2–16, and 11:20–22 for additional shameful behavior).	Acts honorably
"does not insist on its own way [*ou zētei ta heautēs*]" CEB: "doesn't seek its own advantage" MJG: "does not seek its own interest"[211]	"Do not seek your own advantage [*to heautou*], but that of the other" (10:24). "Not seeking my own advantage [*to emautou symphoron*], but that of many" (10:33).	Seeks the good, welfare, and edification of others and the community as a whole

211. This is an important Pauline construction and claim. Literally, it says, love "does not seek its own," with the noun that should follow "its own" being implied. There are similar constructions with missing nouns in 10:24 and in Phil 2:4, 21. The missing noun is made explicit in the parallel text of 10:33: *symphoron*, meaning "advantage," "benefit," "profit."

"Love" Statements from 1 Cor 13:4-7 NRSV (unless otherwise indicated), MJG	Descriptions of the Corinthians' Behavior from Elsewhere in 1 Corinthians NRSV (unless otherwise indicated)	The Implicit Positive Corollaries of the Negatives in 1 Cor 13:4-7
"is not irritable [*ou paroxynetai*]" MJG: "does not provoke [others]"	No explicit parallel, but probably a reference to divisions and rivalries	Acts respectfully and gently toward others
"[is not] resentful [*ou logizetai to kakon*]" NRSVue: "keeps no record of wrongs" MJG: "does not take account of wrong done to it"	No explicit parallel, but probably a reference to lawsuits	Forgives others for their wrongs against oneself

13:6

"does not rejoice in wrongdoing [*ou chairei epi tē adikia*]" MJG: "does not rejoice at injustice"	"When any of you has a grievance against another, do you dare to take it to court before the unrighteous [*adikēn*], instead of taking it before the saints? . . . In fact, to have lawsuits at all with one another is already a defeat for you. Why not rather be wronged [*adikeisthe*]? Why not rather be defrauded? But you yourselves wrong [*adikeite*] and defraud—and believers at that. Or do you not know that wrongdoers [*adikoi*] will not inherit the kingdom of God? Do not be deceived!" (6:1, 7-9b). With near synonyms for *adikia*: "Now these things occurred as examples for us, so that we might not desire evil [*kakon*] as they did" (10:6). "Brothers and sisters, do not be children in your thinking; rather, be infants in evil [*kakia*], but in thinking be adults" (14:20). *See also 5:8, below.*	Delights in goodness, justice, and truthfulness (see next phrase of this verse below)

ADDRESSING LITURGICAL CHAOS

· 8:1–14:40

"Love" Statements from 1 Cor 13:4–7 NRSV (unless otherwise indicated), MJG	Descriptions of the Corinthians' Behavior from Elsewhere in 1 Corinthians NRSV (unless otherwise indicated)	The Implicit Positive Corollaries of the Negatives in 1 Cor 13:4–7
"rejoices in the truth [*synchairei de tē alētheia*]" MJG: "rejoices at the truth"	"Therefore, let us celebrate the festival, not with the old leaven, the leaven of malice and evil [*kakias kai ponērias*], but with the unleavened bread of sincerity and truth [*alētheias*]" (5:8 NRSV alt.). "If one member suffers, all suffer together with it; if one member is honored, all rejoice together with it [*synchairei*]" (12:26; cf. Rom 12:15).	
13:7		
"bears all things [*panta stegei*]"[212] MJG: "endures all things" CEB: "puts up with all things"	"We [Paul and his colleagues] endure [*panta stegomen*] all things" (9:12 MJG). See also Rom 15:1; Gal 6:2, plus the antithesis in 1 Cor 6:7.	
"believes all things [*panta pisteuei*]" "hopes all things [*panta elpizei*]"	Perhaps a reference to Corinthian disbelief in the resurrection of the body as the ground of hope and of endurance (ch. 15). See also 13:13: faith and hope named together.	
"endures all things [*panta hypomenei*]"	Perhaps a reference to "all things" suffered, including the catalog of sufferings in 4:9–13; see also 9:12; 15:30–32, 58; Rom 12:12.	

It is significant that this table shows the contrasts Paul perceives between love and Corinthian behavior. It is also significant, however, that Paul does not go line by line and case by case to make his point; that would be rather

212. If the sense of *panta* in these four phrases is "always" (NIV, NJB) rather than "all things," then this verse is functioning as a transition to the focus on permanence in the following verses. But "all things" is the more likely sense.

334

wooden and artificial. Yet some generalizations (based in specifics) are possible. Above all, it appears, the Corinthians are a community, in contrast to love, that is "puffed up" (13:4 NET) and that "insist[s] on its own way" or seeks its own interest/benefit (*zētei ta heautēs*; 13:5). We have encountered the former problem, and image, several times (4:6, 18–19; 5:2; 8:1). The latter flaw is expressed in an idiom (NAB: "seek[ing] its own interests"; also cf. NIV: "self-seeking") that Paul has already described and denounced in 8:1–11:1, beginning and ending with the slogans and counterslogans that contrast the Corinthian way of life with conformity to Paul's gospel of Christ's cross:

- "Knowledge puffs up, but love builds up" (8:1b).
- "'All things are lawful [permitted],' but not all things are beneficial. 'All things are lawful [permitted],' but not all things build up. Do not seek your own advantage [*mēdeis to heautou zēteitō*], but that of the other" (10:23–24).
- "Just as I try to please everyone in everything I do, not seeking my own advantage [*mē zētōn to emautou symphoron*], but that of many, so that they may be saved. Be imitators of me, as I am of Christ" (10:33–11:1).

This suggests that Paul intends for us to read his description of love, in essence, to mean love edifies and love seeks the good of the other; it does not arrogantly seek its own interest, as Paul also stresses, with very similar language, in texts like Phil 2:1–4: "Let each of you look not to your own interests [*ta heautōn*], but to the interests of others [*ta heterōn*]" (Phil 2:4). Love gives of the self to edify others. Thus, Paul understands "you shall love your neighbor as yourself" (e.g., Lev 19:18) in rather radical ways.[213] Such radical concern for others requires not only humility and sensitivity but also creativity in order to discern and address others' needs.

It is critical to note that practicing this form of love is not a matter of individualistic, heroic altruism but is rather clearly a communal mandate so that individuals' needs are not neglected but are fulfilled by shared loving actions rather than selfish pursuits. Referring back to 10:24, Chrysostom tells us, "For your own profit lies in the profit of your neighbor, and his in yours."[214] This communal, reciprocal perspective is precisely what Paul will offer in his discussion of the exercise of Spirit-ual gifts in chapter 14. But ultimately, here in 1 Corinthians as in Philippians, this sort of love is precisely the sort of love Christ exhibited (for Philippians, see 2:5–11) and which we are now called to

213. See also Matt 19:19; 22:39; Mark 12:31; Luke 10:27; Rom 13:9; Gal 5:14; Jas 2:8; and, applied to the "alien," Lev 19:34.
214. John Chrysostom, *Homilies on 1 Corinthians* 33.3.

ADDRESSING LITURGICAL CHAOS · 8:1–14:40

embody as participants in his Spirit and, thereby, as imitators of Christ. For Paul, there is a necessary correspondence between Christ and the Christian; 1 Cor 13 is about both: Christ's love (as alluded to in 13:3) and ours.

Thus, those who have suggested that the word "love" can be replaced with "Jesus" and, in an aspirational sense, with one's own name have good instincts. This is important, especially since the name of Jesus does not explicitly appear in this passage. There is, however, one caveat to the proposal to substitute one's own name: Paul's implicit and explicit exhortations to love, both in 1 Cor 13 and elsewhere, are always addressed not merely to individuals but especially to communities. This is because Christ lives not only *within individuals* but also *among them in specific Christian bodies.* The African proverb, "I am because we are," might also imply, "I love because we love."

Furthermore, although the Spirit who generates love is not explicitly named in this chapter either, it is important to notice that there are echoes of the fruit of the Spirit from Gal 5:22–23. Love, the first aspect of the fruit listed in Galatians, is of course the main subject here. But we also see the following explicit and implicit parallels:

GAL 5:22–23	EXPLICIT PARALLELS IN 1 COR 13:4–7 (MJG)
love (*agapē*)	love (*agapē*)
joy (*chara*)	"does not rejoice at injustice but rejoices at the truth" (*ou chairei epi tē adikia, synchairei de tē alētheia*)
patience (*makrothymia*)	"acts patiently/with forbearance" (*makrothymei*)[215]
kindness (*chrēstotēs*)	"performs acts of kindness" (*chrēsteuetai*)
faith/faithfulness (*pistis*)	"believes all things" (*panta pisteuei*)

GAL 5:22–23	IMPLICIT PARALLELS IN 1 COR 13:4–7 (MJG)[216]
peace (*eirēnē*)	"does not take account of wrong done to it" (*ou logizetai to kakon*)
generosity/goodness (*agathōsynē*)	"does not seek its own interests or advantage" (*ou zētei ta heautēs*)
gentleness (*prautēs*)	"does not behave shamefully/dishonorably" (*ouk aschēmonei*)
self-control (*enkrateia*)	"does not provoke [others]" (*ou paroxynetai*)

215. See also the similar "endures all things [*panta stegei*]" in v. 7.

216. Since these are conceptual but not linguistic parallels, it would be possible to make slightly different connections between the two passages.

336

13:8–12 · *Love's Permanence and Human Transformation*

These parallels show us that the nouns of Gal 5 have become the verbs and verbal phrases of 1 Cor 13. The fruit of the Spirit is a constellation of loving practices.

Moreover, these practices, so closely connected to the dimensions of the fruit of the Spirit, are ultimately rooted in the character of God as portrayed in Scripture. They are not accidental; love is what God is and does what God does. God is by nature patient and kind, looking out for us, practicing forgiveness and justice and truth. To practice the sort of love we see in these verses means, therefore, becoming more Spirit-filled, Christlike, and Godlike. The process may be called sanctification (becoming holy by the Holy Spirit) or Christosis/Christification (becoming Christlike) or theosis/deification (becoming Godlike). It is to participate in the life of God now in anticipation of the eternality this life of love foreshadows, which Paul takes up next.

13:8–12. Love's Permanence and Human Transformation

The first half of 13:8 repeats the word *agapē* (last heard in 13:4) and functions as a bridge text, concluding the description of love and segueing into the next aspect of Paul's encomium.[217] It is sometimes understood to be the last verse of the description of love, and sometimes (as here) to be the first verse on the topic of love's permanence. To show the importance of love from another angle, in 13:8b–12 Paul moves on to its perpetuity—its eternal character—vis-à-vis the temporary spiritual gifts: "love never ends" (13:8a).

As in the opening of the chapter, here again, in v. 8b, Paul employs a triad of similar phrases, though this time they are quite succinct. Prophecy, tongues, and knowledge—gifts of particular interest at Corinth and already mentioned in 13:1–3—are all temporary and partial. Paul actually uses a stronger word than "cease"; they will be "brought to nothing" (NAB; *katargēthēsetai*) according to vv. 8 and 10. The passive voice (yet another divine passive) indicates God as the agent of their termination, just as the triune God is their source (12:4–6).

These gifts, no matter their value, are provisional because they provide only a partial revelation of God (13:9). They are meant temporarily for the church now, in its immaturity, but not for the time after the parousia and resurrection (13:10)—"when the complete [*to teleion*] comes" (NRSV): the "perfect" (CEB, ESV, NAB). Then the partial and imperfect will also be brought to nothing (13:10; *katargēthēsetai*). The articulation of this theological truth undercuts

---

217. The words *hē agapē* are the first two words in the Greek text of 13:4 and 13:8, and the last two words of 13:13, creating bookends for 13:4–8 and then for 13:8–13.

ADDRESSING LITURGICAL CHAOS   · 8:1–14:40

Corinthian and Corinthian-like claims to knowledge, especially those that divorce knowledge from love (recall 8:1–13).

The perfection to which Paul refers will also be the time when the church, represented by the "I" of the brief, three-part soliloquy in 13:11, reaches its maturity. The contrast between childhood and adulthood offered here is expressed with rich imagery and the use of different Greek tenses (imperfect ["used to do"] versus perfect ["have done"]): "When I was a child, I used to talk like a child, used to think like a child, used to reason like a child; but now that I have become an adult, I have done away with childish things" (13:11 MJG). Paul uses the same verb for terminating childish things as he used for the termination of gifts—*katargeō*.

The apostle's first-person language in vv. 11–12 is less autobiographical and exemplary than it is gnomic, proverb-like, a way to draw readers and auditors in, as in 13:1–3. Paul has earlier criticized the Corinthians for their spiritual immaturity (2:6–3:4); now he actually holds out hope for their present and especially their eschatological maturation. Immature (read Corinthian) speech (uninterpreted public glossolalia?), thinking (absent the mind of Christ), and reasoning (not cross-centered) will end, just as a child's childish ways eventually conclude (13:11).

This future time of perfection, or completeness, will also be when the church, now the "we" of 13:12, will see God fully, "face to face," not as if looking into a poor (by modern standards) ancient mirror in which the reality and the image (knowledge) did not correspond perfectly—that is, "dimly" (NRSV) or "indistinctly" (NAB); see also 2 Cor 3:18.[218]

This future hope is what Christians call the beatific vision, prefigured by Moses' face-to-face encounters with God and inaugurated by our present experience of Christ (2 Cor 4:3–6).[219] Whatever perception and knowledge of God our present experience, reason, and speech provide, they are necessarily imperfect and partial, just like the Spirit-ual gifts themselves. The continuity between the *present* experience of already being fully known by God and the *future* experience of fully knowing God is found in the pursuit not of knowledge but of love (cf. 8:1–3). That is, the eschatological hope must impact behavior now. Neither the Corinthians nor subsequent generations of Christians are permitted to say, "Because we will one day be perfected, we

218. Corinth was known for its production of good bronze mirrors, but even the ancients recognized their inability to portray reality with complete precision and accuracy.

219. For Moses, see Exod 33:11; Num 12:8; Deut 34:10. See also Gen 32:30 (Jacob); Num 14:14 (the people); Deut 5:4 (the people via Moses); Judg 6:22 (Gideon seeing an angel of YHWH).

338

can just carry on as we have been doing today and tomorrow." No—that is not how the gospel works.

If we connect vv. 8–12 with chapter 15, we begin to see the fullness of Paul's eschatological vision and how it unfolds. With respect to humanity, we might refer to it as theosis or deification, as suggested above. This is the process of becoming more like the God who is love by allowing the Spirit of God to manifest God's love, which was displayed most fully on Christ's cross, in and through us—both individually and corporately.

This process of deification involves both our moral and our bodily transformation, the former now and the latter later. As Rom 6 puts it, we experience transformation *in* the body now, and *of* the body later. The process also involves our knowledge and our vision, as we grow in our relationship with God in terms of increasingly intimate knowledge and improved perception. These culminate in the eschatological finale of seeing God face to face and knowing God fully (13:12)—a promise that is almost too good to be true. It is a promise of full salvation that also extends beyond humanity, as we learn in outline form in chapter 15 (vv. 24–28) and in more detail in Rom 8 (vv. 18–39).[220]

It is no accident that Paul employs both first-person-singular ("I") and first-person-plural ("we") verbs (and, in English, pronouns) in these verses. Both moral and corporeal transformation are communal as well as individual realities. Western culture tends to stress the "I" of ethics and eschatology, while other cultures are more communally oriented. Both are needed, and both need to include the rest of creation too. The love of others rooted in the love of God, and oriented toward the ultimate knowledge and vision of God, must encompass the entire good creation that God has made and loves.

13:13. Faith, Hope, and Love's Superiority

The connection between the present and the future leads, at last, to Paul's final claim, which is that love is the greatest of the three things that do "abide," that matter in the long run in this age and, more importantly, survive into the age to come (unlike Spirit-ual gifts). This is, of course, the Pauline triad of faith, hope, and love,[221] a triad the apostle seems to have devised, or (rather)

---

220. In certain circles, eschatological hope has been reduced either to anticipation of the survival of one's bodiless soul (a hope in conflict with 1 Cor 15 and Paul more generally) or to social and political transformation accomplished by human agents (a hope no less in conflict with 1 Cor 15 and Paul more generally).

221. See also 1 Thess 1:3; 5:8; Rom 5:1–5; Col 1:4–5.

ADDRESSING LITURGICAL CHAOS · 8:1–14:40

discovered under the guidance of the Spirit, for the Spirit reveals the truth about God and interprets "Spirit-ual things to those who are Spirit-ual" (2:13 MJG; cf. John 14:26; 16:13).

This triad has already subtly appeared in chapter 13; in v. 7 Paul says that love "believes all things [*panta pisteuei*]" and "hopes all things [*panta elpizei*]." The three theological virtues, as they are known, are thus distinct but inseparable (not unlike the persons of the Trinity), with love portrayed as the driving force even in that earlier verse. And as noted previously, love is the ultimate goal Paul has in mind: "Let all that you do be done in love" (16:14).

Paul does not say a lot about faith in this letter, especially in comparison with letters like Galatians and Romans.[222] It is rather ironic, though, that this chapter that ends in praise of faith begins not with a critique but certainly with a caveat regarding faith: "if I have all faith, so as to remove mountains, but do not have love, I am nothing" (13:2b). Faith, even of the spiritual-gift or the mountain-moving variety mentioned by Jesus himself, without love is dead—to borrow language from James (Jas 2:17, 26). Or as Paul says elsewhere, "in Christ Jesus neither circumcision nor uncircumcision counts for anything; the only thing that counts is faith working through love" (Gal 5:6).

But what Paul does say positively about faith in this letter is critically important. Yes, there is a version of faith that is not granted to all, a Spirit-ual gift (12:9). But faith as a response of the self to the gospel is essential for salvation (1:21; 15:2). It must be grounded in divine, not human, power (2:5), for people are conduits—not objects—of faith (3:5). Especially critical is what Paul says about faith and the resurrection. Belief in the resurrection of Christ is at the heart of one's response to the gospel. The veracity of this event must not be denied (15:11–12), either explicitly or implicitly, the latter by denying resurrection in principle. If there is no such thing as resurrection, then Christ has not been raised and there is no salvation: Christian faith is empty, and we are still in our sins (15: 14, 17). (See further the comments on ch. 15.)

The apostle does not speak frequently about hope in this letter, either, especially (again) in contrast to Romans (esp. Rom 5:1–11; 8:17–39).[223] But, as with faith, what he does say is tied to the resurrection and is absolutely critical. Right here in chapter 13, Paul has just spoken of the hope Christians call the beatific vision. In chapter 15, the theme of hope will burst forth, and it will become clear

---

222. For more on faith in Paul's letters, see Nijay K. Gupta, *Paul and the Language of Faith* (Grand Rapids: Eerdmans, 2020), and Gorman, *Cruciformity*, 95–154.

223. See Gorman, *Cruciformity*, 304–48, for a fuller discussion of Paul's understanding of hope.

340

that this hope is not one merely of knowing God in some vague spiritual, bodiless way. Rather, it involves bodily transformation for immortal life (15:35–57), what Paul elsewhere calls the "redemption" of our bodies (Rom 8:23). And this hope is not merely for humanity but is cosmic in scope, which chapter 15 also stresses (15:20–28, 51–57), as does Romans in a different idiom (Rom 8:19–23).

Hope can be understood, then, as the future tense of faith (see esp. Rom 4); *the faithful are the hopeful.* And for the faithful, hope is the certainty that the ultimate fate of the humiliated, crucified Messiah will also be *their* future. It is this sort of hope that keeps faith and love alive in the present. It is not the power of positive thinking, which propels people to say things like, "I believe everything happens for a reason," or, "I'm sure it will all turn out for good in the end." No, for Christians hope is trust in the God who raised Jesus from the dead, the God who can—and does—"give life to the dead" (Rom 4:17) and make "all things new" (Rev 21:5).

Paul the practical theologian of faith and love is thus also the apocalyptic theologian of hope, and healthy Christian theology keeps the triad united (13:13a). Indeed, their unity in importance and in actual practice is the foundation of Christian community and Christian unity, for faith and hope are just as practical as love.[224] Yet "the greatest of these is love" (13:13b). It endures, as the greatest, because God is love.

Summary

Chapter 13 is representative of Paul's bifocal way of doing theology: love is the present reality of the Christian life, grounded in participatory faith in Christ's cross and resurrection and expectant of a glorious future—of love perfected. In the words of N. T. Wright, "Love is not merely the Christian duty; it is the Christian destiny. . . . To hold the Corinthian church together, Paul needs to teach them love, but to teach them love he needs to teach them eschatology. All the themes of the letter, therefore, are now pointing towards chapter 15."[225]

For the Corinthians and for us, Paul can do no more and no less than extol love (see also the end of the letter: 16:14, 22, 24). Cruciform love is the enduring pattern—the rule—of life in the church. The active content of love

---

224. See especially Geoffrey Wainwright, *Faith, Hope, and Love: The Ecumenical Trio of Virtues* (Waco, TX: Baylor University Press, 2014), who argues that each of these virtues has a particular corresponding Christian practice: baptism (faith), the Lord's Prayer (hope), and the Lord's Supper (love).

225. N. T. Wright, *The Resurrection of the Son of God* (Minneapolis: Fortress, 2003), 296.

ADDRESSING LITURGICAL CHAOS

· 8:1–14:40

has an essentially two-dimensional character. *Negatively*, it does not seek its own advantage or edification. *Positively*, it seeks the good, the advantage, the edification of others. It "entails 'being for someone,'" just as God in Christ is for us (Rom 8:31–39).[226] This is a radical but also a necessarily communal understanding of love, and one that is dependent on the power of the Spirit.

The eloquence of this chapter and the realities that it reveals are meant to lead the hearer or reader of these words both to contemplation of their significance and to praise of the God who is love. In the words of a lovely nineteenth-century hymn: "Since Love is Lord of heaven and earth, How can I [we] keep from singing?"

THE PASSAGE AS A WHOLE: MARRIAGE AND MISSION

This famous text raises at least two practical, theological questions about its contextual significance and its real-life implications for two topics: marriage and mission.

First of all, as nearly every commentator has emphasized, 1 Cor 13 is not about marriage; it is about the exercise of cruciform love in the Christian community, especially in the context of worship, and particularly in the context of using spiritual gifts. So why is it used at weddings? And should it be?

A cynical (or possibly realistic) answer would be that the passage lacks any explicit God talk and might therefore be beautiful but inoffensive for weddings in which some or most of the key participants are not very religious. However, as we have seen, a responsible reading of this rich text requires us to interpret it theologically. At a wedding, pastors or others can emphasize the truths that love is from God, is Christlike and even cross-shaped (self-giving), and is enabled by the grace of God and the power of the Holy Spirit.[227]

Moreover, since the family is a type of community, it is completely appropriate to relate this sort of communal love to a new couple as they begin to create a community of love. This is especially true in the context of Christian marriage and the Christian family, which is sometimes (especially among Roman Catholics) called a domestic church.

---

226. Ciampa and Rosner, *First Letter to the Corinthians*, 640.

227. The sort of (frequently misunderstood) mutually submissive, self-sacrificing marital love that puts one's spouse's needs ahead of one's own is discussed in Eph 5:21–33. For a careful analysis, see Gorman, *Cruciformity*, 261–66.

Second, it is important to see the outward, as well as the inward, focus of this text. That is, the love it describes is not only about what is required within a Christian community; it is the love Christians need to exhibit to others, such as neighbors—and even enemies. Paul has already made this point at the end of chapter 10, where he articulates the principles of cruciform, others-edifying love as the guide for deciding when, where, and how to eat meat with nonbelievers. These principles include the following lines:

- "'All things are lawful [permitted],' but not all things are beneficial. 'All things are lawful [permitted],' but not all things build up" (10:23).
- "But if someone says to you, 'This has been offered in sacrifice,' then do not eat it, out of consideration for the one who informed you, and for the sake of conscience—I mean the other's conscience, not your own" (10:28–29a).
- "Give no offense to Jews or to Greeks or to the church of God, just as I try to please everyone in everything I do, not seeking my own advantage, but that of many, so that they may be saved" (10:32–33).

Individually and together, these verses can be summarized in the words of 1 Cor 13:5, "love does not seek its own interests or advantage" (MJG), and they can be seen in the example of Paul, whose ministry is an imitation of Christ's (1 Cor 11:1).

The last of the bulleted texts listed above is particularly significant for our purposes, since Paul is explicitly saying that the requirement of cruciform love extends beyond the "church of God" to "Jews" and "Greeks." The reference to these two groups clearly signifies *unbelieving* Jews and Greeks, in contrast to the church, which consists of *believing* Jews and Greeks. Furthermore, if we peek ahead to what Paul says in his later letter to the Romans about love (Rom 12:9–21), we can see that it includes not only "mutual affection" (Rom 12:10) and associated behaviors (Rom 12:12–13, 15–16) among Christians but also nonretaliation toward enemies and the blessing of persecutors (12:14, 17–21).

In other words, the love Paul describes in 1 Cor 13 is the sort of love that should characterize the Christian community in all of its life together: its worship, its weddings, and its witness. It is a truly catholic theological virtue and practice.

ADDRESSING LITURGICAL CHAOS · 8:1–14:40

Reflections and Questions for 13:1–13

Spiritual, Pastoral, Missional, and Theological Reflections

1. Christian love is necessarily communal, in part because just as it takes a village to raise a child, **it takes a Christian community of love to raise a loving Christian.** It takes saints to demonstrate what resurrectional, charismatic cruciform love looks like in real life, on the ground, in all sorts of situations.

2. **Eugene Peterson has a lovely rendering of this chapter in** *The Message*; here is 13:1–7:

> If I speak with human eloquence and angelic ecstasy but don't love, I'm nothing but the creaking of a rusty gate.
>
> If I speak God's Word with power, revealing all his mysteries and making everything plain as day, and if I have faith that says to a mountain, "Jump," and it jumps, but I don't love, I'm nothing.
>
> If I give everything I own to the poor and even go to the stake to be burned as a martyr, but I don't love, I've gotten nowhere. So, no matter what I say, what I believe, and what I do, I'm bankrupt without love.
>
> > Love never gives up.
> > Love cares more for others than for self.
> > Love doesn't want what it doesn't have.
> > Love doesn't strut,
> > Doesn't have a swelled head,
> > Doesn't force itself on others,
> > Isn't always "me first,"
> > Doesn't fly off the handle,
> > Doesn't keep score of the sins of others,
> > Doesn't revel when others grovel,
> > Takes pleasure in the flowering of truth,
> > Puts up with anything,
> > Trusts God always,
> > Always looks for the best,
> > Never looks back,
> > But keeps going to the end.

3. C. S. Lewis famously claimed, "Love is not affectionate feeling, but a steady wish for the loved person's ultimate good as far as it can be obtained."[228] This

---

228. C. S. Lewis, *God in the Dock: Essays on Theology and Ethics* (Grand Rapids: Eerdmans, 2014; orig. 1970), 37. Most people do not realize that this popular sentence was

344

sort of statement probably seems extreme to many people, even to many Christians. But read carefully, it rhymes with 1 Cor 13. Neither Lewis nor Paul would deny the value of affection; what each is saying is that love, particularly Christian love (*agapē*), is **something more than affectionate feeling**.

4. Bernard of Clairvaux (ca. 1090–1153), in reflecting on the Song of Songs and on Paul's "puffed up" image, wrote, "There are some who long to know for the sole purpose of knowing, and that is shameful curiosity; others who long to know in order to become known, and that is shameful vanity. . . . There are others still who long for knowledge in order to sell its fruits for money or honors, and this is shameful profiteering; **others again who long to know in order to be of service, and this is charity [*caritas*]**."[229]

5. Jane Goodall, the noted naturalist, and Douglas Abrams have written a volume entitled *The Book of Hope: A Survival Guide for Trying Times*.[230] In many ways quite inspiring, the book defines hope, calls readers to be messengers of hope, and offers four reasons for hope in a time of human and ecological crises: the amazing human intellect, the resilience of nature, the power of young people, and the indomitable human spirit.

    This is clearly a **very secular hope**, placing its confidence primarily in human beings. As we see in 1 Cor 13 and elsewhere in Paul, Christian hope, unlike secular hope, is theocentric rather than anthropocentric, and eschatological. It takes human sin along with God's transforming grace as the dueling realities that both necessitate hope and focus it outside of ourselves, and even outside of time as we know it. This does not mean that we do nothing, or anticipate no good in the near future but only that we depend on one who is more amazing, resilient, powerful, and indomitable than any human.

Questions for Those Who Read, Teach, and Preach

1. How does Paul's view of love reflect or challenge understandings of love in contemporary church(es) and culture(s)?

2. How might taking this chapter seriously affect both the centripetal (inner-

---

penned in response to a question about the compatibility, for Christians, of neighbor love and support for war. Lewis implies that killing (in war) an otherwise unrestrainable person could be an act of love, but he acknowledges he could be wrong.

229. Bernard of Clairvaux, *Commentary on the Song of Songs* 36.3, "The Acquiring of Knowledge," ed. Darrell Wright, 2008, https://tinyurl.com/bdecsxyf.

230. Jane Goodall and Douglas Abrams, with Gail Hudson, *The Book of Hope: A Survival Guide for Trying Times* (New York: Celadon Books, 2021).

ADDRESSING LITURGICAL CHAOS
· 8:1–14:40

oriented) and the centrifugal (outward-oriented) dimensions of the church's mission?

3. How can those responsible for planning and officiating at weddings make sure that, if 1 Cor 13 is read, it is interpreted appropriately?

4. Does the Rev. Dr. Martin Luther King Jr.'s message about love still speak today? If so, how? What is fundamentally the same since he wrote and preached those words? What has changed?

5. In sum, what does this passage urge the church to believe (faith), do (love), and anticipate (hope)?

FOR FURTHER READING

Bailey, Justin Ariel. *Interpreting Your World: Five Lenses for Engaging Theology and Culture*. Grand Rapids: Baker Academic, 2022.

Bauerschmidt, Frederick Christian. *The Love That Is God: An Invitation to Christian Faith*. Grand Rapids: Eerdmans, 2020.

Burnett, Gary W. *Paul's Gospel of Love*. Cambridge: Grove Books, 2023.

Campbell, Douglas A. *Pauline Dogmatics: The Triumph of God's Love*. Grand Rapids: Eerdmans, 2020.

Gupta, Nijay K. *The Affections of Christ Jesus: Love at the Heart of Paul's Theology*. Grand Rapids: Eerdmans, 2025.

———. *Paul and the Language of Faith*. Grand Rapids: Eerdmans, 2020.

Held, Shai. *Judaism Is about Love: Recovering the Heart of Jewish Life*. New York: Farrar, Straus & Giroux, 2024.

King, Martin Luther, Jr. *Strength to Love*. Minneapolis: Fortress, 2010 (orig. New York: Harper & Row, 1963).

Lewis, C. S. *The Four Loves*. New York: HarperCollins, 2017 (orig. 1960).

Mitchel, Patrick. *The Message of Love*. London: Inter-Varsity Press, 2019. (highly accessible)

Roger of Taizé, Brother. *Living for Love: Selected Texts*. Taizé: Les Presses de Taizé, 2010.

Sampley, J. Paul. *Walking in Love: Moral Progress and Spiritual Growth with the Apostle Paul*. Minneapolis: Fortress, 2016.

Wainwright, Geoffrey. *Faith, Hope, and Love: The Ecumenical Trio of Virtues*. Waco, TX: Baylor University Press, 2014.

Wischmeyer, Oda. *Love as Agapē: The Early Christian Concept and Modern Discourse*. Translated by Wayne Coppins. Waco, TX: Baylor University Press, 2021. (technical)

Wright, N. T. *Surprised by Hope: Rethinking Heaven, the Resurrection, and the Mission of the Church*. New York: HarperOne, 2008.

14:1–40. EDIFICATION AND THE USE OF GIFTS IN WORSHIP

If cruciform love is the church's rule of life, and if that entails living always with the edification and salvation of others, individually and corporately, in mind, that rule must be embodied when the church assembles for worship. Paul has already made this point implicitly in 11:17–34 and will now do so explicitly in chapter 14.

In the introduction to chapter 12, we observed the structure of chapters 12–14 as a unit:

A The Church as Christ's Richly Gifted Body (ch. 12)
    B The Rule (Criterion) of Cruciform Love in Eschatological Perspective (ch. 13)
A' The Use of Gifts in Worship (ch. 14)

This chapter, then, is parallel to chapter 12 in its focus on Spirit-ual gifts. It applies the principles of chapters 12 and 13 to the concrete issue of the exercise of gifts, especially glossolalia (speaking in tongues, or simply "tongues"), in the public assembly.

As noted in the comments on chapter 12, scholars have various understandings of precisely what tongues was—other languages, angelic/heavenly languages, unique prayer language(s), or even nonsensical sounds. (I lean toward the angelic/heavenly interpretation in 1 Corinthians; see 13:1.) Whatever the precise experiences, in Paul's estimation, Corinthian worship was chaotic and self-indulgent, certainly anything but cruciform and community oriented, and therefore not actually Spirit-filled, despite Corinthian thoughts to the contrary.

The apostle's basic perspective on the situation can be summarized quite briefly: The church gathers to worship God, to be built up, and to bear witness, so its members must pursue the gifts of the Spirit, and then exercise them publicly, in an orderly way that is worshipful and edifying for all, believers and nonbelievers alike—that is, in love.

This will be a truly catholic, and therefore also apostolic, church, unified and growing in holiness. It will then be truly Spirit-filled; the motif of the *pneuma* (Spirit/spirit) runs throughout the chapter.[231]

---

231. The Greek word *pneuma*, referring sometimes to the divine Spirit and sometimes to the human spirit, occurs seven times in ch. 14: vv. 2, 12, 14, 15 (2×), 16, and 32. The related word *pneumatika* ("spiritual gifts" or "manifestations of the Spirit") also appears, of course (v. 1), as well as *pneumatikos* ("spiritual person" or "Spirit-person") in v. 37.

ADDRESSING LITURGICAL CHAOS

The closely related theme of pursuing the Spirit's gifts—and doing so eagerly, even zealously—reveals the central concern of this chapter, picking up the exhortation of 12:31: "But be zealous for [*zēloute*] the greater grace-gifts [*charismata*]. And I will show you a still more excellent way" (MJG). Explicit expressions of this theme bookend the whole of chapter 14 and anchor it near the middle:

- "Pursue [*diōkete*] love and be zealous for [*zēloute*] the Spirit-ual gifts [*pneumatika*], and especially that you all might prophesy" (14:1 MJG).
- "So also with yourselves: since you are zealous for [*zēlōtai*] manifestations of the Spirit [*pneumatōn*], seek [*zēteite*] to abound in them for the edification [*oikodomēn*] of the church" (14:12 MJG).
- "So, brothers and sisters, be zealous [*zēloute*] to prophesy, and do not forbid speaking in tongues; all things should take place appropriately and in order" (14:39–40 MJG).

Contrary to the interpretations of some, then, Paul is not trying to control, much less extinguish, Spirit-inspired, charismatic activity. After all, even tongues is a gift (12:10). Rather, the apostle wants the Corinthians to marry their charismatic passion with Christ's cruciform love that respects and serves others in the community while bearing proper witness to visitors.

Along with Spirit/spirit and zeal for the Spirit's gifts, then, edification is a central theme and apt image in the chapter, with the "edify" (*oikodom-*) word family appearing seven times.[232] Worship is formational, a critical means of building up the community that is God's building (3:9), the temple of the Holy Spirit (3:16–17), by building on its foundation: Jesus Christ (3:10–15).

As we have repeatedly seen, edification of others is the hallmark of Christian love (8:1; ch. 13) and Christian freedom (9:19; 10:23). Now Paul will say, "Let all things be done for edification" (14:26 RSV). That is, Christian worship must be characterized by Christlike love. As Paul affirmed in chapter 12, the gifts are for the "common good" (12:7). One key result of the centrality of communal edification in this chapter will be a strong emphasis on pursuing the gift of prophecy (14:1–6, 24, 39).

The chapter can be divided into two main sections: 14:1–25 (primarily practical theological principles) and 14:26–40 (concrete practices).

---

232. 14:3, 4 (2×) 5, 12, 17, 26.

348

14:1–25. A Practical Theology of Gifts and Loving Edification

In the first half of chapter 14, Paul offers a practical theology of the relationship between Spirit-ual gifts (especially tongues, on the one hand, and prophecy, on the other) and the edification of the gathered community of both believers/insiders and unbelievers/outsiders.

14:1–5. The Criterion: Loving Edification of the Body

In the first five verses of this chapter, on the basis of the fundamental theological norms enunciated in chapters 12–13, Paul reminds the Corinthians that they should all, as a body, both pursue love and strive zealously for Spirit-ual gifts. Thus, they should seek the gifts that best express love by building up the church (see also v. 12). In both the structure of v. 1 and the structure of Paul's theology, love precedes gifts. The directives in v. 1 once again (as in 12:31) occur with plural verbs—"you all should pursue." Thus gifts should not be pursued to make individuals feel important or more spiritual, or to be recognized as such by others. Rather, they are to be pursued and received in, as, and for the community. The gifts Paul especially wants the Corinthians to seek are the "greater gifts" (12:31) that express the most love for others and their edification, especially prophecy. According to 12:28, prophecy appears to be second only to apostleship, which is restricted to a relative few.

In 14:2–4, the plural verbs in v. 1 give way to singular subjects and verbs in the Greek text, though some recent translations pluralize those subjects and verbs (e.g., NRSV, CEB). Paul presents a comparison of the one who prophesies and the one who speaks in (uninterpreted) tongues. Although Paul has implied in chapter 12 that prophecy is the superior gift (12:10, 28), we learn here that it is not the gift per se that is the issue but rather the individual believer and how he or she uses the gift. Paul's focus is on individual responsibility in a communal context:

THE ONE WHO SPEAKS IN AN UNINTERPRETED TONGUE	THE ONE WHO PROPHESIES
Does not speak to humans but speaks to God—that is, it is a form of prayer (v. 2)	Speaks to people (v. 3)
No one understands (v. 2)	Implied: all understand

THE ONE WHO SPEAKS IN AN UNINTERPRETED TONGUE	THE ONE WHO PROPHESIES
Speaks mysteries in (or by) the Spirit (v. 2)[233]	Speaks edification, both exhortation and consolation (v. 3)[234]
Edifies oneself (v. 4)	Edifies the *ekklēsia* (v. 4)

To summarize, in Paul's own words, "The one who prophesies is greater than the one who speaks [prays] in tongues, unless someone interprets so that the church may be edified" (14:5b MJG). In a word, prophecy (or interpreted tongues) is an act of love. This is a classic Pauline case of self-interest (uninterpreted tongues) versus community interest (prophecy and interpreted tongues). But it is important to recognize that Paul implies that because the speaker is part of the community, he or she will benefit from his or her own prophetic word or interpreted glossolalia, as well as such speech offered by others.

Surprisingly, however, though Paul especially wants *all* the Corinthians to prophesy and thus edify the gathered assembly (14:5),[235] in the same breath, he does say, "I would like all of you to speak in tongues"—even if he would prefer them to prophesy, and even if he immediately notes the need for interpreters (cf. v. 13). Paul values every gift, including glossolalia.

For Paul, then, the gift of glossolalia is a form of prayer, speech *to* God (see also v. 14). As in 11:4–5, prayer (if understandable) pairs well with prophecy. (And 11:4–5 implies that interpreted glossolalia can be practiced by both women and men in the assembly.) Prophecy, as we saw in chapter 12, is speech *from* God: an inspired word of instruction and edification that addresses the community *in the language of the people*. This is why it ranks ahead of uninterpreted tongues and should be zealously sought by the community. In the words of Abraham Joshua Heschel, "The prophet not only conveys; he reveals. . . .

233. As noted in the discussion of 13:2, the mysteries spoken in tongues may refer to the gospel or, more likely, to the Corinthians' witness to heavenly mysteries. In either case, Paul's point is that they cannot be understood, and therefore cannot edify, without interpretation.

234. Paul uses three words in 14:3 to characterize what the one prophesying accomplishes, and most translations have something like this: "upbuilding and encouragement and consolation" (NRSV, NRSVue). It is more likely, however, that the middle term (*paraklēsin*) should be translated here as "exhortation" (so also Brookins and Longenecker, *1 Corinthians 10–16*, 98; cf. KJV, NASB1995), and "exhortation and consolation" understood as two aspects of the first and main word, "edification" ("upbuilding"; *oikodomēn*).

235. Paul here sounds like Moses: "Would that all the LORD's people were prophets, and that the LORD would put his spirit on them!" (Num 11:29).

This is the marvel of a prophet's work: in his words, *the invisible God becomes audible.*[236] Prophecy is both revelatory and formational.

14:6–12. The Necessity of Intelligibility for Edification

In 14:6, Paul continues in first-person ("I") language to ensure that the Corinthians grasp his main concern: the need for intelligibility in the assembly so that communal edification can occur. Uninterpreted tongues will not suffice because they are not intelligible and therefore do not edify. Paul names prophecy and three other prophecy-like gifts that appear to be in the category of gifts that are self-evidently beneficial to the community or are inherently edifying: revelation, knowledge, and teaching (14:6). Paul would add, of course, that they are inherently edifying as long as they are practiced lovingly (see 13:1–3).

Besides prophecy, two of these gifts Paul has named before: knowledge (12:8), even if it can be misused, and teaching (12:28–29), which he will also include in 14:26. Prophecy, the subject of vv. 1–5, is repeated in v. 6, probably both to stress its importance and to show the similarity of the other three gifts to it; that is, their source is God and their goal is edification. New to the discussion of Spirit-ual gifts is "revelation," though Paul has earlier spoken of Spirit-inspired revelation (2:10), and he will also name this gift again in 14:26, 30.[237]

What especially unites these intrinsically edifying gifts is their intelligibility. So Paul offers three analogies from everyday life to reinforce the need for intelligibility in worship. He presents two in vv. 7–8, followed by "So with yourselves" (v. 9), and then another in vv. 10–11, again followed by "So with yourselves" (v. 12).

First, even inanimate musical instruments, such as the flute and the harp, must produce distinct, differentiated tones in order to be recognized (v. 7). Second, a trumpet's summons to battle (e.g., Num 10:9; Josh 6:1–20; Judges 3:27–30) must be clear and recognizable in order for people to prepare (v. 8). Uninterpreted tongues, by contrast, are unintelligible; "you will be speaking into the air" (v. 9). Third, there are many languages in the world, and all are able to convey meaning (v. 10).[238] But there is no communication between persons—they are foreigners

---

236. Heschel, *Prophets*, 1:22.

237. For Paul the ultimate revelation (*apokalypsis*) is Christ and the gospel about him (e.g., Gal 1:16; 2 Cor 12:1, 7; Rom 16:25; Eph 3:3, 5). It would seem, then, as a Spirit-ual gift, revelation is not so much about unveiling something new as it is expounding this foundational revelation.

238. Most translations rightly render forms of the Greek word *phōnē* in vv. 10–11 as "languages," rather than "sounds," found in the NRSV and NRSVue.

ADDRESSING LITURGICAL CHAOS · 8:1–14:40

(*barbaros*: stammering non-Greek barbarian) to each other—unless they know the language (v. 11). So too with uninterpreted tongues (v. 12). Paul's use of first-person ("I") language again, as in vv. 5–6, is more than a rhetorical device; it reveals his personal investment in the issue at hand, and in the community.

Paul follows his three analogies with a practical conclusion: the Corinthians, "zealous" (*zēlōtai*) for "manifestations of the Spirit" (14:12 RSV, ESV),[239] need to seek to abound in those manifestations, or gifts, that build up the community by reason of their intelligibility to all—that is, in prophecy or tongues interpretation, rather than uninterpreted glossolalia, the Corinthian favorite (or perhaps the Corinthian elites' favorite).[240] The call for edification ends this section as it ended 14:1–5.

14:13–19. The Practical Consequence for Tongues Speakers

For the reasons noted repeatedly in the first twelve verses—the critical value of community edification as the embodiment of Christlike love, and the corollary need for intelligibility to effect edification—tongues speakers should pray "for the power to interpret" (14:13), which is a distinct gift (12:10, 30). Verse 13 functions as a sort of thesis for this entire short section, though the main point Paul might be implying is somewhat larger—pray for *someone* to receive the gift of interpretation!

In these verses, Paul once again speaks autobiographically, both as a rhetorical pedagogical device and as an ongoing sign of his deep concern for the community. He wraps a set of questions and statements in the first-person-singular ("I" language; vv. 14, 18–19) around a question and a statement in the second-person-plural ("you [all]" language; vv. 16–17). The main point is clear: the criteria of intelligibility and loving edification mean that, sometimes, tongues speakers must restrain themselves. Hence the need for the gift of interpretation so that such restraint is not necessary.

Paul's characterization of glossolalia in vv. 14–16, echoing v. 2, reveals that it is intended primarily as prayer, including praise, blessing, and thanksgiving, both spoken and sung.[241] He says that uninterpreted tongues involves only a

---

239. It is interesting that Paul does not use the word *pneumatika* here but, instead, *pneumatōn*, "Spirit-manifestations," perhaps more general but still inclusive of the spiritual gifts.

240. As noted in the discussion of 12:31, the verb *zēteite* ("seek") in 14:12 could be either an indicative or an imperative by virtue of its form, but the context makes it clearly an imperative.

241. Paul may also see *interpreted* tongues as a way of God speaking and teaching "to

352

person's spirit (*pneuma*; v. 14), and strongly implies that interpreted tongues also involves a person's mind (*nous*).[242] In v. 15, therefore, Paul asks and answers his own question about what to do: speaking paradigmatically, he says that in the assembly, "I" will engage in prayer that uses both the spirit and the mind simultaneously, for the sake of intelligibility.[243] That is, he will pray in his normal human language, though perhaps this means he will do so until or unless an interpreter can render his glossolalia intelligible.

The immediate rationale for this counsel is supplied in 14:16–17. An "outsider" (NRSV) or "inquirer" (NIV) will not understand the prayer in tongues and will not be able to say "Amen" (v. 16).[244] The prayer is legitimate prayer but not edifying prayer (v. 17). That is, uninterpreted tongues, as Paul says again in 14:23–25, does not have the same missional, potentially salvific impact on outsiders or inquirers as does interpreted glossolalia or, say, prophecy.

It is clear, however, that Paul does not, indeed cannot, disparage or dismiss Spirit-inspired tongues (see also 14:39), which he himself uses frequently—"more than all of you" (14:18)! But, at the same time, out of love and dedication to the entire community's edification, including visitors, in the assembly, he prefers speaking a few words in plain English, so to speak, rather than a long discourse in an unknown language (14:19). This suggests that uninterpreted glossolalia is an appropriate form of private prayer. Paul is not here boasting about his gift but simply restating a principle he enunciated in 8:13 for a different situation: "If food is a cause of their falling [the antithesis of edification], I will never eat meat, so that I may not cause one of them to fall."

With respect to self-restraint in the use of glossolalia, as in other situations he has addressed, Paul exhibits his Christocentric master story of "Although [x] (status), not [y] (selfish exploitation), but [z] (loving, others-oriented ac-

---

instruct others" (14:19), perhaps educating them in how to pray. That is, glossolalia is *definitely* a means of prayer and *may also* be a means of prophecy: speech *to* God (and self; v. 28) and (indirectly?) speech *from* God.

242. In vv. 14–16, there are four occurrences of the word *pneuma*. Although these are probably referring primarily to the human spirit, this is not to the exclusion of the divine Spirit. The Corinthians, Paul has just said, are eager for manifestations of the Spirit (14:12), including prayer in tongues, which is prayer in (or by) the Spirit (14:2). In Paul's theology of prayer, God's Spirit is involved with the human spirit, both when people are praying in tongues and more generally (see Gal 4:6; Rom 8:15–16, 26–27). The CEB interprets *pneuma* as God's Spirit in vv. 15 and 16, and the NIV does so in v. 16.

243. Other interpreters understand v. 15 to refer to sequential prayer (tongues first, then not) or, less likely, private prayer at home (tongues) and public prayer (not tongues).

244. The Greek word for this sort of person is *idiōtēs*, discussed further in the comments on vv. 20–25.

ADDRESSING LITURGICAL CHAOS   · 8:1–14:40

tion)." And he once again expects the Corinthians who speak in tongues to
do likewise:

> Although [x] you have the gift of tongues,
> do not [y] exercise that gift in the assembly without an interpreter (yourself
  or another) because it will not edify the whole community and is therefore
  not loving,
> but rather [z] speak to or for God in intelligible words, such as prayer in hu-
  man language, interpreted tongues, teaching, or prophecy, in order to edify
  both believers and visitors.

Such restraint is not an end in itself but is for the purpose of edification. But
it would be better to have interpreters so that the gift of glossolalia can also
be used for edification.

14:20–25. Missional Maturity in the Exercise of Gifts

There follows in 14:20–25 a confusing section that has, ironically, some major translation problems. The passage, however confusing in itself, is in line
with Paul's basic concern: whatever is done should be done to edify and instruct whoever is present. This would be a sign of spiritual maturity (v. 20),
something the Corinthians don't have, in Paul's estimation (recall 3:1–4).
Once again, Paul's attitude of salvific intentionality emerges; there is a public-
witness dimension to worship, even to glossolalia (cf. 14:15–17). Understandable prophecy might move "outsiders" or unbelievers toward God and the
community (14:24–25).

In 14:21, Paul quotes, partially quotes, or paraphrases Isa 28:11–12, a word of
warning and judgment related to an apathetic response to divine messengers
speaking foreign languages.[245] Whatever Paul's intent in using that quotation,
the following verses are complex, if not undecipherable. Verse 22 seems to indicate that tongues are a sign "for" unbelievers rather than believers, but v. 23
claims that unbelievers and "outsiders" (NRSV; but see below) will think everyone is crazy—hardly a positive, attractive sign. One solution is to interpret
the phrase translated "sign for" in v. 22a to mean "sign against"—a grammatical

---

245. The context for Isaiah was the threat of the (foreign-language-speaking) Assyr-
ians. The wording of 14:21 does not match either the MT or the LXX. The best explanation for the differences is probably that Paul is both quoting and applying (with his own
words) the scriptural text to the concrete situation (so Thiselton, *First Epistle*, 1120–22).

possibility but not one that works well with the parallel phrase in v. 22b (where it must mean "sign for"). Verse 22 remains a puzzle.

Another challenging aspect of this passage is the identity of those about whom Paul is concerned with respect to the impact of uninterpreted tongues. There is one clear group—unbelievers (Gk. *apistoi*) and one unclear group (Gk. *idiōtai*; vv. 23–24).[246] The latter term has been interpreted, for example, as "outsiders" (NRSV; cf. CEB), "the uninstructed" (NAB), "inquirers" (NIV), "uninformed person" (NET), or "some uninitiated people" (NJB). The word means something like "nonspecialist" or "inexperienced," so it likely refers to those new to the community or not fully part of it (perhaps inquirers similar to the Godfearers associated with synagogues), or to those ungifted in glossolalia.

Despite the difficulties in interpreting 14:22–25, five things seem clear:

1. There are visitors to the assembly. How does that happen? It is theoretically possible, of course, that someone just wandered into a villa, insula (apartment building), tavern, or public space where the church was meeting. But it is at least as likely that a community member invited the person and, in so doing, engaged in some form of faith-sharing. Perhaps the sharing involved a simple invitation, such as "Come and see!" (John 1:46), or a more specifically theological statement such as "Jesus is Lord!" (1 Cor 12:3).

2. There is, or should be, a shared evangelistic goal among the believers present (vv. 24–25). The hope for a confession of faith from visitors echoes prophetic hopes about the gentiles acknowledging the one true God (see, e.g., Isa 45:4) and biblical narratives of that sort of confession actually occurring (e.g., Dan 2:46–47).

3. Paul has a concern, which should be shared by the Corinthians (but probably is not), about a possible accusation of mental derangement or delirium within the community (14:23). This is reminiscent of the Pentecost narrative in Acts (Acts 2:1–21, esp. vv. 12–16).

4. Both interpreted tongues and prophecy have their place in the worship of the gathered assembly because they are instruments of God's work in people's lives. At the same time, Paul urges the church not to exercise the gift of (uninterpreted) glossolalia publicly, so that, through interpreted tongues and especially prophecy, there will be a clear message sent both to believers and to any unbelieving visitors or new participants.

---

246. The word *apistoi* can also mean "unfaithful," so a few interpreters think the *apistoi* in this passage are unfaithful Christians, but throughout the letter the word indicates nonbelievers.

ADDRESSING LITURGICAL CHAOS · 8:1–14:40

5.   Thus the loving self-restraint Paul has repeatedly stressed in this letter has a clear centrifugal, as well as centripetal, missional motive: the edification (in the broadest sense of the word) of others. A spirit of catholic salvific intentionality needs to be at work in worship as in other aspects of the Christian life.

14:26–40. Instructions for the Assembly's Worship

Having shared his perspective on the need for loving edification and mature missional sensitivity in the use of Spirit-ual gifts, particularly glossolalia, Paul turns in the second part of the chapter to general instructions for the assembly at worship. As in the first half of the chapter, this will include a call for some communal self-restraint with respect to speaking in the assembly.

14:26–36. Order in Worship

Next, then, come Paul's practical directives about coming together (14:26; the same verb as in 11:17–18, 20), building on the principles in 14:1–25. What he describes seems to be the Christian version of the culture's after-dinner *symposion*, normally a time of discussion, entertainment, and drinking.

Paul starts in v. 26 with the same question he asked in 14:15: "What should be done?" Since the purpose of the assembly is edification—"Let all things be done for building up" (14:26; cf. v. 31b)—the use of gifts cannot be chaotic or unhelpful. Therefore people are to do their various kinds of gifted speaking ("a hymn, a lesson [teaching], a revelation, a tongue, or an interpretation") in an orderly fashion, one at a time (14:26, 30–31, 33; cf. 14:40), while others remain silent (14:28, 30).

A tongues speaker (the Greek subject and verb are again singular, as in 14:2–4) may speak only if someone can interpret (14:27); otherwise that person must be silent and speak only to him- or herself and to God (14:28). Prophets as a group are to be mutually discerning and self-correcting (14:29, 32–33). One who is speaking may even need to become silent if another receives a revelation (14:30). Furthermore, even the number of people speaking in tongues (with interpretation) and prophesying should be limited (14:27, 29); considerations of time may be in play as an act of edifying love. Paul summarizes his main point in a theological assertion that is, for him, axiomatic: God is a God of peace, not chaos (14:33a).

It should be noted that the silence Paul is speaking about is not meant to encourage an individualistic or nonparticipatory approach to the gifts or to worship—quite the opposite, in fact. It is the current Corinthian chaos that is

356

individualistic, unedifying, and, ultimately, nonparticipatory, at least for those not joining in the chaos. The orderly silence while others speak, rather than the Corinthian disorder, has both centrifugal, or outreach, purposes (in light of 14:20–25), and centripetal, or ecclesial, purposes (14:26–33a). Moreover, in Paul's world, silence was one way of exercising self-control and honoring others, especially those deemed to be higher than oneself.[247]

The meaning of silence varies greatly from culture to culture, whether ancient or contemporary. For Paul, the ecclesial purposes for silence are several, starting with embodying the love described in 1 Cor 13. Silence is a position of humility, respect, and teachability. Dietrich Bonhoeffer writes of "the ministry of listening"; he says that "the first service that one owes to others in the fellowship consists in listening to them. Just as love to God begins with listening to His Word, so the beginning of love for the brethren is learning to listen to them. . . . Christians, especially ministers . . . forget that listening can be a greater service than speaking."[248] Furthermore, and relatedly, the purpose of silence is to foster corporate edification and unity. When there is corporate silence during someone's expression of a gift in worship, there is the possibility of the whole church actually praying with the individual and thus being both edified and unified.

One likely exception to the need for silence is the situation when a "hymn" is shared (14:26). Interestingly, although Paul explicitly calls for patient silence during moments of glossolalia, prophecy, and revelation, he does not mention hymns in the same way. This may be because he would hope that the assembly could sing together, as he elsewhere encourages gathered believers to do (e.g., Col 3:16; Eph 5:19). As Bonhoeffer asks and answers, "Why do Christians sing when they are together? The reason is, quite simply, because in singing together it is possible for them to speak and pray the same Word at the same time; in other words, because here they can unite in the Word."[249]

Before the chapter's conclusion, there stands another confusing text, 14:33b–36, requiring women—in some sense—to be silent (echoing the general admonition to silence at certain times mentioned in 14:28, 30). This requirement appears to be reinforced with references to the early church's universal (catholic) practice (vv. 33b, 36). In 14:36, Paul asks rhetorically and

---

247. On silence, speech, and women, see Susan E. Hylen, *Finding Phoebe: What New Testament Women Were Really Like* (Grand Rapids: Eerdmans, 2023), 150–66.

248. Dietrich Bonhoeffer, *Life Together: The Classic Exploration of Christian Community*, trans. and ed. John W. Doberstein (New York: HarperCollins, 1954), 97.

249. Bonhoeffer, *Life Together*, 59.

ADDRESSING LITURGICAL CHAOS · 8:1–14:40

somewhat sarcastically whether the Corinthians are either the source or the only recipients of the word of God. But there are several difficult aspects of this passage to consider.

First, there is the question of authorship. Some scholars believe that 14:34–35 (or perhaps 14:33b–35) is actually a later insertion by someone other than Paul (an interpolation), even though the manuscript evidence for this hypothesis is very thin.[250] If vv. 34–35 are a later addition, then v. 36 follows v. 33b and refers to the universality of the more general admonitions in the chapter.

Second, contrary to the popular impression that Paul wishes to keep women silent, we have already seen that he assumes they will pray and prophesy in the assembly, speaking both to and for God (11:5). Furthermore, the only other Pauline text that includes any explicit restriction on women's speech is 1 Tim 2:11–12, and, as with our text here, its concrete meaning in context and its authorship are debated. Romans 16 certainly demonstrates that Paul did not encourage women's silence as the norm.

Third, then, what precisely does Paul say in vv. 34–35, and what prompts him to say it? Specifically, for instance, how should we interpret words that refer to silence, speech, and subordination? References to the law? And what kind of behavior by (certain) women is the presenting problem?

Some have suggested that Paul is attempting to silence a group of female prophets, or to remind women (specifically wives) of their appropriate public role (submission),[251] or to prevent frenzied speech that might be associated with women in previous pagan cultic activity. Still others, such as Lucy Peppiatt, have suggested that in 14:34–35 Paul is quoting, and in 14:36 rebuking, misguided Corinthians who wish to suppress women's voices in the assembly.[252] But the possible evidence in this passage for something like Corinthian perspectives followed by Pauline rejoinders—as in 6:12–20, 8:1–3, 10:23–24, 10:31–11:1, and possibly elsewhere—is not convincing to all interpreters.

If Paul himself did write these words, we can be certain of at least two things from the context of the chapter and the letter as a whole: (1) that he does not mean that women should be absolutely silent in the assembly; and (2) that the motive for self-restraining silence is love, and its goal is community

250. A few manuscripts place vv. 34–35 at the end of the chapter, which might suggest they are something of an addendum.

251. Both Eph 5:22–23 and Titus 2:5 might be interpreted along these lines, but there are other ways to read those texts too.

252. Peppiatt, *Women and Worship at Corinth,* and Peppiatt, *Rediscovering Scripture's Vision for Women: Fresh Perspectives on Disputed Texts* (Downers Grove, IL: IVP Academic, 2019).

edification, order, and peace. The gist of 14:33b–36 in context, if from Paul, is probably to keep women from adding to the Corinthian chaos by calling out for explanations of prophecies or interpretations of tongues. Their questions should only be temporarily silenced, and discussed with their husbands at home (v. 35a). This would be an honorable expression of both cultural deference and community edification through selective silence.

The problem with this interpretation is that it ignores the dark tone of the passage, at least to modern/Western sensibilities, manifested most clearly in the sentence "it is shameful for a woman to speak in church" (v. 35b). Of course, this problem is somewhat alleviated if "speak" means something like "speak out of turn" or "interrupt." And it is further alleviated, or at least explained, if we recognize (1) that Paul has already told others to be selectively silent (14:28, 30) and (2) that silence was, at times, a culturally appropriate mode of controlling oneself and honoring others.

Perhaps the best we can do with this challenging text is to give the apostle the benefit of the doubt and say the following, on the assumption that Paul did write these words: Paul's counsel arises from a specific cultural and ecclesial context, not fully discernible to us, that requires some women to exercise self-restraint with respect to certain forms of speech that are disruptive. They should do this in order to practice love in a community short on that virtue, and to avoid some sort of shame in a culture of honor and shame. Neither more nor less, in my view, should be concluded.

14:37–40. Summary Exhortations

Whatever we make of 14:33b–36, in 14:37–40 Paul wraps up his words about the chaotic Corinthian worship. The (additional?) rationale for Paul's instructions in chapter 14 comes in vv. 37–38. Any actual prophet or Spirit-ual person (*pneumatikos*) should recognize that Paul's teaching is to be heeded because he is passing on a commandment from the Lord (Jesus).[253] Unless Paul has something like Jesus' command to love one another in mind, perhaps he is referring not to a gospel tradition but to his having the mind of Christ (2:16). As an apostle passing on the Lord's command, Paul speaks with more authority than any who think of themselves as prophetic or Spirit-ual but who defy the Lord's apostle (authoritative messenger) and thereby the Lord himself. They

253. Most translations render *pneumatikos* similarly, including the NRSVue's "spiritual" replacing the NRSV's misguided "have spiritual powers." For misguided self-perception, see also 3:18; 8:2.

should not be acknowledged as what they claim to be. This is not Paul boasting but rather his recalling the divinely appointed order of "first apostles, then prophets" (12:28) and his own divinely granted apostleship (9:1; 15:8–10).

The authoritative instruction to which Paul refers can be summarized as follows: enthusiastically encourage prophecy but don't forbid tongues (as some may have been calling for), which implies, of course, that they should be *interpreted* tongues at the assembly (v. 39). This will contribute to the fulfillment of the proverb-like final sentence: "all things should be done decently and in order" (v. 40). Such decency and order, Paul is certain, will express love and increase edification in the assembly—all in a spirit of catholicity and apostolicity (mission).

REFLECTIONS AND QUESTIONS FOR 14:1–40

Spiritual, Pastoral, Missional, and Theological Reflections

1. Christians and churches today, in all parts of the world, often remain **divided over certain spiritual gifts, especially glossolalia and healing.** Two **significant developments** among some Pentecostal/pentecostal and charismatic churches have been (1) eliminating the expectation that all true Christians will speak in tongues and (2) recognizing the need for the charismatic church to be cruciform rather than oriented toward a form of the prosperity gospel.[254]

2. What is prophecy? It is not only directed to and within the people of God, but it also has a **public, missional function.** Walter Brueggemann perceives this public, missional dimension well. In his book *Reality, Grief, Hope: Three Urgent Prophetic Tasks*, he identifies three critical prophetic tasks for the church, plus a corollary way of life:[255]

   › articulating reality amid ideology
   › performing grief amid denial
   › offering hope amid despair
   › living amid empire as neighborhood

---

254. See, e.g., Cletus L. Hull III, *The Wisdom of the Cross and the Power of the Spirit in the Corinthian Church: Grounding Pneumatic Experiences and Renewal Studies in the Cross of Christ* (Eugene, OR: Wipf & Stock, 2018); Vijay Michael Antony Payyapilly, "Introducing Charismatics to the Spirituality of the Cross: Applying the Spirituality of St. Paul of the Cross within Charismatic Prayer Groups Associated with Vincentian Retreat Centers" (DMin thesis, The Catholic University of America, 2024).

255. Walter Brueggemann, *Reality, Grief, Hope: Three Urgent Prophetic Tasks* (Grand Rapids: Eerdmans, 2014).

He once summarized these as **"to tell the truth in a society that lives in illusion, to grieve loss in a society that practices denial, and to express hope in a society that lives in despair."**[256] The final bullet point indicates an emphasis in all of Brueggemann's writings, and one shared by this book and by the work of many others: the people of God are called to be an alternative culture that offers a different way of being human together.

3. **The missional task of the church** is not to make the gospel *palatable* but to make it *intelligible* (see 14:6–13).

4. **Paul's vision of the church at worship, with every attendee also (at least potentially) an active contributor,** is compelling but often difficult to implement. The many contemporary congregations in which the primary participants, in terms of offering gifts to the gathered body, are normally one celebrant/preacher and a few musicians might do well to rethink how their gatherings can embody the reality of a fully gifted body of Christ.

Questions for Those Who Read, Teach, and Preach

1. What are some contemporary manifestations of the misuse of spiritual gifts in public worship?

2. Is intelligibility the only legitimate criterion for the use of spiritual gifts like glossolalia in public worship?

3. How can a worship service or other Christian gathering properly encourage a visitor's encounter with the living God? How can it also possibly discourage such an encounter?

4. In sum, what does this passage urge the church to believe (faith), do (love), and anticipate (hope)?

For Further Reading

Adewuya, J. A. "Gifts of the Spirit." *DPL*[2] 361–67.
Aune, David E. *Prophecy in Early Christianity and the Ancient Mediterranean World.* Grand Rapids: Eerdmans, 1983. (technical)
Carson, D. A. *Showing the Spirit: A Theological Exposition of 1 Corinthians 12–14.* Grand Rapids: Baker, 1987.

---

256. For the full interview, see T. K. Barger, "Rev. Walter Brueggemann Draws Parallels from Today's Society to Ancient Times," *Blade*, January 11, 2014, https://tinyurl.com/5ezt4esj.

Cavanaugh, William T. *Theopolitical Imagination: Discovering the Liturgy as a Political Act in an Age of Global Consumerism*. London: T&T Clark, 2002.

Cohick, Lynn H. *Women in the World of the Earliest Christians: Illuminating Ancient Ways of Life*. Grand Rapids: Baker Academic, 2009.

Fee, Gordon D. *God's Empowering Presence: The Holy Spirit in the Letters of Paul*. Peabody, MA: Hendrickson, 1994. (technical)

————. *Paul, the Spirit, and the People of God*. Grand Rapids: Baker Academic, 2023 (orig. Peabody, MA: Hendrickson, 1996). (highly accessible)

Forbes, Christopher. *Prophecy and Inspired Speech in Early Christianity and Its Hellenistic Environment*. Tübingen: Mohr Siebeck, 1995. (technical)

Frederick, John. *Worship in the Way of the Cross: Leading Worship for the Sake of Others*. Downers Grove, IL: InterVarsity Press, 2017. (highly accessible)

Heschel, Abraham J. *The Prophets*. Two vols. in one. Peabody, MA: Hendrickson, 2007 (orig. 1962).

Hluan, Anna Sui. *"Silence" in Translation: 1 Corinthians 14:34–35 in Myanmar and the Development of a Critical Contextual Hermeneutic*. Carlisle: Langham, 2022. (technical)

Hull, Cletus L., III. *The Wisdom of the Cross and the Power of the Spirit in the Corinthian Church: Grounding Pneumatic Experiences and Renewal Studies in the Cross of Christ*. Eugene, OR: Wipf & Stock, 2018.

Hylen, Susan E. *Finding Phoebe: What New Testament Women Were Really Like*. Grand Rapids: Eerdmans, 2023. (highly accessible)

Keener, Craig S. *Spirit Hermeneutics: Reading Scripture in Light of Pentecost*. Grand Rapids: Eerdmans, 2016.

Keown, Mark J. *Pneumaformity: Transformation by the Spirit in Paul*. Grand Rapids: Kregel Academic, 2024.

Peppiatt, Lucy. *Rediscovering Scripture's Vision for Women: Fresh Perspectives on Disputed Texts*. Downers Grove, IL: IVP Academic, 2019. (highly accessible)

————. *Women and Worship at Corinth: Paul's Rhetorical Arguments in 1 Corinthians*. Eugene, OR: Cascade, 2015.

Pohl, Christine D. *Making Room: Recovering Hospitality as a Christian Tradition*. Grand Rapids: Eerdmans, 1999.

Turner, Max. *The Holy Spirit and Spiritual Gifts: In the New Testament Church and Today*. Rev. ed. Peabody, MA: Hendrickson, 1996.

SUMMARY OF 1 COR 11:2–14:40

In chapters 11–14, we have seen Paul express several major concerns about Corinthian worship (see also the summary of 8:1–11:1 above):

- The community's worship requires an appropriate combination of freedom, or spontaneity, and order, so that it follows the customs of the churches and ensures the edification of its members.
- The church is the body of Christ, a gifted community of unity-in-diversity that remembers, proclaims, and embodies the cross of its Lord by giving special attention to its poorer and weaker members.
- Cruciform love—love that is patient and kind but not rude or arrogant, not seeking its own interest but bearing and enduring all things—is the most fundamental, essential, and distinguishing feature of the church's life.
- The modus operandi of the church is always Spirit-empowered cruciform love, which gives meaning and shape to its worship life, especially its exercise of Spirit-ual gifts/grace-gifts for the edification of the body and the salvation of outsiders.
- Worship must embody these values if it wishes to be truly catholic in its local manifestations.

REFLECTIONS AND QUESTIONS ON 1 COR 11:2–14:40 AS A WHOLE

1. A key subject in these chapters is the identity of the church and the way that identity gets expressed, or not, in its public worship. What contributions to ecclesiology (the theology of the church) do these chapters make?
2. Another key topic in these chapters is the reality of conflict about, and even during, the church's public worship. Which contemporary issues related to Christian worship are implicitly addressed by these chapters?

15:1–58
ADDRESSING THEOLOGICAL CHAOS: THE APOSTOLIC WITNESS
TO THE RESURRECTION OF CHRIST AND OF BELIEVERS
(ONE, HOLY, CATHOLIC, AND *APOSTOLIC* CHURCH)

Few books of Scripture culminate as dramatically as does 1 Corinthians with its majestic chapter 15. Karl Barth called it the interpretive key to the whole letter.[1] Together perhaps with Rom 8, it represents the pinnacle of Pauline rhetoric and theological argument, and yet, like Rom 8, it does not contain the musings of an armchair theologian. Rather, it embodies the deepest and most practical convictions of someone who believes that what he has to say is a matter of life and death, both for himself and for his readers/hearers. It actually *was* such a matter even as Paul wrote his letters to young churches, because in Corinth, as in Thessalonica, some members of the community had died (1 Cor 11:27–30; 1 Thess 4:13–18), and in both communities, there was confusion about death and resurrection. In fact, the confusion at Corinth was, unsurprisingly, chaos.

The chaos addressed in this chapter is not a chaos like the others at Corinth—simply one problem among several. This issue—the resurrection—constitutes, with the cross, the *foundational* issue at Corinth. For the Corinthians to be one, holy, and catholic, they must above all be apostolic—grounded in the gospel that the apostles, including *their* apostle (Paul), proclaimed. With the resurrection, Paul comes to the topic no one can skirt and call themselves Christian. *To deny or grossly misinterpret the resurrection of Christ and of the dead in Christ spells theological and spiritual shipwreck.*

As a Pharisee (Phil 3:5), Paul would have affirmed the future resurrection of the dead, as did certain other apocalyptically minded Jewish writers of his time. The critical issue was whether God had raised the crucified Jesus now, in advance of that future resurrection. Once Paul met the resurrected Lord, he could only say, "Yes!" and then unpack its significance. For him, Christ's resurrection accomplished the following:

- revealed his identity as
  - the Son of God and Messiah of Israel

---

1. Karl Barth, *The Resurrection of the Dead*, trans. H. J. Stenning (London: Hodder & Stoughton, 1933). In addition to Barth and the commentaries on ch. 15, see especially Wright, *Resurrection of the Son of God*, 312–60.

- the risen, living Lord and Savior of all peoples
- the one who forever remains the crucified Jesus
- the one who, by his Spirit, encounters, inhabits, and transforms individuals and communities

- manifested the nature of justification and salvation as transformative participation in his death and resurrection
- secured immortality for those in him
- guaranteed the significance of all other Christian beliefs, including the saving value of the cross
- furnished the basis of a life of faith, hope, and love
- made possible Spirit-enabled (charismatic) *resurrectional* cruciformity
- elevated the significance of the human body both ethically and eschatologically
- ensured the divine defeat of humanity's metaenemies, Sin and Death[2]
- affirmed the goodness of the entire creation and God's commitment to its ultimate salvation
- inaugurated the new age and new creation, as God's future has penetrated the present
- and much more

For Paul, then, Christ's resurrection is a multivalent topic, as we will discover in some detail, and it is no less significant today than it was in the first century.

As we have repeatedly seen, Paul is ever the bifocal theologian, with an eye on both the past dimension of God's salvation in Christ (the coming, crucifixion, resurrection, and exaltation of Christ) and the future dimension, including the parousia, the resurrection of the dead, the full and final glorification of believers, and the liberation of the entire cosmos. Paul even structures the body of this letter in this bifocal way, bookending it with a deep dive into the significance of the crucified Messiah on the front end (especially 1:18–2:5) and a similar in-depth analysis of the significance of the resurrected Messiah here in chapter 15.

Although when he was first in Corinth the apostle had clearly proclaimed Christ's resurrection as well as his cross (15:3–5), some in the Corinthian church had begun to say, "there is no resurrection of the dead" (15:12). Paul is shocked but probably not surprised. In fact, in addition to concerns about the flat-out deniers, Paul is not so sure that any of the Corinthians grasp the full meaning of resurrection; he finds them eschatologically challenged, to put

---

2. When these words signify cosmic powers, they are often spelled with uppercase initial letters.

THE APOSTOLIC WITNESS TO THE RESURRECTION · 15:1–58

it idiomatically. In bifocal perspective, there is, of course, a close connection between Christ's (past) resurrection and the (future) resurrection of believers, and that bond comes to expression with power and clarity in 1 Cor 15.

But there is also an equally tight link between Christ's resurrection in the past and believers' resurrection to new life in the present. That connection is clear in the present chapter as well. Since the Corinthians were challenged in other ways, not least in their lack of emphasis on the real-life implications of Christ crucified that has led Paul to stress it throughout the letter, one might be tempted to think that the resurrection is of secondary importance to him. May it never be! To be sure, Paul had said early on in the letter that he had "resolved to know nothing among you except the Messiah Jesus, that is, the *crucified* Messiah" (2:2 MJG). Yet for Paul, the crucified Messiah is precisely the resurrected, living Lord, and vice versa. This reality has profound practical implications.

Like the story of Christ, life in him is a *sequential* experience of death and resurrection both initially, in baptism (death to the old life, resurrection to the new), and also eschatologically, as physical death gives way to resurrection and immortality. But life in Christ is also a *simultaneous* experience of death and resurrection precisely because the resurrected Lord remains the crucified Messiah. To be in Christ is to embody continuously and simultaneously Good Friday and Easter. Good Friday—that is, Christ crucified—supplies the *pattern*, while Easter—that is, Christ resurrected and alive—supplies the *power* of this life. This is why cruciformity is best described as *resurrectional*. Resurrectional cruciformity means cross-shaped existence that is infused with the power and the presence of the living, resurrected Lord.

Chapter 15 therefore comes to us as both the culmination and the foundation of what has preceded it. A number of issues already addressed in the letter relate especially to eschatology, as we would expect from Paul's bifocal mode of theologizing: anticipation of the parousia and eschatological life (1:7–8; 2:9); the question of judging apostles and their work (chs. 3, 4, and 9); the man to be delivered to Satan (5:1–13); the lawsuits (6:1–11); sex with prostitutes (6:12–20, focusing on resurrection); the passing away of this age (7:29–31); the threat of condemnation for not discerning the body (11:27–34); and the permanence of love versus gifts (ch. 13). But, as noted above, there is a new problem that may lie behind all of these: resurrection denial.

THE PRESENTING PROBLEM: SOME ARE DENYING THE RESURRECTION OF THE DEAD

What we have in 1 Cor 15 is Paul's rather lengthy exposition of the reality and the implications, for this life and the next, of Christ's bodily resurrection as

366

the firstfruits of believers' bodily resurrection and the key to God's cosmic salvation. Paul is not alone among ancient Jewish writers in anticipating resurrection and divine victory over cosmic powers (see, e.g., Dan 7:9–28; 12:1–4), but his perspective is, of course, shaped by the crucified and resurrected Christ. Much of what Paul says in this chapter appears elsewhere, sometimes more succinctly, in other letters, for example in Rom 8; 2 Cor 3:18; 4:16–5:11; Phil 3:10–21; 1 Thess 4:13–18. Paul, then, does not need denial of believers' future resurrection to prompt him to write about it. Yet because of the chaos at Corinth, the various claims of 1 Cor 15 address major consequences of the potential *unreality* of both our resurrection and Christ's, while also affirming the consequences of the *reality* of both Christ's resurrection and ours.

"Now if Christ is proclaimed as raised from the dead, how can some of you say there is no resurrection of the dead?" (15:12). Perhaps such words were uttered by "some" after members of the community died. This affirmation-with-denial is the presenting problem that Paul seeks to address. It is also the issue that has perhaps most perplexed scholars, especially recently, who have tried to offer explanations from both the evidence of the letter and the realities of Greco-Roman culture.

What is going on? First, the Corinthians have accepted and are continuing to believe the gospel (15:1–2), summarized in a minicreed that they likely recited (15:3–5), which claims that God raised Christ from the dead (15:4). Second, "some"—and we need to stress that it was some, not all—are denying the resurrection of the dead (15:12). (More on what this might mean below.) Third, the Corinthians have an unusual practice of baptizing people "on behalf of the dead" (15:29). In other words, at least some Corinthians are guilty of serious inconsistency, both theological and practical:

- affirming the resurrection of Jesus but denying the resurrection of the dead (theological inconsistency)
- baptizing on behalf of the dead but denying the resurrection of the dead (practical inconsistency)

How is such inconsistency possible, especially the affirmation of Christ's resurrection but the denial of the resurrection of the dead?

We should not look for a consistent, carefully thought-through systematic theology among the "some." Even today, many Christians affirm Christ's resurrection without necessarily understanding it well or properly recognizing the connection between it and personal or cosmic eschatology. Indeed, Paul's main point is that there is confusion, chaos, and inconsistency. After all, there were many different views of the afterlife in the Greco-Roman world. Paul

THE APOSTOLIC WITNESS TO THE RESURRECTION · 15:1–58

Brown names the following perspectives apart from Jewish (especially Pharisaic) beliefs in resurrection:[3]

- continued existence in the earth/grave/tomb
- continued existence in the underworld (Hades)
- immortality of the soul (see, e.g., Plato) and metempsychosis (migration of the soul into other places and beings—essentially reincarnation)
- celestial immortality (deification by becoming a star)
- fleshly immortality (deification in a bodily form—similar to but not the same as the resurrection as Paul teaches it)
- nihilism—no afterlife whatsoever, which was probably the view of the common man[4]

Since any and all of these ideas (and possibly more) could have been floating around Corinth, scholars have debated precisely what the "some" at Corinth denied and affirmed. Three significant options are the following:[5]

1. They denied a *future* eschatological resurrection of believers and affirmed a present, spiritual resurrection. Popular in the late twentieth century but now a minority position, this view is sometimes summarized by saying some Corinthians had an overrealized eschatology.
2. They denied a *bodily* resurrection and affirmed something like the immortality of the soul.
3. They denied an afterlife *altogether* and affirmed that *death is the end.*

Which interpretation is correct? In my view, there is likely some truth in all three.

First of all, the dominant Corinthian spirituality seems to be one in which the present experience of believers—particularly in their ecstatic worship in the Spirit, in their sense of freedom from future judgment, and in their apathy about the physical body—is one of present glory and power, something that Paul himself reserves for the future except in a *cruciform* sense (cross-shaped glory and cross-

---

3. Paul J. Brown, *Bodily Resurrection and Ethics in 1 Cor 15* (Tübingen: Mohr Siebeck, 2014), 28–56. See also Wright, *Resurrection of the Son of God*, 32–84. For biblical and ancient Jewish views, see 85–206 in Wright and, for a different perspective, Greg Carey, *Death, the End of History, and Beyond: Eschatology in the Bible* (Louisville: Westminster John Knox, 2023), 93–134.

4. This is sometimes called annihilation.

5. See Brown, *Bodily Resurrection*, 67–79, although Brown does not think any of these is the actual Corinthian view.

368

shaped power). *Some* Corinthians may well have understood the resurrection of Jesus, and their participation in it, primarily in terms of his presence, by the Spirit, in their worship. This focus on present experience is not, however, best understood precisely as overrealized or collapsed eschatology. Rather, it is a matter of hyperemphasis on the Spirit, but a Spirit decoupled from Christ crucified.

Second, from 6:12–20 we know that Paul has already seen in the Corinthians a disconnect between their behavior and their eschatology regarding the body. One-third of chapter 15 (vv. 35–50) is devoted to the question of bodily resurrection, so it is highly probable that this is a major issue for *some* Corinthians. Whatever they affirmed about the afterlife, it was not bodily resurrection. And they may not have known precisely what Jesus' own resurrection entailed.

Finally, because Paul spends so much time in chapter 15 dealing with the futility of Christian faith and life if there is no resurrection of the dead, it is likely that *some* Corinthians simply denied believers' postmortem existence altogether, with or without understanding all the consequences of that view. Such people would not necessarily deny Christ's resurrection, seeing him as a unique figure with a unique fate.[6]

To summarize, in my view, the Corinthian "some" (1) affirmed the resurrection of Jesus but understood that primarily as a present Spirit-ual experience of the resurrected Jesus (though disconnected from his crucifixion) and (2) denied believers' future (eschatological) bodily resurrection, holding instead to one or the other of the common Greco-Roman views. It is also possible that they believed Jesus' resurrection was in fact bodily but was a unique event, while average people, even believers, simply died—and that was it. But whatever the specific Corinthian view(s), the main issue is that "some" now see no connection whatsoever between the reality and character of Jesus' past death and resurrection and the future experience of believers. Eschatologically speaking, they were functionally pagans, following in the footsteps of Plato, the Epicureans, and the man on the street.

PAUL'S PERSPECTIVE

In response to the denial of future bodily resurrection, Paul affirms the following main points in chapter 15:

---

6. There are various versions of this position. Paul Brown, for instance, believes the Corinthian deniers thought normal humans simply die, but unusual figures and heroes, like those of certain ancient myths (and Jesus), were destined for an afterlife (*Bodily Resurrection*, 79–107).

THE APOSTOLIC WITNESS TO THE RESURRECTION · 15:1–58

1. Christ was raised, bodily, from the dead.
2. Christ's resurrection constitutes the firstfruits of the eschatological bodily resurrection of the dead.
3. If there is no eschatological resurrection of the dead at all, then Christ was not raised as the firstfruits of that eschatological resurrection; Christ is dead. (But you Corinthians know he is not!)
4. If Christ was not raised, then those supposedly "in Christ" will not be raised either; the dead are dead. (You Corinthians don't seem to believe that either!)
5. Since you don't understand bodily resurrection, I will explain it to you by way of scriptural interpretation and analogies from everyday life.
6. The resurrection of the dead signals the culmination of God's plan of salvation, including the defeat of the powers of Sin and Death.

Furthermore, while the primary issue Paul addresses is the Corinthians' problematic denial of future resurrection and the connection of that resurrection to Christ's, this situation does lead him to implicitly deny certain misunderstandings of Christ's resurrection and ours. Healthy Christian theology should also echo Paul's claims.

First, *although Christ's resurrection is in certain ways a mystery, it is not a metaphor.* Ancient peoples had ways of speaking metaphorically about new life as resurrection-like (e.g., Ezek 37), and Paul can actually use such language. In Rom 6 and 8, for example, he speaks of a resurrection *in* the body now (to new life) in anticipation of a resurrection *of* the body later. Our nonmetaphorical (bodily) resurrection is grounded in Christ's nonmetaphorical (bodily) resurrection. Contrary to some voices, even some self-identified Christians, the resurrection of Christ does not mean that he lives on in our hearts or collective memories, like a departed loved one or famous musician.

Second, Christ's resurrection is not a footnote to the cross. Rather, the theology in chapter 15 is foundational for the entire letter, and the short creed at the start of the chapter places equal weight on the saving significance of both Christ's death and his resurrection. With respect to Christ's resurrection and ours, 1 Cor 15 has been foundational and formative for two thousand years of Christian history. Without that resurrection, the chapter exclaims, the cross is not salvific, and Christian faith is both baseless and pointless.

Third, Christians do not believe (merely) in the survival of a believer's soul, but in the resurrection of the body. This conviction is central to 1 Cor 15 even if it is also part of the mystery we cannot fully comprehend. Many influential Greek and Roman philosophers believed in some version of the alliterative Greek phrase *sōma sēma,* meaning the body (*sōma*) is a tomb (*sēma*), a prison for the

370

true self—for the soul. Not so with Paul and the Christian tradition he helped shape: "I believe . . . in the resurrection of the body" (the Apostles' Creed).

One last word of introduction, an affirmation rather than a negation: ultimately, this important chapter is a theological statement about God. *The one true God is the living God, the making-alive God, the God of life and the God of the living.*[7] It is also therefore a statement about the *missio Dei* with respect to humanity: to form those made in the image of Adam into the image of Christ, through whom and in whom they are given life that is purposeful and permanent—a life in full communion with the God who made them and who will ultimately defeat humanity's greatest enemies, Sin and Death. Thus, God will be "all in all" (15:28)—heaven and earth will be fully and finally united. Although Paul does not explicitly use the language of "new creation" here as he does elsewhere (2 Cor 5:17; Gal 6:15), that is what he has in mind, as 1 Cor 10:11 implies.[8] The Christian canon leaves it especially to Revelation to add more apocalyptic images and theological vision about this new creation. But whether we read Revelation or Paul, we see God redeeming the material, bodily creation as such.

The chapter unfolds as follows:

15:1–34   Christ's Resurrection and Its Consequences
    15:1–11   The Common Creed: Christ Has Been Raised
    15:12–34   The Consequences of Christ's Resurrection as Fiction or Fact

15:35–57   The Nature of Believers' Resurrection in Eschatological Perspective
    15:35–50   The Nature of the Resurrection
    15:51–57   The Final Victory

15:58   Concluding Exhortation

15:1–34. Christ's Resurrection and Its Consequences

The first half of chapter 15 begins by focusing on the reality of Christ's resurrection as expressed in what looks like a brief creed (15:1–11). It then considers

---

7. Paul uses the verb "make alive" (*zōopoieō*) in 15:22, 36, 45. See also Rom 4:17; 8:11; 2 Cor 3:6; Gal 3:21.

8. See Wright, *Resurrection of the Son of God*, 312–60; Johnson, "Turning the World Upside Down."

THE APOSTOLIC WITNESS TO THE RESURRECTION · 15:1–58

the consequences of the unreality or reality of the resurrection of the dead generally, and the resurrection of Christ specifically (15:12–34).

15:1–11. The Common Creed: Christ Has Been Raised

The theme of proclamation and acceptance bookends and anchors this passage, as Paul begins the chapter by reminding the Corinthians of the content of the gospel that he received and preached, and that they received and believed (15:1, 3, 11). Thus, this good news is *not* news to the Corinthians. And yet even though they *knew* the gospel, they did not fully *understand* it or know it and its implications existentially. This gospel is the means of their salvation, but only if they hold on to it firmly, for if they do not, their faith will have been in vain (15:2). In fact, the possibility of futile—or empty—belief and behavior is one of the chapter's principal themes (see 15:10, 14, 17, 58; cf. 15:29–32).[9] The apostle is hinting that discarding belief in the future resurrection of the dead threatens a core gospel tenet—Christ's resurrection—and thus the security of one's salvation.

15:1–2. The Gospel and the Corinthians

Paul begins by once again addressing the Corinthians as his siblings (15:1) as he prepares to rehearse the gospel that he "gospelized" to them.[10] His intent is not merely to call to memory but to encourage contemplation and comprehension ("I want you to understand"; 15:1 NRSVue; cf. 12:3; Gal 1:11). Paul says four key things about this gospel:

1. He proclaimed it (see 1:17–21; 2:1–5; 9:14–18, 27).
2. The Corinthians received it—that is, they believed it. (Though Paul does not say so here, receiving the gospel also means they were baptized—though probably not by Paul [1:14–17]—into Christ and his body, were thereby washed of their sins and made holy and just, and received the gift of the Spirit [see 3:5; 6:11; 12:13].)
3. They "stand" in it—that is, they continue to believe it, and it shapes (or should shape) who they are and what they do (see 16:13; Rom 5:2).

9. Paul uses several related words to express this theme, and translations render the terms differently, but the dominant image is emptiness (vv. 10, 14 [2×], 58).
10. The Greek text is *to euangelion ho euēngelisamēn hymin.*

372

4. They are being saved (*sōzesthe*; present tense, as in 1:18; 2 Cor 2:15) by it, that is, by the God whose gospel it is,[11] as long as they hold on to it.

That is, there is both an ongoing and a conditional aspect of salvation. Salvation is an unfolding reality, even a process. In fact, Paul maintains that salvation is as much a future event (e.g., Rom 5:9–10) as a past event: we are saved "in hope" (Rom 8:24). Furthermore, salvation is a gift that must be maintained and nurtured over time, until the time of one's death or Jesus' parousia. It is not a one-and-done experience of accepting the gospel (or Jesus) as if that were, literally, the be-all and the end-all of faith. Such faith is "in vain"—to no avail, purposeless.

This does not mean that people somehow earn or merit their salvation, for that would be the precise opposite situation to the good news that God loves sinners and enemies (Rom 5:1–11). Rather, Paul is describing not the *means* of salvation but the *meaning* of salvation: transferal from the realm of Adam and Sin and Death into the realm of Christ and holiness and life. That is what and where salvation is, past, present, and future: being in, with, and for Christ.

The means of that salvation is none other than the message, the "word" (*logos*; 1 Cor 15:2), which means the word of the cross: "the message [*logos*] about the cross is foolishness to those who are perishing, but to us who are being saved [*sōzomenois*, present tense] it is the power of God" (1:18). That is, Paul can summarize the gospel as "the word" or "the word of the cross," but as he will now say, that message of the cross is also the message of the resurrection. A faith that is not in vain is one that is built on the resurrection of Christ and all that it entails for believers.

15:3–7. The Gospel in Four Acts

Using traditional Jewish language of carefully passing on sacred tradition, as in 11:23 concerning the Last Supper, Paul now reminds the Corinthians of the specific substance of the gospel that he had "received" and then "handed on" to the Corinthians (15:3), which they had then "received" (repeating 15:1).[12] As

---

11. See the phrase "the gospel of God" in Rom 1:1; 15:16; 1 Thess 2:2, 8, 9.

12. "Handed on" translates *paredōka*, as in 11:2, 23. In Gal 1:12, Paul says he did not receive the gospel "from a human source." In Galatians, he is trying to prove the divine origin of his claim about the justification of gentiles—and thus the unity of gentiles and Jews in the Messiah—over against Cephas' (Peter's) recent, misguided practice of separation (Gal 2:11–14) from gentiles. In 1 Cor 15, however, he is trying to demonstrate the continuity, rather than the contrast, between himself and Cephas plus the other apostles.

THE APOSTOLIC WITNESS TO THE RESURRECTION   · 15:1–58

noted above, the contents of the gospel Paul received and conveyed, as presented here, have the appearance of an early creedal statement, likely recited in various churches. It consists of four main points, what we might call articles, or affirmations, or acts in a succinct drama (15:3–5 or 15:3–6a, 7).[13] Each of the four is introduced by the word "that" (*hoti*):

AFFIRMATION/ARTICLE/ACT	INTERPRETATION	ELABORATION
1. "that Christ died" (15:3b)	-"for our sins" -"in accordance with the Scriptures"	
2. "that he was buried" (15:4a)		
3. "that he was raised" (15:4b)		-"on the third day"
	-"in accordance with the Scriptures"	
4. "that he appeared" (15:5) (15:6a, 7)		-"to Cephas" -"then to the Twelve" ... -"to more than five hundred" -"to James" -"to all of the apostles"

This creed is not just a list of historical and theological claims; it is a narrative account of God's salvific activity in Christ, and it is therefore absolutely critical—"of first importance" (15:3). It is sometimes called the *kērygma*, which means "proclamation." We see a similar but longer account in Acts 2:22–36.

The short creed's kerygmatic emphasis clearly lies on the two affirmations, 1 and 3, that are said to be in accord with the Scriptures: the Messiah's death and his resurrection. Here and elsewhere in Paul, these are the main events, fulfilling the Scriptures, while 2 and 4, Christ's burial and postresurrection appearances, confirm the reality of the two central acts, respectively. Nonetheless, for Paul, the sequence actually worked the other way around, experientially: (4) the resurrected Jesus appeared to him, which led him to conclude (3) that God had raised him (2) from his grave and therefore (1) that the reality of Jesus' death by crucifixion was not merely the epitome of shame but the

13. The fourth article may have originally been short (just v. 5) or longer (vv. 5–6a, 7, with v. 6b added by Paul); if the former (my view), Paul has added to the original.

374

scripturally anticipated saving work of God (as he has said in 1:18–25). But we will explore the four parts as the creed presents them.

The beginning of the first affirmation, that Christ died (15:3b), seems at first blush like a simple and basic historical claim. While "Jesus of Nazareth was crucified" (see 1:13, 23; 2:2, 8) would be such a historical claim very few people would deny, that "Christ" (or "the Messiah") died involves an interpretation: the one who was thought by some to be the Jewish Messiah, but by others to be a blasphemer, was in fact the Messiah. This first affirmation also has two explicit, closely related interpretive glosses: that this death was "for our sins" (cf. 11:24—"for us") and that it was "in accordance with the scriptures."[14]

In fact, these two phrases really constitute one claim: this was a death for sins that is in sync with certain scriptural themes or texts and with Scripture as a whole. It is only by faith that we can affirm that Jesus was the Jewish Messiah and that, as such, his cruel crucifixion at the hands of the Romans was salvific. Only by faith can we affirm that Jesus' death was a sacrificial death for sins, and specifically a death for *our* sins: not for his own sins (see 2 Cor 5:21) and not just for the sins of the Jewish people but also for the sins of the world, the sins of the Corinthians and the sins of all.

The specific scriptural text or texts alluded to in 1 Cor 15:3 almost certainly include Isaiah's fourth servant hymn (Isa 52:13–53:12), with lines like the following (all taken from the NETS translation of the Greek Septuagint, or LXX):

- "But he was wounded because of our acts of lawlessness and has been weakened because of our sins; upon him was the discipline [or "punishment"] of our peace; by his bruise we were healed" (Isa 53:5).
- "Because his life is being taken from the earth, he was led to death on account of the acts of lawlessness of my people" (Isa 53:8b).
- "And he himself shall bear their sins" (Isa 53:11d).
- "Because his soul was given over to death, and he was reckoned among the lawless, and he bore the sins of many, and because of their sins he was given over" (Isa 53:12b).

Interestingly, unlike some of the phrases in this prophetic poem, the creed

---

14. As in 1 Corinthians, the rest of the Pauline letters have various ways of conveying the saving significance of Jesus' death, including both that it was for us/our sake (e.g., Rom 5:6–8; 8:32; 2 Cor 5:14–15; Gal 2:20; 1 Thess 5:10; Eph 5:2; 1 Tim 2:5–6; Titus 2:14) and for our sins (e.g., Rom 4:25; Gal 1:4; cf. Rom 8:3; 2 Cor 5:21).

THE APOSTOLIC WITNESS TO THE RESURRECTION · 15:1–58

does not say Christ was wounded or stricken (by God, or by other humans) but that he died; the implication is that he did so of his own accord (cf. Phil 2:6–8).

The second affirmation, that he was buried (15:4a), naturally contains a verb in the passive voice, as others did the burying. The burial confirms the reality of Christ's death. (In addition to the four gospel accounts, see Isa 53:9.) He did not merely appear to die—the claim of the later docetists since, they alleged, God or the Son of God could not succumb to death.[15] There is no facticity to the swoon theory—the conspiratorial attempt to say Jesus did not really die on the cross but was drugged—because Jesus was actually placed in a tomb.

The third affirmation, about the resurrection (15:4b), makes four main claims. First, the passive voice of the verb ("was raised") means that someone—obviously God the Father—raised Christ; he did not simply rise on his own steam (see also 15:15, where God is explicitly named).[16] Second, the tense of the verb is perfect (as also in each verse of 15:12–14), suggesting that Christ was raised *and remains alive*—as the appearances will confirm. Third, this took place on the third day, that is, on the day we call Sunday. And fourth, it happened, like the death, in fulfillment of the Scriptures.

We cannot be sure whether the entire phrase "he was raised *on the third day*," or simply "he was raised," is meant to be understood as in accord with the Scriptures. But given the parallel to the first affirmation about Jesus' death, it is likely that the whole phrase is meant. Early Christian proclamation of the resurrection was buoyed by scriptural texts, such as the beginning and ending of the fourth servant hymn (also quoted above regarding the death) as well as words from certain psalms (once again, quoting the NETS translation of the LXX):

- "See, my servant shall understand [or "prosper"], and he shall be exalted and glorified exceedingly" (Isa 52:13).
- "If you offer for sin, your soul shall see a long-lived offspring, And the Lord wishes to take away from the pain of his soul, to show him light and fill [or "mold"] him with understanding" (Isa 53:10b–11a).

15. The words "docetist" and "docetism" come from the Greek word *dokeō*, which means "seem, appear." The docetists believed that Jesus was not a real human: he only appeared to be incarnate and only appeared to die.

16. A few translations—most surprisingly the CEB—have "he rose" rather than "he was raised" at 15:4. This is a possible but highly unlikely rendering of the Greek verb *egeirō*, especially in light of 15:12–15. In those verses, the same form of *egeirō* appears three times in vv. 12–14, followed by "[God] raised Christ." An active construction, naming God, occurs as well in 6:14; Rom 4:24; 8:11; 1 Thess 1:10. A passive construction appears also in Rom 4:25; 6:4.

376

- "Therefore he shall inherit many [or "he shall cause many to inherit"], and he shall divide the spoils of the strong" (Isa 53:12a).
- "Because you will not abandon my soul to Hades, or give your devout to see corruption" (Ps 16:10).[17]

The reference to the third day is likely an interpretation of Hos 6:2: "After two days he will make us healthy; on the third day we will rise up and live before him" (NETS). There may also be an echo of the Jonah story—"And Ionas [Jonah] was in the belly of the sea monster three days and three nights" (Jonah 2:1b NETS = 1:17 MT)—as in the teaching of Jesus preserved by Matthew's Gospel (Matt 12:40). And all four gospels recount Jesus' prediction of his resurrection on the third day, with Luke 24 including the words of Jesus, "*Thus it is written*, that the Messiah is to suffer and to rise from the dead on the third day" (Luke 24:46; emphasis added).[18] "The third day" is clearly fixed in the mind of the early churches.

Several implicit claims are also present in the third affirmation: that Christ's resurrection validates his death as salvific, liberating us from the power of Sin and the sting of Death; that *his* resurrection is the firstfruit of *our* resurrection, the general resurrection of believers; and that his resurrection means that neither our belief in this good news nor our corollary life of faithful activity is folly. These implications will be drawn out by Paul later in the chapter.

The fourth and final affirmation of this minicreed is parallel to the second and similarly functions as proof of the immediately prior claim: "he appeared" (*ōphthē*). This is actually a form of the verb "see" and means "he was seen by them," not "they had a dreamlike vision of him."[19] He could be seen because he had emerged from the grave, bodily. Christ's postresurrection appearances to people demonstrate the reality of his resurrection (15:5–7). This affirmation is the longest of the four, encompassing five parts:

- two events known from the canonical gospels and undoubtedly part of the original creed (v. 5)

17. For Ps 16:10, see Acts 2:27, 31.

18. See also Matt 16:21; 17:23; 20:19; 26:61; 27:40, 63–64; Mark 8:31; 9:31; 10:34; 14:58; 15:29; Luke 9:22; 13:32; 18:33; 24:7, 21; John 2:19–20. Some have also suggested an echo of the binding of Isaac narrative in Gen 22: "on the third day" of travel, Abraham saw the place God had shown him (Gen 22:4).

19. This passive form of the verb *horaō* ("see") conveys an active sense, indicating that Christ took the initiative. The English word family "appear" can (wrongly, in this case) suggest unreality rather than concrete reality.

THE APOSTOLIC WITNESS TO THE RESURRECTION · 15:1–58

> ‣ an appearance to Cephas/Simon Peter (v. 5a; see Luke 24:34; cf. John 21)
> ‣ an appearance to the Twelve (v. 5b; probably the appearance to the eleven disciples [the Twelve minus Judas] narrated in Matt 28:16–20, and/or John 20:19–23, and/or Luke 24:33–51)
- three events not known from the canonical gospels (vv. 6–7)
> ‣ an appearance to more than five hundred believers at one time (v. 6), most of whom were still alive to bear witness, though some had fallen asleep (a euphemism for death but especially appropriate because their state is temporary)[20]
> ‣ an appearance to James alone (v. 7a)
> ‣ an appearance to "all" the apostles, which is a group larger than the Twelve (v. 7b; this *might* refer to one of the gospel accounts)

The named recipients of these appearances, Cephas and James, are two of the pillars of the earliest Jerusalem church (Gal 2:9), and Cephas was, of course, a significant figure for the Corinthians (1:12; 3:22; 9:5). That both Cephas (v. 5) and Paul (v. 8) saw the resurrected Lord further puts them on equal footing and unifies them, rather than making them the basis for division.

Although one cannot be sure, it is likely that the original creed ended with the references to Peter and the Twelve (v. 5), which would make the fourth article relatively short, like the second (the burial). This would mean that the other three episodes (vv. 6–7), plus the reference to his own experience (v. 8), were added by Paul. There are other appearances in the canonical gospels that are either unknown to Paul (or the composers of the creed), or are intentionally not included for one reason or another.[21] (The empty tomb stories are not noted, but they would not have qualified as solid proofs of the resurrection.)

In any event, what is obviously not mentioned here is an account of Jesus' appearances to one or more women, as we have in three of the canonical gospels (Matt 28:1–10; John 20:11–18; Luke 24:33–53), as well as the longer ending of Mark (Mark 16:9).[22] This lacuna could be accidental, the result of ignorance about the appearances to women, but it is more likely intentional. The rationale in the minds of those who composed the creed would not be to suppress women or undervalue their role in the church, as some have claimed, but for apologetic purposes. In the third century, Origen bears witness to the

20. For the image of sleep, see also 7:39; 11:30; 15:18, 20, 51; 1 Thess 4:13–15.
21. See Luke 24:13–32 (the Emmaus account) and the episodes in John 20:19–29; 21:1–22.
22. The "companions" mentioned in Luke 24:33 certainly included women. Some interpreters also think that the two disciples in Luke 24:13 are Cleopas (see 24:18) and his wife.

378

critique of the pagan Celsus that the Christian story is attractive primarily to the foolish, weak, and stupid like enslaved persons, children, and women (*Against Celsus* 3.44). Celsus especially mocked the Jewish and Christian belief in the resurrection of the body (*Against Celsus* 5.14). A quasi-public text like a creed could be a place to keep such a critique from resulting in easy, but unnecessary, public mockery of the gospel.

At the same time, there is one almost definite and one possible allusion to women in Paul's additions to this basic creed. The word "brothers" (15:6) regularly means both men and women (hence "brothers and sisters" in many translations here); the five hundred *almost certainly* includes women. And since Paul likely counts Junia as one of the apostles (Rom 16:7), the reference to apostles in 15:7 *might* include women. Interestingly, the early eighteenth-century Black female preacher Jarena Lee argued for women's right to preach based on this text and John's Gospel: if the resurrection is central to apostolic Christian faith, and Mary Magdalene was the first preacher of the resurrection (John 20:18), then it must be legitimate for women to proclaim the gospel.[23]

15:8–11. The Gospel, Paul, and the Corinthians

There is still one appearance to be noted: the one to Paul himself. Although 15:8 was not part of the creed, Paul uses the same Greek verb (*ōphthē*) to convey that his experience of the resurrected Christ was of the same genre as the experiences of Cephas, James, and the others. The Lord had appeared to him, and he had seen the Lord (9:1)—and this experience was, for Paul, essential to his vocation of apostleship.[24] Paul's short autobiographical and self-revelatory remarks in these verses recount his sense of unworthiness ("unfit"; 15:9) to be an apostle because he had persecuted God's church (15:9), as both Acts and other Pauline letters also attest.[25]

Thus, Paul had become an apostle in a late, abnormal or untimely way (lit., "as a miscarried or aborted fetus" [15:8 MJG])—perhaps a "traumatic birth."[26] Similar sentiments about unfitness and unworthiness appear elsewhere in the Pauline correspondence.[27] But the accent is on divine grace from start to finish (15:10). Paul was not part of the original witnesses but was "last of all" (15:8) and is "least" of all the apostles (15:9). It was God's grace that allowed him to

---

23. Bowens, *African American Readings of Paul*, 77–78.

24. See also Acts 9:1–31; 22:1–21; 26:2–23.

25. Acts 8:1–3; 9:1–5; 22:3–8; 26:9–15; Gal 1:13–14, 23; Phil 3:6; 1 Tim 1:13.

26. McKnight, *Second Testament*.

27. See, e.g., Gal 1:15; Eph 3:7–10; 1 Tim 1:12–16.

see the resurrected Lord and be called from being a persecutor to being a pro-claimer; this transformation was, in effect, a resurrection from the dead and thus another witness to the gracious, life-giving power of God.[28] It is God's grace that has equipped and enabled Paul to do his ministry, such that he (Paul) worked hard, and yet it was not really him working but God (see 3:5–10).[29]

These claims about Paul's own life ultimately serve his overarching con-cern: that if there is no resurrection, if he did not really encounter the living Christ, then the whole Jesus-as-Messiah project has been in vain—literally, "empty" (15:10; similarly, 15:2). Paul, however, is certain that God has raised Jesus and that all is not in vain. And this apostolic gospel of the Messiah's death and resurrection was precisely what the Corinthians had heard and believed, both from Paul and from any others who had proclaimed the good news in their presence (15:11). There are many gospelizers, but only one gospel.

Believers' Participation in the Story/Reality of the Messiah

In context, the main point of the creed Paul recites and expands is that from the very beginning, the Corinthians have affirmed the gospel Paul proclaimed, and they continue to do so—all four affirmations, including, of course, Christ's resurrection. If God has acted in fulfillment of Scripture, if the Corinthians have believed God raised Jesus, and if apostles and others have encountered the risen Lord, how could some now deny the future resurrection of the dead (15:12)? We will return to this question when we consider 15:12.

But there is another dimension to this minicreed that is not made explicit in 1 Corinthians, though it likely lies behind and undergirds other aspects of the letter. God's salvific activity in Christ is not only a past event and reality with a corollary promise about the future; it is also something in which believers par-ticipate now, beginning with their baptismal death and resurrection *with* and *into* Christ. Although Paul does not spell out the details of this participatory reality here, he hints at it a few times in the letter, using the very participatory liquid image of baptism:

- "Were you baptized in the name of Paul?" (1:13)—no, in Christ's name.
- "All were baptized into Moses in the cloud and in the sea" (10:2)—and now all have been baptized into Christ.
- "In the one Spirit we were all baptized into one body" (12:13)—the body of Christ.

28. I owe this insight to Michelle Rader. Cf. Rom 4:17.

29. On grace in Paul's ministry, see also Rom 1:5; 12:3; 15:15–16; 2 Cor 1:12; 12:9; Gal 1:15; Eph 3:2, 7–8.

380

15:8–11 · *Believers' Participation in the Story/Reality of the Messiah*

In Rom 6, however, Paul does refer to the four-act creed, part by part, as an experience of participation in and with Christ through baptism: death, burial, resurrection, and appearance (or public presentation):[30]

DRAMATIC ACT	THE STORY OF MESSIAH JESUS (1 COR 15 MJG)	THE STORY OF BELIEVERS (ROM 6 MJG)
DEATH	"The Messiah **died** for our sins in accordance with the Scriptures" (15:3)	"We . . . **died** with respect to Sin . . . all of us who have been baptized into the Messiah Jesus, into his **death** were baptized" (6:2–3); "into **death**" (6:4); "we have been **co-joined** with him [*symphytoi gegonamen*] in the likeness of his **death**" (6:5); "our old self was **co-crucified** with him [*synestaurōthē*]" (6:6); "we have **died** with the Messiah [*syn Christō*]" (6:8); "**dead** with respect to Sin" (6:11)
BURIAL	"he was **buried**" (15:4a)	"we have been **co-buried** with him [*synestaphēmen*] by baptism into his death" (6:4)
RESURRECTION	"he was **raised** on the third day in accordance with the Scriptures" (15:4b)	*Present (resurrection to new life):* "just as the Messiah was **raised** [by God] from the dead . . . so we too might **walk in newness of life**" (6:4); "**alive** in relation to God in the Messiah Jesus [*en Christō Iēsou*]" (6:11); "**from death to life**" (6:13) *Future (bodily resurrection):* "we will certainly also be [co-joined with him] in [the likeness of] his **resurrection**" (6:5); "we will also **co-live** with [*syzēsomen*] him" (6:8; cf. "**eternal life**" in 6:22–23)
APPEARANCE	"he **appeared** to Cephas, then to the Twelve" (15:5–9)	"**present** yourselves [make your **appearance**] to God as those who have been brought from death to life, and **present** your members to God as weapons of justice" (6:13; cf. 6:16); "**present** your members as slaves to justice for the purpose of holiness" (6:19)[31]

30. This table is adapted from Gorman, *Romans*, 170–71.

31. Luke has similar language about Jesus' own appearances in Acts 1:3, using the same Greek verb (*paristēmi*) that is translated in Rom 6:13, 16, 19 as "present." Most translations correctly render the first Greek verb in Acts 1:3, which is followed by a reflexive pronoun (as in Rom 6:13, 16), as "he presented himself [*parestēsen heauton*] alive."

381

As James Dunn wrote about the focus on "with" words and phrases here and elsewhere in Paul,

> What was of fundamental importance for Paul was that believers could not simply affirm these foundational beliefs but could *identify with them* in a way and degree hitherto unknown. . . . So it was not simply the belief in Jesus's death and resurrection that was central to Paul's gospel: it was also the sense that those who responded to the gospel could realistically share in what was thus proclaimed, could already experience both a dying of and a dying to their old self-centered nature, and a new life welling up within and giving a new goal and motivation to all they did.[32]

Participation with Christ means that the response of faith begins a present resurrection (to new life) *in* the body now, in anticipation of future resurrection (to glory and eternal life) *of* the body later. This participatory experience is what many Christians have called justification, sanctification, and glorification, or, if these aspects of salvation are seen as one continuous work of God, Christification or deification—becoming like Christ and thus like God. Putting Rom 6 in conversation with 1 Cor 15—not just 15:3–7 but the entire chapter—brings out more fully Paul's understanding of baptism and belief, and of the connection between death and resurrection: both Christ's and ours, both present and future.

15:12–34. The Consequences of Christ's Resurrection as Fiction or Fact

The creed that Paul passed on to the Corinthians and that they likely recited together in worship was clear about Christ's resurrection. Equally clear, it seems, was Paul's insistence on the reality of sharing in Christ's death and resurrection in baptism, in daily life, and in anticipation of eschatological glory. Clarity of public affirmation, instruction, and even experience was apparently, however, no match for the cultural climate in Corinth. Whatever the specific causes and articulations—Stoic, Platonic, Epicurean, hyperspiritualized, or whatever—some Corinthians did not believe in the resurrection of the dead, of *their* dead, of themselves. Paul sets out to name and then correct this critical lack of apostolicity and rejection of basic Christian teaching because it means

---

32. James D. G. Dunn, *Jesus according to the New Testament* (Grand Rapids: Eerdmans, 2019), 111–12.

denying—even if unintentionally—the resurrection of Christ that the creed announces and the Corinthians as a whole (so it seems) affirm.

The veracity or falsity of Christ's resurrection carries enormous consequences, and Paul sets out to identify them for the Corinthians and for us. That is the burden of 15:12–34, which is structured chiastically as follows:

A The Consequences If Christ's Resurrection Is Fiction (15:12–19)
   B The Reality of Christ's Resurrection and Its Consequences (15:20–28)
A′ Paul's *Peroratio*: Further Consequences If the Resurrection Is Fiction, and Concluding Admonitions (15:29–34)

15:12–19. The Consequences If Christ's Resurrection Is Fiction

"Now if Christ is proclaimed as raised from the dead, how can some of you say there is no resurrection of the dead?" (15:12). The first half of this verse summarizes the critical point of the creed and the apostolic gospel: raised (by God—another divine passive) *from the dead*—from among corpses, so to speak. This summary makes it absolutely clear that Christ's resurrection does not entail some sort of vague postmortem existence or an aliveness in believers' memories; it is a *bodily* resurrection. The second half of 15:12 reveals the theological and spiritual contradiction operative among some in Corinth: belief in a proclamation affirming Christ's bodily resurrection from the dead in the recent past (15:1–5) while denying the future bodily resurrection of the dead in the future.

These Corinthians sound more like their pagan counterparts (see, e.g., Acts 17:16–34), which suggests they were in fact reflecting their previous, pre-Christian point of view that they had not yet fully abandoned. A common (especially Epicurean) Greco-Roman sentiment, seen on many graves—"I was not, I was, I am not, I care not"—may well have been present in the church at Corinth. This denial of the future resurrection of the dead by some, in spite of Paul's clear proclamation and the Corinthians' acceptance of Christ's own resurrection from the dead, naturally leads the apostle to identify the consequences if it is in fact the case that there is no resurrection of the dead. First and foremost is this: *there was no resurrection of the dead Christ either.*

It is important to note the different starting points of Paul and the Corinthians. Paul begins with the Pharisees' conviction that God will one day raise the dead. In his worldview, resurrection is a *possibility* or a *promise* that has become a *reality* in God's raising of the crucified Messiah Jesus from the

THE APOSTOLIC WITNESS TO THE RESURRECTION · 15:1–58

dead. He interprets his encounter with the resurrected Lord in the light of his Pharisaic understanding of an eschatological bodily resurrection of the dead. On the other hand, as former pagans steeped in many alternatives to belief in a future, bodily resurrection, some Corinthians deny the resurrection of the dead in principle. They begin, in other words, with the *impossibility* of the bodily resurrection of the dead, which forces them, perhaps unwittingly, into a theological contradiction: *affirming* Christ's past resurrection but *denying* future resurrection. In the introduction to chapter 15 above, we noted various explanations for this contradiction. Perhaps "some" Corinthians saw Jesus' resurrection as a one-off, an exception to the rule, or perhaps they did not understand his resurrection to be bodily. They clearly did not see a connection between the reality or unreality of their future resurrection and the reality or unreality of Christ's. Whatever the precise cause of this disconnect, the fundamental issue and starting point is the possibility or impossibility of the resurrection of the dead, which Paul names twice (15:13, 16).

For Paul, the implications of the unreality of the resurrection of the dead are grave indeed. Appealing to logic, repeatedly saying "if . . . then," he identifies significant theological and practical corollaries in 15:13–19. Using pathos (strong emotion), he adds more existential consequences in 15:29–32.

The first corollaries of the resurrection as unreality are these:

- Most importantly, as just noted, Christ has not been raised (15:13, 16), which means God did not raise him (15:15).
- Paul's preaching (15:14) and the Corinthians' faith (15:14, 17) have been in vain, futile, empty—like the speculations of the so-called wise (3:20).
- Paul's preaching misrepresents God (15:15; lit., they are "false witnesses" [CEB, NAB, NIV]), a serious offense for any Jew.
- Believers—"you" (Paul gets direct and personal)—are "still in your sins" (15:17) because, it is implied, Jesus' death was really just a brutal crucifixion and not a death for sins, as the creed affirms (15:3). The locative language of still being "in" sins suggests that through faith and baptism, people are transferred out of sins and into Christ and his body.[33]
- Believers who have died have perished; they are permanently dead and will not be raised (15:18).
- Apostles and believers alike are the most pitiable souls, for they (it is implied)

33. Similar ideas and language are found in Romans, but with the focus on Sin singular, as a power (see esp. Rom 6:1–2), which reappears as such in 1 Cor 15:56. The plural "sins" here in 15:17 is an echo of the word "sins" in the creedal text (15:3).

384

have endured much cost for what amounts to a hoax full of empty claims and promises—an eschatological scam (15:19).

Paul's logic can be illustrated graphically as follows:

If no resurrection of the dead → Then no resurrection of Christ.
If no resurrection of Christ → Then empty and false apostolic proclamation.
If empty and false apostolic proclamation → Then empty and false faith.
If empty and false faith → Then still in sins (empty present) and death is the end (empty future), and thus the most pitiable of all people.

In other words, without the resurrection of the dead, there is no resurrection of Jesus, in which case the death of Jesus is not salvific. Moreover, if there is no resurrection of the dead, there is no reason for faith, hope, or love—the kind of love that endures suffering. Texts like 1 Cor 13 and Rom 8 make no sense. Death is the ultimate enemy, life nothing other than a meaningless trip to experience, like a college fraternity party or the hookup culture (or a Corinthian Lord's Supper), so . . . carpe diem! For the dead are simply dead; there is no difference between (hoodwinked) believers and nonbelievers (who actually believe the truth, the nonreality of resurrection): the fate of both is to perish (15:18; cf. 1:18; 2:6).

It is quite possible that Paul's presentation of these consequences surprised the Corinthians, even the resurrection deniers. They may not have recognized the connections Paul makes, or their own inconsistency. But Paul has not finished. There are both positive and further negative consequences concerning the truth or falsity of the resurrection to unpack (vv. 20–34), and questions to address (vv. 35–57).

15:20–28. The Reality of Christ's Resurrection and Its Consequences

"But in fact," writes Paul—or rather, "*But now*," (NAB)—"Christ *has been* raised from the dead" (15:20a; emphasis added) and is therefore the living Lord—as Paul knows by personal experience and the Corinthians know by his witness and by their own experience, especially in worship. As in the creed (15:4), which is echoed throughout 15:12–19, the passive verb "has been raised" in 15:20 implies divine action. As a consequence of God's act, all the implications of the potential unreality of the resurrection of the dead are reversed.

Interestingly, Paul does not respond point by point to the logical concerns of the previous verses. Rather, he focuses apocalyptically on the big picture: the fundamental reality of Christ's parousia, or royal arrival and presence

385

THE APOSTOLIC WITNESS TO THE RESURRECTION · 15:1–58

(15:23),[34] which is possible only because of his resurrection, and which signals the future resurrection of the dead and God's ultimate victory over Death:

- Christ is the "firstfruits" of believers who have died (lit., "those who have fallen asleep"), that is, the first of many to be resurrected (15:20–23; cf. Col 1:18; Rev 1:5).[35] *For Paul, the image, or metaphor, of firstfruits is an absolutely critical part of his argument, for it inextricably links Christ's resurrection to that of believers*—precisely the connection "some" Corinthians were missing. In fact, the image has the potential to open up for the Corinthians a brand-new perspective on Christ's resurrection and on theirs—and on how they both fit into the story of God's salvation.[36]
- Christ is the second Adam, who undoes the reign of death initiated by the first Adam (15:21–22; cf. Gen 3; Rom 5:12–21).
- Christ is alive and reigning now as Lord, in the process of defeating all enemies, not with Roman imperial power but with the power of God evidenced in resurrection (15:24–28, citing Pss 8:6; 110:1).
- In God's future, Death—humanity's most powerful enemy—will finally be destroyed (15:26), and the "end," the telos of the *missio Dei*, is achieved (15:24; Gk. *telos*, meaning "goal," not "termination"): God will "be all in all" (15:24–28).

This apocalyptic scenario is one that offers hope but also creates some confusion with respect to (1) its understanding of Christ in relation to the Father and (2) the scope and nature of salvation (Christology and soteriology). A few observations may provide some clarity, focusing first on the latter issue.

Of particular note in 15:20–28 is the recurrence of the word translated "all" or "every"—twelve occurrences of forms of the Greek word *pas*.[37] This suggests the universal scope of sins/Sin, on the one hand, and of Christ's salvation

34. The Greek word *parousia* can signify "arrival" or "presence" in a general sense, but it was also a more technical term for the arrival and presence of a god, king, or emperor. Paul uses *parousia* for Jesus' future royal appearance only five times: here in 15:23, plus 1 Thess 2:19; 3:13; 4:15; 5:23. In 1 Cor 1:7, he uses the word *apokalypsis*, "revelation." In 1 Thess 4:13–18, he offers a bit more detail about the order at the parousia: the dead in Christ are raised first, followed by those who are alive.

35. CEB has "first crop of the harvest" in vv. 20, 23. For various practices involving firstfruits, see, e.g., Exod 23:16, 19; 34:22, 26; Lev 2:12; 19:23–25; 23:10, 17, 20; Deut 18:4; 26:1–15.

36. See Andy Johnson, "Firstfruits and Death's Defeat: Metaphor in Paul's Rhetorical Strategy in 1 Cor 15:20–28," *Word and World* 16 (1996): 456–64.

37. See 15:22 (2×), 24 (2×), 25, 27 (3×), 28 (4×).

386

and rule, directed toward its completion in God the Father, on the other. Paul's anthropology here depicts humanity as either "in Adam" or "in Christ" (15:22), each location and corollary participation resulting in either death or life for "all" therein (see also the parallel phrases in 15:21). Those in Christ don't simply live in the present; the emphasis here is that they will be made alive, or brought to life in the future, at the parousia (15:23)—the passive voice in 15:22 ("will be made alive") implying divine action. *What is going to happen is not simply the natural course of human life*; God must reverse the normal spiral toward nonexistence, for God is the one who "gives life to the dead" (Rom 4:17). But it is the promised telos of those raised to new life in Christ (Rom 6:4–5, 22–23).

What looks at first like a claim of universal resurrection to salvation in parallel to universal death (the double "all" of 15:22) is qualified by the phrase "those who belong to Christ" (lit., "those of Christ"; recall 1:12) in 15:23, which restricts the universalism. A universalist interpretation is also challenged by Paul's words about those who are perishing (1:18; 2:6).[38] We should therefore read 15:22 to mean, "Just as all in Adam die, so also all who are in Christ will be made alive." (It is difficult to write or read those words without hearing Handel's *Messiah* in the background.) *Location is everything; location determines salvation.* Paul's logic is this: we humans share the fate of the one in whom we live; being in Adam means death; being in Christ (the result of faith and baptism) means life. But the divine passive in v. 22 ("will be made alive") again reminds us that God alone is the actor, the Savior, the making-alive one.

But before the parousia, Christ will be reigning as Lord, for he has been given that authority by God the Father (15:27; cf. Phil 2:9–11). And that reign will include the "destruction" of all the powers—three kinds are named in 15:24—that Paul calls "the enemies" (15:25).[39] Although most translations say, "his enemies," Paul's words probably signify the enemies of humanity, of the people Christ came to save; *humanity's* enemies are also *his* enemies (see Ps 110:1, "your enemies"). His death, resurrection, and present reign are the reason those enemies are "under his feet" (15:27, quoting Ps 8:7 LXX [8:6 MT]), a common image in the ancient world that was known not only to the Hebrew psalmist but also to anyone in Paul's day who saw Roman images of soldiers conquering the world.

The promise of Christ's parousia—his royal arrival and presence—and the presence of his reign mean that all other powers, especially social and political

38. See also, e.g., 2 Cor 2:15; 4:3; Phil 1:28.

39. On the powers, see also 1 Cor 2:8; Rom 8:35–39; Eph 6:10–17; Col 1:15–16; and perhaps 1 Cor 10:20–21; 12:2.

powers, that promise a sort of perfect kingdom now pale in comparison to the true Lord. In addition, to the degree that such powers practice injustice or demand uncritical allegiance in exchange for their promises, they commit the sin of idolatry by pretending, explicitly or implicitly, to rule the world. They crucified the Lord himself (1 Cor 2:8) and have murdered many other innocents before and after. They are part of the band of enemies that challenge Christ's rule but over whom he rightly reigns now, and will completely reign, as the world's true Lord. *This does not, however, mean that Christ-followers are charged with somehow dominating the political realm or "ridding the world of evil."* Their function is to bear witness to what *God* has done in Christ's death and resurrection, and what *God* will do at history's climax.

Christ's victorious reign is not due to his having inflicted injustice in the form of suffering or slavery but rather to his having enslaved himself for our benefit and suffered and died for us. The most powerful of the enemies of humanity Christ will destroy is Death (which Paul dramatically personifies), and it is the last to be destroyed by him (15:26). Once again, the word "all" or "every" matters: no enemy will last forever. Even now, those enemies are being subdued, as texts like Ps 8 and Ps 110, noted above and cited in vv. 25 and 27, suggest.[40]

Following the parousia comes what most translations call "the end" (15:24; *to telos*), meaning the culmination. (It is important to note that here and elsewhere Paul speaks of one and only one future coming of Jesus; there is no hidden or secret coming that involves the so-called rapture of the church.) This is the goal toward which the divine project and the human story have been proceeding, which includes Christ being "subjected" to God the Father. In light of the entire letter, and especially 8:6, this cannot mean that Jesus, the eternal Son of God (Gal 4:4), is somehow minimized.

Rather, it suggests that Christ's particular mission—that aspect of the *missio Dei* appropriated to him—has been accomplished and, with the defeat of all the enemies finalized and the reign of Christ over "all things" in place, the story of the world as being *from* God (the Father) and *through* Christ (8:6) has reached its destination by being united with the source of all: God the Father. (Yet again, the word "all" is prominent in 15:24–28.) In other words, this last act does not reflect a vague panentheism or pantheism; rather, it is a claim that

---

40. See esp. Ps 8:7 LXX (8:6 MT), which reads, "And you set him over the works of your hands; you subjected all under his feet" (NETS); Ps 109:1 LXX (110:1 MT): "The Lord said to my lord, 'Sit on my right until I make your enemies a footstool for your feet'" (NETS).

the mission of God in Christ is to draw all people, and indeed all of creation, into the fullness of life in Christ and thus also to make creation full of God's presence and glory (cf. Eph 3:19; Hab 2:14)—full of God's Spirit. Christ the victorious Son and Lord brings glory to the Father (Phil 2:9–11).

Within these verses, then, we find an apocalyptic drama in several ordered acts, expressed in words and phrases like "firstfruits," "in his own order," "then," "after," "until," and "last enemy."[41] The sequence is Christ's death, his resurrection, his reign (i.e., as Lord) and defeat of the powers, his parousia, the resurrection of those in Christ (which will entail transformation: see 15:42–54), the handing of all authority over to the Father, and the reality of God's being "all in all" (15:28). The powers, including "the rulers of this age" such as those who crucified the Lord, are "doomed to perish" (2:6). Prior to that final reality, Christ's death, resurrection, and lordship are a direct challenge, not only to the metapowers of Sin and Death but also to all powers, including political authorities, that in any way oppose the mission of God in the world (15:24–25; cf. Col 2:15). Paul is putting the empire on notice: eternal Rome (*Roma aeterna*) and its various heirs—which themselves are empowered by Sin and Death—will not have the final word about human history and life.

15:29–34. Paul's Peroratio: Further Consequences If the Resurrection Is Fiction, and Concluding Admonitions

As the apostle comes to the conclusion of the first half of his discussion of the resurrection, he increases the rhetoric, especially his use of pathos (emotion), as he poses rhetorical questions, points to real-life experiences, and practically begs the Corinthians—while shaming them—to come to their senses. The potential unreality of the resurrection has further serious consequences:

- The Corinthian ritual of baptism for the dead (which Paul chooses not to condone or condemn, or to describe, but to exploit for his argument) is pointless (15:29).
- Paul's daily danger and suffering (including literal or, more likely, figurative fighting with "wild animals")—his apostolic lifestyle and boast—are absurd and of no gain (15:30–32a).
- Hedonism is the logical lifestyle: "'Let us eat and drink, for tomorrow we die'" (15:32b, citing Isa 22:13).

41. See 15:3–7 for similar language about order and sequence.

THE APOSTOLIC WITNESS TO THE RESURRECTION   · 15:1–58

Paul draws on two experiences—the Corinthians' and his own—to essentially ask, If God does not raise the dead (15:29, 32), what's the point? In 15:29, he twice asks this question rhetorically about the mysterious, unexplained practice of baptism for (*hyper*) the dead. The Corinthians must have known about, and almost certainly engaged in, such a practice. The Greek word *hyper* can mean "on behalf of," "in place of," "on account of," or "concerning," though many translations have simply "for."

Whatever the practice was specifically—and scholars have made dozens of proposals—its likely theological assumption is this: dead people (whether literally or spiritually dead) need salvation, which baptism by the living somehow represents or effects.[42] Paul decides not to challenge the practice but, instead, to use it to make his What's the point? point. If the dead are dead and rotting in their graves forever, or doomed to do so, it is an absurdity to think they need either salvation or baptism. In other words, this Corinthian practice *presupposes* that which (some of) the Corinthians are disbelieving!

Paul then turns in 15:30–32a to the realities of regular, indeed daily (*kath' hēmeran*; v. 31) and even hourly (v. 30), danger and death experienced by himself and his coworkers ("we"). He seems to be thinking about both the possibility of literal death and the reality of being crucified with Christ, and thus to oneself and one's own interests. The temporal references may sound hyperbolic, but the point Paul means to make is that his and others' troubles are persistent, not occasional, as he says also in Rom 8:36, quoting Ps 44:22: "As it is written, 'For your sake we are being killed *all day long*; we are accounted as sheep to be slaughtered.'"[43] And Paul may also know the words of Jesus that discipleship entails taking up one's cross *daily* (*kath' hēmeran*; Luke 9:23).

Paul will sometimes list more fully the sorts of sufferings to which he alludes in vv. 30–32a (see 1 Cor 4:9–13 and other such catalogs),[44] even as he mentions one particular episode in Ephesus of fighting with wild beasts (15:32a). (Some scholars have even suggested that "I die every day" in v. 31 alludes to the gladiato-

---

42. The most common view is that what is going on is vicarious baptism, that is, baptism in place of, or on behalf of, the dead. Such a practice (if that's what it was) is not known anywhere else in the first-century churches. For a range of proposed interpretations, see, e.g., Thiselton, *First Epistle*, 1242–49. In their *Doctrine and Covenants* (e.g., section 128), the Church of Jesus Christ of Latter Day Saints (the Mormons) discuss their practice of baptism for the dead and cite Paul (128.16).

43. Emphasis added. See also 2 Cor 4:10: "always carrying in the body the death of Jesus."

44. See 2 Cor 4:7–12; 6:3–10; 11:23–33 and, more briefly or more focused, Rom 8:35; 2 Cor 1:3–11; 12:10.

rial life.) This might have been in an actual arena with live animals—think of the Roman Colosseum—but is more likely a metaphor for encounters with the cosmic forces (recall 15:24–28) manifested in political powers or other opponents.[45] No matter the specifics, such struggles and sufferings were integral to Paul's vocation and a focus of his boasting (15:31; cf. 9:15; Rom 5:3; 2 Cor 11:16–12:10).[46] And these struggles did sometimes border on death (2 Cor 1:8–11; 11:23). But if the dead are not raised, such fighting was, and is, of absolutely no use or value.

Rather, the logical conclusion is this: Let's party! (15:32b). The prophet Isaiah (Isa 22:13) and many others have known this sentiment. But Paul does not leave the Corinthians hanging to draw their own conclusion, because, of course, Christ *has been* raised and the dead *will be* raised. In light of these truths—and the lifestyle implications they imply—Paul employs a popular proverb originating from the Greek dramatist Menander (died ca. 292 BC) to counsel the Corinthians to separate themselves from bad influences: "Bad company ruins good morals" (15:33). In context, this admonition refers (at least) to avoiding those who deny the resurrection of the dead, either with their explicit theological statements or with their lifestyles (see, e.g., 6:12–20). In this midstream peroration, Paul warns the resurrection deniers and those captivated by their teaching or their lives to sober up (see also 1 Thess 5:6–10) and to end this ignorance of God, this "sin" (15:34). Self-styled wise and knowing people (3:20; 8:1–11) are often lacking precisely that which they claim to have. "All our knowledge brings us nearer to our ignorance, / All our ignorance brings us nearer to death" (T. S. Eliot, "The Rock").

A proper Christian eschatology is not—as some more recent resurrection deniers have mistakenly thought—merely a carrot to entice people to behave properly so they can go to heaven when they die, but it is the basis of an appropriate use of both the mind and the body for the service and glory of God in anticipation of one's telos (13:12). Paul is not afraid to call out, and even shame (15:34), those who, like some of the Corinthians, claimed (and claim) knowledge of God and all things in relation to God but actually revealed (and reveal) their profound ignorance of God and the ways of God.[47] In such fraternal and apostolic correction lies the hope of salvation for more than a few ancient and contemporary Corinthians.

---

45. See 1 Cor 16:8–9; 2 Cor 1:8–11; Acts 19:23–41. Paul's attitude to opposition is counterintuitive, as we will see in the discussion of 16:8–9.

46. Paul understands this boasting in suffering as boasting in the Lord (1 Cor 1:31; 2 Cor 10:17) and specifically in his cross (Gal 6:14).

47. Recall the similar shaming language in 6:5 regarding lawsuits; see also Mark 12:24.

THE APOSTOLIC WITNESS TO THE RESURRECTION · 15:1–58

15:35–57. THE NATURE OF BELIEVERS' RESURRECTION IN ESCHATOLOGICAL PERSPECTIVE

The second, somewhat shorter, half of the chapter is focused on the nature of believers' resurrection in the context of God's final, eschatological victory. These image-rich and apocalyptic verses will lead to the chapter's concluding exhortation in 15:58.

15:35–50. The Nature of the Resurrection

The human body, with all its various activities, has figured prominently in this letter. In one important passage, Paul had declared, "God raised the Lord and will also raise us by his power" (6:14). In good rhetorical form, he now addresses questions (or perhaps objections), either known or anticipated, to his teaching on bodily resurrection.

Specifically, in 15:36–50 Paul considers two issues named in 15:35—the process of resurrection (how) and the nature of the resurrection body (what). He addresses these concerns by providing an analogy from nature (15:36–41) that is then applied to the questions (15:42–49); a summary follows (15:50). Paul's main claim is that resurrection, which must logically be preceded by death, involves postmortem transformation. (In 15:51–53, he will offer an addendum: not all believers will actually die before the parousia, but all will need transformation to inherit the kingdom of God.)

The passage is deeply Trinitarian, with references (using both active and passive verbs) to God as the God of creation and transformation; to Christ as the second Adam/human whose heavenly image believers will bear; and to the Spirit who both animates the resurrected Christ and will animate resurrected believers (implicitly continuing, in a new key, the work of resurrection/giving life).

15:35 Two Questions

Paul's discussion of the nature of believers' resurrection proceeds from two questions posed by what looks like a hypothetical inquirer: "But someone will ask, 'How are the dead raised? With what kind of body do they come?'" It is likely, however, that behind this hypothetical inquirer are real Corinthians and their concerns that Paul has heard about. It is also possible, of course, that believers in other places had raised up similar matters; as noted above, we know that the Thessalonians, for instance, had questions and even worries

392

about the resurrection from the dead (1 Thess 4:13–18). In the case of Corinth, as with Thessalonica, the issues are deeply theological but also practical—and, in fact, perpetual among Christian believers: *how* can the dead be raised, and *what* is the character of the resulting body?

15:36–41. An Analogy from Nature

The corporate tag "Fool" that starts v. 36 implies that the (self-styled "wise") Corinthians should know the answers to the two questions. The analogy Paul offers in vv. 36–41 to illustrate the how and the what of bodily resurrection comes in two parts. First, he draws on the ancient belief that a seed that is sown must die in order to come to life (15:36, the how; cf. John 12:24). He then adds the observation that the resulting plant is a transformation of the original seed: "you do not sow the body that is to be" but a bare (lit., "naked," echoed in 2 Cor 5:3) seed, or kernel (15:37, the what).[48] This is the case for wheat or any other grain. But for Paul, this is not just a natural sequence: as in v. 22, the passive voice of the verb "make alive" (*zōopoieō*) in v. 36 indicates that this transformation is God's work.[49] The seed is "brought to life" (NAB) by God; it does not naturally "come to life" (NRSV, NRSVue, NIV, and most other translations).

In 15:38–41, Paul expands the latter part of the analogy by remarking that God has created a variety of seeds with differing "bodies," as God has assigned (v. 38)—as God does with spiritual gifts (ch. 12). Echoing Gen 1, Deut 4:16–19, and other ancient writings, he maintains that there is a wide variety of "bodies" in creation: for humans, animals, birds, fish (v. 39). These various earthly bodies do not exhaust God's good creation, because there are also heavenly bodies (v. 40): sun, moon, stars (v. 41). And each body has its own distinctive "glory," or divinely given honor and splendor (vv. 40–41). The basic distinction is between the glory of earthly and of heavenly bodies (v. 40), but this God is so creative that there is differentiation of glory among the various types of heavenly bodies and even among the various stars (v. 41). Contrary to some interpretations, which refer to certain somewhat similar pagan and Jewish texts, Paul is not saying that Christ or believers become astral—stars—any more than they become solar or lunar.[50] The

---

48. In vv. 53–54, Paul will use the imagery of getting dressed—putting on imperishability and immortality.

49. And in v. 45, Paul uses the same verb to characterize Christ, the last Adam, as a "life-giving spirit."

50. There may be echoes of such texts, like Dan 12:2–3, without the interpretation of them in terms of deification as starification.

THE APOSTOLIC WITNESS TO THE RESURRECTION · 15:1–58

stars help to demonstrate the diversity of bodies and their glory in God's creation, not the destiny of human bodies.

Thus, the analogy indicates that (1) there is both continuity and discontinuity in the death that effects the transformation from seed to body, and (2) there are different kinds of bodies, each with its own wondrous beauty. The analogy sets the table for Paul to speak theologically about death being followed by resurrection, a transformation from one form of glory (earthly, Adam-shaped) to another (heavenly, Christ-shaped)—as 2 Cor 3:18 suggests.

15:42–49. The Analogy from Nature Applied to Bodily Resurrection

Continuity and discontinuity, and different kinds of bodies: so too, then, with the resurrection of the dead (15:42a). (Given certain appearance narratives in the Gospels, this is exactly what we would expect: Luke 24:13–32; John 20:11–28.) Paul structures his theological interpretation of the analogy in 15:42–49, plus a conclusion in 15:50, with the bookends of the perishable-imperishable (or corruptible-incorruptible; NAB) contrast (vv. 42, 50). In the passage, he addresses both the temporal and the ontological aspects of the transformation; that is, both the process and the nature of the change, though the two aspects are inseparable.

As in the case of a seed and the resulting plant, there is continuity, for that which is sown is also that which is raised. The repeated words "what [is sown]" and "it" in 15:42b–44a accurately convey the sense of the Greek text. But it must also be remembered, again, that the passive verbs in these verses mean that God is the active agent, the one responsible for this continuity. And yet there is also discontinuity.

The discontinuity is also the work of God, expressed in a series of contrasting phrases in vv. 42b–44. Death and resurrection mean transformation: from a body that is perishable, dishonorable, weak, and "natural" into a body that is imperishable, honorable, powerful, and "spiritual."[51] It will then be a glorified heavenly body, and the glory that believers will have is the experience of Christ's bodily, heavenly glory (cf. Phil 3:21, which is a succinct synopsis of 1 Cor 15:35–57).[52] The contrast between these two bodies is unpacked in vv. 45–49 and expressed succinctly in the Greek words *psychikos* and *pneu-*

51. In 15:44, many translations have "natural body" as the opposite of "spiritual body," which is much better than the misleading "physical body" (NRSV, NRSVue).

52. See also Rom 6:5, noted in the table above: "united with him in a resurrection like his."

394

matikos, from *psychē* (soul, being, person) and *pneuma* (spirit/Spirit), respectively (v. 44). The terminology appears also in 2:14–15.[53]

The following verses explain these terms for us. A *psychikos* body is one defined by Adam, the first man/human, who became a living *psychē* (v. 45)—usually translated as "living being" or "living person." Adam, and thus the *psychikos* ("psychic") body, is earthly, from the dust (vv. 47–48); through creation, we have borne his image (v. 49).[54] This is the body of "flesh and blood" (v. 50).[55]

A *pneumatikos* body, on the other hand, is one defined by Christ, the second man/human, the last Adam. He became (or "is"—the Greek phrase lacks a verb) a "life-giving spirit" (v. 45; further discussion in the sidebar on pp. 397–98). Christ, and thus the *pneumatikos* ("pneumatic") body, is from heaven (vv. 47–48), and we will bear his image (v. 49).[56] By "spiritual" or "pneumatic," then, Paul clearly does not mean the absence of the body (as in a free-floating spirit or soul)—which would ruin his analogy—but rather a transformed body, fully enlivened and glorified by the transforming Spirit of God and fully remade in the image of Christ. It is therefore better to understand this "pneumatic" body as a fully en-Spirited body, one in which the person is no longer determined by anything—including Sin and Death—other than the Spirit of Christ, who is the Spirit of God.[57] He or she is now completely Spiritual. Whatever else this means, it means that believers, *as embodied persons*, are conformed to the resurrected, glorified Christ (Rom 8:29).

15:50. Conclusion to the Analogy and Its Application

The transformed body Paul has been describing is no longer "flesh and blood" (15:50), or characterized by normal human existence, because it has

---

53. The repetition suggests that in both places, Paul is contrasting a way of being determined by creation alone (the flesh or merely human; the image of Adam) and a way of being determined by new creation (the Spirit-ual; the image of Christ).

54. "Psychic" in this sense has nothing to do with extrasensory powers.

55. Similarly, the *psychikos* person in 2:14 is "merely human" (NTW), though in that context the word has a more negative connotation.

56. Some manuscripts say, "let us bear the image" (of Christ). The difference in Greek is one letter (omicron versus omega); the eschatological context favors "we will bear."

57. One scholar who uses the term "pneumatic body," Matthew Thiessen, argues that Paul understands *pneuma* in a material sense as the most real, best matter ever. Although I don't share that view of *pneuma*, I agree that the pneumatic body is a real body and think the term is useful to distinguish the resurrected body from the flesh-and-blood "soulish" body. See Thiessen's *A Jewish Paul: The Messiah's Herald to the Gentiles* (Grand Rapids: Baker Academic, 2023), 133–47.

been changed from one kind of glory (the splendor of creation, as flesh and blood) to another (the splendor of resurrection and glorification). This does not mean that that flesh and blood are bad, as if the created order is evil, or the work of someone or something other than the Creator God. Flesh and blood cannot inherit the kingdom of God, not because they are associated with the body but because they represent the body's mortality; they are signs of corruptibility, of the reality of death. The Adamic body of flesh and blood and dust will be transformed but not destroyed, for God is the remaker, not the destroyer, of creation. *Thus, both forms of existence—the* psychikos *and the* pneumatikos—*are bodily*, each with its own splendor, the pneumatic greater than the psychic.[58]

We can summarize much of what Paul has been saying (which he summarizes in 15:50 and will again summarize in 15:53) as follows:[59]

	THE EMBODIED PERSON BEFORE RESURRECTION	THE EMBODIED PERSON AFTER RESURRECTION
15:42b	Perishable	Imperishable
15:43a	Sown in dishonor	Raised in glory
15:43b	Sown in weakness	Raised in power
15:44	Sown a "psychic" body	Raised a "pneumatic" or spiritual (fully en-Spirited) body
15:48	As was the human of dust [Adam = first person], so are those who are of the dust	As is the human of heaven [Christ = last Adam, second person], so are those who are of heaven
15:49	Just as we have borne the image of the man of dust	We will also bear the image of the man of heaven

The main point is clear: inheriting the kingdom of God, which is imperishable, requires a transition from perishability to imperishability (v. 50). This is the logical order from creation to new creation (v. 46). The CEB puts it bluntly: "a rotting body is put into the ground, but what is raised won't ever decay" (15:42b).

Within 15:35–50, we find Paul repeatedly echoing or quoting the early chapters of Genesis: the variety in creation from animals to celestial bodies to

---

58. On eschatological transformation into the image and glory of Christ, see also Rom 8:11, 17, 29–30; 2 Cor 3:17–18; 4:17–5:5; Phil 3:10–11, 20–21; Col 1:27; 3:3–4; 2 Thess 2:13–14.

59. This table is inspired by Nash, *1 Corinthians*, 420.

396

humans (15:38–41; cf. Gen 1); the nature of Adam, the first human, as a living being or soul (*psychēn*) and made of dust (15:45, quoting Gen 2:7; 15:47–49); humanity bearing Adam's image (15:48–49; cf. Gen 5:3). The implication is that the contrast between then and now, Adam and Christ, is ultimately the contrast between creation and new creation, even if Paul does not use that specific term (but see 2 Cor 5:17; Gal 6:15). Salvation is the remedy for humanity's predicament, the creation of a new humanity being remade into the likeness of Christ, "the last Adam" (1 Cor 15:45).

CHRIST THE LIFE-GIVING SPIRIT
AND ESCHATOLOGICAL TRANSFORMATION

It is the overall framework of new creation and of human transformation from *psychikos* body to *pneumatikos* body found in the second half of chapter 15, in conversation with Romans, that helps us understand what Paul means by saying Christ is a "life-giving spirit," or Spirit (*pneuma zōopoioun*; 15:45). Paul is neither suggesting that Christ is now a bodiless spirit nor applying Stoic conceptions of material spirit to Christ. For Paul, Adam is associated not only with life ("a living being," v. 45) but also with Sin and Death (Rom 5:12–21). Even here in 1 Cor 15, sharing in Adam's dust implies perishability, death. In Romans, Paul summarizes the Adam-Christ contrast in terms of Sin and Death versus justification and life: "If, because of the one man's trespass, death exercised dominion through that one, much more surely will those who receive the abundance of grace and the free gift of righteousness exercise dominion in life through the one man, Jesus Christ. Therefore just as one man's trespass led to condemnation for all, so one man's act of righteousness leads to justification and life for all" (Rom 5:17–18).

Later in Romans, Paul further associates the Christ-gift of life with the work of the Holy Spirit, both now and later: "For the law of the Spirit of life in Christ Jesus has set you free from the law of sin and of death. . . . But if Christ is in you, though the body is dead because of sin, the Spirit is life [present] because of righteousness. If the Spirit of him who raised Jesus from the dead [God the Father] dwells in you, he who raised Christ from the dead will give life [future; *zōopoiēsei*] to your mortal bodies also through his Spirit that dwells in you" (Rom 8:2, 10–11). The *present* transformation from Sin and Death to new life in

> Rom 8:2, 10 leads to the *future* transformation from mortality to immortality (implicitly) in Rom 8:11. This transformation involves the Father, the Son, and the Spirit. The same sort of Trinitarian dynamic regarding only the *future* liberation of believers from Sin and Death is at work in 1 Cor 15 (esp. vv. 54–57). God is by nature the one who gives life (*zōopoieō*; 15:22, 36; Rom 4:17), who raises the dead, just as he raised the Son.[60] The result is new creation, which entails the end of the Adam era. Christ the *Resurrected* One is also the *resurrecting* one, the *life-giving* one—but that is something only God can do. Paul's language of "life-giving Spirit" is therefore best understood as shorthand for Christ as the en-Spirited divine agent of this new reality, in contrast to Adam and the realities he introduced. Adam may *have* life, but Christ is much more—as only God can do, he *gives* life.[61]

Throughout this entire section of chapter 15 (15:35–50) and into the next, the repetition of one fundamental point about the new creation makes Paul's focus clear: resurrection means transformation from perishability/corruptibility to imperishability/incorruptibility (15:42, 50, 52–54). That is, to repeat for emphasis, human beings in Christ will be fully conformed to him, fully imbued with God's Spirit, and thus partakers in that most fundamental divine trait of immortality *as embodied persons*. In the Christian tradition, this culmination, or telos, is sometimes called theosis or deification. The process of glorification will be complete (Rom 8:30; 2 Cor 3:18). This reality is closely related to the promise of chapter 13: "For now we see in a mirror, dimly, but then we will see face to face. Now I know only in part; then I will know fully, even as I have been fully known" (13:12). But future transformation is not limited to humans. The "redemption of our bodies" (Rom 8:23) means also the liberation of creation, which has been suffering with us: "the creation itself will be set free from its bondage to decay and will obtain the freedom of the glory of the children of God" (Rom 8:21).

60. Rom 6:4 probably also names the Spirit ("the glory of the Father") as active in Christ's resurrection, and 1 Cor 6:14 ("his power") is likely also a reference to the Spirit's involvement in our, and perhaps also Christ's, resurrection.

61. The Scriptures and Christian tradition identify both the Son and the Spirit with the divine ability to give life (e.g., John 5:21; 6:63; 14:6; 2 Cor 3:6); the Spirit is "the Lord, the giver of life" according to the Nicene Creed.

15:51–57. The Final Victory

Having explained the how and the what of bodily resurrection, Paul shifts from argument by analogy to triumphant apocalyptic proclamation. Joshua Jipp aptly calls the rhetorical center of this passage, 15:54–56, a "poetic gloat over Death's future defeat."[62]

The assumption in 15:35–50 was that we will all die. But the mystery (revelation) of the parousia means that some will not actually die: "We will not all die, but we will all be changed" (15:51; cf. 1 Thess 4:13–18). This transformation affects both living and dead believers because mortal flesh, dead or alive, cannot inherit the kingdom of God (15:50). The word "all" is once again significant, referring to *all* in Christ, no matter their race, gender, or socioeconomic status. In the context of American slavery, some preachers rightly focused on this verse to emphasize that "black bodies belonged to God, not the white slaveholder, and that the bodily transformation prophesied by the apostle included black bodies too," bodies that "had endured so much."[63]

The three passive verbal constructions in 15:51–52 once more indicate divine action; God—probably acting through Christ the life-giving Spirit (15:45)—is the changemaker. Although this change is a radical and definitive one, it is also in continuity with the work of God among believers in the present, from glory to glory (2 Cor 3:18). The theme of vv. 51b–54a is again transformation, echoing 15:42–50: in addition to the promise of 15:51, there is the image of putting on, that is, putting on clothes (15:53–54a).[64] As the preface to the Commemoration of the Dead in the Book of Common Prayer of the Episcopal Church puts it, "For your faithful people, O Lord, life is changed, not ended."[65]

Yet there is still the emphasis on continuity too: the subjects of each sentence—"we" and "this [perishable] body"—indicate continuity of the self in embodied, though transformed, existence. When the trumpet, a standard feature of apocalyptic literature that announces both the divine battle and the divine triumph (e.g., Zech 9:14; cf. Matt 24:31; 1 Thess 4:16), sounds, "in the

---

62. Joshua W. Jipp, *Pauline Theology as a Way of Life: A Vision of Human Flourishing in Christ* (Grand Rapids: Baker Academic, 2023), 95.

63. Bowens, *African American Readings of Paul*, 41.

64. Recall the language of a "naked" seed in 15:37. See also 2 Cor 5:1–4, which uses similar language of nakedness and clothing regarding the resurrection body.

65. See "Proper Prefaces," *The (Online) Book of Common Prayer*, https://tinyurl.com/24xrj5xk. Very similarly, in the Roman Catholic Church, as stated in preface 1 for the dead in the Roman missal: "For your faithful, Lord, life is changed not ended." See "Missal," iBreviary, https://tinyurl.com/yve26sr7.

THE APOSTOLIC WITNESS TO THE RESURRECTION · 15:1–58

blink of an eye" (NAB), the dead will be raised and transformed, and the living will likewise be changed (15:52). This is all God's doing, and it indicates the time of God's final defeat of "the last enemy," Death (15:26, 54–56), which has no ultimate victory or fatal "sting": "'Death has been swallowed up in victory.' 'Where, O death, is your victory? Where, O death, is your sting?'" (15:54b–55). Here Paul quotes (and perhaps tweaks) Isa 25:6–8 and Hos 13:14, saying that these texts are fulfilled when humanity's telos of immortality is reached.[66] The Isaiah text promises not only the defeat of death but also the cessation of tears and a wonderful banquet in death's place, images picked up in the book of Revelation (Rev 19:9; 21:1–4). Paul may well have the eschatological banquet in mind (cf. Matt 8:11; Mark 14:25);[67] such heavenly feasting is the proper alternative to hopeless, hedonistic eating, drinking, and merrymaking now (15:32). The banquet imagery indicates that immortality is more than everlasting existence; it is as much about the character as the duration of life.

This immortality can, of course, occur only because, as John Donne wrote, "Death, thou shalt die":

> Death, be not proud, though some have called thee
> Mighty and dreadful, for thou art not so;
> For those whom thou think'st thou dost overthrow
> Die not, poor Death, nor yet canst thou kill me.
> From rest and sleep, which but thy pictures be,
> Much pleasure; then from thee much more must flow,
> And soonest our best men with thee do go,
> Rest of their bones, and soul's delivery.
> Thou art slave to fate, chance, kings, and desperate men,
> And dost with poison, war, and sickness dwell,
> And poppy or charms can make us sleep as well
> And better than thy stroke; why swell'st thou then?
> One short sleep past, we wake eternally,
> And death shall be no more; Death, thou shalt die.[68]

This victory is the conclusion to the victory of God begun in Christ's death (alluded to in 15:57), through whom believers have been freed from the power

66. For example, the LXX text of Hos 13:14 actually says, "O Death, where is your sentence [*dikē*]" (NETS), or "punishment," rather than *nikē* ("victory"). Paul may have had a slightly different text.

67. As noted in the discussion of 11:17–34, for Paul, the Lord's Supper anticipates the eschatological banquet.

68. "Holy Sonnet 10" ("Death, Be Not Proud"), ca. 1601–10.

400

and consequences of the triumvirate of Sin, Death, and the law (15:56).[69] Now, at the climax of God's salvation in the bodily resurrection of believers, the final enemy (Death) is defeated and can be addressed as the vanquished enemy it is (15:55). The final victory won, the feasting will begin.

The conjunction of Sin and Death is not accidental. Death is the wage Sin pays (Rom 6:23), not only as the ultimate consequence for unholy sinners themselves but as the consequence in the present for so many people who are victims of war, gun violence, and other forms of death-dealing sin. *The certain defeat of Sin and Death means that God will triumph over humanity's addiction to the antithesis of life.* This is the ultimate apostolic (missional) divine act that displays God's own unity, holiness, and catholicity as it ensures that the missional people of God will finally be fully sanctified (holy because they are free of sin and death) and universally united (catholic, one as "God will be all in all," v. 28).

15:58. Concluding Exhortation

In Christ's resurrection, God has defeated humanity's ultimate enemy, Death. For this reason, and this reason alone, Paul writes in a thunderous final exhortation, the Corinthians should be steadfast and faithful in the Lord: 1 Cor 15:58 is the antithesis of 1 Cor 15:32. Christ-participants can joyfully live the life of cruciform, missional love they find in Christ Jesus, see modeled in Paul, and hear about throughout the letter. Why? Because their labor in the body, like Paul's, is not empty and worthless, since Christ has been raised as the firstfruits of their bodily resurrection.

The reality of these "firstfruits" compels us to remember two things.

First, for Christ, death and resurrection "were 'back-to-back,' for the resurrection happened 'on the third day' (1 Cor. 15:4). For believers, however, the twin realities of Jesus' death and God's vindication of him in resurrection create an experiential tension. By identifying with his death, they experience his humiliation; by identifying with his resurrection, they experience the joy of exaltation—but only in part, only in process, and only in paradoxical connection with an ongoing death."[70]

That is, the Christian life is one of charismatic resurrectional cruciformity, of living bifocally, looking back and looking ahead in the power of the Spirit. By God's grace, believers are moving toward the goal of their baptism: being "blameless on the day of our Lord Jesus Christ" (1:8).

---

69. The last of the three, the law, has been co-opted by the other two; see Rom 7:7–25 and discussion in the commentaries (e.g., my *Romans*, 180–89).

70. Gorman, *Cruciformity*, 320.

THE APOSTOLIC WITNESS TO THE RESURRECTION · 15:1–58

Second, Christian mission—whether that of Paul, the Corinthians, the saints and martyrs of the church, or contemporary Christians from Los Angeles to Chicago to Washington, DC to Havana to Dar es Salaam to Baghdad to Kiev to Moscow to rural China and the Amazon rain forest and everywhere in between—is not only not futile, but it is the work of God, a participation in the *missio Dei*, if, and only if, God has raised Christ from the dead and sent the Spirit of his resurrected Son into our hearts. If—rather, *since*—that is true, life is not meaningless, and exhausting work for the kingdom of God is its own reward, both now and in the future. Even if death were to come, the resurrection means that life has not been wasted. As the book of Revelation reports the heavenly perspective, "Write this: 'Blessed are the dead who from now on die in the Lord.' 'Yes,' says the Spirit, 'they will rest from their labors, for their deeds follow them'" (Rev 14:13).

Summary

First Corinthians 15 proclaims loudly and clearly that there is no salvation, no hope, and no purpose without both Christ's resurrection and ours. Even more loudly and more clearly, however, it proclaims that because of the resurrection, we have a *purposeful*, apostolic (missional) life now and will have a *permanent*, eschatological life in the future. Read together with 2 Cor 5 and Rom 8, 1 Cor 15 gives us an inspired glimpse from the apostle into the liberation from Sin and Death of God's entire creation and its glorious, transformed future. In the words of New Testament specialist Andy Johnson, "What God *has done* for the body of Jesus in microcosm in his resurrection, God *is doing* in the ecclesial body of Christ—the current locale of the new humanity and new creation/cosmos—and God *will do* for those in Christ and for the body of the cosmos in macrocosm at the parousia."[71]

Reflections and Questions for 15:1–58

Spiritual, Pastoral, Missional, and Theological Reflections

1. The present spiritual significance of Christ's bodily resurrection in the past and our bodily resurrection in the future can be summarized as follows:[72]

---

71. Andy Johnson, "The Past, Present, and Future of Bodily Resurrection as Salvation: Christ, Church, and Cosmos," in *Cruciform Scripture: Cross, Participation, and Mission*, ed. Nijay K. Gupta et al. (Grand Rapids: Eerdmans, 2021), 207–24 (here 208; cf. 224).
72. Adapted and abbreviated from my *Participating in Christ*, 260–62.

402

15:1–58 · *Reflections and Questions*

> The resurrection to new life we have received is *the life of Christ within us by means of the Spirit*. It is a life of *participation*.

> As the term "resurrectional, charismatic cruciformity" stresses, the resurrection to new life is—paradoxically—*a life shaped by Christ crucified, enabled by the Spirit*.

> The resurrection life is *a countercultural, or altercultural, existence* that values the body as God's temple that is destined for resurrection and transformation; it is a life dedicated in mind and body to the service of God and others.

> The resurrection life is a *missional life*; the resurrection of Jesus provides the incentive and the power to join in the *missio Dei* (the mission of God).

2. In Corinth, the flow of disbelief went from rejection of the eschatological, bodily resurrection of the dead to (implicit or explicit) rejection of Christ's bodily resurrection. In the present, **the flow of disbelief more often works the other way around, starting with the explicit rejection of Christ's resurrection or its reinterpretation as metaphor.** New Testament scholar Richard Hays puts it this way: "On the issue of resurrection, many preachers and New Testament scholars are unwitting partisans of the Sadducees [who denied resurrection]. Because they deny the truth of Scripture's proclamation that God raised Jesus from the dead—or waffle about it—they leave the church in a state of uncertainty, lacking confidence in its mission, knowing neither the Scriptures nor the power of God. . . . The recent history of theology is replete with attempts to reinterpret the meaning of the New Testament's resurrection in ways that will not conflict with a modern scientific worldview."[73]

Hays (and Paul) would concur with the poet John Updike, in his "Seven Stanzas at Easter": "Let us not mock God with metaphor, / analogy, sidestepping, transcendence; / making of the event a parable, a sign painted in the / faded credulity of earlier ages: / let us walk through the door."

3. Jessica Martin, echoing the poet John Updike but writing from a **theological and philosophical perspective**, contends that **Jesus' resurrection**

> **isn't some kind of metaphor.** It's not even, to use [American poet] Patricia Lockwood's words, "a metaphor that is more than a metaphor." It's *bodily*: a body, once dead, now living, proclaiming himself, there and then, as the sign for the intimate re-joining of mortal humanity with the eternal, intangible being of God.
>
> Resurrection re-knits, renews, *re-members*, the life of memory with life in the world of time and space. The risen Jesus ate, drank, cooked and served

---

73. Richard B. Hays, "Reading Scripture in Light of the Resurrection," in *The Art of Reading Scripture*, ed. Ellen F. Davis and Richard B. Hays (Grand Rapids: Eerdmans, 2003), 216–38 (here 216).

THE APOSTOLIC WITNESS TO THE RESURRECTION · 15:1–58

breakfast, walked a day's journey, broke bread, touched and was touched. There is no hint in the Gospels that his resurrection was "just" an *idea*.[74]

And there is no such hint in Paul's letters either.

4. In the words of the great Catholic theologian Karl Rahner, "**Easter is not the celebration of a past event**. The alleluia is not for what was; Easter proclaims a beginning which has already decided the remotest future. The Resurrection means that the beginning of glory has already started."[75]

5. Dr. Patricia Fosarelli, a good friend and longtime colleague, is a pediatrician as well as a professor of spiritual and practical theology. In addition, she has written haiku and other forms of poetry, particularly as a form of prayer when contemplating God in the face of sick and dying children. One such short piece reflects **the hope of resurrection in light of the death of a young girl**; it is inspired by the famous Johns Hopkins statue of Jesus, *The Divine Healer*: "You—Source, Guide, and Goal / Embarking Point, Journey, and / Destination—You."[76]

6. Esau McCaulley, in "What Good Friday and Easter Mean for Black Americans like Me," provides the following powerful reflection on Jesus' cross and resurrection:

> The body that God raised was the same body that was on the cross. . . . His body was transformed and healed, no longer subject to death, but it still had the wounds from his crucifixion. . . .
>
> Jesus' resurrection has implications not just for his body, but for all bodies subject to death. Christians believe that what God did for Jesus, he will do for us. The resurrection of Jesus is the forerunner of the resurrection of our bodies and restoration of the earth. . . .
>
> **When my body is raised, it will be a Black body**. One that is honored alongside bodies of every hue and color. *The resurrection of Black bodies will be the definitive rejection of all forms of racism*. At the end of the Christian story, I am not saved from my Blackness. It is rendered everlasting. Our bodies, liberated and transfigured but still Black, will be the eternal testimony to our worth. . . .
>
> The depiction of the afterlife in which we live apart from our bodies gives physical suffering the final word. *If a Black body can be hanged from a tree and burned, never to be restored again, what kind of victory is the survival of a soul?*[77]

7. On a recent pilgrimage I led in the footsteps of Paul during the Easter season,

---

74. Jessica Martin, *The Eucharist in Four Dimensions: The Meanings of Communion in Contemporary Culture* (London: Canterbury, 2023), 3.

75. Karl Rahner, *Everyday Faith* (London: Herder & Herder, 1968), 71.

76. Cited in Randi Henderson and Richard Marek, *Here Is My Hope: Inspirational Stories from the Johns Hopkins Hospital* (New York: Doubleday, 2001), 96.

77. Esau McCaulley, "What Good Friday and Easter Mean for Black Americans like Me," *New York Times*, April 15, 2022, https://tinyurl.com/3x959ckp (emphasis added).

404

my friend Rev. Randy Cooper offered a Sunday homily to our group that included these **powerful words about Christ's resurrection:**

> I can't begin to imagine or understand how Jesus was bodily raised from Death. I have no idea what a "resurrection body" is like. Yet if I believed that the resurrection of Jesus did not in fact happen, I could not with any integrity remain a Christian. I would have no choice but to renounce my Christian baptism. I would convert to Judaism and live in hope for the coming of the Messiah. If Jesus wasn't raised—which by insistent biblical testimony was a bodily resurrection—then God's promised New Creation hasn't begun or been established in the world. We who bear Jesus's Name "are still in our sins" and are "of all people most to be pitied."
>
> Christians put our lives on the line when we pledge our allegiance to One who "suffered under Pontius Pilate, was crucified, dead, and buried, [and] on the third day . . . rose again," as our Apostles' Creed says. In his resurrection Jesus calls us to live in such an odd, peculiar way that our lives will only make sense if he is risen and leading us as Lord into his New Creation.
>
> If God had raised someone like Alexander the Great or Julius Caesar, God would surely be advancing his Kingdom through military means in our day. Had God raised someone like Winston Churchill, we could expect the Kingdom to advance through political events and developments. If God had raised a great philosopher like Plato or a person of unparalleled intellect like Albert Einstein, our hopes would lie with education and knowledge.
>
> Yet God raised a man who had no place to lay his head, who was himself poor, who healed the sick, who refused violence and political power, and who challenged the dominant powers of his day (and ours). God raised this man, Jesus of Nazareth, thus declaring that his Kingdom would be found in people whose lives resembled Jesus's.

Questions for Those Who Read, Teach, and Preach

1. What intellectual or practical forms of denying the resurrection (Christ's, or ours, or both) exist today, both inside and outside the church? What can be done to challenge these forms of denial? In addition, what can be done to combat the prevalence of belief in the survival of the soul, rather than the resurrection of the body, in spite of Paul's teaching and the content of the historic Christian creeds?

2. What are some of the contemporary implications of the doctrine of bodily resurrection, whether of Christ or of believers?

3. What theological and practical insight can the following honest reflections offer to believers and nonbelievers today? They are part of the obituary for a man, the words written by the deceased himself in anticipation of his death, with instructions for the celebration of his life:

THE APOSTOLIC WITNESS TO THE RESURRECTION · 15:1–58

There can be no religion of any kind at my funeral nor any service in a church. And if anyone claims at the end of my life that I accepted the Lord Jesus Christ as my savior, know that they are lying. I've spent my life as an atheist. That's the way I'll die. And hope that hell has been way oversold. . . . Don't say my life was worthwhile because I inspired one person or . . . changed somebody's life. I don't care if my life was worthwhile and have no illusions it should be. . . . [But] I really loved life.[78]

4. In sum, what does this passage urge the church to believe (faith), do (love), and anticipate (hope)?

FOR FURTHER READING

Barth, Karl. *The Resurrection of the Dead*. Translated by H. J. Stenning. London: Hodder & Stoughton, 1933.

Brown, Paul J. *Bodily Resurrection and Ethics in 1 Cor 15*. Tübingen: Mohr Siebeck, 2014. (technical)

Campbell, Constantine R. *Paul and the Hope of Glory: An Exegetical and Theological Study*. Grand Rapids: Zondervan Academic, 2020.

Carey, Greg. *Death, the End of History, and Beyond: Eschatology in the Bible*. Louisville: Westminster John Knox, 2023.

Graieg, David. *Resurrection Remembered: A Memory Approach to Jesus' Resurrection in First Corinthians*. New York: Routledge, 2024. (technical)

Johnson, Andy. "Firstfruits and Death's Defeat: Metaphor in Paul's Rhetorical Strategy in 1 Cor 15:20–28." *Word and World* 16 (1996): 456–64.

———. "Turning the World Upside Down in 1 Corinthians 15: Apocalyptic Epistemology, the Resurrected Body and the New Creation." *Evangelical Quarterly* 75 (2003): 291–309.

Jones, Beth Felker. *Marks of His Wounds: Gender Politics and Bodily Resurrection*. New York: Oxford University Press, 2007. (technical)

Keller, Timothy. *Hope in Times of Fear: The Resurrection and the Meaning of Easter*. New York: Viking, 2021.

Lorenzen, Thorwald. *Resurrection, Discipleship, Justice: Affirming the Resurrection of Jesus Christ Today*. Macon, GA: Smith & Helwys, 2003.

Madigan, Kevin J., and Jon D. Levenson. *Resurrection: The Power of God for Christians and Jews*. New Haven: Yale University Press, 2008.

Matera, Frank J. *Resurrection: The Origin and Goal of the Christian Life*. Collegeville, MN: Liturgical Press, 2015.

78. Taken from my *Participating in Christ*, 257. Out of respect for the family of the deceased, I am not revealing the man's identity.

O'Reilly, Matt. *Paul and the Resurrected Body: Social Identity and Ethical Practice.* Atlanta: SBL Press, 2020. (technical)

Rae, Murray A. *Resurrection and Renewal: Jesus and the Transformation of Creation.* Grand Rapids: Baker Academic, 2024.

Sandnes, Karl Olav, and Jan-Olav Henriksen. *Resurrection: Texts and Interpretation, Experience and Theology.* Eugene, OR: Pickwick, 2020. (technical)

Stewart, Robert B., ed. *The Resurrection of Jesus: John Dominic Crossan and N. T. Wright in Dialogue.* Minneapolis: Augsburg Fortress, 2006.

Swinburne, Richard. *The Resurrection of God Incarnate.* New York: Oxford University Press, 2003.

Tappenden, Frederick S. *Resurrection in Paul: Cognition, Metaphor, and Transformation.* Atlanta: SBL Press, 2016. (technical)

Williams, Rowan. *The Sign and the Sacrifice: The Meaning of the Cross and Resurrection.* Louisville: Westminster John Knox, 2017.

Wright, N. T. *The Resurrection of the Son of God.* Minneapolis: Fortress, 2003. (technical)

———. *Surprised by Hope: Rethinking Heaven, the Resurrection, and the Mission of the Church.* New York: HarperOne, 2008.

SUMMARY OF 1 COR 15

In 1 Cor 15, Paul demonstrates the following:

- Christ's bodily resurrection is an original and integral part of the gospel.
- If there is no resurrection of the dead, Christ was not raised; the gospel is not good news; and believers' resurrectionally cruciform life of faith, hope, and love is in vain.
- Since Christ was raised, however, he is the firstfruits and guarantor of believers' bodily resurrection, and he provides purpose for life in general and for cruciform, missional living in particular.
- At the parousia, all believers will experience a transformation from a perishable to an imperishable body following the resurrection of the dead; there is thus continuity and discontinuity between pre- and postparousia embodied existence.
- The parousia will lead to the final defeat of all the enemies of God and humanity, including the last enemy, Death itself.

16:1–24
CLOSING: THE APOSTOLIC WITNESS CONTINUES
(ONE HOLY, CATHOLIC, AND *APOSTOLIC* CHURCH)

Having completed the body of the letter, Paul and Sosthenes briefly address a few additional matters regarding their relationship with the Corinthian church, and especially Paul's relationship with the community; there is a lot of first-person-singular ("I") language in this closing chapter. This relationship does not stand in isolation, however, any more than the Corinthian communities are an isolated group, unconnected to the rest of the *ekklēsiai* throughout the empire. The apostolic mission continues, and Paul wants the Corinthians to be part of it as an expression of their own apostolic (missional) identity. Thus, 1 Cor 16 is not a mere appendage to the letter body; it continues Paul's focus on the apostolic witness of both individual believers and Christian communities.

In this chapter, Paul speaks about his own missional activity and that of others in order to garner the following from the Corinthians:

- participation: the collection for Jerusalem (16:1–4)
- understanding: his ministry plans (16:5–9)
- support: of Timothy, Apollos, and local leaders (16:10–12, 15–18)
- ongoing bonds of fellowship (16:19–24)

Ultimately, for Paul none of this is merely human activity. He is writing about the *missio Dei*, the mission of God in the world through human coworkers (cf. 3:5–9).

16:1–4. THE ECUMENICAL COLLECTION FOR JERUSALEM

Paul first calls on the church, in fairly strong language, to participate in the collection for the poor believers in Jerusalem (16:1–4). This was a project of great importance to Paul, who discusses it explicitly in two other letters: in Romans (Rom 15:25–33) and, at length, in 2 Corinthians (2 Cor 8–9). The resurrection, discussed in chapter 15, is the basis for seeing the collection as a form of participation in the *missio Dei* that is not in vain (15:58).[1]

Paul involves, or tries to involve, various Christ assemblies with a majority of gentile participants that he has founded or otherwise knows: in Macedonia

1. I owe this insight to Hunter Brown.

(northern Greece), Achaia (southern Greece), Rome, and perhaps elsewhere. The apostle is engaging in this collection in fulfillment of an agreement made with the Jerusalem leaders (Gal 2:10) that he would remember the poor—though the promise may not have been limited to the Jerusalem poor.[2] Thus, the collection is an act of "ecumenical charity,"[3] of global Christian unity and missional interconnectedness. But it is not a one-way street; it has a reciprocal character: "if the Gentiles have come to share in their spiritual blessings [those that come from "the poor among the saints at Jerusalem"], they ought also to be of service to them in material things" (Rom 15:27).

Paul provides several specific details about the request he is making (16:1–2):

- It is to be done in concert with the Galatians in central Asia, where Paul has previously evangelized and founded communities.[4]
- It is to be done on the first day of the week—that is, at the weekly gatherings on Sunday evenings.[5]
- It is expected that everyone participate, both richer and poorer.
- It is expected that each person give according to their own surplus from the week.
- It should be completed before Paul returns, so that collecting money does not take place while he is there, no doubt because that could wrongly suggest the funds are for his financial support.

Although Paul does not here specify the theological rationale for this collection, he does so in Romans: "At present . . . I am going to Jerusalem in a ministry to the saints; for Macedonia and Achaia have been pleased to share their resources with the poor among the saints at Jerusalem. They were pleased to do this, and indeed they owe it to them; for if the Gentiles have come to share

---

2. See Acts 11:27–30 for a previous collection in which Paul participated.

3. See Hunter Brown, "Christian Division and the Neglect of the Poor: Learning from Paul's Collection for the Poor in Jerusalem" (MA thesis, St. Mary's Ecumenical Institute, 2020).

4. Paul will also ask the Roman and Macedonian communities (see Rom 15:25–29; 2 Cor 8:1–5; 9:1–5) to participate, the latter referring almost certainly to the Philippians, probably also to the Thessalonians, and perhaps to others.

5. Or possibly Saturday evenings, since the Jewish Sabbath ended at sundown. But most interpreters take the reference to "the first day" to be Sunday, since gentiles would be following the Roman, not the Jewish, calendar.

CLOSING: THE APOSTOLIC WITNESS CONTINUES · 16:1–24

in their spiritual blessings, they ought also to be of service to them in material things" (Rom 15:25–27).

Paul thus sees the collection not only as global and ecumenical but also as reciprocal: gentiles and Jews, West and East, richer and poorer. Each party contributes different but necessary gifts to the other, like a *global* body of Christ (1 Cor 12): spiritual blessings from Jerusalem and the Jewish Christ-participants, material blessings from what is modern Turkey, Greece, and Italy and thus the largely gentile Christ-participants. As Paul said in the opening of the letter, there is a common, global bond among all who "in every place call on the name of our Lord Jesus Christ, both their Lord and ours" (1:2). This critical collection was arguably the start of international Christian relief efforts.[6]

Although it is certain from Romans (15:26) that the Corinthians did eventually participate in the collection, they did not do so immediately, as 2 Cor 8–9 makes clear. The Corinthians made a promise but did not deliver until urged again by the apostle, and even gently shamed by him (2 Cor 8; 9:1–5).

Paul seems to have anticipated potential issues with the Corinthians, as he not only wants no collecting to occur when he returns to Corinth, but he also tells the Corinthians that he will send (implying at his cost) representatives chosen by the Corinthians with their gift and his letters of recommendation (16:3). Paul will go with them only if it seems appropriate (16:4), which implies that he will do so only if the Corinthians approve.

16:5–9. PAUL'S MISSIONAL PLANS

The conclusion and delivery of the Corinthians' collection for Jerusalem depend on a future visit from Paul. He therefore informs them of his travel plans and possibilities.[7] His itinerary includes a short visit to Macedonia, or northern Greece (16:5), possibly primarily to collect funds for Jerusalem there too.[8] He hopes, however, to have an extended stay in Corinth, possibly even wintering there, if the Lord permits (16:7; recall 4:19), on his way to who knows where next (16:6). The verb Paul uses in v. 6 for "send me on my way" (*propempō*) from Corinth may imply the provision of financial or other forms of support.

6. A precursor is narrated in Acts 11:27–30.

7. The plans described here have a close parallel in the Acts account of Paul's stay in Ephesus (Acts 19:21–22; 20:1–2).

8. The Macedonian believers were generous despite their poverty and were deployed, successfully it appears (Rom 15:25–27), in Paul's appeal to the Corinthians after he had offered the Corinthians as an example to motivate the Macedonians (2 Cor 9:1–5).

410

16:10–12 ·   *Concerning Timothy and Apollos*

This would not contradict his practice described in chapter 9, since he was willing to accept support of existing Christian communities (see Rom 15:22–24, where Paul uses the same verb *propempō* in v. 24; cf. Phil 4:10–19).

In these verses, Paul hints at a stay that could be close to a year's duration, from some time after the late-spring festival of Pentecost in one year (v. 8) through winter of the next. He is letting the Corinthians know that he wants to both deepen his relationship with them and, no doubt, check up on their progress in becoming the one, holy, catholic, and apostolic community he has written about to them, full of resurrectional, charismatic cruciformity.

In the meantime, however, Paul will stay in Ephesus, on the western coast of the Roman province of Asia (in modern Turkey), until Pentecost. Why? Even if he could travel in the winter or early spring, the opposition and thus also the opportunity in Ephesus are too great for the apostle to leave (16:8–9; cf. 15:32).[9] The passive voice in 16:9—"a wide door for effective work has opened to [or "for"] me"—is Paul's way of saying that God has caused this situation (see the "opened door" language also in 2 Cor 2:12), and Paul is not deterred by opponents to his ministry.

In 15:32, Paul has mentioned fighting with (metaphorical) wild beasts in Ephesus, and in 2 Cor 1:8–11 he recounts a near-death episode in "Asia" (probably meaning Ephesus), in which God rescued him and his coworkers. This attitude of characterizing opposition as a challenge to be undertaken with God's aid is both quintessentially Pauline ("all things to all people, that I might by all means save some"—9:22) and fairly counterintuitive. Most people flee from adversity (perhaps even more rapidly than from idolatry or immorality!). But Paul stays—even, it appears, with great satisfaction, and possibly even joy. That is resurrectional cruciformity in evangelistic mode.

16:10–12. CONCERNING TIMOTHY AND APOLLOS

Paul next writes about the travel plans of two colleagues well known to the Corinthians: his trusted coworker from the original mission in Corinth, Timothy (Acts 18:5),[10] and his successor in Corinth, Apollos (Acts 18:24). Paul

---

9. For Paul in Ephesus, see Acts 18:19–21 (the post-Corinth visit); 19:1–20:1. It is sometimes thought that the reference to the (past) sacrifice of Christ the paschal lamb (1 Cor 5:7–8) suggests that 1 Corinthians was written shortly after Passover/Easter, anticipating the celebration of Pentecost. But the mention of the paschal lamb could simply be a reference to Jesus' death, rather than an allusion to the calendar.

10. According to Acts 18:5, Timothy and Silas came from Macedonia to join Paul in Corinth. Second Corinthians is co-sent by Paul and Timothy (2 Cor 1:1). They are

CLOSING: THE APOSTOLIC WITNESS CONTINUES · 16:1–24

seems to expect some hostility toward Timothy, no doubt because he represents the now more controversial Paul (see 1 Cor 4:17)—even though, like Paul, Timothy is "doing the work of the Lord" (16:10; cf. 15:58). Timothy is either on the way to Corinth or is about to go there, in order to "remind" the Corinthians of Paul's "ways in Christ Jesus" (see 4:17). He may have expressed to Paul his unease, even fear (16:10a), about the mission, so Paul requests a safe and hospitable welcome for Timothy, without any disdain (16:11a).[11] After the visit, there should be a peaceful and supportive send-off (*propempō*, as in v. 7) of Timothy back to Paul (16:11b). ('The phrase "with the brothers" in 16:11b may refer to companions with Timothy or to people with Paul.)

As for Apollos (16:12; first mentioned in 1:12),[12] Paul seems to want the Corinthians to know that the absence of Apollos during these controversies was his own decision, not Paul's, for Paul had urged Apollos to make a visit. On the one hand, Paul is reemphasizing that he and Apollos are not in a competitive but a cooperative relationship vis-à-vis the Corinthians (cf. 3:4–9, 21–23; 4:1–6). On the other, Paul is also stressing that Apollos himself does not want to exacerbate a delicate situation. In other words, both leaders, from different vantage points, see their ministry as collaborative, another instantiation of the truths of 1 Cor 3–4 and 1 Cor 12: different gifts but one God, Lord, and Spirit active in the ministry of God's servants and coworkers. For that reason, Apollos will come later—when the time is right.

16:13–14. SUMMARY EXHORTATIONS

Further personal business will follow, but first Paul recapitulates his letter in five brief exhortations, which can be summarized as an eschatologically oriented appeal to be firm (in faith and hope) and to do everything in love (16:13–14; cf. 1:4–9).

The first four admonitions appear in 16:13, three of which (marked with an asterisk below) are only one word each in Greek (all MJG translations):

---

identified, with Silvanus (Silas), as those who proclaimed the gospel to the Corinthians (2 Cor 1:19).

11. When Paul requests that no one "despise" Timothy, he uses a verb (*exoutheneō*) employed also in 1:28 (for the "despised" God has chosen) and 6:4 (referring to those without standing in the church). The verb is related to the Greek word for "nothing" (*ouden*). For the many references to Timothy in the New Testament, see the note in the discussion of 4:14–21.

12. See also 3:4–6, 22; 4:6; plus Acts 18:24–19:1.

16:13–14 ·   *Summary Exhortations*

- *"Watch!" (NRSV "Keep alert"; CEB "Stay awake")—a verb used in other texts with an eschatological focus as well as texts about staying literally awake with Jesus.[13]
- "Stand firm in the faith!" (NRSV "in your faith")—that is, in the gospel; see also Rom 14:4; Gal 5:1; Phil 1:27; 4:1; 1 Thess 3:8; 2 Thess 2:15.
- *"Man-up!" (NRSV "Be courageous"; ESV "Act like men")—used only here in the New Testament.[14]
- *"Be strong!"— a verb used also in Eph 3:16.

Together these convey the need for an active discipleship that pays attention to the reality of the Lord's coming and, in that time of waiting, perseveres with courage and fortitude. Given the realities at Corinth described in the letter, this form of discipleship will mean an ongoing conversion so that the Corinthians will be "blameless on the day of our Lord Jesus Christ" (1:8) and avoid the errors and evils that have plagued them. At the moment, as we have seen, they are eschatologically challenged and morally immature and weak, even though they think they are mature and strong. But Paul the pastor does not give up on them.

The fifth admonition (16:14) is to the "more excellent way" of love (recall ch. 13). It is in many ways a summary of the letter. The important Greek word *panta*, meaning "all things" ("all" or "everything" in most translations) occurs yet again, echoing its earlier appearances in key texts, including the love chapter: love "bears all things, believes all things, hopes all things, endures all things" (13:7).[15] Thus, Paul again calls the Corinthians to think and live bifocally, rooted in the love found in the gospel story and always alert as they prepare for the parousia.

Paul himself lovingly "endures" all things (9:12) and "becomes" all things to all people (9:22), doing all things for the sake of the gospel (9:23). He exhorts his fellow Christ-participants to do all things to God's glory (10:31), which means, in part, following Paul's Christlike example of pleasing others, rather than self, in all things (10:33). All things, then, should be done in love, to build up the

---

13. See, e.g., 1 Thess 5:6, 10; Mark 13:34, 35, 37; 14:34, 37, 38; Matt 24:42, 43; 25:13; 26:38, 40, 41; Luke 12:37; Rev 16:15.

14. It is possible that the exhortation to "man up" is meant as a call to Christlike, rather than Roman, masculinity, focusing especially on care for the weak. See Brian J. Robinson, *Being Subordinate Men: Paul's Rhetoric of Gender and Power in 1 Corinthians* (Lanham, MD: Lexington/Fortress Academic, 2019), esp. 189–94.

15. See also 2:10, 15; 3:21, 22; 6:12 (3×); 8:6 (2×); 9:12, 22, 23, 25; 10:23 (4×), 31, 33; 11:2, 12; 12:6, 11, 12, 19, 26 (2×); 13:2, 3; 14:26, 40; 15:27 (3×), 28 (3×).

413

CLOSING: THE APOSTOLIC WITNESS CONTINUES · 16:1–24

community (14:26)—which is what Paul essentially says here in 16:14. And he will conclude the letter by sending the Corinthians his own love (v. 24).

16:15–18. CONCERNING CERTAIN CORINTHIANS

In 16:15–18, Paul finds yet another way to connect with the Corinthian community, this time by naming three of their own who have visited him as surrogates for the whole community (16:17): Stephanas ("Crowned"), Fortunatus ("Lucky"), and Achaicus ("Achaia-man"). The household of Stephanas in Corinth had constituted the "first converts" in the province of Achaia (16:15): literally the "firstfruits" (see NAB; cf. CEB).[16] Fortunatus and Achaicus could be members of the household of Stephanas (mentioned in 1:16), even (former?) enslaved persons. Paul feels an emotional tie to them and, through them, with the whole community as the visit effected reciprocal refreshment (16:18). It is quite possible they took Paul's letter back to the Corinthians.

Paul singles out for special mention Stephanas, whom Paul baptized along with members of his household (16:15; cf. 1:16). He commends Stephanas and his household for their devout service (*diakonian*; v. 15), urging the Corinthians in v. 16 to "be subordinate" (NAB, rightly) to them and their coworkers (NRSV: "put yourselves at the service of such people"). This is quite a remarkable admonition, since members of the household would almost certainly have included enslaved persons (not least Fortunatus and Achaicus?), so Paul is probably urging even free persons to honor the servant leadership of enslaved persons or (possibly) formerly enslaved persons.

The principle Paul enunciates here is that leaders in the church are servants, and that as such, somewhat ironically, they are due subordination. This does not mean unquestioning submission but rather respect and recognition (see v. 18; cf. Phil 2:29; 1 Thess 5:12–13a) for their leadership and for their service to both Paul and the Corinthians, none of which—in contrast to some of the so-called wise and gifted—is self-centered and self-serving.

16:19–24. GREETINGS AND FINAL WORDS

The last words of greeting and grace would no doubt be read out to the gathered Corinthian assembly, just like the rest of the letter. Paul continues both

---

16. Paul uses the same image in Rom 16:5 for the first convert in Asia; in 1 Cor 15:20, 23 for Christ as the first to be resurrected; in Rom 8:23 for the Spirit; and in Rom 11:16 for the first portion of God's people.

16:19–24 · Greetings and Final Words

to build his relationship with the assembly (he is "networking," says Richard Hays) and to express the unity and catholicity of the worldwide church.[17]

The greetings begin with a general salutation from the churches of Asia (16:19a), of which Ephesus was the most important city. Paul and his associates, as well as others not part of the Pauline mission, have no doubt ministered widely in the region. The unnamed churches likely include those in Colossae, Hierapolis, and Laodicea (see Colossians as a whole, plus Col 4:13–16), and possibly also others either named in the book of Revelation (Smyrna, Pergamum, Thyatira, Sardis, and Philadelphia) or unknown to us.

Next (16:19b) follow the "many" (i.e., "warm") greetings specifically from Aquila and Prisca (Priscilla), the tent-making Jewish believers originally from Rome who had also worked with Paul in Corinth (Acts 18:2–3). They had also been in Ephesus, where they instructed the eloquent and enthusiastic, but not fully informed, Apollos before he went on to Corinth (Acts 18:24–28). The couple is now probably with Paul in Ephesus, and they are the hosts of a church in their home (see also Rom 16:3–5), whose additional members send greetings too.

Next come greetings from "all" the brothers and sisters (16:20a), a possible allusion to the universality of the church, but especially a reference to the specific assemblies in Ephesus. The final word about greetings is an instruction to the Corinthians to greet one another with a holy kiss (16:20b), a common ritual in the early church,[18] but one that might be a challenge in divided Corinth. Paul is encouraging a practical expression of unity and love.

The apostle continues with a statement about adding a few words in his own hand (16:21) to a letter prepared by a scribe.[19] Four final pronouncements follow and conclude the letter:

- a curse for those who lack love for the Lord (16:22a, using *anathema*, as in 12:3; Rom 9:3; Gal 1:8–9), which functions as a warning more than an actual curse
- a (probably common) early Christian prayer for the parousia (16:22b, using the Aramaic *marana tha* = "Our Lord, come"—only here in the New Testament; cf. Rev 22:20 for the Greek version: *erchou kyrie Iēsou* = "Come, Lord Jesus")
- a benediction of grace (16:23), partially echoing 1:3

---

17. Hays, *First Corinthians*, 290.

18. See also Rom 16:16; 2 Cor 13:12; 1 Thess 5:26; 1 Pet 5:14. It is still practiced in parts of some Christian traditions.

19. See also Gal 6:11; Col 4:18; 2 Thess 3:17; Phlm 19, as well as Rom 16:22.

415

CLOSING: THE APOSTOLIC WITNESS CONTINUES · 16:1–24

- a final offer of apostolic love to *all* (*pantōn*; 16:24), one final occurrence of that small but important word in the letter

Paul extends his love as a reminder of his affection for the Corinthians, in spite of all the correcting he has done throughout the letter (and even in spite of the strong curse warning), and also as a reminder that imitating him will always mean treating others with Christlike love, the ultimate manifestation of God's grace at work in the *ekklēsia*.

Looking back on the letter as a whole, we may perhaps see, with John Chrysostom, why Paul ends this letter focusing on love—both his (v. 24) and especially the Corinthians' (v. 14)—since "all the things which have been mentioned arose from neglect" of love:

> For if this [love] had not been neglected, they would not have been puffed up, they would not have said, "I am of Paul, and I of Apollos." If this had existed, they would not have gone to law before heathens, or rather they would not have gone to law at all. If this had existed, that notorious person would not have taken his father's wife; they would not have despised the weak brethren; there would have been no factions among them; they would not have been vain-glorious about their gifts. Therefore it is that he saith, "Let all things be done in love."[20]

REFLECTIONS AND QUESTIONS FOR 16:1–24

Spiritual, Pastoral, Missional, and Theological Reflections

1. One of the often forgotten but central aspects of Paul's ecclesiology is the **worldwide scope of the church**, and how important it is for Christians from various parts of the world to find ways to know one another and to care for one another, both spiritually and materially. Contemporary international Christian relief agencies constitute but one expression of this catholic *koinōnia*. The collection for Jerusalem is a reminder that the relationship between involved parties should be recognized and practiced as one of reciprocity.

2. It is always somewhat dangerous to reduce Christian ethics or spirituality to one word, but when it is appropriate to do so, **"love" is an excellent candidate for that one word.** Yet that word needs to be filled in with the sort of content we see in 1 Corinthians, especially the substance of Christlike, cruciform, others-edifying action.

20. John Chrysostom, *Homilies on 1 Corinthians* 44.2.

416

Questions for Those Who Read, Teach, and Preach

1. What can churches today learn from Paul's vision of the collection for Jerusalem?
2. How might Paul's attitude to opposition be of value for a contemporary understanding of Christian mission?
3. In sum, what does this passage urge the church to believe (faith), do (love), and anticipate (hope)?

FOR FURTHER READING

Downs, David J. "Collection for the Saints." *DPL*[2] 136–39.

———. *The Offering of the Gentiles: Paul's Collection for Jerusalem in Its Chronological, Cultural, and Cultic Contexts*. Grand Rapids: Eerdmans, 2016. (technical)

Gombis, Timothy G. *Power in Weakness: Paul's Transformed Vision for Ministry*. Grand Rapids: Eerdmans, 2021. (highly accessible)

Longenecker, Bruce W. *Remember the Poor: Paul, Poverty, and the Greco-Roman World*. Grand Rapids: Eerdmans, 2010.

Welborn, L. L. *That There May Be Equality: Paul's Appeal for Partnership in the Collection*. Minneapolis: Fortress, 2023.

Acknowledgments

In a very real sense, this commentary has been in the works for more than two decades. Various publications along the way have expressed some of the interpretations of 1 Corinthians found in these pages. I am grateful to Eerdmans for encouraging and allowing me to expand the minicommentary on the letter in *Apostle of the Crucified Lord* into the present book-length commentary.[1] I am grateful also to Paulist Press for permission to use and expand the essay on Paul's life and theology from *The Paulist Biblical Commentary*.[2] In addition, references to several essays on 1 Corinthians I have published will appear here and there. I am grateful for the invitations to write those pieces, which helped lay the groundwork for this book.

I express my sincere gratitude as well to the pastors and others who made suggestions about what this commentary should look like and do. Likewise, I thank the members of my fall 2022 seminar called First Corinthians as Christian Theology, my students in the English exegesis course on the letter that same term, and my students in the corresponding Greek reading course on the letter during the very same semester. (It was a season of eating, breathing, and living 1 Corinthians!) I mention in particular Zack Holbrook, Zach Watson, and Michelle Newman Rader.

Michelle, who is also my longtime research and teaching assistant, read every word, checked every Scripture reference and citation, contributed to some of the reflections and questions, suggested resources, and permitted the use of a few insights from papers she had written for the above-mentioned

---

1. Michael J. Gorman, *Apostle of the Crucified Lord: A Theological Introduction to Paul and His Letters*, 2nd ed. (Grand Rapids: Eerdmans, 2017), 273–341.

2. Michael J. Gorman, "Paul: His Life and Theology," in *The Paulist Biblical Commentary*, ed. José Enrique Aguilar Chiu et al. (Mahwah, NJ: Paulist, 2018), 1228–33.

ACKNOWLEDGMENTS

seminar. This commentary would not be the same without her input, including assistance with the indexes. In addition, my student Pat Semanie helped with the indexing.

Colleagues in the field provided helpful feedback on various parts of the commentary draft: Michael Barber, Roy Ciampa, Nijay Gupta, Fredrik Hansen, Andy Johnson, Brent Laytham, Lucy Peppiatt, Brian Rosner, Carla Works, and K. K. Yeo. I, of course, hold none of them responsible for remaining errors of fact or judgment.

Once again, I express my thanks to St. Mary's Seminary & University for its support of my teaching and research. I owe a particular debt to the president-rector, Fr. Phillip Brown, and to my present and former deans, Dr. Brent Laytham, Fr. Gladstone Stephens, and Dr. Matthew Dugandzic. I completed the work on this project during a sabbatical, for which I am especially grateful.

I am also thankful to Eerdmans for their belief in this project, with special thanks to James Ernest and Trevor Thompson, as well as Laurel Draper and Justin Howell for their careful, helpful editorial work. Thanks are also due to Jenny Hoffman and to professional indexer Holly Knowles.

I would be remiss not to thank my friend Richard Hays, whose stellar commentary on 1 Corinthians I have read, reread, and assigned to students many times. Although I wrote the draft of this commentary without, for the most part, consulting other works, I soon realized how indebted I was to Richard and that commentary. If there is any unacknowledged similarity between his and mine, it is because his wisdom had gotten into my interpretive veins, and it simply had to bleed out onto the written page. Something similar can be said for the work of the late Gordon Fee (with whom I was privileged to study Greek), on whose commentary I cut my teeth in both writing about and teaching 1 Corinthians.

Finally, I give thanks to and for my family, who are always supportive of my work: my adult children (Mark, Amy, and Brian), and especially my wife, Nancy. She has shown a special interest in this volume and been a much-needed sounding board on more than one occasion. She also assisted with the indexing.

My extended family includes a group of Christian brothers and sisters (Marilyn, Joe, Marsha, Matt, Rick, Darice, Barb, Mary, Kathy, Mary, Ken, and more) who have met weekly in our home, some for more than thirty years. This commentary is dedicated to them.

Index of Names

Abrams, Douglas, 345
Achaicus, 107n12, 414
Adam, 15, 77, 137n71, 281n101, 371, 373, 386–87, 392, 393n49, 394, 395–98
Adewuya, J. Ayodeji, 298n138
Agosto, Efraín Agosto, 5, 254–55
Alkier, Stefan, 126n53
Ambrose, 248n41
Anthony the Great, 223
Apollos, 44, 52, 53, 56, 73, 89, 105, 106, 124, 133, 140, 144, 145, 147, 151–53, 160, 245, 408, 411–12, 415, 416
Aquila, 44, 51, 106, 415
Aquinas, Thomas, 33n10, 93n14, 102, 105n8, 196, 281n101, 305
Aristotle, 308
Augustine, xviii, 261n66, 305
Augustus (Caesar), 13, 169n8, 228

Bakhtin, Mikhail M., 28n6
Balthasar, Hans Urs von, 78n99, 118–19
Barber, Michael P., 295n131, 303nn147–48
Barclay, John M. G., 6, 114, 187n37, 317
Barnabas, 243–45
Barnett, Paul, 164n1
Barram, Michael, 43n37, 45–46, 73, 214nn71–72, 241n28, 270n87
Barth, Karl, 27, 364
Bassler, Jouette, 282n102
Bates, Matthew W., 309n161
Batibuka, Pontien Ndagijimana, 107n11
Becker, Eve-Marie, 153n100

Beker, J. Christiaan, 5
Bender, Kimlyn J., 40n31
Bennema, Cornelis, 160n111
Bernard of Clairvaux, 345
Bernier, Jonathan, 9n5
Berrigan, Daniel, 204
Blackwell, Ben, 6
Bolz-Weber, Nadia, 201–2
Bonhoeffer, Dietrich, 12, 92, 126, 187, 203, 298n137, 357
Bowens, Lisa M., 122n46, 141n82, 217n79, 328n201, 379n23, 399n63
Brendsel, Daniel J., 41n36
Brookins, Timothy A., 55, 118n35, 133n65, 260n61
Brower, Kent E., 164n1
Brown, Amberle, 317n174
Brown, Hunter, 408n1, 409n3
Brown, Paul J., 368n3, 368n5, 369n6
Brown, Raymond E., 30
Brueggemann, Walter, 360–61
Burroughs, Presian Renee, 302n145

Cailing, Rolex, 47, 308n158, 320
Calvin, John, 4, 330n209
Campbell, Douglas A., 5, 9n5, 324n192
Campbell, Ted A., 297n134
Carey, Greg, 368n3
Cavanaugh, William T., 301n144
Celsus, 379
Cephas (Peter), 8, 42, 52, 53, 105, 106,

INDEX OF NAMES

140, 144, 151, 152, 174, 244n34, 245, 293, 373n12, 374, 378, 379, 381

Chloe, 57, 105

Chrysostom. *See* John Chrysostom

Ciampa, Roy E., 58n66, 79n104, 114n23, 208n57, 209n58, 210n61, 226n1, 261n66, 267n84, 330n207, 342n226

Cicero, 112–13, 169n8, 242

Claudius, 7, 50, 51

Clement of Rome, 74n87

Cohick, Lynn, 6

Collins, Raymond F., 67

Cone, James H., 113n21

Cooper, Randy, 405

Craddock, Fred B., 31n4, 46

Crispus, 51, 107

Davis, Ellen F., xviii

Deasley, Alex R. G., 97n23

Donne, John, 400

Dunn, James D. G., 4, 22, 382

Eastman, Susan Grove, 6, 31, 39, 122n47, 231, 322

Edwards, Dennis R., 154n100

Ehrensperger, Kathy, 6

Ekem, John D. K., 285

Elaw, Zilpha, 122

Eliot, T. S., 391

Elliott, Neil, 5

Engels, Donald, 49n47

Epictetus, 172, 193

Fee, Gordon D., 40

Fiensy, D. A., 50n51

Flett, John G., 35

Fortunatus, 107n12, 414

Fosarelli, Patricia, 400

Fowl, Stephen E., 272, 273

Francis (Pope), 324n194

Fredriksen, Paula, 5

Gaius, 52, 107

Gallio, 7, 8, 50, 51

Gaston, Thomas, 234n16

Gaventa, Beverly Roberts, 5, 6n4, 27

George, Roji T., 5

Glahn, Sandra L., 284n107

Gombis, Timothy G., 115n26, 157

Goodall, Jane, 345

Goode, Scott, 43n37, 45n39, 171n11, 214nn70–71, 241n28

Gorman, Brian, 130, 420

Gorman, Mark, 77n97, 420

Gorman, Michael J., 92n6, 92n8, 114n22, 129n62, 132n64, 155n103, 180n26, 184n34, 187n36, 193n43, 202n49, 203n52, 226n2, 247n40, 249n42, 251n51, 252n52, 255n58, 272–73, 340n223, 342n227, 401n70, 406n78

Green, Joel B., xx, 27nn4–5, 68n81

Gupta, Nijay, 6, 340n222

Hammon, Jupiter, 122

Hannah, 121, 123n49, 126

Harland, Philip A., 289n117

Hays, Richard B., xx, 5, 6n4, 27, 37, 40n30, 61n69, 63n70, 68n81, 91n4, 94n16, 116n27, 121n43, 147n91, 151, 168n7, 177n22, 214, 232, 235, 241n27, 255, 289n114, 294n130, 307n157, 314, 319, 403, 415, 415n17, 420

Heil, John Paul, 41n35

Heilig, Christoph, 5

Heschel, Abraham Joshua, xviii, 179, 350–51

Hill, Wesley, 19n22

Holbrook, Zack, 41n36, 108n14, 419

Holmes, Michael W., 203n52

Hooker, Morna, 6

Horrell, David, 6

Horsley, Richard, 5

Hughes, Frank W., 58n65

Hull, Cletus L., III, 360n254

Hurtado, Larry W., 167, 234n16

Hylen, Susan E., 357n247

Ignatius of Antioch, 304n152

Ignatius of Loyola, 130

James, 8, 244n34, 293, 374, 378, 379

Jervis, L. Ann, 60n68

Jewett, Robert, 58n65

Jipp, Joshua W., 19, 20n24, 399

422

Index of Names

John Chrysostom, 91, 107, 123, 147, 175, 188n39, 200, 210, 232n11, 303, 329, 335, 416
John Paul II (Pope), 100
Johnson, Andy, 93n12, 137n74, 164n2, 371n8, 386n36, 402
Jones, Beth Felker, 167
Josephus, 49n46, 112–13
Jüngel, Eberhard, 128

Käsemann, Ernst, 33n13, 126
Keesmaat, Sylvia, 5
Kim, Yung Suk, 32, 160n110, 308, 317n177
Kincaid, John A., 295n131, 303n148
King, Martin Luther, Jr., 12, 118, 129, 319–20, 328–29, 346

Last, Richard, 93n10
Laytham, D. Brent, 77n98, 78n99, 79n103
Lewis, C. S., 203, 344–45
Lewis, John, 11
Lincicum, David, 239
Loader, William, 167n6
Longenecker, Bruce W., 260n61, 350n234
Lucian of Samosata, 287
Luther, Martin, 4

MacDonald, Margaret, 6
Maggay, Melba Padilla, 128
Malcolm, Matthew R., 79n104
Martin, Jessica, 403–4
Martyn, J. Louis, 5
Matera, Frank J., 68
Mbiti, John S., 128–29
McCaulley, Esau, 400
McKnight, Scot, xviii, 4, 14, 39, 118n34, 216n77, 231n6, 330, 379n26
Meeks, Wayne A., 112
Menander, 391
Meng, Xiangjiao, 299n139
Miller, Patrick D., 330n209
Mitchell, Margaret, 74n87
Moltmann, Jürgen, 128
Moo, Douglas, 4
Morales, Isaac Augustine (Rodrigo J.), 41n34, 107n11
Musonius Rufus, 210n62

Nanos, Mark, 5
Nash, Robert Scott, 37, 63n70, 105, 396n59
Nero, 49
Norris, Kathleen, 272

Oakes, Peter, 6
Octavia, 228

Pascal, Blaise, 121
Paul, Pathipati Victor, 320
Payyapilly, Vijay Michael Antony, 360n254
Peppiatt, Lucy, 6, 283–84, 358
Perkins, Pheme, 34n18, 37–38, 63n70, 68, 105n6
Perry, Andrew, 234n16
Peter. *See* Cephas (Peter)
Peterson, Eugene, 344
Piper, John, 4
Pitre, Brant, 295n131, 303n148
Plato, 308, 368, 369, 405
Pliny the Younger, 290–91
Plyming, Philip, 130n63
Priscilla (Prisca), 44, 51, 106, 415
Punt, Jeremy, 5

Quintilian, 113

Rader, Michelle Newman, 56n60, 120n42, 166n4, 215n75, 279n97, 318n180, 380n28, 419
Rahner, Karl, 404
Rhodes, Michael J., 303
Robinson, Brian J., 59n67, 413n14
Rosner, Brian, xxin8, 43n37, 58n66, 67, 79n104, 114n23, 169n10, 208n57, 209n58, 210n61, 226n1, 261n66, 267n84, 330n207, 342n226
Runesson, Anders, 5
Rutledge, Fleming, 127

Sanders, E. P., 4
Schnelle, Udo, 118n36
Schreiner, Thomas, 4
Silas (Silvanus), 51, 160n112, 411n10
Silverman, Eric J., 203n51
Simon, Mark, xxin8, 67

423

INDEX OF NAMES

Smith, Dennis E., 287nn110–11, 289n116
Sosthenes, 51, 57, 66, 75, 89, 90, 93, 107n12, 117, 119, 132, 133, 137, 138, 143, 152, 164, 168, 227, 237, 275, 408
Stanley, Christopher, 5
Starling, David I., 115n25, 158
Stendahl, Krister, 4
Stephanas, 107, 414
Stott, John, 320–21
Streett, R. Alan, 287n110, 301n144
Sunquist, Scott W., 38n26
Swarup, Paul, 143n83

Theodoret of Cyrus, 74
Thiessen, Matthew, 5, 20n26, 138, 395n57
Thiselton, Anthony C., 67, 74, 97n23, 119n39, 128, 155n104, 235n18, 255, 260n61, 265, 266n81, 293n128, 300n142, 311n164, 321, 354n245, 390n42
Thompson, Dion, 129n60
Thompson, James W., 38, 97n22, 112n18, 162, 299

Timothy, 44, 51, 56, 73, 90n1, 133, 144n84, 145, 160, 161, 408, 411–12
Tucker, J. Brian, 34nn15–16

Vespasian, 49n46
Volf, Miroslav, 127

Wainwright, Geoffrey, 341n224
Watson, Zach, 78n102, 419
Wesley, John, 109
Westerholm, Stephen, 4
Westfall, Cynthia Long, 281n101
Winter, B. W., 48n45
Works, Carla Swafford, 120n40, 140n81
Wright, N. T., 4, 6n4, 13, 17, 19, 67n76, 70, 341, 364n1, 368n3, 371n8

Yeo, K. K., 240
Young, Stephen E., 217n78

Zhao, Lin, 12
Zizioulas, John D., 305

Index of Subjects

abortion, 203–4, 239, 255, 256

accommodation, missional, 246–53. *See also* salvific intentionality

accountability: of believers, 137n73, 138, 176, 295; of ministers, 151, 152–54, 157, 162, 175

adiaphora. See essentials and nonessentials

African American interpretation of Paul, 122, 141, 217, 328–29, 379, 399

African interpretation of Paul, 141, 298, 336

age to come, 17, 60–61, 263, 304, 339. *See also* creation: new

allegiance: to Christ, 16, 18, 107, 190, 239, 267, 274, 297, 309–10, 405; misguided, 53, 105–6, 119, 140, 151, 162–63, 388. *See also* faith/faithfulness

alterculture, Christian, 19, 21, 69–70, 203, 308, 361. *See also* holiness

anathema, 288, 310–11, 415

ancestor worship/veneration, 239–40

antiwitness, 163, 169, 174, 175, 178–79, 188–89, 215, 227, 235, 304, 384, 388. *See also* witness

apostleship, 71, 143–44, 150, 157, 162, 237, 242–55, 269, 313, 318, 349, 359–60, 378, 379; false, 109. *See also* Paul: apostleship of

apostolicity, xx–xxi, 6, 35, 36, 38, 45, 46, 47, 56, 58, 59, 63, 68, 70, 72–74, 76–80, 82, 93, 99, 150, 160, 174, 225, 226, 271, 325, 360, 364, 382–83, 402, 408. *See*

also marks of the church; *missio Dei*: church's participation in

assembly. *See* church (*ekklēsia*): as assembly

banquets, 53, 192, 235, 286–87, 289n117, 290, 291, 301, 320, 400. *See also* eating; idol meat; Lord's Supper

baptism, 18, 33n10, 41, 51, 52, 64, 73, 110, 111, 178, 181, 184, 186–88, 190, 198, 215n73, 259–61, 276, 297, 299, 303, 308, 314, 315, 341n224, 372, 380, 384, 387, 401, 405; on behalf of the dead, 367, 389–90; and division, 52–53, 69, 102, 105, 106–8; and the story of Jesus, 61, 107, 110, 122, 265, 300, 366, 381–82

beatific vision, 37, 97, 338, 340. *See also* glorification: eschatological; immortality; theosis/deification

bifocal perspective, xxi–xxii, 40, 47, 60–63, 138, 161–62, 165, 168, 171, 173, 178, 181, 183, 185, 199–200, 207, 222, 224, 245, 254, 287, 294, 304, 326, 341, 365–66, 401, 413

blamelessness, 38, 39–40, 61, 95–97, 99, 102, 161, 401, 413

boasting, 11, 122–23, 144, 151, 153; misdirected (puffed-up), 54, 123, 153, 161, 169, 174, 175, 231, 307, 323n189, 327–29, 335, 345, 416; Paul's, 124, 146–47, 156n106, 246–47, 389

body (human): resurrection of, 17, 53, 61, 196–201, 325, 334, 339, 364–71, 379,

425

INDEX OF SUBJECTS

382, 392–407; significance of, 193, 196–99, 206; as temple of Holy Spirit, 19, 171, 173, 191–205, 214. *See also* church (*ekklēsia*): as body of Christ; church (*ekklēsia*): as temple of Holy Spirit; flesh; glorification: eschatological; immortality; resurrection (of believers); weakness: of the body

care, mutual, 20, 21, 22, 69, 74–75, 250n49, 276, 281, 298, 299, 301, 315–17, 321, 322, 325, 343, 356, 416

catholicity, 35, 68, 71–72, 77–78, 80, 98, 99, 160, 215, 226–27, 237, 238, 254, 261, 269–70, 271, 279, 282–84, 294, 296, 297n134, 299, 317, 319, 343, 357–58, 363, 416; macro, 71; micro, 71–72. *See also* marks of the church

celibacy. *See* singleness

chaos in Corinth, 31, 52–57, 79–82, 356–57; ecclesial, 102–63; liturgical, 164, 226–363; about the Lord's Supper, 289, 297; moral, 164–225; sexual, 191–93; theological, 364–407

charismatic community. *See* church (*ekklēsia*): as charismatic community

charismatic cruciformity. *See* cruciformity: resurrectional/charismatic character

charismatic gifts. *See* spiritual (Spirit-ual) gifts

charisms. *See* spiritual (Spirit-ual) gifts

chastity, 202–3, 213n69, 280. *See also* marriage; same-sex relations; sex/sexual immorality

choice. *See* freedom

Christ. *See* Jesus Christ

Christian nationalism, 129–30, 272–73

Christification/christosis. *See* Christoformity; cruciformity; theosis/deification

Christlikeness. *See* Christoformity; cruciformity

Christoformity, xviiin3, 14, 39, 105, 155, 157, 158, 269. *See also* cruciformity; theosis/deification

Christology. *See* Jesus Christ

Christophany: church as, 319; Jesus' death as, 15, 117, 162, 319

Christosis. *See* Christoformity; cruciformity; theosis/deification

church (*ekklēsia*): as assembly, 3n1, 9, 11, 19, 35, 51–52, 90–91; as body of Christ, 23, 92–93, 149, 187, 195, 199, 237, 258–59, 264–65, 296, 298, 301, 306–21, 327, 361, 363, 410; as charismatic community, xxi, 33–35, 38, 51, 63–65, 97, 99, 125, 227, 307, 348, 360; as Christophany, 319; as family, 19, 52, 159, 161, 178, 181, 182, 184, 185, 187–88, 230, 236, 298, 303, 310, 321, 342–43; global/universal (ancient), 35, 68, 71–72, 78n99, 91, 98, 117, 160, 215, 269–70, 279, 409–10, 415; global/universal (contemporary), xx, 6n4, 71–72, 78n99, 99, 109, 110, 129, 189, 239, 256, 272; marks of the, xx–xxii, 34–35, 63, 67–82; multicultural, 35, 99, 317, 319, 285; as temple of Holy Spirit, 19, 69, 146, 148–50, 162, 226, 267, 348. *See also* chaos in Corinth; divisions; embodiment: of gospel, by church; Jew and gentile; *missio Dei*: church's participation in; spirituality (Spirit-uality): communal; worship

circumcision, 4, 10, 32, 174, 216, 340

collection, for Jerusalem, 44, 71, 73, 244n35, 408–10, 416, 417

communion. *See* koinōnia; Lord's Supper; participation

contextualization, 22, 206, 251, 256

conversion, 44, 59, 74, 125, 127, 188, 214; corporate, 41; of the imagination, 40, 41, 151; ongoing, 34–35, 39, 59–60, 187, 413; Paul's, 8, 9–10, 23

Corinth: chaos in, 31, 52–57, 79–82, 356–57; composition of church, 119–22; description, 48–50, 227–28; divisions and scandals, 52–57; Paul's mission in, 50–52. *See also* divisions

Corinthians, First Letter to the: character of, 31–48; as contemporary text, 46–47; as formational text, 38–40; as liturgical text, 41–43; as missional text, 43–46; as pastoral text, 31, 38–40; story behind, 48–58; story within, 58–81; structure of, 79–82; as subversive text, 59; themes in, 34–38; as theological text, 31–38

covenant, 4, 15, 18, 43, 75, 76–77, 166, 169, 210, 264, 270, 292; marriage as, 196, 210, 211n65, 213, 222; new, 13, 14, 17, 32, 42, 44, 258, 293–95, 299, 300, 304

coworkers (Paul's and God's), 11, 50, 73, 90, 144–46, 152, 155, 181, 264, 278, 390, 408, 411–12, 414. *See also* partnership

creation, 94, 151, 166n4, 168, 233, 235, 270, 282, 284, 305, 339, 365, 371, 389, 392–98, 402; new, xxii, 13, 17, 18–19, 32, 44, 60, 120, 137n74, 149, 216, 301, 325, 365, 371, 395n53, 396–98, 402, 405

creed: Apostles', 67, 371, 405; early, 71, 72, 276, 367, 370–71, 372–85; as interpretive lens, xx–xxi, 28, 34–35; Nicene (Niceno-Constantinopolitan), xx–xxi, 28–29, 67–68, 80n105, 398n61

cross. *See* crucifixion/cross, of Jesus

crucifixion/cross, of Jesus, 9, 13, 15, 16–17, 20, 33, 47, 59, 107, 112–13, 119, 120, 126, 134, 156n105, 161–62, 173, 242, 365–66, 369, 374–75, 384, 388–89, 404–5; and composition of Corinthian community, 119–24; as divine power and wisdom, 92, 102–3, 108, 112–19, 122, 124, 129–30, 133, 134–36, 147, 151, 154; as divine self-revelation, 15, 114–30, 132–38, 140; as divine subversion, 67, 115–17; as sacrifice, 41, 57, 173, 265–66, 302–3, 375, 411n9; and the Spirit, 23, 31–34, 54, 56, 134–41, 369. *See also* Jesus Christ: death and resurrection

cruciformity, 20–21, 132–40, 234–38, 308, 322–45; apostolic/ministerial, 123–27, 142–58, 241–55; and justice, 178, 183–90, 224; resurrectional/charismatic character, xxi, 21, 23, 33–35, 38, 39, 47, 59–60, 63, 65–67, 79, 97, 125, 126, 227, 237, 240, 252, 269, 303, 344, 365, 366, 401, 403, 407, 411. *See also* hierarchy: cruciform; love; x-y-z pattern

culture, engaging, 35, 44–45, 47, 220, 254, 255, 285. *See also* apostolicity; salvific intentionality; witness

Dead Sea Scrolls. *See* Qumran

death: confusion about, 364, 368; defeat of, 97, 386, 388, 399–402, 407; nature of, 393–94, 396–98, 405–6; as power/enemy (Death), 5, 15, 17, 97, 151, 218, 365, 370, 371, 373, 377, 385, 386, 388–89, 395, 397–402, 407. *See also* crucifixion/cross, of Jesus; Jesus Christ: death and resurrection; victory, final

deconstruction and reconstruction, 59, 70, 112, 117, 142–43

deconversion, 184

deification. *See* Christoformity; theosis/deification

demons, 76, 134, 258–59, 266–67. *See also* Satan

disabilities, 317, 320

discipleship, 110, 156, 175, 201, 207, 222, 247, 251, 257–58, 325, 390, 413. *See also* cruciformity

discipline: apostolic/ecclesial, 176, 276, 288; divine, 295–96, 304; spiritual, 253. *See also* excommunication; judgment

divisions, 30–32, 46, 52–57, 64, 68–69, 74n87, 80, 99, 102–11, 132–33, 138–40, 150–51, 153, 156, 161–63, 164, 177, 227, 287, 289, 291–92, 314, 319–20, 333, 378

divorce, 45, 71, 208, 212–14, 219. *See also* marriage

docetism, 201, 376

eating: in homes, 192, 214, 227, 229, 258, 270–71, 291; at pagan temples, 53, 148, 191–92, 227–30, 234–38, 252, 257–58, 266–67, 270, 302. *See also* banquets; idol meat; Lord's Supper; meat markets

ecclesiology. *See* church (*ekklēsia*)

ecclesiophany, 319

edification, 43, 58, 170, 220, 231, 236, 268, 271, 275–76, 282, 307–8, 312–14, 318, 335, 342–43, 347–60, 363, 416

ekklēsia. *See* church (*ekklēsia*)

elite and nonelite, 49, 50, 51, 54–56, 106,

INDEX OF SUBJECTS

107n12, 120, 133, 134, 155n102, 169, 177, 182, 185, 192, 227, 231, 241, 242, 249, 250, 258, 284, 290, 352. *See also* poor; weak (powerless)

embodiment: of God, by Christ, 118, 122, 123, 136, 161; of gospel, by church, 14, 21, 22, 29, 31–32, 43–45, 59, 65, 70, 72, 76, 137, 152, 160, 164, 188–89, 245–46, 252, 255, 258, 298, 300–302, 316–17, 319–20, 323, 336, 347, 352, 361, 363, 366; of gospel, by Paul, 125, 162, 234, 245–55, 323n190; and resurrection, 395–99, 407. *See also* Jesus Christ: incarnation

engaged couples, 218–19, 221. *See also* chastity; marriage; sex/sexual immorality; singleness

Ephesus, 8, 11, 44, 50, 51, 56–57, 89, 106, 107n12, 390–91, 410n7, 411, 415

epistemology, 112, 124, 137, 325; of the cross, 112, 124. *See also* knowledge

equality, 207, 210, 213, 216n76, 218, 222, 277–81, 285, 290, 299, 307, 314, 315, 378. *See also* care, mutual; marriage: mutuality in

eschatology, 13, 17, 36–37, 76–77, 79n104, 97–99, 135, 141, 145, 150, 154n102, 162, 181, 182, 185, 253, 259, 287, 301, 325–26, 364–70, 382–85, 391–405, 412–13; and devotion to Christ, 219–21; and love, 337–41; and marriage, 219–21. *See also* bifocal perspective; death; glorification; hope; immortality; judgment: divine; parousia; resurrection (of believers)

essentials and nonessentials, 72, 216, 235

Eucharist. *See* Lord's Supper

excommunication, 169, 171, 176, 302. *See also* discipline: apostolic/ecclesial

exodus, new, 13, 15, 17, 294, 299

faith/faithfulness: of believers, 16–19, 47, 73, 91, 95, 98, 99, 108n15, 113–14, 115, 126, 127, 145, 148, 152, 154, 157, 162, 187, 190, 218, 246, 264–65, 299–300, 326–28, 336, 339–41, 355, 370, 372–73, 375, 377, 382, 384, 385, 401; of Christ, 15, 22, 65, 95, 251, 261, 328; of God, 13, 14–15, 75, 91,

95–96, 264; as spiritual gift, 311, 312. *See also* faith, hope, and love as triad

faith, hope, and love as triad, xviii, 19, 39, 43, 77, 330, 339–41, 365, 385, 407

family. *See* church (*ekklēsia*): as family; marriage

fellowship. *See koinōnia*

flesh: as anthropologically negative, 40, 119, 132–33, 138–41, 171–72, 203; as anthropologically neutral, 265, 278, 328, 395–96, 399; and marital unity, 196, 211. *See also* body (human)

foolishness: apostolic, 62, 148, 155, 156–57, 264; divine, 11, 66, 114, 115–18, 120, 121, 129, 136, 156–57, 373; human, 65, 114, 115–16, 142, 147, 151, 203, 379, 393. *See also* wisdom

freedom, 55, 63, 78, 192–93, 240, 275; of believers, 195–98, 200–205, 207, 217–19, 227–28, 230, 235–36, 259, 267–71, 274, 348, 362; eschatological, 398, 400–401; misguided, 170, 172, 197, 200–205, 209n58, 255–56, 314, 368; Paul's, 46, 241–43, 246–54

gifts, spiritual. *See* spiritual (Spirit-ual) gifts

glorification: eschatological, 33n10, 39, 61, 70n84, 77n96, 114, 135, 138, 161, 168, 341, 365, 382, 394–99; of God, 43, 110, 197–200, 224, 268–71, 389, 391, 413. *See also* beatific vision; body (human): resurrection of; immortality; theosis/deification; worship

glory: human, 280–81, 283, 393–94; present, 54, 154, 368–69, 404

glossolalia (speaking in tongues), 41, 54, 64, 212, 276, 307, 312–13, 318, 326–27, 337, 347–56, 359, 360. *See also* spiritual (Spirit-ual) gifts

Godfearers, 10, 51, 355

gospel, 13–14, 18, 55–56, 110, 113–14, 127, 245, 407; false, 154, 172, 273, 360; summary of, 300, 372–82. *See also* embodiment: of gospel, by church

grace, 10, 16, 17–18, 33n10, 67, 93–99,

118, 153, 186–87, 302, 324, 345, 414–16. *See also* spiritual (Spirit-ual) gifts: as grace-gifts

guns, 147, 204, 239, 256, 401

hairstyles/head coverings, 278–85

headship, 278, 280–81, 283

hedonism, 16, 389, 400

hierarchy: cruciform, 307–8, 316, 318–19, 320, 321; and marriage, 210n60, 278–82, 284n107

holiness, 21, 45, 68–70, 75, 78, 80, 91–93, 99, 100, 102, 122, 150, 161, 164, 178, 181, 186–87, 191, 214, 220, 224, 337, 372, 401; definition of, 35, 60, 69–70; of God, 77–78. *See also* alterculture, Christian; body (human): as temple of Holy Spirit; cruciformity; Holy Spirit; marks of the church

holy kiss, 41, 277, 415

Holy Spirit, 17, 19, 39–40, 64, 68–69, 198; and revelation, 132–41, 148. *See also* body (human): as temple of Holy Spirit; church (*ekklēsia*): as charismatic community; church (*ekklēsia*): as temple of Holy Spirit; spiritual (Spirit-ual) gifts; spirituality (Spirit-uality)

homosexual relations. *See* same-sex relations

honor: to God/Christ, 14, 98, 123, 164, 196, 199–200, 289, 309, 316, 318, 320; misguided, 96, 122; and Paul, 155, 246; Roman, 155n104, 236, 300, 301, 357; to the weak, 66, 69, 72, 121, 233, 298–99, 359, 414. *See also* shame

hope, 77n96, 99, 110, 141, 189, 199, 294, 295, 301, 303–4, 334, 338–41, 345, 360–61, 373, 386, 391, 402, 404–5, 412–13. *See also* eschatology; faith, hope, and love as triad

humility, 59, 64, 65, 104, 153, 158, 231, 331, 335, 357; divine, 242; interpretive, xviii, 279, 285. *See also* cruciformity; love

idolatry, 14, 41, 43, 48, 50, 76, 119, 134, 158, 166–67, 173–74, 186, 191, 197, 200, 204,

226, 242, 255, 258–64, 266–67, 270–74, 295, 310, 388

idol meat, 53, 68–69, 226–40, 250n48, 270–71, 323. *See also* eating; idolatry

Ignatian exercises, 130

imitation: of Christ, 144, 183–84, 220, 237, 239, 256, 267–70, 323n190, 335–36; of Paul, 35, 46, 59, 73, 102, 150, 183–84, 209, 220, 226, 237, 267–70, 323n190, 335, 343, 416. *See also* cruciformity; participation; Paul: as imitator of Christ

immaturity, 105, 132–41, 235, 337, 338, 413

immortality, 39, 253, 304, 341, 365, 366, 368, 393n48, 398, 400; of soul, 368. *See also* beatific vision; body (human): resurrection of

incarnation. *See* Jesus Christ: incarnation

incest, 165, 167, 168–75. *See also* sex/sexual immorality

inclusion. *See* catholicity

inculturation. *See* contextualization

individualism, 66, 298

injustice, 14, 17, 80, 166, 176–91, 224, 230, 288, 295, 330, 388. *See also* justice

integrity, 125, 129, 174, 245, 300, 304, 405; ministerial, 125

intercultural communication. *See* culture, engaging; salvific intentionality; witness

interdependence, 279, 281–83, 285, 307–8, 316. *See also* care, mutual; equality

Israel: God's covenant with, 14–15, 17; prefiguration of church, 76, 258–67, 295, 302–3; as YHWH's congregation, 90–91, 148–49, 196

Isthmian games, 50, 253

Jerusalem, collection for. *See* collection, for Jerusalem

Jesus Christ: death and resurrection, 13, 15–16, 18, 135, 364–66, 369, 380, 382, 388, 401; as foundation, 143, 146–48; as God's self-exegesis, 117n33, 118, 137, 140; incarnation, 15, 16, 20, 61, 65, 70n83, 122, 162, 199, 221, 249, 254, 308; as life-giving spirit, 393n49, 395, 397–99; as Lord, 5, 16–17, 61, 72, 75, 144, 276,

429

INDEX OF SUBJECTS

297, 299, 302, 309–11, 355, 388; as Lord of glory, 61, 114, 133–36, 183; reign, 18, 126n52, 386–89; self-emptying/self-enslavement, 11, 108, 247, 248, 251, 253, 308, 388. *See also* crucifixion/cross, of Jesus; resurrection (of Christ)

Jew and gentile, 10, 11, 15, 19, 45–46, 64, 69, 113–14, 116–17, 207, 216, 243, 249–50, 260, 266n80, 268–71, 294, 310, 343, 373n12, 410

judgment: among believers, 137, 152–53, 165, 178–84, 271, 320, 366; apostolic, 169–71, 173–74, 289–92; divine, 14, 143, 150, 161, 262, 289, 295–96, 302, 304–5; final, 17, 21, 60–61, 96–97, 98, 99, 102n1, 148, 152–53, 162, 171, 178, 200n48, 368; of outsiders, 175; by pagan courts, 176–88. *See also* discipline; lawsuits

justice, 46, 56, 176–91, 205, 225; and baptism, 178, 181, 184, 186–88, 190; by believers, 18–19, 186–90, 264n72, 292, 333, 337, 381; cruciform, 178, 183–90, 224; of God/Christ, 15, 17, 70, 118, 122–23, 161, 179–81, 301, 316; and justification, 4–5, 18, 30, 70, 91–92, 107, 176–89, 372; Roman/worldly, 17, 179, 184. *See also* injustice

justification, 4, 5, 18, 70, 107, 176–89, 312, 365, 372, 373n12, 382, 397–98. *See also* justice: and justification

kingdom of God, 161, 170–71, 178, 185–86, 235, 305, 392, 396, 399, 402, 405

knowledge, 54, 95, 125, 228; and God, 116, 127, 134, 149, 231–33, 325–38, 391; and love, 66, 230–32, 235, 239–40, 257, 268, 274, 323, 325–38, 345; and rights, 229, 230, 234–38; as spiritual gift, 311–12, 351. *See also* epistemology

koinōnia: among believers, 20, 62, 74–77, 95, 97–98, 104, 132, 265, 287, 291, 297–99, 323n190, 416n1; with Christ, 20, 60, 62, 74–77, 79, 97–98, 104, 257–67, 274, 287, 291; and the marks of the church, 74–77. *See also* Lord's Supper; mutual indwelling; participation

Last Supper, 71, 265, 279, 288, 292–95, 297, 299–300, 373. *See also* Lord's Supper

law of Christ, 250–51

lawsuits, 53, 62, 165, 176–89, 201, 333, 391n47

leadership, 47, 53, 56, 129, 132, 140, 141, 143–44, 147, 150–52, 157–58, 162, 175, 227, 276, 311, 313, 318, 330, 412, 414; and wisdom, 150–53, 158

lived theology, xviii

Lord's Supper, 20, 33n10, 37, 41, 52, 70, 72, 97, 164, 173–74, 261, 286–306, 315n172, 317, 341n224; malpractice of, 53, 288–92, 295–96, 330, 385; and participation, 20, 259, 261, 264–67, 287, 297–99; theology and practice of, 286–88, 297–306, 400n67. *See also* Last Supper

love: cruciform character of, 226, 329–36; divine, 118, 323–24, 326, 328, 329; and edification, 231, 347–60; and emotions, 317, 322, 329–30, 344–45, 414, 416; and eschatology, 337–41; and freedom/rights, 226–40; for God, 231–32, 323n189, 325–26; and knowledge, 66, 230–32, 235, 239–40, 257, 268, 274, 323, 325–38, 345; necessity of, 326–29; permanence of, 337–39; superiority of, 339–40; tough, 161. *See also* faith, hope, and love as triad

love feast, 297. *See also* Lord's Supper

male-female relations. *See* equality; marriage: mutuality in; marriage: to nonbelievers; women: in the assembly

manna, 260

marks of the church: in 1 Corinthians, xxi, 34–35, 63, 67–82; and God's character, 77–79; as interpretive lens, xx–xxii; and letter's structure, 79–82. *See also* apostolicity; catholicity; holiness; unity

marriage, 169n8, 206–23; and 1 Cor 13, 322, 342–43; as Christian community, 342–43; confusion about, 53, 68; as discipleship, 207, 219–21, 222; and divorce, 213; and engaged couples, 218–19,

430

Index of Subjects

221–22; and eschatology, 219–21; as gift/ vocation, 207, 211–12, 213, 215, 221, 222, 244; and love, 342–43; mixed, 213–15; mutuality in, 206–11, 222, 224–25, 278, 283, 342n227; to nonbelievers, 213–15; Pauline privilege, 215n73; remarriage, 212n68, 219n82, 221–22; and sex, 199, 208–10, 212; and sin, 219, 225, 244, 332; as spiritual image, 75, 165, 196; theology of, 207, 221–22, 223, 224–25; witness in, 213–15, 224–25, 342–43. *See also* persistence; singleness; widowhood
maturity. *See* immaturity
meals. *See* banquets; eating; Lord's Supper
meat markets, 228, 229, 270. *See also* eating
memory, and the Lord's Supper, 294, 299–300, 301, 304
men, Corinthian, 54, 58–59, 155n102, 192, 208–9, 212, 219, 221–22, 282–84, 290, 413. *See also* elite and nonelite; equality; women
messianic banquet, 301
mind of Christ, 20, 103, 104, 133, 136–38, 158, 338, 359
ministry, accountability in, 151, 152–54, 157, 162, 175; cruciform, 123–27, 142–58, 241–55; and rights, 71, 73, 241–55; and stewardship, 144n84, 152–54, 246. *See also* apostleship; apostolicity; partnership; Paul: apostleship of
missio Dei, xx, xxii, 29, 38, 39, 44, 46, 73, 76, 93, 146, 222, 255, 308, 371, 386, 388, 401, 402, 403, 408; church's participation in, 23, 38, 39, 46, 97, 222, 226, 241–42, 249, 270, 302, 345–46, 356, 357, 402, 408
missional commentary, definition of, xvii–xviii, xx, 27–29
mission of the church. *See* apostolicity; justice; *missio Dei*: church's participation in; salvific intentionality; witness
modesty, 279–80, 282
Muratorian Canon (Fragment), 74
mutual care. *See* care, mutual

mutual indwelling, 20, 23, 237, 299, 301–2, 315. *See also koinōnia*; participation
mystery, 100, 124–25, 134–35, 319, 370–71, 399. *See also* Paschal Mystery

nationalism. *See* Christian nationalism
new covenant. *See* covenant: new
new creation. *See* creation: new
new exodus. *See* exodus, new
Nicene (Niceno-Constantinopolitan) Creed. *See* creed: Nicene (Niceno-Constantinopolitan)
nonbelievers. *See* marriage: to nonbelievers; outsiders; witness; worship: visitors to
nonessentials. *See* essentials and nonessentials

one-anothering. *See* care, mutual
outsiders, 45, 46, 73, 74, 93n10, 174, 175, 179, 181, 183n32, 186, 236, 322, 349, 353–55, 363. *See also* worship: visitors to
overlap of the ages, 17, 60, 168, 219n83 220, 263

parousia: of Christ, xxi–xxii, 17, 47, 96–97, 148, 162, 168, 207, 219–20, 224, 287, 294, 304, 337, 365, 366, 373, 385–89, 392, 399, 402, 407, 413, 415; of Paul, 159–60. *See also* bifocal perspective; eschatology; victory, final
participation: in Christ and his story, 4, 18, 73, 122, 141, 160, 177, 302–3, 380–82; communal, 73, 74, 265, 298, 308; exclusive, 16–17, 76, 209–10, 233, 258–67, 274, 297, 299, 309; and transformation, xxii, 6, 19–21, 70n84, 365. *See also koinōnia*; *missio Dei*: church's participation in; partnership; salvation; Trinity: participation in
partnership, 74–76, 97–98, 148, 157, 252n53, 258, 266. *See also* coworkers (Paul's and God's); *koinōnia*; participation
Paschal Mystery, 15, 47
pastoral commentary, definition of, xvii–xxii, 27–29

431

INDEX OF SUBJECTS

patronage, 53, 91, 151, 152, 235, 242, 249, 290

Paul: African American interpretation, 122, 217, 328–29, 379, 399, 404; apostleship of, 3, 9–12, 21, 32–33, 46, 66, 72, 89–90, 92, 103, 107–8, 124–27, 144, 150, 154–57, 159–61, 169, 180–81, 221, 237, 241–55, 359–60, 364, 373n12, 379–80, 408–11; approaches to interpretation, 3–6; call/conversion/transformation of, 8, 9–10, 23; as father, 12, 21, 40, 51, 60, 72, 102, 103, 139, 159–60, 269; freedom of, 46, 241–43, 246–54; grace to, 146–47, 246, 379–80; as imitator of Christ, 11, 46, 59n67, 73, 102, 159–61, 209, 221, 252; Jesus and, 22, 155–56, 169–70, 196, 207, 213, 218–19, 222, 248n41, 251; letters to Corinthians, 57–58; as letter writer, 11–12; life of, 6–11; as mother, 12, 21, 40, 139–40; as pastor/pastoral theologian, 12, 14, 21–22, 33, 35, 38–43, 50, 60, 97n22, 138, 168, 193, 195, 219–20, 223, 252, 327, 413; as slave, 46, 73, 78, 144nn84–85, 157, 242, 247–54; spirituality of, 19–23; suffering of, 11, 155, 389, 390–91; theology of, 13–19. *See also* Scripture, Paul's interpretation of

Pauline privilege, 215n73

peace, 13, 17, 19, 93, 95, 98, 109, 161, 215, 234, 299, 301, 336, 356, 359, 412

persistence, 206, 207, 212–13, 215–18, 222

perspectives on Paul. *See* Paul: approaches to interpretation

Platonism/Platonists, 55, 70n84, 137, 201, 308, 368, 369, 382

pneumatology. *See* Holy Spirit

poor, 11, 53, 121–22, 130, 180, 182–85, 189, 239, 272, 289–90, 291, 296, 301–3, 306, 320, 329, 363, 408–10. *See also* elite and nonelite; preferential option; weak (powerless)

possessions, 220, 326–27

power, 11, 128; of the cross, 102, 108, 110, 112–18, 125, 134–35, 137, 154; cruciform, 16, 47, 58–59, 65, 70, 79, 108, 129–30, 249–50, 324, 368–69; of God, 13, 15, 59, 92, 113–19, 124, 126–27, 133, 156, 161, 291,

373, 380; love and, 328–29; misuse of, 54, 56, 59, 108, 110, 120–21, 134, 142–43, 155, 157–58, 163, 230, 239–40; resurrection, 16, 21, 56, 70, 126, 154, 366; of the Spirit, xx–xxi, 20n25, 21, 32–33, 58, 278, 308, 342, 401. *See also* death: as power/enemy (Death); elite and nonelite; principalities and powers; sin: as power (Sin); weak (powerless)

prayer, 41–42, 97, 130, 206n56, 209, 215, 276–82, 285, 312, 321, 347, 349–50, 352–53, 357–58, 404, 415; and women, 276–82, 285, 286

preferential option, 36, 121–22, 130, 185, 230, 239, 301, 316. *See also* poor; weak (powerless)

pride. *See* boasting

principalities and powers, 5, 128, 134, 151, 175, 218, 266n82, 365n2, 367, 370, 387–89, 391, 405. *See also* death: as power/enemy (Death); sin: as power (Sin); victory, final

prophecy, 360–61; in assembly, 41, 212, 276, 287, 312, 349–60; as spiritual gift, 318, 326–28, 337, 348; and women, 206n56, 277–86, 350, 357–59

prostitutes. *See* sex/sexual immorality

Qumran, 143n83, 149n97

racism, 122, 128, 129, 404. *See also* White supremacy

redemption, 15–16, 17, 70, 107, 113n21, 118, 122, 127, 138, 161, 198, 199–200, 279; of bodies, 341, 398. *See also* resurrection (of believers): bodily; salvation

resurrection (of believers), 61, 195–97, 392–99; analogies for, 392, 393–98; bodily, 17, 53, 61, 196–201, 325, 334, 339, 364–71, 379, 382, 392–407; denial of, 53, 69, 80, 108, 200, 340, 364, 366–70, 380, 383–84, 391, 405. *See also* body (human): resurrection of; immortality; theosis/deification

resurrection (of Christ), 15–16, 33, 47, 61, 135, 308, 340, 364–92; bodily, 366–67, 369–70, 377, 383, 402–3, 404, 407; consequences of, 367, 369, 372, 382–91; as

432

Index of Subjects

fiction or fact, 382–91; misunderstanding of, 154–55; participation in, 6, 21, 23, 33–35, 38, 39, 47, 59–60, 63, 65–67, 79, 97, 110, 125, 126, 227, 237, 240, 252, 269, 303, 344, 365, 366, 401, 403, 407, 411; witnesses to, 243, 377–80, 384, 385
resurrectional cruciformity. *See* cruciformity: resurrectional/charismatic character
revelation, 70n84, 96, 142, 351; cross as, 15, 114–30, 132–38, 140; and the Spirit, 132–41, 148; as spiritual gift, 276, 351, 356–57
reversal, as divine action, 67, 122, 150–51, 181, 182, 184, 250, 291, 387
rhetoric, Paul and, 12, 40, 50, 58, 89–90, 95, 97, 103, 105, 106–8, 110, 112n17, 113, 116, 118, 122, 124, 127, 130, 139, 153–54, 155, 161, 175, 177, 183, 188, 192, 193, 210n60, 211, 241, 243, 244, 264–67, 271, 283, 284, 289, 291–92, 310, 314, 316, 318, 326–27, 352, 357–58, 364, 386n36, 389, 390, 392, 399, 413n14
righteousness, 397; of believers, 18, 180, 218; eschatological, 17; of God/Christ, 15, 113, 122–23, 161. *See also* holiness; justice
rights, 200–201, 204, 229, 234–38; civil/human, 11, 239; culture of, 239; forgoing, 237, 238, 246, 252, 258; and love, 230, 234–40; marital, 208, 211; of ministers, 71, 73, 241–55. *See also* justice; love; x-y-z pattern
Roman Empire/emperor, 5, 7, 10, 11, 17, 31, 48, 49, 50, 58, 71n86, 228, 266, 301, 317, 386n34, 389, 408

sacraments, 33n10, 100, 261–62, 297, 302, 305. *See also* baptism; Lord's Supper
salvation, 10, 13, 16, 60, 73, 79, 91, 96–98, 114, 116, 123, 127, 130, 135, 171–75, 186n35, 199, 201, 232, 253, 270, 301, 309, 339, 340, 365, 372–73, 386–87, 397, 402. *See also* justification; participation; redemption; theosis/deification
salvific intentionality, 43n37, 45, 73, 171, 207, 213–15, 220, 222, 238, 241–55, 257,

270–71, 273, 274, 354, 356. *See also* marriage: witness in; witness
same-sex relations, 167, 178, 186, 222
sanctification. *See* Christoformity; cruciformity; holiness; Holy Spirit; theosis/deification
Satan, 171, 266, 366. *See also* demons
scandals, 52, 53, 110, 127
Scripture, Paul's interpretation of, 4–5, 13, 15, 22, 78, 90, 91, 96–98, 112, 116, 120–23, 135, 136, 148, 151, 153, 166–67, 169, 182, 197, 207, 211, 213, 221, 233, 244, 245, 250, 255, 259, 262, 270, 296, 309, 324, 337, 354n245, 370, 374–76, 380
Second Coming. *See* parousia
Second Vatican Council, 110
segregation, 291, 320
self-examination, 130, 148, 153, 258, 295–96, 300
self-exegesis, Christ as God's, 117n33, 118, 128, 137, 140. *See also* theophany, Jesus' death as
self-sacrifice. *See* cruciformity
self-sufficiency, 55, 154n102
separation, marital. *See* divorce
sex/sexual immorality: and chaos, 191–93; and incest, 165, 167, 168–75; and marriage, 199, 208–10, 212; and prostitutes, 48n44, 53, 167, 170, 186, 191–200; and same-sex relations, 167, 178, 186, 222; and worship, 197–200
shame: divine act, 11, 66, 120, 291; human behavior, 301, 330, 332, 336, 345, 359; human state, 113, 182, 202, 280; and Jesus' death, 15, 120, 249, 374–75; Paul and, 177, 182, 242, 391, 410. *See also* honor
Shema, 42, 72, 78n101, 233–34
signs, 114, 116–17
sin, 17, 56, 166, 170, 172–73, 201, 262, 273, 391, 401; against God/Christ, 166, 197–98, 237, 315; against one's body, 194, 197–98; against sibling/neighbor, 166, 237, 315; marriage and, 219, 225, 244, 332; "mortal," 237–38; as power (Sin), 5, 14–15, 18, 56, 187n35, 218, 365, 370, 371, 373, 377, 381, 384n33, 386, 389,

433

395, 397–98, 401, 402. *See also* death: as power/enemy (Death); idolatry; injustice; sex/sexual immorality

singing, 41, 128–29, 276, 341, 357

singleness, 207, 209, 211–13, 216, 220, 222, 223, 225

slavery/enslaved persons, 49, 112, 160n109, 209n58, 242, 249, 290; in the church, 11, 19, 51, 57, 64, 69, 105–6, 141, 169, 207, 216, 260, 278, 290, 379, 414; to God/Christ, 218, 381; metaphorical, 90, 157, 187n35, 220, 236, 247; Paul's attitude, 217–19; sin as, 170, 172, 195, 197–98, 200, 201; in the United States, 122, 399. *See also* Jesus Christ: self-emptying/self-enslavement; Paul: as slave

slogans, 105, 140, 192–95, 197–98, 230–31, 233, 236, 258, 267–68, 282–83, 314, 335

soul, immortality of. *See* immortality: of soul

spirit, human, 64, 135, 345, 347n231, 353n242

spiritual food and drink, 259, 261

spiritual (Spirit-ual) gifts, 19, 34, 35, 66, 99, 125, 136, 138–39, 153, 261n63, 276, 286, 303, 307–21, 323, 326, 338–40, 347–61, 412, 416; and edification/love, 322, 324–29, 335, 349–52, 363; as grace-gifts, xx, xxin9, 63–64, 93–98, 138n77, 211n66, 276, 309, 311–14, 317–18, 326, 348, 363; impermanence of, 337–39, 366; marriage as, 211; in worship, 347–61

spirituality (Spirit-uality), 20, 33, 40, 103, 132–38, 140–41, 162, 237, 240, 261n63, 308, 309n160, 359–60, 369; communal, 63–65; and eschatology, 395; Paul's, 19–23. *See also* church (*ekklēsia*): as charismatic community; cruciformity; Holy Spirit; mutual indwelling; participation; spiritual (Spirit-ual) gifts; theosis/deification; Trinity: participation in

status, 18, 47, 66, 129, 131, 162, 231, 235, 320, 326; Corinthians and, 31, 50, 51, 54, 58, 96, 120, 155n102, 216, 236n19, 280,

283, 301, 317, 318, 330; Paul and, 11, 107, 248, 252, 269, 308; subversion of, 37, 59, 122, 250, 299, 301, 316. *See also* x-y-z pattern

stewardship, and ministry, 144n84, 152–54, 246

Stoicism/Stoics, 55, 70n84, 112n17, 124, 133n65, 137, 154, 172, 192–93, 210n62, 216, 235, 382, 397

stumbling block, 114, 117, 128, 129, 236, 238, 270

subversion: 1 Corinthians and, 59; cross as, 115–18; Lord's Supper as, 301

suffering: of believers, 97, 155, 276, 300, 317, 334, 385, 404; of creation, 398; of humanity, 320; of Jesus, 15, 114, 130, 168, 377, 388, 405; of Paul, 11, 155, 389, 390–91

symposium, 53, 275–76, 287, 289n116, 290, 356. *See also* banquets; Lord's Supper

synagogue, 10, 51, 52, 89, 107n12, 355

temples, pagan. *See* banquets; church: as temple of Holy Spirit; eating: at pagan temples; idolatry; idol meat

theological commentary, definition of, xvii–xxii, 27–29

theophany, Jesus' death as, 15, 117, 128, 140, 162, 319. *See also* self-exegesis, Christ as God's

theosis/deification, 28, 39, 70, 79, 298n136, 337, 339, 368, 382, 393n50, 398. *See also* beatific vision; body (human): resurrection of; Christoformity; cruciformity; holiness; immortality

tolerance, 53, 172, 175

tongues, speaking in. *See* glossolalia (speaking in tongues); spiritual (Spirit-ual) gifts

transformation, 22, 37–39, 47, 64, 70, 186–87, 269, 303, 339; eschatological, 389, 392–401, 403, 407

Trinity, 19, 28, 36, 94, 133, 136, 137n75, 140, 143, 149, 234n17, 340; participation in, 16, 19–20, 60, 70n84, 77n96, 79, 96,

133, 337; and salvation, 187, 199, 392, 398; and spiritual gifts, 311–12
typology, 260–64, 266

union with Christ. *See koinōnia*; mutual indwelling; participation
unity, 59–60, 64, 67–69, 72, 74–75, 77, 78n100, 91, 99, 100, 102–6, 109–10, 141, 142, 157, 161, 164, 169, 202, 227, 265, 291, 296, 305, 325n195, 331, 341, 357, 373n12, 409; in diversity, 153, 312–16, 319, 321, 363. *See also* divisions; equality; marks of the church
universalism, 387

victory, final, 241, 367, 386, 392, 399–401, 404. *See also* death: defeat of; principalities and powers
violence, 9, 127, 189, 204, 255–56, 287, 401, 405. *See also* abortion; guns
virgins. *See* marriage: and engaged couples
vocation, 22, 71, 207, 215–18, 219, 222. *See also* Paul: apostleship of

weak (powerless), 11, 56, 58, 228, 229–30, 234–38, 240, 249–50, 379; divine preference for, 11, 66, 119–22, 185, 289, 300–301; treatment of, 72, 185, 292, 295, 300–301, 303, 308, 316–18, 363, 413n14, 416. *See also* elite and nonelite; poor; preferential option
weakness, 229–30, 240, 249–50; of the body, 394, 396; of the cross, 114, 116–18, 190; of God, 103, 116–18, 156–57; of Paul and ministers, 46, 59n67, 106, 124–27, 156–57, 242, 249–50, 254; and power, 70, 238; and spiritual gifts, 307, 316–17. *See also* elite and nonelite; power; weak (powerless)
White supremacy, 113n21, 129. *See also* racism
widowhood, 180, 212, 221–22, 264n72. *See also* marriage

wisdom, 54; Christ crucified as God's, 15, 59, 70, 102, 112–23, 128, 129, 134–38, 142–43, 147–48, 156–57, 161–62, 190; cruciform, 65, 132; human/Corinthian, 54, 59, 108, 111–12, 116–17, 120, 130, 133, 137, 140–41, 154, 155, 158, 163, 177, 182, 185, 188; and leadership, 150–53, 158; Paul and, 124–26, 147–48, 155; as spiritual gift, 311, 312, 313n168. *See also* foolishness; power
witness, 11, 43–45, 59, 100, 129, 136, 150, 189, 190, 303, 343; in the assembly, 44–45, 277, 307, 347–48, 353–56, 361; in marriage, 213–15, 224–25, 342–43; in private homes, 229, 258, 270–71. *See also* antiwitness; salvific intentionality
women: in the assembly, 11, 51, 69, 71, 275–86, 303, 307, 310, 315, 320, 350, 357–59; and the resurrection, 378–79. *See also* equality; marriage
worship, 30, 37, 46, 54, 64, 72, 119, 130, 132, 154, 163, 164, 199, 233–34, 266–67, 268, 273, 275–77, 288, 305–6, 309–10, 323, 327, 342–43, 347–48, 354, 361–63; and 1 Corinthians, 41–43; and commentary writing, xviii, 28; evening, 275n92, 290, 409; order in, 281, 282, 285, 307, 347, 348, 356–60, 362–63; practices of, 275–77, 287; and spiritual gifts, 63–65, 72, 99, 206n56, 276, 277, 286, 307, 312–13, 318, 324–25, 342, 347–61, 368–69; visitors to, 44–45, 277, 307, 348, 353–56, 361. *See also* ancestor worship/veneration; chaos in Corinth: liturgical; creeds; Lord's Supper; women: in the assembly

x-y-z pattern, xxi, 65–66, 184–85, 199, 210–11, 238, 247–49, 251, 253, 256, 269, 301, 307, 353–54. *See also* cruciformity

zeal: for gifts, 95n17, 318, 348–50, 352; misguided, for leaders, 144; Paul's, 9

Index of Scripture and Other Ancient Sources

For 1 Corinthians, only citations that are out of their natural order in the commentary are included.

OLD TESTAMENT

Genesis

1	393, 397
1:27	281, 283
2:7	397
2:21–25	196
2:24	211
3	386
5:3	397
6:1–4	281
22:24	377n18
32:30	338n219
39:7–20	196–97
39:12	197
39:18	197

Exodus

6:6–7	198
6:7	75n91
12:14	299
12:21–28	173
12:23	262, 263
13:7	173
13:21–22	260
14:21–29	260
16	260

17:1–7	260, 261
18:13–27	179
19:6	91
20:14	167
23:16	386n35
23:19	386n35
24	294
24:5–8	293
24:8	300
32	261
32:6	262–63
33:11	338n219
34:6	324n193
34:22	386n35
34:26	386n35

Leviticus

2:12	386n35
6:14–18	245n37
7:9	266
7:15	266
11:45	77
18	166, 167
18:3	167
18:8	168n8
18:20	164
18:22	186

19:2	69, 77, 91
19:14	236n21, 237n24
19:18	335
19:23–25	386n35
19:29	167
19:34	335n213
20:10	167
20:11	168n8
20:13	186
20:26	69, 164
23:10	386n35
23:17	386n35
23:20	386n35
26:11–12	149n97
26:12	75n91

Numbers

10:9	351
11	260
11:29	350n235
12:8	338n219
14:2	263
14:14	338n219
14:36	263
15	262
16:41–49	263
18:1–19	245n37

Index of Scripture and Other Ancient Sources

18:29–32	245n37	32:17	266	78:20	261n65
20:2–13	260–61	32:18	261n65	78:35	261n65
21:4–6	263	32:30–31	261n65	80:8–10	245n36
21:4–9	262–63	34:10	338n219	86:5	91n3
25	262–63			86:7	91n3
25:1	263	**Joshua**		86:15	324n193
25:1–2	261	6:1–20	351	89:11	270n88
25:1–9	261			92:7	102n1
25:6–13	9	**Judges**		92:9	102n1
25:9	262, 263	3:27–30	351	93:5	150
		6:22	338n219	94:4	172
Deuteronomy				94:11	151
1:9–18	179	**1 Samuel**		95	261n65
4	166	2:1–10	123n49	103:8	324
4:16–19	393	2:4	121	105	261n62
4:24	267	2:8	121	106	261n62
4:34	233n13			106:24–27	263
4:39	233n13	**1 Kings**		106:30–31	9
5:4	338n219	18:24	91n3	109:1 LXX	
5:9	267			[110:1 MT]	388n40
5:18	167	**1 Chronicles**		109:28	156
6:4	233	16:8	91n3	110	388
6:15	267	28:8	90n2	110:1	386, 387
7:9	96			113:4–8	121
13:5	173n16	**Job**		114:2	149n97
16:1–8	173	2:6	171	115	310
16:18	182	5:13	151	116:2	91n3
16:18–20	179	42:1–17	171	116:7	91n3
17:1–13	173n16			116:13	91n3
18:1–8	245n37	**Psalms**		133:1	105
18:4	386n35	8	388	139:1–6	231–32, 325
19:15–21	173n16	8:6	386	145:8	324
21:18–21	173n16	8:7 LXX [8:6 MT]	387,	145:14	121
22:13–30	167		388n40		
22:20–24	173n16	16:10	377	**Proverbs**	
22:22	168n8	24:1	270	6:23–7:27	166
22:30	168n8	34:2	123	6:27–28	212
23:18	167	35:3	123		
24:7	173n16	44:22	390	**Ecclesiastes**	
25:4	244	50:13	270n88	3:3	112
26:1–15	386n35	52:1	172		
27:20	168n8	63:4	91n3	**Song of Solomon**	
29:13	75n91	78	261n62	2:16	210n61
32:4	261n65	78:15–16	261n65	6:3	210n61
32:15	261n65			7:10	210n61
32:16–21	267				

437

INDEX OF SCRIPTURE AND OTHER ANCIENT SOURCES

Isaiah

1:16–17	264n72
1:17	180
1:18	264
1:21	180
1:23c	180
2:2	10
2:12	96n21
5:1–7	245n36
11:2	313n167
12:4	93
13:6	96n21
22:13	389, 391
25	292n123
25:6–8	400
28:11–12	354
28:16	147
29:9–12	116
29:13–14	116
40:13	136
42:6	10, 150n98
43:16–21	294
44	310
44:25	116
45:4	355
45:23	16
46	166
49:5–6	10
49:6	10, 150n98
51:9–11	294
52:13	376
52:13–53:12	15, 375–77
53:5	375
53:6	292n125
53:7–9	183
53:8b	375
53:9	376
53:10b–11a	376
53:11d	375
53:12	292n125
53:12a	377
53:12b	375
55	292n123
55:8	136, 267
55:8–9	232
57:15	122
58:4	288
58:6–7a	288
58:10	288, 301
61	180
61:8a	184
64:4 [64:3 LXX]	135

Jeremiah

1:4–8	10
7:23	75n91
9:23–24 [9:22–23 LXX]	123
11:4	75n91
20:9	246
23:6	123
30:22	75n91
31:31–34	14, 294
32:40	294

Lamentations

3:45	156

Ezekiel

13:5	96n21
16	196
36:28	75n91
37	17, 149, 370
40–48	149

Daniel

2:46–47	355
7:9–28	367
7:22	181n28
12:1–4	367
12:2–3	393n50

Hosea

1–3	196
6:2	377
13:14	400

Joel

1:15	96n21
2:1	96n21
2:11	96n21
2:13	324n193
2:28	315n172
2:31	96n21
2:32	91n3
2:32 [LXX 3:5]	16
3:14	96n21
3:28–29	278

Amos

5:18–20	96n21
5:24	180

Jonah

2:1b [1:17 MT]	377

Micah

6:8	180

Habakkuk

2:14	389
2:18–20	310

Zechariah

2:6	196
9:14	399
14:1–21	96n21

Malachi

1:6–14	267n83
3:13–4:6	96n21

Wisdom

3:8	181n28
13:14	166

1 Maccabees

1:15	216

2 Maccabees

1:10	93n13

NEW TESTAMENT

Matthew

4:2	155
5:3–12	156
5:13–16	93

438

Index of Scripture and Other Ancient Sources

5:14–16	150n98	27:63–64	377n18	4:2	155
5:31–32	213	28:1–10	378	4:18–19	180
5:32	213	28:16–20	378	6:27–36	156
5:38–48	156	28:19	187	8:16	150n98
5:39b–40	183			9:22	377n18
6:1–4	328	**Mark**		9:23	390
8:11	400	3:31–35	244n34	9:58	156
8:20	156	7:18–19	270n88	10:7	245
10:10	245	7:19b	235	10:27	335n213
11:25	121	8:11–12	117n30	11:14–16	117n30
12:38–45	117n30	8:31	377n18	11:29–30	117n30
12:40	377	8:34–37	254	11:42	180
13:55	244n34	9:31	377n18	12:37	413n13
16:1–4	117n30	9:42	236n21, 237n24	13:32	377n18
16:21	377n18	10:2–12	213	14:7–24	292n123
17:20	327n198	10:7–8	196	16:18	213
17:23	377n18	10:8	211	17:6	327n198
18:6	236n21	10:11–12	213	18:33	377n18
18:15–21	170	10:34	377n18	21:5–7	117n30
18:17	170	10:38–39	300	22:15–20	265n76, 293
18:20	170	10:42b–45	247	22:16	294
18:21–35	184	10:43–45	144n84	22:18	294
19:3–9	213	10:45	251	22:19b	293
19:5–6	196, 211	11:12	155	22:19b–20	293n126
19:6	213	11:23	327n198	22:20	300
19:9	213	12:1–12	245n36	22:20b	293
19:19	335n213	12:24	391n47	22:24–27	300
19:28	181n28	12:31	335n213	22:25b–27	247
20:19	377n18	13:3–8	117n30	22:30	181n28
20:25b–28	247	13:32	96n21	23:34	183
21:21	327n198	13:34	413n13	24:7	377n18
22:39	335n213	13:35	413n13	24:13	378n22
23:23	180	13:37	413n13	24:13–32	378n21, 394
24:1–3	117n30	14:22–25	265n76	24:18	378n22
24:31	399	14:25	294, 400	24:21	377n18
24:42	413n13	14:34	413n13	24:33	378n22
24:43	413n13	14:37	413n13	24:33–51	378
25:13	413n13	14:38	413n13	24:33–53	378
25:31–46	237	14:58	377n18	24:34	378
26:26–29	265n76	14:65	156	24:36–49	126
26:29	294	15:29	377n18	24:46	377
26:38	413n13	16:9	378		
26:40	413n13			**John**	
26:41	413n13	**Luke**		1:5	150n98
26:61	377n18	1:46–55	120	1:9	150n98
26:67	156	2:32	150n98	1:46	355
27:40	377n18			2:12	244n34

INDEX OF SCRIPTURE AND OTHER ANCIENT SOURCES

2:12–22	149n94
2:18	117n30
2:19–20	377n18
3:19–21	150n98
4:48	117n30
5:21	398n61
5:35	150n98
6:30	117n30
6:63	398n61
7:37–38	315n172
8:12	150n98
9:5	150n98
10:10	15
11:9	150n98
12:24	393
12:35–36	150n98
12:46	150n98
13:35	325
14:6	398n61
14:26	340
15:1–8	245n36
16:13	340
17	103, 319
17:23	325n195
19:28	155
20:11–18	378
20:11–28	394
20:18	379
20:19–23	378
20:19–29	126, 378n21
21	378
21:1–22	378n21

Acts

1:3	381n31
2:1–18	312
2:1–21	355
2:12–16	355
2:17–18	315n172
2:22–36	374
2:27	377n17
2:31	377n17
8:1–3	9, 379n25
9	10
9:1–5	9, 379n25

9:1–31	379n24
9:4	315
9:10–16	10n6
9:27	243n32
9:30	8
11:19–30	243n32
11:27–30	8, 409n2, 410n6
12:25	243n32
13–21	9
13:1–15:41	243n32
13:47	10n6, 150n98
15	8
15:28–29	228
15:36–18:22	50
16:1–3	160n112
16:6–17:14	51
16:7	32n8
17	125
17:1–9	10
17:14–15	160n112
17:15–18:1	51
17:16–34	117n30, 383
18	8
18:1–4	51
18:1–18	144
18:2–3	415
18:3	11, 249
18:5	56, 90n1, 160n112, 411
18:5–6	51
18:7–8	51
18:8	107n12
18:11	8, 50
18:12–17	7, 8, 50, 51
18:17	51, 89
18:19–21	411n9
18:24	411
18:24–26	106
18:24–28	144, 415
18:24–19:1	52, 412n12
18:26	106
18:27–28	106
19	8
19:1	106
19:1–20:1	411n9
19:8	8

19:10	8
19:21–22	410n7
19:22	160n112
19:23–41	391n45
20:1–2	410n7
20:3	8
20:4	160n112
20:31	8
20:33–35	245
20:35	245–46n39
21:25	228
21:27–36	8
22:1–21	379n24
22:3–8	379n25
23:6	9
26:2–23	379n24
26:5	9
26:9–15	379n25
26:23	150n98
28	8

Romans

1:1	13, 144n84, 373n11
1:5	10, 10n6, 18, 380n29
1:16	270n86
1:16–17	10, 13, 114
1:18–25	110
1:18–27	262n67
1:18–32	14n19, 48, 166n4, 186
1:18–3:20	14, 114
1:19–22	116
1:22	116n29
1:26–27	186
2:9–10	270n86
2:14–16	14
2:19	150n98
2:25–29	216n76
3:9	270n86
3:9–20	204
3:20	15
3:21–26	15, 122
3:24	198
3:27–31	18, 216n76
3:29	270n86

Index of Scripture and Other Ancient Sources

4:1–22	216n76	8:5–17	20	11:34	136
4:1–25	18	8:9	17, 32n8, 147	12:1	33, 200
4:13	15	8:10–11	397	12:1–2	21, 42, 69, 199,
4:17	120, 341, 371n7,	8:11	371n7, 376n16,		204, 219, 268, 303
	380n28, 387, 398		396n58, 398	12:2	60n68
4:23–24	xvii	8:15	19	12:3	153, 380n29
4:24	376n16	8:15–16	353n242	12:3–10	35n21
4:25	292, 375n14, 376n16	8:17	136, 317n176,	12:4–5	196, 265n78,
5:1–5	339n221		396n58		314n170
5:1–11	15, 16, 302, 340, 373	8:17–39	340	12:4–8	19
5:2	372	8:18–25	17	12:6	311, 312
5:3	391	8:18–39	339	12:6–8	153, 313
5:5	232n9	8:19–23	341	12:7–8	313
5:6	238	8:21	398	12:8	313
5:6–8	324, 375n14	8:23	200, 341, 398,	12:9–13	276
5:8	15, 232n9		414n16	12:9–21	343
5:9–10	373	8:24	373	12:10	20n27, 343
5:12–21	15, 386, 397	8:26–27	353n242	12:12	334
5:15	94n15	8:28	232n9	12:12–13	343
5:17–18	397	8:29	395	12:13	212n68
6	107, 276, 300, 339,	8:29–30	396n58	12:14	183n32, 343
	370, 381–82	8:29–35	136	12:14–21	156
6:1–2	384n33	8:30	398	12:15	220, 317n176, 334
6:1–11	18	8:31–39	342	12:15–16	343
6:2–3	381	8:32	15, 292, 375n14	12:16	20n27
6:3	107	8:34	319	12:17–21	183n32, 256, 343
6:4	376n16, 381, 398n60	8:35	11, 50n49, 155n103,	13:8	20n27
6:4–5	387		390n44	13:9	335n213
6:5	381, 394n52	8:35–37	15	13:11	220
6:6	172, 218n80, 381	8:35–39	232n9, 387n39	13:14	301, 315
6:8	381	8:36	390	14:1–15:13	35n21, 216n76,
6:11	381	8:38	134n67		226, 288n113
6:12–13	196	8:38–39	151	14:4	413
6:12–23	200	8:39	15	14:13	20n27, 236n21
6:13	186n35, 381	9–11	249n44	14:13b	237n24
6:16	381	9:1–5	250n47	14:14	270n88
6:16–22	218n80	9:3	415	14:15	237n23, 239
6:17–18	186n35	9:24	270n86	14:17	161, 185, 235
6:19	196, 381	9:31–33	117	14:18–27	166
6:22–23	381, 387	10:5–13	16	14:19	215
6:23	401	10:9	16	14:20	237n23, 237n24,
7:7–25	401n69	10:12	270n86		270n88
7:7–8:4	15	10:12–13	309	14:20–21	236n21
8	364, 367, 370, 385, 402	10:12–14	91n3	15:1	250n46, 334
8:2	397–98	11:16	414n16	15:1–3	220
8:3	269, 375n14	11:25	327n199	15:1–4	268

441

INDEX OF SCRIPTURE AND OTHER ANCIENT SOURCES

15:4	xvii, 244, 276
15:5	20n27
15:7	20n27, 295
15:8	144
15:14	20n27
15:15–16	380n29
15:15–21	10n6
15:16	13, 373n11
15:18	147
15:18–19	125
15:18–20	96
15:22–24	411
15:24	411
15:25–27	410
15:25–29	409n4
15:25–33	408
15:26–27	244n35
15:27	409
15:33	94
16	278n96, 358
16:1	144n84
16:3	145n87
16:3–5	415
16:5	414n16
16:7	244n34, 379
16:9	145n87
16:16	20n27, 90n2, 415n18
16:20	94, 94n15
16:21	145n87, 160n112
16:22	12–13n13, 90, 415n19
16:23	52, 107n12, 290
16:25	327n199, 351n237
16:25–27	134
16:26	10n6, 18

1 Corinthians

1–4	68, 79–80, 102, 142, 162–63
1–6	61n69
1:1	51, 75, 89–90, 157, 242
1:1–3	80, 89–95
1:1–9	75, 80, 89–101, 102, 103, 107, 139
1:1–3:4	61
1:2	xvii, 19, 21, 41, 51, 67, 69n82, 71, 75, 78, 90–93, 95, 103, 117, 119, 122, 123, 140, 146, 181, 298, 410
1:2b	70
1:3	19, 41, 93–95, 128, 415
1:4	92, 94, 123
1:4–9	80, 94, 95–98, 412
1:5	92, 123, 327n197
1:7	63n71, 64, 94n16, 148, 211n66, 386n34
1:7–8	17, 60, 61, 161, 366
1:8	21, 38, 58, 148, 161, 171, 401, 413
1:9	20, 41, 60, 75, 79, 91, 114, 117, 119, 216, 264
1:10	58, 67, 68, 74–75, 102, 139, 265, 287, 289, 316
1:10–11	40
1:10–12	103–6
1:10–16	143
1:10–17	81, 103–11
1:10–4:21	75n92, 79, 81, 102–63
1:11	56, 57
1:12	52, 53, 102, 140, 144, 151, 244n34, 378, 387, 412
1:13	41, 61, 69, 78, 138, 161, 375, 380
1:13–14	52
1:13–17	41, 106–8
1:14	51, 52, 290
1:14–16	276
1:14–17	372
1:16	51, 414
1:17	114, 115, 124
1:17–21	372
1:17–25	61
1:18	32n6, 108, 112, 126, 373, 385, 387
1:18–20	115–16

1:18–25	9, 13, 81, 103, 108, 110, 113–19, 121, 123–24, 128, 134, 147, 155, 156, 161, 249, 294, 319, 375
1:18–31	15, 95, 185, 238
1:18–2:5	81, 91–92, 102–3, 111–32, 140, 237, 269, 292, 307, 308, 365
1:21	340
1:21–25	116–18
1:22	310n162
1:22–24	270
1:23	41, 126, 375
1:23–24	112
1:23–25	129
1:24	59, 61, 92, 93n11, 119, 122, 310n162
1:25	124, 229
1:26	40, 51, 93n11, 107n12, 115, 148, 216
1:26–27	66
1:26–28	291
1:26–29	11, 49n48, 117, 119–22
1:26–31	67, 72, 81, 103, 112, 119–24, 156, 298, 316
1:27	115, 229
1:27b	291
1:28	103, 134, 182, 412n11
1:29	102, 126, 156
1:29–31	331
1:30	69n82, 70, 93, 115, 118, 134, 187, 198
1:30–31	122–24
1:31	102, 116n27, 126, 144, 151, 156, 391n46
2:1	115, 139, 327
2:1–5	81, 103, 106, 112, 124–27, 134, 249, 294, 372
2:2	16, 31, 59, 61, 147, 155, 161, 366, 375
2:3	115, 229
2:4	115, 161
2:5	115, 340

Index of Scripture and Other Ancient Sources

2:6	115, 120n41, 385, 387, 389	3:4–9	412	4:6	52, 54, 106, 140, 144, 161, 169, 231, 323n189, 331, 335, 412n12
2:6–10	133	3:5	340, 372		
2:6–13	134–36	3:5–6	106, 140	4:7	331
2:6–16	132–38, 139	3:5–9	44, 106, 143, 144–46, 244–45, 408	4:7–13	157
2:6–3:4	81, 103, 112, 132–42, 179, 338			4:8	96
		3:5–10	152, 380	4:8–13	11, 143, 154–57
2:7	115, 124	3:5–4:13	62, 81, 103, 142–59	4:9	181, 244n34
2:7a	133			4:9–13	62, 162, 334, 390
2:7b	133	3:6	51, 311	4:10	115, 159, 229, 238, 264
2:8	61, 114, 133, 161, 183, 375, 387n39, 388	3:8	148		
		3:9	143, 157, 348	4:11	252
2:9	61, 133, 141, 161, 232, 323n189, 366	3:9–15	143	4:11–12a	50
		3:10	51, 94, 115	4:12–13	183
2:10	351, 413n15	3:10–15	145, 146–48, 152, 348	4:14	177
2:10a	133			4:14–21	81, 103, 159–61, 412n11
2:10b	133	3:10–17	146–50		
2:11	133	3:11	115, 143	4:15	40, 51
2:11–12	198	3:12–15	143	4:16	78, 102, 269, 323n190
2:11–13	133	3:13	96n20, 152		
2:11–14	137n75	3:13–14	153	4:16–17	150
2:12	133	3:13–15	62, 162	4:17	56, 71, 215n74, 412
2:12–13	64, 222	3:16	40n32, 43, 64, 69, 140, 152, 298	4:18	54, 153, 169, 231
2:13	115, 133, 261, 340			4:18–19	323n189, 332, 335
2:13–3:5	172	3:16–17	19, 69, 70, 143, 146, 148–50, 164, 198–99, 226, 292, 348		
2:14	65, 115, 133, 395n55			4:18–7:40	79n104
		3:17	69n82, 78, 102, 143, 237	4:19	54, 115, 153, 169, 231, 410
2:14–15	395				
2:14–16	133, 136–38, 139	3:18	115, 359n253	4:20	115, 185
2:15	152n99, 261, 413n15	3:18–23	143, 150–52	4:21	323n189
		3:19	115	5–6	206
2:16	103, 133, 222, 359	3:20	115, 384, 391	5:1	165, 191
2:16a	133	3:21	102, 144, 156, 331, 413n15	5:1–2	332
2:16b	133			5:1–2a	332
3	366	3:21–23	143, 412	5:1–5	43, 168–72
3:1	40, 65, 115, 136, 261, 261n63	3:22	52, 102, 105n5, 106, 140, 144, 244n34, 378, 412n12, 413n15	5:1–8	53
				5:1–11	68
3:1–3	12n11, 137n73			5:1–13	35n19, 62, 81, 165, 167, 168–76, 179, 191, 206, 211, 227, 262, 276–77n95, 279, 303n149, 366
3:1–4	44, 105, 132, 133, 138–40, 143, 354	4	366		
		4:1	106, 124, 144n84, 327		
3:2	115, 144–45n86	4:1–2	246		
3:2–3a	40	4:1–4	89		
3:3	141, 287, 331	4:1–6	242, 412	5:1–7:40	70, 79–80, 81, 164–225
3:4	144, 151	4:1–7	143, 152–54		
3:4–5	53, 102	4:2	218	5:2	54, 153, 231, 323n189, 335
3:4–6	52, 412n12	4:5	62, 148, 162		

443

INDEX OF SCRIPTURE AND OTHER ANCIENT SOURCES

5:3	165	6:7b–8	177n22	7:1–40	6, 53, 68, 81, 206–24
5:5	62, 96n20	6:8	177, 181	7:2	165, 208
5:6	40n32, 149n95, 165, 331	6:9	40n32, 62, 149n95, 165, 177, 187, 188, 193n42, 229	7:2–4	196, 207
5:6–13	172–75			7:2–5	209–11, 220
5:7	57, 62, 169, 183, 294, 299	6:9–10	161, 171, 177, 185–86, 191, 211	7:2–16	207, 209–15, 222
5:7–8	302, 411n9	6:9–11	14, 188, 227	7:3	208
5:7b–8a	41	6:11	18, 41, 42, 59, 64, 69n82, 70, 91, 107, 108, 122, 165, 177, 181, 184, 186–88, 198, 199, 214, 276, 300, 372	7:3–4	213
5:8	333, 334			7:4	208
5:9	57, 165, 186			7:5	184n33, 207
5:9–10	45, 220			7:6	207
5:9–11	213			7:6–7	211–12
5:9–13	53	6:12	54, 192, 220, 221, 227, 267–68, 314, 413n15	7:7	63n71, 94n16, 207, 209, 221
5:10	165, 229				
5:11	165, 186, 229	6:12–18a	193–97	7:8	207, 209, 213, 222
5:12	165	6:12–20	53, 62, 81, 165, 170, 172, 191–205, 206, 208, 209, 211, 220, 227, 239, 262, 279, 282, 284, 332, 358, 366, 369, 391	7:8–9	211, 212, 218, 221
5:12–13	176			7:9	207, 221
5:13	169			7:10	71, 207, 208
5:13b	169			7:10–11	212–13, 219
6:1	69n82, 165, 177, 187, 333			7:10–12	207
		6:13	120n41, 165, 192, 193n42, 210, 235	7:10–16	220
6:1–6	179–82, 185			7:11	207, 217
6:1–7	177	6:14	62, 376n16, 392, 398n60	7:12	207, 218
6:1–8	43			7:12–13	207, 208
6:1–11	53, 62, 68, 81, 165, 166, 173n17, 176–91, 193, 236, 331, 366	6:14a	200	7:12–14	207
		6:15	19, 40n32, 149n95, 165, 192, 193, 199, 237, 308	7:12–16	207, 213–15
6:1–20	14n19			7:13–14	45
6:2	40n32, 69n82, 149n95, 165, 177, 188			7:14	69n82, 165, 208
		6:15–17	209, 210	7:15	94, 207, 208, 216, 217
6:2–3	62	6:16	40n32, 43, 149n95, 165, 171, 193, 211	7:15–16	216
6:2–6	188			7:16	45, 207, 208, 251, 281
6:2–8	188	6:17	298, 308		
6:3	40n32, 149n95, 165, 177, 188	6:18	43, 165, 166, 193n42, 264, 282n103	7:17	71
		6:18a	198	7:17–24	93n11, 207, 215–18, 219
6:4	165, 177, 178n23, 412n11	6:18b–20	193–95, 197–99		
		6:19	19, 40n32, 64, 69n82, 78, 148, 149, 149n95, 164, 165, 171, 193, 214	7:18–19	207
6:5	165, 177, 296, 391n47			7:19	174
6:5–8	188			7:20	207
6:6	165, 177			7:21–23	207
6:6–8	185	6:20	15, 62, 217, 268	7:22–23	198, 207
6:7	20n27, 62, 165, 334	7–15	61n69	7:23	15, 207
6:7–8	177n21, 183–85	7:1	56, 57, 206, 207, 208–9, 282	7:24	207
6:7–9	177			7:25	206, 207, 221, 222
6:7–9b	333	7:1–5	199, 211, 227	7:25–28	218–19, 221
6:7–11	183–88	7:1–16	278, 284	7:25–40	207, 218–22
				7:26	207

444

Index of Scripture and Other Ancient Sources

7:26–28	207, 212	8:7	228, 229, 230, 271	9:18	230, 235–36n19, 241, 244, 245
7:27	215	8:7–12	250	9:18–19	73
7:28	221	8:7–13	234–37	9:18c	248
7:28a	207, 208	8:7a	228	9:19	63, 78, 235–36n19, 242, 245, 254, 348
7:29–31	207, 216, 366	8:7b–10	228	9:19–23	13, 46, 73, 214, 241, 247–53, 254, 269
7:29–35	207, 218, 219–21	8:8	282	9:19–27	152
7:31	245, 246	8:9	228, 230, 241, 244, 245, 270, 327n198	9:21	183
7:32–34	207, 208	8:9–11	228	9:22	230, 238, 411, 413, 413n15
7:32–35	207, 212, 222	8:9–13	246	9:22–25	254
7:33–34	210	8:10	227, 228, 229, 230, 231, 231n7	9:23	76, 258, 413, 413n15
7:34	69n82, 165, 207, 218n81, 221	8:11	230, 249	9:24	40n32, 149n95
7:36	207, 212, 218n81, 219, 332	8:11–13	230, 239	9:24–27	241, 246, 247, 253
7:36–37	207	8:12	228, 230, 298, 315	9:25	63, 413n15
7:36–38	218	8:13	66, 73, 229n4, 232n12, 245, 353	9:27	372
7:36–40	218, 221–22	9:1	10, 63, 235–36n19, 360, 379	10:1	149n95, 259, 266n80
7:37	165, 218n81, 230	9:1–2	243, 246	10:1–4	259
7:38	207, 212, 218n81	9:1–14	241, 242–45	10:1–11	295
7:39	207, 213, 378n20	9:1–27	66, 81, 125, 241–57, 366	10:1–14	260–64
7:39–40	212, 218	9:3	242	10:1–22	15, 16, 41, 97, 229, 237, 258, 259–67, 288
7:40	207, 212, 218	9:3–14	71, 243–45, 246		
8:1	54, 66, 102, 153, 169, 206, 220, 228, 229, 236, 268, 318, 335, 348	9:3–18	11	10:1–11:1	81, 257–74
		9:4	230, 235–36n19, 241	10:2	41, 380
8:1–3	231–32, 338, 358	9:5	52n54, 105n5, 209, 230, 235–36n19, 241, 252, 378	10:3–4	301
8:1–6	228, 230–34			10:6	259, 333
8:1–11	391	9:6	230, 235–36n19, 241	10:6–14	14n19
8:1–13	53, 59, 68, 72, 81, 230–41, 242, 247, 267, 331, 338	9:10	xvii	10:7	166, 229
		9:11	253, 261	10:9	258
8:1–11:1	35n21, 81, 160n110, 164, 165n3, 185, 201, 206, 226, 227–75, 288, 307, 335	9:12	73, 230, 235–36n19, 239, 241, 246, 247, 253, 334, 413, 413n15	10:11	xvii, 17, 220, 244, 259, 371
		9:12b	73, 248	10:13	96
8:1–14:40	41, 43, 79n104, 80, 81, 164, 226–63	9:12c	248	10:14	43, 166, 229
		9:13	40n32, 149n95	10:14–21	173, 299
8:1a	323n189	9:14	245–46n39, 258	10:15–22	258, 264–67, 286, 297
8:1b	323, 332, 335	9:14–15	156		
8:2	359n253	9:14–18	372	10:16	20, 42, 60, 75, 79, 97
8:3	138, 323n189, 325	9:15	73, 209, 245, 247, 391		
8:4	229, 231	9:15–18	241, 246–47	10:16–17	298
8:4–6	16, 78n101, 232–34, 266, 311	9:15–27	246–53	10:16–21	258–59, 297, 298, 301
8:6	19, 42, 72, 94, 297, 309, 388, 413n15	9:15a	73, 248		

INDEX OF SCRIPTURE AND OTHER ANCIENT SOURCES

10:16–22	20
10:17	259, 314
10:18	76, 259, 302
10:18–20	302
10:18–21	227
10:19	229
10:19–20	134
10:20	76
10:20–21	387n39
10:23	54, 192, 195, 259, 314, 343, 348, 413n15
10:23–24	220, 258, 267–70, 335, 358
10:23–30	227
10:23–11:1	59, 174, 214, 226, 229, 242, 267–71, 323n189
10:24	59, 78, 105, 332, 335
10:25–30	267, 269, 270–71
10:26	235
10:27–29a	45
10:28	229
10:28–29a	343
10:29	235–36n19
10:29–30	282
10:30	259n60
10:31	413, 413n15
10:31–33	45
10:31–11:1	46, 258, 267–70, 358
10:32	19, 90n2, 271, 310
10:32–33	78, 271, 343
10:32–11:1	105
10:33	59, 73, 221, 332, 413, 413n15
10:33–11:1	73, 220, 335
11:1	45, 59, 78, 159, 160, 183, 209, 226, 300, 323n190, 343
11:2	51, 71, 288, 373n12, 413n15
11:2–16	6, 41, 69, 81, 276, 277–86, 287, 315, 332

11:2–14:40	52, 81, 226, 275–363
11:4–5	72, 350
11:5	315, 358
11:7–34	276
11:12	413n15
11:14	276
11:16	71, 90n2, 215n74
11:17	304
11:17–18	356
11:17–22	288–92, 295
11:17–34	20, 41, 53, 69, 70, 72, 81, 97, 164, 173, 174, 185, 264n73, 265, 276n93, 277, 279, 286–306, 307, 347, 400n67
11:18	57, 68, 69, 316
11:19	282n104
11:20	266, 286, 298, 356
11:20–22	331, 332
11:22	19, 90n2, 288, 298
11:23	373, 373n12
11:23–25	71, 72, 276
11:23–26	42, 51, 265, 279, 288, 290, 292–95
11:24	293, 299, 375
11:24–26	298
11:25	13n14, 14, 32n9, 293, 299, 300
11:26	300
11:27	298
11:27–29	298
11:27–30	364
11:27–34	288, 289, 295–96, 331, 366
11:28	300
11:29	298, 307, 314
11:30	378n20
11:31	300
11:32	304
11:33	20n27, 40, 289, 331
11:34	289
12:1	40, 63, 64n72, 94n16, 149n95, 206, 308
12:1–3	309–11
12:1–6	19

12:1–11	153, 234n17
12:1–31	18, 19, 35n21, 58, 81, 105, 107, 120, 276, 277, 306–22, 347, 410
12:1–14:40	53, 165n3, 206, 277
12:2	51, 229, 387n39
12:3	16, 42, 69n82, 72, 276, 297, 355, 372, 415
12:4	63n71, 94n16, 211n66, 308
12:4–5	275
12:4–6	95, 337
12:4–11	72, 311–14
12:6	413n15
12:7	66, 94–95n16, 268, 348
12:7–11	95
12:8	136, 351
12:8–10	327n197
12:9	63n71, 94n16, 211n66, 308, 340
12:10	296, 348, 349, 352
12:11	64, 413n15
12:12	78, 149n94, 196, 199, 237, 319, 413n15
12:12–13	69, 314–15
12:12–31	19
12:13	41, 64, 260, 276, 310n162, 372, 380
12:14–26	314, 315–17
12:19	413n15
12:21–26	315
12:22–24	58
12:22–26	72, 230, 276
12:24	66
12:24b–25	69
12:25	20n27, 68, 314
12:26	220, 334, 413n15
12:27	196, 265n78, 314
12:27–31	314, 316, 318–19
12:28	63n71, 94n16, 211n66, 308, 312, 313, 349, 360
12:28–29	351

Index of Scripture and Other Ancient Sources

12:28–30	312, 313	14:6	312, 313	15:1–5	51, 383
12:30	63n71, 94n16,	14:6–12	351–52	15:1–8	292
	211n66, 308, 312, 313, 352	14:6–13	361	15:1–11	82, 371, 372–80
12:31	63n71, 94n16,	14:12	64, 66, 318n179,	15:1–12	279
	211n66, 308, 323,		347n231, 348, 348n232,	15:1–34	81–82, 200,
	324, 348, 349, 352n240		349, 353n242		371–91
13:1	312, 347	14:13	350	15:1–58	18, 60, 80, 81–82,
13:1–3	313, 323, 326–29,	14:13–19	352–54		126, 185, 364–407
	337, 338, 351	14:14	347n231, 350	15:2	114, 340, 380
13:1–7	344	14:14–17	312	15:3	15, 292, 293, 372,
13:1–13	35n21, 39, 58–59,	14:15	41, 276,		381, 384, 384n33
	63, 81, 277, 322–46, 347,		347n231, 356	15:3–4	13
	348, 357, 366	14:15–17	73, 354	15:3–5	42, 71, 72, 300,
13:2	350n233, 413n15	14:16	276, 347n231		365, 367
13:2b	340	14:17	348n232	15:3–7	279, 373–79,
13:3	413n15	14:18	64		382, 389n41
13:4	54, 153, 169, 231	14:20	138, 333	15:3–8	276
13:4–7	323, 329–37	14:20–25	353n244,	15:3–9	125
13:5	59, 63, 105, 183,		354–56, 357	15:4	367, 385, 401
	220, 221, 268, 343	14:21–25	303	15:4a	381
13:6	183, 317n176	14:23	52	15:4b	381
13:7	245, 253, 340, 413	14:23–25	45, 353	15:5	52n54, 105n5,
13:8	120n41, 313	14:24	348		244n34
13:8–12	323, 337–38	14:26	72, 276, 314, 348,	15:5–7	244n34
13:10	76, 120n41		348n232, 351, 413n15, 414	15:5–9	381
13:11	120n41	14:26–31	276	15:7	244n34
13:12	63, 76, 97, 325,	14:26–36	356–59	15:8	10, 378
	391, 398	14:26–40	348, 356–60	15:8–10	18, 89, 360
13:13	xviii, 19, 300, 323,	14:28	352–53n241	15:8–11	379–80
	334, 337n217, 339–41	14:29	296	15:9	9, 19, 90n2
14:1	63, 64, 94n16, 308,	14:29–33	276	15:9–10	10
	309n160, 318, 318n179,	14:30	351	15:10	94, 108n15,
	347n231, 348	14:32	347n231		146, 372
14:1–5	349–51, 352	14:33	69n82, 94, 282	15:11	372
14:1–6	348	14:33–35	71, 215n74	15:11–12	340
14:1–25	348, 349–56	14:33–36	284n107	15:12	53, 57, 69, 154, 200,
14:1–40	6, 41, 64, 81,	14:33b–35	276n94		365, 367, 380
	276, 277,	14:34b–36	315	15:12–14	376
	327n197, 347–62	14:36–38	309	15:12–15	376n16
14:2	312, 327n199,	14:37	63–64, 64n72,	15:12–19	383–85
	347n231, 352, 353n242		347n231	15:12–34	16, 82, 371,
14:2–4	356	14:37–40	359–60		382–91
14:3	348n232	14:39	318n179, 348, 353	15:14	108, 340, 372
14:4	66, 348n232	14:39–40	64, 348	15:15	376
14:4–5	318	14:40	282, 356, 413n15	15:17	340, 372
14:5	64, 348n232	15:1–2	367, 372–73	15:18	378n20

447

INDEX OF SCRIPTURE AND OTHER ANCIENT SOURCES

15:20	378n20, 414n16	15:48	396	16:19–20a	44
15:20–27	17	15:48–49	397	16:19–24	73, 82, 408,
15:20–28	341, 383,	15:49	396		414–16
	385–89	15:50	185, 394, 395–97,	16:20	20n27, 69n82
15:20–34	385		398, 399	16:21	12–13n13
15:21–22	15	15:51	327, 378n20	16:22	42, 72, 138, 232,
15:22	77, 393, 398	15:51–53	392		276, 311n164, 341
15:23	148, 414n16	15:51–57	82, 151, 341, 371,	16:22b	97
15:24	120n41,		399–401	16:23	42, 93, 94n15
	134n67, 185	15:52–54	398	16:24	341, 414
15:24–28	339, 391	15:53	396		
15:26	120n41, 151,	15:53–54	393n48	**2 Corinthians**	
	400, 410	15:54–55	97	1–7	242n30
15:27	413n15	15:54–57	398	1:1	19, 90n1, 90n2,
15:28	78, 283, 371,	15:56	384n33		160n112, 411n10
	401, 413n15	15:58	82, 334, 371,	1:3–11	155n103, 390n44
15:29	41, 367		372, 392, 401–2, 408, 412	1:8–11	391, 411
15:29–32	372, 384	16:1	69n82, 206	1:12	380n29
15:29–34	383, 389–91	16:1–4	44, 71, 73, 82,	1:14	96n20, 96n21
15:30–32	334		408–10	1:19	160n112, 411–12n10
15:32	155n104, 400,	16:1–7	56	1:20	17
	401, 411	16:1–24	80, 82, 408–17	1:22	17
15:35	392–93	16:2	275	1:24	145n87
15:35–50	82, 196, 369,	16:5–9	44, 73, 82, 408,	2:1	57
	371, 392–98, 399		410–11	2:2–3	243n31
15:35–57	82, 341, 371, 385,	16:7	412	2:3–4	57
	392–401	16:8	8, 51, 56	2:5	57
15:36	371n7, 398	16:8–9	57, 391n45	2:5–11	171n12, 276–77n95
15:36–41	392, 393–94	16:9	57	2:6	276–77n95
15:36–50	392	16:10–11	56, 90n1, 160,	2:12	411
15:37	399n64		160n112	2:14	155
15:42	398	16:10–12	44, 73, 82, 408,	2:15	373, 387n38
15:42–49	392, 394–95		411–12	3:6	13n14, 14, 32n9,
15:42–50	399	16:11	94		144n84, 295, 371n7,
15:42–54	253, 389	16:12	52, 56, 106, 206		398n61
15:42b	396	16:13	372	3:17–18	21, 396n58
15:43	135	16:13–14	82, 412–14	3:18	135, 338, 367, 394,
15:43a	396	16:13–18	44		398, 399
15:43b	396	16:14	58, 70, 102, 325,	4:3	387n38
15:44	396		340, 341, 416	4:3–4	114
15:44–46	137n70	16:15	51, 69n82, 107n12	4:3–6	338
15:45	137n71, 371n7,	16:15–18	73, 82, 408, 414	4:4	171
	393n49, 397, 399	16:17	56, 57	4:5	144n84, 144n85
15:45–49	15	16:17–18	107n12	4:5–12	124
15:46	396	16:19	8, 278n96		
15:47–49	397	16:19–20	41		

Index of Scripture and Other Ancient Sources

4:7–12	11, 155n103, 390n44	11:1–12:10	156n106	1:15–17	10
4:10	390n43	11:2–3	196	1:16	10n6, 351n237
4:11	292n124	11:4	273	1:17	8
4:14	196	11:5–11	242n30	1:18–19	8
4:16–5:11	367	11:5–15	245–46n39	1:19	244n34
4:17–18	135	11:6	106	1:21	8
4:17–5:5	396n58	11:15	144n84	1:23	379n25
5	402	11:16–12:10	391	2	288n113
5:1–4	399n64	11:22–33	242n30	2:1–10	8, 10n6
5:3	393	11:23	144n84, 391	2:1–13	243n32
5:5	17	11:23–33	11, 155n103, 390n44	2:1–21	216n76
5:11–21	16	11:24–26	10	2:9	378
5:14	15, 232n9, 325	11:27	50n49	2:10	409
5:14–15	15, 375n14	11:30	124	2:11–14	373n12
5:14–21	18, 302	12:1	292, 351n237	2:12	174
5:17	13n14, 32n9, 219, 371, 397	12:5–10	124, 242n30	2:15–21	18
5:18–21	122	12:7	292, 351n237	2:19–20	20, 32, 141, 299
5:19	184	12:9	380n29	2:20	15, 186n35, 232n9, 324, 328, 375n14
5:20	59, 269	12:10	11, 155n103, 390n44	2:23	9
5:21	123, 188, 375	12:13	242n30	3:1–5	96, 125
6:1	146	12:15	242n30	3:6–14	16
6:3–10	11, 155n103, 390n44	12:19	269	3:7	259
6:4	144n84	13:1	56n61	3:13	310n163
6:4–5	50n49	13:5	295	3:21	15, 371n7
6:10	50n49	13:10	169	3:24–25	160n109
6:14–16	267n83	13:11	20n27, 324n192	3:25–28	19
6:14–7:1	57n62, 214	13:11b	94	3:26–28	315
6:16	75n91, 148, 199	13:12	415n18	3:27	107, 186n35, 301, 315
7:8	57	13:13	19, 94n15, 232n9	3:27–28	299
8	120n40			3:28	11, 207, 210, 216, 270n86, 278, 281, 283, 315
8–9	408, 410	**Galatians**		4:4	269, 388
8:1–5	409n4	1:4	15, 375n14	4:4–6	78, 140, 149
8:9	96	1:6	94n15	4:6	19, 32n8, 147, 353n242
8:23	145n87	1:6–9	109, 273	4:9	232
9:1–5	409n4, 410	1:8–9	415	4:13–14	124
10–13	57n63, 242	1:10	144n84	4:18–19	12n11
10:1	106, 242n30	1:11	372	4:19–20	40, 139n80
10:5	40n31, 138	1:11–12	13	5	313n167
10:8–10	242n30	1:11–16	18	5:1	413
10:10	106, 124	1:12	373n12	5:1–12	216n76
10:12	20n27	1:13	9, 19, 90n2	5:5–6	19
10:17	391n46	1:13–14	9, 379n25	5:6	141, 216, 340
11:1–14	109	1:15	94n15, 379n27, 380n29		
		1:15–16	10		

INDEX OF SCRIPTURE AND OTHER ANCIENT SOURCES

5:9	172
5:11	114
5:13	20n27, 141, 218n80
5:13–26	21, 139
5:14	335n213
5:15	20n27
5:16	139, 172
5:16–26	19
5:19–21	172, 186
5:19–21a	141
5:21	161, 185
5:22	323, 325
5:22–23	77, 313, 336
5:24	141
5:26	20n27
6:1	161, 176
6:2	20n27, 212n68, 250n49, 321, 334
6:3	231
6:11	415n19
6:12–16	216n76
6:14	123, 125, 391n46
6:15	13n14, 32n9, 216, 371, 397
6:16	266n80

Ephesians

1:4	120
1:9	327n199
1:13–14	17
1:21	134n67, 266n82
2:1–10	18
2:2	134n67, 266n82
2:4	232n9
2:20	147n90
2:21–22	149
3:1	10n6
3:2	380n29
3:3	351n237
3:3–5	327n199
3:5	351n237
3:7	144n84
3:7–8	10, 380n29
3:7–10	147n89, 379n27
3:8	10n6

3:9	327n199
3:10	134n67
3:16	413
3:19	389
4:2	20n27
4:4	314n170
4:4–6	91, 311n165
4:5	276
4:7–16	19
4:11	312, 313
4:11–13	276
4:11–16	140n81
4:12	314
4:13	265n78
4:16	265n78
4:25	20n27
4:32	20n27, 276
5:2	232n9, 375n14
5:16	276
5:19	276, 357
5:20	276
5:21	20n27
5:21–33	210n60, 284n107, 342n227
5:21–6:9	217n78
5:22–23	358n251
5:25	232n9
5:29–32	196
5:30	314n170
5:31	211
6:10–17	387n39
6:11–12	134n67
6:12	266n82
6:18	276
6:19	327n199
6:21	144n84
6:24	232n9

Philippians

1:1	144n84, 160n112
1:3–2:18	19
1:5	20
1:6	96, 96n20
1:9	276
1:10	96n20, 97

1:19	32n8, 147
1:27	104, 413
1:27–2:16	104
1:27–2:18	249
1:28	387n38
2:1	20
2:1–4	104, 141, 276, 335
2:1–5	104
2:1–11	20
2:2	265n78
2:3	153
2:4	59, 268, 332n211, 335
2:5	20, 137
2:5–8	15
2:5–11	335
2:6	251–52
2:6–8	73, 78, 184, 247, 376
2:6–11	104, 108, 247–49, 276
2:6a	248
2:6b	248
2:7	144n84
2:7–8	59, 248
2:9–11	16, 98, 123, 297, 309, 387, 389
2:11	16, 276
2:15–16	104
2:17	317n176
2:17–18	220
2:18	317n176
2:19	160n112
2:21	59, 268, 332n211
2:25	145n87
2:29	414
3:3–14	10
3:5	9, 364
3:5–8	250n47
3:6	9, 379n25
3:8–10	21–22
3:10	20, 97
3:10–11	396n58
3:10–14	21, 152
3:10–21	367
3:12	10
3:12–14	39, 253n54
3:17	160, 269

450

Index of Scripture and Other Ancient Sources

3:20–21	396n58
3:21	136, 394
4:1	413
4:2–3	278n96
4:3	145n87
4:9	94
4:10–14	50
4:10–19	411
4:23	94n15

Colossians

1:1	157, 160n112
1:4–5	339n221
1:5	77n96
1:7	157
1:9–11	77n96
1:15–16	387n39
1:15–17	233n15
1:15–20	17
1:16	134n67
1:18	386
1:19	77n96
1:23	77n96
1:25–29	135
1:26–27	327n199
1:27	77n96, 396n58
2:2	327n199
2:3	117n31
2:7	146n88
2:9–10	77n96
2:10	134n67
2:15	134n67, 389
3:3–4	396n58
3:4	77n96
3:9	20n27
3:11	270n86, 281, 315
3:13	20n27, 276
3:15	265n78
3:16	20n27, 276, 357
3:17	268
3:18–4:1	217n78
4:3	327n199
4:11	145n87
4:12	144n84
4:13–16	415

4:15	278n96
4:16	276
4:18	415n19

1 Thessalonians

1:1	160n112
1:3	19, 339n221
1:4	232n9
1:5	125
1:6	160
1:9–10	166
1:10	376n16
2:1–12	241
2:2	13, 373n11
2:5–8	12n11, 139n80
2:7–8	40
2:8	373n11
2:9	11, 156, 245n38, 373n11
2:12	185
2:19	386n34
3:2	145, 160n112
3:6	160n112
3:8	413
3:12	20n27, 322
3:13	21, 97, 386n34
4:1–8	166
4:3–8	166–67, 203, 206
4:4	210n62
4:5	21
4:9	20n27
4:13–15	378n20
4:13–18	17, 364, 367, 386n34, 393, 399
4:15	386n34
4:16	319, 399
4:18	20n27
5:1–10	96n21
5:2	96n20
5:4	96n20
5:6	413n13
5:6–10	391
5:8	19, 339n221
5:10	375n14, 413n13
5:11	20n27
5:11–15	276

5:12	313
5:12–13a	414
5:15	20n27, 183n32
5:17–18	276
5:19–21	276, 312
5:21	276
5:23	21, 94, 386n34
5:23–24	97
5:24	96
5:26	415n18
5:27	276
5:28	94n15

2 Thessalonians

1:1	160n112
1:3	20n27
1:5	185
1:10	96n20
1:12	94n15
2:2	96n20
2:3	96n20
2:13–14	396n58
2:15	413
2:16	232n9
3:5	232n9
3:6	174
3:7–9	11
3:8	156
3:8–9	245n38
3:16	94
3:17	415n19
3:18	94n15

1 Timothy

1:12–16	379n27
1:12–17	18, 147n89
1:13	9, 379n25
1:20	171
2:5–6	375n14
2:7	10n6
2:9–15	277
2:11–12	358
2:11–15	276n94, 284n107
3:5	90n2
3:8	144n84

INDEX OF SCRIPTURE AND OTHER ANCIENT SOURCES

3:9	327n199	3:1	214n72	**Augustine**	
3:12	144n84	3:9	183		
3:16	10n6	5:14	415n18	*City of God*	
4:3	209			18.48	261n66
4:6	144n84	**2 Peter**			
5:18	244	3:9–15	96n21	**Bernard of Clairvaux**	
5:19–20	157	3:16	xviii		
				Commentary on	
2 Timothy		**1 John**		*the Song of Songs*	
1:12	96n20	2:19	289n115	36.3	345n229
1:18	96n20	4:8	324	**Cicero**	
2:6	244	4:16	324		
2:24	144n84			*Against Verres*	
3:16	27	**Revelation**		2.5.64	112
4:7–8	96n21, 253n54	1:5	386	2.5.66	112
4:8	96n20	2:12–17	288n113	*De officiis*	
4:17	10n6	2:14	228	1.150	242n29
		2:20	228	*Pro Cluentio*	
Titus		3:14–21	154n101	5	168–69n8
2:5	358n251	3:20	302		
2:11	94n15	5	126	*Pro Flacco*	
2:14	375n14	7	319	18	242n29
3:3	20n27	12–13	266		
		14:13	402	**1 Clement**	
Philemon		16:15	413n13	1.1	74n87
1	145n87, 157, 160n112	18:4	100	47	74n87
19	415n19	19:9	400		
23	157	21–22	185	**Dead Sea Scrolls**	
24	145n87	21:1–4	400	1QS [Rule of the	
25	94n15	21:5	341	Community]	
		22:20	276, 415	VIII, 5	143n83
Hebrews				XI, 7–8	143n83
6:6	237	## OTHER ANCIENT SOURCES		**Didache**	
13:20	94			9	261n64
James				**Epictetus**	
2:1–7	292n123	**Aelius Aristides**			
2:8	335n213			*Discourses*	
2:17	340	*Orations*		4.1.1	172, 193n41
2:26	340	46.24	49		
				Epistle to Diognetus	
1 Peter		**Ambrose of Milan**		5.1	203
1:11	32n8	*Letters to Priests*		6–8	203
1:16	77	54	248n41		

Index of Scripture and Other Ancient Sources

Gaius

Institutes

1.63   168–69n8

Ignatius of Antioch

Letter to the Ephesians

20   304n152

John Chrysostom

Homilies on 1 Corinthians

1.1	91n5
3.5	107n9
5.4	123n48
8.7	147n92
16.2	175n20
16.8	188n39
17.3	200n48
19.2	210n63
20.2	232n11
27.6–7	303n150
33.1	329n203

33.3	335n214
44.2	416n20

Josephus

Jewish War

3.540	49n46
7.203	113

Jubilees

33.10–13   168–69n8, 173n16

Lucian of Samosata

Symposium (The Carousel)

287

Origen

Against Celsus

3.44	379
5.14	379

Pliny the Younger

To Avitus (Ep 2.6)   290–91

Pseudo-Phocylides

179	168–69n8
194	201

Quintilian

Lesser Declamations

274   113

Strabo

Geography

8.6.20   48

Theodoret of Cyrus

Commentary on the First Epistle to the Corinthians

167   74n88